International Accounting

Third Edition

A.K. DAS MOHAPATRA
Former Vice-Chancellor, Odisha State Open University, and Professor,
Department of Business Administration, Sambalpur University, Odisha

PHI Learning Private Limited
Delhi-110092
2025

In fond memory of ***Shri Asoke K. Ghosh*** *(October 1942 – February 2024), Founder Chairman and Managing Director of PHI Learning, whose vision endlessly inspires.*

The Legacy Continues. . . .

Published by Pushpita Ghosh, PHI Learning Private Limited, Rimjhim House, 111, Patparganj Industrial Estate, Delhi-110092 and Printed by Syndicate Binders, A-20, Hosiery Complex, Noida, Phase-II Extension, Noida-201305 (N.C.R. Delhi).

₹995.00

INTERNATIONAL ACCOUNTING, Third Edition
A.K. Das Mohapatra

ISBN-978-93-5443-983-4 (Print Book)
ISBN-978-93-5443-726-7 (e-Book)

The export rights of the book are vested solely with the publisher.

To
My loving Parents and revered Teachers

Contents

Preface

The first edition of the book was brought out primarily to help the learners such as the students and professionals to gain knowledge and proficiency over a rather intricate and highly technical subject, the International Accounting. The other objective of the first edition was to facilitate the teachers and academic institutions who were willing to launch International Accounting as a specialised course in finance but were not able to do so because of non-availability of a standard textbook which presents the concepts and rules lucidly and systematically, and illustrates with examples how to implement these rules which even a learner without having prior exposure to basics of accounting can understand.

The second edition was presented based on the feedback and appreciations received from the users of the first edition and the development at international forums that stressed on harmonization of accounting practices across the globe by implementing IFRS as the only business language the world over. Besides updated texts, additional illustrations and practice questions, the other key features of the second edition was inclusion of four new chapters on International Financial Management which is also a complex area of accounting and finance that has gained importance in recent years, especially in the post liberalization, privatization and globalization era. These four chapters were: introduction to international financial management, exchange rate forecasting, measurement of foreign exchange exposure, and management of foreign exchange exposure. These chapters were added to help those who find it difficult to make an inroad into International Financial Management because of its inherent complexities, and also, because they have direct link with international accounting.

The third edition is a further revised and enlarged edition, based on the feedback received from the users of the second edition as well as the demand enquiry received from many prospective users; and also the changes that have occurred over the last decade with regard to financial reporting and disclosure, especially due to adoption and/or convergence of country specific GAAP to IFRS, which necessitated a revision and updating of the book. For instance, out of the forty one IAS, at least seven IAS, namely, IAS 3, 4, 5, 6, 9, 13 and 25 have been either withdrawn or superseded by others. Similarly, the number of IFRS has got increased from 8 in 2012 to 17 in 2023–24. In the Indian context, the Ministry of Corporate Affairs, Government of India has notified in 2015 the Companies (Indian Accounting Standards

[Ind AS] Rules 2015. This notification has mandated for the adoption and applicability of Ind AS in a phased manner beginning from Accounting period 2016–17 by the Indian companies. Indian Accounting Standards (Ind AS) are standards that have been harmonized with the IFRS through adoption and convergence to make reporting by Indian companies more accessible globally. Furthermore, the Ministry of Corporate Affairs has come up with three Amendment Rules, one each in year 2016, 2017, and 2018 to amend the 2015 rules. Moreover, there have been several other changes such as the withholding tax rates in the international taxation front, and so also the Double Tax Avoidance Treaties (DTA). Keeping these factors in mind, the third edition is a revised edition that has come up with presentation of updated rules and provisions, along with inclusion of over 105 additional illustrations and practice questions.

While revising the book I have referred to the work of other authors and the circulars and notifications of the policy documents and proclamations of rules by different standard setting and regulating bodies like the IFRS organization, Ministry of Corporate Affairs, Government of India, and Institute of Chartered Accountants of India. I would like to record my sincere thanks, gratitude and indebtedness to those authors, regulatory and policy formulating bodies, including IFRS organization whose work and documents I have referred to and who have directly or indirectly encouraged me for completion of the present work. I would also record my sincere appreciations to the encouragements that I have received from many other experts and well-wishers, such as Prof K.B. Das, Vice-Chancellor, Central University of Jharkhand; Prof Nageswar Rao, Vice-Chancellor, IGNOU; Prof Ami Upadhyaya, Vice-Chancellor, Dr Babasaheb Ambedkar Open University, Ahmedabad; Prof Arun K Pujari, former Vice-Chancellor of Sambalpur University, and Rajasthan Central University; Prof Bishnu Charan Barik, former Vice-Chancellor of Sambalpur University; Prof C.R. Tripathy, former Vice-Chancellor of Sambalpur University and Biju Pattnaik University of Technology; Prof G.D. Sharma, former Vice-Chancellor, Nagaland University, and Bilaspur University; Prof K.C. Sinha, Vice-Chancellor, Nalanada Open University, Bihar; Prof Sanjay Tiwari, Vice-Chancellor, MP Bhoj Open University, Madhya Pradesh; Prof Karamjeet Singh, Vice-Chancellor, Punjab Open University; Prof T N Sahu, Vice-Chancellor, Jharkhand Open University; Prof Amit Gautam, Institute of Management, BHU; Prof Ananda Mohan Pal, Calcutta University; Prof Debasish Sur, Burdwan University; Prof Pradipta Banerjee, SKB University, Puruliya; Prof Arindam Gupta and Prof Abhijit Sinha of Vidya Sagar University; Prof B Mishra, NEHU; Prof J Pataria, Institute of Management, Guru Ghasidas University, Bilashpur; Prof S N Dhar, University of North Bengal, Darjeeling; to list a few.

I am thankful to the publisher PHI Learning Private Limited and their associated officials, especially Sri Malaya Ranjan Parida and the editorial and production staff for their support and encouragement in bringing out the third edition of the book.

I hope this new edition will be as useful to the target audience as the earlier ones. I will be pleased to receive suggestions at *akdm_2002@yahoo.com* for improvement in the subsequent editions.

A.K. Das Mohapatra

1

International Accounting
An Overview

LEARNING OBJECTIVES

After Studying this chapter, you will be able to:

- Define International Accounting
- Identify the factors that have contributed to the development of International Accounting as a separate branch of study
- Understand the scope of International Accounting
- Recognize the dimensions of International Accounting
- Appreciate the significance of International Accounting
- Understand the difficulties encountered in International Accounting

INTRODUCTION

Accounting is aptly called as the language of business. It is through accounting that a business communicates to its stakeholders. Accounting acts as the basic source of information for business and economic decisions. The important categories of information contained in accounting are operating information, financial accounting information, management accounting information and tax accounting information. Operating information is needed for effective conduct of the day-to-day activities of the business. A store's records, for example, helps the store manager to assess on a daily basis the availability of certain items of stock for taking appropriate action to ensure that neither the production nor the sales get affected due to stock out. Financial accounting information is required for the internal stakeholders such as the managers, employees, owner and the external stakeholders like the creditors and government agencies. An investor, for instance, would like to decide to buy, hold or sell the security issued by a firm based on information on the firm's economic performance and cash flows. Management accounting information is needed for effective planning, implementation, evaluation and control of the firm's strategic and tactical operations. Tax accounting information is required for effective tax planning and meeting the legal requirements.

The purpose of accounting thus is to provide information that is useful for decision making. As long as the business continues to operate within its national boundaries, generating accounting information as above is never a challenge, for the accountant has to follow the same accounting standard, and operate in the same social, political, economic and legal environment. Over the last few decades however, businesses have grown more globalized. Multinational corporations have emerged in a bigger way both in quantum and size. Trade and commerce between nations have been on rise. Cross-border transactions involving flow of goods, services and capital are in an ever increasing spree. With the increasing pace of globalization and economic liberalization particularly towards the end of twentieth century, executives are called upon to make decisions based on financial information originating from other countries. These decisions range from evaluating the performance of foreign subsidiary(ies), affiliates, joint ventures, to making credit decisions on customers belonging to other countries, and making investment and financing decisions based on opportunities in other countries. Since countries have their own set of socio-economic, political, legal, cultural, technological and linguistic environment, financial reporting diversities are quite eminent. With diverse financial reports in hand, the decision makers find it difficult to making effective decisions. To overcome this difficulty and to have a more uniform and harmonized financial reporting across the globe, the concept of 'international accounting' has gained momentum.

INTERNATIONAL ACCOUNTING

International accounting has been viewed differently by different authors. Some of these views are:

'There is nothing new about international accounting, accounting has always been international, from the time it emerged some thousands of years ago, because of its concern with international trade and because of the spread of ideas across countries' [1].

'The heritage of accounting is indisputably international. So, today's concern with multinational accounting is more a renaissance than a new idea' [2].

'International accounting extends general-purpose nationally oriented accounting in its broadest sense to (a) international comparative analysis, (b) accounting measurement and reporting issues unique to multinational enterprises, (c) accounting needs of international financial markets, and (d) harmonization of worldwide accounting and financial reporting diversity via political, organizational, professional and standard-setting activities' [3].

'International accounting would involve accounting for international transactions, the operational aspects of international firms, comparison of accounting principles and practices found in foreign countries and the procedures by which they were established' [4].

'International accounting is that branch of accounting which analyses the different accounting principles and practices prevalent around the globe, deals with the specific technical problems encountered by individuals and MNCs in international operations and as its ultimate goal, attempt to develop a universal system of accounting that would receive acceptance the world over' [5].

The above views are indicative of the diverse dimensions of 'international accounting', ranging from recording of foreign transactions to the preparation and presentation of consolidated and comparative foreign financial statements for the use of decision makers.

International accounting may thus be defined as that branch of accounting which deals with the recording and translation of foreign transactions, preparation and presentation of consolidated foreign financial statements, and presentation of international financial reporting in accordance with international GAAP and auditing practices.

DEVELOPMENT OF INTERNATIONAL ACCOUNTING

The factors which have contributed towards development of international accounting are:

- Expansion of world trade
- Emergence of Multi National Corporations
- Increase in international flow of capital
- Historical evolution of accounting
- Need for harmonization of accounting practices

Expansion of World Trade

Over the past couple of decades, countries have become increasingly interdependent in terms of goods, services and flow of capital. Unlike the early caravans who used to cross national boundaries selling their wares, the past three and half decades have envisaged a surge in the volume of international trade between countries as a result of modern means of transport and communication. The value of world export, for example, has increased from 3495.69 Billion USD in 1990 to 6452.32 Billion USD in 2000, 15297.25 Billion USD in 2010, 17648.37 Billion USD in 2020, and 24904.59 Billion USD[6] in 2022 as shown in Exhibit 1.1 and Figure 1.1.

EXHIBIT 1.1 Trends in global export value of trade in goods from 1950 to 2022 (in Billion USD)

Year	*Amount (in Billion USD)*	*Year*	*Amount (in Billion USD)*
1950	61.81	2009	12557.46
1955	93.92	2010	15297.25
1960	130.09	2011	18335.03
1965	189.62	2012	18504.18
1970	318.02	2013	18942.48
1975	876.89	2014	18999.68
1980	2049.41	2015	16554.29
1985	1964.84	2016	16035.88
1990	3495.69	2017	17740.89
1995	5176.20	2018	19549.33
2000	6452.32	2019	19014.31
2005	10502.73	2020	17648.37
2006	12127.84	2021	22343.93
2007	14021.11	2022	24904.59
2008	16147.77		

Source: https://www.statista.com/statistics/264682/worldwide-export-volume-in-the-trade-since-1950/

It is evident from Exhibit 1.1 that the global trade value of goods exported throughout the world was over 24.90 trillion U.S. dollars at current prices, which was a little over 6.45 trillion U.S. dollars in 2000. This exponential growth in the value of goods exported around the world reflects the expansion that has taken place in the world trade, supported by globalization and technological advancement.

Consequently, the complexities involved in accounting practices because of the involvement of so many countries have increased. This has necessitated establishing harmony in accounting practices across nations and therefore the development of international accounting.

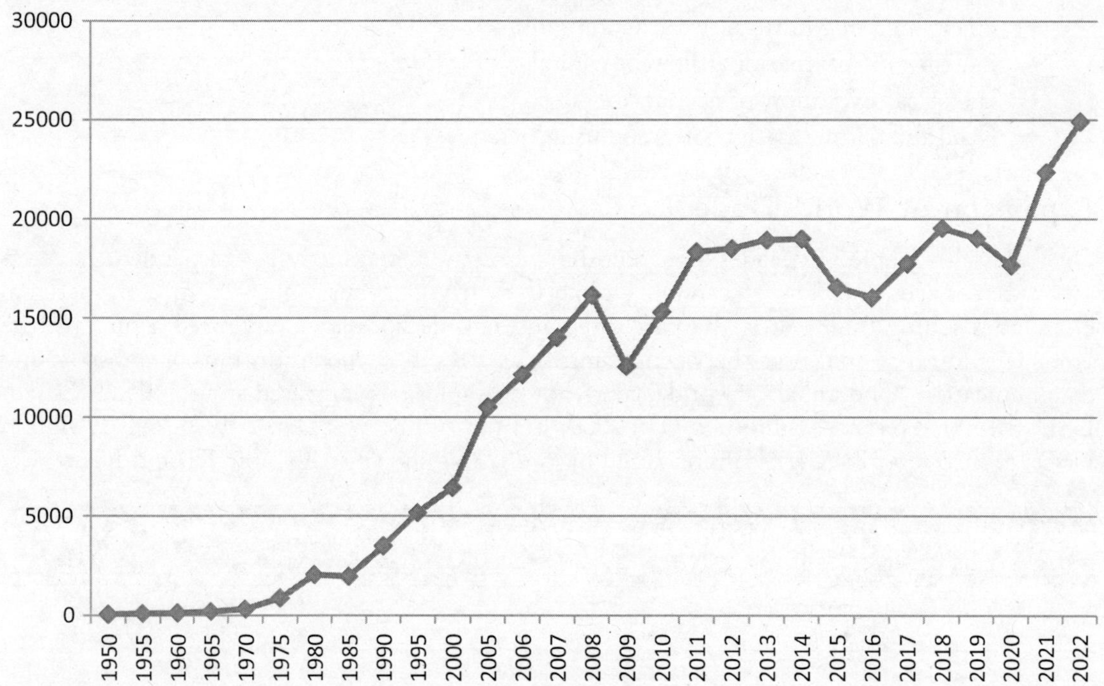

Figure 1.1 Trends in global export value of trade in goods from 1950 to 2022 (in Billion U.S. dollars)

Emergence of Multinational Corporations

Proliferations of multinational corporations has been seen as an important contributory factor towards the development of international accounting as a distinct discipline. Multinational corporations operate under differential tariffs, taxes, government regulations, political risks, inflations, currencies, and accounting policies/standards. As such, consolidation of the financial statements of subsidiaries becomes difficult in the absence of a uniform accounting methods, which in fact is fulfilled by international accounting.

International Flow of Capital

International flow of capital has been on the rise over the past years. For instance, the amount of debt capital raised in the international capital markets totaled over $328 billion in 1989 compared to $50 billion in 1980. Another example of the international flow of capital is evident in the fact that by the end of 1997 as many as 343 non-US companies from 46 nations with an aggregate market capitalization of US $ 3 trillion, as against a total market capitalization of US $ 11.6 trillion, were listed to the New York stock exchange [7].

Similarly, in terms of foreign direct investment (FDI) as an indicator of global flow of capital, the aggregate value of global FDI in the year 1990 was 204.89 Billion USD, which increased to 1356.69 Billion USD, 1393.01 Billion USD, and 2056.42 Billion USD, in the year 2000, 2010 and 2015, respectively. In 2022 the aggregate value of global FDI was 1294.74 Billion USD which is approximately 1.3 trillion USD [8] as shown in Exhibit 1.2A and Figure 1.2.

EXHIBIT 1.2-A Trends in global FDI from 1990 to 2022

Year	*FDI in Billion USD*	*Year*	*FDI in Billion USD*	*Year*	*FDI in Billion USD*
1990	204.89	2009	1173.74	2016	2003.45
1995	345.14	2010	1393.01	2017	1644.87
2000	1356.69	2011	1613.47	2018	1375.44
2005	954.07	2012	1469.07	2019	1707.83
2006	1413.37	2013	1468.37	2020	961.98
2007	1906.64	2014	1411.83	2021	1478.14
2008	1488.31	2015	2056.42	2022	1294.74

Source: https://hbs.unctad.org/foreign-direct-investment/

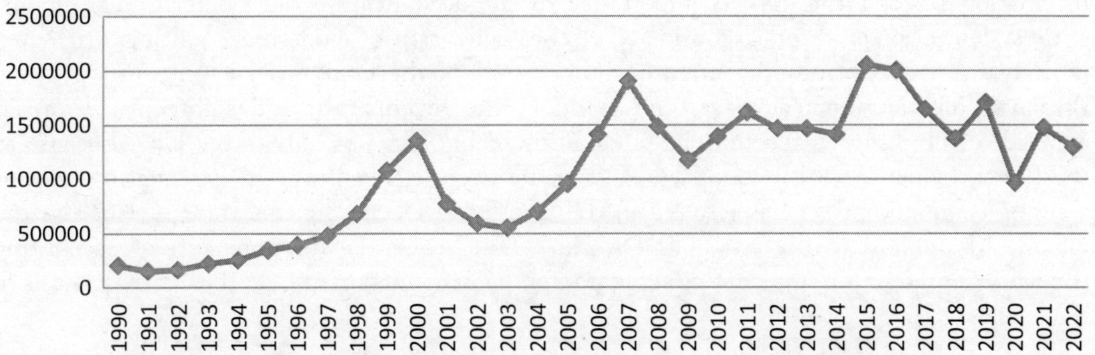

Figure 1.2 Trends in global FDI from 1990 to 2022

Further, the top three recipients of FDI in 2022 were the USA, China and Singapore who attracted 285 billion USD, 189 billion USD, and 141 billion USD, respectively. The other seven countries in the same order were China, Hong Kong SAR, Brazil, Australia, Canada, India, Sweden and France. Exhibit 1.2B contains a list of top 20 countries with highest inflow of FDI in 2022.

EXHIBIT 1.2B Top 20 economies with highest FDI inflows in 2022

Rank	*Country*	*Amount (in Billion USD)*	*Rank*	*Country*	*Amount (in Billion USD)*
1	USA	285	11	Mexico	35
2	China	189	12	Spain	35
3	Singapore	141	13	Japan	33
4	China, Hong Kong SAR	118	14	Poland	29
5	Brazil	86	15	Israel	28
6	Australia	62	16	UAE	23
7	Canada	53	17	Indonesia	22
8	India	49	18	Italy	20
9	Sweden	46	19	Chile	20
10	France	36	20	Republic of Korea (South Korea)	18

Source: http://hbs.unctad.org/foreign-direct-investment/

This increasing dependence on international money and capital markets has warranted for comparable and reliable financial information for the present and potential investors spread across the globe. International accounting by virtue of harmonization of accounting practices, helps produce more reliable and comparable financial information, and therefore is a boon in this direction.

Historical Evolution

International accounting has its importance in the accounting evolution itself. The double entry system of book keeping, considered as the foundation of modern accounting, originated in Italy in 1493, spread to Germany, France and Netherlands in the sixteenth century. Britain's political supremacy over the world in the seventeenth and eighteenth centuries enabled it to transfer its accounting and auditing technology not only to the USA but also to the British Commonwealth countries. And in the twentieth century, the emergence of US as a strong economic power has resulted in the transfer of US accounting thought (such as the US GAAP) almost to the rest of the world. These sequential developments of accounting thoughts represent an international character of accounting irrespective of nationalistic tendencies.

Need for Harmonization

The need for harmonization of accounting practices has also led to the development of international accounting. Harmonization refers to the process of minimization of diversities in financial reporting practices that exist among nations so as to make the financial statements comparable and useful to decision makers. Diversities in accounting practices act as a hindrance to the international flow of capital for its efficient and productive use. This is because international investors find it difficult to read the accounting figures of other nations which are prepared based on a different set of accounting rules and language of the nation. It is through the harmonization of accounting practices that these barriers are removed to a greater extent.

Development of international accounting in itself is the manifestation of harmonization of accounting practices across the globe. Over and above, most economies in the world have agreed to adopt the International Financial Reporting Standards (IFRS) as the base for reporting financial performance of their companies which in itself will result in removal of disparities in financial reporting. In India, for example, companies which were part of NSE Index—Nifty 50, or companies which were part of BSE Sensex—BSE 30, or companies whose shares or other securities were listed on a stock exchange outside India, and companies, whether listed or not, but having paid up capital or net worth of ₹1,000 crore or more were to adopt IFRS from April 2011. This date was subsequently shifted and applicability of Indian Accounting Standards (or Ind AS) was made in a phased manner from 1st April, 2015 with further details as given in Exhibit 1.3.

EXHIBIT 1.3 Applicability of Indian Accounting Standards (Ind AS)

The Ministry of Corporate Affairs, Government of India, in 2015, had notified the Companies (Indian Accounting Standards (Ind AS)) Rules 2015, which stipulated the adoption and applicability of Ind AS in a phased manner beginning from the Accounting period 2016-17.

However, the Ministry of Corporate Affairs has since issued three Amendment Rules, one each in year 2016, 2017, and 2018 to amend the 2015 rules. The Ind AS are basically standards that have been harmonised with the IFRS to make reporting by Indian companies more globally accessible.

Phase-I

Mandatory applicability of Ind AS to all companies from 1st April 2016, provided:

- It is a listed or unlisted company
- Its net worth is greater than or equal to ₹500 crore*

*Net worth shall be checked for the previous three Financial Years (2013–14, 2014–15, and 2015–16

Phase-II

Mandatory applicability of Ind AS to all companies from 1st April 2017, provided:

- It is a listed company or is in the process of being listed (as on 31.03.2016)
- Its Net worth is greater than or equal to ₹250 crore but less than ₹500 crore (for any of the below mentioned periods)

Net worth shall be checked for the previous four Financial Years (2014-14, 2014-15, 2015-16, and 2016-17

Phase-III

Mandatory applicability of Ind AS to all Banks, NBFCs, and Insurance companies from 1st April 2018, whose:

- Net worth is more than or equal to INR 500 crore with effect from 1st April 2018.

Insurance Regulatory and Development Authority (IRDA) of India shall notify the separate set of Ind AS for Banks & Insurance Companies with effect from 1st April 2018. Non-Banking Finance Companies (NBFCs) include core investment companies, stock brokers, venture capitalists, etc. Net worth shall be checked for the past 3 financial years (2015–16, 2016–17, and 2017–18).

Phase-IV

All NBFCs whose net worth is more than or equal to ₹250 crore but less than ₹500 crore shall have Ind AS mandatorily applicable to them with effect from 1st April 2019.

(*Contd.*)

Note:

1. Since Indian companies have a far wider global reach now as compared to earlier, the need to converge reporting standards with international standards was felt, which has led to the introduction of Ind AS.
2. If Ind AS becomes applicable to any company, then Ind AS shall automatically be made applicable to all the subsidiaries, holding companies, associated companies, and joint ventures of that company, irrespective of individual qualification of such companies. In case of foreign operations of an Indian Company, the preparation of stand-alone financial statements may continue with its jurisdictional requirements and need not be prepared as per the Ind AS. However, these entities will still have to report their Ind AS adjusted numbers for their Indian parent company to prepare consolidated Ind AS accounts.

Source: https://cleartax.in/s/applicability-ind-as

SCOPE OF INTERNATIONAL ACCOUNTING

The scope of international accounting is both wide and vast included in which are recording of foreign transactions, translation of foreign currency, adjustment of foreign financial statements against inflation, consolidation of foreign financial statements, financial reporting and disclosure, segment reporting, multinational transfer pricing, international budgeting, performance evaluation of subsidiaries, foreign exchange risk management, international taxation, analysis of foreign financial statements, accounting for newer financial instruments like options, swaps and other derivative products, international joint ventures, environmental accounting, and integration of ethics into accounting. When clubbed into major groups, the scope of international accounting covers financial accounting, management accounting and social and allied accounting activities as depicted in Exhibit 1.4.

EXHIBIT 1.4 Scope of International Accounting

Financial Accounting	*Management Accounting*	*Social and allied accounting activities*
♦ Recording of foreign transactions ♦ Foreign currency translation ♦ Accounting for foreign inflation ♦ Consolidation of foreign financial statements, reporting and disclosure ♦ Segment and interim reporting	♦ Analysis of foreign financial statements ♦ Multinational transfer pricing ♦ Budgeting and performance evaluation of foreign subsidiaries ♦ Management of foreign exchange risk ♦ International taxation	♦ Social accounting ♦ Accounting for newer financial instruments ♦ Accounting for Mergers and acquisitions ♦ Global joint ventures ♦ Environmental and social disclosure ♦ Integration of ethics into accounting curriculum

Each of the components of international accounting dimensions as depicted in Exhibit 1.4 may be briefly discussed as follows:

Recording of Foreign Transactions

International accounting essentially begins with recording of foreign transactions. A transaction, in relation to importing, exporting, foreign borrowings and lending, and forward contracts, taking place between parties belonging to two different countries, is said to be an international (foreign) transaction. If a British firm, for example, decides to import goods from an Indian counterpart and agrees to pay in pounds, then the transaction becomes an international transaction for the Indian firm as foreign currency is involved. The same transaction does not amount to a foreign transaction for the British firm as the payment by the said firm is made by pounds, the firm's own currency. International Accounting Standard (IAS) 21 provides that 'transactions whose terms are denominated in a foreign currency or which require settlement in a foreign currency' are international (or foreign currency) transactions. IAS 21 further states that foreign currency transactions arise when an enterprise (a) buys or sells on credit goods or services whose prices are denominated in foreign currency, (b) borrows or lends funds and the amounts payable or receivable are denominated in foreign currency, (c) is a party to an unperformed foreign exchange contract, or (d) for other reasons, acquires or disposes of assets or incurs or settles liabilities denominated in foreign currency.

As far as recording of foreign transactions is concerned, two approaches–single transaction approach and the dual transaction approach are found to be popular. The date(s) of the transaction such as (i) the initial transaction date, (ii) the interim reporting date, and (iii) the settlement date too have bearings on the recording process.

Foreign Currency Translation

Foreign currency translation refers to the change in the monetary expression of the financial data contained in the financial statements. For example, figures of the balance sheet and income statement expressed in rupees when restated in dollar equivalent or in other similar foreign currency, a foreign currency translation is said to have occurred.

The need for translation of currencies arises for consolidation of financial statements of the subsidiary(ies) located in countries other than the parent's country of domicile with the financial statements of the parent company(ies). Translation is also needed in order to facilitate performance evaluation of the subsidiaries globally by restating their financial data into a common currency, i.e., the currency of the parent country. Further, translation is needed for better decision making by the stakeholders. Independent company, domiciled in one country, may also undertake translation of financial statements in a view to reaching out to the global audience of interest.

The major issues vis-à-vis steps involved in foreign currency translation are: (1) recognition and recording of foreign currency transactions, (2) recording of forward exchange contracts, (3) translation (methods) of foreign currencies, and (4) understanding the international GAAP on foreign currency translation.

Foreign Inflation

Price level changes refer to the increase or decrease in the purchasing power of money. Purchasing power, in turn, refers to the ability of a given sum of money to buy a certain amount of goods or services now in comparison to what the same sum of money could have bought at a previous date. The common manifestation of the changes in the purchasing power of money worldwide these days is the decrease in the purchasing power of money, called inflation.

Financial statements prepared as per the traditional methods are based on the basic assumption that the purchasing power of money is always stable. Given this assumption, and as long as it holds well, the financial statements prepared under the traditional (historical cost) method will provide useful and valid information to the decision makers. However, as the monetary unit does not remain stable due to inflation, the information contained in the financial statements without adjustments for inflation becomes highly distorted owing to misrepresentation of elements like cost of goods sold, depreciation, deferred expenses and purchasing power gains and losses. Generally, profit as revealed by the profit and loss account prepared under the historical cost method has a tendency to be overstated in times of rising prices (inflation). As a consequence, corporate firms lend up with, among others, paying higher taxes. Taxation of overstated profits in real term amounts to tax on capital. Financial statements too lose their credibility and interpretative benefits for overstatement of values of assets, inflated rate of return on capital, lenient distribution of dividend, higher wage payments and poor liquidity, all due to inflated profits. These reasons causing distortions to financial statements, with the associated consequences call for adjustment of financial statements against price level changes.

Consolidation of Foreign Financial Statements

Consolidation basically refers to the preparation and presentation of 'integrated financial statements', popularly known as consolidated statements, by incorporating the financial data of the subsidiary(ies), to the extent of the controlling interest, in the financial statement of the parent company in a view to giving the stakeholders information as regards the economic resources being controlled by the group. Consolidated financial statements essentially convey the results of operations and the financial position of a group companies as if they were a single economic entity regardless of any legal distinctions that exist among the separate corporate entities. The purpose of consolidation is to report to the users of the financial statement the economic resources controlled by the group and also the group's obligations.

International Accounting Standard 27 provides for the presentation of consolidated financial statements in situations where one entity controls another entity. Control is said to exist when the parent owns, directly or indirectly through subsidiaries, more than one-half of the voting power over an enterprise. It may also exist even in the absence of this level of ownership if the parent has more than one-half of the voting power as a result of a voting trust or similar arrangement; the power to govern the financial and operating policies of the enterprise by operation of law or by means of an agreement, the power to appoint or remove the majority of the directors or equivalent governing persons, or the power to cast a majority of votes at the meetings of the directors or its equivalent.

Indian Accounting Standard 21 too deals with the provisions for preparation of consolidated financial statements by parent companies except when (1) a parent acquires the controlling right in the subsidiary (through investment), which is intended to be temporary as the investment (controlling interest) is to be disposed of in the near future; and (2) the subsidiary operates under severe long term restrictions for which its ability to transfer the funds to parent is significantly weakened. It also states that consolidated financial statements are not the substitute for separate financial statements of a parent and its subsidiary(ies).

Segment and Interim Reporting

Segment reporting refers to the reporting of financial information in relation to different business activities of the firm classified as business segment or geographical segment. The bases of classification have been stipulated in International Accounting Standard 14 and also in the Indian Accounting Standard (AS) 13 which has now been replaced by Ind AS 108. The purpose of such classification and reporting is to disclose all relevant facts the non-availability of which will adversely affect the quality of investors' decisions.

Interim reporting refers to the presentation of financial statements of the enterprise covering periods of less than a full financial year. The purpose of such presentation of financial statements is to provide the decision makers with frequent and timely information for taking investment and credit decisions, based on their ability to predict full year's financial results from the interim results. IAS 34 issued by International Accounting Standards Committee (IASC) contains detailed provisions as regards interim financial reporting. The Institute of Chartered Accountants India ICAI too has issued guidelines through pronouncement of AS 25 which has now been replaced by Ind AS 34 for interim reporting by Indian firms.

Foreign Financial Statement Analysis

Financial statement analysis refers to an information processing system that is meant for providing financial data which are appropriate and useful to decision makers who are concerned with evaluating the economic situation of the firm and predicting its future course. The information in context is derived basically from the published financial statements such as the income statement and the balance sheet of the firm. Non-accounting information like stock prices and economic indicators are also used in the process of financial statement analysis. The decision makers include a variety of stakeholders prominent being the investors, creditors, employees, regulatory agencies, environmentalists, social activists, researchers, and the management itself. Investors, for example, are concerned with portfolio decisions; creditors for determining the firm's creditworthiness; and employees for establishing economic bases for collective bargaining. The regulatory and policy formulating bodies of the state are interested in 'controlling' decisions; environmentalists and social activists on 'social accounting' issues; researchers for studying firm vis-à-vis industry behaviour; and the management for evaluating the operational and financial efficiency of the firm and its subunits.

The purpose of financial statement analysis, as stated above, from the users or decision makers' perspective, be it a domestic company or a foreign company is the same. Therefore, the tools used for analyzing the financial statements of domestic company and for the MNCs would be basically the same. The most widely used techniques of financial statement analysis are: vertical or common-size analysis and ratio analysis. A few modern techniques like the Economic Value Added (EVA), Market Value Added (MVA) and Multiple Discriminate Analysis (MDA) are also used for effective analysis of the financial statements. The choice and use of any or all of these techniques would depend on the analyst's own objective and the terms of reference.

Budgeting and Performance Evaluation

Firms use budgeting and performance evaluation as tools for strategic planning and control. For multinational corporations it is essential that these budgeting and performance evaluation tools are chosen appropriately so as to fit to the environment of the country(ies) of their own domicile and also of the foreign country(ies). The budget should be prepared in a manner as would lead to employees' motivation and goal congruence between the employees and the organization. Performance evaluation should also be appropriately designed keeping in view the domestic and the international environment in which the subsidiaries and affiliates operate. 'If the budget is to motivate the employees and to help create goal congruence between the employees and organization, then it must set appropriate criteria and provide reasonable targets for the employees to attain. Along with all the budgeting and performance evaluation issues that organization must contend with in the purely domestic context, there are additional considerations that must be factored into designing budget and performance evaluation systems for subsidiaries and affiliated entities located in other countries'. [9]

Transfer Pricing

Transfer pricing relates to the pricing of goods and services that change hands between entities engaged in inter-firm trade. Transfer price is the price at which goods or services are transferred between affiliated entities within an organization. IAS 14 on segment reporting defines transfer pricing as 'the pricing of products or services between industry segments or geographic areas'. The term transfer price is more popular among multinational corporations than the domestic firms for transfer of materials, parts or finished products and services.

The need for transfer pricing system arises primarily to communicate data that will lead to goal-congruent decisions. Appropriate evaluation of segment vis-à-vis managerial performance and avoidance of foreign currency restrictions and quotas, minimization of taxes and tariffs, minimization of exchange risks, avoidance of profit repatriation restrictions and enhancement of shares of profits in joint ventures are some of the other important objectives which are accomplished through transfer pricing mechanism.

The methods used for transfer pricing are cost-based prices, market-based prices and negotiated prices.

Exchange Risk Management

Exchange risk management aims at monitoring and managing the firm's foreign exchange exposure so as to maximize its profitability, cash flow and market value. Foreign exchange exposure primarily assumes three forms: Translation exposure, transaction exposure, and economic exposure.

Translation exposure refers to the potential of an increase or decrease in the parent company's net worth and reported net income due to fluctuations in the exchange rates. In contrast, transaction exposure arises due to sensitivity of the firm's contractual cash flows denominated in foreign currency to exchange rate fluctuations.

Translation exposure arises from (1) buying and selling on credit goods or services whose prices are contractually denominated in foreign currency, (2) borrowing and lending funds in foreign currency, (3) forward exchange contracts, (4) acquisition or disposal of assets denominated in foreign currency, and (5) settlement of liabilities denominated in foreign currency.

Economic exposure refers to the extent to which the value of the firm would be impacted by unexpected changes in the exchange rates. The managerial efforts to manage economic exposure would be to formulate long-term strategies so as to enhance and preserve its value in the event of unexpected exchange rate fluctuations.

International Taxation

International taxation is a complex phenomenon that affects all aspects of multinational operations including foreign investments, transfer pricing, marketing of product and services, cost of capital and capital structure. It is, therefore, imperative for multinational corporations in particular to understand the diversities that exist in relation to corporate tax laws in different countries for better (tax) planning and decision making.

Accounting for Newer Financial Instruments

Newer financial instruments such as derivatives have become more popular in recent years. As defined by IAS 39, a derivative is a financial instrument which has the following characteristics:

1. Its value changes in response to the change in a specified interest rate, security price, commodity price, foreign exchange rate, index of prices or rates, a credit rating or credit index, or similar variable called the underlying.
2. It requires no initial net investment or little initial net investment relative to other types of contracts that have a similar response to changes in market conditions.
3. It is settled at a future date.

Derivatives in general are of four types: Option, swap, futures and forward. Options can be of call or put options in the form of bond option, purchased or written currency option, purchased or written commodity option and purchased or written stock option. Swaps can be of interest rate swap, currency swap, commodity swap, equity swap, credit swap and total return swap. Futures may take the form of treasury futures (i.e., interest rate futures linked to government debt), currency futures and commodity futures; and forward may be in the form of treasury forward, currency forward, commodity forward and equity forward.

Global Joint Venture

IAS 31 deals with the accounting procedure of investments in joint ventures. For accounting purposes, joint ventures have been classified as jointly controlled operations, jointly controlled assets, and jointly controlled entities. IAS 31 prescribes for distinct set of reporting and disclosure guidelines in respect of each of the three kinds of joint ventures.

Environmental Disclosures

Environmental disclosures by companies have increasingly become a matter of interest not only to the environmentalists but also to stakeholders like the investors, employees, customers, regulatory agencies and the society at large. Major environmental disasters of the recent past and the government regulations in certain countries such as the USA have further necessitated for corporate environmental reporting. The nature and extent of environmental disclosures however vary from country to country depending upon the strength of the country's own environmental regulations and the pressure exerted by the stakeholders. Few companies, in a bid to be good corporate citizen and also to meet the expectations of the stakeholders have nevertheless demonstrated greater environmental disclosures. Others need to follow the suit. 'As various constituents, including investors, demand greater disclosure of companies' environmental impact and any resulting liabilities, companies will have to take this aspect of financial disclosure more seriously. In deed there is evidence that a number of companies are already beginning to do just that' [10].

Social Disclosure

Social disclosure primarily aims at informing the general public about the social welfare measures taken by the firm and their effects on the society. The firm's ability and success in discharging social obligations also gets reflected in the process of social disclosure.

Public enterprises in India like the Bharat Heavy Electrical Ltd. (BHEL), Steel Authority of India Ltd. (SAIL), and Oil and Natural Gas Corporation (ONGC) Ltd. have been publishing social income statement and social balance sheet, over and above the conventional and statutory financial reports, for the use of the stakeholders. The social income statement discloses information as regards (1) net social income to employees, (2) net social income to community, and (3) net social income to general public. The social balance sheet reports (1) the organization's equity, and (2) the social equity contribution by the employees as the total liabilities, and (1) social capital investments, (2) other social assets and (3) human assets as the total assets. Exhibit 1.5-A and 1.5-B contain the format of and the list of items generally included in the social income statement and social balance sheet as found in vogue.

EXHIBIT 1.5-A Social Income Statement

Particulars	*This year (₹)*	*Previous year (₹)*
I. Social Benefits and Costs to Staff		
A *Social Benefits to Staff:*		
1. Medical and hospital facilities	—	—
2. Educational facilities	—	—
3. Canteen facilities	—	—
4. Recreation, entertainment and cultural activities	—	—
5. Housing and township facilities	—	—
6. Water supply, concessional electricity and transport	—	—
7. Training and career development	—	—
8. Provident fund, gratuity, bonus, insurance benefits	—	—
9. Holiday, leave encashment and leave-travel benefits	—	—
10. Other benefits		
Total benefits to Staff	—	—
B. *Social Costs to Staff:*		
1. Lay off and involuntary termination	—	—
2. Extra hours put in by officers voluntarily	—	—
Total cost of staff	—	—
Net social income to staff-I (A–B)	—	—
II. Social Benefits & Cost to Community		
A. *Social Benefits to Community*		
1. Local taxes paid to panchayat/municipality	—	—
2. Environmental improvements	—	—
3. Generation of job potential	—	—
4. Generation of business		
Total social benefits to community	—	—

Particulars	*This year* (₹)	*Previous year* (₹)
B. *Social Costs to Community:*		
Increase in cost of living in the firm's Vicinity	—	—
Net social income to community-II (A–B)	—	—
III. Social Benefits and Costs to General Public		
A. *Social Benefits to General Public:*		
1. Taxes, duties, etc. paid to the state governments	—	—
2. Taxes, duties, etc. paid to the central government	—	—
Total benefits to general public	—	—
B. *Social Costs to General Public:*		
1. State services consumed:		
Electricity services	—	—
2. Central services consumed:		
Telephone, telegrams, postal services and banking	—	—
Total social benefits to general public-III(A–B)	—	—
Net Social Income to Staff Community and General Public (I+II+III)	—	—

Source: Public Interest Accounting, RBSA (India), pp. 86–88.

EXHIBIT 1.5-B Social Balance Sheet

Liabilities	₹		Assets	₹	
	As at 31-3-	As at 31-3-		As at 31-3-	As at 31-3-
(I) Organization Equity	—	—	(I) Social Capital Investment	—	—
(II) Social Equity Contribution by staff	—	—	(1) Township land	—	—
			(2) Buildings		
			(i) Residential and welfare buildings	—	—
			(ii) Canteen buildings	—	—
			(3) Township water supply and sewerage		
			(4) Township-roads	—	
			(5) Township-electrification -	—	
			(II) Other social Assets		
			(1) Hospital equipment	—	—
			(2) Hospital vehicle/ Ambulance	—	—
			(3) School equipments	—	—
			(4) Club equipments	—	—
			(5) Playground/park	—	—
			(6) School buses	—	—
			(7) Others	—	—
Total	—	—	Total	—	—

Source: Public Interest Accounting, RBSA (India), p. 88.

Like environmental disclosure, social disclosure too has become imperative for companies especially the MNCs for owning the confidence of investors and other stakeholders.

IMPORTANCE OF INTERNATIONAL ACCOUNTING

The importance of International accounting lies with its advantages. The advantages associated with international accounting are as follows:

1. It facilitates achieving harmonization of accounting practices across nations.
2. It helps reaching out to global investors.
3. It helps taking informed decisions.
4. It helps mobilizing global resources.
5. It helps establishing uniformity in global financial reporting and disclosures practices.
6. It helps professionalization of accounting education world over.
7. It helps inculcating ethics and transparency into accounting practices.

DIFFICULTIES IN INTERNATIONAL ACCOUNTING

The major difficulties associated with international accounting are its operational complexities and diversities owing to the socio-economic, political, cultural, technological and perceptual differences that exist among nations worldwide. The nature and extent of these diversities vary not only across countries but also from trivial to sustentative in terms of intensity. Trivial differences are for example what is called sales in the US is turnover in the UK. A major difference in terms of accounting philosophy is found in Germany where, among others, the emphasis is laid on 'creditor's protection' and accordingly the accounting reporting. 'German accounting is heavily influenced by the desire to protect creditors, and income taxes in Germany are based primarily on externally reported accounting profit, so there are strong legal and economic pressures to report income and asset values conservatively. Consequently, German accounting standards require that allowances be made for all possible losses. Since virtually anything can be deemed possible, management has considerable flexibility when determining the appropriate allowance' [11].

Exhibit 1.6 and Exhibit 1.7 which have been constructed based on the work of Leftwich [12] 'on contrasts in accounting philosophy' and 'accounting treatments across the globe' amply demonstrate the prevalent diversities in world accounting.

EXHIBIT 1.6 Contrasts in accounting philosophy

	On the one hand	*On the other*
Primary purpose of external financing reporting	Provide information to stockholders (e.g. US and UK).	Protect creditors; guard against reporting information that will harm the company competitively (e.g. Japan and Germany).
Guidance provided by standards	Very specific operational and implementation details (e.g. US).	Broad principles only, allowing management considerable discretion for many transactions (e.g. Japan and Germany).
Topics covered by standards	Specific individual standards provide extensive coverage of major and minor business activities, including, for example how to account for the costs of modifying computer software to cope with the year 2000 (US).	No specific individual standards for some major business activities (e.g. post employment health benefits in Canada, Germany and Netherlands).

	On the one hand	On the other
Relationship to income tax laws	External reporting and tax reporting based on such different rules that there are essentially two sets of books (e.g. Australia, Canada, US and Netherlands).	Income taxes based heavily on externally reported income (e.g. Germany, France and UK).
Reporting frequency	Quarterly (US, Canada, Mexico and Israel).	Semi-annually (UK, France, Netherlands, Germany and Japan).
Disclosure of accounting adjustments (transparency)	Extensive footnote and narrative discussion of: choices and applications of accounting methods, estimation techniques, transfers to and from reserves and provisions, and other accounting adjusting entries (e.g. Australia, New Zealand, US, Canada, and UK).	Considerable aggregation of asset and liability classes, few footnotes, and, at most, cryptic comments about: how accounting standards are applied, transfers to and from reserves, and the basis for various accounting adjustments (e.g. France, Japan, Germany and Switzerland).
Charges against owners' equity	Clean surplus – virtually all charges, including the cumulative effects of changes in accounting choices, must flow through the income statement (e.g. US and, with more exceptions, the UK).	No clean surplus – some charges, especially those associated with the prior-period effect of changes in accounting methods, can be made directly against retained earnings (e.g. Germany).

EXHIBIT 1.7 Accounting treatments across the globe

Event or transaction	Range of alternatives
Asset revaluation	Allowed (Australia, Hong Kong, India, UK) Allowed under some circumstances (France, Italy, Sweden) Not allowed (Canada, Germany, Japan, US).
Funds statement	Report sources and uses of cash (US, UK, Israel, Korea) Report sources and uses of working capital (Mexico, Sweden, Singapore) Not required (France, Germany, Netherlands, Switzerland).
Inflation accounting	Required (Argentina, Brazil, Israel, Mexico) Optional supplementary information (UK, Australia, Netherlands, US) Not required (Canada, Indonesia, Japan, Germany, Korea).
Goodwill	Capitalize and write-off against owners' equity (Italy, Singapore, South Africa and UK) Capitalize and write-off through income statement (Australia, Canada, France, US).
Research and development costs	Expense (US, Germany, Mexico) Capitalize (Argentina, Korea, Norway, Netherlands) Capitalize Development Costs, Expense Research (UK, Canada, Denmark, Israel, Nigeria) Not specified (China, Ireland).
Segment reporting	Sales, profits, and assets by industry and geographic segment (Canada, UK, Israel, Italy and Singapore) Sales by industry and geographic segment (France, Germany, Belgium, Netherlands) Sales and profits by industry (Korea) Not specified ((India, Indonesia, Norway, and Switzerland).

(Contd.)

Event or transaction	Range of alternatives
Non-operating leases	Capitalization required (Belgium, Hong Kong, Israel, US) Capitalization optional, or allowed under highly specific circumstances (Denmark, Sweden, France, Japan) Expense (India, Italy).
Other post-employment benefits	Accrue expenses (Indonesia, Nigeria, UK, US) Cash basis (Australia, Germany, Hong Kong, Japan)
Pension plans	Recognize unfunded liability (US, Mexico) Ignore unfunded liability (Canada, Germany, Netherlands, UK) Not specified (Hong Kong, New Zealand, Belgium).

SUMMARY

Accounting is aptly called as the language of business. It is through accounting that a business communicates to its stakeholders. Accounting acts as the basic source of information for business and economic decisions. The important categories of information contained in accounting are operating information, financial accounting information, management accounting information and tax accounting information.

With the increasing pace of globalization and economic liberalization particularly towards the end of twentieth century, executives are called upon to make decisions based on financial information originating from other countries. These decisions range from evaluating the performance of foreign subsidiary (ies), affiliates, joint ventures, to making credit decisions on customers belonging to other countries, and making investing and financing decisions based on opportunities in other countries. Since countries have their own set of socio-economic, political, legal, cultural, technological and linguistic environment, financial reporting diversities are quite eminent. With diverse financial reports in hand, the decision makers find it difficult to making effective decisions. To overcome this difficulty and to have a more uniform and harmonized financial reporting across the globe, the concept of 'international accounting' has gained momentum.

International accounting refers to that branch of accounting which deals with the recording and translation of foreign transactions, preparation and presentation of consolidated foreign financial statements, and presentation of international financial reporting in accordance with international GAAP and auditing practices.

The scope of international accounting ranges from recording of foreign transactions to foreign currency translation, adjustment of foreign financial statements against inflation, consolidation of foreign financial statements, financial reporting and disclosure, segment reporting, multinational transfer pricing, international budgeting, performance evaluation of subsidiaries, foreign exchange risk management, international taxation, analysis of foreign financial statements, accounting for newer financial instruments such as derivatives, international joint ventures, environmental accounting, and integration of ethics into accounting.

International accounting has both advantages and limitations. Its major advantages relate to achieving harmonization of accounting practices across nations, reaching out to global investors, making informed decisions, mobilizing global resources, establishing uniformity in global financial reporting and disclosures practices, professionalizing accounting education world over and inculcating ethics and transparency into accounting practices. Its limitation lie with effect that a uniform accounting practices world over is difficult if not impossible due to the presence of socio-economic, political, cultural, technological and perceptual differences among nations.

KEY TERMS

International accounting: International accounting may be defined as that branch of accounting which deals with the recording and translation of foreign transactions, preparation and presentation of consolidated foreign financial statements, and presentation of international financial reporting in accordance with international GAAP and auditing practices.

Foreign currency translation: Foreign currency translation refers to the change in the monetary expression of the financial data contained in the financial statements.

Transfer pricing: Transfer pricing relates to the pricing of goods and services that change hands between entities engaged in inter-firm trade.

Segment reporting: Segment reporting refers to the reporting of financial information in relation to different business activities of the firm classified as business segment or geographical segment.

Exchange risk management: Exchange risk management aims at monitoring and managing the firm's foreign exchange exposure so as to maximize its profitability, cash flow and market value. Foreign exchange exposure primarily assumes three forms: Translation exposure, transaction exposure and economic exposure.

Translation exposure: Translation exposure refers to the potential of an increase or decrease in the parent company's net worth and reported net income due to fluctuations in the exchange rates.

Transaction exposure: Transaction exposure arises due to sensitivity of the firm's contractual cash flows denominated in foreign currency to exchange rate fluctuations. It arises from (1) buying and selling on credit goods or services whose prices are contractually denominated in foreign currency, (2) borrowing and lending funds in foreign currency, (3) forward exchange contracts, (4) acquisition or disposal of assets denominated in foreign currency, and (5) settlement of liabilities denominated in foreign currency.

Economic exposure: Economic exposure refers to the extent to which the value of the firm would be impacted by unexpected changes in the exchange rates. The managerial efforts to manage economic exposure would be to formulate long-term strategies so as to enhance and preserve its value in the event of unexpected exchange rate fluctuations.

Social disclosure: Social disclosure primarily aims at informing the general public about the social welfare measures taken by the firm and their effects on the society. The firm's ability and success in discharging social obligations also gets reflected in the process of social disclosure.

REVIEW QUESTIONS

1. Define International Accounting and discuss its significance especially in the context of modern business.
2. Discuss the factors that have contributed to the development of international accounting. Which of these factors, in your opinion, can be considered as the most influential and why?
3. Discuss the scope of international accounting. Cite example(s) to supplement your answer.
4. What do you mean by international dimensions of accounting? Discuss the impediments for internationalization of the accounting profession.
5. State the importance of 'International Accounting' in recent years. Discuss the financial accounting aspects of 'International Accounting'.
6. Write a detailed note on corporate social reporting. Why corporate social reporting became so important these days?
7. State and explain the difficulties encountered in international accounting practices. Suggest measures to overcome these difficulties.
8. Explain the need for international accounting.
9. 'Even though international business has been conducted for centuries, it has become truly significant in terms of its importance in the twentieth century' – Comment.
10. Discuss the reasons as to why accounting practices differ among individual nations. Do you subscribe to the continuation of these differences? Justify your views.
11. Given the ongoing economic policy changes in India which dimension(s) of the International accounting, in your opinion, is/ are going to be affected and how? Explain.
12. Write explanatory notes on:
    (a) Social Income Statement
    (b) Social Balance Sheet
    (c) Exchange risk management
    (d) Social disclosure
13. Critically examine the role of International accounting in establishing harmony in accounting practices across nations.
14. 'With increased globalization of business and economy, International accounting has become a necessity'—Do you agree. Justify your answer.
15. 'The advantages of international accounting outplays its limitations' – Ilucidate.

REFERENCES

[1] Samuels, J.M. and Piper, A.G., *International Accounting: A Survey*, Croom Helm Ltd., London, 1985.

[2] Choi, F.D.S. and Mueller, G.G., *Essentials of Multinational Accounting: An Anthology*, Ann Arbor, Michigan, 1979.

[3] Choi, F.D.S. and Mueller, G.G., *International Accounting, 2nd Ed.*, Prentice-Hall Inc., Englewood Cliffs, NJ, 1992.

[4] Evans, T.G., Taylor, M.E. and Holzmann, O., *International Accounting and Reporting*, McMillan, NY, 1985.

[5] Shirin, R., *International Accounting*, PHI Learning, New Delhi, 1996.

[6] https://www.statista.com/statistics/264682/worldwide-export-volume-in-the-trade-since-1950/

[7] NSE Fact Book, 1997.

[8] https://unctad.org, 'Global investment flows flat in 2019, moderate increase is expected in 2020'.

[9] Saudagaran, S.M., *International Accounting—A User Perspective*, Taxman India, 2001, p. 192.

[10] Beets, S.D. and Souther, C.C., *Corporate environmental reports: The Need for Standard and an Environmental Assurance Service*, Accounting Horizon, 13(2): 129–145 (1999).

[11] Leftwich, R., *International Accounting Standards*, *Mastering Finance*, Pearson, p. 103.

[12] Ibid, pp.102-4.

E-resources

https://www.statista.com/statistics/264682/worldwide-export-volume-in-the-trade-since-1950/

http://hbs.unctad.org/foreign-direct-investment/

https://cleartax.in/s/applicability-ind-as

2

Foreign Currency Translation

LEARNING OBJECTIVES

After Studying this chapter, you will be able to:

- Define foreign currency transaction and translation
- Appreciate the need for and the issues involved in foreign currency translation
- Know the process of recording foreign (international) transactions
- Know the accounting treatment of forward exchange contracts
- Understand the techniques of foreign currency translations
- Know the treatment of translation gains and losses
- Comprehend the International, Indian and US GAAP on foreign currency translation

INTRODUCTION

Translation in the context of foreign currency refers to the change in the monetary expression of the financial data contained in the financial statements. For example, figures of the balance sheet and income statement expressed in rupees when restated in dollar equivalent or in similar other foreign currency, a *translation* is said to have occurred. Translation does not result in physical exchange of currencies. Physical exchange of one currency with another is termed as conversion.

NEED FOR TRANSLATION

Translation of currencies is required for *consolidation* of financial statements of the subsidiaries located in countries other than the parent company(ies) country(ies) of domicile with the financial statements of the parent companies. Multinational corporations while preparing consolidated financial statements translate the figures of the financial statements of the subsidiary(ies) into units of common currency depending upon the location of the multinational corporations concerned. For example, figures of the financial statements of an Indian subsidiary denominated in 'Rupees' are expressed in equivalent Yen, under the process of translation, given that the MNC is a Japanese company.

Translation is also needed in order to facilitate *performance evaluation* of the subsidiaries globally by restating their financial data into a common currency, i.e., the currency of the parent's country.

Translation too is needed for *better decision making* by the stakeholders such as the investors and the management. This is because fluctuations in exchange rates, called the currency gyrations, have the potential of increasing or decreasing the reporting firm's net worth and the profits due to exchange gains and losses. It is by virtue of translation that a true and fair view of the financial performance of the reporting firm could be possible which would aid to effective decision making.

Independent company, domiciled in one country, may also undertake translation of financial statements in a view to reaching out to global audience of interest. This is particularly true in the context of globalization and economic liberalization where firms are looking for foreign investments.

ISSUES IN FOREIGN CURRENCY TRANSLATION

The important issues involved in foreign currency translation are:

1. International transactions and their recording.
2. Forward exchange contracts and their recording.
3. Diversity in the translation methods.
4. International GAAP on foreign currency translation.

International Transaction

A transaction, in relation to importing, exporting, foreign borrowings and lending, and forward contracts, taking place between parties belonging to two different countries, is said to be an international (foreign) transaction. If a British firm, for example, decides to import goods from an Indian counterpart and agrees to pay in £, then the transaction becomes an international transaction for the Indian firm as foreign currency is involved. The same transaction does not amount to a foreign transaction for the British firm as the payment by the said firm is made by £, the firm's own currency.

Foreign currency transactions as defined under IAS 21 are 'transactions whose terms are denominated in a foreign currency or which require settlement in a foreign currency'. Foreign currency transactions arise when an enterprise:

(a) buys or sells on credit goods or services whose prices are denominated in foreign currency,

(b) borrows or lends funds and the amounts payable or receivable are denominated in foreign currency,

(c) is a party to an unperformed foreign exchange contract, or

(d) for other reasons, acquires or disposes of assets or incurs or settles liabilities denominated in foreign currency.

Recording of Foreign (International) Transactions

Recording of foreign transactions depends on two broad issues:

1. The date(s) of the transaction such as (i) the initial transaction date, (ii) the interim reporting date, and (iii) the settlement date; and
2. The recording methods such as (i) the single transaction approach, and (ii) dual transaction approach. Exhibit 2.1 contains the profile of these issues.

EXHIBIT 2.1 Issues affecting recording of foreign transactions

Date of transaction			*Recording approaches*	
Date of initiation	*Interim date of reporting*	*Date of settlement*	*Single transaction approach*	*Dual transaction approach*
It is the date on which the transaction was first initiated between the parties.	It is the date on which either or all the parties to the transactions report its (their) financial and operating results.	It is the date on which the transaction referred to under the date of initiation is settled.	It is based on the assumption that a transaction and its subsequent settlement are a single event. Accordingly, difference due to exchange rate fluctuations are credited to the cost of goods purchased or to an export sale.	It is based on the assumption that foreign exchange involved in an international transaction is separate from that of the cost of goods purchased or sold. Accordingly, the losses or gains due to fluctuations in exchange rates are treated separately by opening a loss (or gain) on foreign exchange account, keeping the goods purchased or sold recorded at the prevailing rate of exchange on the date of such purchase or sale.

Journal Entries: As stated before, journal entries for recording foreign transactions, in the books of the buyer, can be made by adopting *either the single transaction approach* or *the dual transaction approach.* The journal entries made for recording foreign transactions under the single transaction approach has been given in Exhibit 2.2-A.

EXHIBIT 2.2-A Recording of foreign transactions in the books of the buyer under the single transaction approach

Date and nature of transaction	*Journal entries*	
Date of initiation (i.e., the date on which goods are purchased on credit)	Purchase A/c To Accounts payable/Supplier's A/c (Quantity purchased *multiplied* by the exchange rate prevailing on the date of purchase)	Dr

Date and nature of transaction	*Journal entries*	
Interim date of reporting, (i.e., the date on which the accounting year of the buying firm ends)	Purchases A/c To Accounts payable/Supplier's A/c (Quantity multiplied by the difference between the exchange rate on the interim date and the date of initial transaction)	Dr
Settlement date (i.e., the date on which actual payment is made to settle the account)	Inventories A/c To Accounts payable/Supplier's A/c (Quantity multiplied by additional change in the exchange rate between settlement date and interim date)	Dr
	Accounts payable/Supplier's A/c To Cash/Bank (For settling the payment)	Dr

Similarly, journal entries made for recording foreign transactions under the dual transaction approach has been given in Exhibit 2.2-B as under:

EXHIBIT 2.2-B Recording of foreign transactions in the books of the buyer under the dual transaction approach

Date and nature of transaction	*Journal entries*	
Date of initiation (i.e., the date on which goods are purchased on credit)	Purchase A/c To Accounts payable/Supplier's A/c (Quantity purchased *multiplied* by the exchange rate prevailing on the date of purchase)	Dr
Interim date of reporting, (i.e., the date on which the accounting year of the buying firm ends)	Loss on foreign exchange A/c To Accounts payable/Supplier's A/c (Quantity multiplied by the difference between the exchange rate on the interim date and the date of initial transaction) *Note:* Reverse will be the entry for gain on foreign exchange	Dr
Settlement date (i.e., the date on which actual payment is made to settle the account)	Loss on foreign exchange A/c To Accounts payable/Supplier's A/c (Quantity multiplied by additional change in the exchange rate between settlement date and interim date)	Dr.
	Accounts payable/Supplier's A/c To Cash/Bank (Quantity multiplied by exchange rate prevailing on the date of settlement)	Dr

ILLUSTRATION 2.1

On 1st February, 2023, Horizon Green Ltd., an Indian firm, purchased goods worth £ 5,000 from M/s Straw and Straw of UK, on a 3 months term. Horizon Green Ltd. closes its account on 31st March every year.

If the exchange rate per 1 £ remained at ₹100.00, ₹100.25 and ₹100.55 respectively on 1st February, 2023, on 31st March, 2023 and on 1st May, 2023, how will you record the above transactions in the books of Horizon Green Ltd. under (i) the single transaction approach, and (ii) the dual transaction approach?

SOLUTION

(i) Recording under single transaction approach: As already mentioned in Exhibit 2.1, the single transaction approach is based on the assumption that a transaction and its subsequent settlement are a single event. Therefore, differences due to exchange rate fluctuations are credited to the cost of goods purchased or to an export sale. Accordingly, the journal entries to the given transactions in the books of Horizon Green Ltd. will be as follows:

Journal entries in the Books of Horizon Green Ltd. under the single transaction approach

Date	*Particulars*		*L/f*	*Dr* (₹)	*Cr* (₹)
01.02.2023	Purchase A/c	Dr		5,00,000	
	To Straw & Straw A/c				5,00,000
	(Being goods worth £ 5000 purchased on credit recorded at ₹100/£, i.e., £ 5000 × ₹100)				
31.03.2023	Purchase A/c	Dr		1,250	
	To Straw & Straw A/c				1,250
	(Being the change in initial exchange rate of ₹ 0.25 recorded, i.e., £ 5000 × ₹ 0.25)				
01.05.2023	Inventories A/c	Dr		1,500	
	To Straw & Straw A/c				1,500
	(Being further change in exchange rate recorded, i.e., £ 5000 × (₹100.55 – ₹100.25)				
01.05.2023	Straw & Straw A/c	Dr		5,02,750	
	To Cash/Bank A/c				5,02,750
	(Being the payment made i.e., £ 5000 @ ₹100.55 settled)				

Note: Under the single transaction approach, the initial transaction is recorded on the date of initiation, i.e., on 1st February, 2023. On the date on which the company closes its books of account, called the interim reporting date, i.e., 31st March, 2023 in case of Horizon Green Ltd, the carrying value of the goods is increased and so also the corresponding liability since the exchange rate has increased from ₹100.00/£ to ₹100.25/£. On the settlement date, i.e., on 31.05.2023, the exchange rate has further increased from ₹100.25/£ to ₹100.55/£ and hence the carrying value of the goods and the corresponding liability has been further increased. Similar will be the process for recording a transaction of sale where the value of sales will be proportionately increased.

(ii) Recording under dual transaction approach: It has already been stated in Exhibit 2.1 that the dual transaction approach is based on the assumption that foreign exchange involved in an international transaction is separate from that of the cost of goods purchased (or sold). As such the losses or gains on account of fluctuations in exchange rates are treated separately by opening a 'loss (or gain) on foreign exchange account', keeping the goods purchased or sold recorded at the prevailing rate of exchange on the date of such purchase or sale. Further the loss or gain on foreign exchange would appear in the income statement separately at the end of the year.

The entries **under dual transaction** approach shall therefore be as follows:

Journal entries in the Books of Horizon Green Ltd.under the dual transaction approach

Date	*Particulars*		*L/f*	*Dr (₹)*	*Cr (₹)*
01.02.2023	Purchase A/c To Straw & Straw A/c (Being goods purchased recorded at £ 5000 × ₹100)	Dr		5,00,000	 5,00,000
31.03.2023	Loss on foreign exchange A/c To Straw and Straw A/c (Being the increase in initial exchange rate recorded, i.e., £ 5000 × (₹100.25 – ₹100)	Dr		1,250	 1,250
01.05.2023	Loss on foreign exchange A/c To Straw and Straw A/c (Being further loss transferred, i.e., £ 5000 × (₹100.55 – ₹100.25)	Dr		1,500	 1,500
01.05.2023	Straw & Straw A/c To Cash/Bank A/c (Being the payment settled, i.e., £ 5000 × ₹100.55 paid)	Dr		5,02,750	 5,02,750

Note: Like the single transaction approach, under dual transaction approach too recordings are made corresponding to the date of initial transaction, date of interim reporting and the date of settlement. The exchange rate loss (or gain) however does not increase or decrease the cost of goods purchased and instead the cost of goods purchased continues to maintain its individuality, and so also the loss or gain due to fluctuations in the exchange rates.

ILLUSTRATION 2.2

Dolphin India Ltd. which closes its books of account on 31st March every year purchased goods from Wheels International Ltd. of Australia on 30.01.2023 amounting to Australian dollar (AUD) 12,000 on a four months term. The exchange rate of 1 AUD has been as follows:

30.01.2023 1 AUD = ₹43.00

31.03.2023 1 AUD = ₹43.45

30.05.2023 1 AUD = ₹43.75

How will the transactions be recorded in the books of Dolphin India Ltd. under (a) the single transaction approach, and (b) the dual transaction approach?

SOLUTION

(a) Journal entries in the books of Dolphin India Ltd. under the single transaction approach

Date	Particulars		L/f	Dr (₹)	Cr (₹)
30.01.2023	Purchase A/c To Wheels International Ltd. A/c (Being goods worth AUD 12,000 purchased @ ₹43/AUD	Dr		5,16,000	 5,16,000
31.03.2023	Purchase A/c To Wheels International Ltd. A/c (Being the increase in exchange rate recorded, i.e., AUD 12,000 × ₹0.45)	Dr		5,400	 5,400
30.05.2023	Inventories A/c To Wheels International Ltd. A/c (Being further increase in exchange rate recorded, i.e, AUD 12,000 × ₹0.30)	Dr		3,600	 3,600
30.05.2023	Wheels International Ltd. A/c To Cash/Bank A/c (Being the payment settled, i.e., AUD 12,000 × ₹43.75 paid)	Dr		5,25,000	 5,25,000

(b) Journal entries in the books of Dolphin India Ltd. under the dual transaction approach

Date	Particulars		L/f	Dr (₹)	Cr (₹)
30.01.2023	Purchase A/c To Wheels International Ltd. A/c (Being goods purchased recorded, i.e., AUD 12,000 purchased @ ₹43/AUD	Dr		5,16,000	 5,16,000
31.03.2023	Loss on foreign exchange A/c To Wheels International Ltd. A/c (Being the increase in initial exchange rate recorded, i.e., AUD 12,000 × ₹0.45)	Dr		5,400	 5,400
30.05.2023	Loss on foreign exchange A/c To Wheels International Ltd. A/c (Being further increase in exchange rate recorded, i.e., AUD 12,000 × ₹ 0.30)	Dr		3,600	 3,600
30.05.2023	Wheels International Ltd. A/c To Cash/Bank A/c (Being the payment settled, i.e., AUD 12,000 × ₹43.75 paid)	Dr		5,16,000	 5,16,000

ILLUSTRATION 2.3

SystemsZ India Ltd. procured goods worth 10,000 Singapore Dollar (SGD) from Informatics Universal Ltd. of Singapore on 25.01.2023 on a two months term. On 30.01.2023, SystemsZ India Ltd. also purchased goods worth 10,000 USD on a three months term from Robinson Inc. of the USA. The exchange rates of 1 SGD and 1 USD were as follows:

Date	*SGD against INR*	*USD against INR*
25.01.2023	1 SGD= ₹52.00	1 $ = ₹76.50
30.01.2023	1 SGD= ₹52.20	1 $ = ₹76.60
25.03.2023	1 SGD = ₹52.35	1 $ = ₹76.75
31.03.2023	1 SGD = ₹52.50	1 $ = ₹76.85
30.04.2023	1 SGD = ₹52.60	1 $ = ₹76.95

You are required to record the above transactions in the books of SystemsZ India Ltd. under (1) the single transaction approach and (2) the dual transaction approach, assuming that SystemsZ India Ltd. closes its books of account on 31st March every year.

SOLUTION

(1) Journal entries in the Books of SystemsZ India Ltd. under the single transaction approach

Date	*Particulars*	*L/f*	*Dr (₹)*	*Cr. (₹)*
25.01.2023	Purchase A/c Dr To Informatics Universal Ltd. A/c (Being goods purchased from Informatics Universal Ltd recorded, i.e., 10,000 SGD × ₹52)		5,20,000	 5,20,000
30.01.2023	Purchase A/c Dr To Robinson Inc. A/c (Being goods purchased from Robinson Inc. recorded, i.e.,10,000 $ × ₹76.60)		7,66,000	 7,66,000
25.03.2023	Purchase A/c Dr To Informatics Universal Ltd. A/c (Being the increase in exchange rate recorded, i.e., 10,000 SGD × ₹0.35)		3,500	 3,500
25.03.2023	Informatics Universal Ltd. A/c Dr To Cash/Bank A/c (Being amount due paid, i.e., 10,000 SGD × ₹52.35)		5,23,500	 5,23,500
31.03.2023	Purchase A/c Dr To Robinson Inc. A/c (Being increase in exchange rate recorded, i.e., 10,000 $ × ₹0.25)		2,500	 2,500
30.04.2023	Inventories A/c Dr To Robinson Inc. A/c (Being further increase in exchange rate recorded, i.e., 10,000 $ × ₹ 0.10		1,000	 1,000
30.04.2023	Robinson Inc. A/c Dr To Cash/Bank A/c (Being the amount due paid, i.e., 10,000 $ × ₹76.95)		7,69,500	 7,69,500

(2) Journal entries in the books of SystemsZ India Ltd. under the dual transaction approach

Date	*Particulars*		*L/f*	*Dr (₹)*	*Cr. (₹)*
25.01.2023	Purchase A/c	Dr		5,20,000	
	To Informatics Universal Ltd. A/c				5,20,000
	(Being goods purchased from Informatics Universal Ltd. recorded, i.e., 10,000 SGD × ₹52)				
30.01.2023	Purchase A/c	Dr		7,66,000	
	To Robinson Inc. A/c				7,66,000
	(Being goods purchased from Robinson Inc. recorded, i.e.,10,000 $ × ₹76.60)				
25.03.2023	Loss on foreign exchange A/c	Dr		3,500	
	To Informatics Universal Ltd. A/c				3,500
	(Being the increase in exchange rate recorded, i.e., 10,000 SGD × ₹0.35)				
25.03.2023	Informatics Universal Ltd. A/c	Dr		5,23,500	
	To Cash/Bank A/c				5,23,500
	(Being amount due paid, i.e., 10,000 SGD × ₹52.35)				
31.03.2023	Loss on foreign exchange A/c	Dr		2,500	
	To Robinson Inc. A/c				2,500
	(Being increase in exchange rate recorded, i.e., 10,000 $ × ₹0.25)				
30.04.2023	Loss on foreign exchange A/c	Dr		1,000	
	To Robinson Inc. A/c				1,000
	(Being further increase in exchange rate recorded, i.e., 10,000 $ × ₹0.10)				
30.04.2023	Robinson Inc. A/c	Dr		7,69,500	
	To Cash/Bank A/c				7,69,500
	(Being the amount due paid, i.e., 10,000 $ × ₹76.95)				

ILLUSTRATION 2.4

Orbit India Ltd. purchased goods from Global Inc. of Germany on a 60 days' term on 11.03.2023 at €5,000. The exchange rates of 1€ as on 11.03.2023, 31.03.2023 and 11.05.2023 have remained ₹82.25, ₹82.65 and ₹82.85, respectively. Orbit India Ltd. closes its books of account on March 31 every year.

Show how will you record the above transactions in the books of Orbits India Ltd. under the (a) single transaction approach, and (b) the dual transaction approach given that Orbit India has paid off the dues on account on 31.03.2023.

SOLUTION

(a) Journal entries in the books of Orbit India Ltd. under the single transaction approach:

Date	Particulars	L/f	Dr (₹)	Cr. (₹)
11.03.2023	Purchase A/c Dr To Global Inc A/c (Being goods purchased recorded at €5,000 × ₹82.25)		4,11,250	4,11,250
31.03.2023	Purchase A/c Dr To Global Inc A/c (Being the increase in exchange rate, i.e., ₹82.65 – ₹82.25 multiplied by €5,000 recorded).		2,000	2,000
31.03.2023	Global Inc A/c Dr To Cash/Bank A/c (Being the amount due paid, i.e., €5,000 × ₹82.65)		4,13,250	4,13,250

(b) Journal entries in the books of Orbit India Ltd. under the dual transaction approach

Date	Particulars	L/f	Dr (₹)	Cr. (₹)
11.03.2023	Purchase A/c Dr To Global Inc A/c (Being goods purchased recorded at €5,000 × ₹82.25)		4,11,250*	4,11,250
31.03.2023	Loss on Foreign Exchange A/c Dr To Global Inc A/c (Being the increase in exchange rate, i.e., ₹82.65 – ₹82.25 multiplied by €5,000 recorded).		2,000**	2,000
31.03.2023	Global Inc A/c Dr To Cash/Bank A/c (Being the amount settled)		4,13,250	4,13,250

Notes:

* If the whole purchase remains unsold by the end of the year, the value of closing stock will be taken at ₹4,11,250. For goods remaining partially unsold, the value shall be determined proportionately taking the initial purchase price (i.e., ₹4,11,250 above) as the base.

** The loss on foreign exchange (account) shall be closed by charging it to the year's profit and loss account. The corresponding entry shall be:

Profit and loss A/c Dr
To loss on foreign exchange A/c

Forward Exchange Contracts

A forward exchange contract is a contract wherein a buyer agrees to buy a certain amount of foreign exchange at a future date and at a predetermined price. Conversely, a forward exchange contract is a contract where a seller agrees to sell a certain sum of foreign exchange at a future date and at a price agreed upon in advance. In a forward exchange contract the amount of the transaction, the maturity date, and the exchange rate are all determined in advance, but no money changes hands until the settlement date. Moreover, one of the parties to the forward contract may not perform on the date of maturity thus indicating towards the underlying risk (disadvantage) of a forward contract. But for the associated advantages, forward exchange contracts are used as a mechanism to minimize exchange risk. Exporters, importers, borrowers, and lenders find forward contracts very useful. Speculators too use forward contracts to benefit from anticipated movements in exchange rates.

Accounting Treatment

Accounting treatment of forward contracts has always invited controversies as regards the treatment of (i) forward premium or discount, and (ii) foreign exchange gain or loss on the forward variation. Forward premium occurs when the forward rate is higher than the spot rate and forward discount when the spot rate is higher than the forward rate. Similarly, foreign exchange gain or loss occurs when the exchange rate on the date of closure of accounts is higher than the deferred rate, i.e., the rate prevailing on the date of initial transaction.

Forward premium or discount may be treated as a part of the base of the related item or alternatively written off against income over the life of the forward contract. The foreign exchange gain or loss on the forward contract may also be recognized as current income or deferred as part of the base of the related item. *The actual practice however varies from country to country depending upon the accounting standard issued by the Standard Setting Body to the effect.* The related provisions issued by the Accounting Standards Board (ASB) of India (issued in March, 1989 and revised in December, 1994) read as follows:

'An enterprise may enter into a forward exchange contract, or another financial instrument that is in substance a forward exchange contract, to establish the amount of the reporting currency required or available at the settlement date of a transaction. The difference between the forward rate and the exchange rate at inception of the forward exchange contract should be recognized as income or expense over the life of the contract, except in respect of liabilities incurred for acquiring fixed assets, in which case, such difference should be adjusted in the carrying amount of the respective fixed assets. Any profit or loss arising on cancellation of a forward contract should be recognized as income or as expense for the period, except in case of a forward exchange contract relating to liabilities incurred for acquiring fixed assets, in which case, such profits or losses should be adjusted to the cost of the respective fixed asset'.

Journal Entries: Journal entries in the books of the buyer for a forward exchange contract under taken for purchase of fixed assets *under deferral method* shall be as follows:

1. On entering into forward contract (i.e., on initiation)	Dr	Foreign currency receivable (with the agreed purchase price of the asset represented at spot rate)
	Dr	Deferred cost on forward contract (with the amount of forward premium, i.e., agreed purchase price of the asset multiplied by the difference between forward rate and spot rate)
	Cr	Accounts payable/Seller's account (with the agreed purchase price of the asset multiplied by forward rate)

2. On reporting date (if it is earlier to the settlement date) for the gain on foreign currency	Dr	Foreign currency receivable (with the agreed purchase price of the asset multiplied by the difference between exchange rate on the reporting date and the spot rate)
	Cr	Deferred foreign exchange gain*
3. On settlement		
(a) Closing of forward contract	Dr	Accounts payable/seller's account
	Cr	Cash/Bank account (closing forward contract account as per 1 above)
(b) Receipt of foreign currency as part of forward contract	Dr	Investment in foreign currency
	Cr	Foreign currency receivable (with the agreed purchase price of the asset multiplied by the exchange rate on the date of settlement)
(c) Recording current value of asset/ closing investment in foreign currency	Dr	Asset Account
	Cr	Investment in Foreign currency Account (with the agreed purchase price of the asset multiplied by exchange rate on the date of settlement)
(d) Closing deferred cost on forward contract	Dr	Deferred foreign exchange gain (with the amount as per 2 above)
	Dr	Asset Account (with the differential amount)
	Cr	Deferred cost on forward contract (with the amount as per 1 above)

* *for loss reverse is the entry*

ILLUSTRATION 2.5

KNS India Ltd. agreed on 10th January, 2023 to purchase a plant from Crax Inc. of Italy at € 8,000 with the term that 25% of the purchase consideration shall be paid instant and the balance on delivery on 10th June, 2023. KNS India Ltd. entered into a forward contact on 10th January, 2023 to purchase €. On 10th January, 2023 the forward rate prevalent was ₹84.50/€ and the spot rate was ₹81.85/€. The exchange rates prevalent on 31st March, 2023 and on 31st May 2023 were ₹82.05/€ and ₹82.35/€, respectively. On 10th June, 2023 the rate is expected to be ₹82.35/€.

If KNS Ltd. happens to close its books of account on March end every year, how the above transactions should be recorded in the books of KNS Ltd. under the deferral system?

SOLUTION

Journal entries in the books of KNS Ltd. under the deferral system

Date	Particulars		L/f	Dr (₹)	Cr. (₹)
10.01.2023	Crax Inc. A/c To Cash/Bank (Being part of the purchase price paid for purchase of plant, i.e., 25% of €8,000 @ ₹81.85 paid)	Dr		1,63,700	 1,63,700
10.01.2023	EUR(€) Receivable A/c (6,000 € @ ₹81.85) Deferred cost on forward [6,000 € @ (₹84.50–₹81.85)] To Crax Ltd. (6,000 € @ ₹84.50) (Being forward contact and forward premium recorded)	Dr Dr		4,91,100 15,900	 5,07,000
31.03.2023	EUR(€) Receivable A/c To Deferred foreign exchange gain [Gain in value of forward contract, i.e., 6,000 € × (₹82.05 – ₹81.85) recorded]	Dr		1,200	 1,200
10.06.2023*	EUR(€) Receivable A/c To deferred foreign exchange gain [Being further gain in value of forward contract, i.e., 6,000 € x (₹82.35 – ₹82.05) recorded]	Dr		1,800	 1,800
10.06.2023	Crax Inc. A/c To Cash/Bank (Being forward contract record closed)	Dr		5,07,000	 5,07,000
10.06.2023	Investment in EUR(€) A/c To € receivable (Being € received as part of forward contract, with 6,000 € × ₹82.35)	Dr		4,94,100	 4,94,100
10.06.2023	Plant A/c [2,000 € × 81.35)+(6,000€ × ₹82.35)] To investment in EUR(€) (For the amount paid on delivery, i.e. 6,000 € × ₹82.35) To Crax Inc. (For adjustment of the amount paid as advance on 10.01.2021) (Being the cost of machinery recorded)	Dr		6,57,800	 4,94,100 1,63,700
10.06.2023	Deferred foreign exchange gain A/c Plant A/c (with the difference) To deferred cost on forward (Being the final cost of plant recorded)	Dr Dr		3,000 12,900	 15,900

**Further movement in the exchange rate is recorded.*

ILLUSTRATION 2.6

On 1st April, 2023, Victor India Ltd. agreed to purchase a machine from Mellon Inc. of USA at USD 1,000. The machine was agreed to be delivered on 21st April, 2023 and the payment to be made on delivery. Victor India Ltd. entered into a forward contract on 01.04.2023 to purchase USD. The forward rate prevalent on 01.04.2023 per USD was ₹79 and the spot rate per USD was ₹78.50. Victor India Ltd. closes its books on 31st March every year. The exchange rate prevalent on 31st March, 2023 was ₹78.80/USD and the same rate is expected to prevail on 21.04.2023.

Show how these transactions will be recorded in the books of Victor India Ltd. under the deferral system.

SOLUTION

Journal entries in the Books of Victor India Ltd.

Date	*Particulars*		*L/F*	*Dr (₹)*	*Cr. (₹)*
01.04.2023	Dollar receivable A/c (1000 × ₹78.50)	Dr		78,500	
	Deferred cost on forward [(1000 × (₹79 – ₹78.50)]	Dr		500	
	To Mellon Inc.				79,000
	(Being premium on forward deferred recorded)				
31.03.2023	Dollar receivable A/c			300	
	To deferred foreign exchange gain [Gain in value of forward contract, i.e., 1000 x (₹78.80 – ₹78.50)]				300
21.04. 2023	Mellon Inc. A/c	Dr		79,000	
	To Cash/Bank (Closing of forward contract records)				79,000
21.04. 2023	Investment in Dollar A/c	Dr		78,800	
	To Dollar receivable (Receipt of dollar as part of forward contract)				78,800
21.04. 2023	Machinery A/c	Dr		78,800	
	To investment in Dollar (Cost of machine at current value recorded)				78,800
21.04. 2023	Deferred foreign exchange gain A/c	Dr		300	
	Machinery (difference) A/c	Dr		200	
	To deferred cost on forward (Final cost of equipment recorded)				500

Foreign Currency Translation

Foreign currency translation as stated earlier refers to the change in the monetary expression of the financial data contained in the financial statements. The term is widely used in and is associated with the process of consolidation of foreign financial statements with the domestic financial statements in a single currency by adopting an appropriate translation method.

There are basically *four* methods, namely, the current rate method, the Current/Non-current method, the Monetary/Non-monetary method and the Temporal method, which are found to be in use for translation of the balance sheet items across nations. Exhibit 2.3 displays these methods along with their distinct features. The guidelines followed for translation of items of income statement are given in Exhibit 2.4.

EXHIBIT 2.3 Methods for translation of Balance Sheet items

Single rate method (Also known as current rate method)	*Multiple rate method*		
	Current/Non-current method	*Monetary/Non-monetary method*	*Temporal method*
Under the single rate method business of the subsidiary is viewed as an investment and not as a part of the business operation of the parent company. Therefore, all the assets and liabilities of the subsidiaries are translated at *current exchange rate*, i.e., the exchange rate prevailing on the date of preparation of the balance sheet. IAS 21 has pronounced for the use of current rate method for translation.	Under the Current/ Non-current method, current assets and current liabilities are translated at *current rate* and the non-current assets and non-current liabilities are translated at *historical rate*. Indian Accounting Standard 11 has prescribed for the use of the Current/Non-current method for translation of integral operations.	Under the Monetary/ Non-monetary method, monetary assets i.e., most liquid assets or near cash items and monetary liabilities i.e., all liabilities except owners' equity or ownership capital are translated at *current rates* and the rest i.e., non-monetary assets and non-monetary liabilities are translated at *historical rate*. Indian Accounting Standard 11 has provided for the use of Monetary/ Non-monetary method for translation of non-integral operations.	Under the temporal method, items of the balance sheet carried at present or future prices such as the cash and accounts receivable and payables are translated at *current rate* and the remaining assets and liabilities are translated at *historical rate*. Use of this (temporal) method was mandatory under the US GAAP as per provisions of SFAS 8 until it was superseded by SFAS 52 which requires the use of current rate at present. Temporal method is used only for re-measure from foreign currency to functional currency (as per SFAS 52) these days.

EXHIBIT 2.4 Methods and guidelines for translation of items of Income Statement

Single rate or Current rate method	*Multiple rates*		
	Current/Non-current method	*Monetary/Non-monetary method*	*Temporal method*
All items of revenue and expenses are translated at the prevailing rates when these items were recognized. Alternatively, weighted average of the current rates for the period may also be used.	*Cost of goods sold* is translated at current rate. *Depreciation* is translated at historical rate. *Operating expenses* are translated at average rate for the period covered by the expenses. Sales and other revenues are also translated at average rate prevailing during the period covered by the revenues.	*Cost of goods sold* is translated at historical rate. *Depreciation* is also translated at historical rate. *Operating expenses* are translated at average rate. *Sales and other revenues* are also translated at average rate prevailing during the period covered by the revenues and expenses.	*Cost of goods sold* is translated at historical rate. *Depreciation* is translated at historical rate. *Operating expenses* are translated at average rate. *Sales and other revenues* are translated at average rate prevailing at the period covered by the revenues and expenses.

ILLUSTRATION 2.7

The Balance Sheet of Smith & Smith of UK, an Indian subsidiary, as on 31.03.2023 is as follows:

Liabilities	*GBP(£)*	*Assets*	*GBP(£)*
Equity	4,000	Land and building	3,500
Reserves	2,000	Plant and equipment	5,000
Profit	1,000	Furniture and fixture	2,000
Bonds and debentures	6,000	Inventories (at market value)	2,500
Accounts payable	1,500	Accounts receivable	1,000
		Cash	500
Total	14,500	Total	14,500

You are required to translate the above Balance Sheet into Indian rupees as it would appear under the single rate method of translation given that the historical rate of exchange was ₹ 90.75 and the current rate is ₹91.15.

SOLUTION

Translated Balance Sheet of Smith & Smith under *single rate method*

Liabilities	*GBP (£)*	₹	*Assets*	*GBP (£)*	₹
Equity	4,000	3,64,600	Land and building	3,500	3,19,025
Reserves	2,000	1,82,300	Plant and equipment	5,000	4,55,750
Profit	1,000	91,150	Furniture and fixture	2,000	1,82,300
Bonds and debentures	6,000	5,46,900	Inventories (at market value)	2,500	2,27,875
Accounts payable	1,500	1,36,725			
			Accounts receivable	1,000	91,150
			Cash	500	45,575
Total	14,500	13,21,675	Total	14,500	13,21,675

Note: As per current rate method, all the items in the Balance Sheet have been translated by a single rate, i.e., current rate, which is ₹91.15

ILLUSTRATION 2.8

The Balance Sheet of David International Inc., USA, a subsidiary of Robotics India Ltd., as on 31.03.2023 is as under:

Liabilities	($)	*Assets*	($)
Equity	6,000	Land and building	6,500
Reserves	3,000	Plant and equipment	8,500
Profit	2,000	Furniture and fixture	1,500
Bonds and debentures	8,000	Inventories (at market value)	2,500
Accounts payable	2,500	Accounts receivable	3,000
Outstanding	1,500	Cash	1,000
Total	23,000	Total	23,000

Translate the above Balance Sheet into Indian rupees as it would appear under the Current/Non-current method of translation given further that the exchange rate was ₹80.75/$ on April 1, 2022 and ₹81.50/$ on March 31, 2023.

SOLUTION

Translated Balance Sheet of David International Inc. under Current/Non-current method

Liabilities	($)	₹	*Assets*	($)	₹
Equity share capital	6,000	4,86,375	Land and building	6,500	5,24,875
Reserves	3,000	2,42,250	Plant and equipment	8,500	6,86,375
Profit	2,000	1,61,500	Furniture and fixture	1,500	1,21,125
Debentures	8,000	6,46,000	Inventories (at market value)	2,500	2,03,750
Accounts payable	2,500	2,03,750	Accounts receivable	3,000	2,44,500
Outstanding	1,500	1,22,250	Cash	1,000	81,500
Total	23,000	18,62,125	Total	23,000	18,62,125

Note: As per Current/Non-current method, (i) Current assets and current liabilities have been translated at current rate, i.e., ₹ 81.50/$; and (ii) the non-current assets and non-current liabilities, except Equity share capital have been translated at historical rate which is ₹ 80.75/$. Further, the differential amount in the balance sheet after translation of all other items except Equity share capital have been attributed to Equity share capital.

ILLUSTRATION 2.9

The Balance Sheet of Hamilton Inc., Germany, a subsidiary of Promise India Ltd., as on 31.03.2023 is as under:

Liabilities	(€)	*Assets*	(€)
Equity share capital	16,000	Land and building	9,000
Reserves	6,000	Plant and equipment	17,000
Profit	4,000	Furniture and fixture	4,000
Bonds and debentures	18,000	Inventories (at market value)	8,000
Accounts payable	7,500	Accounts receivable	12,000
		Cash	1,500
Total	51,500	Total	51,500

You are required to translate the above Balance Sheet into Indian rupees as it would appear under the Monetary/Non-monetary method of translation, given further that the exchange rate was ₹70.75/€ on April 1, 2022 and ₹71.40/€ on March 31, 2023.

SOLUTION:

Translated Balance Sheet of Hamilton Inc. under Monetary/Non-monetary method

Liabilities	(€)	₹	*Assets*	(€)	₹
Equity	16,000	11,27,200	Land and building	9,000	6,36,750
Reserves	6,000	4,22,700	Plant and equipment	17,000	12,02,750
Profit	4,000	2,81,800	Furniture and fixture	4,000	2,83,000
Debentures	18,000	12,85,200	Inventories (at market value)	8,000	5,66,000
Accounts payable	7,500	5,35,500	Accounts receivable	12,000	8,56,800
			Cash	1,500	1,07,100
Total	51,500	36,52,400	Total	51,500	36,52,400

Workings: Cash, and Accounts Receivable in the asset side, and Accounts Payable, and Debentures in the liabilities side are the monetary items which have been translated at the current rate of ₹ 71.40/€.

Similarly, Inventories (at market value), Furniture and fixture, Plant and equipment, Land and building are non-monetary items, hence have been translated at the historical rate of ₹70.75/€.

Translated value of Owner's equity = Translated value of total assets – the translated value of outsiders' liabilities. Therefore, the translated value of Owner's equity should be equal to: ₹36,52,400 – (₹5,35,500 + ₹12,85,200) or ₹18,31,700.

Even if the items of owner's equity such as 'Profit' and 'Reserves and Surpluses' in the instant case are translated by multiplying them with historical rate of ₹70.75 for being non-monetary items, and then the difference in the balance sheet is attributed to 'Equity Share Capital' as the translated value, the sum total of these three items, namely, profit, reserves and surpluses, and equity share capital after translation would have been the same ₹18, 31,700.

Now, this translated value of owner's equity which is ₹18, 31,700 has been proportionately distributed among profit, reserves and surpluses, and equity share capital, taking their pre-translated value as the basis, i.e, 4,000:6,000:16,000, or 2:3:8.

ILLUSTRATION 2.10

The Balance Sheet of Multi-Rose Inc. Hong Kong, a subsidiary of Treasure India Ltd., as on 31.03.2023 is as under:

Liabilities	(HKD)	*Assets*	(HKD)
Equity	70,000	Land and building	79,000
Profit	18,000	Plant and equipment	47,000
Bonds and debentures	52,000	Inventories (at market value)	32,000
Accounts payable	80,000	Accounts receivable	44,000
		Cash	18,000
Total	2,20,000	Total	2,20,000

You are required to translate the above balance sheet into Indian rupees as it would appear under the 'temporal method' of translation given that the exchange rate was ₹7.75/HKD on April 1, 2022 and ₹8.25/HKD on March 31, 2023.

SOLUTION

Translated Balance Sheet of Multi-Rose Inc. under Temporal method

Liabilities	*(HKD)*	₹	*Assets*	*(HKD)*	₹
Equity	70,000	5,23,500	Land and building	79,000	6,12,250
Profit	18,000	1,39,500	Plant and equipment	47,000	3,64,250
Debentures	52,000	4,29,000	Inventories (at market value)	32,000	2,64,000
Accounts payable	80,000	6,60,000	Accounts receivable	44,000	3,63,000
			Cash	18,000	1,48,500
Total	2,20,000	17,52,000	Total	2,20,000	17,52,000

Note: As per temporal method, (i) items carried at present or future values, namely, Cash, Accounts receivable, Inventories (at market value), Accounts payable, and Debenture have been translated at the current rate, i.e., ₹8.25/HKD; and (ii) the rest except Equity share capital have been translated at historical rate of 7.75/HKD, with Equity share capital carrying the differential amount.

ILLUSTRATION 2.11

The Balance Sheet of Simon & Co. of Canada, an Indian subsidiary, as on 31.03.2023 is as follows:

Liabilities	*Canada* (C $)	*Assets*	*Canada* (C $)
Equity & reserves	10,000	Land and building	10,000
Bonds and debentures	12,000	Plant and equipment	6,000
Accounts payable	8,000	Inventories (at market value)	8,000
		Accounts receivable	4,000
		Cash	2,000
Total	30,000	Total	30,000

You are required to translate the above Balance Sheet into Indian rupees as it would appear under (a) the single rate, and (b) the multiple rate methods, assuming the historical rate and current rate of 1 C $ is equal to ₹52 and ₹53, respectively.

SOLUTION

(a) Translated Balance Sheet of Simon & Co. under *single rate method*

Liabilities	(C $)	₹	*Assets*	(C $)	₹
Equity and reserves	10,000	5,30,000	Land and building	10,000	5,30,000
Bonds and debentures	12,000	6,36,000	Plants and equipments	6,000	3,18,000
Accounts payable	8,000	4,24,000	Inventories (at market value)	8,000	4,24,000
			Accounts receivable	4,000	2,12,000
			Cash	2,000	1,06,000
	30,000	15,90,000		30,000	15,90,000

(b) Translated Balance Sheet of Simon & Co. under *Current/Non-current method*

Liabilities	(C $)	₹	*Assets*	(C $)	₹
Equity and reserves	10,000	5,26,000*	Land and building	10,000	5,20,000
Bonds and debentures	12,000	6,24,000	Plants and equipments	6,000	3,12,000
Accounts payable	8,000	4,24,000	Inventories (at market value)	8,000	4,24,000
			Accounts receivable	4,000	2,12,000
			Cash	2,000	1,06,000
	30,000	15,74,000		30,000	15,74,000

**represents the balance amount.*

(c) Translated Balance Sheet of Simon & Co. under *Monetary/Non-monetary method*

Liabilities	(C $)	₹	*Assets*	(C $)	₹
Equity and reserves	10,000	5,06,000*	Land and building	10,000	5,20,000
Bonds and debentures	12,000	6,36,000	Plants and equipments	6,000	3,12,000
Accounts payable	8,000	4,24,000	Inventories (at market value)	8,000	4,16,000
			Accounts receivable	4,000	2,12,000
			Cash	2,000	1,06,000
	30,000	15,66,000		30,000	15,66,000

* *represents the balancing amount.*

(d) Translated Balance Sheet of Simon & Co. under *Temporal method*

Liabilities	(C $)	₹	*Assets*	(C $)	₹
Equity and reserves	10,000	5,14,000*	Land and building	10,000	5,20,000
Bonds and debentures	12,000	6,36,000	Plants and equipments	6,000	3,12,000
Accounts payable	8,000	4,24,000	Inventories (at market value)	8,000	4,24,000
			Accounts receivable	4,000	2,12,000
			Cash	2,000	1,06,000
	30,000	15,74,000		30,000	15,74,000

**represents the balancing amount*

Comparative view of the translated Balance Sheet of Simon & Co. under all the four methods of translation

		Single rate	*Multiple rates*		
	(C $)	*Current rate* (₹)	*Current/ Non-current* (₹)	*Monetary/Non-monetary* (₹)	*Temporal* (₹)
Assets					
Land and building	10,000	5,30,000	5,20,000	5,20,000	5,20,000
Plants and equipment	6,000	3,18,000	3,12,000	3,12,000	3,12,000
Inventories (at market value)	8,000	4,24,000	4,24,000	4,16,000	4,24,000
Accounts receivable	4,000	2,12,000	2,12,000	2,12,000	2,12,000
Cash	2,000	1,06,000	1,06,000	1,06,000	1,06,000
Total	30,000	15,90,000	15,74,000	15,66,000	15,74,000
Liabilities					
Equity and reserves	10,000	5,30,000	5,26,000*	5,06,000*	5,14,000*
Bonds and debentures	12,000	6,36,000	6,24,000	6,36,000	6,36,000
Accounts payable	8,000	4,24,000	4,24,000	4,24,000	4,24,000
Total	30,000	15,90,000	15,74,000	15,66,000	15,74,000

ILLUSTRATION 2.12

The following Balance Sheet related to MaxiMin Ltd. of France, an Indian subsidiary, as on 31.03.2023:

Liabilities	€	*Assets*	€
Accounts payable	38,000	Cash	14,000
Short-term loans	70,000	Receivables	28,000
Fixed deposits	40,000	Inventories (at market value)	1,10,000
Bonds	1,12,000	Land and building	1,20,000
Reserves	40,000	Plant and machinery	1,28,000
Equity capital	1,00,000		
	4,00,000		4,00,000

If the historical rate and current rate of 1 € is ₹79.50 and ₹80.00, respectively, translate the above balance sheet into Indian rupees using the single rate and the multiple rates approach to translation.

SOLUTION

(a) Translated Balance Sheet of MaxiMin Ltd. under the **single rate** approach

Liabilities	€	₹	Assets	€	₹
Accounts payable	38,000	30,40,000	Cash	14,000	11,20,000
Short-term loans	70,000	56,00,000	Receivables	28,000	22,40,000
Fixed deposits	40,000	32,00,000	Inventories (at market value)	1,10,000	88,00,000
Bonds	1,12,000	89,60,000	Land and building	1,20,000	96,00,000
Reserves	40,000	32,00,000	Plant and machinery	1,28,000	1,02,40,000
Equity capital	1,00,000	80,00,000			
	4,00,000	3,20,00,000		4,00,000	3,20,00,000

(b) Translated Balance Sheet of MaxiMin Ltd. under the Current/Non-current approach

Liabilities	€	₹	Assets	€	₹
Accounts payable	38,000	30,40,000	Cash	14,000	11,20,000
Short-term loans	70,000	56,00,000	Receivables	28,000	22,40,000
Fixed deposits	40,000	31,80,000	Inventories (at market value)	1,10,000	88,00,000
Bonds	112,000	89,04,000	Land and building	1,20,000	95,40,000
Reserves	40,000	31,80,000	Plant and machinery	1,28,000	1,01,76,000
Equity capital	1,00,000	79,72,000*			
	4,00,000	3,18,76,000		4,00,000	3,18,76,000

**Represents the balancing figure.*

(c) Translated Balance Sheet of MaxiMin Ltd. under the Monetary/Non-monetary approach

Liabilities	€	₹	Assets	€	₹
Accounts payable	38,000	30,40,000	Cash	14,000	11,20,000
Short-term loans	70,000	56,00,000	Receivables	28,000	22,40,000
Fixed deposits	40,000	32,00,000	Inventories (at market value)	1,10,000	87,45,000
Bonds	1,12,000	89,60,000	Land and building	1,20,000	95,40,000
Reserves	40,000	31,48,857*	Plant and machinery	1,28,000	1,01,76,000
Equity capital	1,00,000	78,72,143*			
	4,00,000	3,18,21,000		4,00,000	3,18,21,000

Note: The balancing amount has been proportionately transferred to Reserves and Equity, i.e, in the ratio of 2:5.

(d) Translated Balance Sheet of MaxiMin Ltd. under the Temporal approach

Liabilities	€	₹	Assets	€	₹
Accounts payable	38,000	30,40,000	Cash	14,000	11,20,000
Short-term loans	70,000	56,00,000	Receivables	28,000	22,40,000
Fixed deposits	40,000	32,00,000	Inventories (at market value)	1,10,000	88,00,000
Bonds	1,12,000	89,60,000	Land and building	1,20,000	95,40,000
Reserves	40,000	31,64,571*	Plant and machinery	1,28,000	1,01,76,000
Equity capital	1,00,000	79,11,429*			
	4,00,000	3,18,76,000		4,00,000	3,18,76,000

Note: The balancing amount has been proportionately transferred to Reserves and Equity, i.e, in the ratio of 2:5.

Comparative view of the translated Balance Sheet of MaxiMin Ltd. under all the four approaches to translation

Liabilities	€	*Current rate* (₹)	*Current/ Non-current* (₹)	*Monetary/ Non-monetary* (₹)	*Temporal* (₹)
Accounts payable	38,000	30,40,000	30,40,000	30,40,000	30,40,000
Short term loans	70,000	56,00,000	56,00,000	56,00,000	56,00,000
Fixed deposits	40,000	32,00,000	31,80,000	32,00,000	32,00,000
Bonds	1,12,000	89,60,000	89,04,000	89,60,000	89,60,000
Reserves	40,000	32,00,000	31,80,000	31,48,857*	31,64,571*
Equity capital	1,00,000	80,00,000	79,72,000*	78,72,143*	79,11,429*
	4,00,000	3,20,00,000	3,18,76,000	3,18,21,000	3,18,76,000
Assets					
Cash	14,000	11,20,000	11,20,000	11,20,000	11,20,000
Receivables	28,000	22,40,000	22,40,000	22,40,000	22,40,000
Inventories (at market value)	1,10,000	88,00,000	88,00,000	87,45,000	88,00,000
Land and building	1,20,000	96,00,000	95,40,000	95,40,000	95,40,000
Plant and machinery	1,28,000	1,02,40,000	1,01,76,000	1,01,76,000	1,01,76,000
	4,00,000	3,20,00,000	3,18,76,000	3,18,21,000	3,18,76,000

ILLUSTRATION 2.13

The Income Statement of Fair and Foul Inc. of Spain, a subsidiary of ABC India Ltd. for the year ended 31.03.2023 is as under:

(Figures in €)

Sales	2,00,000	
Other incomes	30,000	
Total income		2,30,000
Less: Cost of goods sold		
Opening stock	20,000	
Add: Purchases	1,00,000	
Less: Closing stock	10,000	1,10,000
Gross profit		1,20,000
Less: Operating expenses		
(a) Administrative		
Office	40,000	
Depreciation	5,000	
(b) Selling		
Advertising	15,000	
Depreciation	10,000	70,000
Profit before tax		50,000
Less: Tax(15%)		7,500
Profit after tax		42,500

Additional information:

(i) The current rate is ₹84/€ and the historical rate was ₹80/€.
(ii) Sales generated were €80,000, €50,000 and €70,000 at ₹82, ₹83 and ₹84 per €.
(iii) Purchases were made in two equal lots at ₹82 and ₹83 per €.
(iv) Office and selling expenses have been incurred at ₹82 and ₹83, respectively.

Translate the income Statement of Fair and Foul Inc. into Indian currency under the Single rate method.

SOLUTION

Translation of income statement items of Fair and Foul Inc. under Single rate method

	€	€	*Rate(s) used for translation*	*Translated value (₹)*
Sales	2,00,000	–	80,000 × ₹82 70,000 × ₹83 50,000 × ₹84	1,65,70,000
Other incomes[1]	30,000	–	30,000 × ₹84	25,20,000
Total income	–	**2,30,000**		1,90,90,000
Less: Cost of goods sold	–	–	–	–
Opening stock[2]	20,000	–	20,000 × ₹80	–
Add: Purchases	1,00,000	–	50,000 × ₹82 50,000 × ₹83	
Less: Closing stock	10,000	1,10,000	10,000 × ₹84	90,10,000
Gross profit	–	1,20,000	–	**1,00,8,000**
Less: Operating expenses	–	–	–	–
(a) Administrative	–	–	–	–
Office	40,000	–	40,000 × ₹82	–
Depreciation[3]	5,000	–	5,000 × ₹84	–
(b) Selling	–	–	–	–
Advertising	15,000	–	15,000 × ₹83	–
Depreciation	10,000	70,000	10,000 × ₹84	57,85,000
Profit before tax	–	**50,000**	–	42,95,000
Less: Tax(15%)	–	7,500	–	6,44,250
Profit after tax	–	42,500	–	36,50,750

Note:

1. Other income is assumed to have accrued at the end of the year and hence multiplied by the current rate of ₹84.
2. Opening stock and closing stock has been valued at ₹80 and ₹84, respectively.
3. Depreciations have been valued at ₹84 as they are recognized at the end of the year.

ILLUSTRATION 2.14

Following is the income statement of Freedom Inc. of Hong Kong, a subsidiary of Universal Services India Ltd. for the year ended 31.03.2023:

(*Figure in HKD*)

Sales	15,80,000	
Other income	5,20,000	
Total income		21,00,000
Less: Cost of goods sold		
Opening stock	4,50,000	
Add: Purchase	8,30,000	
Less: Closing stock	2,10,000	10,70,000
Gross profit		10,30,000
Less: Operating expenses		
(a) Administrative		
Office	1,40,000	
Depreciation	15,000	
(b) Selling		
Delivery Services	25,000	2,80,000
Profit before tax		7,50,000
Less: Tax(10%)		75,000
Profit after tax		6,75,000

You are required to translate the above income statement into Indian currency under the single rate method taking into consideration the following additional information:

(i) The current rate is ₹ 9.70/HKD and the historical rate was ₹9.10.

(ii) Purchases were made in three lots in the ratio of 2:3:5 at ₹9.20, ₹9.30 and ₹9.40 per HKD, respectively.

(iii) Office and selling expenses have been incurred at ₹9.35 and ₹9.55 per HKD, respectively.

SOLUTION

Translation of income statement of Freedom Inc. under Single rate method

Sales	15,80,000 × ₹ 9.70	1,53,26,000
Other income[1]	5,20,000 × ₹ 9.70	50,44,000
Total income		2,03,70,000
Less: Cost of goods sold		98,01,900
Opening stock[2]	4,50,000 × ₹ 9.10	
Add: Purchase (8,30,000)	1,66,000 × ₹ 9.20	
	2,49,000 × ₹ 9.30	
	4,15,000 × ₹ 9.40	
Less: Closing stock	2,10,000 × ₹ 9.70	
Gross profit		1,05,68,100
Less: Operating expenses		
(a) Administrative		
Office	1,40,000 × ₹ 9.35	
Depreciation[3]	15,000 × ₹ 9.70	
(b) Selling		
Salesmen's commission	25,000 × ₹ 9.55	16,93,250
Profit before tax		88,74,850
Less: Tax(10%)		8,87,485
Profit after tax		79,87,365

Notes:

1. Other income is assumed to have accrued at the end of the year and hence multiplied by the current rate.
2. Opening stock and closing stock has been valued at historical rate and current rate, respectively.
3. Depreciation has been valued at current rate as they are recognized at the end of the year.

Treatment of Translation Gains and Losses

There is no single agreement as regards treatment of translation gains or losses which arise due to currency variations. However, the *three* basic methods known for the purpose are:

1. Immediate recognition and reflection in the income statement.
2. Deferral method.
3. Deferral and amortization.

Immediate recognition: The immediate recognition method is also known as *no deferral method*. It is based on the traditional approach of 'conservatism'. Under this method translation gains and losses are recognized as soon as they occur. Consequently, they find a place in the income statement of the reporting firm in the same period in which they occur.

The immediate recognition method in considered superior to 'deferral method' insofar as it immediately recognizes the exchange rate 'behaviour' and communicates it to the users of the financial statements. Opponents to this method however hold the opinion that immediate recognition and reflection of translation gains and losses in the income statement causes significant fluctuations to the earnings of the firm as a result of which the interpretative value of the statements goes down.

Deferral method: As opposed to the immediate recognition, under the *deferral method* translation gains and losses are allowed to accumulate separately as 'consolidated equity' and instead of being transferred to the income statement. The argument behind so doing is that translation gains and losses are never realized until the foreign operations are closed down and all the (net) assets are distributed to the parent company. 'The gains or losses will not become realized until the foreign operations are closed down and all the net assets are distributed to the parent, that at or before such time the changes in the exchange rate may be reversed, i.e., that no gain or loss will ever be realized' [1].

The method is considered favourable to firms who otherwise would be to report significant losses in the consolidated financial statements due to currency fluctuations if the immediate recognition method is adopted. The method receives further support on the ground that changes in the subsidiary's net assets due to currency fluctuations are unrealized and further that such changes do not affect the subsidiary's cash flows. Hence it is improper to include them in the reporting firm's current income.

Non-recognition of the exchange rate losses in the income statement of the relevant year and deferring of such losses and gains amounts to violation of accounting principles of conservatism and full disclosure, the critics hold.

Deferral and amortization: The third method followed for treatment of translation gains and losses is called the deferral and amortization method. This method is more a hybrid of the deferral and no deferral methods discussed above. Under the deferral and amortization method, translation gains and losses are amortized over the life of the concerned balance sheet items. The argument for so doing is that 'the cost of an asset includes the sacrifice required to discharge the related liabilities. The translation loss, if any, is therefore treated as part of the related asset cost and amortized to expenses over its useful life' [2]. Further, since fixed assets are normally translated at historical rates of exchange, and the amount of depreciation charged to income statement is lower than what would have been charged at current rates, the higher income so derived would be offset by the reduced income due to amortization of deferred translation losses.

This method has been criticized on the ground that it lacks logical consistency and ignores the dual aspect of the transaction.

Choosing the Appropriate Method

Each of the methods discussed above for treatment of translation gains and losses has its own merits and demerits. Hence, use of any of the methods would depend on the objective to be accomplished from such translation. For instance, the parent company would favour adjustment of translation gains and losses against current income (no deferral approach), whereas the subsidiary(ies) would favour the deferral approach.

INTERNATIONAL GAAP ON FOREIGN CURRENCY TRANSLATION

IAS 21 (revised 1993) primarily deals with the provisions of foreign currency translations and transactions. The standard, i.e., IAS 21 (revised), while superseding IAS 21 of 1983 on 'Accounting for the Effects of Changes in Foreign Exchange Rates', applies to:

(a) accounting for foreign currency transactions which are denominated in currency other than the functional currency of the enterprise; and
(b) translation of foreign currency financial statements of branches, divisions, subsidiaries and other investees that are incorporated in the financial statements of an enterprise by consolidation, proportionate consolidation, or by the equity method.

Functional currency is a term used under the US GAAP which, in the context of foreign currency translation, refers to the currency of the primary economic environment in which the enterprise operates. In other words, it is the currency of the environment in which an entity primarily generates and expends cash. Similarly, foreign currency transactions are transactions whose terms are denominated in a foreign currency or which require settlement in a foreign currency. Such transactions occur when an enterprise:

- buys and sells on credit goods or services whose prices are denominated in foreign currency,
- borrows or lends funds and the amounts payable or receivable are denominated in foreign currency,
- is a party to an unperformed foreign exchange contract, or
- for other reasons acquires or disposes of assets or incurs or settles liabilities denominated in foreign currency.

Applicability of IAS 21

IAS 21 in relation to *translation* of financial statements stipulates that the methods to be adopted for such translation would depend on whether the foreign operation is (a) *integral* to the operations of the reporting entity or is (b) *nonintegral* to the operation of the reporting entity. Foreign operation here refers to the 'activities' of the subsidiary, associate, joint venture, or branch of the reporting enterprise which are conducted in a country other than the country where the reporting enterprise is domiciled.

The foreign operations will be considered as *non-integral* to the operations of the reporting enterprise if the following characteristics/factors are found present:

1. The foreign operations are carried out with significant autonomy.
2. The foreign enterprise's transactions with the reporting enterprise are not of very high proportion.
3. The foreign enterprise's activities are financed principally from its own sources or through local borrowings instead of the reporting enterprise's funds.
4. The foreign enterprise's cost of labour, material and other components are paid primarily in the local currency and not in the currency of the reporting enterprise.
5. The sales are primarily made in currency(ies) other than the reporting currency. Where reporting currency is the currency in which an enterprise denominates its financial statements.
6. The day-to-day activities of the foreign operation do not directly affect the cash flows of the reporting enterprise.

Classification of foreign operations into integral or non-integral warrants greater care to be exercised as often such classification would involve subjective judgments. 'The classification of a foreign operation is to be based on the facts surrounding each case, and sometimes this could be quite subjective and unclear. Thus, a degree of caution is to be exercised in judgments relating to classification of boarder line cases, since on such classification will depend the method that will ultimately be used to translate the foreign operation's financial statements into the reporting currency'. [3]

Provisions for Translation for Integral Operations

Foreign operations that are integral to the operations of the reporting enterprise are taken as if they are the transactions of the reporting enterprise itself. Therefore, these operations should be translated in line with the provisions contained in IAS 21 for translation and reporting of foreign currency items of an enterprise's own transactions, unless any rules otherwise specifically override these provisions. The rules thus contained in IAS 21 for translations of foreign operations are as follows:

1. Foreign currency monetary items should be reported at the closing exchange rate. Closing rate refers to the spot rate of exchange, i.e., exchange rate for immediate delivery of currencies exchanged on the balance sheet date. Monetary items are cash and claims that entitle receipt and payment obligations of fixed amount of cash.
2. Foreign currency non-monetary items if carried at historical costs should be reported at the rate(s) as prevalent on the date(s) of the transaction. Given further that foreign

currency non-monetary items if carried at fair values such as revalued property, plant and machineries as per alternative treatments provided under IAS 16 should be reported at exchange rates that existed when such fair values were determined.

Non-monetary items are all the items of the balance sheet except cash and cash obligations.

3. Items of all incomes and expenses should be reported at the same rates as were prevalent on the dates of the transactions. In practice, a rate such as the monthly average rates that approximates the actual rates of exchange on the dates of transactions may be used for translating all items of expenses and incomes except depreciation which should be translated using either the rate that prevailed on the date of purchase of the asset or if the asset is carried at fair value, the rate that existed on the date of such revaluation.
4. Exchange differences occurring due to reporting of monetary items should be recognized as income or expense during the reporting period.

   In case such differences are in relation to the reporting enterprise's investment in a foreign entity, they should be classified as a separate component of equity and shown in the reporting enterprise's financial statement until disposal of the net investment when the ultimate loss or gain will be recognized. A similar treatment shall be made for the differences which arise on a foreign liability accounted as a hedge of the reporting enterprise's net investment in a foreign entity.
5. Inventories should be reported at the rates prevalent on the dates of procurement. However, if they are carried at a lower realizable value, then at the exchange rate prevailing on the date when such lower realizable value was determined.

Provisions for Translation of Non-integral Operations

The following rules have been pronounced for translation of financial statements in case of foreign operations that are not integral to the reporting enterprise's operations:

1. All assets and liabilities, irrespective of whether monetary or non-monetary, should be translated at the closing rate.
2. Items of expenses and incomes should be translated at the rates as were prevalent on the dates of the transactions except when the foreign entity reports in a currency under hyperinflationary economy in which the translations should be at the closing rates.
3. Exchange differences should be classified as a separate component of equity of the reporting enterprise until the net investment in foreign entity is disposed off.

Special Provisions

The important additional provisions contained in IAS 21 in relation to translation are follows:

1. The accumulated exchange differences resulting from translation attributable to the *minority interest* should be allocated to minority interest and reported accordingly instead of being shown as a separate component of equity.
2. *Goodwill* arising from acquisition of foreign entity should be treated either as an asset (or a liability in case of negative goodwill) of the foreign entity and translated at the closing rate; or as an asset (or a liability for negative goodwill) of the reporting

entity which is either already expressed in the reporting currency or is converted to the reporting currency and translated at the rate as on the date of transaction.

3. On consolidation, exchange differences arising from *intergroup* monetary items should be recognized as income or expenses and shown separately as equity until the disposal of the net investment, instead of being eliminated against corresponding amounts arising on other inter group balances.
4. Any reversal to the initial classifications of foreign operations into integral and non-integral at a subsequent date due to fulfillment or non-fulfillment of related conditions, the translation procedure applicable to the revised classification should be applied from the date of such change in the classification.

Disclosure Requirements

IAS 21 stipulates on the following disclosures on foreign currency translation:

1. The amount of exchange differences included in the net income or loss for the period, exchange differences that are included in the carrying value of an asset and those which are classified as equity together with the reconciliation of the opening and closing balance in the cumulative exchange difference account carried as part of equity should be disclosed.
2. In case of any change in the classification of foreign operations, the nature and reasons of such change and its impact on the current year as well as each of the previous years reporting should be stated.
3. In case the reporting currency is different from the currency of the country of reporting enterprise's domicile, the reason(s) behind such use of a different currency now, and also of any subsequent changes thereof should be mentioned.
4. The method used to translate goodwill and fair value adjustments arising out of acquisition of foreign entity should be indicated.
5. The foreign currency risk management policy of the reporting enterprise should also be disclosed.

INDIAN GAAP ON FOREIGN CURRENCY TRANSLATION

Indian Accounting Standard 11 (AS 11, revised 2003) on 'Effects of changes in foreign exchange rates' contains specific provisions as regards translation and accounting of foreign currency. Application of this standard, which supersedes AS 11 (of 1994) has been made mandatory in India with effect from April 1, 2004 with the exception that accounting for transactions in foreign currencies entered into by the reporting enterprises itself or through its branches before April 1, 2004 will continue to be done under AS 11 (of 1994).

Applicability

AS 11 (Revised 2003) will apply to:

1. Accounting for transactions in foreign currencies.

2. Translation of financial statements of foreign operations which are integral as well as non-integral to the reporting enterprise's operations.
3. Accounting for forward exchange contracts.

The standard will *not* apply to:

1. Restatement of an enterprise's financial statements from its reporting currency to another currency for the convenience of users accustomed to that currency.
2. Presentation in the cash flow statement of cash flows arising from transactions of cash flows of foreign operations.
3. Exchange differences arising from foreign currency borrowings to the extent they are regarded as an adjustment to interest cost as given in AS 16.

Classification of Transactions

For the purpose of accounting treatment of the effects of changes in exchange rates, the following categorization shall be made of the transactions:

1. *Category I:* Foreign currency transactions.
   This would include buying or selling of goods and services, lending and borrowing in foreign currency, and acquisition and disposition of assets denominated in foreign currency.
2. *Category II:* Foreign operations.
   This would include integral and non-integral operations of foreign branch, associate, joint venture and foreign subsidiary.
3. *Category III:* Forward exchange contracts.
   This would include forward exchange contract for managing risk (hedging) and for trading and speculation.

Accounting Treatment for Category I Transactions, i.e., Foreign Currency Transactions

AS 11 provides the following guidelines in respect of accounting treatment of foreign currency transactions:

1. *Initially* foreign currency transactions should be recorded at an exchange rate as prevalent on the date of such transaction, or at a weekly or monthly average exchange rate provided that there is no significant fluctuation in the exchange rates.
2. *Monetary items* such as debtors, creditors and loans should be converted and reported at the closing rate, i.e., the rate of exchange prevalent on the balance sheet date.
   Incase the closing rate is unrealistic and it is not possible to effect an exchange at that rate, then at a rate most likely to be realized.
3. *Non-monetary* items such as the fixed assets and long-term investments carried at historical rates should be reported at the same actual (historical) rate(s) on the balance sheet date.
4. *Non-monetary* items such as inventory and short-term investments carried at fair value should be converted and reported at the exchange rate which was prevailing at the

time of determination of such fair value. Normally, fair value is determined on the date of balance sheet and hence it is the rate as prevalent on the balance sheet date.

5. Exchange differences resulting in gains and/or losses should be transferred to the profit and loss account for the period.
6. Contingent liabilities should be reported at the exchange rate of the balance sheet date.

Accounting Treatment for Category II Transactions, i.e., Foreign Operations

AS 11 provides separate sets of rules for treatment of integral and non-integral operations. The rules for reporting of *integral foreign operations* are as follows:

1. Individual items of the financial statements of the foreign operation should be translated at the actual rate on the date of transaction. The standard permits for use of 'average rate' as an alternative to the actual rate(s).
2. If the tangible fixed assets are carried at cost on the date of balance sheet, then the associated cost and depreciation should be translated at the exchange rate on the date of purchase of the assets.
3. If the tangible fixed assets are carried at fair value, the translation should be made at the rate as was prevalent on the date of determination of such fair value.
4. The cost of inventories should be translated at the rate that existed when the cost of the inventory was incurred. The realizable value should be the closing rate, i.e., the rate as prevalent on the balance sheet date.
5. Exchange difference should be charged to profit and loss account of the period.
6. The tax effect on exchange difference should be dealt with as per provisions of AS 22.

The accounting treatment for *non-integral foreign operations* shall be as under:

1. Balance sheet items irrespective of monetary or non-monetary should be translated at closing rate.
2. Items of incomes and expenses should be translated at actual exchange rates on the date of transactions. Average rate may also be applied subject to materiality.
3. Exchange differences should continue to accumulate in a 'foreign currency translation reserve account', until the net investment in non-integral foreign operation by the reporting enterprise is disposed off.

   On partial disposal of the foreign operation, a proportionate amount of the foreign currency translation reserve should be recognized as income or expenses, and on full disposal, the entire foreign currency reserve should be recognized as income or expenses and transferred to the profit and loss account of the period.

   Disposal of non-integral foreign operation results from sale, liquidation, repayment of share capital, or abandonment of all or part of the foreign operation by the reporting enterprise. A partial disposal is said to have occurred if dividend is paid by such non-integral operation to the reporting enterprise with the latter considering such dividend as return on investment.

4. Contingent liability should be reported at closing rate.
5. Tax effects on exchange differences should be dealt with as per AS 22.

Reversal of Integral to Non-integral and the vice versa

AS 11 provides the following for treatment when an integral operation subsequently becomes non-integral, or a non-integral operation becomes integral:

Integral to non-integral

1. The translation procedure applicable to non-integral should be followed from the date of such change.
2. The exchange difference arising on the translation of non-monetary items on the date of reclassification should be allowed to accumulate in the foreign currency reserve account.

Non-integral to integral

1. The translation procedure as applicable to integral operations should be followed from the date of such change.
2. The translated amount of non-monetary items on the date of change should be taken at historical cost.
3. The exchange difference accumulated in foreign currency translation reserve account should continue to remain as such and not treated as income or expense until the disposal of the operation.

Accounting Treatment for Category III Transactions, i.e., Forward Exchange Contracts

For accounting purposes, forward exchange contracts are classified into (1) contracts that are entered into for managing risk, popularly known as hedging and (2) contracts that are entered for making profits out of trading or speculation in foreign exchange.

Where the forward contract is taken as a risk managing mechanism, premium on such contract is treated as an expense over the term of the contract. The corresponding exchange gain or loss is transferred to the profit and loss account of the period. Profit or loss arising out of cancellation of the contract or renewal of the same too is transferred to profit and loss account for the period. In case the forward contract is for speculative motive, the forward premium or discount is not recognized. The market value of the contract is shown in the balance sheet on the reporting date and the corresponding profit or loss is transferred to the profit and loss account.

Disclosure Requirements

AS 11 requires an enterprise to disclose the following:

1. The amount of accumulated foreign exchange translation reserve, along with reconciliation of the opening and closing balances of the translation reserve.
2. The amount of exchange differences included in the net profit or loss.

3. In case the reporting currency is different from the currency of the reporting enterprise's country of domicile, the reasons for such difference.
4. In case there is a change in the classification of foreign operation, the nature, reason, and effect of such change on shareholders' fund and on the reported net profit or loss for the period.
5. The enterprise's foreign currency risk management policy.

DEFINITION OF THE TERMS USED IN AS 11

Foreign operations: Foreign operations refer to the operational activities, in the form of subsidiary, associate, joint venture or a branch of the enterprise, conducted in a country other the country of domicile of the reporting enterprise.

Reporting Currency: Reporting currency refers to the currency of the country in which the financial statements are prepared.

Foreign currency: Foreign currency refers to the currency other than the reporting currency.

Exchange rate: Exchange rate refers to the rate at which foreign currency is converted to the reporting currency.

Forward rate: Forward rate refers to the agreed exchange rate between two parties, the buyer and the seller, for the exchange of two currencies at a specified future date.

Closing rate: Closing rate refers to the exchange rate on the date of balance sheet

US GAAP ON FOREIGN CURRENCY TRANSLATION

The Financial Accounting Standard Board (FASB) had issued its statement of Financial Accounting Standards No. 8 (SFAS No. 8) making the use of temporal method as mandatory for the US firms for translation of foreign currency amounts for preparing consolidated financial statements with effect from January 1, 1976. The FASB later came up with the pronouncement of SFAS No. 52 with effect from December 15, 1982 with the incorporation of the concept called functional currency. As against SFAS No. 82 'parent company perception for all transactions', i.e., transactions of the parent's and therefore a single method (the temporal method) of translation; the SFAS No. 52 recognizes the transactions of the subsidiary and the parent as distinct and hence requires a two step translation process. First, the subsidiary's financial statements are to be converted from the local currency to the functional currency using the temporal method and then translated from the functional currency to the US dollar using the current rate method[4].

Exhibit 2.5 depicts the sequence of the translation process to be followed for translation of subsidiary's financial statements into US dollar.

Besides SFAS No. 52, the FASB has also come up with SFAS No. 133 covering voluminous details of the accounting for derivatives and hedging activities effectively from June 15, 2000.

EXHIBIT 2.5 Translation process as per SFAS No. 52

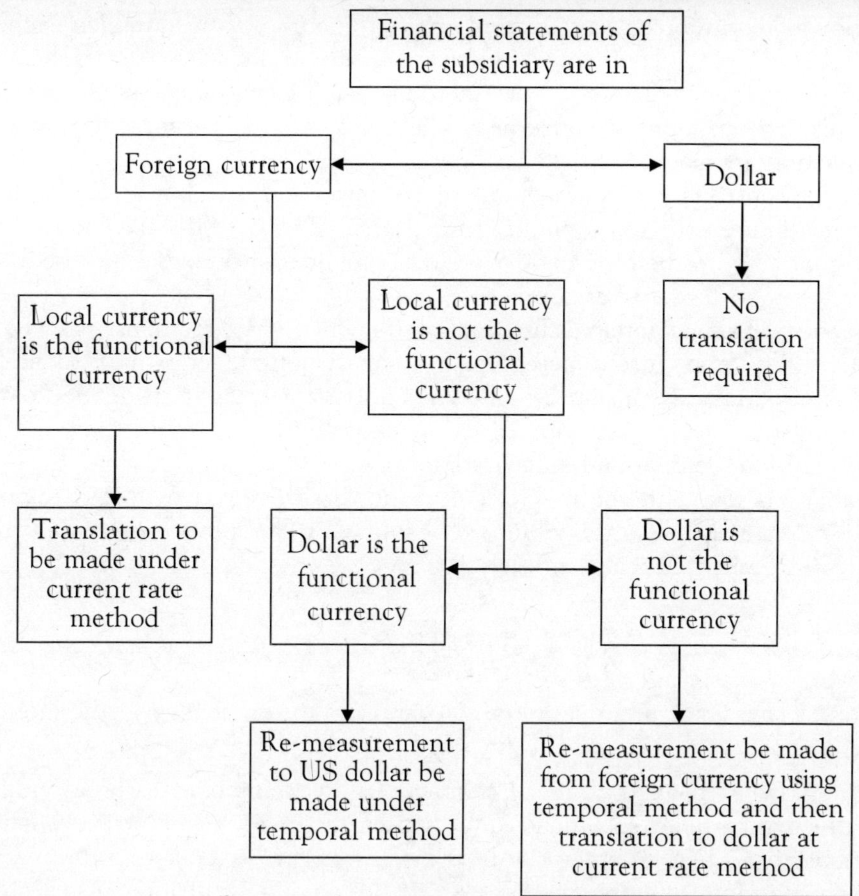

SUMMARY

Foreign currency translation refers to the change in the monetary expression of the financial data contained in the financial statements. Translation of foreign currency(ies) is required primarily for consolidation of financial statements of the subsidiary(ies) with that of the parent company. The other advantages associated with translation are performance evaluation of the subsidiary(ies), informed decision making by the stakeholders and communication to the global audience.

The broader issues involved in translation of foreign currencies are fourfold:

Understanding the nature of foreign transactions and their recording, understanding forward exchange contracts and their recording, understanding the various translation methods and the international issues involved in foreign currency translation.

IAS 21 provides that foreign currency transactions are 'transactions whose terms are denominated in a foreign currency or which require settlement in a foreign currency'. Foreign currency transactions arise where an enterprise buys or sells on credit goods or services whose prices are denominated in foreign currency; borrows or lends funds and the amounts payable or receivable are denominated in foreign currency; is a party to an unperformed foreign exchange contract; or for other reasons, acquires or disposes of assets or incurs or settles liabilities denominated in foreign currency. There are two methods found in vogue across nations as far as recording of foreign transactions is concerned. These are the single transaction approach and the dual transaction approach.

Forward exchange contracts are contracts in which a buyer agrees to buy a certain sum of foreign exchange at a future date and a predetermined price. The core issues associated with forward exchange contracts are the treatment of forward premium or discount and the foreign exchange gains or losses on forward variation.

As far as the translation of foreign currency is concerned, four methods, namely, the current method/the current/non-current method, the monetary/non-monetary method, and the temporal method, are found to be in use by different nations for translation of the financial statement items. Similarly, for treatment of translation gains and losses, the methods followed are: immediate recognition, deferral and amortization.

Given the variations found in the practices of nations with regard to foreign currency translations, the International Accounting Standard Board (AISB) has pronounced standardized procedure to deal with foreign currency translation.

KEY TERMS

Foreign currency translation: Foreign currency translation refers to the change in the monetary expression of the financial data contained in financial statements.

Foreign currency transactions: Foreign currency transactions are 'transactions whose terms are denominated in a foreign currency or which require settlement in a foreign currency'. Foreign currency transactions arise when an enterprise buys or sells on credit goods or services whose prices are denominated in foreign currency; borrows or lends funds and the amounts payable or receivable are denominated in foreign currency; is a party to an unperformed foreign exchange contract; or for other reasons, acquires or disposes of assets or incurs or settles liabilities denominated in foreign currency.

Forward exchange contracts: A forward exchange contract is a contract wherein a buyer agrees to buy a certain amount of foreign exchange at a future date and at a predetermined price. Conversely, a forward exchange contract is contract where a seller agrees to sell a certain sum of foreign exchange at a future date and at a price agreed upon in advance.

REVIEW QUESTIONS

1. What is foreign currency translation? What is its significance? Discuss.
2. Briefly discuss the core issues involved in foreign currency translation.
3. What are the needs for foreign currency translation? State the accounting issues involved in this. Discuss the single transaction approach with an example.

4. Discuss the process of foreign currency translation.
5. Define international transaction and state how such transactions are recorded in the books of the buyer.
6. What are forward exchange contracts? How will you record the losses or gains and the forward premium or discount associated with such contracts?
7. What do you mean by exchange gains and losses? How are they treated in accounting? Explain the features of forward exchange contracts.
8. What are the different techniques of recording foreign currency translation? Explain their features.
9. Explain the provisions of IAS 21 as regards foreign currency translation.
10. Explain the provisions as contained in the Indian GAAP as regards treatment foreign currency translation.
11. Give a comparative picture of the International, Indian and the US GAAP on foreign currency translation.
12. XYZ Ltd. of India purchased goods from ABC Ltd. of Spain on 16.01.2023 for 20,000 € payable four months hence. The exchange rate per € was ₹82.10, ₹82.45 and ₹82.85 as on 16.01.2023, 31.03. 2023 and 16.05. 2023, respectively.

    If XYZ closes the books of account on 31st March every year, show how you will record the above transactions in the books of XYZ Ltd. under the single transaction approach and the dual transaction approach.
13. The following transactions have occurred to RSM India Ltd:

    12.3.2023: Purchased goods from virtual Inc. of USA for 22,500 USD. Twenty five percent of the purchase price was paid in cash and the balance payable 3 months hence.

    20.4.2023: Purchased goods from Jinx & Jinx of UK at £ 18,000 of which 70% were on a 60 days' credit.

    Assume that RSM India Ltd. closes its books of account on every March end.

    Assume further that the following were the rates of exchange:

Date	*₹ per USD($)*	*₹ per £*
12.03. 2023	75.10	90.20
31.03. 2023	75.15	90.45
20.04. 2023	75.35	90.65
12.06. 2023	75.40	90.72
20.06. 2023	75.43	90.74

    Show how you will record the above transactions in the books of RSM India Ltd. under the dual transaction approach.
14. Consider the transactions given in question number 10 above. Show how such transactions will be journalized in the books of RSM Ltd. under the single transaction approach.
15. XYZ Ltd. of India purchased goods from ABC Ltd. of Singapore on 26.01.2023 for 20,000 SGD payable five months hence. The exchange rate per SGD was ₹52.10,

₹52.45 and ₹52.85 as on 26.01.2023, 31.03.2023 and 26.06.2023, respectively. If XYZ closes its books of account on 31st March every year, how you will record the above transactions in the books of XYZ Ltd. under the single transaction approach and the dual transaction approach? Show the entries.

16. Shiva India and Co. agreed on 10.03.2023 to purchase an equipment costing USD 55,000 from Whitnor Inc. of the USA. The machine was agreed to be delivered on 10.08.2023 and the payment was to be made on delivery.

Shiva India and Co. entered into a forward contract on 10.03.2023 to purchase USD. The forward rate prevalent on 10.03.2023 per USD was ₹76.80 and the spot rate was ₹75.40. The exchange rate prevailing on 31.03.2023 and 10.08.2023 was ₹75.75 and ₹76.10 per USD, respectively.

Show how the above transactions will be journalized in the books of Shiva Enterprise under the deferral system.

17. ET India Ltd. purchased goods amounting to 2,500 £ from Max Ltd. of UK on 25th January, 2023 on a six months term. The exchange rate of 1£ as on 25th January,2023, 31st March, 2023 and 25th July, 2023 was ₹89.15, ₹89.95 and ₹90.25, respectively.

How will ET Ltd., which closes its books of account on 31st March every year, record the above transactions under the single transaction approach and the dual transaction approach?

18. The following balance sheet relates to ABC Inc. of France, an Indian subsidiary as on 31.03.2023:

Liabilities	€	*Assets*	€
Equity	8,000	Land and building	6,000
Reserves	12,000	Plant and equipment	14,000
Bonds and debenture	20,000	Long-term investment	8,000
Term loans	14,000	Inventories at market price	15,000
Creditors	6,000	Debtors	12,000
		Cash	5,000
	60,000		60,000

Assuming that the historical rate of 1 € was ₹89.55 and the current rate is ₹89.90, translate the above balance sheet as it would appear under the 'Current rate method'.

19. The following balance sheet relates to ABC Inc. of Italy, an Indian subsidiary as on 31.03. 2023:

Liabilities	€	*Assets*	€
Equity	9,500	Land and building	10,700
Reserves	6,600	Plant and equipment	11,200
Profit	8,500	Furniture and Fixtures	4,300
Bonds and debenture	15,000	Long-term investment	12,100
Term loans	11,000	Inventories at market price	7,900
Creditors	6,000	Debtors	4,400
Outstanding	3,200	Short-term investments	6,600
		Cash	2,600
	59,800		59,800

If the current rate of exchange is ₹80.15 and the historical rate is ₹79.75 per €, translate the above balance sheet as it would appear under the 'Current/Non-current' method.

20. The following balance sheet relates to XYZ Ltd. of Japan, an Indian subsidiary as on 31.03.2023:

Liabilities	€	*Assets*	€
Equity	2,18,000	Land and building	4,16,000
Reserves	1,12,000	Plant and equipment	3,14,000
Bonds and debenture	4,20,000	Long-term investment	1,18,000
Term loans	1,14,000	Inventories at market price	1,20,000
Creditors	2,26,000	Debtors	1,25,000
Outstanding	50,000	Cash	47,000
	11,40,000		11,40,000

Assuming that the historical rate of 100 ¥ was ₹70.55 and the current rate is ₹70.90, translate the balance sheet under 'Current and Non-current rate' method.

21. Following is the balance sheet of Movers and Racers UK Limited, a subsidiary of Slow and Steady India Ltd, as on 31.03.2023:

Liabilities	£	*Assets*	£
Equity	28,000	Land and building	26,000
Reserves	12,000	Plant and equipment	14,000
Bonds and debenture	20,000	Long-term investment	8,000
Term loans	14,000	Inventories at market price	15,000
Payables	16,000	Receivables	22,000
		Cash	5,000
	90,000		90,000

You are required to translate the above balance sheet under 'Monetary and Non-monetary' method taking the historical rate of 1 £ as ₹89.55 and the current rate as ₹90.90.

22. The following balance sheet relates to ABC Ltd. of UK, an Indian subsidiary as on 31.03.2023:

Liabilities	£	*Assets*	£
Equity	12,800	Land and building	9,900
Reserves	8,200	Plant and Machinery	17,700
Profit	4,100	Furniture and fittings	3,200
Bonds and debenture	12,500	Long-term investment	8,800
Term loans	9,900	Inventories at market price	7,900
Payables	5,500	Receivables	4,100
Outstanding	1,300	Short-term investments	1,800
		Cash	900
	54,300		54,300

Translate the above balance sheet under the 'Monetary and Non-monetary' method taking the historical rate of 1 £ as ₹88.90 and the current rate as ₹90.50.

23. The following balance sheet relates to Star Ltd. of Oman, an Indian subsidiary as on 31.03.2023:

Liabilities	*Real*	*Assets*	*Real*
Equity	1,28,000	Land and building	66,000
Reserves and surpluses	12,000	Plant and equipment	44,000
Bonds	20,000	Long-term investment	58,000
Debenture	14,000	Inventories at market price	35,000
Term loans	26,000	Debtors	12,000
Creditors	40,000	Cash	25,000
	2,40,000		2,40,000

Given that the historical rate was ₹19.50/Real and the current rate is ₹20.50, translate the balance sheet under the:

(a) Current rate,
(b) Current and Non-current rate,
(c) Monetary and Non-monetary, and
(d) Temporal method of translation method.

24. Translate the following balance sheet of Richardson Ltd. of UK, a subsidiary of Affluence India Ltd. as on 31.03.2023 under the (a) Current rate, (b) Current and Non-current rate, (c) Monetary and Non-monetary, and (d) Temporal method of translation given further that the historical rate of 1 £ was ₹ 90.15 and the current rate is ₹90.35.

Liabilities	£	*Assets*	£
Equity	22,800	Land and building	19,900
Reserves	16,400	Plant and Machinery	24,700
Profit	14,100	Furniture and fittings	5,200
Bonds and debenture	16,500	Long-term investment	17,800
Term loans	11,900	Inventories at market price	9,900
Payables	6,500	Receivables	8,200
Outstanding	3,250	Short-term investments	3,800
		Cash	1,950
	91,450		91,450

25. The income statement of Priority Ltd. of Ireland, a subsidiary of XYZ India Ltd. for the year ended 31.03.2023 is as under:

		(Fig. in €)
Gross Sales	15,00,000	
Other incomes	30,000	
Total income		15,30,000
Less: Cost of goods sold		
Opening stock	40,000	
Add: Purchases	11,00,000	
Less: Closing stock	10,000	11,30,000
Gross profit		4,00,000
Less: Operating expenses		
(a) Administrative		
Office	1,10,000	

(b) Depreciation	15,000	
Selling		
Advertising	25,000	
Salesmen's Commission	20,000	1,70,000
Profit before tax		2,30,000
Less: Tax(20%)		46,000
Profit after tax		1,84,000

Additional information:

(i) The current rate is ₹40/€ and the historical rate was ₹ 38/€.

(ii) Sales generated were €8,00,000 and €7,00,000 at ₹ 36 and ₹37 per €, respectively.

(iii) Purchases were made in two lots in the ratio of 2:3 at ₹35 and ₹36 per €, respectively.

(iv) Office and selling expenses have been incurred at ₹37 and ₹36, respectively.

Translate the income statement of Priority Ltd. into Indian currency under the multiple rates method.

26. Discuss the specific provisions contained in the US GAAP for translation of foreign currency(ies).

27. Write explanatory notes on:

(a) Integral operations

(b) Forward exchange contracts

(c) Foreign currency translation

(d) Treatment of translation gains and losses

28. Given the following income statement of Cavendor International of Germany, a subsidiary of Fine Tracks India Ltd. for the year ended 31.03.2023 and the additional information beneath, you are required to translate the income statement into Indian currency under the multiple rates method.

		(Fig.in €)
Gross Sales	35,80,000	
Other incomes	3,25,000	
Total income		39,05,000
Less: Cost of goods sold		
Opening stock	4,40,000	
Add: Purchases	18,30,000	
Less: Closing stock	8,10,000	14,60,000
Gross profit		24,45,000
Less: Operating expenses		
(a) Administrative		
Office	2,40,000	
Depreciation	45,000	
(b) Selling		
Advertising	75,000	
Delivery van expenses	20,000	3,80,000
Profit before tax		20,65,000
Less: Tax(25%)		5,16,250
Profit after tax		15,48,750

Additional information:

(i) The current rate is ₹80/€ and the historical rate was ₹78/€.

(ii) Sales generated were €8,00,000; €11,80,000; €9,00,000 and €7,00,000 at ₹78, ₹78.25, ₹78.90and ₹79.30 per €, respectively.

(iii) Purchases were made in three lots in the ratio of 1:2:3 at ₹78.30, ₹78.80 and ₹79.40 per €, respectively.

(iv) Office and selling expenses have been incurred at ₹79 and ₹80 per €, respectively.

29. Following is the income statement of Scientific Generic Inc. of USA, a subsidiary of Endeavours Universal of India Ltd. for the year ended 31.03.2023:

		(*Fig. in* $)
Sales	35,80,000	
Other income	3,25,000	
Total income		39,05,000
Less: Cost of goods sold		
Opening stock	4,40,000	
Add: Purchase	18,30,000	
Less: Closing stock	8,10,000	14,60,000
Gross profit		24,45,000
Less: Operating expenses		
(a) Administrative		
Office	3,40,000	
Depreciation	45,000	
(b) Selling		
Advertising	75,000	
Delivery van expenses	20,000	4,80,000
Profit before tax		19,65,000
Less: Tax(25%)		4,91,250
Profit after tax		14,73,750

You are required to translate the above income statement into Indian currency under the multiple rates method keeping in view the following additional information:

(i) The current rate is ₹80/$ and the historical rate was ₹78/$.

(ii) Sales generated were $8,00,000; $11,80,000; $9,00,000 and $7,00,000 at ₹78, ₹78.25, ₹78.90 and ₹79.30 per €, respectively.

(iii) Purchases were made in three lots in the ratio of 1:2:3 at ₹78.30, ₹78.80 and ₹79.40 per $, respectively.

(iv) Office and selling expenses have been incurred at ₹79 and ₹80 per $, respectively.

REFERENCES

[1] Parkinson, M.R., *Translation of Foreign Currencies*, CICA, Toronto, 1972.

[2] Rathore, S., *International Accounting*, PHI Learning, New Delhi, 1996, p. 68.

[3] Barry, J.E. and Abbas, A.M., IAS 2002, John Wiley & Sons, Inc., p. 867.

[4] Saudagaran, S.M., *International Accounting—A User Perspective*, Taxman, India (2001), p. 74.

3

Consolidation of Financial Statements

LEARNING OBJECTIVES

After Studying this chapter, you will be able to:

- Understand the concept of and the need for consolidation
- Describe the provisions contained in IAS 27 in relation to consolidation
- Describe the provisions of Indian Accounting Standard 21 on consolidation
- Know the techniques followed for consolidation

INTRODUCTION

Consolidation basically refers to the preparation of integrated financial statements, popularly known as consolidated statements, by incorporating the financial data of the subsidiary(ies), to the extent of the controlling interest in the parent company in a view to giving the stakeholders information as regards the economic resources being controlled by the group. In other words, consolidation is an exercise by which the operating results and financial position of the parent company and its subsidiary(ies) are represented in a consolidated manner as if the group were a single economic entity. Consolidated financial statements essentially convey the results of operations and the financial position of a group companies as if they were a single economic entity regardless of any legal distinctions that exist among the separate corporate entities[1]. The purpose of consolidation is to report to the user of the financial statements the economic resources controlled by the group and also the group's obligations.

IAS 27 AND CONSOLIDATION

IAS 27 has stipulated for the presentation of consolidated financial statements in situations where one entity controls another entity. 'Control is deemed to be existing when the parent owns, directly or indirectly through subsidiaries, more than one-half of the voting power over an enterprise. It may also exist even in the absence of this level of ownership if the parent has more than one-half of the voting power as a result of a voting trust or similar arrangement; the power to govern the financial and operating policies of the enterprise by operation of law or by means of an agreement, the power to appoint or remove the majority of the director or equivalent governing peons, or the power to cast a majority of votes at the meetings of the director or its equivalent' [2].

Presentation of consolidated financial statements is mandatory even for non-homogeneous operations. For example, a parent unit engaged in manufacturing might exclude a service subsidiary from its consolidated financial statements for the reason that such inclusion may lead to inappropriate inferences of the results from dissimilar operations. To this effect, IAS 27 provides that 'such reasons are no longer acceptable; if the consolidated statements need further explanation from them to be meaningful, supplementary consolidating statements, showing details for each constituent entity, or detailed footnote schedules can be used to satisfy this need' [3].

Inter-company Transactions

IAS 27 provides that inter-company transactions and balances due from and to the member unit be excluded from the consolidated statements as such transactions and balances do not represent economic events with outside parties and their inclusion would only give a larger appearance of the enterprise than what it is. The standard further stipulates that 'unrealized profit' through an arm's length transaction, i.e., on transfer of assets among the controlled units, be excluded from the consolidated financial statements.

Different Fiscal Periods of Parent and Subsidiary

If the subsidiaries have different fiscal year, they are required to prepare updated information as per the parent's year-end for the purpose of consolidation. IAS 27 permits consolidation of financial data on different dates till the discrepancy does not exceed three months (In India, the permissible discrepancy is up to six months, as per AS 21).

Consistent Accounting Policy

The subsidiaries and the parent included in the consolidated group are required to follow the same accounting policies to account similar transactions and events. In practice, however, this may not happen as the acquired subsidiary may be following, for example, LIFO method of inventory valuation and the parent company the FIFO method. IAS 27 in such case requires adequate disclosure to be made as regards the accounting policies employed.

The standard further provides that if a subsidiary was acquired or disposed of during the period under the acquisition method of accounting, the results of the operations of the subsidiary shall be included in the consolidated financial statements only for the period it was owned.

Minority Interest

If the parent company acquires some, and not all, of the voting shares in the subsidiary, the shares held by third parties represent a minority interest. IAS 27 requires this minority interest to be shown in the consolidated financial statements, in addition to showing the full amount of assets and liabilities and income and expenses of the subsidiary(ies).

Disclosure Requirements

IAS 27 requires that for consolidated financial reporting, the names, countries of incorporation or residence, proportion of ownership interests, and if different, voting interests held be disclosed for all significant subsidiaries. Further, if any subsidiary is not included in the consolidated financial statements, the reasons must be set forth. If an entity over which the parent does not have majority voting control is included in the consolidated financial statements, the reason for this must also be recorded. If the subsidiary was acquired or disposed of during the period covered in the reporting, the effect of the event on the consolidated financial statements should be stated. If parent only financial statements are being presented as permitted, the method of accounting for interest in subsidiaries be disclosed.

INDIAN ACCOUNTING STANDARD 21 (AS 21) AND CONSOLIDATION

Indian Accounting Standard 21 (AS 21) has provided for preparation of consolidated financial statements by parent companies except when (1) a parent acquires the controlling right in the subsidiary (through investment), which is intended to be temporary as the investment (controlling interest) is to be disposed of in the near future; and (2) the subsidiary operates under severe long-term restrictions for which its ability to transfer the funds to parent is significantly weakened. It also states that consolidated financial statements are not the substitute for separate financial statements of a parent and its subsidiary(ies).

As regards disclosure to be made in the consolidated financial statements, AS 21 provides that name(s) of the subsidiary(ies); proportion of ownership interest; nature of relationship between parent and subsidiary such as whether direct control or control through subsidiary(ies); name(s) of the subsidiary(ies) of which reporting date(s) is/are different; the accounting policies adopted for consolidation; and the reasons for non-inclusion of subsidiary(ies), if any, in the consolidated statements, be disclosed.

The Institute of Chartered Accountants of India (ICAI) has offered certain interpretations/ clarifications on AS 21 in relation to consolidation of financial statements. In case a subsidiary has two parents, (i.e., controlled by two enterprises) one controls by holding majority voting power and the other controls by virtue of controlling of the composition of Board of Directors, both the holding enterprises (parents) should consolidate their financial statements by incorporating the same subsidiary. As regards voting power of shares which are held as stock in trade, ICAI clarifies that such stocks should not be included in the consolidated financial statement. Where an enterprise owns majority of voting power by virtue of ownership of the shares of another enterprises and all these shares are held as stock in trade with a view to their subsequent disposal in the near future, then control will be considered temporary and therefore no consolidation of financial statements are required to be prepared [4].

NEED FOR CONSOLIDATION

The basic reason for consolidation of financial statements is to provide the stakeholder with a comprehensive view of the economic resources under the control of the group and the group's obligations. Consolidated financial statements provide an overall financial view of a group of companies so that users are saved the bother of putting together reports of the individual subsidiaries [5]. Thus consolidation of financial statements has an utilitarian value attached to it which can be considered as the single most important advantage of consolidation.

There are legal values attached to consolidated financial statements as well. The Securities and Exchange Board of India (SEBI), for instance, has made consolidation mandatory by virtue of an amendment to its *listing agreement* with effect from April 1, 2001. ICAI, the Accounting Standards setting body in India, too has provided for the inclusion of consolidated financial statements in the Indian financial reporting system. The guidelines and disclosure requirements stated under IAS 27 earlier with regard to presentation of consolidated financial statement are in itself indication of the significance attached to consolidation. In Germany, consolidation of accounts is a statutory requirement and so also in France. The US is, however, pioneer in this respect.

Consolidation of financial statements prevents companies from resorting to 'off the balance sheet financing', the presence of which misleads investors. Off the balance sheet is a mechanism of availing a source of finance which is not statutorily required to be shown as a liability in the balance sheet. In the absence of consolidated financial statements, captive finance subsidiaries may be created to mislead the user of the financial statements. Narayanswamy [6] had reported that the absence of the requirement for presentation of consolidated financial statements has led to the creation of captive finance subsidiaries that are wholly or almost wholly owned by manufacturing or trading firms.

Despite of the advantages associated with presentation of consolidated financial statements for which countries are striving, objections to consolidation are never new. Some thinkers consider this (consolidation) to be redundant. Hylton [7], for example is of the opinion that '... consolidated financial statements are not superior to separate statements. Rather, from separately reported information, an interested reader can determine what really is going on in the parent company. Ratios would no longer be distorted, creditors and stakeholders of the parent company would discover the kind and amount of assets in which they hold an interest and sources and amounts of earnings would be apparent'.

CONSOLIDATION TECHNIQUES

Consolidation techniques found to be in use by different countries may broadly be put as:

1. Line-by-line consolidation
2. One-line consolidation
3. *Pro rata* consolidation

Line-by-Line Consolidation

The line-by-line consolidation is also known as the gross method of consolidation. It has been propagated under IAS 27. Under the line-by-line consolidation technique, all assets and liabilities of the subsidiary company are added to the assets and liabilities of the parent company on a 'one to one' basis. In case the controlling interest of the parent company in the subsidiary company is less than 100 percent, the balancing amount is taken as 'minority interest' and shown as liability in the consolidated balance sheet. The minority interest represents proportional values of assets and liabilities belonging to the shareholders outside the group.

As regards income statement, all income and expenditure and the profit (or loss) of the subsidiary are added to the profit and loss account of the parent company to arrive at the consolidated income statement. Minority's share in the profit too is calculated and adjusted against the net income of the group to find out the share of parent in the net income.

ILLUSTRATION 3.1

Hudson India Ltd. acquired 75% of the equity share capital of James & Co. of USA on 1st April, 2023. The balance sheets of the two companies as on 31st March, 2024 were as follows:

Hudson India Ltd.

Liabilities	₹	*Assets*	₹
Equity shares of ₹10 each	3,00,000	Land and building	2,00,000
Reserves	5,00,000	Plant and machinery	3,00,000
Payables	25,000	Investment in James & Co. Ltd.	75,000
		Stock	80,000
		Receivables	1,20,000
		Cash	50,000
Total	8,25,000	Total	8,25,000

James & Co. Ltd.

Liabilities	₹	*Assets*	₹
Equity shares of ₹10 each	80,000	Plant and machinery	50,000
Reserves	40,000	Furniture and fittings	25,000
		Stock	30,000
		Cash	15,000
Total	1,20,000	Total	1,20,000

You are required to prepare a consolidated Balance Sheet under the line-by-line (gross) method of consolidation.

SOLUTION

Consolidated Balance Sheet

Liabilities	₹	*Assets*	₹
Equity share capital	3,00,000	Goodwill*	15,000
Reserves (₹5,00,000 + 75% of ₹40,000)	5,30,000	Land and building	2,00,000
Payables	25,000	Plant and machinery (₹3,00,000 + ₹50,000)	3,50,000
Minority interest**	30,000	Furniture and fittings	25,000
		Stock (₹80,000 + ₹30,000)	1,10,000
		Receivables	1,20,000
		Cash (₹50,000 + ₹15,000)	65,000
Total	8,85,000	Total	8,85,000

Workings:

1. *Calculation of Goodwill: ₹
   Investment in James & Co. Ltd. 75,000
   Less: Value of equity shares acquired in James & Co. Ltd.,
   (i.e., 75% of ₹80,000) 60,000
   15,000

   Note: In case the value of investment exceeds the cost of investment the resultant figure is taken as capital reserve and reflected in the balance sheet as liability.
2. **Minority interest has been calculated as:
   25% of equity share capital accruing to minority,
   (i.e., 25% of ₹80,000) 20,000
   Plus: Minority's share in the reserves, i.e., 25% of ₹40,000 10,000
   30,000
3. Calculation of group reserves: ₹
   Parent's own reserve 5,00,000
   Add: Parent's share in the reserves of the subsidiary after acquisition,
   i.e.,75% of 40,000 25,000
   Total 5,25,000
4. All other assets and liabilities are added on one to one basis except the equity capitals. Equity capital of the parent alone will be shown in the consolidated balance sheet.

ILLUSTRATION 3.2

Sunderson India Ltd. acquired 80% of the equity share capital of Kimco Ltd. of Japan on 1st April, 2023 for a consideration of ₹92,000. Balance sheets of the two companies as on 31st March, 2024 were as follows:

Hudson India Ltd.

Liabilities	₹	*Assets*	₹
Equity shares of ₹10 each	2,75,000	Land and buildings	2,00,000
Reserves	2,50,000	Plant and machinery	2,00,000
Creditors	1,25,000	Investment in Kimco Ltd.	92,000
Payables	50,000	Debtors	95,000
		Receivables	1,13,000
Total	7,00,000	Total	7,00,000

James & Co. Ltd.

Liabilities	₹	*Assets*	₹
Equity shares of ₹10 each	1,00,000	Land and buildings	1,00,000
Reserves (including ₹10,000 as on 01.04.2023)	50,000	Plant and machinery	75,000
		Debtors	50,000
Creditors	60,000	Receivables	25,000
Payables	40,000		
Total	2,50,000	Total	2,50,000

You are required to prepare a consolidated balance sheet as it would appear under the gross (or line-by-line) consolidation approach.

SOLUTION

Consolidated Balance Sheet

Liabilities	₹	*Assets*	₹
Equity share capital of ₹10 each	2,75,000	Goodwill[1]	4,000
Reserves[2]	2,82,000	Land and building	
Creditors		(₹2,00,000 + ₹1,00,000)	3,00,000
(₹1,25,000 + ₹60,000)	1,85,000	Plant and machinery (₹2,00,000 + ₹75,000)	2,75,000
Payables (₹50,000 + ₹40,000)	90,000	Debtors (₹95,000 + ₹50,000)	1,45,000
Minority interest[3]	30,000	Receivables (₹1,13,000 + ₹25,000)	1,38,000
Total	8,62,000	Total	8,62,000

Workings:

1. Calculation of goodwill:

	₹	₹
Cost of investment in Kimco Ltd.		92,000
Less: Value of investment		
(a) 80% of the value of equity shares of Kimco as on 01.04.2023, (i.e., 80% of ₹1, 00,000)	80,000	
(b) 80% of Kimco's reserve on 01.04.2022, (i.e., 80% of 10,000)	8,000	
		88,000
Goodwill		4,000

2. Calculation of reserves:

	₹
Sunderson's balance of reserve as on 31.03.2024	2,50,000
Plus: 80% of Kimco's reserve after acquisition, {i.e., 80% of (₹50,000 – ₹10,000)}	32,000
	2,82,000

3. Calculation of minority interest:

	₹
20% of share capital accruing to minority, (i.e., 20% of ₹1, 00,000)	20,000
Plus: Minority's share in the reserves of Kimco (i.e. 20% of ₹50,000)	10,000
	30,000

ILLUSTRATION 3.3

Super Max India Pvt. Ltd. has acquired controlling interest in Free Max Inc. of Sweden on April 1, 2023. The balance sheets of the two companies as on March 31, 2024 are given below. You are required to determine the economic resources under the control of the group using the Gross method of consolidation.

Balance sheet of Super Max India Pvt. Ltd. as on March 31, 2024

Liabilities	₹	*Assets*	₹
Equity	12,28,000	Land and building	19,66,000
Reserves and surpluses	8,12,000	Plant and equipment	33,34,000
Profit	10,50,000	Investment in Free Max Inc.	
Bonds	14,20,000	(15,000 shares)	17,10,000
Debenture	16,14,000	Inventories	12,35,000
Term loans	18,26,000	Debtors	8,70,000
Creditors	12,40,000	Cash	75,000
	91,90,000		91,90,000

Balance sheet of Free Max Inc. as on March 31, 2024

Liabilities	₹	*Assets*	₹
Equity (20,000 shares of ₹100 each)	20,00,000	Land and building	22,19,000
Reserves (including ₹2,00,000 as on		Plant and Machinery	24,25,000
1.04.2023)	4,18,000	Furniture and fittings	4,35,000
Profit	6,14,000	Inventories	8,19,000
Bonds	13,16,000	Receivables	12,09,000
Debenture	10,00,000	Short-term investments	3,48,000
Term loans	15,10,000	Cash	2,83,000
Payables	8,07,000		
Outstanding	73,000		
	77,38,000		77,38,000

SOLUTION

The basic purpose of preparing a consolidated financial statement is to determine the economic resources under the control of the parent and its subsidiary/subsidiaries. Hence, the consolidated balance sheet for the group is prepared as under by using the line-by-line (or Gross) method of consolidation.

Consolidated balance sheet as on 31.03.2024

Liabilities	₹	*Assets*	₹
Equity share capital	12,28,000	Goodwill[1]	60,000
Reserves[2a]	9,75,500	Land and building	
Profit[2b]	15,10,500	(₹19,66,000 + ₹22,19,000)	41,85,000
Bonds		Plant and machinery (₹33,34,000 +	
(₹14,20,000 + ₹13,16,000)	27,36,000	₹24,25,000)	57,59,000
Debenture		Furniture and fittings	4,35,000
(₹16,14,000 + ₹10,000)	26,14,000	Inventories (₹12,35,000+ ₹8,19,000)	20,54,000
Term Loans		Debtors	8,70,000
(₹18,26,000 + ₹15,10,000)	33,36,000	Receivables	12,09,000
Creditors		Short-term investment	3,48,000
Payables	12,40,000	Cash (₹75,000+ ₹2,83,000)	3,58,000
Outstanding	73,000		
Minority interest[3]	7,58,000		
Total	1,52,78,000	Total	1,52,78,000

As is evident from the consolidated balance sheet as above, the economic resources under the control of the parent and its subsidiary is found to be ₹1,52,78,000, when determined under the Gross method of consolidation.

Workings:

	₹	₹
1. *Calculation of goodwill:*		
Cost of investment in Free Max Inc.	17,10,000	
Less: Value of investment		
(a) 75% of the value of equity shares of Free Max Inc. as on 01.04.2023, (i.e., 75% of ₹20,00,000)	15,00,000	
(b) 75% of Free Max Inc.'s reserve on 01.04.2023, (i.e., 75% of 2,00,000)	1,50,000	
		16,50,000
Goodwill		**60,000**
2. *Calculation of Reserves and Profit*		
2a. Calculation of reserves		₹
Super Max India Pvt. Ltd.'s balance of Reserve as on 31.03.2024		8,12,000
Plus: 75% of Free Max Inc.'s reserve after acquisition, {i.e., 75% of (₹4,18,000 – ₹2,00,000)}		1,63,500
		9,75,500
2b. Calculation of Profit		
Super Max India PvtLtd's balance of Profit as on 31.03.2024		10,50,000
Plus: 75% of Free Max Inc.'s Profit after acquisition, (i.e., 75% of ₹ 6,14,000)		4,60,500
		15,10,500
3. *Calculation of minority interest:*		
25% of Free Max Inc.'s share capital accruing to the minority shareholder, (i.e., 25% of ₹ 20, 00,000)		5,00,000
Plus: Minority's share in the Reserves and Profits of Free Max Inc (i.e. 25% of ₹4,18,000 + ₹6,14,000)		2,58,000
		7,58,000

Steps in Consolidation under Gross Method

The steps followed for consolidation under the gross (or line-by-line) method may be summarized as follows:

Step 1 Fixed assets except investment in subsidiary and the current assets are added on a 'one to one' basis.

Step 2 Fixed liabilities except owner's equity including reserves and surpluses and current liabilities are added also on a 'one to one' basis.

Step 3 Goodwill is calculated by deducting from the cost of investment (A), the sum total of the cost of equity share acquired (B) and the proportionate share of the reserves of the subsidiary on the date of acquisition (C). Thus, goodwill = A – (B + C).

Note: Cost of investment is the amount paid for acquiring equity shares in the subsidiary company.

Step 4 Group reserves are calculated by adding to the parent company's own reserve, a proportionate share in the reserves of the subsidiary company after acquisition.

Step 5 Minority interest is calculated, in case the parent company does not hold 100% controlling interest in the subsidiary, by adding I and II as follows:

I: Share capital accruing to the minority (i.e., proportionate share belonging to the minority shareholders), and

II: Minority's share in the reserves of the subsidiary as on the date of consolidation.

Step 6 Equity share capital of the parent alone appears in the consolidated balance sheet.

One-Line Consolidation

The one-line consolidation technique is also known as the equity method of consolidation. The technique is found in use mostly in Britain. Contrary to the line-by-line method, under the one-line technique the assets and liabilities and income expenditure of the associated (subsidiary) company are not shown in the consolidated financial statements. Instead, value of investment in the associate is taken at cost plus a proportionate share of the retained earnings including profits from the date of acquisition. Proportionate share of the associate's profit before tax and extra ordinary items are also shown in the consolidated statement.

ILLUSTRATION 3.4

The Balance Sheets of India Inc. and its French subsidiary BH International as on 31.03.2024 were as follows:

India Inc.

Liabilities	₹	*Assets*	₹
Equity shares of ₹10 each	8,00,000	Fixed assets	6,00,000
Retained earnings	2,00,000	Investment in BH International	
Current liabilities	1,00,000	(12,000 shares)	1,50,000
		Current assets	3,50,000
Total	11,00,000	Total	11,00,000

BH International

Liabilities	₹	*Assets*	₹
Equity shares of ₹10 each	2,00,000	Fixed assets	3,50,000
Reserves (including ₹50,000 on		Current assets	1,50,000
01.04.2023)	2,50,000		
Total	5,00,000	Total	5,00,000

Prepare a consolidated balance sheet following the one-line method of consolidation.

SOLUTION

Consolidated Balance Sheet

Liabilities	₹	*Assets*	₹
Equity share capital of ₹10 each	8,00,000	Fixed assets	6,00,000
Reserves[2]	3,20,000	Investments[1] in BH International	2,70,000
Current liabilities	1,00,000	Current assets	3,50,000
Total	12,20,000	Total	12,20,000

Workings

1. *Calculation of investment in BH International (BHI):* ₹
   Cost of (12,000) shares acquired in BHI 1,50,000
   Add: Proportionate share of BHI's retained earnings (reserves) after acquisition,
   i.e., (12,000 share ÷ 20,000 share) × (₹2,50,000 – ₹50,000) = 1,20,000
   2,70,000
2. *Calculation of reserves on consolidation:* ₹
   Existing amount of retained earnings 2,00,000
   Add: proportionate share of BHI's retained earnings after acquisition (calculated as above) 1,20,000
   3,20,000

Note: Other items of assets and liabilities of the parent company (i.e., India Inc.) will continue to be reflected as such in the consolidated statement.

ILLUSTRATION 3.5

Given the following balance sheets of Peter India and its foreign associates Fitter Inc. as on 31.03.2024, and the additional information beneath, prepare a consolidated balance sheet as it would appear under the equity method of consolidation:

Balance sheet of Peter India as on 31.03.2024 *(Fig. in ₹'000)*

Liabilities	₹	*Assets*	₹
Equity share capital (20,000 shares of ₹100 each)	2000	Land and building	900
Reserves and surpluses	500	Plant and machinery	700
Profits	100	Furniture and fittings	300
Debentures	200	Vehicles	150
Creditors	50	Investments in Fitter Inc.	350
Payables	30	Stock	150
Outstanding expenses	20	Debtors	150
		Receivables	200
Total	2900	Total	2900

Balance sheet of Fitter Inc. as on 31.03.2024 *(Fig. in ₹'000)*

Liabilities	₹	*Assets*	₹
Equity share capital (8000 shares of ₹100 each)	800	Land and buildings	450
Reserves and surpluses	200	Plant and machinery	350
Profits	100	Stock	200
Creditors	150	Receivables	250
Total	1250	Total	1250

Additional Information

Peter India had acquired 3,000 equity shares of Fitter Inc. on 01.04.2023 when the latter had ₹1, 40,000 to the credit of its Reserves Account.

SOLUTION

Consolidated Balance Sheet *(Fig. in ₹'000)*

Liabilities	₹	*Assets*	₹
20,000 equity shares of ₹100 each	2000	Land and building	900
Reserves and surpluses[2]	660	Plant and machinery	700
Debentures	200	Furniture and fittings	300
Creditors	50	Vehicles	150
Payables	30	Investment in Fitter Inc.[1]	410
Outstanding	20	Stock	150
		Debtors	150
		Receivables	200
Total	2960	Total	2960

Workings:

	₹
1. *Calculation of investments:*	
Cost of investment	350
Add: Proportionate share in Fitters retained earnings after acquisition, i.e., (3000 equity share ÷ 8,000 equity share) × ₹{(200 – 140) + 100}	60
	410

Note: Retained earnings include reserves and surplus and profits.

2. *Reserves and surpluses:*	
Existing reserves and surplus	500
Plus: Existing profit	100
Plus: Proportionate share in Fitter Inc.'s retained earnings after acquisition	60
	660

ILLUSTRATION 3.6

XYZ India Ltd. has acquired 60% controlling interest in ABC Inc. of Australia on April 1, 2023. The balance sheets of the two companies as on 31.03.2024 are as follows:

Balance sheet of XYZ India Ltd. as on 31.03.2024

Liabilities	₹	*Assets*	₹
Equity		Land and building	61,90,000
(72,800 shares of ₹100 each)	72,80,000	Plant and machinery	77,70,000
Reserves	18,20,000	Furniture and fittings	20,33,000
Profit	14,10,000	Investment in ABC Inc.	18,23,000
Bonds and debenture	52,50,000	Inventories	24,38,000
Term loans	39,90,000	Receivables	16,00,000
Payables	25,50,000	Cash	4,46,000
	2,23,00,000		2,23,00,000

Balance sheet of ABC Inc. as on 31.03.2024

Liabilities	₹	*Assets*	₹
Equity		Land and building	23,00,000
(25,000 shares of ₹100 each)	25,00,000	Plant and equipment	14,00,000
Reserves	9,00,000	Furniture and fixtures	8,00,000
Profit	3,00,000	Inventories	15,00,000
Bonds and debenture	20,00,000	Receivables	22,00,000
Term loans	14,00,000	Cash	5,00,000
Accounts Payable	16,00,000		
	87,00,000		87,00,000

Determine the total economic resources under the control of the group using the 'Equity' method of consolidation.

SOLUTION

The economic resources being controlled by a group at any given point of time can be determined through consolidated financial statements, and in the present case through a consolidated balance sheet. Hence, the consolidated balance sheet for the group has been prepared as under by using the one-line (or Equity) method of consolidation.

Consolidated balance sheet as on 31.03.2024

Liabilities	₹	*Assets*	₹
Equity		Land and building	61,90,000
(72,800 shares of ₹100 each)	72,80,000	Plant and machinery	77,70,000
Reserves[2]	23,60,000	Furniture and fittings	20,33,000
Profit[3]	15,90,000	Investment in ABC Inc.[1]	25,43,000
Bonds and debenture	52,50,000	Inventories	24,38,000
Term loans	39,90,000	Receivables	16,00,000
Payables	25,50,000	Cash	4,46,000
	2,30,20,000		2,30,20,000

As is evident from the consolidated balance sheet above, the economic resources under the control of the parent and its subsidiary is found to be ₹2,30,20,000 when determined under the Equity method of consolidation.

Workings:

1. *Calculation of investments:*

	₹
Cost of investment	18, 23,000
Add: Proportionate share in ABC Inc.'s retained earnings after acquisition, i.e., 60% of Reserves and 60% of Profit = (₹9,00,000+3,00,000)	7,20,000
	25,43,000

Note: Retained earnings include reserves and surplus and profits.

2. *Reserves*

Existing Reserve	18, 20,000
Plus 60% of the reserve of ABC Inc. after acquisition or 60% of 9,00,000	5,40,000
	23,60,000

3. Profit

Existing profit	14,10,000
Plus: 60% of ABC Inc.'s profit after acquisition= 60% of 3,00,000	1,80,000
	15,90,000

Steps in Consolidation under One-line (or Equity) Method

The steps followed for consolidation under the one-line method may be summarized as follows:

Step 1: All the assets and liabilities of the parent company except investment in the subsidiary, Equity capital and reserves and surpluses are shown in the consolidated balance sheet at the same value as they appear in the parent's balance sheet.

Step 2: Value of investment in the associate is increased by adding to it a proportionate share of the retained earnings of the subsidiary/associate from the date of acquisition. This is done based on the fact that the value of investment in associate is equal to the cost of investment (i.e., the purchase price of the investment in the associate as contained in the parent's balance sheet) *plus* a proportionate share (to the extent of minority interest) of the retained earnings including profits of the associate from the date of acquisition.

Step 3: Retained earnings of the parent are increased by adding to it the share (to the extent of controlling interest) in the retained earnings including profits of the subsidiary/associate from the date of acquisition.

Step 4: Equity capital of the parent alone will appear in the consolidated balance sheet.

Pro rata Consolidation

The *pro rata* technique of consolidation is found to be in use in the UK and France. Under this technique, all the items of assets and liabilities and income and expenditure of the subsidiary except share capital are added to the corresponding items of the parent company, to the extent of controlling interest, in order to get the consolidated financial statements. The difference between cost of shares acquired in the subsidiary, and the value of the share acquired plus proportionate share of the parent company in the reserves and surpluses of the subsidiary before acquisition will result in goodwill.

ILLUSTRATION 3.7

Prepare a consolidated balance under the *pro rata* method from the two balance sheets given below in respect of KNG Ltd. of India and its foreign subsidiary Reccon & Co. of Malaysia as on 31.03.2024:

KNG Ltd. (*Fig. in* ₹' 000)

Liabilities	₹	*Assets*	₹
Equity capital (shares of ₹10 each)	200	Fixed assets	250
Reserves and surpluses	200	Investment in Reccon & Co. (9000 shares)	110
Current liabilities	100	Current assets	140
Total	500	Total	500

Reccon & Co. *(Fig. in ₹' 000)*

Liabilities	₹	*Assets*	₹
Equity capital (shares of ₹10 each)	150	Fixed assets	150
Reserves and surpluses (as on 01.04.2023)	30	Current assets	60
Current liabilities	30		
Total	210	Total	210

SOLUTION

Consolidated Balance Sheet *(Fig. in ₹' 000)*

Liabilities	₹	*Assets*	₹
Equity share capital	200	Goodwill [110 – {90+ (3/5) × 30}]	2
Reserves	200	Fixed assets [(250) + (3 ÷ 5)] × 150	340
Current liabilities [(100) + (3 ÷ 5) × 30]	118	Current assets [(140)] + (3 ÷ 5) × 60]	176
Total	518	Total	518

ILLUSTRATION 3.8

Given below are the balance sheets of ABC Ltd. of India and its subsidiary XYZ Ltd. of Sweden as on 31.03.2024:

ABC Ltd. *(Fig. in ₹' 000)*

Liabilities	₹	*Assets*	₹
Equity share capital	300	Plant and machinery	250
Reserves and surpluses	150	Furniture and fittings	100
Long term loan	50	Investment in XYZ Ltd. (9000 shares)	108
Sundry creditors	120	Sundry debtors	115
		Receivables	47
Total	620	Total	620

XYZ Ltd. of Sweden *(Fig. in ₹' 000)*

Liabilities	₹	*Assets*	₹
Equity share capital (shares of ₹10 each)	120	Plant and machinery	100
Reserves	36	Sundry Debtors	60
Creditors	24	Receivables	20
Total	180	Total	180

Prepare a consolidated balance sheet under the *pro rata* method assuming that on 1st April, 2023 ABC Ltd. acquired 75% of the shares of XYZ Ltd. and on which date the later had ₹16,000 to the credit of its reserve account.

SOLUTION

Consolidated Balance Sheet *(Fig. in ₹' 000)*

Liabilities	₹	*Assets*	₹
Equity share capital	300	Goodwill[1]	6
Reserves and surpluses[2]	165	Plant and machinery [(250) + (3 ÷ 4) × 100]	325
Long-term loan	50	Furniture and fittings	100
Sundry creditors [(120) + (3 ÷ 4) × 24]	138	Sundry debtors [(115) + (3 ÷ 4) × 60]	160
		Receivables [(47) + (3 ÷ 4) × 20]	62
Total	653	Total	653

Workings

1. *Goodwill:* ₹

	₹
Cost of shares acquired	108
Less: Value of investment	90
Less: Proportionate share of reserves in XYZ Ltd. on 01.04.2024 i.e., $\left(\frac{3}{4} \times 16 =\right)$	12
	06

2. *Reserves and surpluses:*

Existing reserves	150
Add: Proportionate share in the reserves of XYZ Ltd. after acquisition, i.e., $\left[\frac{3}{4} \times (36 - 16) =\right]$	15
	165

ILLUSTRATION 3.9

Brown Valley India Ltd. has acquired 20,000 Equity shares in Green Valley Ltd. of Sri Lanka on 1.4.2023.

The balance sheets of the two companies as on 31.03.2023 are as follows:

Balance sheet of Brown Valley India Ltd. as on 31.03.2024

Liabilities	₹	*Assets*	₹
Equity	42,18,000	Land and building	26,16,000
Reserves	9,12,000	Plant and equipment	22,14,000
Term loans	22,24,000	Investment in Green Valley Ltd.	
Creditors	24,26,000	(20,000 Shares)	22,18,000
Outstanding	1,50,000	Inventories	10,20,000
		Debtors	16,25,000
		Cash	2,37,000
Total	99,30,000	Total	99,30,000

Balance sheet of Green Valley Ltd. as on 31.03.2024

Liabilities	₹	*Assets*	₹
Equity (30,000 shares of ₹100 each)	30,00,000	Land and building	20,06,000
Reserves (including ₹2,60,000 as on 1.4.2022)	4,40,000	Plant and equipment	16,14,000
Term loans	20,20,000	Inventories	15,00,000
Creditors	8,80,000	Debtors	11,10,000
Outstanding	2,60,000	Cash	3,70,000
Total	66,00,000	Total	66,00,000

You are required to find out the economic resources under the control of the group using the '*pro rata*' method.

SOLUTION

The economic resources under the control of the parent and its subsidiaries (i.e., the group) can be determined through consolidation of the balance sheets. Hence, the consolidated balance sheet has been prepared under the *pro rata* method as under:

Consolidated Balance sheet as on 31.03.2024

Liabilities		₹	*Assets*		₹
Equity share capital		42,18,000	Goodwill[1]		44,667
Reserves and surpluses[2]		10,32,000	Land and Building	26,16,000	
Term loans	22,24,000		*Plus* 2/3 of 20,06,000	13,37,333	39,53,333
Plus 2/3 of	20,20,000	35,70,667	Plant and Equipment	22,14,000	
Creditors	24,26,000		*Plus* 2/3 of 16,14,000	10,76,000	32,90,000
Plus 2/3 of	8,80,000	30,12,667	Inventories	10,20,000	
Outstanding	1,50,000		*Plus* 2/3 of 15,00,000	10,00,000	20,20,000
Plus 2/3 of	2,60,000	3,23,333	Debtors	16,25,000	
			Plus 2/3 of 11,10,000	7,40,000	23,65,000
			Cash	2,37,000	
			Plus 2/3 of 3,70,000	2,46,667	4,83,667
		1,21,56,667			1,21,56,667

As is evident from the consolidated balance sheet, the economic resources controlled by the group is found to be ₹1,21,56,667.

Workings

1. *Calculation of goodwill:*

	₹	₹
Cost of shares acquired in Green Valley Ltd.		22,18,000
Less: Book Value of the shares acquired	20,00,000	
Less: Proportionate share in the reserves of Green Valley Ltd. on 01.04.2023 =2/3 of ₹2,60,000.	1,73,333	21,73,333
		44,667

2. *Reserves and surpluses:*

	₹
Existing reserves	9,12,000
Add: 2/3 of reserves of Green Valley Inc. after acquisition, i.e., 2/3 of ₹1,80,000	1,20,000
	10,32,000

Steps in Consolidation under Pro Rata Method

The steps adopted in *pro rata* consolidation may be summarized as follows:

Step 1: All assets and liabilities except investment, reserves and surpluses, and equity capital of the parent are shown in the consolidated balance sheet by adding to them a proportionate value in the concerned assets and liabilities of the subsidiary.

Step 2: Goodwill is calculated by deducting the cost of investment in the subsidiary from the sum total of the value of investment and a proportionate share in the retained earnings of the subsidiary before acquisition.

The value of investment is equal to the proportionate amount (to the extent of controlling interest) of the book value of subsidiary's share capital. The cost of investment in turn is the price paid to acquire the controlling interest, i.e., the value of investment in subsidiary as shown in the parent's book.

Step 3: Reserves and surpluses are taken as the reserves and surpluses of the parent plus proportionate share in the reserves and surplus of the subsidiary after acquisition.

Step 4: Equity capital of the parent alone is shown in the consolidated balance sheet.

Consolidation Techniques at a Glance

Gross (or line-by-line consolidation)	*One-line or equity*	*Pro rata or proportional*
1. All the assets and liabilities of the subsidiary company are added to the parent company irrespective of the share of controlling interest.	1. The detailed assets and liabilities and revenue and expenses of the subsidiary/associate are not shown in the consolidated financial statements.	1. All the assets and liabilities and income and expenditure of the subsidiary company are shown in the consolidated balance sheet and income statement in proportion to the investment in it by the parent company.
2. Goodwill is calculated by deducting from the cost of investment (A), the sum total of the cost of equity share acquired (B) and the proportionate share of the reserves of the subsidiary on the date of acquisition (C). Thus, goodwill = A – (B + C).	2. Instead, the value of subsidiary/associate is shown in the consolidated balance sheet at '*the cost of investment*' *plus proportionate share in the retained earnings* of the subsidiary/associate from the date of acquisition	2. Goodwill is calculated by deducting the cost of investment in the subsidiary from the sum total of the value of investment and a proportionate share in the retained earnings of the subsidiary before acquisition.
3. Group reserves are calculated by adding to the parent company's own reserve, a proportionate share in the reserves of the subsidiary company after acquisition.	3. Similarly, the figure of proportionate share in the subsidiary/associates' profit before tax and extra-ordinary items are shown in the consolidated income statement.	3. Reserves and surpluses are taken by adding to the parent's reserves and surpluses a proportionate share in the reserves and surplus of the subsidiary after acquisition.

Gross (or line-by-line consolidation)	One-line or equity	Pro rata or proportional
4. If the 'controlling interest' in the subsidiary company is less than 100 percent, 'minority interest' is shown as a liability in the consolidated balance sheet.	4. Retained earnings of the parent are increased by adding to it the share (to the extent of controlling interest) in the retained earnings including profits of the subsidiary/associate from the date of acquisition.	
5. All income and expenditure including profit or loss of the subsidiary(ies) are added to the profit and loss account of the parent company.		
6. Minority's share in the profit is calculated and adjusted against the income of the group to find out the share of the parent company in the net income.		

SUMMARY

Consolidation of financial statements is an exercise by which operating results and financial position of the parent and its subsidiaries are presented in a combined manner as if they were a single economic entity.

The objective of consolidation is to facilitate the investors and other stakeholders getting a comprehensive picture of the economic resources controlled by the group and the group's obligations. Consolidation of financial statements has got utilitarian and legal values attached to it as well.

The methods of consolidation practiced by nations are broadly divided into three: line-by-line (or gross) consolidation, one-line consolidation and *pro rata* consolidation. IAS 27 has stipulated for the use of line-by-line consolidation method.

KEY TERMS

Consolidation: Consolidation refers to the presentation of the operating and financial results of the parent company and its subsidiary(ies) in a consolidated manner so as to help the users of the financial statements getting a comprehensive view of the economic resources controlled by the group and also the group's obligations.

Minority interest: Minority interest refers to the proportion of values of assets and liabilities that belongs to shareholders outside the group.

Line-by-line consolidation: Line-by-line consolidation is a technique of consolidation of financial statements wherein all the assets and liabilities of the subsidiary company are added to the corresponding items of the parent company. In case the parent company does not hold

100 percent controlling interest than minority interest is determined and shown in the balance sheet.

One-line consolidation: One-line consolidation is a technique of consolidation in which value of investment in subsidiary is determined and shown in the consolidated balance sheet unlike the line-by-line method.

Pro-rata consolidation: pro rata consolidation refers to a technique of consolidation financial statements wherein all the assets and liabilities and income and expenditure of the subsidiary are shown in the consolidated balance sheet and income statement in proportion to the controlling interest.

REVIEW QUESTIONS

1. What do you mean by consolidation of financial statements? What are its advantages and drawbacks? Explain.
2. Explain the significance of consolidation of financial statements. State the reasons of objection against consolidation.
3. 'Consolidation of financial statements can do more harm than good'—Do you agree with the statement? Justify your answer.
4. Briefly explain the different methods of consolidation of financial statements. Which of the methods do you recommend for your company and why?
5. Explain the features of line-by-line consolidation. In what respect does it vary from one-line consolidation?
6. Explain how the 'equity method' of consolidating financial statements?
7. Discuss the provisions of IAS 27 in relation to consolidation.
8. Compare and contrast between the provisions of Indian Accounting Standard 21 (AS 21) and IAS 27 in relation to consolidation of financial statements.
9. Explain the utility of consolidated financial statements from the stakeholders' point of view.
10. What do you understand by the term 'limited restatements'? Do such restatements improve the value of the financial information provided to the foreign user?
11. HI India acquired 80% of the equity share capital of JKS of Canada on 1st April, 2023. The balance sheets of the two companies as on 31st March, 2024 were as follows:

HI India

Liabilities	₹	*Assets*	₹
Equity shares of ₹10 each	3,00,000	Land and building	3,00,000
Loans	5,00,000	Plant and machinery	4,00,000
Reserves	2,50,000	Investment in James & Co. Ltd.	80,000
Payables	1,10,000	Stock	1,80,000
		Receivables	1,50,000
		Cash	50,000
Total	11,60,000	Total	11,60,000

JKS Canada

Liabilities	₹	Assets	₹
Equity shares of ₹10 each	1,20,000	Plant and machinery	50,000
Reserves	1,40,000	Furniture and fittings	1,25,000
		Stock	70,000
		Cash	15,000
Total	2,60,000	Total	2,60,000

You are required to prepare a consolidated balance sheet following the line-by-line method of consolidation.

12. S. India Ltd. acquired 90% of the equity share capital of Kings Ltd. of Japan on 1st April, 2023 for a consideration of ₹90,000. Balance sheets of the two companies as on 31st March, 2024 were as follows:

S. India Ltd.

Liabilities	₹	Assets	₹
Equity shares of ₹10 each	5,75,000	Land and buildings	5,00,000
Reserves	7,50,000	Plant and machinery	7,00,000
Creditors	2,25,000	Investment in Kings Ltd.	90,000
Payables	1,50,000	Debtors	2,05,000
		Receivables	2,05,000
Total	17,00,000	Total	17,00,000

Kings Ltd.

Liabilities	₹	Assets	₹
Equity shares of ₹10 each	1,00,000	Land and buildings	1,00,000
Reserves (including ₹20,000 as on 01.04.2023)	80,000	Plant and machinery	75,000
Creditors	60,000	Debtors	80,000
Payables	40,000	Receivables	25,000
Total	2,80,000	Total	2,80,000

You are required to prepare a consolidated balance sheet as it would appear under the gross consolidation approach.

13. The Balance Sheets of India Inc. and its foreign subsidiary BH International as on 31.03.2024 were as follows:

India Inc.

Liabilities	₹	Assets	₹
Equity shares of ₹10 each	9,50,000	Fixed assets	5,50,000
Retained earnings	1,00,000	Investment in BH International (15,000 shares)	2,00,000
Current liabilities	50,000	Current assets	3,50,000
Total	11,00,000	Total	11,00,000

BH International

Liabilities	₹	*Assets*	₹
Equity shares of ₹10 each	3,50,000	Fixed assets	2,50,000
Reserves (including ₹70,000 on 01.04.2023)	1,50,000	Current assets	2,50,000
Total	5,00,000	Total	5,00,000

Prepare a consolidated balance sheet under the one-line method of consolidation.

14. Given the following balance sheets of PQ India and its foreign associates SM Inc. as on 31.03.2024, and the additional information beneath, prepare a consolidated balance sheet as it would appear under the equity method of consolidation:

Balance sheet of PQ India as on 31.03.2024 (*Fig. in ₹'000*)

Liabilities	₹	*Assets*	₹
Equity share capital (20,000 shares of ₹100 each)	2000	Land and building	950
		Plant and machinery	700
Reserves and surpluses	550	Furniture and fittings	300
Profits	150	Vehicles	150
Debentures	150	Investments in SM Inc.	350
Creditors	100	Stock	200
Payables	30	Debtors	150
Outstanding expenses	20	Receivables	200
Total	3000	Total	3000

Balance sheet of SM Inc. as on 31.03.2024 (Fig. in ₹'000)]

Liabilities	₹	*Assets*	₹
Equity share capital (80000 shares of ₹10 each)	800	Land and buildings	550
		Plant and machinery	350
Reserves and surpluses	250	Stock	250
Profits	150	Receivables	300
Creditors	250		
Total	1450	Total	1450

Additional Information:

PQ India had acquired 30,000 equity shares of SM Inc. on 01.04.2023 when the latter had ₹2, 20,000 to the credit of its Reserves Account.

15. Prepare a consolidated Balance Sheet under the *pro rata* method from the two Balance Sheets given below in respect of GN Ltd. of India and its foreign subsidiary KN &Co. of Singapore as on 31.03.2024:

Balance Sheet of GN Ltd. as on 31.03.2024 (*Fig. in ₹' 000*)

Liabilities	₹	*Assets*	₹
Equity capital (shares of ₹10 each)	350	Fixed assets	300
Reserves and surpluses	250	Investment in KN& Co. (8000 shares)	110
Current liabilities	150	Current assets	340
Total	750	Total	750

Balance Sheet of KN & Co. as on 31.03.2024 (*Fig. in* ₹'000)

Liabilities	₹	*Assets*	₹
Equity capital (shares of ₹10 each)	150	Fixed assets	180
Reserves and surpluses (as on 01.04.2023)	130	Stock	60
		Cash	70
Current liabilities	30		
Total	310	Total	310

16. The balance sheets of S&P India and its foreign associates Jasmine Inc. of Philippines as on 31.03.2024 are as follows:

Balance Sheet of S&P India (*Fig. in* ₹'000)

Liabilities	₹	*Assets*	₹
Equity share capital (10,000 shares of ₹100 each)	1000	Land and building	750
Reserves and surpluses	400	Plant and machinery	300
Profits	150	Vehicles	150
Debentures	250	Investments in	350
Payables	50	Jasmine Inc.	175
		Stock	125
		Receivables	
Total	1850	Total	1850

Balance Sheet of Jasmine Inc. (*Fig. in* ₹'000)

Liabilities	₹	*Assets*	₹
Equity share capital (75000 shares of ₹10 each)	750	Land and buildings	250
		Plant and machinery	350
Reserves and surpluses	150	Stock	250
Profits	50	Receivables	200
Creditors	100		
Total	1050	Total	1050

Assuming that S&P India acquired 25,000 equity shares of Jasmine Inc. on 01.04.2023 when the latter had ₹1, 20,000 to the credit of its Reserves Account, prepare a consolidated balance sheet as it would appear under the equity method.

17. Jayco India Ltd. acquired 80% of the equity shares of Suyu Ltd. of Japan on 1st April, 2023 for a consideration of ₹115,000. The balance sheets of the two companies as on 31st March, 2024 were as follows:

Jayco Ltd. (*Fig. in* ₹'000)

Liabilities	₹	*Assets*	₹
Equity capital (shares of ₹10 each)	800	Gross block *less* Depreciation	1200
Reserves and surpluses	320	Investments in Suyu Ltd.	115
Profit	120	Inventory	105
Term loan	180	Receivables	200
Payables	150		
Outstanding expenses	50		
Total	1620	Total	1620

Suyu Ltd. ***(Fig. in ₹' 000)***

Liabilities	₹	*Assets*	₹
Equity capital (shares of ₹10 each)	100	Gross block *less* depreciation	260
Reserves and surpluses (including ₹20,000 as on 01.04.2023)	150	Receivables	140
Payables	150		
Total	400	Total	400

You are required to prepare the consolidated balance sheet for the group under a method of consolidation that you feel as the best.

18. SME India Ltd. acquired 80% of the equity shares of Yu Ltd. of Malaysia on 1st April, 2023 for a consideration of ₹1,05,000. The Balance Sheets of the two companies on 31st March, 2024 were as follows:

Balance Sheet of SME India Ltd. *(Fig. in ₹' 000)*

Liabilities	₹	*Assets*	₹
Equity capital (shares of ₹5 each)	600	Gross block *less* depreciation	1075
General Reserves Surpluses	200	Investments in Yu Ltd.	105
Profit	220	Inventory	165
Term loan	280	Receivables	135
Payables	150	Bank	20
Outstanding	50		
Total	1500	Total	1500

Balance Sheet of Yu Ltd. (Fig. in ₹' 000)

Liabilities	₹	*Assets*	₹
Equity capital (shares of ₹5 each)	100	Gross block *less* depreciation	360
General Reserves	150	Receivables	140
Surpluses (including ₹60,000 as on 01.04.2023)	100	Cash	50
Payables	120		
Outstanding	80		
Total	550	Total	550

You are required to prepare the consolidated balance sheet for the group under a method of consolidation that you feel the most appropriate.

19. Welcome India Ltd. acquired 90% voting rights in Hospitality Thailand Ltd. on 1st April, 2023. The Balance Sheets of the two companies on 31st March, 2024 were as follows:

Balance Sheet of Welcome India Ltd. *(Fig. in ₹' 000)*

Liabilities	₹	*Assets*	₹
Equity capital (shares of ₹5 each)	1600	Gross block *less* depreciation	1575
General Reserves	600	Investments	1165
Capital reserve	520	Inventory	765
Profit	280	Receivables	255
Term loan	450	Bank	120
Payables	250		
Outstanding	180		
Total	3880	Total	3880

Balance Sheet of Hospitality Ltd. *(Fig. in ₹' 000)*

Liabilities	₹	*Assets*	₹
Equity capital (shares of ₹5 each)	1100	Gross block *less* depreciation	1260
General Reserves	450	Investments	140
Surpluses (including ₹1,60,000 as on 01.04.2023)	100	Receivables	300
		Cash	150
Payables	120		
Outstanding	80		
Total	1850	Total	1850

You are required to prepare the consolidated balance sheet for the group under a method of consolidation that you feel the most appropriate.

20. Write explanatory notes on:
   (a) Line-by-line consolidation
   (b) One-line consolidation
   (C) *Pro rata* consolidation

21. Pacific India Ltd. acquired controlling interest in Dolphin Premiers (Philippines) Ltd. on 1st April, 2023. The balance sheets of the two companies as on 31st March, 2024 are as follows:

Balance Sheet of Pacific India Ltd as on 31.03.2024

Liabilities	₹	*Assets*	₹
Equity capital (80,000 shares of ₹100 each)	80,00,000	Land and building	62,00,000
		Plant and machinery	84,40,000
Reserves and surpluses	18,00,000	Investment in Dolphin (18,000 shares)	12,80,000
Profit	14,00,000		
Bonds and Debenture	59,60,000	Inventories (at market value)	27,20,000
Accounts payable	30,40,000	Receivables	30,40,000
Short term loans	26,00,000	Cash	11,20,000
Total	2,28,00,000	Total	2,28,00,000

Balance sheet of Dolphin Premiers (Philippines) Ltd as on 31st March,2024

Liabilities	₹	*Assets*	₹
Share Capital (24,000 shares of ₹50 each)	12,00,000	Land and building	6,90,000
		Plant and machinery	10,58,000
Reserves (Including ₹ 1,80,000 as on 31.3.2023)	2,40,000	Furniture and fixtures	1,60,000
		Inventories (at market value)	2,28,000
Profit	1,10,000	Receivables	2,64,000
Bonds	8,20,000	Cash	1,07,000
Accounts payable	62,000		
Short term loan	75,000		
Total	25,07,000	Total	25,07,000

Prepare a consolidated balance sheet for the group under 'line-by-line' method of consolidation.

22. Curvex India Ltd. acquired 68,000 shares of Circular Systems (Japan) Ltd. on 1st April, 2023. The balance sheets of the two companies as on 31st March, 2021 are as follows:

Balance Sheet of Curvex India Ltd. as on 31.03.2024

Liabilities	₹	*Assets*	₹
Equity share capital	45,25,000	Land and building	51,20,000
Reserves and surpluses	14,75,000	Plant and machinery	78,40,000
Profit	11,80,000	Furniture and fixture	10,80,000
Bonds and Debenture	71,80,000	Investment in Circular Systems	
Fixed Deposits	30,10,000	(Japan) Ltd.	19,10,000
Creditors	22,70,000	Inventories	25,20,000
Short-term loans	11,95,000	Receivables	21,40,000
Outstanding	3,55,000	Cash	5,80,000
Total	2,11,00,000	Total	2,11,90,000

Balance Sheet of Circular Systems (Japan) Ltd. as on 31st March, 2024

Liabilities	₹	*Assets*	₹
Share Capital		Land and building	9,90,000
(80,000 shares of ₹25 each)	20,00,000	Plant and machinery	14,58,000
Reserves (Including ₹2,10,000 as on		Furniture and fixtures	2,10,000
1.4.2023)	2,90,000	Inventories (at market value)	4,08,000
Profit	1,10,000	Receivables	3,24,000
Bonds	8,70,000	Cash	1,47,000
Accounts payable	1,62,000		
Short term loan	1,05,000		
Total	35,37,000	Total	35,37,000

You are required to prepare a consolidated balance sheet for the group under '*pro rata*' method of consolidation, clearly showing your workings.

23. Sea Green India Ltd. acquired 2/3rd of the controlling interest in Butterfly Ltd. of Netherlands on 1st April, 2023. The balance sheets of the two companies as on 31st March, 2024 are as follows:

Balance Sheet of Sea Green India Ltd. as on 31.03.2024

Liabilities	₹	*Assets*	₹
Equity share capital	35,25,000	Land and building	31,20,000
Reserves and surpluses	13,65,000	Plant and machinery	48,40,000
Profit	11,90,000	Furniture and fixture	8,80,000
Bonds and Debenture	41,55,000	Investment in Butterfly Ltd.	9,15,000
Creditors	22,20,000	Inventories	15,20,000
Short-term loans	6,40,000	Receivables	16,40,000
Outstanding	3,50,000	Cash	5,30,000
Total	1,34,45,000	Total	1,34,45,000

Balance Sheet of Butterfly Ltd. as on 31.03.2024

Liabilities	₹	*Assets*	₹
Share Capital		Land and building	18,25,000
(60,000 shares of ₹20 each)	12,00,000	Plant and machinery	13,15,000
Reserves (Including ₹1,20,000 as on		Furniture and fixtures	3,40,000
1.4.2023)	1,80,000	Inventories (at market value)	8,20,000
Profit	2,90,000	Receivables	2,30 ,000
Bonds and Debenture	15,60,000	Cash	1,10,000
Accounts payable	3,40,000		
Short-term loan	4,50,000		
Outstanding	6,20,000		
Total	46,40,000	Total	46,40,000

You are required to prepare a consolidated balance sheet for the group under a method of consolidation you feel the best, showing your workings clearly.

24. Hamilton India Ltd. acquired 36,000 shares of Libra International Ltd. of Philippines on 1st April, 2023. The balance sheets of the two companies as on 31st March, 2024 are as follows:

Balance Sheet of Hamilton India Ltd. as on 31.03.2024

Liabilities	₹	*Assets*	₹
Equity share capital	34,25,000	Land and building	31,20,000
Reserves and surpluses	8,75,000	Plant and machinery	28,10,000
Profit	7,80,000	Furniture and fixture	10,80,000
Bonds and Debenture	31,80,000	Investment in Circular Systems (Japan) Ltd.	19,10,000
Creditors	21,50,000	Inventories	12,20,000
Short-term loans	8,95,000	Receivables	10,40,000
Outstanding	2,55,000	Cash	3,80,000
Total	1,15,60,000	Total	1,15,60,000

Balance sheet of Libra International Ltd. as on 31st March, 2024

Liabilities	₹	*Assets*	₹
Share Capital		Land and building	8,00,000
(80,000 shares of ₹10 each)	8,00,000	Plant and machinery	8,50,000
Reserves (Including ₹90,000 as on		Furniture and fixtures	2,10,000
1.4.2022)	1,50,000	Inventories (at market value)	3,20,000
Profit	1,40,000	Receivables	2,25,000
Debentures	6,90,000	Cash	1,75,000
Accounts payable	2,20,000		
Short-term loan	3,80,000		
Outstanding	2,00,000		
Total	25,80,000	Total	25,80,000

You are required to prepare a consolidated balance sheet for the group under (a) 'line-by-line' method and (b) '*pro rata*' method of consolidation, showing details of your workings.

25. Rosemary and Sons (India) Pvt. Ltd. acquired 60% of the controlling interest in Marigold Universal of Switzerland on 1st April, 2023. Prepare a consolidated balance sheet for the group under (a) 'line-by-line' method and (b) 'equity' method of consolidation from the financial data contained in the balance sheets of the two companies as on 31st March, 2024 as given below:

Balance Sheet of Hamilton India Ltd. as on 31.03.2024

Liabilities	₹	*Assets*	₹
Equity share capital	74,25,000	Land and building	31,15,000
Reserves and surpluses	18,55,000	Plant and machinery	69,35,000
Profit	11,15,000	Furniture and fixture	9,60,000
Bonds and Debenture	51,25,000	Investment in Circular Systems	
Creditors	21,95,000	(Japan) Ltd.	20,05,000
Outstanding	2,35,000	Inventories	21,25,000
		Receivables	23,45,000
		Cash	4,65,000
Total	1,79,50,000	Total	1,79,50,000

Balance Sheet of Libra International Ltd. as on 31st March, 2024

Liabilities	₹	*Assets*	₹
Share Capital		Land and building	8,00,000
(80,000 shares of ₹10 each)	8,00,000	Plant and machinery	8,50,000
Reserves (Including ₹90,000 as on		Furniture and fixtures	2,10,000
1.4.2023)	1,50,000	Inventories (at market value)	3,20,000
Profit	1,40,000	Receivables	2,25,000
Debentures	6,90,000	Cash	1,75,000
Accounts payable	2,20,000		
Short term loan	3,80,000		
Outstanding	2,00,000		
Total	25,80,000	Total	25,80,000

26. Adventure India Ltd. has acquired 3/4th controlling interest in Smart Move International Inc. of Germany on April 1, 2023. The balance sheets of the two companies as on March 31, 2024 are given beneath. You are required to prepare a consolidated balance sheet as it would appear under the 'line-by-line' and' one-line' methods.

Balance sheet of Adventure India Ltd. as on 31.03.2024

Liabilities	₹	*Assets*	₹
Equity	50,95,000	Land and building	31,25,000
Reserves	16,40,000	Plant and equipment	72,14,000
Profit	11,25,500	Furniture and fixtures	14,34,000
Bonds and debenture	44,15,000	Investment in Smart Move	
Term loans	28,11,000	International Inc.	7,97,000
Creditors	17,26,000	Inventories at market price	22,17,000
		Debtors	18,40,000
		Cash	1,85,500
Total	1,68,12,500	Total	1,68,12,500

Balance sheet of Smart Move International Inc. as on 31.03.2024

Liabilities	₹	*Assets*	₹
Equity	8,00,000	Land and building	16,00,000
Reserves	1,20,000	Plant and equipment	17,80,000
Bonds and debenture	12,00,000	Inventories at market price	1,50,000
Term loans	11,40,000	Debtors	7,20,000
Creditors	6,60,000	Cash	50,000
Short-term loan	3,80,000		
Total	43,00,000	Total	43,00,000

27. Secure India Pvt. Ltd. has acquired controlling interest in Heaven's Inc. of Italy on April 1, 2023. The balance sheets of the two companies as on March 31, 2020 are given below. You are required to prepare a consolidated balance sheet as it would appear under the '*pro rata*' and 'one-line' methods of consolidation.

Balance sheet of Secure India Ltd. as on 31.03.2024

Liabilities	₹	*Assets*	₹
Equity	55,95,000	Land and building	31,25,000
Reserves	16,40,000	Plant and equipment	72,14,000
Profit	11,25,500	Furniture and Fixtures	14,34,000
Bonds and debenture	44,15,000	Investment in Heaven's Inc.	
Term loans	28,11,000	(25,000 Shares)	27,97,000
Fixed deposits	17,66,000	Inventories	22,17,000
Creditors	10,00,000	Debtors	18,40,000
Outstanding	4,60,000	Cash	1,85,500
Total	1,88,12,500	Total	1,88,12,500

Balance sheet of Heaven's Inc. as on 31.03.2021

Liabilities	₹	*Assets*	₹
Equity share capital		Land and building	22,50,000
(35,000 shares of ₹100 each)	35,00,000	Plant and equipment	37,25,000
Reserves (including ₹2,50,000 as		Furniture	8,80,000
on 1.4.2023)	3,75,000	Inventories at market price	12,50,000
Profit	5,50,000	Debtors	11,25,000
Bonds and debenture	20,55,000	Cash	50,000
Creditors	19,30,000		
Short-term loan	8,70,000		
Total	92,80,000	Total	92,80,000

28. Super MaxIndia Pvt. Ltd. has acquired controlling interest in Free Max Inc. of Sweden on April 1, 2023. The balance sheets of the two companies as on March 31, 2024 are given below. You are required to prepare a consolidated balance sheet under the (i) Gross method, (ii) Equity method, and (iii) '*pro rata*' method of consolidation.

Balance Sheet of Super Max India Pvt. Ltd. as on 31.03.2024

Liabilities	₹	*Assets*	₹
Equity Share Capital	1,85,95,000	Land and building	1,31,25,000
Reserves	86,40,000	Plant and equipment	1,82,14,000
Profit	51,25,000	Furniture and Fixtures	44,34,000
Bonds and debenture	1,24,15,000	Vehicle	32,52,000
Term loans	1,38,11,000	Investment in Heaven's Inc. (75,000 Shares)	87,87,000
Fixed deposits	50,66,000	Inventories	58,15,000
Accounts Payable	30,00,000	Receivables	1,18,40,000
		Cash	11,85,000
Total	6,66,52,000	Total	6,66,52,000

Balance Sheet of Free Max Inc. as on 31.03.2024

Liabilities	₹	*Assets*	₹
Equity share capital (95,000 shares of ₹100 each)	95,00,000	Land and building	62,50,000
		Plant and equipment	57,25,000
Reserves (including ₹6,50,000 as on 1.4.2023)	10,75,000	Furniture and fittings	14,80,000
		Inventories	32,50,000
Profit	9,50,000	Receivables	11,25,000
Bonds and debenture	24,55,000	Cash at bank	6,75,000
Term Loan	11,30,000		
Accounts payable	12,70,000		
Short-term loan	10,00,000		
Total	1,73,80,000	Total	1,73,80,000

29. Open Sky India Ltd. has acquired 40% controlling interest in Pacific Global Inc. of Holland on April 1, 2023. The balance sheets of the two companies as on March 31, 2024 are given below. Determine the economic worth under the control of the group as on March 31, 2024 using the (i) Gross method, and (ii) '*pro rata*' method of consolidation.

Balance Sheet of Open Sky India Ltd. as on 31.03.2024

Liabilities	₹	*Assets*	₹
Equity Share Capital	1,45,95,000	Land and building	1,11,72,000
Preference share capital	98,00,000	Plant and machinery	1,62,18,000
Reserves	36,40,000	Furniture and fixtures	33,65,000
Profit	21,60,000	Loose tools	12,17,000
Bonds and debenture	1,05,15,000	Vehicle	42,13,000
Term loans	78,11,000	Investment in Pacific Global Inc.	58,15,000
Accounts Payable	33,20,000	Inventories	38,40,000
Short-term Loan	19,80,000	Receivables	51,85,000
		Short-term investment	19,60,000
		Cash	8,36,000
Total	5,38,21,000	Total	5,38,21,000

Balance Sheet of Pacific Global Inc. as on 31.03.2024

Liabilities	₹	*Assets*	₹
Equity share capital (1,25,000shares of ₹100 each)	1,25,00,000	Land and building	70,50,000
Reserves (including ₹6,50,000 as on 1.4.2020)	8,40,000	Plant and equipment	87,60,000
Profit	10,50,000	Furniture and fittings	12,40,000
Bonds and debenture	34,25,000	Inventories	28,20,000
Term Loan	28,28,000	Receivables	21,30,000
Accounts payable	12,70,000	Cash at bank	5,70,000
Outstanding	6,57,000		
Total	2,25,70,000	Total	2,25,70,000

30. Good Luck India Pvt. Ltd. has acquired controlling interest in Fortune Inc. of Maxico on April 1, 2023. The balance sheets of the two companies as on March 31, 2024 are given below.

Balance Sheet of Good Luck India Pvt. Ltd. as on 31.03.2024

Liabilities	₹	*Assets*	₹
Equity Share Capital	1,25,60,000	Land and building	81,82,000
Reserves	16,30,000	Plant and machinery	71,72,000
Profit	11,75,000	Furniture and fixtures	21,22,000
Bonds and debenture	1,15,00,000	Loose tools	11,12,000
Term loans	58,01,000	Vehicle	23,32,000
Accounts Payable	32,10,000	Investment in Fortune Inc. (60,000 shares)	65,64,000
		Inventories	38,47,000
		Receivables	35,34,000
		Cash at bank	10,11,000
Total	3,58,76,000	Total	3,58,76,000

Balance Sheet of Fortune Inc. as on 31.03.2024

Liabilities	₹	*Assets*	₹
Equity share capital (80,000 shares of ₹100 each)	80,00,000	Land and building	40,50,000
Reserves (including ₹ 4,50,000 as on 1.4.2023)	6,40,000	Plant and equipment	51,60,000
Profit	15,50,000	Furniture and fittings	11,30,000
Bonds and debenture	24,25,000	Loose tools	8,22,000
Term Loan	18,58,000	Inventories	22,10,000
Accounts payable	9,67,000	Receivables	16,40,000
Outstanding	2,50,000	Cash at bank	6,78,000
Total	1,56,90,000	Total	1,56,90,000

You are required to determine the economic worth under the control of the group as on March 31, 2024 by using the (i) Gross method, (ii) '*pro rata*' method, and (iii) the one-line method of consolidation.

REFERENCES

[1] Choi, F.D.S. and Mueller, G., *International Accounting*, Prentice Hall Inc., Englewood Cliffs, NJ, 1984.

[2] Epstein, B.J. and Murza, A.A., *Interpretation and Application of International Accounting Standards*, Wiley, 2002, p. 486.

[3] *Ibid*, p. 487.

[4] Rawat, D.S., *Accounting Standards*, Taxmann, 6th Ed., p. 243.

[5] Rathore, S., *International Accounting*, PHI Learning, 1996, p. 86.

[6] Narayanswami, R. *Off Balance Sheet Financing: A threat to financial reporting*, The Chartered Accountant, Vol. 37, No. 2, Aug 1988, pp. 121–126.

[7] Hylton, D.P., *On the Usefulness of Consolidated Financial Statements, The CPA Journal*, Vol. 58, October 1988, pp. 74–77.

4

Accounting for Price Level Changes

LEARNING OBJECTIVES

After Studying this chapter, you will be able to:

- Explain the concept and forms of price level changes
- Appreciate the need for price level change adjustments
- Identify the causes and consequences of distortions in accounting profit vis a vis financial statements
- Describe the techniques of price level change adjustments
- Discuss the merits and limitations of different techniques of price level change adjustments

INTRODUCTION

Financial data contained in the income statement and balance sheet prepared under the traditional accounting method based on the accounting principle of 'cost concept' becomes unreliable in the event of a change in the purchasing power of money. Income and the financial position as reported in the financial statements prepared under the traditional accounting system continue to be distorted in the absence of an adjustment to the effect of the price level changes on the items of revenue and expenses and so also the assets and liabilities. Inflation in particular has become the world order today. It is therefore necessary to adjust the financial statements of the firms against inflation so as to arrive at the true financial positions, in addition to overcoming other limitations associated with distorted profits.

PRICE LEVEL CHANGE

Price level changes refer to the changes in the value of monetary unit. Put differently, price level changes refer to the increase or decrease in the purchasing power of money. Purchasing power in turn refers to the ability of a given sum of money to buy a certain amount of goods or services now, in comparison to what the same sum of money could have bought at a previous date.

TYPES OF PRICE LEVEL CHANGE

Price level changes may assume the following three forms:

1. General price level changes
2. Specific price level changes, and
3. Relative price level changes.

General Price Level Changes

General Price level changes refers to the increase or decrease in the value of monetary unit measured in terms of a price index. Say, for example, if the price index for consumer goods was 100 on 1.4.2022 and 150 on 1.4.2023, the change in the general price level is 50%, i.e. $\frac{150-100}{100}\times 100$.

Specific Price Level Changes

Specific price level changes amount to the changes in the prices of a specific good or service. For example if the price of steel per ton was ₹200 on 1.4.2022 and ₹250 on 1.4.2023, the change in the price of steel is 25%, i.e., $\frac{250-200}{200}\times 100$.

Relative Price Level Changes

Relative price level changes results from the change in the prices of one commodity in relation to the changes in the prices of all commodities and services taken together. For example, if the change in the specific price level is 20% and that of the general price level is 10%, the relative change in price level would be: $\frac{120-110}{110}\times 100$ or 9.09%.

COMMON PHENOMENON OF PRICE LEVEL CHANGES

The changes in the value of monetary unit or simply price level changes can occur due to inflation or deflation. Whereas inflation refers to a continuous increase in the general price level, deflation refers to a decrease in the general price level. The value of money falls under inflationary situation and rises under deflationary situation. Consequently, more amount of money will be needed to buy the same commodity under inflation than under deflation.

Over the past, the price level changes world over have assumed an inflationary trend. As such, we will limit our discussion including accounting treatment on price level changes to inflationary situation only.

NEED FOR PRICE LEVEL CHANGES ADJUSTMENT

Financial statements prepared under the traditional methods are based on the basic assumption that the purchasing power of money is always stable. Given this assumption and as long as the assumption continues to hold good, the financial statements prepared above (i.e., under the traditional or historical cost method) would provide useful and valid information to the decision makers. However, as the monetary unit does not remain stable due to inflation, the information contained in the financial statements without adjustments for inflation becomes highly distorted owing to misrepresentation of certain elements like cost of goods sold, depreciation, deferred expenses and purchasing power gains and losses. Generally, profit as revealed by the profit and loss account prepared under the historical cost method has a tendency to be overstated in times of rising prices. As a consequence, corporate firms lend up with, among others, paying higher tax. Taxation of overstated profits in real term amounts to tax on capital [1]. Financial statements too lose their credibility and interpretative benefits for overstatement of value of assets in the balance sheet, inflated rate of return on capital, generous distribution of dividend, higher wage payments and poor liquidity, all due to inflated profits.

The above listed reasons which cause distortions to financial statements prepared under the historical cost methods and the associated consequences which have been discussed with reasonable details below, call for adjustment of financial statements against price level changes.

FACTORS CAUSING DISTORTIONS TO ACCOUNTING PROFIT VIS-A-VIS FINANCIAL STATEMENTS

Broadly speaking, four factors cause distortions to financial results as reported under historical of accounting method. These are:

1. Cost of goods sold
2. Depreciation
3. Deferred expenses
4. Purchasing power gains and losses.

Cost of Goods Sold

It is a common business phenomenon that goods are purchased on a date prior to the date of their sales. As such, a sale, i.e., revenue, which mostly appears at current money value, is compared with cost mostly in the form of cost of goods sold appearing at historical cost. This uneven comparison of cost with revenue results in overstatement of profits.

Depreciation

Depreciation is charged on depreciable fixed assets over a series of years based on the price(s) at which the assets were initially acquired. As the purchasing power of money at the time of acquisition of the assets was different than the price prevailing now, the amount of depreciation thus calculated under historical cost method and charged to income statement falls short of the cost of the assets consumed as well as becomes insufficient for replacement of the assets. Further, the understatement of depreciation results in overstatement of profit to the extent depreciation is under-recovered.

Deferred Expenses

Heavy advertising expenses, preliminary expenses and alike are often deferred to be written off in future year(s). When such expenses are written off it amounts to matching a previous cost which was at different purchasing power with current revenue. This phenomenon will again lead to getting inflated profits under the historical cost method of accounting.

Purchasing Power Gains and Losses

Purchasing power gains and losses occur on account of treatment of trade debtors and creditors under inflationary situation. Debtors stand to gain from inflation whereas creditors loose due to inflation. Conversely, debtors' gain is the enterprise's loss and the creditors' loss is the enterprise's gain. In traditional accounting however these purchasing power gains and losses are not recognized. As a result only a distorted profit is reported.

CONSEQUENCES OF DISTORTED PROFITS

The major impacts of distorted profits are:

1. Payment of higher taxes
2. Payment of enhanced dividends
3. Payment of higher wages
4. Reduction in the credibility of financial statements
5. Reduction in liquidity position.

Under-recovery of depreciation, as mentioned in the aforesaid paragraphs, leads to overstatement of profits. Overstated profits in turn attract levy of higher taxes on the firm. As a result, tax burden of the firm goes up. Further, inflated profits result in the payment of higher rates of dividend. Workers too will demand for enhanced wage payments due to higher profits.

The credibility of the financial statements goes down under inflationary situation as investors get unrealistic impression about the performance of the firm. For instance, overstated profits will amount to a higher rate of return on investment (ROI), a measure of business performance. Liquidity position of the firm too gets affected due to liberal dividend policy and under recovery of depreciation.

TECHNIQUES OF PRICE LEVEL ADJUSTMENTS

In order to enhance the interpretive value of financial statements of firms which have foreign subsidiary(ies), adjustments against price level changes has become a necessity. Two techniques, not withstanding their relative merits and demerits, have been suggested for the purpose. They are:

1. Restate–Translate, and
2. Translate–Restate.

Under the 'restate–translate' method, proposed by Zenoff and Zwick [2], financial statements of the subsidiaries are first restated to reflect the changes in the purchasing power of the foreign currency(ies) and then translated at the closing rate of exchange corresponding to the parent company's currency. The other proponents of this method are Parkinson [3], Shevayder [4] and the American Accounting Association Committee on International Accounting [5] who have suggested that the financial statements of subsidiaries be restated to general purchasing power (GPP) using a foreign index and then translated at the closing rate of exchange.

Contrary to the above, the translate – restate method mentioned above, emphasizes that financial statements of foreign subsidiaries be first translated into domestic currency of the parent company and then restated for inflation using the parent country index. Translate – restate method was first suggested by the American Accounting Principles Board (APB) statement 3.

As stated earlier, each of the two methods namely, restate–translate and translate–restate has its own merits and demerits. For example, restate–translate method is considered superior to translate–restate method insofar as the former gives a better measure of performance of the subsidiary than the latter. The restate–translate method too has been criticized for being inconsistent as compared to translate–restate method.

Given the choice between the two, it is the restate–translate method which is always preferred to translate–restate method.

Restate–Translate Mechanism

As the name suggests, under restate–translate method, financial statements of the foreign subsidiary(ies) are first restated to GPP using a foreign index and then the restated financial statements are translated into the parent company's own currency. And later, the translated financial statements are consolidated. Thus, the three phases involved in the restate–translate mechanism are:

Whereas translation (i.e., phase II) has been discussed at length in Chapter 2, consolidation (i.e., Phase III) has been discussed in Chapter 3. It is the 'restatement' (i.e., Phase I) which is discussed here.

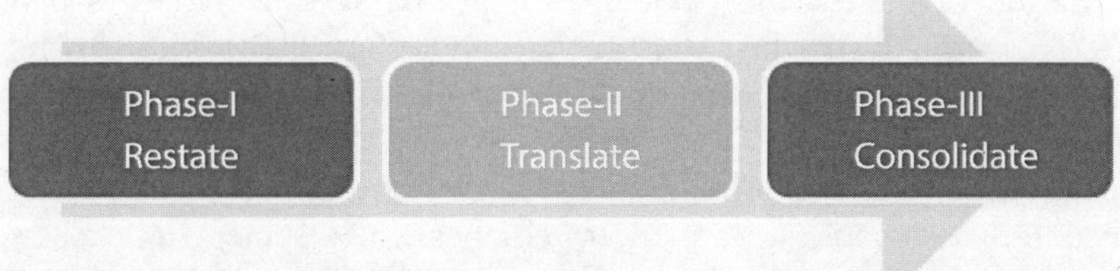

TECHNIQUES OF RESTATEMENT OF FINANCIAL STATEMENTS

Broadly speaking, there are two 'restatement' techniques available for giving effect to changes in price level. These are:

1. Current Purchasing Power Technique (also known as General Purchasing Power Technique), and
2. Current Cost Accounting Technique.

Although several other techniques such as (i) 'creation of reserves' out of profits available for distribution annually to avoid over-distribution of profits, (ii) 'revaluation of capital assets' in order to disclose the current cost of assets used by the firm, and (iii) 'LIFO method' of inventory valuation for adjustment of rising prices are also found to be prevalent in certain countries, they have been excluded from present discussion on the ground that they are considered to be 'incomplete' in nature. Thus, the CPP (or GPP) and the CCA techniques are discussed here.

Current Purchasing Power (CPP) Technique

The CPP technique, which is also known as General Purchasing Power (GPP) technique has found its base way back in 1911 with the publication of Irving Fisher's work 'the purchasing power of money [6]. The CPP is a popular technique found extensively in use in USA, Germany and Australia, by companies for adjusting financial statements against inflation. The basic idea behind CPP technique is to convert items of the financial statements prepared under historical accounting method to their corresponding current costs by adopting and applying 'general purchasing power' as the unit of money measurement.

The entire process followed for such conversion may be divided into the following three steps:

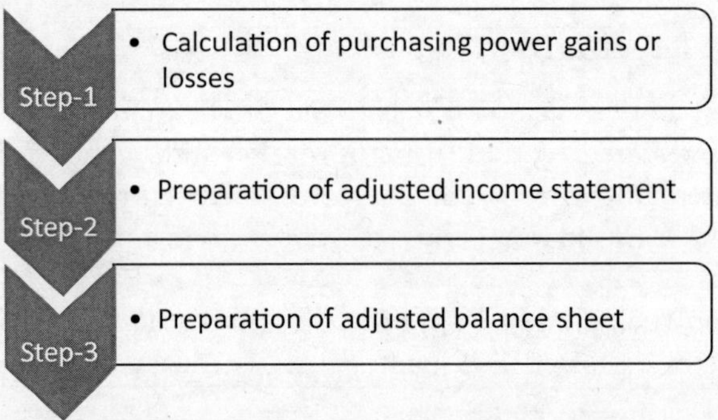

***Step 1:* Calculation of purchasing power gains or losses:** Calculation of purchasing power gains or losses is essentially the first step in the conversion of historical financial statements to price level adjusted financial statements based on the CPP technique. And the first step in calculating purchasing power gains or losses is to classify all assets and liabilities contained in the balance sheet into two categories, namely, monetary and non-monetary.

Monetary assets and liabilities are those which are not subject to reassessment of their recorded values due to changes in the purchasing power of money. In other words, monetary assets and liabilities carry fixed amounts in terms of money by virtue of contract or otherwise, irrespective of change in the general price level. Some of the examples of monetary assets are debtors, bills receivables, outstanding income and cash; and monetary liabilities are creditors, bills payable, outstanding expenses and loans. Monetary liabilities represent obligations to pay a fixed sum of money at a future date irrespective of any change in the value of the monetary unit.

Non-monetary assets and liabilities are those which are subject to reassessment of their values due to changes in the purchasing power of money. Non-monetary assets include inventory, land, building, plant and machinery and alike whose values in terms of monetary units are likely to change over time. Non-monetary liabilities include items like retained earnings and equity capital whose values would change owing to the changes in the purchasing power of money.

Once the assets and liabilities are classified as stated above, the non-monetary items of assets and liabilities are then converted to their respective current purchasing power values using appropriate index/indices.

Having classified the items of assets and liabilities into monetary and non-monetary categories and further having converted the non-monetary items into their corresponding

CPP values, the next step is to find out the net gain or loss arising out of holding monetary assets and liabilities, simply called as purchasing power gains or losses. The process followed to finding out purchasing power gains or losses is to offset all losses on monetary assets against the gains on monetary liabilities owing to inflation, for it is known that inflation is beneficial to debtors and detrimental to creditors.

ILLUSTRATION 4.1

Given the following Balance Sheet of XYZ & Co. Ltd. as on 31.03.2023 and the additional information beneath, determine the purchasing power gains or losses on monetary items:

Balance Sheet of XYZ & Co. Ltd. as on 31.03.2023

Liabilities	₹	*Assets*	₹
Equity Capital	10,00,000	Land and building (net of depreciation)	10,00,000
Long-term loan	10,00,000	Plant and machinery (net of depreciation)	4,00,000
Creditors	4,00,000	Bills receivable	8,00,000
Bills payable	2,00,000	Cash	4,00,000
Total	26,00,000	Total	26,00,000

The general price index as on 31.03.2023 is 225 which was 150 corresponding to the dates on which the fixed assets and long-term loan were acquired.

SOLUTION

The monetary items in XYZ & Co. Ltd. are bills receivable and cash (as assets) and long-term loan, creditors and bills payable (as liabilities). Let us now find out the losses and gains due to changes in the purchasing power of money in respect of these monetary assets and liabilities as follows:

Calculation of purchasing power gains or losses

Monetary items Col. 1	*Value before conversion Col. 2*	*Conversion factor Col. 3*	*Value after conversion Col. 4 (i.e. Col.2 × Col.3)*	*Loss (–) or gain (+) due to conversion Col. 5 (i.e. Col.2 – Col.4)*
Bill receivable	8,00,000	225/150	12,00,000	(–)4,00,000
Cash	4,00,000	225/150	6,00,000	(–)2,00,000
Long-term loan	10,00,000	225/150	15,00,000	+5,00,000
Creditors	4,00,000	225/150	6,00,000	+2,00,000
Bills payable	2,00,000	225/150	3,00,000	+1,00,000
Net purchasing power gains (₹)				2,00,000

Note: It is assumed that the company will lose ₹4, 00,000 and ₹2, 00,000 respectively for holding monetary assets, namely, bills receivable and cash. Similarly the company will gain ₹5, 00,000, ₹2, 00,000 and ₹1, 00,000 respectively for holding monetary liabilities such as loan, creditors and bills payable. The underlying argument is that the company will receive only ₹8,00,000 from the debtors as bills receivable and not ₹12,00,000 as it would have been had the changing prices been taken into account. Thus the loss to the company is assumed to be ₹4, 00,000 on account of bills receivable. A similar argument holds good for monetary liabilities where the company stands to gain. For example, the company would be required to payback ₹10, 00,000 towards loan and not ₹15, 00,000 (i.e., the amount after conversion), thus gaining ₹5, 00,000 on the transaction. The overall gain to the company would therefore be ₹2, 00,000 as stated above.

ILLUSTRATION 4.2

Given the summarized Balance Sheet of XYZ Ltd. as on 31.03.2023, and the additional information below, find out the amount of purchasing power gains or losses associated with monetary assets and liabilities:

Balance Sheet of XYZ Ltd. as on 31.03.2023

Liabilities	₹	*Assets*	₹
Equity capital	11,00,000	Fixed assets less depreciation	14,00,000
Long term debts	7,00,000	Cash and accounts receivable	13,00,000
Short term debts	9,00,000		
	27,00,000		27,00,000

If the current price index is 290 and the price index at which the fixed assets and long-term debts were acquired is 160.

SOLUTION

Purchasing power gains and losses are always associated with monetary assets and monetary liabilities when converted into current purchasing power. In the given illustration, the monetary assets are cash and accounts receivables and monetary liabilities are both long-term and short-term debts.

Given the above backdrop, the net purchasing power gains or losses can be determined as follows:

Calculation of Purchasing Power Gains or Losses

Monetary items Col. 1	*Value before adjustment Col. 2*	*Conversion factor Col. 3*	*Value after conversion Col. 4 (i.e. Col.2 × Col.3)*	*Gain or loss on conversion Col. 5 (i.e. Col.2 – Col.4)*
Cash and accounts receivable	13,00,000	290/160	23,56,250	(–)10,56,250
Current debts	9,00,000	290/160	16,31,250	(+)7,31,250
Long term debts	7,00,000	290/160	12,68,750	(+)5,68,750
Net purchasing power gains (₹)				2,43,750

ILLUSTRATION 4.3

From the Balance Sheet of Blue Moon Ltd. as on 31.03.2023 given below and the additional information beneath, determine the purchasing power gains or losses:

Balance Sheet of Blue Moon Ltd. as on 31.03.2023

Liabilities	₹	*Assets*	₹
Equity Capital	18,00,000	Land and building (net of depreciation)	10,00,000
Reserves	5,00,000	Plant and Machinery (net of depreciation)	14,00,000
Profit	4,00,000	Furniture and fixture	8,00,000
Debentures	12,00,000	Loose tools	4,00,000
Term loan	13,00,000	Inventories	6,00,000
Creditors	8,00,000	Bills receivable	10,00,000
Bills payable	3,00,000	Cash at bank	9,00,000
		Cash in hand	2,00,000
Total	63,00,000	Total	63,00,000

The general price index as on 31.03.2023 is 225, which was 150 corresponding to the dates on which the fixed assets and long-term loan were acquired.

SOLUTION

Calculation of Purchasing Power Gains or Losses

Monetary items Col. 1	*Value before conversion* Col. 2	*Conversion factor* Col. 3	*Value after conversion* Col. 4 (i.e. Col.2 × Col.3)	*Loss (–) or gain (+) due to conversion* Col. 5 (i.e. Col.2 – Col.4)
Bill receivable	10,00,000	225/150	15,00,000	(–)5,00,000
Cash at bank	9,00,000	225/150	13,50,000	(–)4,50,000
Cash in hand	2,00,000	225/150	3,00,000	(–)1,00,000
Debentures	12,00,000	225/150	18,00,000	(+)6,00,000
Term loan	13,00,000	225/150	19,50,000	(+)6,50,000
Creditors	8,00,000	225/150	12,00,000	(+)4,00,000
Bills payable	3,00,000	225/150	4,50,000	(+)1,50,000
Net purchasing power gains (₹)				7,50,000

Note: Bills receivable, Cash at bank and Cash in hand are monetary assets; and Debentures, Term loan, Creditors, and Bills payable are monetary liabilities.

ILLUSTRATION 4.4

Consider the Balance Sheet of Black and Berry Ltd. as on 31.03.2023 and the additional information given below and determine the net purchasing power gains or losses associated with monetary items for the company:

Balance Sheet of Black and Berry Ltd. as on 31.03.2023

Liabilities	₹	*Assets*	₹
Equity Capital	1,18,00,000	Land and building (net of depreciation)	1,20,00,000
Reserves	35,00,000	Plant and Machinery (net of depreciation)	1,44,00,000
Profit	24,00,000	Furniture and fixture	38,00,000
Debentures	1,12,00,000	Loose tools	24,00,000
Term loan	1,13,00,000	Inventories	56,00,000
Creditors	38,00,000	Bills receivable	50,00,000
Bills payable	25,00,000	Cash at bank	29,00,000
Outstanding	5,00,000	Cash in hand	9,00,000
Total	4,70,00,000	Total	4,70,00,000

(i) General Price index prevalent on 31.03.2023 is 225.

(ii) The company had acquired the fixed assets and long-term loan on 31.03.2022 when the General Price index was 200.

SOLUTION

Statement showing calculation of purchasing power gains or losses of Black and Berry Ltd.

Monetary items Col. 1	*Value before conversion* Col. 2	*Conversion factor* Col. 3	*Value after conversion* Col. 4 (*i.e.* Col.2 × Col.3)	*Loss (–) or gain (+) due to conversion* Col. 5 (*i.e.* Col.2 – Col.4)
Bill receivable	50,00,000	225/200	56,25,000	(–)6,25,000
Cash at bank	29,00,000	225/200	32,62,500	(–)3,62,500
Cash in hand	9,00,000	225/200	10,12,500	(–)1,12,500
Debentures	1,12,00,000	225/200	1,26,00,000	(+)14,00,000
Term loan	1,13,00,000	225/200	1,27,12,500	(+)14,12,500
Creditors	38,00,000	225/200	42,75,000	(+)4,75,000
Bills payable	25,00,000	225/200	28,12,500	(+)3,12,500
Outstanding	5,00,000	225/200	5,62,500	(+)62,500
Net purchasing power gains (₹)				25,62,500

Note: Bills receivable, Cash at bank and Cash in hand are monetary assets; and Debentures, Term loan, Creditors, and Bills payable, and outstanding are monetary liabilities.

***Step 2:* Preparation of adjusted income statement:** So far we have seen how purchasing power gains or losses are calculated. It is important to remember that the aggregate of purchasing power gains or losses forms a part of the converted balance sheet items. Now, as the second major step to preparing price level adjusted financial statements, we need to adjust the income statement.

Whereas the basic process followed for adjustment of the items of income statement is the conversion of the individual items of the statement into their current values using appropriate conversion factor(s), special attention needs to be given to the following three items:

1. Treatment of inventory,
2. Treatment depreciation, and
3. Treatment of revenues and expenses not evenly occurring throughout the year (accounting period).

Treatment of inventory: A proper valuation of inventory is a prerequisite to adjustment of income statement. The value of inventory included in the adjusted income statement should be based on conversion factor (price index) in consonance with the method of inventory valuation. If for example, FIFO is the method of inventory valuation followed by a firm, then the price index at the end of the sales period or an average of the indices for the concerned sales period should be used to determine the value of the inventory.

Treatment of depreciation: Depreciation recovered on assets should be adjusted in accordance with the price index appropriate to the date(s) of purchase of the asset(s). The loss or gain on sale of any such asset(s) would also warrant a similar treatment.

Treatment of revenues and expenses not evenly occurring: It is assumed that the revenues (sales) are earned and expenses incurred evenly throughout the accounting year and hence an average price index is considered prudent for the conversion of revenues and expenses in the income statement. In case of specific information as regards the date(s) of occurrence of any items of revenue or expenses, such items would be converted based on price index as available on the date(s) of their occurrence.

ILLUSTRATION 4.5

The income statement of ABC Ltd. for the year ended 31.03.2023 is as under:

	(Fig in ₹)
Sales	9,50,000
Less: Cost of goods sold	5,10,000
Operating income	4,40,000
Less: Expenses	1,20,000
Less: Depreciation	40,000
Net income	2,80,000

Other relevant additional information are:

(i) The price index as on 31.03.2023 was 150.

(ii) Sales were made and expenses incurred when the price index was also 150.

(iii) Inventory was valued on FIFO basis.

(iv) Goods were purchased during the year in three lots of ₹2,50,000, ₹2,00,000 and ₹1,50,000 with the prevailing price index of 120, 125 and 132, respectively.

(v) There was no opening inventory. Closing inventory was valued at ₹90,000.

(vi) The fixed assets were acquired on 1st April, 2022 when the general price index was 120.

(vii) Show how the adjusted income statement would appear.

SOLUTION

Price level adjusted income statement of ABC Ltd. for the year 31.03.2023

Items *Col. 1*	*Value before adjustment* *Col. 2*	*Conversion factor* *Col. 3*	*Value after adjustment* *Col. 4* *(i.e. Col.2 × Col.3)*
Sales	9,50,000	(×)150/150	9,50,000
Less: Cost of goods sold comprising of			
(i) Goods of 1st lot	2,50,000	(×)150/120	3,12,500
(ii) Goods of 2nd lot	2,00,000	(×)150/125	2,40,000
(iii) Goods of 3rd lot (i.e. ₹1,50,000 – closing stock of ₹90,000)	60,000	(×)150/132	68,182
Operating income	4,40,000	—	3,29,318
Less: Expenses	1,20,000	150/150	1,20,000
Less: Depreciation	40,000	150/120	50,000
Net income ₹	2,80,000		1,59,318

Thus, the price level adjusted income for ABC Ltd. is found to be ₹1,59,318 as against the pre-adjusted income of ₹2,80,000.

ILLUSTRATION 4.6

Given the income statement of Blinking Star Ltd. for the year ended 31.03.2023 and the additional information is as under, prepare a price-level adjusted income statement:

	(Fig in ₹)
Sales	99,90,000
Less: Cost of goods sold	45,10,000
Operating income	54,80,000
Less: Expenses	
Office	12,25,000
Selling and Distribution	11,40,000
Less: Depreciation	4,15,000
Net income	27,00,000

Other relevant additional information is:

(i) The price index as on 31.03.2023 was 150, and on 13.3.2022 was 135.

(ii) Sales were made and expenses incurred when the price index was 140 and 145, respectively.

(iii) Inventory was valued on FIFO basis.

(iv) Goods were purchased during the year in three lots of ₹20,00,000, ₹15,00,000 and ₹10,00,000 with the prevailing price index of 138, 140 and 142, respectively.

(v) The opening stock of materials was of ₹8,00,000 and theclosing stock was valued at ₹7,90,000.

(vi) The fixed assets were acquired on 1st April, 2020 when the general price index was 135.

SOLUTION

Price level adjusted income statement of Blinking Star Ltd. for the year 31.03.2023

Items Col. 1	*Value before adjustment* Col. 2	*Conversion factor* Col. 3	*Value after adjustment* Col. 4 (i.e., Col.2 × Col.3)
Sales	99,90,000	(×)150/140	1,07,03,570
Less: Cost of goods sold comprising of			
(i) Opening stock	8,00,000	(×)150/135	8,88,888
(ii) Goods of 1st lot	20,00,000	(×)150/138	21,73,913
(iii) Goods of 2nd lot	15,00,000	(×)150/140	16,07,143
(iv) Goods of 3rd lot (i.e. ₹10,00,000 – closing stock of ₹7,90,000)	2,10,000	(×)150/142	2,21,831
Operating income	54,80,000	–	58,11,795
Less: Expenses			
(i) Office	12,25,000	(×)150/145	12,67,241
(ii) Selling and Distribution	11,40,000	(×)150/145	11,79,310
Less: Depreciation	4,15,000	(×)150/142	4,38,380
Net income ₹	27,00,000		29,26,864

ILLUSTRATION 4.7

Given the income statement of Hill-View Ltd. for the year ended 31.03.2023 and the additional information is as under, prepare a price-level adjusted income statement:

	(Fig in ₹)
Sales	45,45,000
Less: Cost of goods sold	20,55,000
Operating income	24,90,000
Less: Expenses	
(a) Manufacturing	6,30,000
(b) Office	3,25,000
(c) Selling and Distribution	2,40,000
Less: Depreciation	2,15,000
Net income	10,80,000

Other relevant information is:

(i) The price index as on 31.03.2023 was 150, and on 31.3.2022 was 135.

(ii) Sales were made and expenses incurred when the price index was 145 and 140, respectively.

(iii) Inventory was valued on FIFO basis.

(iv) Goods were purchased during the year in three lots of ₹7,50,000, ₹10,25,000 and ₹5,00,000 with the prevailing price index of 140, 145 and 150, respectively.

(v) There was no opening stock and the closing stock was valued at ₹2,20,000.

(vi) The fixed assets were acquired on 1st April, 2022 when the general price index was 135.

SOLUTION

Price level adjusted income statement of Hill-View Ltd. for the year 31.03.2023

Items *Col. 1*	*Value before adjustment* *Col. 2*	*Conversion factor* *Col. 3*	*Value after adjustment* *Col. 4* (*i.e. Col.2 × Col.3*)
Sales	45,45,000	(×)150/145	47,01,724
Less: Cost of goods sold comprising of			
(i) Goods of 1st lot	7,50,000	(×)150/140	8,03,571
(ii) Goods of 2nd lot	10,25,000	(×)150/145	10,60,345
(iii) Goods of 3rd lot (i.e. ₹5,00,000 – Closing stock of ₹2,20,000)	2,80,000	(×)150/150	2,80,000
Operating income	24,90,000		
Less: Expenses		–	25,57,808
(i) Manufacturing	6,30,000	(×)150/140	6,75,000
(ii) Office	3,25,000	(×)150/140	3,48,214
(iii) Selling and Distribution	2,40,000	(×)150/140	2,57,143
Less: Depreciation	2,15,000	(×)150/135	2,38,889
Net income ₹	10,80,000		10,38,562

***Step 3:* Preparation of adjusted balance sheet:** The third step in the process of conversion of historical financial statements into price level adjusted financial statements is the preparation of a price level adjusted balance sheet. Conversion of the values of traditional balance sheet

items through appropriate conversion factor(s) into price level adjusted values is thus the task beforehand.

While converting the balance sheet items due considerations to the following as mentioned against each be given:

1. **Fixed assets:** All fixed assets are to be converted at the price index corresponding to the date(s) of their acquisition.
2. **Inventories:** Inventories to be adjusted appropriately in the income statement and also in the balance sheet as per prevailing price index.
3. **Monetary assets and liabilities:** Monetary assets and liabilities are to appear at their respective closing values, i.e., they do not need any adjustment as they already appear at the year end purchasing power of money.
4. **Equity capital:** Equity share capital to be converted at the price index as was prevalent at the time of its issue.
5. **Purchasing power gains and losses:** Purchasing power gains or losses are to be directly reflected in the balance sheet.
6. **Adjusted income:** Income, as per adjusted income statement, will find a place in the balance sheet. Existing retained earnings are to be converted at the prevailing price index/indices they were created.

Alternatively, and in the absence of an adjusted income statement, the balancing figure in the balance sheet shall be considered as retained earnings.

Illustration 4.8, 4.9, and 4.10 demonstrate how price level adjusted balance sheets are prepared.

ILLUSTRATION 4.8

From the Balance Sheet of Synergy Ltd. as on 31.03.2023 and the additional information given beneath, prepare a price level adjusted Balance Sheet:

Balance Sheet of Synergy Ltd. as on 31.03.2023

Liabilities	₹	*Assets*	₹
Equity capital	8,00,000	Fixed assets net of depreciation	10,00,000
Preference share capital	3,00,000	Investments	4,00,000
Debentures	10,00,000	Debtors	6,00,000
Creditors	4,00,000	Receivables	2,00,000
		Cash	3,00,000
	25,00,000		25,00,000

Additional information

The general price index as on 31.03.2023 was 200 and the same was 160 on 31.03.2022, the date of acquisition of fixed assets and issue of share capital.

SOLUTION

Price level adjusted Balance Sheet of Synergy Ltd. as on 31.03.2023

Liabilities	₹	*Assets*	₹
Equity capital 8,00,000 × (200/160)	10,00,000	Fixed assets net of depreciation 10,00,000 × (200/160)	12,50,000
Purchasing power of gains	50,000	Investments	4,00,000
Preference share capital	3,00,000	Debtors	6,00,000
Debentures	10,00,000	Receivables	2,00,000
Creditors	4,00,000	Cash	3,00,000
	27,50,000		27,50,000

Notes:

1. Investments and preference share capital have been considered as monetary assets and monetary liability, respectively. This is because regardless of the changes in the purchasing power of money, the amount receivable on investments will be the same except the periodic interest earnings. And for preference share capital the amount redeemable will be the same ₹3,00,000.
2. Debtors, receivables and cash are clearly the other items of monetary assets, and debentures and creditors are monetary liabilities.
3. The monetary assets and liabilities as explained under 1 and 2 above give rise to a purchasing power gains of ₹50,000 as shown below:

Calculation of purchasing power gains or losses

Monetary items Col 1	*Pre-adjusted values Col. 2*	*Conversion factor Col. 3*	*Post-adjusted values Col. 4 (i.e., Col.2 × Col. 3)*	*Gains or losses Col. 5 (i.e., Col. 2 – Col. 4)*
Investments	4,00,000	200/160	5,00,000	(–)1,00,000
Debtors	6,00,000	200/160	7,50,000	(–)1,50,000
Bills receivable	2,00,000	200/160	2,50,000	(–)50,000
Cash	3,00,000	200/160	2,75,000	(–)75,000
Preference share capital	3,00,000	200/160	2,75,000	(+)75,000
Debentures	10,00,000	200/160	12,50,000	(+)2,50,000
Creditors	4,00,000	200/160	5,00,000	(+)1,00,000
Net purchasing power gains ₹				50,000

ILLUSTRATION 4.9

Given the Balance Sheet of Orbit Orientation Ltd. as on 31.03.2023 and the additional information given beneath, draw a price level adjusted Balance Sheet for Orbit Orientation Ltd:

Balance Sheet of Orbit Orientation Ltd. as on 31.03.2023

Liabilities	₹	*Assets*	₹
Equity	20,00,000	Land and building	22,00,000
Reserves	4,00,000	Plant and machinery	24,25,000
Profit	6,00,000	Furniture and fittings	4,35,000
Bonds	13,10,000	Inventories	8,00,000
Debenture	10,00,000	Receivables	12,00,000
Term loans	15,08,000	Short-term investments	3,48,000
Payables	8,00,000	Cash	2,80,000
Outstanding	70,000		
	76,88,000		76,88,000

Additional information:

(i) The general price index on 31.03.2023 andon 31.03.2022 was 180 and 160, respectively.
(ii) Fixed assets were acquired when the price index was 160.
(iii) Equity capital, bonds, debentures and term loans were raised on 1.4.2022.

SOLUTION

Price level adjusted Balance Sheet of Orbit Orientation Ltd as on 31.03.2023

Liabilities	₹	*Assets*	₹
Equity {20,00,000 × (180/160)}	22,50,000	Land and building {22,00,000 × (180/160)}	24,75,000
Reserves** {4,00,000 × (180/160)}	4,50,000	Plant and Machinery {24,25,000 × (180/160)}	27,28,125
Profit** {6,00,000 × (180/160)}	6,75,000	Furniture and fittings {4,35,000 × (180/160)}	4,89,375
Bonds	13,10,000	Inventories* {8,00,000 × (180/160)}	9,00,000
Debenture	10,00,000		
Term loans	15,08,000	Receivables	12,00,000
Payables	8,00,000	Short-term investments	3,48,000
Outstanding	70,000	Cash	2,80,000
Purchasing power gains***	3,57,500		
	84,20,500		84,20,500

Notes: *Inventories has been taken as non-monetary item; hence converted accordingly.

** The converted value of Reserves and Profit can also be determined as follows:

The converted value of assets is ₹84,20,500. The converted value of liabilities excluding retained earnings (i.e., Reserves and Profit) is ₹72,95,500. The difference between these two is ₹11,25,000. This may be taken as the converted value of retained earnings, i.e., Reserves and Profit taken together; and then this can be distributed between these two items of retained earnings in proportion to their values before conversion which is 4:6.

***Calculation of purchasing power gains or losses is as under:

Purchasing power gains or losses of Orbit Orientation Ltd.

Monetary items Col 1	*Pre-adjusted values* Col. 2	*Conversion factor* Col. 3	*Post-adjusted values* Col. 4 (*i.e.*, Col. 2 × Col. 3)	*Gains or losses* Col. 5 (*i.e.*, Col.2 – Col.4)
Receivables	12,00,000	180/160	13,50,000	(–)1,50,000
Short-term investment	3,48,000	180/160	3,91,500	(–)43,500
Cash	2,80,000	180/160	3,15,000	(–)35,000
Bonds	13,10,000	180/160	14,73,750	(+)1,63,750
Debenture	10,00,000	180/160	11,25,000	(+)1,25,000
Term loans	15,08,000	180/160	16,96,500	(+)1,88,500
Payables	8,00,000	180/160	9,00,000	(+)1,00,000
Outstanding	70,000	180/160	78,750	(+)8,750
Net purchasing power gains ₹				3,57,500

ILLUSTRATION 4.10

The balance sheet of Regency Ltd. as on 31.03.2023 is as under:

Liabilities	₹	*Assets*	₹
Equity Share capital	25,00,000	Land and building	23,50,000
Preference Share Capital	12,00,000	Plant and equipment	15,00,000
Profit	20,50,000	Furniture and fixtures	8,25,000
Bonds and debenture	14,00,000	Inventories	15,00,000
Term loans	16,50,000	Debtors	22,25,000
Creditors	9,00,000	Bills Receivables	11,00,000
Bills Payables	3,00,000	Cash	5,00,000
	1,00,00,000		1,00,00,000

You are required to prepare a price level adjusted balance sheet for Regency Ltd., after taking into consideration the following additional information:

(a) The general price index on 31.03.2023 and on 31.03.2022 was 180 and 160, respectively.

(b) Fixed assets were acquired when the price index was 160.

(c) Equity and Preference share capital were raised on 1.4.2022 and so also term loans and bonds and debentures.

SOLUTION

Price level adjusted balance sheet for Regency Ltd. as on 31.03.2023

Liabilities	₹	*Assets*	₹
Equity Share capital		Land and building	
{25,00,000 × (180/160)}	28,12,500	{23,50,000 × (180/160)}	26,43,750
Preference Share Capital	12,00,000	Plant and equipment	
Profit**		{15,00,000 × (180/160)}	16,87,500
{20,50,000 × (180/160)}	23,06,250	Furniture and fixtures	
Bonds and debenture	14,00,000	{8,25,000 × (180/160)}	9,28,125
Term loans	16,50,000	Inventories*	
Creditors	9,00,000	{15,00,000 × (180/160)}	16,87,500
Bills Payables	3,00,000	Debtors	22,25,000
Purchasing power gains	2,03,125	Bills Receivables	11,00,000
		Cash	5,00,000
	1,07,71,875		1,07,71,875

Notes: * Inventories has been taken as non-monetary item; hence converted accordingly.

** The converted value of 'Profit'is also equal to the difference between the converted value of assets (i.e., ₹ 1,07,71,875) and the converted value of liabilities excluding 'profit' (i.e, ₹84,65,625). This difference is attributed to 'retained earnings' and in the instant case profit will be considered as retained earnings (in the absence of any other components of retained earnings).

Calculation of Purchasing Power Gains or Losses

Monetary items Col 1	Pre-adjusted values Col. 2	Conversion factor Col. 3	Post-adjusted values Col. 4 (i.e., Col. 2 × Col. 3)	Gains or losses Col. 5 (i.e., Col. 2 – Col. 4)
Debtors	22,25,000	180/160	25,03,125	(–)2,78,125
Bills Receivable	11,00,000	180/160	12,37,500	(–)1,37,500
Cash	5,00,000	180/160	5,62,500	(–)62,500
Preference Share Capital	12,00,000	180/160	13,50,000	(+)1,50,000
Bonds and Debenture	14,00,000	180/160	15,75,000	(+)1,75,000
Term loans	16,50,000	180/160	18,56,250	(+)2,06,250
Creditors	9,00,000	180/160	10,12,500	(+)1,12,500
Bills payable	3,00,000	180/160	3,37,500	(+)37,500
Net purchasing power gains ₹				2,03,125

Advantages of Current Purchasing Power (CPP) Technique

Following are the main advantages of CPP technique:

1. It uses a single price index to measure the changes in purchasing power of money.
2. It does not depart from the basic historical cost system of maintaining accounts, expect for an objective restatement of such costs.
3. It keeps the calculations relatively simple and verifiable because of the use of a single conversion factor.
4. It gives a summarized (i.e., overall) picture of the effect of price level changes.

Limitations of Current Purchasing Power (CPP) Technique

Following are the major drawbacks of the CPP technique:

1. Selection of an appropriate single index for adjustment is difficult. Gynther[7], for example, feels that there is nothing such which can be called as generalized purchasing power of money and hence no single conversion index.
2. By using general price index, CPP approach fails to recognize the effect of price level changes on specific items.
3. CPP accounting is likely to have limited long-term managerial applicability insofar as assessment of the firm's past performance and future planning are concerned. This is because of, among others, the inclusion of purchasing power gains (and losses) in the periodic income and its probable distributions.

CURRENT COST ACCOUNTING TECHNIQUE

The Sandilands Committee [8] of UK, constituted under the chairmanship of F.E.P. Sandilands to tackle the problems of inflation, while rejecting the use of CPP method, had recommended in September, 1975 the use of current cost accounting (CCA) technique for the purpose.

Features of CCA Technique

1. Fixed assets (other than land and building) are shown in the balance sheet at their *value to the business* and not at historical cost as reduced by depreciation. Value to the

business of an asset is its written down current *replacement cost*, i.e., estimated cost of acquiring a new asset of the same productive capacity at current prices less estimated depreciation since acquisition.

If the written down current replacement cost of the asset as stated above is higher than both its *economic value* (i.e., the sum of the discounted future cash flows expected from the use of the asset during its useful life) and *net realizable value* (i.e., the estimated selling price of the asset less reasonably predictable costs of completion and disposal), value to the business of the asset shall be taken as the economic value or net realizable value which ever is higher.

It may be noted that the interpretations to the value to business as given above is based on the Sandilands Committee's adoption of Bonbright's [9] formula.

2. Inventories are shown in the balance sheet at their 'value' prevailing on the date of balance sheet, and not at cost or market value whichever is less as is done in case of historical accounting.
3. Marketable securities are shown in the balance sheet at their market values as on the balance sheet date.
4. Special assets like patent, goodwill, deferred expenses are kept beyond the valuation purview and therefore shown in the balance sheet at par with historical accounting system.
5. Land and building are valued at 'existing use basis'.
6. Depreciation is charged on current value of assets.
7. The difference between the depreciated current replacement value and the depreciation calculated under historical accounting is transferred to *Revaluation Reserve Account* which is not available for declaration of dividend.
8. The cost of goods sold during the year is determined on the basis of prices prevailing on the date of consumption and not on the date of purchase.
9. All items of expenses and revenue are shown at their current prices.
10. Liabilities are shown at par with historical accounting system as they do not change value during inflation.
11. The income for the year shall be the firm's operating profit *less* all holding gains.

The operating profit (i.e., current cost operating profit) is arrived at by adjusting the historical profit against value to the business consumed during the year. This is done by adjusting the historical cost profit against:

(a) Depreciation, (b) cost of sales and (c) monetary working capital.

In addition, a forth adjustment, known as 'gearing adjustment', is also often done to determine the current cost profit attributable to shareholders. All these adjustments have been dealt with in the following paragraphs:

Depreciation Adjustment

The purpose of depreciation adjustment is to find out the value to the business of the part of fixed assets consumed in earning the revenues for the given period. And the process of adjustment is simply to find out the difference between the values to the business of the part of fixed assets consumed during the accounting period and the amount of depreciation charged on the same on historical cost basis. The following illustration will clarify the process of depreciation adjustment:

ILLUSTRATION 4.11

A plant was purchased on 1st April, 2022 for ₹50,000 and was depreciated at 10% p.a. straight line. On 31st March, 2023 the price of the same plant went up to ₹65,000.

How would the plant appear in the balance sheet under CCA method and how would the depreciation be adjusted?

SOLUTION

	Under historical cost	*Under current cost*
Value of the plant (₹)	50,000	65,000
Depreciation 10% (straight line)	5,000	6,500
	45,000	58,500

Under the CCA method, the value of the plant will appear in the balance sheet at ₹58,500. Further, the increase in the value of the plant less increase in the amount of depreciation, i.e., (₹15,000 – ₹1,500) = ₹13,500 shall appear in the liability side of the balance sheet as *current cost reserve*.

Cost of Sales Adjustment

The purpose of cost of sales adjustment (COSA) is to bring the cost of sales to its current value so as to make it comparable with the revenues which are already in the current form, ensuring thereby that current costs are matched with current revenues. The amount of COSA is found by deducting from the 'value to the business' of the stocks used as on the date of sales, the historic costs of such stocks. Value to the business of the stock shall normally be the stock's replacement cost on the date of its consumption. In real-life situation there can be numerous sales in the year and hence it would be tedious and almost impracticable to calculate value to the business in respect of stocks at each point of sales. Therefore, for calculation of COSA and average stock price index is normally used. And based on an average stock price index, the following formula may be used to calculate COSA:

$$\text{COSA} = \left[(\text{HCS} - \text{HOS}) - \text{AI}\left(\frac{\text{HCS}}{\text{CSI}} - \frac{\text{HOS}}{\text{OSI}}\right)\right]$$

where,

HCS ⇒ Historical Cost of Closing Stock
HOS ⇒ Historical Cost of Opening Stock
AI ⇒ Average Index for the year (i.e., simple average of the opening stock index and the closing stock index of the year)
CSI ⇒ Closing Stock Index
OSI ⇒ Opening Stock Index

ILLUSTRATION 4.12

The historical cost of opening stock, closing stock and purchases of a certain commodity are ₹5,000, ₹11,000 and ₹55,000, respectively. If the price index of the opening stock is 100 and that of the closing stock is 110, what is the value of cost of sales adjustment?

SOLUTION

We have $$\text{COSA} = \left[(\text{HCS} - \text{HOS}) - \text{AI}\left(\frac{\text{HCS}}{\text{CSI}} - \frac{\text{HOS}}{\text{OSI}}\right)\right]$$

Where,

HCS ⇒ Historical Cost of Closing Stock

HOS ⇒ Historical Cost of Opening Stock

AI ⇒ Average Index for the year (i.e., simple average of the opening stock index and the closing stock index of the year)

CSI ⇒ Closing Stock Index

OSI ⇒ Opening Stock Index

So, $$\begin{aligned}\text{COSA} &= (11{,}000 - 5{,}000) - 105 \times \left(\frac{11000}{110} - \frac{5000}{100}\right)\\ &= 6{,}000 - 105 \times (100 - 50)\\ &= 6{,}000 - 5{,}250\\ &= ₹750\end{aligned}$$

Alternatively, COSA can be calculated by adopting the following three steps:

Step 1: Revising the opening stock and closing stock of the period to their average costs at average index as under:

$$\text{Average cost of opening stock} = ₹5{,}000 \times \frac{105}{100} = ₹5{,}250$$

$$\text{Average cost of closing stock} = ₹11{,}000 \times \frac{105}{100} = ₹10{,}500$$

Step 2: Calculating cost of sales by using the above revised value of opening and closing stock as under:

	₹
Opening stock	5,250
Add: purchases	55,000
	60,250
Less: closing stock	10,500
Cost of sales (current cost)	49,750

Step 3: Calculating COSA as under:

	₹
Current cost of sales	49,750
Historical cost of sales (5,000 + 55,000 – 11,000)	49,700
	750

Monetary Working Capital Adjustment

The purpose of monetary working capital adjustment (MWCA) is to determine the effects of inflation on the financing requirements of working capital used in the day-to-day operations of the business. Monetary working capital generally includes stock not subjected to COSA, trade debtors, receivables, repayments and trade bills *less* trade creditors. The MWCA would represent the amount of additional (or reduced) finance needed for monetary working capital as a result of changes in the input prices used and financed by the business.

Operationalisation of MWCA is considered to be a difficult affair. The desirability of MWCA too has remained a question mark among various thinkers due to the conceptual flaws associated with it. This is because MWCA considers the additional amount of finance needed for monetary working capital as an expense which ultimately reduces the operating profit.

Gearing Adjustment

The purpose of gearing adjustment is to make an equitable distribution of the total current cost adjusted amount (i.e., depreciation adjustment + COSA + MWCA) as would be attributable to equity holders. The basic logic behind so doing is that a business is financed normally through equity and debt, and therefore the burden of current cost adjustment should not entirely fall on the equity shareholders.

The following formula however is used to determine the amount of gearing adjustment as would be attributable to equity shareholders:

$$\text{Gearing adjustment} = [\{D \div (D + E)\} \times A]$$

where,

D ⇒ Net total borrowing (i.e., total of long-term and short-term borrowings less cash which does not enter MWCA.

E ⇒ Shareholders' fund (i.e., equity capital plus reserves and surpluses).

A ⇒ Total of current cost adjusted amount (i.e., depreciation adjustment plus COSA plus MWCA).

A simple case of gearing adjustment is given in illustration (4.7) 4.13.

ILLUSTRATION 4.13

From the following data, compute gearing adjustment:

	As on 1.4.2022	*As on* 31.3.2023
Share capital (₹)	1,00,000	1,20,000
Reserves and surpluses (₹)	30,000	40,000
Debentures (₹)	50,000	60,000
Bank overdraft (₹)	20,000	30,000

Others:

	₹
Depreciation adjustment	5,000
COSA	15,000
MWCA	10,000

SOLUTION:

Gearing adjustment [{D ÷ (D + E)} × A]

where,

D ⇒ Net total borrowing (i.e., total of long-term and short-term borrowings less cash which does not enter MWCA.

E ⇒ Shareholders' fund (i.e., equity capital plus reserves and surpluses).

A ⇒ Total of current cost adjusted amount (i.e., depreciation adjustment plus COSA plus MWCA).

In the given illustration,

D = Average of opening and closing balances of debentures and bank overdraft which is equal to $\left(\frac{50{,}000+60{,}000}{2}\right)+\left(\frac{20{,}000+30{,}000}{2}\right) = 55{,}000 + 25{,}000 = ₹80{,}000$

E = Average of opening and closing balances of share capital and reserves and surpluses which is equal to $\left(\frac{1{,}00{,}000+1{,}20{,}000}{2}\right)+\left(\frac{30{,}000+40{,}000}{2}\right) = 1{,}10{,}000 + 35{,}000 = ₹1{,}45{,}000$

A = Depreciation adjustment + COSA + MWCA, which is equal to 5,000 + 15,000 + 10,000 = ₹30,000

So, Gearing adjustment = {80,000 ÷ (80,000 + 1,45,000) × ₹30,000} = ₹10,667 (approx.)

The gearing adjustment too has been criticized on the grounds of its operational difficulty and desirability particularly when the 'current cost profit' attributable to shareholders cannot be distributed as dividend because such profits are not backed by equivalent amount of cash inflows.

Working of CCA technique

Given the above mentioned guidelines for current cost accounting technique illustration (4.8)4.14 may be taken to illustrate how CCA works:

ILLUSTRATION 4.14

Following is the Balance Sheet of XYZ Ltd. as on 1.4.2022:

Liabilities	₹	*Assets*	₹
Equity share capital Debentures	2,00,000 1,40,000	Plant and machinery Stock Cash	2,00,000 1,00,000 40,000
	3,40,000		3,40,000

XYZ Ltd.'s profit and loss account for the year ended 31.3.2023 and the balance sheet as on that date are as follows:

Profit and loss A/c for the year ended 31.03.2023

Liabilities	₹	*Assets*	₹
To opening stock	1,00,000	By sales	7,20,000
To purchases	5,00,000	By closing stock	80,000
To operating expenses	80,000		
To depreciation	20,000		
To net profit	1,00,000		
Total	8,00,000	Total	80,000

Balance Sheet of XYZ Ltd. as on 31.03.2023

Liabilities	₹	*Assets*		₹
Equity share capital	2,00,000	Plant and machinery	2,00,000	
Profits	1,00,000	*Less:* Depreciation	20,000	1,80,000
Debentures	1,40,000	(10% straight line)		
Loans	60,000	Stock		80,000
		Debtors		2,00,000
		Cash		40,000
Total	5,00,000	Total		5,00,000

How will XYZ Ltd.'s profit and loss A/c and balance sheet appear under the Current Cost Accounting (CCA) method, if the following additional information is made available?

(i) Closing stock includes 1,000 units purchased at ₹80 per unit. These stocks can be replaced @ ₹90 per unit on 31.03.2023.

(ii) The replacement cost of goods sold as on the date of sales amounts to ₹5,90,000.

(iii) The replacement cost of the plant and machinery has increased to ₹2,20,000.

SOLUTION

Statement showing calculation of profit under CCA

	₹
Sales	7,20,000
Less: Replacement cost of goods sold	5,90,000
	1,30,000
Less: (i) Operating expenses	80,000
(ii) Depreciation on replacement cost of plant and machinery (10% of 2,20,000)	22,000
	1,02,000
Operating profit as per CCA	28,000
Add: Realized holding profit:	
(i) On closing stock Replacement cost of goods sold *less* historical cost of goods sold, i.e., 5,90,000 – 20,000)	70,000
(ii) On plant and machinery (Depreciation on replacement cost *less* depreciation under historical cost, i.e., (22,000 – 20,000)	2,000
Historical profit	1,00,000

Add: Unrealized holding profit:	
(i) On closing stock (Replacement cost of closing stock *less* historical cost of closing stock, i.e., 1,000 units @ ₹90 minus 1,000 units @ ₹80 = ₹90,000 – ₹80,000 = ₹10,000)	10,000
(ii) On plant and machinery (Replacement cost *less* realized holding profit on plant and machinery, i.e., ₹2,20,000 –₹2,00,000 – ₹2,000 = ₹18,000)	18,000
Current cost accounting profit	1,28,000

Balance sheet of XYZ Ltd. as on 31.03.2023 under CCA method

Liabilities	₹	*Assets*		₹
Equity share capital	2,00,000	Plant and machinery	2,20,000	
CCA profit	1,28,000	*Less:* depreciation	22,000	1,98,000
Debentures	1,40,000	Stock		90,000
Loans	60,000	Debtors		2,00,000
		Cash		40,000
	5,28,000			5,28,000

Advantages of CCA technique

The important advantages of CCA technique are:

1. CCA when operates with replacement cost basis exhibits a fair view of the financial position of the firm thereby providing a more useful information for decision making.
2. CCA helps in differentiating between operating profits and holding gains, thus helping the investors better assess the firm's performance.
3. CCA makes a realistic valuation of the assets as they are represented at current market prices.
4. CCA adopts specific price level approach as against CPP's general price level.
5. Profit is determined under CCA by matching the cost and revenue at current prices.

Disadvantages of CCA technique

The important disadvantages of CCA may be enumerated:

1. CCA depends more on subjective adjustments.
2. CCA fails to recognize all aspects of inflation.
3. Determination of economic value of assets as required under CCA is a difficult task.
4. Fast changing technology which promises better assets makes the use of current replacement cost of the old asset consumed for income generation virtually 'redundant'.
5. Involvement of too much calculations makes CCA operationally difficult.
6. Profits disclosed by CCA and under inflation adjustment as a whole is not acceptable to tax authorities, at least in India.

SUMMARY

Financial statements prepared under the historical cost accounting method tend to loose their interpretative value due to price level changes which cause distortions to the reported financial results of the firms. In order to provide the decision makers with credible financial statements therefore that the concept and phenomena of accounting for price level changes has been developed.

The process followed for adjustment of foreign financial statements against inflation is three-fold:

1. Restatement of the financial data as contained in the financial statements of the affiliates according to the chosen technique of price-level adjustment (such as CCP or CCA);
2. Translation of the related financial data of the affiliates into the home currency; and
3. Consolidation of the translated financial data/statement of the affiliate(s) with the financial statement of the parent company in accordance with the translation and consolidation methods adopted.

The techniques available for price level adjustments are basically two:

1. Current Purchasing Power (CPP) or General Purchasing Power (GPP)
2. Current Cost Accounting (CCA) technique with each one having its own set of merits and demerits.

Under the CPP technique, purchasing power gains or losses are first calculated by adjusting non-monetary items of assets and liabilities such as inventory, land and building, plant and machinery and retained earnings and equity capital whose values are subject to change due to changes in the purchasing power of money. Secondly, the income statement is adjusted after giving due considerations to the treatment of inventory, depreciation, and revenue and expenses not evenly occurring throughout the year. Thirdly, price level adjusted balance sheet is prepared by converting the values of the traditional balance sheet items through appropriate conversion factors.

Under the CCA technique the important adjustments done to the traditional financial statements are with respect to depreciation, cost of sales monetary working capital and gearing adjustments.

KEY TERMS

Price level change: Price level changes refer to the changes in the value of monetary unit of simply the increase or decrease in the purchasing power of money.

Purchasing power of money: Purchasing power of money refers to the ability of a given sum goods or services now, in comparison to the amount of goods or services that the same sum of money could not buy at a an earlier date.

General price level changes: General price level changes refers to the increase or decrease in the value of monetary unit measured in terms of a price index.

Specific price level changes: Specific price level changes amounts to the changes in the prices of a specific good or service.

Relative price level changes: Relative price level change refers to the changes in the prices of one commodity in relation to the changes in the prices of all commodities and services taken together.

Purchasing power gains and losses: Purchasing power gains and losses occur on account of the treatment of trade debtors and creditors under inflationary situation.

Current Purchasing Power (CPP) technique: CPP is a technique of adjusting financial statements against inflation. It is also known as the General Purchasing Power (GPP) technique.

Monetary assets and liabilities: Monetary assets and liabilities are those assets and liabilities which are not subject to reassessment of their recorded values due to changes in the purchasing power of money.

Non-monetary assets and liabilities: Non-monetary assets and liabilities are those which are subject to reassessment of their values due to changes in the purchasing power of money.

Cost of sales adjustment (COSA): COSA is an adjustment of the sales value in the context of price level accounting wherein the cost of sales as reported in the historical cost accounting method is brought to its current value.

Current Cost Accounting (CCA) technique: CCA is a technique suggested by Sandilands statements against price level changes.

Gearing adjustment: Gearing adjustment refers to the equitable distribution of COSA

REVIEW QUESTIONS

1. From the following balance sheet of SL Ltd. as on 31.03.2023 and the additional information given beneath, determine the amount of purchasing power gains or losses on monetary items:

Liabilities	₹	*Assets*	₹
Equity share capital	5,00,000	Plant and machinery	
Bonds and debentures	3,00,000	(net of depreciation)	8,00,000
Public deposits	2,00,000	Vehicles	1,00,000
Creditors	1,00,000	Debtors	1,50,000
Bills payable	50,000	Bills receivable	75,000
Outstanding wages	25,000	Cash	50,000
Total	11,75,000	Total	11,75,000

Additional information:

The general price index as on 31.03.2023 is 210 as against the corresponding index of 180 a year back when the fixed assets and long-term liabilities were acquired.

2. The balance sheet of Simplex Ltd. as on 31st March, 2023 is as follows:

Liabilities	₹	*Assets*	₹
Equity share capital (10,000 shares of ₹10 each)	1,00,000	Goodwill	30,000
Preference share capital (50,000 shares of ₹10 each)	5,00,000	Land and building (net of depreciation)	4,00,000
Reserves and surpluses	1,75,000	Plant and machinery *less* depreciation	3,00,000
Long-term borrowings	2,25,000	Furniture and fittings *less* depreciation	1,50,000
Creditors	1,50,000	Stock	80,000
Bills payable	80,000	Debtors	1,70,000
Outstanding expenses	30,000	Bills receivables	70,000
		Cash	60,000
Total	12,60,000	Total	12,60,000

What is the purchasing power gains or losses on monetary items of the company (?) given that the general price index as on 31.03.2023 is 185 as against 145 as the general price index as on 31.03.2022, the date when fixed assets and liabilities were acquired.

3. Analysis of the books of account of OPC Ltd. reveals the following for the year ended 31.03.2023:

Sales ₹11,00,000 Cost of goods sold ₹6,00,000

Other expenses ₹1,40,000 Depreciation ₹60,000

Other relevant information obtained from the books is:

(a) Fixed assets were purchased on 01.04.2022 at a prevailing general price index of 130.
(b) Goods were purchased in three lots of ₹2,00,000, ₹3,00,000 and ₹1,50,000 with a corresponding price index of 130, 140 and 150.
(c) There was no opening stock.
(d) Closing stock was valued at ₹50,000 on FIFO basis.
(e) Sales were made at a price index of 145. Expenses too were incurred at price index of 145.
(f) Price index measured on 31st March, 2023 is 150.

Prepare a price level adjusted income statement for OPC Ltd.

4. The income statement of Rising Star for the year ended 31.03.2023 was as follows:

Sales	15,50,000
Less: Cost of goods sold	8,10,000
Operating profit	7,40,000
Less: Expenses	2,10,000
Less: Depreciation	80,000
Net income	4,50,000

Verification of the company's record further reveals that

(a) Goods were purchased in four separate lots ₹90, 000, ₹2, 50,000, ₹3,50,000 and ₹1,50,000 with a corresponding price index of 120, 125, 135 and 150.

(b) There were opening and closing stocks amounting to ₹60,000 and ₹90,000, respectively.
(c) Stocks were priced under FIFO method.
(d) Sales and expenses were booked at the same price index of 145.
(e) Price index prevalent on 31.03.2023 was 150 and on 31.03.2022 was 125.
(f) Fixed assets were acquired on 31.03.2022.

Prepare a price level adjusted income statement for Rising Star & Co. Ltd.

5. From the following balance sheet and the additional information, prepare a price-level adjusted balance sheet for ZBC Ltd.

Liabilities	₹	*Assets*		₹
Equity share capital	6,00,000	Fixed assets	12,00,000	
Preference share capital	4,00,000	Less: Depreciation	3,00,000	9,00,000
Bonds and debentures	8,00,000	Long-term investments		5,00,000
Creditors	4,00,000	Stock		1,00,000
Outstanding expenses	1,50,000	Debtors		4,00,000
		Bills receivables		3,00,000
		Cash at bank		1,00,000
		Cash in hand		50,000
Total	23,50,000	Total		23,50,000

Additional information:

(a) The general price index on 31.03.2023 was 180 as against 160 on 31.03.2022.
(b) The fixed assets were purchased on 31.03.2022.
(c) The shares, and bonds and debentures were issued also on 31.03.2022. .

6. The balance sheet of Sun Rise Ltd. as on 31.03.2023 was as follows:

(*Fig. in* ₹'000)

Liabilities	₹	*Assets*		₹
Equity share capital		Gross block:	2000	
(1,00,000 shares of ₹10 each)	1,000	Less: Depreciation	200	1,800
Preference share capital		Long-term investment		400
(50,000 shares of ₹10 each)	500	Stock		200
12% 10,000 Debentures of ₹100		Sundry debtors		300
each	1,000	Bills receivables		250
Long-term loans	300	Cash at bank		125
Sundry creditors	200	Cash in hand		75
Bills payable	100			
Misc. current liabilities	50			
Total	3,150	Total		3,150

Prepare a price level adjusted balance sheet for Sun Rise Ltd. after taking into consideration the following:

(a) The general price index was 200 on 31.03.2023.
(b) The fixed assets were purchased on 01.04.2022 when the general price index was 185.

(c) Equity shares, preference shares and debentures were issued on 01.04.2022.
(d) Long-term loans and investments were undertaken on 01.04.2022.

7. The balance sheet of James Ltd. as on 31.03.2023 was as follows:

(*Fig. in ₹'000*)

Liabilities	₹	*Assets*		₹
Equity share capital		Gross block:	1,800	
(80,000 shares of ₹10 each)	800	*Less:* Depreciation	200	1,600
Preference share capital		Long-term investment		400
(40,000 shares of ₹10 each)	400	Stock		200
10% 10,000 Debentures of ₹100 each	1,000	Sundry debtors		120
Sundry creditors	200	Cash at bank		150
Bills payable	100	Cash in hand		80
Misc. current liabilities	50			
Total	2,550	Total		2,550

Prepare a price level adjusted balance sheet for James Ltd. after taking the following into consideration:

(a) The general price index is 190 on 31.03.2023.
(b) The fixed assets were purchased on 01.04.2022 when the general price index was 175.
(c) The equity shares, preference shares and debentures were issued on 01.04.2022 and the investment was undertaken on 31.03.2022.

8. (a) Discuss the concept and process of depreciation adjustment in price-level accounting.
(b) A plant was purchased on 1st January, 2023 at ₹85,000 by M/s S.S & Co. Ltd. which follows the practice of charging depreciation at 20% p.a. straight line. If the price of the same plant has gone up by ₹15,000 as on 31st January, 2023, how will you determine the value of the plant and adjust the depreciation under the current cost accounting method?

9. Two plants—P_1 and P_2—were purchased by M/s Makers and Breakers on 01.01.2023 and 01.07.2022 at ₹8, 80,000 and ₹6,75,000, respectively. The prices of P_1 and P_2 have gone up 20% as on 31.03.2023.

If M/s Makers and Breakers depreciate the plants at 10% straight line, how would the plants appear in the balance sheet and how would you adjust the depreciation under the current cost accounting method?

10. What do you understand by cost of sales adjustment (COSA)? What significance does it hold to inflation accounting? Illustrate your answer?

11. The historical costs of opening stock, purchases, returns outward and closing stock of a certain commodity are given at ₹20,000, ₹1,75,000, ₹15,000 and ₹30,000, respectively. If the price index of the opening stock is 110 and that of the closing stock is 120, what is the value of cost of sales adjustment (COSA)?

12. What is monetary working capital? How is it computed? What significance does it hold to accounting for price level changes? Explain.

13. What is gearing adjustment? How and why is it calculated? Explain.

14. State the essential features of the CPP technique. State also its advantages and limitations.

15. Outline the features of Current Cost Accounting (CCA) technique. Bring out its merits and demerits as well.

16. Bring out the basic source(s) of difference between the CPP and the CCA method. Which of the two methods, in your opinion, promises superior result and why?

17. Explain the concept and usefulness of Cost of Sales Adjustment (COSA) in CCA. Illustrate your answer.

18. Explain the following:
   (a) Depreciation adjustment
   (b) Monetary working capital adjustment
   (c) Gearing adjustment

19. The balance sheets of Super Sales Corporation Ltd. as on 31.03.2022 and 31.03.2023 were as follows:

Liabilities	31.03.2022 ₹	31.03.2023 ₹	*Assets*	31.03.2022 ₹	31.03.2023 ₹
Equity share capital	5,00,000	5,00,000	Plant and machinery net		
Profits	50,000	50,000	of depreciation	3,50,000	3,90,000
Bonds	2,00,000	2,00,000	Furniture and fittings		
Debentures	1,00,000	3,00,000	net of depreciation	2,10,000	2,70,000
Loans	—	50,000	Stock	1,50,000	2,50,000
Creditors	1,50,000	2,00,000	Debtors	2,40,000	3,00,000
			Bills receivable	30,000	70,000
			Cash	20,000	20,000
Total	10,00,000	13,00,000	Total	10,00,000	13,00,000

The profit and loss account of the firm for the year ended 31.03.2023 was as follows:

Profit and Loss A/c (*Fig. in* ₹)

Dr.	₹	*Cr.*	₹
To opening stock	1,50,000	By sales	10,70,000
To purchases	8,00,000	By closing stock	2,50,000
To operating expenses	2,20,000		
To depreciation:			
Plant and machinery 60,000			
Furniture and fittings 40,000	1,00,000		
To net profit	50,000		
Total	13,20,000	Total	13,20,000

Additional information:

(a) Closing stock includes 2,500 units purchased at ₹100 per unit. These stocks can be replaced at ₹120 per unit on 31.03.2023.

(b) The replacement cost of goods sold as on the date of sales ₹7,80,000.

(c) Depreciation on plant and machinery, and furniture and fittings has been charged at 10% p.a. straight line.

(d) Included in the value of plant and machinery on 31.03.2023 were a plant purchased on 01.04.2021 at ₹5,00,000 and another plant purchased on 01.04.2022 at ₹1,00,000.

(e) Included in the value of furniture and fittings on 31.03.2023were furniture purchased on 01.04.2021 and on 01.04.2022 at ₹3,00,000 and ₹1,00,000, respectively.

(f) Replacement costs of the plant and machinery and furniture and fittings as on 31.03.2023 have gone up by 20% each against their acquired prices.

You are required to show how the firm's profit and loss account and balance sheet will appear under the current cost accounting method.

20. Black & Ball Ltd. furnishes the following balance sheets, income statement and additional information and requests you to prepare an income statement and balance sheet as would appear under the CCA method of price level adjustment:

Balance sheets

(Fig. in ₹)

Liabilities	*As on 31.03.2022*	*As on 31.03.2023*	*Assets*	*As on 31.03.2022*	*As on 31.03.2023*
Equity share capital	2,00,000	2,00,000	Fixed assets net of depreciation	2,70,000	2,40,000
Preference share capital	1,00,000	1,50,000	Stock	80,000	1,20,000
Profits	—	70,000	Debtors	60,000	1,80,000
Bonds and debenture	1,50,000	1,50,000	Cash at bank	50,000	90,000
Long-term loans	—	80,000	Cash in hand	30,000	70,000
Creditors	40,000	50,000			
Total	4,90,000	7,00,000	Total	4,90,000	7,00,000

Income statement (P/L A/c) of Black and Ball for the year ended 31.03.2023

Liabilities	₹	*Assets*	₹
To opening stock	80,000	By sales	7,00,000
To purchases	4,00,000	By closing stock	1,20,000
To operating expenses	2,40,000		
To depreciation	30,000		
To net profit	70,000		
Total	8,20,000	Total	8,20,000

Additional information:

(a) Closing stock includes 6000 units purchased at ₹20 per unit. These stocks can be replaced at ₹25 per unit on 31.03.2023.

(b) The replacement cost of goods sold as on the date of sale was ₹4,20,000.

(c) The replacement cost of fixed assets as on 31.03.2022 has gone up by ₹70,000.

21. The balance sheet of Black and Berry Ltd. as on 31.03.2023 is as follows:

Balance sheet of Black and Berry Ltd. as on 31.03.2022

Liabilities	₹	*Assets*	₹
Equity Capital	1,18,28,000	Land and building (net of	
Reserves	35,35,000	depreciation)	1,20,25,000
Profit	24,24,000	Plant and Machinery (net of	
Debentures	1,12,12,000	depreciation)	1,44,34,000
Term loan	1,13,13,000	Furniture and fixture	38,28,000
Creditors	38,38,000	Loose tools	24,38,000
Bills payable	25,50,000	Inventories	56,46,000
Outstanding	5,25,000	Bills receivable	50,15,000
		Cash at bank	29,29,000
		Cash in hand	9,10,000
Total	4,72,25,000	Total	4,72,25,000

The general price index as on 31.03.2023 is 225, which was 200 corresponding to the dates on which the fixed assets and long-term loan were acquired. What are the net purchasing power gains or losses on monetary items by Black and Berry Ltd? Show your calculations.

22. The balance sheet of Blue Moon Ltd. as on 31.03.2023 is as follows:

Balance sheet of Blue Moon Ltd. as on 31.03.2023

Liabilities	₹	*Assets*	₹
Equity Capital	18,13,000	Land and building (net of	10,25,000
Reserves	5,12,000	depreciation)	14,15,000
Profit	4,30,000	Plant and Machinery (net of	8,15,000
Debentures	12,25,000	depreciation)	4,25,000
Term loan	13,15,000	Furniture and fixture	6,05,000
Creditors	8,05,000	Loose tools	10,05,000
Bills payable	3,15,000	Inventories	9,15,000
		Bills receivable	2,10,000
		Cash at bank	
		Cash in hand	
Total	64,15,000	Total	64,15,000

The general price index as on 31.03.2022 is 220, which was 160 corresponding to the dates on which the fixed assets and long-term loan were acquired. What are the purchasing power gains or losses on monetary items held by *Blue Moon Ltd.*?

23. The balance sheet of Black and White Ltd. as on 31.03.2023 is as follows:

Balance sheet of Black and White Ltd. as on 31.03.2023

Liabilities	₹	*Assets*	₹
Equity Capital	97,18,000	Land and building (net of depreciation)	80,25,000
Reserves	26,45,000		
Profit	13,24,000	Plant and machinery (net of depreciation)	73,22,000
Term loan	94,13,000		
Creditors	17,38,000	Furniture and fixture	27,28,000
Bills payable	16,20,000	Loose tools	14,38,000
Outstanding	5,45,000	Inventories	25,46,000
		Bills receivable	31,15,000
		Cash	18,29,000
Total	2,70,03,000	Total	2,70,03,000

The general price index as on 31.03.2023 is 225, which was 200 corresponding to the dates on which the fixed assets and long-term loan were acquired. What are the purchasing power gains or losses on monetary items?

24. The balance sheet of MoonLight Ltd. as on 31.03.2023 is as follows:

The balance sheet of Moonlight Ltd. as on 31.03.2023

Liabilities	₹	*Assets*	₹
Equity Capital	1,18,13,000	Land and building (net of depreciation)	1,10,24,000
Reserves	45,12,000		
Profit	24,30,000	Plant and machinery (net of depreciation)	1,14,16,000
Debentures	52,25,000		
Term loan	53,15,000	Furniture and fixture	38,17,000
Creditors	58,06,000	Loose tools	14,23,000
Bills payable	33,14,000	Inventories	56,06,000
		Bills receivable	40,04,000
		Cash	11,25,000
Total	3,84,15,000	Total	3,84,15,000

The general price index as on 31.03.2023 is 225, which was 175 corresponding to the dates on which the fixed assets and long-term loan were acquired. What are the purchasing power gains or losses on monetary items?

25. Given the income statement of XYZ Ltd. for the year ended 31.03.2023 and the additional information as under, prepare a price-level adjusted income statement:

	(Fig in ₹)
Sales	89,90,000
Less: Cost of goods sold	45,10,000
Operating income	44,80,000
Less: Expenses	
(i) Office	12,18,000
(ii) Selling and Distribution	11,37,000

Less: Depreciation	4,10,000
Net income	17,15,000

Other relevant information is:

(a) The price index as on 31.03.2023 was 225, and on 31.3.2022 was 200.

(b) Sales were made and expenses incurred when the price index was 142 and 148, respectively.

(c) Inventory was valued on FIFO basis.

(d) Goods were purchased during the year in three lots of ₹20,00,000, ₹15,00,000 and ₹10,00,000 with the prevailing price index of 140, 142 and 145, respectively.

(e) The opening stock of materials was of ₹8, 00,000 and the closing stock was valued at ₹7,90,000.

(f) The fixed assets were acquired on 1st April, 2020 when the general price index was 140.

26. Given the income statement of BQ Ltd. for the year ended 31.03.2023 and the additional information as under, prepare a price-level adjusted income statement:

	(Fig in ₹)
Sales	45,45,000
Less: Cost of goods sold	20,55,000
Operating income	24,90,000
Less: Expenses	
(a) Manufacturing	6,30,000
(b) Office	3,25,000
(c) Selling and Distribution	2,40,000
Less: Depreciation	2,15,000
Net income	10,80,000

Other relevant information is:

(a) The price index as on 31.03.2023 was 250, and on 31.3.2022 was 200.

(b) Sales were made and expenses incurred when the price index was 145 and 140, respectively.

(c) Inventory was valued on FIFO basis.

(d) Goods were purchased during the year in three lots of ₹7,50,000, ₹10,25,000 and ₹5,00,000 with the prevailing price index of 140, 145 and 150, respectively.

(e) There was no opening stock and the closing stock was valued at ₹2,20,000.

(f) The fixed assets were acquired on 1st April, 2022 when the general price index was 200.

27. Given the income statement of SH Ltd. for the year ended 31.03.2023 and the additional information is as under, prepare a price-level adjusted income statement:

	(Fig in ₹)
Sales	1, 89,89,000
Less: Cost of goods sold	85,25,000
Operating income	1,04,64,000
Less: Expenses	
(a) Office	22,25,000
(b) Selling and Distribution	18,40,000
(c) Misc. expenses	17,000
Less: Depreciation	24,15,000
Net income	39,67,000

Other relevant information is:

(a) The price index as on 31.03.2023 was 250, and on 31.3.2022 was 220.

(b) Sales were made and expenses incurred when the price index was 160 and 175, respectively.

(c) Inventory was valued on FIFO basis.

(d) Goods were purchased during the year in three lots of ₹38,00,000, ₹ 26,00,000 and ₹20,42,000 with the prevailing price index of 160, 175 and 180, respectively.

(e) The opening stock of materials was of ₹18,00,000 and the closing stock was valued at ₹17,17,000.

(f) The fixed assets were acquired on 1st April, 2022.

28. Given the income statement of IPU Ltd. for the year ended 31.03.2023 and the additional information as under, prepare a price-level adjusted income statement:

	(Fig in ₹)
Sales	55,45,350
Less: Cost of goods sold	20,19,180
Operating income	35,26,170
Less: Expenses	
(a) Manufacturing	7,36,300
(b) Office	6,26,100
(c) Selling and Distribution	3,42,400
Less: Depreciation	2,22,100
Net income	15,99,270

Other relevant information is:

(i) The price index as on 31.03.2023 was 250, and on 31.3.2020 was 220.

(ii) Sales were made and expenses incurred when the price index was 175 and 190, respectively.

(iii) Inventory was valued on FIFO basis.

(iv) Goods were purchased during the year in three lots of ₹9,58,500, ₹12,02,000 and ₹4,03,080 with the prevailing price index of 175, 185 and 220, respectively.

(v) There was no opening stock and the closing stock was valued at ₹5,44,400.

(vi) The fixed assets were acquired on 1st April, 2022.

29. The balance sheet of OxyFresh Ltd. as on 31.03.2023 is as under:

Liabilities	₹	*Assets*	₹
Equity	20,05,000	Land and building	22,10,000
Reserves	4,30,000	Plant and machinery	24,15,000
Profit	6,15,000	Furniture and fittings	4,55,000
Bonds	13,20,000	Inventories	8,25,000
Debenture	10,25,000	Receivables	12,15,000
Term loans	15,08,000	Short term investments	3,68,000
Payables	8,03,000	Cash	2,92,000
Outstanding	74,000		
	77,80,000		77,80,000

You are required to prepare a price level adjusted balance sheet for OxyFresh Ltd., after taking into consideration the following additional information:

(a) The general price index on 31.03.2023 and on 31.03.2022 was 250 and 220, respectively.

(b) Fixed assets were acquired when the price index was 225.

(c) Equity capital, bonds, debentures and term loans were raised on 1.4.2022.

30. The balance sheet of Revolution Ltd. as on 31.03.2023 is as under:

Liabilities	₹	*Assets*	₹
Equity Share capital	22,30,000	Land and building	21,50,000
Preference Share Capital	13,15,000	Plant and equipment	13,75,000
Profit	21,50,000	Furniture and fixtures	8,25,000
Bonds and debenture	12,25,000	Inventories	15,10,000
Term loans	13,50,000	Debtors	20,25,000
Creditors	8,15,000	Bills receivables	11,07,000
Bills Payables	4,10,000	Cash	5,03,000
	94,95,000		94,95,000

You are required to prepare a price level adjusted balance sheet for Revolution Ltd., after taking into consideration the following additional information:

(a) The general price index on 31.03.2023 and on 31.03.2022 was 250 and 220, respectively.

(b) Fixed assets were acquired when the price index was 225.

(c) Equity and Preference share capital were raised on 1.4.2022 and so also term loans and bonds and debentures.

31. The balance sheet of Fresh Rose Ltd. as on 31.03.2023 is as under:

Balance sheet of Fresh Rose Ltd. as on 31.03.2023

Liabilities	₹	*Assets*	₹
Equity	24,05,250	Land and building	24,10,500
Reserves	6,30,100	Plant and machinery	26,15,000
Profit	8,15,150	Furniture and fittings	8,55,200
Bonds	12,20,100	Inventories	10,25,000
Debenture	12,25,000	Receivables	14,15,100
Term loans	17,08,000	Short-term investments	13,68,000
Payables	18,03,175	Cash	4,92,050
Outstanding	3,74,075		
	1,01,80,850		1,01,80,850

You are required to prepare a price level adjusted balance sheet for Fresh Rose Ltd., after taking into consideration the following additional information:

(a) The general price index on 31.03.2023 and on 31.03.2022 was 240 and 220, respectively.

(b) Fixed assets were acquired when the price index was 230.

(c) Equity capital, bonds, debentures and term loans were issued on 1.4.2022.

32. The balance sheet of Arch Inclusive Ltd. as on 31.03.2023 is given below. You are required to prepare a price level adjusted balance sheet for the company, after taking into account the additional information beneath.

Balance sheet of Arch Inclusive Ltd. as on 31.03.2023

Liabilities	₹	*Assets*	₹
Equity Share capital	1,22,30,000	Land and building	1,01,50,000
Preference Share Capital	83,15,000	Plant and equipment	1,93,75,000
Reserves	43,20,000	Furniture and fixtures	48,25,000
Profit	21,50,000	Inventories	45,10,000
Bonds and debenture	1,12,25,000	Debtors	52,25,000
Creditors	63,50,000	Bills Receivables	28,07,000
Bills Payables	38,15,000	Cash	15,13,000
	4,84,05,000		4,84,05,000

Additional information:

(i) The general price index on 31.03.2023 and on 31.03.2022 was 250 and 220, respectively.

(ii) Fixed assets were acquired when the price index was 225.

(iii) Equity and Preference share capital were raised on 1.4.2022 and so also term loans and bonds and debentures.

REFERENCES

[1] Rathore, S., *International Accounting*, p. 131.

[2] Zenoff, D.B. and Zwick, J., *International Financial Management*, Prentice Hall, Englewood Cliffs, NJ, 1969.

[3] Parkinson, M.R., *Translation of Foreign Currencies*, *The Canadian Institute of Chartered Accounts*, Toronto, 1972.

[4] Shwayder, K.R., *Accounting for Exchange Rate Fluctuations*, *The Accounting Review*, Vol. 47, pp. 747–760, October, 1972.

[5] American Accounting Association, Committee on International Accounting, Report of the Committee on International Accounting, *the Accounting Review*, Supplement to Vol. 48, 1973.

[6] Fisher, I., *The Purchasing power of Money*, Macmillan, New York, 1911.

[7] Gynther, R.S., 'Why use general purchasing power?' *Accounting and Business Research*, Spring 1974, pp. 141–156.

[8] Sandilands Committee on Inflation Accounting, London, 1975.

[9] Bonbright, J.C., *Valuation of Property*, McGraw-Hill, New York, 1937.

5

Harmonization of Accounting Practices

LEARNING OBJECTIVES

After Studying this chapter, you will be able to:

- Describe the process of harmonization
- Draw up the list of International Accounting Standards (IAS), International Financial Reporting Standards (IFRS) and Indian Accounting Standards (AS) that are in place
- Compare between International Accounting Standards (IAS) and Indian Accounting
- Standards (AS)
- Explain the manner of convergence of Indian Accounting Standard (AS) with International Accounting Standards (IAS) and IFRS
- Discuss the Institutional efforts to achieving harmonization
- Describe the Impediments to harmonization
- Narrate suggested accounting models for harmonization

INTRODUCTION

Harmonization of accounting practices aims at bringing down the disparities that exist in the financial reporting system practiced by different countries owing to their own set of socio-economic, political, cultural and legal systems. The purpose of harmonization is to increase the comparability of accounting practices as followed by different nations across the globe. Standardization, often used as synonymous to harmonization, too aims at reducing disparities in accounting practices, but not without a set of rigid rules and policy guidelines as compared to harmonization. It is the process of harmonization which is preferred to standardization, as harmonization still allows nations to enjoy certain degrees of freedom while preparing financial reports than under the standardization. Nevertheless, it is mostly through standardization that harmonization of accounting practices is achieved.

NEED FOR HARMONIZATION

The important reasons which necessitate harmonization of accounting practices are well contained in the observation made by Sandagaran [1]. 'While the initial efforts at harmonization were mainly championed by political bodies and professional accounting organizations, current pressures to harmonize are driven by investor groups who use financial statements, multinational companies which prepare financial statements, regulators who monitor capital markets, the securities industry (including stock exchanges) which views itself as being significantly impacted by the global diversity in financial reporting requirements, and developing countries that often lack the resources to develop indigenous accounting standards'. These reasons may broadly be put as:

1. Global flow of capital
2. Emergence of MNCs
3. Internationalization of accounting profession
4. Administrative requirements
5. Diversities in measurement of business income

Global Flow of Capital

Harmonization of accounting practices is a necessity to getting enhanced flow of international capital. It is a well-known fact that from ancient times to the recent euphoria of globalization that businesses never remained confined to national boundaries. As such, the flow of capital investments across nations is both a fact and a necessity. The flow however gets checked owing to international diversity in accounting practices. To quote International Organization of Securities Commissions (IOSCO), 'the primary impediment to an international offering of securities is that different countries have different accounting standards' [2]. Harmonization of accounting practices is therefore needed to help international investors get comparable financial information. The greatest benefit that would flow from harmonization would be the comparability of international financial information. Such comparability would eliminate the current misunderstanding about the reliability of foreign financial statements and remove one of the most important impediments to the flow of international investment observes J.N.Turner [3]. As harmonization would result in a more uniform financial reporting across nations, global investors will find it easy to understand the financial data and decide about their investment destinations.

Emergence of MNCs

Harmonization of accounting practices would greatly reduce the efforts, energy and money that otherwise are required by MNCs to put in for presenting financial reports as per country specific requirements. In other words, different countries follow different set of accounting rules for presentation of financial reports and as such MNCs operating in different countries will have to prepare multiple sets of financial reports to meet the legal requirements of each individual country in which they operate thus incurring additional expenses. Through harmonization of accounting practices, however these expenses can be reduced as then only one set of reports may be just enough to meet the requirements of every country in which the MNCs have presence.

Internationalization of Accounting Profession

Harmonization of accounting practices will help in internationalizing the accounting profession. As harmonization aims at reducing the disparities in accounting practices across nations, accounting professionals operating in one nation will find it easy to operate in another nation as well.

Administrative Requirements

Different countries have different regulatory and administrative requirements as regards financial reporting of MNCs. For instance, in the US, foreign firms are required to furnish financial information in line with the domestic firms and in accordance with the US GAAP. Consequently, non-US firms will have to translate and reconcile their financial reports as per US accounting principles. But for the harmonization of accounting practices that not only such translations would be avoided but also government and regulatory authorities would be in a better position to understand the financial reports of MNCs and control their operations.

Diversities in Measurement of Business Income

Diversities exist in measurement of business income due to differences in accounting practices across nations. For example, for the same set of business transactions the profits as per Indian GAAP will be different from that calculated under the US GAAP. By virtue of harmonization of accounting practices, this difference in profit determination is likely to get substantially reduced.

HARMONIZATION PROCESS

Notwithstanding the fact that harmonization of accounting practices has many advantages as stated above, a complete harmonization would be difficult to achieve due to the socio-economic, political, legal, environmental and cultural diversities that exist in different countries. However, endeavors have been made in the past and the efforts are still on both at the international and national levels to minimize the deviations in accounting practices across the globe by formulating, adopting and implementing standardized accounting procedures in the form of proclaimed policy guidelines called *accounting standards*.

Accounting Standards

Accounting standards are 'policy documents' issued by professional accountancy bodies at national and international levels, in relation to different aspects of measurement, treatment, disclosure and presentation of accounting information. The basic purpose behind issuance of accounting standards from time to time is to minimize the effects on financial statements of the diversities in accounting practices that exist between nations due to their own socio-economic, political, legal, cultural, technological and environmental set up. By providing standardized accounting policies thus accounting standards help in achieving international harmony in the preparation and presentation of accounting information for use by various stakeholders.

At the international level, 41 accounting standards called IAS as shown in Exhibit 5.1 and 17 International Financial Reporting Standards called IFRS as shown in Exhibit 5.2

have been issued till date. Of the forty one IAS, thirty four are in use now. The remaining seven IAS have been either merged with these 34 or done away with keeping pace with the changing business environment. At the national level, i.e., in India, 32 accounting standards (AS), and 41 Indian Accounting Standards called Ind AS have been issued by the Institute of Chartered Accountants of India (ICAI). Exhibit 5.3A and Exhibit 5.3B respectively displays list of these thirty two AS and forty one Ind AS.

EXHIBIT 5.1 List of International Accounting Standards (IAS)

IAS	*Broad Title/Theme*
IAS 1	Presentation of Financial Statements (Revised Dec. 2003)
IAS 2	Inventories (Revised Dec. 2003)
IAS 3*	Consolidated Financial Statements (IAS 3 has been superseded by IAS 27 and IAS 28 in 1989)
IAS 4*	Depreciation Accounting (IAS 4 has been withdrawn from 1999)
IAS 5*	Information to be Disclosed in Financial Statements (IAS 5 has been superseded by IAS 1 with effect from July 1, 1998)
IAS 6*	Accounting Responses to Changing Prices (IAS 6 has been superseded by IAS 15 in 2003)
IAS 7	Cash Flow Statements
IAS 8	Accounting Policies, Changes in accounting Estimates and Errors (Revised Dec. 2003)
IAS 9*	Accounting for Research and Development Activities (IAS 9 has been superseded by IAS 38 effect from July 1, 1999)
IAS 10	Events after the Balance Sheet Date (Revised Dec. 2003)
IAS 11	Construction Contracts
IAS 12	Income Taxes
IAS 13*	Presentation of Current Assets and Current Liabilities (IAS 13 has been superseded by IAS 1 effect from July 1, 2009)
IAS 14	Segmental Reporting
IAS 15	Information Reflecting the Effects of Changing Prices
IAS 16	Property, Plant and Equipment (Revised Dec. 2003)
IAS 17	Leases (Revised Dec. 2003)
IAS 18	Revenue
IAS 19	Employee benefits
IAS 20	Accounting for Government Grants and Disclosure of Government Assistance
IAS 21	The Effects of Changes in the Foreign Exchange Rate (Revised Dec. 2003)
IAS 22	Business Combination (now withdrawn and replaced by IFRS 3: Business Combination)
IAS 23	Borrowing Costs
IAS 24	Related Party Disclosures (Revised Dec. 2003)
IAS 25*	Accounting for Investments (IAS 25 has been superseded by IAS 39 and IAS 40 effective from 2001)
IAS 26	Accounting and Reporting by Retirement Benefits Plans
IAS 27	Consolidated and Separate Financial Statements (Revised Dec. 2003)
IAS 28	Investments in associates (Revised Dec. 2003)
IAS 29	Financial Reporting in Hyper Inflationary Economics
IAS 30	Disclosure in the Financial Statements of the Banks and Similar Financial Institutions
IAS 31	Interests in Joint Ventures (Revised Dec. 2003)

(*Contd.*)

IAS	Broad Title/Theme
IAS 32	Financial Instruments: Disclosure and Presentation (Revised Dec. 2003)
IAS 33	Earnings Per Share (Revised Dec. 2003)
IAS 34	Interim Financial Reporting
IAS 35	Discontinuing Operations
IAS 36	Impairment Assets
IAS 37	Provisions, Contingent Liabilities and Contingent Assets
IAS 38	Intangible Assets
IAS 39	Financial Instruments: Recognition and Measurement (Revised Dec. 2003)
IAS 40	Investment Property (Revised Dec. 2003)
IAS 41	Agriculture

[*Note:* IAS 3,4,5,6,9,13 and 25 marked star (*) have either been withdrawn or superseded by others as indicated in the Exhibit 5.1 itself]

EXHIBIT 5.2 List of International Financial Reporting Standards (IFRS)

IFRS	Broad Title/Theme
IFRS-1	First-time Adoption of International Financial Reporting Standards. IFRS 1 applies when an entity adopts IFRSs for the first time by an explicit and unreserved statement of compliance with IFRSs.
IFRS-2	Share-based Payment IFRS 2 applies to transactions in which shares, share options or other equity instruments are granted to employees or other parties. It also applies to transactions to be settled in cash or other assets that are share-based because the payment amount is based on the price of the entity's shares.
IFRS-3	Business Combinations
IFRS-4	Insurance Contracts The publication of this IFRS provides, for the first time, guidance on accounting for insurance contracts, and marks the first step in the IASB's project to achieve the convergence of widely varying insurance industry accounting practices around the world.
IFRS-5	Non-current Assets held for Sale and Discontinued Operations.
IFRS-6	Exploration for and Evaluation of Mineral Resources
IFRS-7	Financial Instruments: Disclosures
IFRS-8	Operating Segments
IFRS-9	Financial Instruments
IFRS-10	Consolidated Financial Statements
IFRS-11	Joint Arrangements
IFRS-12	Disclosure of Interests in Other Entities
IFRS-13	Fair Value Measurement
IFRS-14	Regulatory Deferral Accounts
IFRS-15	Revenue from Contracts with Customers
IFRS-16	Leases
IFRS-17	Insurance Contracts

International Accounting Standards (IAS) and IFRS

It was in 1904 that the idea of setting up international accounting standards emerged in the first International Congress of Accountants held at St. Louis. In the tenth International

Congress however, leading accounting bodies of *ten* nations, namely, Australia, Canada, France, Germany, Japan, Mexico, the Netherlands, United Kingdom, Ireland and the USA, agreed to form the International Accounting Standards Committee (IASC) in the year 1973. The IASC, before being restructured to be called as International Accounting Standards Board (IASB) with effect from 2001, had issued forty one accounting standards, popularly known as International Accounting Standards or IAS. The IASB, while deciding to retain all the pronouncements of accounting policies made by IASC in the name as International Accounting Standards, also decided to call its own pronouncements of policies as International Financial Reporting Standards (IFRS). The IASB has so far issued 17 IFRS. Lists of the 41 IAS and the 17 IFRS are given in Exhibit 5.1 and 5.2, respectively.

Indian Accounting Standards (AS) and Ind AS

The Institute of Chartered Accountants of India (ICAI) has issued 32 accounting standards (AS) as shown in Exhibit 5.3-A and 41 Ind AS which have been shown in Exhibit 5.3-B. With the withdrawal of AS 8 (on R & D) consequent upon the issuance of AS 26 (on intangible assets) that the effective number of AS remained at 31. These accounting standards aim at bringing the financial reporting system of India at convergence with the international reporting system. Section 211 (3A) of the Indian Companies (Amendment) Act, 1999 made it mandatory for firms to comply with accounting standards for reporting their financial results.

In 2015, the Ministry of Corporate Affairs, Government of India had further notified the Companies (Indian Accounting Standards [Ind AS] Rules 2015. This notification stipulated for the adoption and applicability of Ind AS in a phased manner beginning from Accounting period 2016-17. The Ministry (of Corporate Affairs) has thereafter issued three Amendment Rules, one each in year 2016, 2017, and 2018 to amend the 2015 rules. Basically, Ind AS are standards that have been harmonized with the IFRS through adoption and convergence that will make reporting by Indian companies more globally accessible.

EXHIBIT 5.3-A List of Indian Accounting Standards (AS)

AS	*Broad Title/Theme*
AS-1	Disclosure of Accounting Policies
AS-2	Valuation of Inventories
AS-3	Cash flow Statement
AS-4	Contingencies and Events Occurring After the Balance Date
AS-5	Net Profit or Loss for the Period, Prior Period and extraordinary Items and changes in Accounting Policies
AS-6	Depreciation Accounting
AS-7	Construction Contracts
AS-8*	Accounting for Research and Development
AS-9	Revenue recognition
AS-10	Accounting for Fixed Assets
AS-11	Accounting for the Effects of Changes in Foreign Exchange Rates
AS-12	Accounting for Government grants
AS-13	Accounting for Investments
AS-14	Accounting for Amalgamation

(*Contd.*)

AS	*Broad Title/Theme*
AS-15	Accounting for Retirement Benefits in the Financial Statements of Employers
AS-16	Borrowings Costs
AS-17	Segmental Reporting
AS-18	Related Party Disclosures
AS-19	Leases
AS-20	Earnings Per Share
AS-21	Consolidated Financial Statements
AS-22	Accounting for Taxes on Income
AS-23	Accounting for Investment in Associates in Consolidated Financial Statements
AS-24	Discontinuing Operations
AS-25	Interim Financial Reporting
AS-26	Intangible Assets
AS-27	Financial Reporting of Interest in Joint Venture
AS-28	Impairment of Assets
AS-29	Provisions, Contingent Liabilities and Contingent Assets
AS-30	Financial Instruments: Recognition and Measurement and Limited Revisions to AS-2, AS-11 (Revised 2003), AS-21, AS-23, AS-26, AS-27, AS-28 and AS-29
AS-31	Financial Instruments: Presentation
AS-32	Financial Instruments: Disclosures, and limited revision to AS-19, Leases

* AS-8 is not I use now.

EXHIBIT 5.3-B List of Indian Accounting Standards (Ind AS)

Ind AS	*Broad Title/ Theme*
Ind AS 1	Presentation of Financial Statements
Ind AS 2	Inventories
Ind AS 7	Statement of Cash Flows
Ind AS 8	Accounting Policies, Changes in Accounting Estimates and Errors
Ind AS 10	Events occurring after Reporting Period
Ind AS 11	Construction Contracts – Amendment Rules, 2018
Ind AS 12	Income Taxes
Ind AS 16	Property, Plant, and Equipment
Ind AS 18	Revenue
Ind AS 19	Employee Benefits
Ind AS 20	Accounting for and disclosing government grants
Ind AS 21	The Effects of Changes in Foreign Exchange Rates
Ind AS 23	Borrowing Costs
Ind AS 24	Related Party Disclosures
Ind AS 27	Separate Financial Statements
Ind AS 28	Investments in Associates and Joint Ventures
Ind AS 29	Financial Reporting in Hyperinflationary Economies
Ind AS 32	Financial Instruments: Presentation
Ind AS 33	Earnings Per Share
Ind AS 34	Interim Financial Reporting
Ind AS 36	Impairment of Assets
Ind AS 37	Provisions, Contingent Liabilities, and Contingent Assets
Ind AS 38	Intangible Assets
Ind AS 40	Investment Property

Ind AS	*Broad Title/ Theme*
Ind AS 41	Agriculture
Ind AS 101	Ind AS is being used for the first time
Ind AS 102	Shared Payment
Ind AS 103	Business Combination
Ind AS 104	Insurance Contracts
Ind AS 105	Non-current Assets Held for Sale and Discontinued Operations
Ind AS 106	Exploration for and Evaluation of Mineral Resources
Ind AS 107	Financial Instruments & Disclosures
Ind AS 108	Operating Segments
Ind AS 109	Financial Instruments
Ind AS 110	Consolidated Financial Statements
Ind AS 111	Joint Arrangements
Ind AS 112	Disclosure of Interests in Other Entities
Ind AS 113	Fair Value Measurement
Ind AS 114	Regulatory Deferral Accounts
Ind AS 115	Revenue from Contracts with Customers (Applicable from April 2018)
Ind AS 116	Leases–Applicable from April 2019

International Accounting Standards (IAS) and the Indian Accounting Standards at a Glance

A comparative picture of the International Accounting Standards and Indian Accounting Standards (AS) has been given in Exhibit-5.4(A). Similarly, Exhibit-5.4(B) contains a comparative presentation of the International Accounting Standards and Indian Accounting Standards, called Ind AS.

EXHIBIT 5.4(A) International and the Indian Accounting Standards (AS) at a Glance

IAS	*Corresponding Indian GAAP (AS)*	*Broad Title/Theme*
IAS 1	AS-1 & AS-31	Presentation of Financial Statements
IAS 2	AS-2	Inventories
IAS 7	AS-3	Cash Flow Statements
IAS 8	AS-5	Accounting Policies, Changes in accounting Estimates and Errors
IAS 10	AS-4	Events after the Balance Sheet Date
IAS 11	AS-7	Construction Contracts
IAS 12	AS-22	Income Taxes
IAS 14	AS-17	Segmental Reporting
IAS 15	—	Information Reflecting the Effects of Changing Prices
IAS 16	AS-10 & AS-6	Property, Plant and Equipment
IAS 17	AS-19	Leases
IAS 18	AS-9	Revenue
IAS 19	AS-15	Employee benefits
IAS 20	AS-12	Accounting for Government Grants and Disclosure of Government Assistance
IAS 21	AS-11	The Effects of Changes in the Foreign Exchange Rate

(*Contd.*)

IAS	*Corresponding Indian GAAP (AS)*	*Broad Title/Theme*
IAS 22	AS-14	Business Combination (now withdrawn and replaced by IFRS 3: Business Combination)
IAS 23	AS-16	Borrowing Costs
IAS 24	AS-18	Related Party Disclosures
IAS 26	AS-15	Accounting and Reporting by Retirement Benefits Plans
IAS 27	AS-21	Consolidated and Separate Financial Statements
IAS 28	AS-23	Investments in associates
IAS 29	—	Financial Reporting in Hyper Inflationary Economics
IAS 30	As per RBI Guidelines	Disclosure in the Financial Statements of the Banks and Similar Financial Institutions
IAS 31	AS-27	Interests in Joint Ventures
IAS 32	AS-13 & AS-30	Financial Instruments: Disclosure and Presentation
IAS 33	AS-20	Earnings Per Share
IAS 34	AS-25	Interim Financial Reporting
IAS 35	AS-24	Discontinuing Operations
IAS 36	AS-28	Impairment Assets
IAS 37	AS-4 & AS-29	Provisions, Contingent Liabilities and Contingent Assets
IAS 38	AS-26	Intangible Assets
IAS 39	AS-13 & AS-32	Financial Instruments: Recognition and Measurement
IAS 40	AS-13	Investment Property
IAS 41	—	Agriculture

EXHIBIT 5.4(B) International Accounting Standards (IAS) and the Indian Accounting Standards (Ind AS) at a glance

IAS	*Broad Title/Theme*	*Ind AS*	*Broad Title/Theme*
IAS 1	Presentation of Financial Statements	Ind AS 1	Presentation of Financial Statements
IAS 2	Inventories	Ind AS 2	Inventories
IAS 7	Statement of Chas Flows	Ind AS 7	Statement of Chas Flows
IAS 8	Accounting Policies, Changes in accounting Estimates and Errors	Ind AS 8	Accounting Policies, Changes in accounting Estimates and Errors
IAS 10	Events after the Balance Sheet Date	Ind AS 10	Events occurring after Reporting Period
IAS 11	Construction Contracts	Ind AS 11	Construction Contracts
IAS 12	Income Taxes	Ind AS 12	Income Taxes
IAS 14	Segmental Reporting	Ind AS 108	Operating Segments
IAS 15	Information Reflecting the Effects of Changing Prices	Ind AS 29	Information Reflecting the Effects of Changing Prices
IAS 16	Property, Plant and Equipment	Ind AS 16	Property, Plant and Equipment
IAS 17	Leases	Ind AS 116	Leases Applicable from April 2019
IAS 18	Revenue	Ind AS 18	Revenue
IAS 19	Employee benefits	Ind AS 19	Employee benefits
IAS 20	Accounting for Government Grants and Disclosure of Government Assistance	Ind AS 20	Accounting for and disclosing Government Grants
IAS 21	The Effects of Changes in the Foreign Exchange Rates	Ind AS 21	The Effects of Changes in the Foreign Exchange Rates

IAS	Broad Title/Theme	Ind AS	Broad Title/Theme
IAS 22	Business Combination (now withdrawn and replaced by IFRS 3: Business Combination)	Ind AS 103	Business Combination (now withdrawn and replaced by IFRS 3: Business Combination)
IAS 23	Borrowing Costs	Ind AS 23	Borrowing Costs
IAS 24	Related Party Disclosures	Ind AS 24	Related Party Disclosures
IAS 26	Accounting and Reporting by Retirement Benefits Plans	Ind AS 19	Accounting and Reporting by Retirement Benefits Plans
IAS 27	Consolidated and Separate Financial Statements	Ind AS 27	Separate Financial Statements
IAS 28	Investments in Associates	Ind AS 28	Investments in Associates and Joint ventures
IAS 29	Financial Reporting in Hyper Inflationary Economics	Ind AS 29	Financial Reporting in Hyper Inflationary Economics
IAS 30	Disclosure in the Financial Statements of the Banks and Similar Financial Institutions	—	—
IAS 31	Interests in Joint Ventures	—	—
IAS 32	Financial Instruments: Disclosure and Presentation	Ind AS 32	Financial Instruments: Presentation
IAS 33	Earnings Per Share	Ind AS 33	Earnings Per Share
IAS 34	Interim Financial Reporting	Ind AS 34	Interim Financial Reporting
IAS 35	Discontinuing Operations	Ind AS	Discontinuing Operations
IAS 36	Impairment of Assets	Ind AS 36	Impairment of Assets
IAS 37	Provisions, Contingent Liabilities and Contingent Assets	Ind AS 37	Provisions, Contingent Liabilities and Contingent Assets
IAS 38	Intangible Assets	Ind AS 38	Intangible Assets
IAS 39	Financial Instruments: Recognition and Measurement	—	—
IAS 40	Investment Property	Ind AS 40	Investment Property
IAS 41	Agriculture	Ind AS 41	Agriculture

Convergence of Indian Accounting Standard (AS) with IAS

In order to achieve harmonization of accounting practices, convergence of national accounting standards with that of international accounting standards is essential. As stated earlier, the Indian accounting standards operate in convergence with the international accounting standards so that the Indian financial reporting system is at per with the international practice. Exhibit 5.3 though presents an overview of the International Accounting Standards' equivalent Indian Accounting Standards, a detailed analysis of the provision and guidelines of each of the standards would reveal the nature and extent of real convergence. However, as detailed presentation of the provisions of the accounting standards, both national and international, is beyond the scope of this book; a comparative view of the provisions of a few standards, namely, IAS 1, IAS 2, and ISA 7 along with their corresponding Indian Standards, AS 1, AS 2 and AS 3 has been given here under as an example of convergence.

IAS 1 Vs AS 1

IAS 1: Presentation of Financial Statements

The purpose of presenting financial statements as outlined by the International Accounting Standards Committee (IASC) in its framework for the preparation and presentation of financial statements is to provide information regarding an enterprise's financial position, performance, and changes in financial position to a broad spectrum of users so as to enable them to make rational and informed economic decisions. Keeping this in view, IAS 1 sets the objective of presenting the general purpose financial statements as to 'providing information about an enterprise's financial position, its performance and its cash flows. According to IAS 1 this information be presented through a complete set of financial statements comprising of:

1. The balance sheet
2. An income statement
3. Another statement showing either
   (a) all changes in equity, or
   (b) changes in equity other than those arising from capital transactions with owners and distributions to owners
4. A cash flow statement
5. Accounting policies and other explanatory notes

On the inclusion of items in the financial statements, IAS 1 further states that 'to be included in the financial statements, an item must meet the *definitional* requirements, *recognition* requirements and *measurement* requirements'. Accordingly, three important items of the balance sheet, namely assets, liabilities and equity which relate to the status (and not performance) of an entity at a particular point of time, have been defined by IAS 1 as follows:

Assets: Probable future economic benefits obtained or controlled by a particular entity as a result of past transactions or events.

An item in order to be called as an asset must satisfy three characteristics:

1. The asset must provide probable future economic benefit that enables it to provide future net cash inflows;
2. The entity is able to receive the benefit and restrict other entities' access to that benefit; and
3. The event that provides the entity with the right to the benefit has occurred.

Liabilities: Probable future sacrifices of economic benefits arising from present obligations of a particular entity to transfer assets or provide services to other entities in the future as a result of past transactions or events.

To be called as a liability, an item must satisfy three characteristics:

1. A liability requires that the entity settles a present obligation by the probable future transfer of an asset on demand when a specified event occurs or at a particular date;
2. The obligation cannot be avoided; and
3. The event that obligates the entity has occurred.

Equity: The residual interest in the assets that remains after deducting its liabilities. In a business enterprise, the equity is the ownership interest.

Classification of assets, liabilities and equity: IAS 1 provides that the assets, liabilities and stockholders' equity be separated in the balance sheet so as to exhibit important relationships and focus attention on the subtotals. Accordingly, the assets have been classified into:

- ***Current assets*** comprising of cash, trading investments, receivables, inventories and prepaid expenses;
- ***Non-current assets*** comprising of held-to-maturity investments, investment property, property, plant and equipment, intangible assets comprising of goodwill, trademarks, patents, copyrights and organizational costs and other assets such as deferred and prepaid expenses.

According to IAS 1, *current asset* is one that:

(a) is expected to be realized in, or is held for sale or consumption in the normal course of the enterprise's operating cycle; or

(b) is held primarily for trading purposes or for the short-term, and is expected to be realized within twelve months of the balance sheet date; or

(c) is cash or a cash equivalent asset that is not restricted in its use.

Non-current assets, as defined by IAS 1, are tangible, intangible, operating and financial assets of a long-term nature.

A liability, according to IAS 1, is current if

(a) It is expected to be settled in the normal course of the enterprise's operating cycle, or

(b) It is due to be settled within twelve months of the balance sheet date.

Non-current liabilities are obligations that are not expected to be liquidated within the current operating cycle including obligations arising out of:

(a) Acquisition of assets such as the issuance of bonds, long-term notes and lease obligations;

(b) Normal course of operations such as pension obligations; and

(c) Contingent obligations involving uncertainty as to possible losses.

The standard further provides that for long-term liabilities, the maturity date, nature of obligation, rate of interest and description of any security pledged to support the agreement should be clearly shown.

Equity, as defined in IAS 1, represents the interest of the stockholders in the assets of the firm. It shows the cumulative net results of past transactions and other events. Further, it includes share capital and retained earnings. Share capital includes the par and stated value of preferred and common shares, excluding the preference capital that is redeemable at the option of the holder which is of course shown as a separate item. The number of shares authorized, issued and outstanding and the features of the preference share capital should be displayed clearly.

Retained earnings represent the accumulated earnings of the firm since its inception, less any earnings distributed to owners as dividends.

Disclosure Principles

Disclosure principles basically aim at making the financial statements free from misleading because of non-inclusion of certain items/information. The important disclosure principles as contained in IAS 1 are:

1. Parenthetical explanations
2. Footnotes
3. Supporting schedules
4. Cross references
5. Valuation accounts

Parenthetical explanations are used to disclose supplemental information appropriate to the balance sheet item. For example, information regarding share capital in the balance sheet may look like:

Equity share capital ₹1,20,000
(of ₹10 each, 20,000 shares authorized and 12,00 shares issued)

Footnotes are used when additional information are not possible to be disclosed in a short and concise parenthetical explanation. For giving adequate details as regards certain balance sheet items, supporting schedules are used. Cross-references are necessary in case two or more items of the balance sheet are directly related. For example, bank loan secured by stock in trade ₹35,000. Valuation accounts are used to indicate the reduced or increased value of an item of the balance sheet. Depreciation, for example, reduces value of a depreciable asset, say machinery. The said machinery is therefore shown in the balance sheet as:

	₹
Machinery	50,000
Less: Depreciation	5,000
	45,000

Accounting policies: IAS 1 requires financial statements to disclose clearly the significant accounting policies that have been used in their preparation. This may be in line with (1) selection from available alternatives, (2) principles and methods peculiar to the industry, (3) unique application of IAS.

The standard has an 'allowance clause' as well which is often called as the 'fairness exception clause' by some experts. It states that 'while the use of IAS will result in virtually all circumstances in financial statements that achieve a fair presentation, in some instances this may not be the case'. In such eventualities, IAS 1 permits ***departure*** from the standards to achieve the greater good of fair presentation provided however that the enterprise discloses the following:

1. That management has concluded that the financial statements fairly present the entity's financial position, financial performance and cash flows;
2. That the entity has compiled in all material respects with applicable IAS except that it departed from a standard to achieve a fair presentation; and
3. The standard from which the entity has departed; the nature of the departure; including the accounting treatment which the standard would have required; the reason why that treatment would have been misleading in the circumstances; the alternative treatment

which was in fact applied; and the financial impact of the departure on profit or loss, assets, liabilities, equity, and cash flows for each period represented.

Reporting format: IAS 1 does not prescribe any format as such in which the assets and liabilities are to be represented except to the fact that at least previous year's figure in respect of the concerned balance sheet items is displayed to increase the usefulness of financial statements. As a matter of convention, balance sheets are found to be prepared in two forms—the report form and the account form.

AS 1: Disclosure of Accounting Policies

The principles adopted by the enterprise in preparation and presentation of financial statements are referred to be called as accounting policies. AS 1 requires the enterprises to disclose the accounting policies they have followed for preparation and presentation of their financial statements. This disclosure is essential because there are many items such as the methods of depreciation, treatment of expenditure during construction, translation of foreign currency, valuation of inventories, treatment of retirement benefits, valuation of fixed assets and investments, treatment of contingent liabilities, and alike have alternative treatments which can influence the values contained in the financial statements in respect of such items. *AS 1 therefore puts forth that all significant accounting policies followed in the preparation of financial statements be disclosed at one place so as to facilitate the reader taking informed decisions*.

For selection of the accounting policies, AS 1 provides that polices that would result in the exhibition of a true and fair view of the financial statements be selected. The standard has provided three basic guidelines, namely, *prudence*, *substance over form*, *and materiality*, for the selection of accounting policies. Prudence refers to making estimates under conditions of uncertainty, say for example, with regard to uncertainty in collectivity of receivables. Substance over form refers to recording of the transactions in accordance with their actual happenings and economic reality rather than their legal forms. For example, assets on hire purchase are to be shown in the books of the hire purchaser even if the last installment is not paid, meaning thereby that the seller continues to be the legal owner of the asset. Materiality refers to disclosure of all such facts whose presence or absence is likely to influence the decisions of stakeholders.

As regards changes in accounting policies, AS 1 stipulates the following two conditions under which the enterprise can bring a change to the adopted policies:

(a) If there is a change in the statutory provision(s) and/or there is a requirement to comply with an Accounting Standard.

(b) If it is considered that such a change would result in more appropriate presentation of financial statements.

For example, companies in India have been required to revise their accounting policy as regards valuation of inventory by including applicable fixed production overheads following the issuance of mandatory AS 2 by the Institute of Chartered Accountants of India (ICAI).

IAS 2: Inventory Valuation

IAS 2 deals with the definition, valuation and classification of inventories. Inventories, according to this standard, are 'items held for sale in the ordinary course of business; in the process of production of such sale; or in the form of materials or supplies to be consumed in the production process or in the rendering of services.

For valuation of inventories and cost of goods sold, IAS 2 has recommended for the use of 'specific techniques' which means that the production and/or acquisition costs be allocated to the specific goods to which they relate. As specific identification is not practicable in general, for product tend to loose its identity as it passes through the production and sales process, IAS 2 suggests for use of *three* alternative techniques: **FIFO, Weighted average and LIFO.** The standard further provides for valuation of certain kind of inventories at selling price *less* disposal costs. The inventories included under this category are livestock, agricultural and forest products, and mineral ores whose costs are difficult to determine; whose market prices are available and whose marketability is assured.

As far as classification of inventories is concerned, IAS 2 puts the inventories into four types: Merchandise, raw material, work in progress and finished goods. Whereas, merchandise inventory relates to the merchandising entity such as a retailer or whole seller who maintains a single inventory account, the other three relate to the manufacturing entity.

IAS 2 has further set forth certain *disclosure requirements* in relation to inventory accounting. They are:

1. The accounting policies adopted in measuring inventories, including the costing method (FIFO, Weighted average, or LIFO) employed.
2. The total carrying amount of inventories and carrying amount in classifications appropriate to the enterprise.
3. The carrying amount of inventories carried at net realizable value.
4. The amount of any reversal of any previous write-down that is recognized in earnings for the period.
5. The circumstances or events that led to the reversal of a write-down of inventories to net realizable value.
6. The carrying amount of inventories pledged as security for liabilities.

AS 2: Inventory Valuation

The purpose of AS 2 is to formulate method of computation of cost of inventories and to determine the value of closing stock as would appear in the balance sheet till it is not sold and recognized as revenue.

Inventories as defined by AS 2 are:

1. Items held for sale in the ordinary course of business, i.e., finished products.
2. Items in the process of production of such sale, i.e., raw materials and work in progress.
3. Items in the form of materials or supplies to be consumed in the production process or in the rendering of services, i.e., stores, spare raw materials and consumables.
4. Spares which can be used only in connection with an item of fixed assets and whose use is irregular.

Inventories of the following specifications have been excluded from the applicability of AS 2:

1. Work in progress arising under construction contract including those related to services contract.

2. Work in progress arising in ordinary course of business for service providers, e.g. incomplete consultancy services, incomplete medical services and incomplete merchant bank(ing) services.
3. Financial instruments such as shares, bonds and debentures held as stock-in-trade.
4. Producer's inventories like livestock, agricultural and forest products, mineral ores, oil and gas.

Valuation of Inventories

AS 2 provides that the value of inventories shall be the *least of* cost and *net realizable value* of the inventories, compared items by item or in group.

The cost of inventories shall include:

1. *Cost of purchase*, comprising of purchase price, duties and taxes, freight inward and other expenditure directly attributable to the purchase *less* discount and rebate, duties and taxes recoverable from the tax authorities, and similar other items.
2. *Cost of conversion*, comprising of cost directly attributable to the unit, i.e., direct material, direct labour and direct expenses; and systematic allocation of fixed and variable production overheads that are incurred in converting material into finished products.
3. *Other costs*, comprising of cost in incurred in bringing the inventories to their current location and condition.

AS 2 provides for the *exclusion* of abnormal loss due to wastage of materials, labour or other production cost; storage cost; administrative, selling and distribution overheads; and interest and borrowing cost (unless and otherwise AS 16 provides for such inclusion of interest and borrowing cost).

For determining the cost formula, AS 2 provides that *specific identification method* be followed for determining the cost of inventories and where specific identification is not feasible, the FIFO and weighted average cost methods be followed.

Net realizable value, as per AS 2, is the estimated selling price per unit in ordinary course of business *less* estimated cost of completion and estimated cost necessary to make the sale.

AS 2 sets forth the following disclosure norms in the financial statements in relation to inventories:

1. The accounting policies adopted for measuring the value of inventories;
2. The cost formula used; and
3. The classification of inventories (into finished goods, raw materials, work in progress, and spares) along with their carrying values.

IAS 7 Vs AS 3

IAS 7: Cash Flow Statement

The purpose of cash flow statements are basically twofold: providing information as regards the inflow and outflow of cash during a given period and providing an insight into the investing and financing activities of the firm. Keeping this in view, IAS 7 has outlined the perceived benefits of presenting cash flow statement in addition to the balance sheet and the income statement as follows:

1. It provides an insight into the financial structure of the enterprise including its liquidity and solvency and its ability to affect the amount and timing of cash flows in order to adapt to changing circumstances and opportunities.
2. It provides additional information to the users of financial statements for evaluating changes in assets, liabilities and equity of an enterprise.
3. It enhances the comparability of reporting of operating performance by different enterprises by eliminating the effects of using different accounting treatments for the same transactions and events.
4. It serves as an indicator of the amount, timing and certainty of future cash flows.

IAS 7 has accordingly recommended for the preparation of cash flow statement as follows:

Cash inflows	
Operating	1. Sale of goods and services.
	2. Sales of loans, debt or equity instruments carried in trading portfolio.
	3. Interest on loan and dividend on equity securities received.
	4. Collection of loan principals and sale of other debt instruments.
Investing	5. Sale of investments and returns from investments.
Financing	6. Sale of plants and equipment/fixed assets.
	7. Issue of share capital and debt instruments.
Cash outflows	
Operating	1. Purchase of goods and services.
	2. Purchase of loans, debt or equity instruments carried in trading portfolio.
	3. Payment of taxes, interest and payment to or on behalf of employees.
	4. Purchase of plant and equipment
	5. Repayment of loans and purchase of other debt instruments.
Investing	6. Purchase of equity instruments.
Financing	7. Payment of dividends, repayment of loans and repurchase of company shares.

IAS 7 also stipulates on *two* categories of disclosure norms:

1. Required disclosure
2. Recommended disclosure

Under the *required disclosure*, it states that the amount of significant cash and cash equivalent balances held by an enterprise that are not available for use by the group should be disclosed along with the comments from the management.

Under the *recommended disclosure*, included are:

(a) The amount of undrawn borrowing facilities, indicating restrictions on their use (if any).

(b) In case of investments in joint ventures, which are accounted for using prorate consolidation, the aggregate amount of cash flows from operating, investing and financing activities that are attributable to the investment in the joint venture.

(c) Aggregate amount of cash flows that are attributable to the increase in operating capacity separately from those cash flows that are required to maintain operating capacity.

(d) Amount of cash flows segregated by reported industry and geographical segments.

AS 3: Cash Flow Statement

AS 3 stipulates that enterprises with annual turnover of more than ₹50 crore (500 million) and the listed companies shall have to present cash flow statements, a statement of incoming and outgoing of cash in addition to other financial statements, in order to enable the users of these statements assess the liquidity and solvency positions of the enterprises through their abilities to generate and utilize cash. The standard requires listed companies to prepare the cash flow statement under the indirect method as prescribed by the standard.

The flow of cash as per AS 3 shall be on account of *operating activities, investing activities and financing activities*. Cash would mean cash in hand and demand deposits, and cash equivalent comprising of risk free highly liquid investments with maturity less than three months and which can be readily converted into cash without any loss of value. The flow of cash for example shall be as follows:

Inflow	
Operating activities	Cash receipts from sale of goods and services, royalties, fees, commission and similar other revenues like refund of tax, receipt of dividend.
Investing activities	Cash receipts from disposal of fixed assets including intangibles, shares, warrants, debt instruments in other enterprises and disposal of interests of joint ventures.
Financing activities	Issue of shares, debentures and long term loans.
Outflow	
Operating activities	Cash payments to employees and on behalf of employees, payment of taxes.
Investing activities	Cash payments for purchase of fixed assets including intangibles, acquiring shares, warrants, debt instruments of other enterprises and interests in joint ventures.
Financing activities	Redemption of shares, debentures, repayment of loans, buy back of shares and payment of interest and dividend.

AS 3 required enterprises to disclose:

1. The component of cash and cash equivalents along with reconciliation of the amount shown in the cash flow statement with the equivalent items reported in the balance sheet.
2. The amount of significant cash and cash equivalent balance held (by the enterprise) that is not available for use by it with management explanation.

From the comparative representations of the provisions of IAS 1, IAS 2, IAS 7 and their corresponding Indian Accounting Standards AS 1, AS 2 and AS 3, it is evident that the provisions contained in the Indian Accounting Standards in respect of presentation of financial statements and disclosure of accounting policies, valuation of inventories and preparation and presentation of cash flow statements, are mostly in line with the International Accounting Standards.

INTERNATIONAL FINANCIAL REPORTING STANDARDS

International Financial Reporting Standards (IFRS) are 'principles based' set of standards, interpretations and framework for the preparation and presentation of financial statements. The broad components of IFRS are:

International Financial Reporting Standards (IFRS)—standards issued after 2001
International Accounting Standards (IAS)—standards issued before 2001
Interpretations originated from the International Financial Reporting Interpretations Committee (IFRIC)—issued after 2001
Standing Interpretations Committee (SIC)—issued before 2001
Conceptual Framework for the Preparation and Presentation of Financial Statements (2010)

IFRS requires entities to prepare:

(i) a Statement of Financial Position,
(ii) a Statement of Comprehensive Income or two separate statements comprising an Income Statement and separately a Statement of Comprehensive Income, which reconciles Profit or Loss on the Income statement to total comprehensive income,
(iii) a Statement of Changes in Equity (SOCE),
(iv) a Cash Flow Statement or Statement of Cash Flows, and
(v) notes, including a summary of the significant accounting policies

IFRS also requires 'Comparative Information' for the prior reporting period stated under IAS 1, para 36. IFRS further specifies that an entity preparing IFRS accounts for the first time must apply IFRS in full for the current and comparative period, although there are transitional exemptions as provided under IFRS 1, para 7.

The IASB has issued a revised IAS 1 'Presentation of Financial Statements' on 6 September 2007 making it effective for annual periods beginning on or after 1 January 2009 or a date prior to this. The revised IAS 1 requires each entity to:

(i) present all non-owner changes in equity (i.e., 'comprehensive income' either in one 'statement of comprehensive income' or in two statements (a separate income statement and a statement of comprehensive income). Components of comprehensive income may not be presented in the Statement of changes in equity;
(ii) present a statement of financial position (balance sheet) as at the beginning of the earliest comparative period in a complete set of financial statements when the entity applies the new standard;
(iii) present a statement of cash flow; and
(iv) make necessary disclosure by the way of a note.

Adoption of IFRS by Different Counties

IFRS when adopted worldwide will benefit investors and other users of financial statements by reducing the costs of comparison between alternative investments and by enhancing the quality of information for available for decision making. Keeping this in view and to reduce the disparities in financial reporting across nations that IFRS are now used in many countries including the European Union, Canada, Hong Kong, Australia, Malaysia, Russia, South Africa, Singapore and Turkey, India not being an exception. Over 140 countries around the world, including all of Europe, currently require or permit IFRS reporting. Nearly 93 of these countries require IFRS reporting for all domestic and listed companies. The US too is readying towards convergence with IFRS. The Securities Exchange Commission of US, for example, has started progressively shifting its requirement of disclosure from the exclusive US GAAP to accepting IFRS and making IFRS standards as the only disclosure norms in the long run, expected to be by the end of financial year 2014. The Canadian publicly accountable profit-oriented enterprises, including public companies and other "profit-oriented enterprises that are responsible to large or diverse groups of shareholders are adopting IFRS for financial periods beginning on or after 1 January 2011". IFRS have been made effective from beginning 2010 in Hong Kong. Japan has made it mandatory from beginning 2012. The Turkish companies listed to Istanbul Stock Exchange are already preparing IFRS reports from 2006 and so also the companies listed to the Johannesburg Stock Exchange (South Africa) from January 1, 2005. Russia started for full transition to IFRS from 2011.

Taiwan chalked out the following plans for adoption of IFRS:

Phase-I: All listed companies and financial institutions supervised by the Financial Supervisory Commission, except for credit cooperatives, credit card companies and insurance intermediaries:

(i) They will be required to prepare financial statements in accordance with Taiwan-IFRS starting from January 1, 2013.

(ii) Firms that have already issued securities overseas, or have registered an overseas securities issuance with the FSC, or have a market capitalization of greater than NT$10 billion, will be permitted to prepare additional consolidated financial statements in accordance with Taiwan-IFRS starting from January 1, 2012. If a company without subsidiaries is not required to prepare consolidated financial statements, it will be permitted to prepare additional individual financial statements on the above conditions.

Phase-II: All unlisted public companies, credit cooperatives and credit card companies:

They will be required to prepare financial statements in accordance with Taiwan-IFRS beginning January 1, 2015. They will also be permitted to apply Taiwan-IFRS starting from January 1, 2013.

Pre-disclosure: Pre-disclosure about the IFRS adoption plan, and the impact of adoption:

To prepare properly for IFRS adoption, domestic companies should propose an IFRS adoption plan and establish a specific taskforce. They should also disclose the related information from 2 years prior to adoption, as follows:

Phase I companies:

(i) They will be required to disclose the adoption plan, and the impact of adoption, in 2011 annual financial statements, and in 2012 interim and annual financial statements.

(ii) Early optional adoption: (a) Companies adopting IFRS early will be required to disclose the adoption plan, and the impact of adoption, in 2010 annual financial statements, and in 2011 interim and annual financial statements. (b) If a company opts for early adoption of Taiwan-IFRS after January 1, 2011, it will be required to disclose the adoption plan, and the impact of adoption, in 2011 interim and annual financial statements commencing on the decision date.

Phase II companies: Phase II companies will be required to disclose the related information from 2 years prior to adoption, as stated above.

The year-wise work plan: The following was the year-wise work plan for adoption of IFRS in Taiwan:

2008	♦ Establishment of IFRS Taskforce
2009-2011	♦ Acquisition of authorization to translate IFRS.
	♦ Translation, review, and issuance of IFRS.
	♦ Analysis of possible IFRS implementation problems, and resolution thereof.
	♦ Proposal for modification of the related regulations and supervisory mechanisms.
	♦ Enhancement of related publicity and training activities.
2012	♦ IFRS application permitted for Phase I companies.
	♦ Study on possible IFRS implementation problems, and resolution thereof.
	♦ Completion of amendments to the related regulations and supervisory mechanisms.
	♦ Enhancement of the related publicity and training activities.
2013	♦ Application of IFRS required for Phase I companies, and permitted for Phase II companies.
	♦ Follow-up analysis of the status of IFRS adoption, and of the impact.
2014	♦ Follow-up analysis of the status of IFRS adoption, and of the impact.
2015	♦ Applications of IFRS required for Phase II companies.

Adoption of IFRS is going to benefit the Taiwan firms in the following ways:

- More efficient formulation of domestic accounting standards, improvement of their international image, and enhancement of the global rankings and international competitiveness of the local capital markets;
- Better comparability between the financial statements of local and foreign companies;
- No need for restatement of financial statements when local companies wish to issue overseas securities, resulting in reduction in the cost of raising capital overseas;

- For local companies with investments overseas, use of a single set of accounting standards will reduce the cost of account conversions and improve management efficiency.

IFRS and India

The Institute of Chartered Accountants of India (ICAI) had announced that IFRS will be mandatory in India for financial statements for the periods beginning on or after 1 April 2011 for all listed companies with paid capital of ₹1,000 crore. This will be done by revising existing accounting standards to make them compatible with IFRS. Reserve Bank of India too has made financial statements of banks IFRS-compliant for periods beginning on or after 1 April 2011.

The phase wise application of IFRS shall be as follows:

2011	Phase-1	Opening balance sheet as at 1 April 2011* (i) Companies which are part of NSE Index – Nifty 50 (ii) Companies which are part of BSE Sensex – BSE 30 (a) Companies whose shares or other securities are listed on a stock exchange outside India (b) Companies, whether listed or not, having net worth of more than ₹1,000 crore
2012	Phase-2	Opening balance sheet as at 1 April 2012* Companies not covered in phase 1 and having net worth exceeding INR 500 crore
2014	Phase-3	Opening balance sheet as at 1 April 2014* Listed companies not covered in the earlier phases

(*If the financial year of a company commences at a date other than 1 April, then it shall prepare its opening balance sheet at the commencement of immediately following financial year)

Applicability of Indian Accounting Standards (or Ind AS) was further shifted and made mandatory for implementation in a phased manner from 1st April, 2015. Details of the revised date(s) and manner of implementation have already been given in Exhibit 1.3 in Chapter 1.

IFRS in Practice by Indian Firms

To get an insight into how Indian companies are readying themselves to adopt IFRS in practice, the financial statements prepared by Infosys Technologies India Limited may be taken into account which has made its financial statements IFRS compliant before date, i.e., April 1, 2011, an abstract of which is as under:

Audited Consolidated financial results of Infosys Technologies Limited and subsidiaries for the quarter and half-year ended September 30, 2010 prepared in compliance with International Financial Reporting Standards (IFRS) as issued by International Accounting Standards Board (IASB).

(Fig. in ₹ Crore, except per share data)

Particulars	*Quarter ended September 30,*		*Half—year ended September 30,*		*Year ended March 31,*
	2010	2009	2010	2009	2010
Revenues	**6,947**	**5,585**	13,145	11,057	22,742
Cost of sales	3,971	3,203	7,619	6,342	13,020
Gross profit	**2,976**	2,382	5,526	4,715	9,722
Selling and marketing expenses	380	276	719	537	1,184
Administrative expenses	498	413	954	841	1,628
Operating profit	**2,098**	1,693	3,853	3,337	6,910
Other income	267	239	506	508	990
Profit before income taxes	**2,365**	1,932	4,359	3,845	7,900
Income tax expense	628	397	1,134	785	1,681
Net profit	**1,737**	1,535	3,225	3,060	6,219
Paid-up equity share capital (par value ₹5 each, fully paid)	286	286	286	286	286
Share premium, retained earnings and other components of equity	26,039	21,227	26,039	21,227	23,787
Earnings per share (par value ₹5 each)					
Basic	30.40	26.91	56.47	53.67	109.02
Diluted	30.40	26.87	56.45	53.60	108.90
Dividend per share (par value ₹5 each) (Refer Note 5 & 6)					
Interim dividend	10.00	10.00	10.00	10.00	10.00
30th year special dividend	30.00	—	30.00	—	—
Final dividend	—	—	—	—	15.00
Total dividend	40.00	10.00	40.00	10.00	25.00
Total public shareholding#					
Number of shares	37,21,19,179	37,25,67,451	37,21,19,179	37,25,67,451	37,48,64,267
Percentage of shareholding	64.82	64.99	64.82	64.99	65.32
Promoters and Promoter Group Shareholding					
Pledged/Encumbered	—	—	—	—	—
Number of shares	—	—	—	—	—
Percentage of shares (as a % of the total shareholding of promoter and promoter group)	—	—	—	—	—
Percentage of shares (as a % of the total share capital of the company)	—	—	—	—	—
Non-encumbered	—	—	—	—	—
Number of shares	9,20,85,078	9,44,84,978	9,20,85,078	9,44,84,978	9,20,84,978
Percentage of shares (as a % of the total shareholding of promoter and promoter group)	100.00	100.00	100.00	100.00	100.00
Percentage of shares (as a % of the total share capital of the company)	16.04	16.48	16.04	16.48	16.05

Total Public Shareholding as defined under Clause 40A of the Listing Agreement excludes shares held by founders and American Depositary Receipt Holders.

1. The audited financial statements have been taken on record by the Board of Directors at its meeting held on October 15, 2010. The statutory auditors have expressed

on unqualified audit opinion. The information presented above is extracted from the audited financial statements as stated. The financial statements are prepared in accordance with International Financial Reporting Standards as issued by International Accounting Standards Board (IFRS).

2. The Securities Exchange Board of India (SEBI) vide its circular dated April 5, 2010 permitted listed entities having subsidiaries **to voluntarily submit** the consolidated financial statements as per IFRS. Consequent to this, the company has voluntarily prepared and published audited consolidated IFRS Financial Statements for the quarter and half-year ended September 30, 2010 as well as for fiscal year 2010.

3. Other information (Consolidated–Audited)

(Fig. in ₹ crore)

Particulars	*Quarter ended September 30,*		*Half-year ended September 30,*		*Year ended March 31,*
	2010	2009	2010	2009	2010
Staff costs	3,682	2,984	7,064	5,862	12,093
Items exceeding 10% of aggregate expenditure	–	–	–	–	–
Details of other income:					
Interest on deposits with banks and others	257	198	494	424	779
Income from available-for-sale financial assets/ investments	2	23	22	33	160
Miscellaneous income, net	3	4	5	6	21
Gains/(losses) on foreign currency	5	14	(15)	45	30
Total	**267**	**239**	**506**	**508**	**990**

4. Audited financial results of Infosys Technologies Limited (standalone information)

(Fig. in ₹ crore)

Particulars	*Quarter ended September 30,*		*Half-year ended September 30,*		*Year ended March 31,*
	2010	2009	2010	2009	2010
Revenues	6,425	5,201	12,183	10,305	21,140
Profit before tax and exceptional item	2,237	1,824	4,156	3,661	7,472
Profit after tax before exceptional item	1,641	1,438	3,072	2,902	5,755
Profit after tax and exceptional item	1,641	1,438	3,072	2,902	5,803

4. The final dividend of ₹15 per equity share for fiscal 2010 was approved by the shareholders at the Annual General Meeting of the company held on June 12, 2010 and the same was paid subsequently.

5. The Board declared an interim dividend of ₹10 per equity share and a 30th year special dividend of ₹30 per equity share. The record date for the payment of interim dividend and 30th year special dividend is October 22, 2010. The interim dividend declared in the previous year was ₹10 per share.

6. Information on investor complaints pursuant to Clause 41 of the Listing Agreement for the quarter ended September 30, 2010.

Nature of complaints received	*Opening balance*	*Additions*	*Disposal*	*Closing balance*
Net receipt of dividend/Annual Report related	–	192	192	–

8. Mr. Claude Smadja, independent director retired from the Board with effect from August 30, 2010. The Board expressed its appreciation for the services rendered by Mr. Claude Smadja during his tenure as director.

9. **Matters relating to Subsidiaries:**
   Infosys Technologies (China) Co. Limited
   During the quarter and half-year ended September 30, 2010, additional investments of US $9 million (₹42 crore) was made in Infosys Technologies (China) Co. Limited, which is a wholly owned subsidiary. As of September 30, 2010, the company has invested in equity, an aggregate of US $23 million (₹107 crore) in the subsidiary.

10. **Statement of assets and liabilities (IFRS)**

(*Fig. in ₹ crore*)

Particulars	*As at*	
	September 30, 2010 (Audited)	*September 30, 2009 (Unaudited)*
Assets		
Cash and cash equivalents	15,401	10,624
Other current assets	1,860	1,333
Trade receivables	4,171	3,366
Investments		
Available-for-sale financial assets	38	3,222
Investments in certificates of deposits	1,949	–
Property, plant and equipment	4,529	4,554
Other non-current assets	2,345	1,835
Total	**30,293**	**24,934**
Liabilities and Equity		
Liabilities		
Provisions	81	
Other current liabilities	3,630	
Non-current liabilities	257	
Equity attributable to equity holders of the company		
Share capital	286	
Share premium	3,059	
Retained earnings	22,894	
Other components of equity	86	
Total	30,293	24,934

The above disclosure is in compliance with Clause 41 (v)(h) of the Listing Agreement. ***The disclosure is an extract of the audited IFRS Balance Sheet*** *as at September 30, 2010.*

11. Segment reporting

(*Fig. in ₹ crore*)

Particulars	*Quarter ended September 30,*		*Half-year ended September 30,*		*Year ended March 31,*
	2010	2009	2010	2009	2010
Revenue by industry segment					
Financial services	2,462	1,871	4,700	3,678	7,731
Manufacturing	1,314	1,080	2,522	2,201	4,506
Telecom	927	902	1,803	1,824	3,661
Retail	1,001	787	1,816	1,510	3,035
Others	1,243	945	2,304	1,844	3,809
Total	**6,947**	**5,585**	**13,145**	**11,057**	**22,742**
Less: Inter-segment revenue	—	—	—	—	—
Net revenue from operations	**6,947**	**5,585**	**13,145**	**11,057**	**22,742**
Segment profit before tax, depreciation and non-controlling interest:					
Financial services	828	649	1,569	1,248	2,710
Manufacturing	425	299	804	649	1,374
Telecom	329	351	601	718	1,451
Retail	337	283	565	523	1,025
Others	398	345	741	657	1,301
Total	**2,317**	**1,927**	**4,280**	**3,795**	**7,861**
Less: Other un-allocable expenditure (excluding un-allocable income)	219	234	427	458	951
Operating profit before tax and non-controlling interest	**2,098**	**1,693**	**3,853**	**3,337**	**6,910**

Notes on segment information

Principal segments

The company's operations predominantly relate to providing technology services, delivered to clients globally, operating in various industry segments. Accordingly, revenues represented along industries served constitute the primary basis of the segmental information set out above.

Segmental capital employed

Fixed assets used in the company's business or liabilities contracted have not been identified to any of the reportable segments, as the fixed assets and support services are used interchangeably between segments. Accordingly, no disclosure relating to total segment assets and liabilities has been made.

By order of the Board
For Infosys Technologies Limited

Bangalore, India	S.D. Shibulal	S. Gopalakrishnan
October 15, 2010	Chief Operating Officer	CEO and Managing Director

The Board has also taken on record the unaudited consolidated results of Infosys Technologies Limited and subsidiaries for the three months and six months ended September

30, 2010, prepared as per International Financial Reporting Standards (IFRS). A summary of the financial statements is as follows:

(Fig. in US$ Million, except per ADS data)

Particulars	*Three month ended September 30,*		*Six month ended September 30,*		*Year ended March 31,*
	2010	2009	2010	2009	2010
Revenues	1,496	1,154	2,854	2,276	4,804
Cost of sales	855	662	1,655	1,305	1,749
Gross profit	641	492	1,199	971	2,055
Net profit	374	317	700	630	1313
Earnings per American Depositary Share (ADS)					
Basic	0.65	0.56	1.23	1.10	2.30
Diluted	0.65	0.56	1.23	1.10	2.30
Total assets	6,742	5,188	6,742	5,188	6,148
Cash and cash equivalents including available-for-sale financial assets and certificates of deposit	3,869	2,878	3,869	2,878	3,532

Statements in connection with this release may include forward-looking statements within the meaning of U.S. Securities laws intended to qualify for the 'safe harbor' under the Private Securities Litigation Reform Act. These forward-looking statements are subject to risks and uncertainties including those described in our SEC filings available at www.sec.gov including our Annual Report on Form 20-F for the year ended March 31, 2010, and our other recent filings, and actual results may differ materially from those projected by forward-looking statements. We may make additional written and oral forward-looking statements but do not undertake, and disclaim any obligation, to update them.

(*Source:* The Times of India, October 16, 2010)

REPORTING UNDER IND AS

The Ministry of Corporate Affairs (MCA), Government of India, on 16th February, 2015 had notified the Companies (Indian Accounting Standards) Rules, 2015 for phase-wise adoption and applicability of Indian Accounting Standards (Ind AS). In the first phase, all listed and unlisted companies with net worth of ₹500 Cr or more, including the parent or subsidiaries of such companies, were to prepare their financial statements following the Ind AS with effect from 1st April 2016, with comparative periods beginning 1st April 2015. TCS, with a net worth above threshold, had to publish its financial statements prepared under Ind AS with effect from 1st April 2016. Exhibit 5.5 shows key figures of the Profit and Loss Account of TCS prepared under the IFRS, Indian GAAP (or AS), and Ind AS for the Year 2015-16. Calculation of other financials of TCS upon adoption of Ind AS for the year 2015-16 has been given in Appendix-1 at the end of this Chapter. It is apparent from Exhibit 5.5 that the figures under IFRS and Ind AS are very close to each other, and in fact in the instant case they are the same, but under the Indian GAAP or AS the values slightly differs.

EXHIBIT 5.5: Profit and Loss Account of TCS under the Indian GAAP (or AS), IFRS and Ind AS for the Year 2015-16

Particulars in brief	*IFRS*	*Indian GAAP or AS*	*Ind AS*
Revenues	108,646	108,646	108,646
Profit Before Taxes	31,840	31,676	31,840
Taxes	7,502	7,301	7,502
Profit after Taxes before non-controlling interest	24,338	24,375	24,338

Source: https://www.tcs.com/content/dam/tcs/pdf/discover-tcs/investor-relations/key-events/TCS_IND_AS_Adoption.pdf

Since Ind AS are the IFRS-converged Indian Accounting Standards, the results reported under IFRS and Ind AS are expected to be very close to each other, except for certain carve-outs that were required to make the standards suitable to Indian business conditions. In fact, the Government of India, in consultation with the ICAI, had decided to converge and not to adopt the IFRS issued by the IASB. Accordingly, while formulating IFRS-converged Indian Accounting Standards (Ind AS), due care has been taken to keep these Standards (Ind AS) as far as possible in line with the corresponding IFRS, except for some departures where considered absolutely necessary for the Indian business and economic environment. Some of these changes are due to the terminology used in the Indian law such as 'Statement of Profit and Loss' in place of 'Statement of Comprehensive Income' and 'Balance Sheet' in place of 'Statement of Financial Position'. While converging with IFRS to issue Ind AS, the ICAI had also taken into account the carveouts made in the Ind AS finalized in 2011; while deciding not to continue with some of the carve-outs; and to make certain new carveouts/carve-in based on the feedback received from various stakeholders.

INSTITUTIONAL EFFORTS IN HARMONIZATION

There are many organizations and institutional bodies who are associated with bringing harmony to global financial reporting. Prominent among them are:

1. International Accounting Standards Committee (IASC)
2. International Federation of Accountants (IFAC)
3. International Organization of Securities Commissions (IOSCO)
4. United Nations
5. Organization for Economic Cooperation and Development (OECD)
6. Association of South East Asian Nations Federation of Accountants (AFA)
7. IFRS Interpretations Committee (IFRIC)

International Accounting Standards Committee (IASC)

The IASC is an independent private body. It was formed in 1973 in the 10th International Congress of Accountants held at St. Louis by leading accounting bodies of ten nations, namely, Australia, Canada, France, Germany, Ireland, Japan, Mexico, the Netherlands, United Kingdom, and the USA. The body has over 140 professional accounting bodies at present from over 100 countries across the globe. IASC has been restructured and renamed as International

Accounting Stands Board (IASB) with effect from 2001. The IASC has pronounced forty one Accounting standards called IAS (Exhibit 5.1) and the IASB has pronounced eight International Financial Reporting Standards called IFRS. The IASB while deciding to retain the IAS pronounced by IASC has decided to name its own pronouncements as IFRS (Exhibit 5.2).

The objectives set before IASC which of course continue as the objectives of IASB were:

1. To formulate and publish in the public interest accounting standards to be observed in the presentation of financial statements and to promote their worldwide acceptance and observance.
2. To work generally for the improvement and harmonization of regulations, accounting standards and procedures relating to the presentation of financial statements.

The IASC in its early days used to issue accounting standards with so many alternative accounting treatments. As a result, the comparability part of the 'IAS complied' financial statements used to be missing and so also the harmony part. But with the feedback and criticism received, IASC reduced the number of alternatives in various IAS issued by it through revision or otherwise so as to ensure compatibility in global financial reporting.

International Federation of Accountants (IFAC)

IFAC was formed in 1977. It is a body of the national professional accounting organizations represented by accountants employed in public, private and government institutions including the education, to frequently interface with the profession. At present IFAC has over two million accountants from as many as 150 member organizations in over 100 countries.

IFAC basically issues International Standards on Auditing (ISA) in order to harmonize international auditing practices. The other additional activities performed by IFAC are as follows:

1. It works towards reducing differences in the requirements to qualify as a professional accountant in the member countries.
2. It issues code of Ethics for Professional Accountants in the line of their independence, objectivity and integrity.
3. It works for providing the governments worldwide *international public sector standards* for improving their financial management and reporting practices.

International Organization of Securities Commissions (IOSCO)

IOSCO was formed in 1983 with the following objectives:

1. To promote high standards of regulation in order to maintain just, efficient and sound (capital) markets.
2. To establish standards and effective surveillance of international securities transaction.
3. To promote the integrity of the markets by a rigid application of enforcement of the standards.

IOSCO is represented by over 115 securities regulatory agencies of the world; having a coverage of 85% of the world's capital markets. As regards harmonization of accounting practices, IOSCO is more stringent on IAS for the fact that it has endorsed only around 50% of the IAS issued by IASC and has tended conditional support to the remaining IAS till the IASC does not produce a comprehensive high quality core standards. IOSCO's work on developing international disclosure standards has been well received by stock exchanges and securities agencies worldwide.

United Nations

The UN's role in harmonization of accounting practices has been rather limited. The list of financial and non-financial disclosures to be made by MNCs as suggested by its Group of Experts on International Standards of Accounting and Reporting in the year 1977 was not well accepted by most of the industrialized nations. The list of disclosures was comprehensive including information on transfer pricing, segment performance, R & D, employment. As most of these are considered as priority information which countries did not want to part with and as UN has no enforcing authority, its recommendation did not work. However, the UN's recent efforts in bringing harmony in international accounting practices in the line of IASC and environmental reporting has been seen as a success.

Organization for Economic Cooperation and Development (OECD)

OECD, which has 29 member countries who produce two-third of the world's goods and services, was formed in 1960 by 24 developed nations in order to serve as a forum for officials of these nations to meet and discuss problems of mutual interest and to harmonize their policies in important international issues.

In the context of accounting, OECD formed an Ad hoc Working Group on Accounting Standards in 1979 to:

1. Support current efforts by international, regional and national bodies towards harmonization of accounting practices;
2. Function as a forum for the exchange of views on UN efforts on accounting and disclosure standards; and
3. Provide technical clarification to the terms used in disclosure guidelines.

In 1976, OECD had issued a code of conduct entitled 'Declaration on International Investment and Multinational Enterprises' for financial reporting by MNCs.

Association of South East Asian Nations Federation of Accountants (AFA)

The ASEAN regional organization was formed in 1977 as a regional accounting body comprising of five South East Asian countries – Indonesia, Malaysia, Philippines, Thailand and Singapore. Countries subsequent to join the ASEAN regional forum were Brunei, Vietnam, and Laos and Myanmar respectively in the year 1984, 1995 and 1997.

The primary objectives set for AFA were:

1. To provide an organization for the ASEAN accountants for furtherance of the cause of accounting profession in the region.

2. To establish an ASEAN philosophy on the accounting profession.
3. To establish a medium for closer relations, regional cooperation and assistance among ASEAN accounts.
4. To work in cooperation with ASEAN business regional groupings whose economic development efforts may be completed by ASEAN Accountants.

In 1979, AFA issued the first accounting standard and in 1980 the first auditing standard, in a view to bringing greater harmony in the accounting and auditing practices in ASEAN countries.

IFRS Interpretations Committee (or IFRIC)

IFRIC Interpretations are developed by the IFRS Interpretations Committee, previously the International Financial Reporting Interpretations Committee (IFRIC), and are issued after approval by the International Accounting Standards Board (IASB). IFRIC works with the IASB in maintaining and supporting the consistent application of IFRS Accounting Standards. The Committee (IFRIC) has 14 voting members, appointed by the Trustees under section 16(c) for renewable terms of three years. The Trustees shall select members of the Interpretations Committee so that it comprises of a group of people representing, within that group, the best available combination of technical expertise and diversity of international business and market experience in the practical application of IFRS Accounting Standards and analysis of financial statements prepared in accordance with those Standard.

IFRIC has been mandated to interpret the application of IAS and IFRS and provide timely guidance on financial reporting issues which have not been specifically addressed in the IAS and IFRS, and to carry out other tasks as required by the IASB. When a stakeholder submits a question to IFRIC, the Committee may address the question via standard setting, e.g., through Amendment to an existing standard or through issuance of an interpretation to a standard. Exhibit 5.6 contains the list of 'interpretations' issued by IFRIC of date.

EXHIBIT 5.6 List of 'interpretations' issued by IFRIC

IFRIC 1	Changes in Existing Decommissioning, Restoration and Similar Liabilities
IFRIC 2	Members' Shares in Co-operative Entities and Similar Instruments
IFRIC 3	Emission Rights (Withdrawn June 2005)
IFRIC 4	Determining Whether an Arrangement Contains a Lease
IFRIC 5	Rights to Interests arising from Decommissioning, Restoration and Environmental Rehabilitation Funds
IFRIC 6	Liabilities Arising from Participating in a Specific Market-Waste Electrical and Electronic Equipment
IFRIC 7	Applying the Restatement Approach under IAS 29 Financial Reporting in Hyperinflationary Economies
IFRIC 8	Scope of IFRS 2 (Withdrawn effective 1 January 2010)
IFRIC 9	Reassessment of Embedded Derivatives
IFRIC 10	Interim Financial Reporting and Impairment

IFRIC 11	IFRS 2: Group and Treasury Share Transactions (Withdrawn effective 1 January 2010)
IFRIC 12	Service Concession Arrangements
IFRIC 13	Customer Loyalty Programmes (Superseded by IFRS 15 from 1 January 2018)
IFRIC 14	IAS 19 – The Limit on a Defined Benefit Asset, Minimum Funding Requirements and their Interaction
IFRIC 15	Agreements for the Construction of Real Estate (Superseded by IFRS 15 from 1 January 2017)
IFRIC 16	Hedges of a Net Investment in a Foreign Operation
IFRIC 17	Distributions of Non-cash Assets to Owners
IFRIC 18	Transfers of Assets from Customers
IFRIC 19	Extinguishing Financial Liabilities with Equity Instruments
IFRIC 20	Stripping Costs in the Production Phase of a Surface Mine
IFRIC 21	Levies
IFRIC 22	Foreign Currency Transactions and Advance Consideration
IFRIC 23	Uncertainty over Income Tax Treatments

Source: https://www.iasplus.com/en/standards/ifric

IMPEDIMENTS TO HARMONIZATION

The major obstacles to achieving harmonization in global financial reporting and accounting practices are:

1. Absence of professional accounting bodies
2. Economic consideration
3. Nationalism
4. Object of financial reporting
5. Legal environment

Absence of Professional Accounting Bodies

The absence of strong professional accounting bodies in a number of countries [4] is an obstacle to accounting harmonization. This is because IASC operates and implements its standards through professional accounting bodies of the nations as its members, and in the absence of such accounting bodies implementation of IAS in such countries becomes difficult, for implementation of these standards would require necessary amendments to the existing laws of the land to be made by the Government of the respective countries which may not do it by itself without being lobbied or persuaded by such professional bodies.

Economic Consideration

Empirical evidences have shown that harmonization is opposed by nations due to its impact on the countries' economy and/or the specific segment of the economy. Guenther and Hussein [5] for instance have found through their studies that 'the support for LIFO method of inventory valuation (IAS 2) originated from countries where use of LIFO provided clear tax advantage to the companies. Grinyer and Russell [6] too have reported about the 'lobbying; in UK for accounting for goodwill.

Another aspect of economic consideration that affects harmonization of accounting practices is the economic gap between developed and developing nations. Given the fact that 'accounting is the language of the business', if the business itself is less developed (in the context of developing countries), accounting is bound to be less developed. An example to the effect is the concept of leasing and derivatives coming to India late in the Eighties and Nineties and consequently the ICAI coming up with issuance of AS 19 and bringing modifications to AS 3 to provide for their accounting and reporting.

Nationalism

Nationalism has been another obstacle to harmonization of accounting practices. National pride prevents an accountant from willingly accepting the idea that his accounting principles are inferior to those of another country, even though the accountant may be a strong proponent of harmonization[7]. Nationalism represents a political obstacle to harmonization [7]. As in many other areas, countries are wary of ceding control of their accounting regulation to outsiders, particularly if it is perceived as replacing their own accounting regulations with those of the other countries [8].

Objects of Financial Reporting

The objectives of financial reporting are often found to be different in different countries and therefore the reporting practices. For example, the Securities and Exchange Board of India (SEBI) requires companies to disclose relevant information in the financial statement so as to help the investors take informed decision, thus making the 'investors' the prime audience for the accounting reports. In France and Germany, the prime clients traditionally were the revenue authorities and the governments' economic and statistical agencies. This variation in the focus group of stakeholders has resulted in reporting variation across nations.

Legal Environment

The legal system prevailing in a country does have effect on harmonization of accounting practices. There are countries like France and Germany whose legal system is based on a civil code which is more prescriptive in nature and which prescribes precise rules as regards income measurement, asset valuation and the format of financial reporting, leaving hardly any scope for subjective treatment. Contrary to this, there are countries like England whose legal system is based on common law with flexible rules, leaving thereby scope for alternative treatment and fair presentation of the financial statements. The variations in the legal systems prevalent in different countries are sure to cause diversities in the accounting and reporting practices across nations.

ACCOUNTING MODELS

It is seen that diversity persists in global financial reporting system owing to country specific issues in relation to political, economic, social and legal environment. In order to eliminate or at least to reduce this diversity, efforts are needed to address to these core issues which pose as hindrance to achieving global harmony in financial reporting.

However, experts have suggested *three* accounting models which if accepted and implemented would result in harmonization of accounting practices. These models are called *accounting uniformity models*. Al Hashim and Arpan [9] have reported them as:

1. Absolute uniformity model
2. Circumstantial uniformity model
3. Purposive uniformity model

The *absolute uniformity model* proposes an all purposive 'one set' of accounting and reporting methods irrespective of the audience to whom the reporting is meant or the circumstances under which the report is prepared. Obviously the model if practiced will establish total harmony in global accounting practices; but for its rigidity and inflexibility is unlikely to be acceptable to all the nations.

The *circumstantial uniformity model* holds its ground to the practice of medicine which provides for different treatments to different patients having same disease based on attached circumstances. The model thus allows variation in accounting practices based on circumstances.

The *purposive uniformity model* encourages flexibility to accommodate both circumstances and the purpose of reporting.

SUMMARY

Harmonization of accounting practices aims at bringing down the disparities that exist in the financial reporting system worldwide due to socio-economic, political cultural and legal diversities among nations. The need for harmonization of accounting practices arises to facilitate flow of capital across nations, standardization of financial reporting by MNCs, reduction of diversities in income measurement, internationalization of accounting profession and to fulfill administrative requirements.

There are many international institutions and bodies who have been working all through to achieving harmony in global financial reporting. Prominent among these institutions are the International Accounting Standards Committee (IASC), the International Federation of Accountants (IFAC), the International Organization of Securities Commission (IOSCO), the United Nations (UN), the Organization of Economic Cooperation and Development (OECD) and the Association of South East Asian Nations Federation of Accountants (AFC).

Despite the continual efforts by these organizations to achieve international harmony in accounting and financial reporting, a complete harmony has not been possible so far owing to factors like the absence of strong professional accounting bodies in some nations, economic considerations, nationalism, varied objectives of financial reporting and prevalence of different legal system in different countries.

In the efforts of establishing harmony in international financial reporting, experts have opined three different models of accounting which when practiced is expected to eliminate the existing diversities in the reporting practices. These models are named as 'absolute uniformity', 'circumstantial uniformity' and 'purposive uniformity' models.

KEY TERMS

Harmonization: Harmonization in the context of accounting practices refers to bringing down the disparities that exist in the financial reporting system practiced by nations. Harmonization is as good as standardization but with a certain degree of allowances.

Standardization: Standardization in accounting context refers to complete elimination of the disparities in accounting practices and reporting, buy adopting a set of rigid rules and policy guidelines.

Accounting standards: Accounting standards are policy documents issued by professional accountancy bodies at national and international level, in relation to different aspects of measurement, treatment, disclosure and presentation of accounting information. The erstwhile International Accounting Standards Committee (IASC) has issued 41 IAS and the present International Accounting Standards Board (IASB) has issued 6 IFRS so far at the international level and the Institute of Chartered Accounts of India (ICAI) has issued 29 Accounting Standards in India as of now.

IAS: IAS are International Accounting Standards issued by IASC.

IFRS: IFRS (International Financial Reporting Standards) are accounting standards issued by IASB (the changed name of IASC after its restructuring).

AS: AS are Indian Accounting Standards issued by ICAI.

Convergence: Convergence in the context harmonization of practices refers to bringing the accounting standards of a nation (say India) at par with the International Accounting Standards.

Assets: Assets, as defined by IAS 1, are probable future economic benefits to be obtained or controlled by a particular entity as a result of past transactions or events.

Liabilities: Liabilities, as defined by IAS 1, are probable future sacrifices of economic benefits arising from present obligations of a particular entity to transfer assets or provide services to other entities in the future as a result of past transactions or event.

Equity: Equity as prescribed in IAS 1 are the residual interest in the assets that remains after deducting its liabilities. In a business enterprise the equity is the ownership interest.

Net realizable value: Net realizable value in the context of inventory valuation as provided in IAS[2] is the difference between net estimated selling price per unit (of the items of stock) in the ordinary course of business and the estimated cost of completion and estimated cost necessary to make the sale.

Specific Identification Method: Specific Identification Method is a method of determining the cost of inventory as per IAS 2.

Absolute Uniformity Model: Absolute Uniformity Model is a model suggested for preparing accounting and financial reports, without leaving any scope for alternative treatment of transactions and/or events, thus resulting in global harmony in accounting and financial reporting. The model is difficult to apply in practice for its rigidity.

Circumstantial Uniformity Model: Circumstantial Uniformity Model has been suggested as the second model for accounting practices in order to achieve international harmony in financial reporting. The model leaves scope for certain alternative treatment of transactions depending upon the circumstances.

Purposive Uniformity Model: Purposive Uniformity Model is the third model suggested for accounting practices in the context of harmonization. The model leaves scope for alternative treatment of certain transactions and events depending upon both the circumstances and the purpose.

REVIEW QUESTIONS

1. What do you understand by harmonization of accounting practices? What are its need and impediments? Explain.
2. Discuss the concept and process of harmonization of accounting practices.
3. Discuss the factors that cause diversities in global accounting practices. Suggest remedial measures for the same.
4. 'Diversity in accounting principles and practices complicates the efforts of the analyst to assess comparative investor potential in companies abroad'. Comment.
5. Discuss the institutional arrangements to establishing accounting harmony in the light of the efforts of international organizations.
6. Discuss the role of International Accounting Standards Committee (IASC) in harmonization of accounting practices.
7. Explain the specific provisions of IAS 1 as regards presentation of financial statements.
8. Explain the provisions of IAS 2 and its equivalent India GAAP.
9. Distinguish between standardization and harmonization of accounting practices. Which of these you will prefer and why?
10. Discuss the various accounting models as talked about in bringing global harmony in financial reporting. Which of these models you will favour and why?
11. Explain the important provisions of IAS 7.
12. Explain the process of inventory valuation as contained in AS 3.
13. Give an account of the nature and extent of convergence of Indian Accounting Standards with the International Accounting Standards.
14. What is the need for convergence of National Accounting Standards with the International Accounting Standards? Can there be a total convergence?
15. Explain the disclosure norms as prescribed by IAS 1. Explain.
16. Compare and contrast between the salient provisions of IAS 7 and AS 3.
17. Write notes on:

    (a) IASC (b) IOSCO

18. Write notes on:

(a) IAFC (b) OECD (c) ASEAN Federation of Accountants

19. Which of the main models of international classification of accounting do you prefer? Explain your reasoning.

20. Examine the different practices prevalent among MNCs to cater to the financial information needs of the foreign audiences of interest. Which approach would you consider the best and why?

21. "The basic cause of international differences in financial reporting practices is the different degree of interference by governments in accounting". Discuss.

22. Discuss the arguments for and against the process of international harmonization of accounting.

23. Convergence with IFRS is a step forward to achieving international harmony in financial reporting—Comment.

REFERENCES

[1] Saudagaran, S.M., *International Accounting—A User Perspective*, Taxmann India, 2000, p. 33.

[2] IASC News, Vol. 18, No. 1, January 1989, London.

[3] Turner, J.N., International Harmonization: A Professional Goal, *Journal of Accounting*, Vol. 155, January 1983, pp. 58-66.

[4] Nobes, C., and Parker R., *Comparative International Accounting*, London, Prentice Hall, 1991.

[5] Guenther, D.A., and Hussein, M.E., Accounting Standards and national tax laws: The IASC and the ban on LIFO, *Journal of Accounting and Public Policy*, 14(1): 115 – 141.

[6] Grinyer, J.R., and Russell, A., National Impediments to International Harmonization: Evidence of Lobbying in the UK, *Journal of International Accounting, Auditing and Taxation*, 1(1): 13 – 31.

[7] Rathore, S., *International Accounting*, PHI, 1996, p. 194.

[8] Saudagaran, Op. Cit, p. 36.

[9] AlHashim, D.D., and Arpan, J.S., *International Dimensions of Accounting*, 2nd Ed., PWS – Kent Publishing Company, Boston, 2nd Ed., 1988.

Annexure-I
ADOPTION OF IND AS
(*Effective April 1, 2016*)

1. BACKGROUND

The Ministry of Corporate Affairs (MCA) has issued a notification dated 16th February 2015, announcing the Companies (Indian Accounting Standards) Rules, 2015 for phase-wise roadmap for adoption and applicability of Indian Accounting Standards (Ind AS). As per these rules, in the first phase, listed and unlisted companies with net worth of ₹500 Cr or more including the parent or subsidiaries of such companies will have to prepare their financial statements following Ind AS with effect from 1st April 2016 with comparative periods beginning 1st April 2015. Since TCS' net worth is above this threshold, TCS is required to publish its financial statements prepared under Ind AS with effect from 1st April 2016.

2. IND AS

The accounting standards issued by the MCA under the rules on the recommendation of National Advisory Committee on Accounting Standards (NACAS) is a result of convergence exercise that the Institute of Chartered Accountants of India (ICAI) and International Accounting Standards Board (IASB) undertook. The standards have been converged from the International Financial Reporting Standards (IFRS) as issued by IASB except for certain carve-outs that were required to make the standards suitable to Indian business conditions.

3. IND AS IN TCS CONTEXT

TCS has been publishing its financial statements prepared under Indian GAAP and IFRS. There were very few areas of difference between IFRS and Indian GAAP. With the adoption of Ind AS, almost all of the differences would disappear and only those differences which would result due to different dates of adoption of the standards would remain. These differences would largely remain in the balance sheet while the statement of profit and loss on a periodic basis would be similar.

However, there are many areas of difference between Indian GAAP and Ind AS. The areas which are of significant interest to TCS are as follows:

- **Dividend:** Under Ind AS, dividend to holders of equity instruments is recognized as a liability in the period in which the obligation to pay is established. In Indian GAAP, dividend payable is recorded as a liability in the period to which it relates.
- **Consolidation of Employee welfare trusts:** Ind AS 110 – Consolidated financial statements defines control and establishes control as the main basis for consolidating the entities. An investor controls an investee when it is exposed, or has rights, to variable returns from its involvement with the investee and has the ability to affect those returns through its power over the investee, in light of which we are required to consolidate employee welfare trusts of the Group. In Indian GAAP, the entities were not required to be consolidated.

- **Employee benefits:** In Indian GAAP, actuarial gains and losses were recognized in profit and loss. Under Ind AS, the actuarial gains and losses form part of remeasurement of net defined benefit liability/asset which is recognized in other comprehensive income in the respective periods.
- **Depreciation:** In April 2014, the Group revised its method of depreciation from written down value to straight-line basis. Under Ind AS, the Group has elected to apply Ind AS 16–Property, plant and equipment from the date of acquisition. This change in method was retrospectively adjusted in Indian GAAP.
- **Reorganization of entities under common control:** The Group under Ind AS 103–Business combination has accounted the transfer of the shareholding of Tata Sons Limited in CMC Limited and Tata America International Corporation to Tata Consultancy Services Limited on the historical cost basis and the consideration paid in excess of carrying cost of these entities, as on the date of transfer, has been recorded as a reduction to equity. In Indian GAAP, the transfer was accounted for on fair value basis.
- **Acquisition of non-controlling interest:** The group has issued shares to the non-controlling interest shareholders of CMC Ltd. in the Scheme of amalgamation of CMC Ltd. with the Company. Under Ind AS 103 – Business combinations, the difference between the nominal value of the shares issued and the carrying value of the non-controlling interest has been recognized in retained earnings.
- **Obligation to acquire non-controlling interests:** The Group under Ind AS-103 – Business Combination has recognized a liability for the present value of the redemption amount towards call option and the non-controlling interest's put option which collectively contains an obligation for the Group to acquire non-controlling interest's equity ownership. Indian GAAP do not have any such requirement.
- **Impact of retrospective application of Ind AS 103 to prior business combinations:** In Indian GAAP, the business combination was accounted at the book value, under Ind AS the acquiree's identifiable assets, liabilities and contingent liabilities that meet the condition for recognition are recognized at their fair values at the acquisition date. Consequently intangible assets have been created and amortization of the same has resulted in an adjustment to the equity.
- **Fair valuation of investments:** In Indian GAAP, current investments were measured at lower of cost or fair value and long-term investments were measured at cost less diminution in value. Under Ind AS, investment in debt securities have been measured at fair value with changes in fair value accounted in other comprehensive income. All other investments other than debt securities have been measured at fair value to profit and loss.
- **Tax adjustments:** In Indian GAAP, in the consolidated financial statements, the tax expense of the parents and group companies were added line- by-line and no adjustments were made/additional deferred taxes recognized or reversed on consolidation. Under Ind AS, deferred tax on account of undistributed profits of the subsidiaries has been recognized in statement of profit and loss. Further tax adjustments are also made for deferred tax impact on account of differences between Indian GAAP and Ind AS.

Process followed to adopt Ind AS

First time adoption of Ind AS involves the following:

- Selection of appropriate options as per Ind AS 101, which contains the transition provisions for an entity to adopt Ind-AS for the first time.
- Preparation of opening balance sheet as at 1st April 2015 under Ind AS
- Preparation of quarterly financials of all four quarters of FY16
- Preparation of financial statements under Ind AS from Q1 FY17

We have analysed the options available to preparers under Ind AS 101 in the areas of business combinations, fair-valuation of assets, exchange rate fluctuation reserves, etc. and have followed the options that takes the base financials in Indian GAAP close to IFRS financials without causing major changes to the balance sheet under Indian GAAP. An opening balance sheet as on 1st April 2015 of the TCS un-consolidated entity and TCS Consolidated entity has been prepared under Ind AS along with a reconciling statement between Indian GAAP and Ind AS in respect of Shareholders Equity as at that date.

4. FINANCIALS STATEMENTS PREPARED UNDER IND AS

A comparison of key Profit & Loss account metrics from the financial statements prepared under Indian GAAP, IFRS and Ind AS for the financial year ended 31st March, 2016 is given in Annexure I. The reconciliation statements of the Equity as at 31st March, 2015 under Indian GAAP and Ind AS is given in Annexure II. The Balance Sheet of TCS Ltd – Unconsolidated and Consolidated as at 1st April 2015 and 31st March 2016, prepared under Ind AS is given in Annexure III. Quarterly Profit & Loss account under Ind AS for all four quarters of FY16 – Consolidated and Unconsolidated is given in Annexure IV.

The financial information in Annexures below are not audited financials and are being given only to facilitate early dissemination of comparative historical data. An excel version of these previous period financial statements will also be available on the company website.

Annexure I

PROFIT AND LOSS ACCOUNT COMPARISON UNDER INDIAN GAAP, IFRS & IND AS FOR FY16

(Amounts in ₹ crore)

	TCS Consolidated Profit and Loss Account for FY 2016		
	Indian GAAP	*IFRS*	*Ind AS*
Revenues	108,646	108,646	108,646
Profit before Taxes	31,676	31,840	31,840
Taxes	7,301	7,502	7,502
Profit after Taxes before non-controlling interest	24,375	24,338	24,338

Comprehensive income reconciliations for consolidated financials:

(₹ *in crores*)

	For quarter ended June 30, 2015	*For quarter ended Sept 30, 2015*	*For quarter ended Dec 31, 2015*	*For quarter ended March 30, 2016*
Net income under Indian GAAP attributable to:				
TCS Limited	5,711	6,085	6,083	6,413
Non-controlling interests	30	23	20	10
Net income under Indian GAAP	5,741	6,108	6,103	6,423
Actuarial loss recognised in other comprehensive income	11	32	34	37
Effect on consolidation of employee trusts	8	(3)	8	2
Effect of change in depreciation method	17	15	13	12
Obligation to acquire non-controlling interests	(3)	(3)	(4)	(5)
Change in fair value of investments in mutual funds	27	(18)	10	(21)
Tax adjustments	(27)	(38)	(34)	(101)
Others	–	–	(5)	–
Profit for the period under Ind AS	5.773	6,093	6,125	6,347
Other comprehensive income	53	55	16	145
Total comprehensive income under Ind AS	5,826	6,148	6,141	6,492
Attributable to:				
TCS Limited	5,763	6,133	6,127	6,475
Non-Controlling interests	63	15	14	17

Annexure-II
EQUITY RECONCILIATION

Unconsolidated

(₹ *in crores*)

	As on April 1, 2015
As reported under Indian GAAP	45,416
Adjusted effect of CMC Merger	810
Adjusted equity under Indian GAAP	46,226
Proposed dividend (including dividend tax) reversed	5,724
Credit on account of change in method of depreciation reversed	(537)
Tax adjustments	132
Fair value of investments in mutual funds and other equity investments	9
Other	(1)
Equity under Ind AS	51,553

	As on April 1, 2015
Consolidated	
Equity under Indian GAAP attributable to:	
TCS Limited	50,635
Non-controlling interests	1,128
Adjusted equity under Indian GAAP	51,763
Proposed dividend (including tax on dividend) reversed	5,649
Effect on consolidation of employee trusts	168
Effect of change in depreciation method	(537)
Obligation to acquire non-controlling interests	(240)
Reorganisation of entities under common control accounted under pooling of interest method	(167)
Fair valuation of investments	9
Tax adjustments	(25)
Amortisation of intangible asset resulting from election to apply fair value accounting for business combination on or after April 1, 2013	(47)
Amalgamation of subsidiary under common control	(296)
Others	(2)
Equity under Ind AS	56,275
Attributable to:	
TCS Limited	56,052
Non-controlling interests	223

Annexure-III
BALANCE SHEET

Unconsolidated

TATA CONSULTANCY SERVICES LIMITED BALANCE SHEET

(₹ *in crores*)

	As at March 31, 2016	*As at April 1, 2015*
I. **ASSETS**		
Non-current assets		
(a) Property, plant and equipment	9,054	7,628
(b) Capital work-in-progress	1,640	2,741
(c) Intangible assets	24	31
(d) Financial assets		
(i) Investments	2,228	2,283
(ii) Loans	2,435	1,590
(iii) Other financial assets	1,176	1,077
(e) Advance income Tax asset–non-current	4,230	3,956
(f) Deferred tax assets (net)	2,528	2,321
(g) Other non-current assets	720	843
Total Non-current assets	24,034	22,471

	As at March 31, 2016	As at April 1, 2015
Current assets		
(a) Inventories	9	15
(b) Financial assets		
(i) Investments	21,930	971
(ii) Trade receivables	19,058	17,392
(iii) Cash and cash equivalents	4,383	461
(iv) Other bank balances	423	16,074
(v) Unbilled revenue	2,712	2,631
(vi) Loans	2,523	1,337
(vii) Other financial assets	866	884
(c) Other current assets	1,473	1,503
Total Current assets	53,379	41,268
TOTAL ASSETS	77,413	68,739

TATA CONSULTANCY SERVICES LIMITED CONSOLIDATED BALANCE SHEET

(₹ *in crores*)

	As at March 31, 2016	As at April 1, 2015
I. EQUITY AND LIABILITIES		
Shareholder' funds		
(a) Share capital	197	196
(b) Other equity	64,817	51,358
TOTAL EQUITY	65,014	51,553
Non-current liabilities		
(a) Financial liabilities		
(i) Borrowings	50	65
(ii) Other financial liabilities	293	411
(b) Employee benefit obligation	48	56
(c) Provisions	40	94
(d) Deferred tax liabilities (net)	366	271
(e) Other non-current liabilities	298	281
Non-current liabilities	1,095	1,178
Current liabilities		
(a) Financial liabilities		
(i) Borrowings	113	186
(ii) Trade payables	5,371	6,856
(iii) Other financial liabilities	2,083	1,001
(b) Income received in advance	1,068	870
(c) Current income tax liabilities (net)	536	350
(d) Employee benefit obligation	1,164	982
(e) Provisions	115	103
(f) Other current liabilities	855	661
Total current liabilities	11,304	11,007
TOTAL EQUITY AND LIABILITY	77,413	63,739

Consolidated

(₹ *in crores*)

	As at March 31, 2016	As at April 1, 2015
I. **ASSETS**		
Non-current Assets		
(a) Property, plant and equipment	9,971	8,641
(b) Capital work-in-progress	1,669	2,762
(c) Intangible assets	136	220
(d) Goodwill	1,669	1,572
(e) Financial assets		
(i) Investments	344	253
(ii) Loans	2,475	1,584
(iii) Other financial assets	1,322	1,231
(f) Advance Income Tax asset	4,464	4,093
(g) Deferred tax assets (net)	2,910	2,633
(h) Other non-current assets	926	1,075
Total Non-current assets	25,886	24,064
Current assets		
(a) Inventories	17	15
(b) Financial assets		
(i) Investments	22,479	1,501
(ii) Trade receivables	24,073	20,440
(iii) Unbilled revenue	3,992	3,827
(iv) Cash and cash equivalents	6,294	1,862
(v) Other bank balances	493	16,696
(vi) Loans	2,743	1,493
(vii) Other financial assets	916	909
(c) Advance Income Tax asset	32	75
(d) Other current assets	2,175	2,083
Total Current assets	63,214	48,901
TOTAL ASSETS	89,100	72,965

TATA CONSULTANCY SERVICES LIMITED CONSOLIDATED BALANCE SHEET

(₹ *in crores*)

	As at March 31, 2016	As at April 1, 2015
I. **EQUITY AND LIABILITIES**		
Shareholder' funds		
(a) Share capital	197	196
(b) Other equity	70,875	55,856
Equity attributable to shareholders of TCS Limited	71,072	56,052
Non-controlling interest	355	223
TOTAL EQUITY	71,427	56,275
Non-current liabilities		
(a) Financial liabilities		
(i) Borrowings	82	115
(ii) Other financial liabilities	493	662

(*Contd.*)

	As at March 31, 2016	As at April 1, 2015
(b) Employee benefit obligation	237	203
(c) Provisions	40	94
(d) Deferred tax liabilities (net)	805	540
(e) Other non-current liabilities	443	404
Total Non-current liabilities	2,100	2,018
Current liabilities		
(a) Financial liabilities		
(i) Borrowings	113	186
(ii) Trade payables	7,541	8,832
(iii) Other financial liabilities	2,364	1,245
(b) Income received in advance	1,359	1,062
(c) Current income tax liabilities (net)	805	546
(d) Employee benefit obligation	1,635	1,356
(e) Provisions	115	103
(f) Other current liabilities	1,641	1,342
Total current liabilities	15,573	14,672
TOTAL EQUITY AND LIABILITY	89,100	72,965

Annexure IV
QUARTERLY PROFIT AND LOSS ACCOUNT UNDER IND AS

Unconsolidated

TATA CONSULTANCY SERVICES LIMITED UNCONSOLIDATED INCOME STATEMENT

(₹ *in crores*)

	For the quarter ending June 30, 2015	*For the quarter ending Sep. 30, 2015*	*For the quarter ending Dec 31, 2015*	*For the quarter ending Mar 31, 2016*
I. Revenue from operations	20,349	21,636	21,621	22,258
II. Other income (net)	991	679	1,148	939
III. **TOTAL REVENUE**	**21,340**	**22,315**	**22,769**	**23,197**
IV. Expenses:				
(a) Employee cost	10,104	10,318	10,809	11,189
(b) Other operating expenses	3,752	4,247	4,019	4,372
(c) Finance costs	1	3	4	5
(d) Depreciation and amortisation expense	348	362	365	384
TOTAL EXPENSES	14,205	**14,930**	**15,197**	**15,950**
V. PROFIT BEFORE TAX	7,135	7,385	7,572	**7,247**

	For the quarter ending June 30, 2015	*For the quarter ending Sep. 30, 2015*	*For the quarter ending Dec 31, 2015*	*For the quarter ending Mar 31, 2016*
VI. **Tax expense:**				
(a) Current tax	1,535	1,635	1,613	1,594
(b) Deferred tax	(33)	27	(35)	(72)
VII. **PROFIT FOR THE PERIOD**	**5,633**	**5,723**	**5,994**	**5,725**
(A) (i) Items that will be reclassified subsequently to profit and loss:				
(a) Net gains on financial assets other than equity shares carried at fair value through OCI	–	–	–	82
(b) Net change in fair value of intrinsic value of cash flow hedges	(131)	26	53	(21)
(c) Net change in fair value of time value of cash flow hedges	(59)	24	20	(6)
(ii) Income tax on items that will be reclassified to profit or loss	26	(6)	(9)	(25)
(B) (i) Items that will not be reclassified subsequently to profit and loss				
(a) Net gains/(losses) on equity shares carried at fair value through OCI	–	0	1	–
(b) Remeasurement of defined employee benefit plans	(8)	(15)	(26)	(73)
(ii) Income tax on items that will not be reclassified to profit or loss	–	–	5	10
IX. **TOTAL OTHER COMPREHENSIVE INCOME NET OF TAXES**	**(172)**	**29**	**44**	**(33)**
X. **TOTAL COMPREHENSIVE INCOME FOR THE PERIOD**	**5,461**	**5,752**	**6,038**	**5,692**

Unconsolidated

TATA CONSULTANCY SERVICES LIMITED UNCONSOLIDATED INCOME STATEMENT

(₹ *in crores*)

	For the quarter ending June 30, 2015	*For the quarter ending Sep 30, 2015*	*For the quarter ending Dec 31, 2015*	*For the quarter ending Mar 31, 2016*
I. Revenue from operations	25,668	27,165	27,364	28,449
II. Other income (net)	778	683	707	915
III. **TOTAL REVENUE**	26,446	27,848	28,071	29,364
IV. Expenses:				
(a) Employee cost	13,291	13,623	14,011	14,423
(b) Other operating expenses	5,174	5,720	5,606	6,119
(c) Finance costs	8	8	8	10
(d) Depreciation and amortisation expense	453	469	471	495
TOTAL EXPENSES	18,926	19,820	20,096	21,047
V. PROFIT BEFORE TAX	7,520	8,028	7,975	8,317
VI. **Tax expense:**				
(a) Current tax	1,796	1,886	1,871	1,955
(b) Deferred tax	(49)	49	(21)	15
VII. **PROFIT FOR THE PERIOD**	5,773	6,028	6,125	6,347
VIII. **OTHER COMPREHENSIVE INCOME**				
(A) (i) Items that will be reclassified subsequently to profit and loss:				
(a) Net gains on financial assets other than equity shares carried at fair value through OCI	–	–	–	82
(b) Net change in fair value of intrinsic value of cash flow hedges	(131)	26	53	(21)
(c) Net change in fair value of time value of cash flow hedges	(59)	24	20	(6)
(d) Exchange differences on translation of financial statements of foreign operations	227	39	(22)	158
(ii) Income tax on items that will be reclassified to profit or loss	26	(6)	(9)	(25)
(B) (i) Items that will not be reclassified subsequently to profit and loss				
(a) Net gains/(losses) on equity shares carried at fair value through OCI	–	–	1	–

	For the quarter ending June 30, 2015	*For the quarter ending Sep 30, 2015*	*For the quarter ending Dec 31, 2015*	*For the quarter ending Mar 31, 2016*
(b) Remeasurement of defined employee benefit plans	(11)	(32)	(34)	(37)
(ii) Income tax on items that will not be reclassified to profit or loss	1	4	7	(6)
IX. **TOTAL OTHER COMPREHENSIVE INCOME NET OF TAXES**	53	55	16	145
X. **TOTAL COMPREHENSIVE INCOME FOR THE PERIOD**	5,826	6,148	6,141	6,492
XI. **Profit attributable to:**				
Owners of the Company	5,747	6,073	6,109	6,341
Non-controlling interests	26	20	16	6
XII. **Total comprehensive income for the period attributable to:**				
Owners of the Company	5,763	6,133	6,127	6,475
Non-controlling interests	63	15	14	17

6

Transfer Pricing

LEARNING OBJECTIVES

After Studying this chapter, you will be able to:

- Explain the concept of transfer pricing
- Describe the significance of transfer pricing
- Discuss the factors which govern transfer pricing policies of firms
- Explain the methods of transfer pricing
- Compare and contrast between different methods of transfer pricing
- Highlight the transfer pricing methods in practice
- Describe the process of fixing 'minimum' transfer price
- Discuss the process of fixing transfer pricing for services

INTRODUCTION

The phenomenal growth of domestic and multinational companies over the past few decades has given rise to the popularization of the concept called 'transfer pricing'. As companies grew in size and structure, their activities got expanded beyond geographical territories. This expansion led to the divisionalisation of their activities and decentralization of power and authority. Each division so created was then expected to act as a responsibility centre in the form of cost, revenue, profit or investment. Consequently, measurement of the divisional performance became imperative which was best met through the adoption of the transfer pricing mechanism.

Transfer pricing is a key technique of divisional performance measurement particularly when the products or services of one division (or sub-unit/department) are transferred to another division of the same company for further processing or treatment before they are passed on to the hands of the customers as final product. It is therefore important to understand the transfer pricing mechanism in vogue. The present chapter is devoted to meeting this end.

TRANSFER PRICING

Transfer pricing relates to the pricing of goods and services that change hands between entities engaged in inter-firm trade [1]. The price that one segment (subunit, department, division) of an organization charges for a product or service supplied to another segment of the same organization is known as transfer price [2]. Transfer price is the price at which goods or services are transferred between affiliated entities within an organization [3]. IAS 14 on segment reporting defines transfer pricing as "the pricing of products or services between industry segments or geographic areas [4]. The term transfer price is more popular among MNCs than the domestic firms for transfer of materials, parts or finished products and services. Naisbitt [5] observes, a multinational company can produce its products anywhere, using resources from anywhere, by a subsidiary located anywhere, to a quality found anywhere, to be sold anywhere. Inter-firm trade and transfer pricing are thus closely associated and hence the growth in inter-firm trade has resulted in increased focus on transfer pricing.

NEED FOR TRANSFER PRICING

Transfer pricing system exists primarily to communicate data that will lead to goal-congruent decisions. Appropriate evaluation of segment vis-à-vis managerial performance and avoidance of foreign currency restrictions and quotas, minimization of taxes and tariffs, minimization of exchange risks, avoidance of profit repatriation restrictions and enhancement of shares of profits in joint ventures are some of the other important objectives which are accomplished through transfer pricing mechanism.

Rathore [6], in the context of importance of transfer pricing, has observed "... transfer pricing developed as a logical result of the movement towards divisionalisation of operations by large business organizations like General Motors and General Electric in America during the early part of the present (20th) century. Highly centralized operations were decentralized by establishing numerous profit centers in search for more productivity. The delegation of increased authority to local managers in turn gave rise to the need for a mechanism of internal pricing that would serve the dual purpose of, on one hand optimizing allocation of corporate resources and on the other, motivating the divisional managers to operate their units at a high degree of efficiency so that goal congruence prevails between divisional and corporate management. At the same time it served as a device for monitoring the performance of divisional managers".

FACTORS GOVERNING TRANSFER PRICING POLICY

The important factors which govern transfer pricing policy of firms may be enumerated as follows:

1. Employees
2. Shareholders/owners
3. Management
4. Domestic government agencies
5. Foreign government agencies

6. Competitors
7. Joint venture partners
8. Supplies/creditors
9. Customers

Employees

Employees of the different divisions of the firm can be affected by the transfer pricing policy particularly when their performance is measured in terms of profitability of their divisions. Therefore, employees of the selling division would like to have a higher transfer price whereas those of the buying division a lower transfer price. The transfer pricing policy of the firms can thus affect and be affected by their employees.

Shareholders/Owners

Shareholders and owners of the firm, like the employees, can influence and be influenced by the transfer pricing policy. If the firm adopts a very aggressive transfer pricing policy to increase its profitability, it may attract close scrutiny by tax administrators, penalty, negative publicity and higher taxes, which in turn would not be liked by the shareholders. The shareholders therefore would prefer such transfer pricing policy which would enhance the firm's overall earnings and reduce its global tax liability.

Management

Management of the firm especially at the senior level would prefer such transfer pricing policy as would help the firm maximize its consolidated earnings especially when their compensation is linked to the firm's overall performance. To this effect therefore the firm's transfer pricing policy is likely to influence and be influenced by senior management of the firm.

Domestic Government Agencies

Transfer pricing policy of the firm is likely to attract the attentions of at least three kinds of government agencies – the tax authorities, the custom authorities and the law enforcement and enacting bodies. The tax authorities for example would like not to see that firms use transfer pricing as a mechanism to 'shift' income and reduce their tax liability. The custom authorities would like to see that firms pay appropriate duties on all exports to and imports from the affiliated entities as per provisions of the nation. The law enforcement and enacting bodies of the nation would like to ensure that firms do not use transfer pricing mechanism as an escape route to defy law of the land. They are also to review the impact of existing law on the tax collection as a source of revenue to the government and to bring about appropriate modifications so as to make the laws compatible with other nations.

Foreign Government Agencies

The tax and custom authorities, among others, of the foreign countries do have similar concerns like the domestic government agencies in terms of collection of duties and taxes from firms especially the MNCs who have multiple locations across the globe, as these firms are apprehended to be shifting their profits globally to avail tax advantage.

Competitors

Transfer pricing policy of firms can affect the market competition insofar as a multinational corporation can charge artificially low transfer price for the goods or services supplied to its affiliates in the foreign country thereby enabling the affiliates offer its products at a price lesser than the competition. Consequently the competitors would take up anti-dumping measures as provided under the WTO regime forcing the MNC to alter its pricing policy.

Joint Venture Partners

MNCs with joint venture partners may like to charge higher transfer prices for the goods transferred to the joint venture units and lower transfer prices for the goods transferred from the joint venture units. This is so because by charging lower transfer prices, the MNCs would eventually share less profits with the joint venture partners. The joint venture partners in turn would prefer a reverse process, i.e., they would like to charge higher transfer prices for products transferred out of it to maximize profit and lower transfer price for products transferred to it in a view to reduce costs. In the process, joint venture partners would influence and be influenced by the transfer pricing policy.

Suppliers/Creditors

The transfer pricing policy adopted by MNCs can have influence on suppliers both at home country and abroad. Creditors, for example, would like to stay away from MNCs and firms who are under scrutiny by government agencies for violation of state laws with regard to conducting business such as income-shifting or tax evasions. These kinds of creditors would be affected by the MNCs'/firms' transfer pricing policies and they may therefore try to prevail upon such firms to adopt pricing policy that would suit them.

Customers

Customers too are likely to be affected by the transfer pricing policies of firms when 'higher prices' are charged on products transferred to affiliates which are in turn passed on to the customers. This can happen when the products have virtually no or limited competition to face with.

Given the above, management of the firms have to judiciously fix transfer pricing policies which would protect the interests of all those who are directly or indirectly affected as discussed above and which would also result in maximizing the corporate objective(s). Surveys conducted by Tang [7] and Elliott [8] indicate that multinational transfer pricing policies in practice are influenced, in order of importance, by (1) income tax rate and other tax differences among countries, (2) total income of the company, (3) restrictions on income or dividend repatriation, (4) availability of market price information, and (5) the competitive positions of the subunits/subsidiaries in their respective markets. And for decisions on domestic transfer pricing, the influencing factors, in order of importance, are (1) maximizing consolidated after tax profits, (2) performance evaluation, (3) management motivation, (4) pricing and product mix, and (5) external market recognition.

METHODS OF TRANSFER PRICING

The various transfer pricing methods practiced by different countries across the globe can be broadly divided into three broad categories:

1. Cost-based transfer prices
2. Market-based transfer prices
3. Negotiated transfer prices

The choice of any of these categories of methods or a combination of them would depend on their relative merits and demerits, company's own policy and such other internal and external factors which would influence and would get influenced by the pricing policy chosen.

Cost-based Transfer Prices

A company may choose to charge its product or services that change hands between sub-units based as cost price. The cost price in consideration may be actual or budgeted. It may be based on 'full cost', partial cost or adjusted (modified) full cost. The 'full cost' here includes cost of production and the attributable part of other functional costs such as R & D, marketing, distribution, engineering, and customer care.

Cost-based transfer prices are considered to be suitable to situations where market prices for similar products are not available or are not suitable otherwise. Divisions of the company considered as 'cost centre' too favour cost-based pricing methods for better control, decision making and performance evaluation.

ILLUSTRATION 6.1

M/S Infinite International, manufacturer of a standard equipment for use in the aviation industry, has three Divisions, namely, A, B and C. As a corporate policy, the output of Division A is transferred to Division B, and that of Division B to Division C for further processing and completion as finished product which are then sold in the open market at ₹20,10,000 per unit. During the month of January, the firm has produced and sold 100 units with the following further details:

Particulars	*Division A*	*Division B*	*Division C*
Product variable cost per unit (in ₹)	4,80,000	—	—
Process variable cost per unit (in ₹)	2,25,000	2,50,000	2,80,000
Fixed cost (in ₹)	5,40,000	4,60,000	3,10,000

If Division A decides to transfer its output to Division B at Cost plus 25%, and Division B decides to transfer its output to Division C at Cost plus 20%, determine the profits generated by the firm and its three Divisions.

SOLUTION

Calculation of profits of **M/S Infinite International** and its three Divisions under cost-based transfer pricing method

(Fig. in ₹'000)

	Divisions			*Firm*
	A (₹)	B (₹)	C (₹)	*M/S Arvind International* (₹)
(X) Revenue A = Cost+25%, B = cost + 20%, and C = Selling price × total quantity	**88,800**	**1,37,112**	**2,01,000**	**2,01,000**
Less: **(Y) Expenses**				
1. Product variable costs (100 units @ ₹480)	48,000	Nil	Nil	48,000
2. Process variable costs (100 units @ ₹225/₹250/₹280)	22,500	25,000	28,000	75,500
3. Division fixed costs	540	460	310	1,310
4. Transfer price (Cost plus 25% for B/Cost plus 20% for C)	Nil	88,800	1,37,112	Nil
Total expenses (1 + 2 + 3 + 4)	71,040	1,14,260	16,5422	1,41,810
Total operating income (X – Y)	17,760	22,852	35,578	76,190

Notes:

1. Products passing through Division C are the final products which are sold to external buyers at ₹ 20, 10,000 per unit. Hence, the company's revenue should be equal to the revenue of the Division C, i.e., 100 units @ ₹ 20,10,000 per unit (or ₹ 20,10,00,000).
2. Operating income of the three divisions taken together should be the operating income of the company.

It is obvious from the above calculations that the profits of Division **A, B and C** have been ₹1,77,60,000; ₹2,28,52,000 and ₹3,55,78,000, respectively; and that of the firm M/S Infinite International has been ₹7,61,90,000.

ILLUSTRATION 6.2

Pro Care Ltd., manufactures and sells specified medical equipment at ₹20,95,000 per unit. The company has four Divisions—D_1, D_2, D_3 and D_4. The output of D_1 gets transferred to D_2, that of D_2 to D_3 and from D_3 to D_4 for further performance and completion as finished product for sale. The firm has produced and sold 50 such equipment during the month of February. The other relevant information concerning manufacture and sell of the equipment is as follows:

Particulars	*Division D_1*	*Division D_2*	*Division D_3*	*Division D_4*
Product variable cost per unit (in ₹)	4,10,000	—	—	—
Process variable cost per unit (in ₹)	2,20,000	1,10,000	1,80,000	1,45,000
Fixed cost (in ₹)	2,40,000	2,60,000	2,80,000	3,00,000

You are required to determine profits of the firm Pro Care Ltd. and its four divisions, if Division D_1 transfers its output to Division D_2 at Cost plus 25%, Division D_2 transfers its output to Division D_3 at Cost plus 20%, and Division D_3 transfers its output to Division D_4 at Cost plus 10%.

SOLUTION

Calculation of profits of **Pro Care Ltd.** and its four Divisions under cost based transfer pricing method.

(Fig. in ₹'000)

	Divisions				Firm
	D_1 (₹)	D_2 (₹)	D_3 (₹)	D_4 (₹)	Pro Care (₹)
(X) Revenue D_1 = Cost + 25%, D_2 = Cost + 20%, D_3 = Cost + 10%, and D_4 = Selling price × total quantity	39,675	54,522	70,182.2	1,04,750	**1,04,750**
Less: **(Y) Expenses**					
1. Product variable costs (50 units @ ₹410)	20,500	Nil	Nil	Nil	**20,500**
2. Process variable costs (50 units @ ₹220/ ₹110/₹180/₹145)	11,000	5,500	9,000	7,250	**32,750**
3. Division fixed costs	240	260	280	300	**1,080**
4. Transfer price (Cost + 25% for D_2/Cost + 20% for D_3/ Cost +10% for D_4)	Nil	39,675	54,522	70,182.2	
Total expenses (1 + 2 + 3 + 4)	31,740	45,435	63,802	77,732.2	54,330
Total operating profit (X – Y)	7,935	9,087	63,80.2	27,017.8	50,420

Notes:

1. Products passing through Division D_4 are the final products which are sold to external buyers at ₹20,95,000 per unit. Hence, the company's revenue should be equal to the revenue of the Division D_4, i.e., 50 units @ ₹20,95,000 per unit (or ₹10,47,50,000).
2. Operating income of the three divisions taken together should be the operating income of the company.

It is clear from the above calculations that the profits of **Divisions—D_1, D_2, D_3 and D_4** have been ₹79,35,000; ₹90,87,000 and ₹63,80,200, ₹2,70,17,800, respectively; and that of Pro Care Ltd. has been ₹5,04,20,000.

ILLUSTRATION 6.3

ABC Company Ltd. is a leading manufacturer of a certain consumer durable product. The company has two divisions—Engineering and Assembly. The output of the Engineering division are transferred to Assembly division for further processing and assembling before they are sold to the customer as complete product.

Verification of the company's records reveals that the variable cost per unit of the product for Engineering and Assembly are ₹250 and ₹300, respectively. The fixed cost of Engineering division is ₹15,000 and that of the Assembly division is ₹10,000. The product variable cost per unit of Engineering division is ₹400, and the total output is 100 units which are sold to customer on completion @ ₹2000 per unit.

If the Engineering division decides to charge its transfers to Assembly division at cost plus 50%, what will be ABC's overall profit and the profits of its two divisions?

SOLUTION

Calculation of ABC Company Ltd.'s overall profit and profits of its two divisions – Engineering and Assembly under cost based transfer pricing method.

Items of expenses and revenue	*Divisions*		*Total revenue, expenses and income of the company*
	Engineering	*Assembly*	
A. **Revenue**	₹	₹	₹
150% of cost, i.e., 150% of (B) for Engineering division, and the Market price for Assembly division	1,20,000	2,00,000	2,00,000
Less: B. **Expenses:**			
1. Product variable cost (₹400 × 100 units)	40,000	—	40,000
2. Transferred cost	25,000	1,20,000	55,000
3. Division variable cost	15,000	30,000	25,000
4. Division fixed cost	—	10,000	—
Total expenses (1 + 2 + 3 + 4)	80,000	1,60,000	1,20,000
Operating income (A – B)	40,000	40,000	80,000

Notes:

1. Products passing through the Assembly division are the final products which are sold to external buyers at ₹2,000 per unit. Hence, the company's revenue should be equal to the revenue of the Assembly division, i.e., 100 units @ ₹2,000 per unit (or ₹2,00,000).
2. Operating income of the two divisions taken together should be the operating income of the company. Evidently the two divisions' income has been the same at ₹40,000 and the company's income has been ₹80,000.

ILLUSTRATION 6.4

XYZ Co. Ltd. is the manufacturer of a certain electronic product. The company has three divisions – D_1, D_2 and D_3. Output of D_1 is transferred to D_2 and that of D_2 to D_3 for further processing and assembling before they are passed on to the hands of the customer as final product.

The company reports that variable costs per unit of the product for D_1, D_2 and D_3 are ₹300, ₹200 and ₹100, respectively. The fixed costs for the three divisions respectively are ₹20,000, ₹15,000 and ₹10,000. The product variable cost per unit is ₹400 for division D_1. If the total output of the company for a certain period is 1,000 units, which are sold to the customer at ₹1,400 per unit, and if division D_1 decides to charge its transfers to D_2 at cost plus 20% and D_2 to D_3 at cost plus 10%, what is the company's total profit and the profits of its divisions?

SOLUTION

Calculation of total profit and the profits of the three divisions D_1, D_2 and D_3 of XYZ Ltd. under cost based transfer pricing method.

	D_1	D_2	D_3	*Total*
A. **Revenue**	(₹)	(₹)	(₹)	(₹)
D_1 = 120% of cost, D_2 = 110% of cost and D_3 = Market price × total quantity	8,64,000	11,86,900	14,00,000	15,00,000
Less: B. **Expenses**				
1. Product variable costs (1000 units @ ₹400)	4,00,000	—	—	4,00,000
2. Division variable costs (1,000 units @ ₹300/₹200/₹100)	3,00,000	2,00,000	1,00,000	6,00,000
3. Division fixed costs	20,000	15,000	10,000	45,000
4. Transfer costs (Cost plus 20%/10%)	—	8,64,000	11,86,900	—
Total expenses (1 + 2 + 3 + 4)	7,20,000	10,79,000	12,96,900	10,45,000
Total operating profit (A – B)	1,44,000	1,07,900	1,03,100	3,55,000

It is obvious from the above calculations that the divisional profits for D_1, D_2 and D_3 have been ₹1,44,000, ₹1,07,900 and ₹1,03,100 respectively, and the company's total profit has been ₹3,55,000.

Market-based Transfer Prices

A company may choose to adopt prices of similar products or services as available in the market to price all transfer of products and services between its subunits, departments or divisions. The market price so charged may be the actual market price prevailing at a particular point of time or it can be a modified market price.

Market-based transfer prices are considered useful to companies having more decentralized operations. Market-based prices too help in distinguishing between profitable and non-profitable operations/centres. 'A transfer price system based on market price has considerable appeal. It seems a fair, objective measure of the value of the product transferred. It introduces external competitiveness pressure and standards, and it measures divisional profits in terms of external opportunities' [9]. 'By using market-based transfer prices in perfectly competitive markets, a company can achieve (1) goal congruence, (2) management effort, (3) subunit performance evaluation, and (4) subunit autonomy' [10].

Whereas use of market-based transfer prices aims at cost control and efficiency enhancement, the optimal outcome would however depend on the satisfaction of three conditions, that 'the market for the intermediate product is perfectly competitive, interdependencies of subunits are minimal, and there are no additional costs or benefits to the company as a whole from buying or selling in the external market instead of transacting internally' [11].

ILLUSTRATION 6.5

Everything else in Illustration 6.1 remaining unchanged, if Division A decides to price its transfers to Division B at the prevailing (current) market rate of a similar product which is ₹9, 12,000 per unit, and Division B decides to price its transfers to Division C at the prevailing market price of a similar product which is ₹13,75,000, what will be the company's overall profit and the profits of its three divisions?

SOLUTION

Calculation of profits of **M/S Infinite International** and its three Divisions A, B and C under Market-based transfer pricing method.

(*Fig. in* ₹'000)

Details	*Divisions*			*Firm*
	A (₹)	B (₹)	C (₹)	*M/S Infinite International* (₹)
(X) **Revenue** A = 100 units @₹9, 12,000; B = 100 units @ **₹13, 75,000,** and C = 100 units @Selling price, i.e., **₹20,10,000**	**91,200**	**1,37,500**	**2,01,000**	**2,01,000**
Less: **(Y) Expenses**				
1. Product variable costs (100 units @ ₹480)	48,000	Nil	Nil	48,000
2. Process variable costs (100 units @ ₹225/₹250/₹280)	22,500	25,000	28,000	75,500
3. Division fixed costs	540	460	310	1,310
4. Transfer price	Nil	91,200	1,37,500	Nil
Total expenses (1 + 2 + 3 + 4)	71,040	1,16,660	1,65,810	1,41,810
Total operating income (X – Y)	20,160	20,840	35,190	76,190

Notes:

1. Products passing through Division C are the final products which are sold to external buyers at ₹ 20, 10,000 per unit. Hence, the company's revenue should be equal to the revenue of the Division C, i.e., 100 units @ ₹ 20,10,000 per unit (or ₹ 20,10,00,000).
2. Operating income of the three divisions taken together should be the operating income of the company.

It is obvious from the above calculations that the profits of Division A, B and C have been ₹2,01,60,000; ₹2,08,40,000 and ₹3,51,90,000, respectively; and that of the firm M/S Arvind International has been ₹7,61,90,000.

ILLUSTRATION 6.6

All other things given in Illustration 6.2 remaining unchanged, if Division D_1 decides to price its transfers to Division D_2 at the prevailing market price of a similar product which is ₹7,25,000 per unit, Division D_2 decides to price its transfers to Division D_3 at the prevailing market price of a similar product which is ₹10,10,000, and Division D_3 decides to price its transfers to Division D_4 at the prevailing market price of a similar product which is ₹14,90,000 per unit, what is the company's overall profit and the profits of its four divisions?

SOLUTION

The basic information provided is that Pro Care Ltd. manufactures and sells certain medical equipment at ₹20,95,000 per unit which the company manufactures through its four Divisions—D_1, D_2, D_3 and D_4. The output of D_1 gets transferred to D_2, that of D_2 to D_3 and from D_3 to D_4 for further performance and completion as finished product for sale. The company has produced and sold 50 units of such equipment during the month of February. The other relevant information concerning manufacture and sell of the equipment is as follows:

Particulars	*Division* D_1	*Division* D_2	*Division* D_3	*Division* D_4
Product variable cost per unit (in ₹)	4,10,000	—	—	—
Process variable cost per unit (in ₹)	2,20,000	1,10,000	1,80,000	1,45,000
Fixed cost (in ₹)	2,40,000	2,60,000	2,80,000	3,00,000

We are required to determine the company's overall profit and profits of its four divisions D_1, D_2, D_3 and D_4 given that Division D_1 transfers its output to Division D_2 at the prevailing market price of ₹7,25,000 per unit, Division D_2 transfers its output to Division D_3 at the prevailing market price of ₹10,10,000 per unit, and Division D_3 transfers its output to Division D_4 at the prevailing market price of ₹14,90,000 per unit.

With the above background, we may prepare a table as under to compute the profit of Care International and its four divisions D_1, D_2, D_3 and D_4:

Calculation of profits of Pro Care Ltd. and its four Divisions D_1, D_2, D_3 and D_4 under Market-based transfer pricing method.

(Fig. in ₹'000)

Details	*Divisions*				*Firm*
	D_1 (₹)	D_2 (₹)	D_3 (₹)	D_4 (₹)	*Pro Care Ltd.* (₹)
(X) **Revenue** D_1 = 50@₹ 725, D_2 = 50@1010, D_3 = 50@1490, and D_4 = Selling price × total quantity	36,250	50,500	74,500	1,04,750	1,04,750
Less:					
(Y) **Expenses**					
1. Product variable costs (50 units @ ₹410)	20,500	Nil	Nil	Nil	20500
2. Process variable costs (50 units @ ₹220/₹110/₹180/₹145)	11,000	5,500	9,000	7,250	32,750
3. Division fixed costs	240	260	280	300	1,080
4. Transfer price	Nil	36,250	50,500	74,500	—
Total expenses (1 + 2 + 3 + 4)	31,740	42,010	59,780	82,050	54,330
Total operating profit (X – Y)	4,510	8,490	14,720	22,700	50,420

Notes:

1. Products passing through Division D_4 are the final products which are sold to external buyers at ₹20, 95,000 per unit. Hence, the company's revenue should be equal to the revenue of the Division D_4, i.e., 50 units @ ₹20,95,000 per unit (or ₹10,47,50,000).
2. Operating income of the three divisions taken together should be the operating income of the company.

It is clear from the above calculations that the profits of Divisions—D_1, D_2, D_3 and D_4 have been ₹45,10,000; ₹84,90,000 and ₹1,47,20,200, ₹2,27,00,000, respectively; and that of Care International Ltd. has been ₹5,04,20,000.

ILLUSTRATION 6.7

All other things given in Illustration 6.3 remaining unchanged, if the Engineering division decides to price its transfers to Assembly division at the prevailing (current) market rate of

₹1,000 per unit for similar products, what is the company's overall profit and also profits of the two divisions?

SOLUTION

Calculation of profits of profits of ABC Company Ltd. and its two divisions under market-based transfer pricing method.

Items of expenses and revenue	*Divisions*		*Total revenue, expenses and income of the company*
	Engineering ₹	*Assembly* ₹	₹
A. Revenue (100 units: @ ₹1000/@ ₹2000)	1,00,000	2,00,000	2,00,000
Less:			
B. Expenses			
1. Product variable cost: (100 units @ ₹400 per unit)	40,000	—	40,000
2. Transferred cost: (100 units @ ₹1000 per unit)	—	1,00,000	—
3. Division variable cost: (100 units @ ₹250/@ ₹300)	25,000	30,000	55,000
4. Division fixed cost:	15,000	10,000	25,000
Total expenses (1 + 2 + 3 + 4)	20,000	60,000	1,20,000
Operating income (A – B)	20,000	60,000	80,000

Notes:

1. Product passing through the Assembly division is the final product. Hence revenue for the company should be the revenue of the assembly division, i.e., 100 units sold to external customers @ ₹2,000 per unit.
2. Operating income of Engineering division and Assembly division together is the operating income of the company.
3. Alternatively, the total revenue of the company, i.e., ₹2,00,000 *less* total expenses of the company, i.e, product variable cost plus divisions' variable cost and divisions' fixed cost or ₹1,20,000 is the company's operating income.

ILLUSTRATION 6.8

All other things in Illustration 6.4 remaining constant, if division D_1 decides to charge its transfers to D_2 and D_2 to D_3 at current market prices per unit of ₹850 and ₹1200 respectively, what will be the change in the profits earned by the company and its divisions in comparison to the cost-based transfer prices?

SOLUTION

The cost-based transfer pricing profits for the company XYZ Ltd. and its three divisions D_1, D_2 and D_3 have been found as ₹3,55,000, ₹1,44,000, ₹1,07,900 and ₹1,03,100, respectively, as in Illustration 6.4.

To find out the profits under market-based transfer pricing so as to know the changes in the profits earned under the market-based pricing system and the cost-based transfer pricing system, the following Table may be constructed:

Calculation of profits of XYZ Co. Ltd. and its three divisions' under market-based transfer pricing.

	D_1 (₹)	D_2 (₹)	D_3 (₹)	*Total* (₹)
A. **Revenue** (Output × market rates = 1,000 units × ₹850/₹1200/₹1400)	8,50,000	12,00,000	14,00,000	14,00,000
Less:				
B. **Expenses**				
1. Product variable costs (1,000 units × ₹400)	4,00,000	—	—	4,00,000
2. Division variable costs (1,000 × ₹300/₹200/₹100)	3,00,000	2,00,000	1,00,000	6,00,000
3. Division fixed costs	20,000	15,000	10,000	45,000
4. Transfer costs (at market price)	—	8,50,000	12,00,000	—
Total expenses (1 + 2 + 3 + 4)	7,20,000	10,65,000	13,10,000	10,45,000
Operating income (as per market price)	1,30,000	1,35,000	90,000	3,55,000
Operating income as per cost price	1,44,000	1,07,900	1,03,100	3,55,000

It is evident from the above table that the profit under market-based transfer pricing have been ₹3,55,000, ₹1,30,000, ₹1,35,000 and ₹90,000 respectively for the company XYZ Ltd. and its three divisions D_1, D_2 and D_3. Whereas the total profits earned by the company under both the methods (cost price and market price) remain the same, the profits earned by the divisions vary.

Distress Prices

Distress price refers to the temporary fall in market price in comparison to the historical average due to a situation where supply exceeds demand. As such, when distress price prevails, care should be taken to price the transfers at such 'adjusted' market price(s) as would be appropriate to measure the performance of the division.

Negotiated Transfer Prices

A company may adopt the policy of charging such price(s) as would be fixed through negotiations between the subunits involved for the transfer of products or services. The subunits (or departments/divisions) of the company may be set free to negotiate the price at which they would like to transfer the products or services between themselves and then to decide if they would buy or sell internally or deal with external agencies. The subunits concerned may use information as regards cost price and market price of the products or services under consideration for transfer while determining the negotiated price although the price ultimately fixed may not hold any relationship with such cost or market price.

Negotiated transfer prices are considered ideal for adoption when the market is volatile. Further, negotiated transfer prices are the outcome of the bargaining process between the selling and the buying subunits. As such the negotiated prices are indicative of the bargaining strengths of the subunits involved.

ILLUSTRATION 6.9

All other things given in Illustration 6.1 remaining unchanged, if Division A and Division B agree that the transfers from Division A to Division B shall be priced at ₹10,80,000 per unit; and further that Division B and Division C agree that the transfers from Division B to Division C shall be priced at ₹16,30,000 per unit, what will be the company's overall profit and the profits of its three divisions?

SOLUTION

The basic information provided is hat M/S Infinite International is a manufacturer of standard equipment which is used in the aviation industry. The Company has three Divisions, namely, A, B and C. As a matter of corporate policy, the output of Division A is transferred to Division B, and that of Division B to Division C for further processing and completion as finished product which are then sold in the open market at ₹20,10,000 per unit. During the month of January, the company has produced and sold 100 units of the equipment, with the other relevant information made available being:

Particulars	*Division A*	*Division B*	*Division C*
Product variable cost per unit (in ₹)	4,80,000	—	—
Process variable cost per unit (in ₹)	2,25,000	2,50,000	2,80,000
Fixed cost (in ₹)	5,40,000	4,60,000	3,10,000

We are required to determine the company's overall profit and profits of its three divisions A,B and C given that Division A transfers its output to Division B at an agreed price of ₹10,80,000 per unit, and Division B transfers its output to Division C at an agreed price of ₹16,30,000 per unit.

With the above background, we may prepare a table as under to compute the profit of Arvind International and its three divisions A, B and C:

Calculation of profits of M/S Infinite International and its three Divisions A, B and C under Market-based transfer pricing method.

(*Fig. in* ₹'000)

	Divisions			*Firm*
	A (₹)	B(₹)	C(₹)	*M/S Infinite International* (₹)
(X) Revenue A = 100 units @ ₹10,80,000; B = 100 units @ ₹16,30,000, and C = 100 units @ Selling price, i.e., ₹ 20,10,000	**1,08,000**	**1,63,000**	**2,01,000**	**2,01,000**
Less:				
(Y) Expenses	48,000	Nil	Nil	48,000
1. Product variable costs (100 units @ ₹ 480)	22,500	25,000	28,000	75,500
2. Process variable costs (100 units @ ₹225/₹250/₹280)	540	460	310	1,310
3. Division fixed costs	Nil	1,08,000	1,63,000	Nil
4. Transfer price				
Total expenses (1 + 2 + 3 + 4)	71,040	1,33,460	1,91,310	1,41,810
Total operating income (X – Y)	36,960	29,540	9,690	76,190

Notes:

1. Products passing through Division C are the final products which are sold to external buyers at ₹20,10,000 per unit. Hence, the company's revenue should be equal to the revenue of the Division C, i.e., 100 units @ ₹20,10,000 per unit (or ₹20,10,00,000).
2. Operating income of the three divisions taken together should be the operating income of the company.

It is obvious from the above calculations that the profits of Division **A, B and C** have been ₹3,69,60,000; ₹2,95,40,000 and ₹96,90,000, respectively; and that of the firm M/S Infinite International has been ₹7,61,90,000 under the negotiated transfer pricing method.

ILLUSTRATION 6.10

All other things given in Illustration 6.2 remaining unchanged, if **Division D_1** and Division D_2 agree that the transfers from Davison D_1 to Division D_2 shall be priced at ₹11,11,000 per unit; Division D_2 and Division D_3 agree that the transfers from Davison D_2 to Division D_3 shall be priced at ₹14,14,000 per unit, and similarly Division D_3 and Division D_4 agree that the transfers from Division D_3 to Division D_4 shall be priced at ₹17,10,000 per unit, what will be the company's overall profit and the profits of its four divisions?

SOLUTION

The basic information provided is that Pro Care Ltd. manufactures and sells certain medical equipment at ₹20,95,000 per unit which the company manufactures through its four Divisions—D_1, D_2, D_3 and D_4. The output of D_1 gets transferred to D_2, that of D_2 to D_3 and from D_3 to D_4 for further processing and completion as finished product for sale. The company has produced and sold 50 units of such equipment during the month of February. The other relevant information concerning manufacture and sell of the equipment is as follows:

Particulars	*Division D_1*	*Division D_2*	*Division D_3*	*Division D_4*
Product variable cost per unit (in ₹)	4,10,000	—	—	—
Process variable cost per unit (in ₹)	2,20,000	1,10,000	1,80,000	1,45,000
Fixed cost (in ₹)	2,40,000	2,60,000	2,80,000	3,00,000

We are required to determine the company's overall profit and profits of its four divisions **D_1, D_2, D_3 and D_4** given that **Division D_1** transfers its output to Division **D_2** at an agreed price of ₹11,11,000 per unit, Division **D_2** transfers its output to **Division D_3** at an agreed price of ₹14,14,000 per unit, and **Division D_3** transfers its output to **Division D_4** at an agreed price of ₹17,17,000 per unit.

Given the above background, we may prepare a table as under to compute the profit of Pro Care Ltd. and its four divisions D_1, D_2, D_3 and D_4:

Calculation of profits of Pro Care Ltd. and its four Divisions D_1, D_2, D_3 and D_4 under negotiated price method.

(*Fig. in* ₹'000)

	Divisions				*Firm*
	D_1 (₹)	D_2 (₹)	D_3 (₹)	D_4 (₹)	*Care International* (₹)
(X) Revenue					
D_1 = 50@₹11,11,000, D_2 = 50@14,14,000, D_3 = 50@17,17,000, and D4 = Selling price × total quantity	55,550	70,700	85,850	1,04,750	**1,04,750**
Less:					
(Y) Expenses					
1. Product variable costs (50 units @ ₹410)	20,500	Nil	Nil	Nil	**20,500**
2. Process variable costs (50 units @ ₹220/ ₹110/₹180/₹145)	11,000	5,500	9,000	7,250	32,750
3. Division fixed costs	240	260	280	300	1,080
4. Transfer price	Nil	55,550	70,700	85,850	Nil
Total expenses (1+2+3+4)	31,740	61,310	79,980	93,400	54,330
Total operating profit (X – Y)	23,810	9,390	5,870	11,350	50,420

Notes:

1. Products passing through Division D_4 are the final products which are sold to external buyers at ₹20,95,000 per unit. Hence, the company's revenue should be equal to the revenue of the Division D_4, i.e., 50 units @ ₹20, 95,000 per unit (or ₹10,47,50,000).
2. Operating income of the three divisions taken together should be the operating income of the company.

It is clear from the above calculations that the profits of Divisions—D_1, D_2, D_3 and D_4 have been ₹2,38,10,000; ₹93,90,000, ₹58,70,000, ₹1,13,50,000, respectively; and that of Pro Care Ltd. has been ₹5,04,20,000.

ILLUSTRATION 6.11

All other things in Illustration 6.3 remaining unchanged, if the two divisions bargain to fix ₹1,150 per unit at which Engineering division should price its transfers to Assembly division, what will be the profits of the two divisions vis-à-vis that of the company?

SOLUTION

Calculation of profits of ABC Co. Ltd. and its two subdivisions under negotiated transfer pricing method.

Items of expenses and revenue	*Divisions*		*Total revenue, expenses and income of the company* (₹)
	Engineering ₹	*Assembly* ₹	
A. **Revenue:** (Engineering – 100 @ ₹1,150, Assembly – 100 @ ₹2,000	1,15,000	2,00,000	2,00,000
Less:			
B. **Expenses:**			
1. Product variable cost	40,000	–	40,000
2. Transferred cost	–	1,15,000	–
3. Division variable cost	25,000	30,000	55,000
4. Division fixed cost	15,000	10,000	25,000
Total expenses (1 + 2 + 3 + 4)	80,000	1,55,000	1,20,000
Operating income (A – B)	35,000	45,000	80,000

ILLUSTRATION 6.12

All other things in Illustration 6.4 remaining unchanged, if the three divisions D_1, D_2 and D_3 of the company bargain and decide that division D_1 will charge ₹835 per unit on its transfers to division D_2 and that division D_2 will charge ₹1,160 per unit on its transfers to division D_3, what will be the divisions' profits under the changed situation and also the profit of the company?

SOLUTION

Determination of profits under negotiated price method for XYZ Co. Ltd. and its three divisions.

	D_1 (₹)	D_2 (₹)	D_3 (₹)	Total (₹)
A. Revenue (1000 units @ ₹835/₹1160/₹1400	8,35,000	11,60,000	14,00,000	14,00,000
B. Expenses:				
1. Product variable costs (1,000 × ₹400)	4,00,000	—	—	4,00,000
2. Division variable costs (1,000 × ₹300/₹200/₹100)	3,00,000	2,00,000	1,00,000	6,00,000
3. Division fixed costs	20,000	15,000	10,000	45,000
4. Transfer costs (negotiated)	—	8,35,000	11,60,000	-
Total expenses (1 + 2 + 3 + 4)	7,20,000	10,50,000	12,70,000	10,45,000
Operating income (A – B)	1,15,000	1,10,000	1,30,000	3,55,000

The company's profit and the profits of its three divisions—D_1, D_2 and D_3 under the negotiated transfer price method are found to be ₹3,55,000, ₹1,15,000, ₹1,10,000 and ₹1,30,000, respectively.

TRANSFER PRICING METHODS—A COMPARISON

When the three recognized methods of transfer pricing are compared with each other, one can easily observe that the operating profit of the firm remains unchanged irrespective of whether it is a cost-based method of transfer pricing or market-based or even the negotiated transfer pricing method. The income of the Divisions however varies when the method is changed from Cost-based to market-based or to negotiated and the vice versa. Exhibit 6.1, 6.2, 6.3 and 6.4 constructed below clearly indicate so.

EXHIBIT 6.1 Comparison of incomes under Cost-based, Market-based and Negotiated transfer pricing method for M/S Infinite International and its Divisions

Firm →	M/S Infinite International				Remarks
Method ↓	Division A	Division B	Division C	Firm	
Cost-based	1,77,60,000	2,28,52,000	3,55,78,000	7,61,90,000	Illustration 6.1
Market-based	20,11,60,000	2,08,40,000	3,51,90,000	7,61,90,000	Illustration 6.5
Negotiated	3,69,60,000	2,95,40,000	96,90,000	7,61,90,000	Illustration 6.9

EXHIBIT 6.2 Comparison of incomes under Cost-based, Market-based and Negotiated transfer pricing method for Pro Care Ltd. and its Divisions

Firm →	Pro Care Ltd.					Remarks
Method ↓	Division A	Division B	Division C	Division D	Firm	
Cost-based	79,35,000	90,87,000	63,80,200	2,70,17,800	5,04,20,000	Illustration 6.2
Market-based	45,10,000	84,90,000	1,47,20,000	2,27,00,000	5,04,20,000	Illustration 6.6
Negotiated	2,38,10,000	93,90,000	58,70,000	1,13,50,000	5,04,20,000	Illustration 6.10

EXHIBIT 6.3 Comparison of incomes under Cost-based, Market-based and Negotiated transfer pricing method for ABC Ltd. and its Divisions

Items of revenue and expenses of the divisions	*Cost-based transfer pricing (Ref. Illustration 6.3)*	*Market-based transfer pricing (Ref. Illustration 6.7)*	*Negotiated transfer pricing (Ref. Illustration 6.11)*
Engineering	₹	₹	₹
1. Revenue:			
(i.e., 100 units @ ₹1200/₹1000/₹1150	1,20,000	1,00,000	1,15,000
2. Expenses:			
(i) Product variable cost	40,000	40,000	40,000
(ii) Division variable cost	25,000	25,000	25,000
(iii) Division fixed cost	15,000	15,000	15,000
I. Division operating income (1–2)	40,000	20,000	35,000
Assembly			
1. Revenue:			
(100 × ₹2000)	2,00,000	2,00,000	2,00,000
2. Expenses:			
(i) Transferred cost	1,20,000	1,00,000	1,15,000
(ii) Division variable cost	30,000	30,000	30,000
(iii) Division fixed cost	10,000	10,000	10,000
II. Division operating income	40,000	60,000	45,000
Company operating income (I+II)	80,000	80,000	80,000

It is quite evident from Exhibit 6.3 that the operating income of the company is the same, i.e., ₹80,000 irrespective of whether the transfer pricing method is cost-based, market-based or negotiated. The operating incomes of the two divisions, namely, Engineering and Assembly, however vary with regard to the method adopted. For example, the operating income of Engineering division is the highest under cost-based transfer pricing method, followed by the negotiated pricing method and the market-based pricing method. Contrary to this, the operating income of Assembly division is highest under market price method, followed by the negotiated price and the cost price method. Given this, and given further that if profit maximization were the sole objective of the concerned division(s) on the basis of which their performance would be measured, Engineering division would certainly prefer a cost based transfer pricing to market based, if the choice were to be made between cost based and the market based methods. The reverse would be the choice of the Assembly division. Further, if the market price and/or cost prices are likely to fluctuate, the 'divisions' of the company may go for a negotiated price which will optimize their individual objectives vis-à-vis the company objectives.

A similar interpretation can also be made for XYZ Co Ltd. on the basis of Exhibit 6.4 as under:

EXHIBIT 6.4 Comparison of incomes under Cost-based, Market-based and Negotiated transfer pricing method for Care International Ltd and its Divisions

Firm →	*XYZ Co. Ltd.*				*Remarks*
Method ↓	*Division* D_1	*Division* D_2	*Division* D_3	*Firm*	
Cost-based	1,44,000	1,07,900	1,03,100	3,55,000	Illustration 6.4
Market-based	1,30,000	1,35,000	90,0000	3,55,000	Illustration 6.8
Negotiated	1,15,000	1,10,000	1,30,000	3,55,000	Illustration 6.12

Therefore, the firms may be indifferent as regards choice of any particular method of transfer pricing by the divisions/segment/units of the firm because the total income will remain the same for the firms. But, the choice of a particular method of transfer pricing by the divisions will be influenced by factors like Employees, Shareholders/owners, management, domestic and foreign government agencies, competitors, Joint venture partners, supplies/creditors and customers as has been already discussed.

TRANSFER PRICING METHODS IN PRACTICE

Transfer prices generate income for the selling division and corresponding expenses or costs for the buying division of the company which of course get 'off set' when divisions' results are consolidated to determine the overall income of the company. Efforts in real term have however been made to fix transfer prices that would benefit both the selling and the buying divisions of the company as well as the company itself. Of course although any single preferred method is yet to emerge. The observation made by Sharav [12] in context is worth noting: 'What, if any, is the preferred method of transfer pricing? No method that has emerged to date, be it cost—or market based, has been immune from criticism. The practices of actual companies involved in transfer pricing demonstrate a consistent rejection of any dogmatic and singular approach, no matter how theoretically superior it may have been proclaimed. Users and uses determine the transfer pricing technique to be selected'.

Expert studies have revealed that for domestic transfer pricing, managers in all countries use cost based transfer prices more frequently than market based transfer prices; and for multinational transfer pricing, managers use both cost based and market-based methods equally often. Many multinational companies have market-based transfer prices in some divisions and cost based transfer prices in others [13]. A research study on the US MNCs has revealed that large firms tend to choose market-based transfer pricing methods [14]. Exhibit 6.5 depicts a comparative view of the frequency of different transfer pricing methods used in practice by different domestic companies and MNCs in the US, UK, Canada and India.

Exhibit 6.5 Transfer pricing practices in selected countries (in terms of percentage of times they are used by companies)

	Countries			
	US[15]	*UK*[16]	*Canada*[17]	*India*[18]
A. Domestic Companies				
1. Cost based	53	49	46	53
(of which full cost)	(49)	(38)	(37)	(47)
2. Market-based	26	26	34	47
3. Negotiated	17	24	18	—
4. Others	04	01	02	—
	100	100	100	100
B. MNCs				
1. Cost based	42	38	33	—
(of which full cost)	(42)	(28)	(26)	—
2. Market-based	35	31	37	—
3. Negotiated	14	20	26	—
4. Others	08	11	04	—
	100	100	100	100

Source: Compiled from sources put as references 15, 16, 17 and 18.

Evidently, as shown in Exhibit 6.5, cost-based transfer pricing followed by market-based and negotiated transfer pricing have been the techniques used by companies to price their transfer. Further, of the cost-based pricing, full cost has been the primary technique of pricing.

TRANSFER PRICING AND FULFILLMENT OF COMPANY OBJECTIVES

The purpose of transfer pricing mechanism, as already mentioned, is goal congruence, performance evaluation, managerial motivation and subunit autonomy to the desired level. Any method(s) of transfer pricing chosen by the company should therefore be ideally fulfilling these objectives. Exhibit 6.9 indicates the extent to which these objectives are achieved under various methods of transfer pricing.

EXHIBIT 6.6 Transfer Pricing Methods and Fulfillment of Company Objectives

Transfer pricing methods	*Fulfillment of objective criteria*			
	Goal congruence	*Performance evaluation*	*Managerial motivation*	*Subunit autonomy*
Cost-based	Mostly, though not always	Possible when transfer price exceeds full costs	Possible if the transfer price is based on budgeted cost	Normally not
Market-based	Yes, in case of competitive market	Yes, in case of competitive market	Yes	Yes
Negotiated	Yes	Yes, though sometimes get affected by bargaining strengths	Yes	Yes

It is evident from Exhibit 6.6 that no single method of transfer pricing is capable of meeting all the objectives criteria. Therefore, the choice of any transfer pricing method(s) by a company will depend on its economic circumstances and the decision at hand.

FIXING A MINIMUM TRANSFER PRICE

Horngreen, Datar and Foster [19] have recommended a minimum transfer price, for a perfectly competitive market with the selling division having no idle capacity, as "the sum of incremental cost per unit incurred up to the point of transfer" and 'the opportunity cost per unit to the selling division'. The incremental cost is the additional cost of producing and transferring the products or services; and the opportunity cost is the maximum contribution margin forgone by the selling division if the products or services are transferred internally. Thus,

Minimum transfer price = Incremental cost per unit incurred upto the point of transfer *plus* opportunity cost per unit to the selling division.

The minimum transfer price per unit for the Engineering division in Illustration 6.2, for example, would be ₹1,000. This is because the contribution forgone by this division for not able to sell the product to outside parties instead, and supplying it internally to Assembly division is ₹200 (i.e., selling price – full cost, or ₹1,000 – ₹800) and the incremental cost the Assembly division otherwise would be required to incure to manufacture the product is ₹800.

While fixing the minimum transfer price per unit appropriate care needs to be taken in situations where (i) competitive market exists but the selling division has idle capacity, and (ii) where no market exists for the intermediate products. Whereas, in the later case contribution will be zero for no market and no sales, in the former case contribution will be less as in order to utilize the idle capacity, production will have to be increased and correspondingly selling price to be lowered.

TRANSFER PRICING METHODS FOR SERVICES

Pricing the transfers of services has remained all the difficult as regards choosing an appropriate transfer pricing method due mainly to the fact that services are intangibles and the buyers and sellers find it difficult to determine what exactly to buy or sell. A study conducted by Keegan and Haward [20] on transfer prices of services however reveals that 'historically services have been transferred at cost or at a mandated market price, equivalent to standard cost plus a mark up. As establishing an external market price for transfers in general is difficult, more so for customized services, it is always ideal to go for a negotiated price for such transfer of services. With large number of players operating in the services market in recent years, market prices of specified services may be relatively easier to get for adoption.

SUMMARY

Transfer pricing relates to the pricing of goods and services that change hands between entities engaged in inter-firm trade. Transfer pricing system exists primarily to communicate data that will lead to goal congruent decisions. The other objectives accomplished by transfer pricing system are evaluation of segment (subunit, department, division) vis-à-vis managerial performance, avoidance of foreign currency restrictions, minimization of taxes, tariffs and exchange risks, avoidance of profit repatriation restrictions and increase in the shares of joint venture profits.

It is found that transfer pricing techniques fall into three broad categories: (1) cost price based, (2) market price based, and (3) negotiated price based. The selling division of the firm prices its transfers to the buying division at 'cost plus a margin' under the cost based transfer pricing method. The cost here can be actual, budgeted, full cost or modified full cost. The advantages associated with cost-based transfer pricing are better control and evaluation of divisional performance. Besides, cost-based pricing is useful to situations where market prices for similar products are not available.

When the selling division prices its transfers to the buying division at a price as is prevalent in the market for such products, the pricing amount to market based pricing. The prices so charged can be a modified market price as well. The greatest advantage of market-based transfer pricing is that it helps in distinguishing between profitable and non profitable divisions. Market-based pricing is equally useful to companies having more decentralized operations. Companies using market-based transfer pricing may confront with situations of distress prices. To over come this, they need to price their transfers at an adjusted market price as would be appropriate to measure the divisional performance. Distress price here refers to the temporary fall in the market price of the product in comparison to its historical average.

If the market is volatile, negotiated price is the option for pricing the transfers. Negotiated price is the price agreed upon, through bargaining process, between the subunits at which the transfers would be priced. The advantages associated with negotiated transfer pricing is the bargaining process by itself which indicates the strength, i.e., bargaining power as well as skills, of the subunits involved.

Of the three suggested categories of techniques available for pricing the transfers between subunits, it is found that mostly the cost based followed by the market based and negotiated transfer pricing are in use worldwide by both the domestic companies and the MNCs. Given further that transfer prices generate income for the selling division and results in a corresponding expenses (cost) for the buying division, efforts should be made to fix transfer prices that would benefit both the buying and the selling divisions. In the context, a minimum transfer price, worked out as 'incremental cost per unit incurred up to the point of transfer plus opportunity cost per unit to the selling division, may be useful. While exercising the minimum transfer price, due care must be taken in situations where competitive market exists but the selling division has idle capacity and where no market exists for the intermediate products.

KEY TERMS

Transfer price: The price that one segment (subunit, department, division) of an organization charges for a product or service supplied to another segment of the same organization.

Transfer pricing: Pricing of goods and services that change hands between entities engaged in inter-firm trade.

Distress price: The temporary fall in market price in comparison to the historical average owing to a situation where supply exceeds demand.

Minimum transfer price: Incremental cost per unit incurred up to the point of transfer *plus* opportunity cost per unit to the selling division.

REVIEW QUESTIONS

1. What is transfer pricing? Why is transfer pricing necessary?
2. Examine the role of transfer pricing in national and multination business operations. Briefly analyze the current practices relating to transfer pricing adopted by multinational corporations.
3. What are the various factors that influence transfer pricing policies of firms? Explain.
4. What are the different methods of transfer pricing in vogue? Which of these methods are practiced by contemporary MNCs and why?
5. Give a comparative analysis of the various techniques of transfer pricing with their relative merits and demerits.
6. Explain, with suitable example(s) the cost-based transfer pricing method.
7. How is the negotiated transfer pricing different from market-based transfer pricing? Explain with examples(s).
8. 'Transfer pricing facilitates goal congruent decisions' – Elucidate.
9. How should a minimum transfer price be fixed? What factors should be considered while fixing the minimum transfer price? Explain with suitable example(s).
10. "The use of market prices for transfer pricing may lead to dysfunctional decisions by some employees" – Comment.
11. 'An appropriate in house pricing mechanism serves as a monitoring device in the evaluation of decentralized divisional performance'. Comment.
12. Considered that a firm has two divisions—A and B. The products produced by A transferred to B for further processing. Division A does not have an external market for its output. Division B can not buy the product produced by division A from any other sources either. What transfer pricing method should you recommend for the situation and why?
13. SDC Co. Ltd. has two divisions—D_1 and D_2. The output of division D_1 passes through D_2 for further treatment and completion before they are finally sold to customers at ₹1,450 per unit.

    The company reports that its product variable cost per unit (for D_1) has been ₹500 per unit whereas its process variable costs per unit has been ₹300 and ₹250 for D_1 and D_2, respectively, with a corresponding fixed costs of ₹30,000 and ₹45,000 for D_1 and D_2.

If the total units produced by the company are 2,000 and if division D_1 decides to charge its transfers to D_2 at 25% above cost, what is the company's total profit and also the profits of its two divisions?

14. Kedia Associates has three divisions – X_1, X_2 and X_3. The output of X_1 passes through X_2 and of X_2 through X_3 for further processing and completion which are then sold at ₹1,050 per unit.

The company reveals that the variable cost per unit for X_1, X_2 and X_3 has been ₹200, ₹145 and ₹105 respectively, and the fixed costs for the divisions are in the order of ₹25,000, ₹45,000 and ₹50,000. The variable cost of the product for X_1 is ₹300. If the total output of the company is 1250 units and if the divisions follow market-based transfer pricing with X_1 and X_2 charging ₹575 and ₹795 respectively on their transfers, what is the profit earned by the company and its three divisions?

15. M/s Agrawal and Agrawal, manufacturer of standard audio-visual products, has two divisions—S_1 and S_2. Output of S_1 passes through S_2 for completion. During a certain period, the firm has manufactured 2,500 units of the product which are sold at ₹1,050 per unit. The variable costs per unit for S_1 and S_2 are ₹280 and ₹200 respectively. The fixed costs of S_1 are ₹1,05,000 and of S_2 are ₹1,35,000. The two divisions bargained to fix ₹745 per unit at which S_1 will price its transfers to S_2. If the product variable costs per unit for S_1 are ₹320, what are the firm's profit and the profits of its two divisions S_1 and S_2?

16. Plasto Co. Ltd. has two divisions—D_1 and D_2. Division D_1 which operates at 100% capacity level has been required by the company management to supply its products to division D_2 which is at present operational at 60% capacity. Division D_2 needs the product produced by D_1 for supplementing its main product and is willing to pay ₹200 per unit as against ₹300 per unit which D_1 can charge to external customers. D_1's full cost per unit is ₹200 whereas its variable cost is ₹170 per unit. D_2's cost per unit after purchase from D_1 is ₹2000 with the following break up:

Parts purchased from outside vendors	₹900
Parts purchased from division D_1	₹200
Other variable costs	₹500
Fixed costs (per unit)	₹400

D_2 can fix a selling price per unit full cost plus 10%.

Required:

You are the manager of division D_1. Would you recommend the sales to D_2? Will the sale be in the overall interest of Plasto Ltd.? What alternative transfer pricing would according to you lead to goal congruent decisions?

17. A company fixes the inter-divisional transfer prices for its products on the basis of cost plus 25% return on investment in its divisions. The budgetary provisions of Division A for the year 2005–06 is given below:

	₹
Fixed assets	50,000
Current (excluding debtors)	30,000
Debtors	20,000
Annual fixed cost of the division	80,000
Variable cost per unit (or product)	10
Volume of production per year (units)	40,000

You are required to determine the transfer price per unit for Division A.

18. P.D. Ltd. has two divisions. Division A manufactures a component which is used by Division B to produce a finished product. Output and costs have been budgeted for a period as follows:

	Division A	*Division B*
Component units	5,000	—
Finished units	—	5,000
Total variable costs	₹25,000	₹60,000
Fixed costs	₹15,000	₹20,000

If the transfer from Division A to Division B is made at full cost, what is the maximum price that Division B could sell the finished product for, and would this price be in the best interest of the organization as a whole?

19. Cox Ltd. has two divisions. Division P manufactures a component which is used by Division Q to produce a finished product. The budgeted costs and output for a certain period have been given as follows:

	Division P	*Division Q*
Component units	15,000	—
Finished units	—	15,000
Total variable costs	₹75,000	₹60,000
Fixed costs	₹20,000	₹30,000

If the transfer from Division P to Division Q is made at full cost

(i) what is the maximum price that Division Q could sell the finished product for, and

(ii) would this price be in the best interest of the organization as a whole?

20. Write explanatory notes on:

(a) Transfer pricing of services.

(b) Distress prices.

(c) Importance of transfer pricing.

(d) Factors governing transfer pricing.

21. VST Ltd. has two divisions—A_1 and A_2. The output of division A_1 passes through A_2 for further processing and completion, before they are sold in the open market as finished products at ₹12,500 per unit.

The company has revealed that its product variable cost per unit has been ₹4,000 whereas its process variable costs per unit have been ₹2,800 and ₹2,500 for A_1 and A_2, respectively. It is also revealed that the fixed costs for A_1 and A_2 have been ₹3,00,000and ₹4,50,000, respectively.

If the total units produced and sold by VST Ltd. are 4,000 units, and if division A_1 decides to price its transfers to A_2 at cost plus 25%, what are the profits earned by VST Ltd. and its two divisions?

22. Marvel Inc. has three divisions—D_1, D_2 and D_3. The output of D_1 passes through D_2 and that of D_2 through D_3 for completion sell at ₹11,250 per unit.

    The company revealed that the variable cost per unit for D_1, D_2 and D_3 has been ₹2,000, ₹1,450 and ₹ 1,050, respectively, and the fixed costs for the divisions are in the order of ₹1,25,000, ₹ 1,45,000 and ₹1,50,000. The variable cost of the product has been ₹3,000 per unit. If the company has produced and sold 1200 units of the product and if the divisions follow market-based transfer pricing, with D_1 and D_2 charging ₹5,700 and ₹7,950 respectively on their transfers, determine the profits earned by Marvel Inc and its three divisions, D_1, D_2 and D_3.

23. Regalia Universe, manufacturer of standard audio-visualequipment, has two divisions—A_1 and A_2. Output of A_1 passes through A_2 for completion. During a certain period, the firm has manufactured 3,500 units of the product which were sold at ₹1,850 per unit. The variable costs per unit for A_1 and A_2 are ₹380 and ₹300, respectively. The fixed costs of A_1 were ₹1,65,000 and that of A_2 was ₹1,95,000. The two divisions bargained to fix ₹945 per unit at which A_1 will price its transfers to A_2. If the product variable costs per unit for A_1 were ₹445, what are the firm's profit and the profits of its two divisions A_1 and A_2?

24. ESBQ Ltd. has two divisions—D_1 and D_2. The output of division D_1 passes through D_2 for further treatment and completion before they are finally sold to customers at ₹11,450 per unit.

    The company reports that its product variable cost per unit (for D_1) has been ₹3,500 whereas its process variable costs per unit have been ₹2,800 and ₹2,250 for D_1 and D_2, respectively. Further, the fixed costs corresponding D_1 and D_2 have been ₹1,30,000 and ₹1,45,000.

    If the total units produced by the company are 4,000 and if division D_1 decides to charge its transfers to D_2 at 25% above cost, what is the company's total profit and also the profits of its two divisions?

25. Continental Inc. has three divisions — X_1, X_2 and X_3. The product of X_1 passes through X_2 and of X_2 through X_3 for further processing and completion as finished products which are then sold at ₹9,050 per unit.

    The company reveals that the variable cost per unit for X_1, X_2 and X_3 has been ₹1,800, ₹1,545 and ₹1,440 respectively, and the fixed costs for the divisions are in the order of ₹1,20,000, ₹1,95,000 and ₹2,25,000. The variable cost of the product is ₹3,300. If the total units produced and sold by the company is 1110 units and if the divisions adopt market-based transfer pricing method by wich X_1 and X_2 charge ₹5,750 and ₹7,950 respectively on their transfers, what is the profit earned by the company and its three divisions?

26. Imaging Services Inc., manufacturer of standard audio-visual products, has two divisions—A_1 and A_2. Output of A_1 gets transferred to A_2 for further processing and

completion. During the month of March, the firm has manufactured 5000 units of the product which were sold at ₹15,700 per unit. It has been ascertained that the variable costs per unit for A_1 and A_2 have been ₹2,800 and ₹3,200, respectively. The fixed costs of A_1 were ₹4,44,000 and of A_2 were ₹5,15,000. The two divisions bargained to fix ₹7,450 per unit at which A_1 will price its transfers to A_2. If the product variable costs per unit for A_1 have been ₹4,600, determine the firm's profit and the profits of its two divisions A_1 and A_2?

27. Blue Berry International Inc. manufactures and sells health care equipment. It has four Divisions—D_1, D_2, D_3 and D_4 to jointly manufacture the equipment. Given the nature of the equipment and the corporate policy, output of D_1 is transferred to D_2, that of D_2 to D_3 and from D_3 to D_4 for further processing, performance and completion as finished product. The firm has produced and sold 250 such equipment during the months January to March @ ₹16,60,000 per unit.

Other relevant information relating to the manufacture and sell of the equipment is as follows:

Particulars	*Division D_1*	*Division D_2*	*Division D_3*	*Division D_4*
Product variable cost per unit (in ₹)	3,10,000	—	—	
Process variable cost per unit (in ₹)	1,20,000	2,10,000	1,30,000	2,40,000
Fixed cost (in ₹)	4,50,000	5,60,000	3,30,000	2,10,000

Determine profits of the firm and its four divisions, if Division D_1 transfers its output to Division D_2 at Cost plus 15%, Division D_2 transfers its output to Division D_3 at Cost plus 20%, and Division D_3 transfers its output to Division D_4 at Cost plus 25%.

28. Disha Ltd. has three Divisions— A, B and C. The output of Division A is transferred to Division B, and that of Division B to Division C for further processing and completion as finished product. The poducts are sold in the open market at ₹25,25,800 per unit. During the month of January-March, the firm has produced and sold 80 units of the product, with the following further details:

Particulars	*Division A*	*Division B*	*Division C*
Product variable cost per unit (in ₹)	6,60,550	—	—
Process variable cost per unit (in ₹)	4,25,570	3,70,350	2,60,280
Fixed cost (in ₹)	4,80,200	5,30,300	3,90,100

If Division A decides to transfer its output to Division B at the prevailing market price of a similar product which is ₹14,44,000 per unit, and Division B and C agree that Division B will transfer its output to Division C at ₹20,21,210 per unit, find out the profits the firm and its three Divisions.

29. Star Ltd. is a manufacturer of consumer durable products. It has three divisions—Manufacturing, Forging and Assembly. The output of Manufacturing is transferred to Forging and that of Forging to Assembly for further performance before they are sold to the customers as finished product.

Verification of the company's records show that the variable cost per unit of the product for Manufacturing, Engineering and Assembly has been ₹2500 and ₹3000,

₹3,500, respectively. The fixed costs are in the order of ₹5,50,000, ₹6,60,000 and ₹7,70,000 for the divisions. If the product variable cost per unit is ₹8,80,000, total output is 145 units and the price charged to customers is ₹30,30,300 per unit, determine the performance of the divisions and the company using the method(s) you feel the best .

30. XYZ Co. Ltd. is the manufacturer of a certain electronic product. The company has three divisions—X, Y and Z. The output of Division X is transferred to Y and that of Y to Z for further processing and assembling before they are passed on to the hands of the customer as final product.

The company reports that variable costs per unit of the product for divisions – X, Y and Z have been ₹7,300, ₹8,600 and ₹4,400, respectively. The fixed costs for the three divisions respectively were ₹12,00,800, ₹14,00,800 and ₹10,00,100. The product variable cost per unit has been ₹5,76,000.

If the total output of the company for a certain period is 500 units, which are sold to the customersat ₹26,12,400 per unit, and if division D_1 decides to charge its transfers to D_2 at cost plus 20%, and D_2 to D_3 at cost plus 10%, what is the company's total profit and the profits of its divisions?

REFERENCES

[1] Whitman, M.V., *Domestic Myths on Globalization*, *Wall Street Journal*, October 27, 1995, A 14.

[2] Horngreen, C.T. and Foster, G., *Cost Accounting: A Managerial Emphasis*, 7th Ed., PHI, New Delhi, 1991.

[3] Saudagaran, S.M., *International Accounting*, Taxman India, 2001, p. 194.

[4] Barry J. Epstein, et al., *Wiley IAS 2002*, John Wiley & sons, Inc., p. 783.

[5] Naisbitt, J., *Global Paradox*, New York: William Morrow & Co., 1994, p. 50.

[6] Rathore, S., Op cit., p. 244.

[7] Tang, R., *Canadian Transfer Pricing in the 1990s*, 'Management Accounting, Feb. 1992.

[8] Elliott, J., *International Transfer Pricing, a survey of UK and Non-UK Groups*, Management Accounting, CIMA, Nov. 1998.

[9] Shillinglaw, G. and Burton, J.C., *Materials Management and Profit Centre Concept*, Management Bulletin 4, American Management Association, 1964.

[10] Horngreen, T., et al., *Cost Accounting—A Managerial Emphasis*, Pearson Education, 2003, p. 762.

[11] *Ibid.*

[12] Sharav, I., *Transfer Pricing—Diversity of Goals and Practices*, *The Journal of Accountancy*, Vol. 165, No. 3, March 1988, pp. 96–103.

[13] Horngreen, et al., op. cit., p. 767.

[14] El-Eryani, et al., *Transfer Pricing Determinants of US Multinationals*, *Journal of International Business Studies*, 3rd quarter, 1990, pp. 409–425.

[15] Tang, R., *Transfer Pricing Systems Management: Practical Issues and Cases*, Montvale, NJ: Institute of Management Accountants, 2001.

[16] Mostafa, et al., *Transfer Pricing—A Survey Using Discriminant Analysis*, Omega, 12, No. 5, 1984.

[17] Tang, R., *Canadian Transfer Pricing in the 1990s*, Management Accounting, Feb 1992.

[18] Govindarajan, V., and Ramamurty, B., *Transfer Pricing Policies in Indian Companies: A Survey*, Chartered Accountant, Nov. 1983.

[19] Horngreen, et al., Op cit., p. 768.

[20] Keegan, D.P., and Howard, P.D., *Making Transfer Prices Work for Services*, *Journal of Accountancy*, Vol. 165, No. 3, pp. 96–103, 1988.

7

Foreign Financial Statement Analysis

LEARNING OBJECTIVES

After studying this chapter, you will be able to:

- Explain the concept and purpose of foreign financial statement analysis
- Give an overview of the various techniques of financial statement analysis in vogue
- Describe the process and utility of horizontal analysis
- Describe the process and utility of vertical analysis
- Discuss the process of ratio analysis
- Discuss the modern techniques used in financial statement analysis
- Explain the difficulties encountered in analyzing foreign financial statements

INTRODUCTION

Financial statement analysis refers to an information processing system that is meant for providing financial data which are appropriate and useful to decision makers who are concerned with evaluating the economic situation of the firm and predicting its future course. The information in context is derived basically from the published financial statements such as the income statement and the balance sheet of the firm. Non-accounting information like stock prices and economic indicators are also used in the process of financial statement analysis. The decision makers include a variety of stakeholders prominent among them being the investors, creditors, employees, regulatory agencies, environmentalists, social activists, researchers, and the management itself. Investors, for example, are concerned with portfolio decisions; creditors for determining the firm's credit worthiness; and employees for establishing economic bases for collective bargaining. The regulatory and policy formulating bodies of the state are interested in 'controlling' decisions; environmentalists and social activists on 'social accounting' issues; researchers for studying firm vis-à-vis industry behaviour; and the management for evaluating the operational and financial efficiency of the firm and its subunits.

Table 7.1 shows the different decision makers and the kinds of decisions they are concerned with.

TABLE 7.1 Decision makers and the kind of decisions they are interested in

Investors	Portfolio decisions
Creditors	Firm's credit worthiness
Employees	Establishing economic rationale
Regulatory and Policy formulating bodies	Controlling decisions
Environmentalists and Social activists	Sòcial Accounting issues
Researchers	Studying the firm and industry behavior
Management	Evaluating operational and financial performance

The purpose of financial statement analysis, as stated above, from the users (decision makers) perspective be it a domestic company or a foreign company is the same. Therefore, the tools used for analyzing the financial statements of domestic company and for the MNCs would be basically the same. The only precaution that an analyst dealing with foreign financial statements has to take is to see that consolidated balance sheets and income statements are made available for analysis. This is so because financial statements of the subsidiaries/affiliates located at different countries will have financial data represented at different currencies than that of the parent company which unless translated and consolidated will lose their interpretive values.

TECHNIQUES OF FINANCIAL STATEMENT ANALYSIS

The techniques most widely used for financial statement analysis in the traditional category are:

1. Horizontal (or trend) analysis,
2. Vertical (or common-size) analysis, and
3. Ratio analysis.

A few *modern techniques* like the Economic Value Added (EVA), Market Value Added (MVA) and Multiple Discriminate Analysis (MDA) are also used for effective analysis of the financial statements.

The choice and use of any or all of these techniques would depend on the analyst's own objective and the point of reference. Further, analysts and researchers have evidently combined statistical tools like measures of central tendencies, dispersion, correlation and regression with these techniques in general and with the ratios in particular in order to enhance the predictive and interpretive values of the financial performance of the firms.

Horizontal Analysis

Horizontal analysis, also known as the trend analysis or dynamic analysis, is one under which financial statements of a number of years of the firm are analyzed against a 'common base'. Figures of the initial year of the periods for which the analysis is made are normally taken as the base and converted into percentage which facilitates easy comparison. Horizontal analysis is considered suitable for intra-firm comparison. The trend as would emerge out of the analysis will indicate the improvement or deterioration in the performance of the firm.

ILLUSTRATION 7.1

Following is the abstract of the financial statements of JMJ International for the year ended 2019, 2020, 2021, 2022, 2023 and 2024.

(*Fig. in* ₹'000)

Year	*2019*	*2020*	*2021*	*2022*	*2023*	*2024*
Sales	280	308	322	350	378	420
EBIT	120	126	150	180	198	204
Debt	150	150	195	240	255	270
Equity	110	121	132	143	165	165
Fixed assets	200	204	250	240	350	380

You are required to make a trend (horizontal) analysis of the performance of the JMJ taking year 2019 as the base.

SOLUTION

Given that year 2019 is to be taken as the base year, the figures in respect of Sales, EBIT, Debt, Equity and Fixed assets each will be taken as 100 against which respective figures of all other years will be compared. That is, if sales of year i.e., 2019 which is ₹2,80,000 is taken as 100, sales of 2020 which is ₹3,08,000 will be equal to (100 ÷ 2,80,000 × 3,08,000 or) 110. In the same manner all other figures can be calculated and arranged as shown in Exhibit 7.1.

EXHIBIT 7.1 Horizontal analysis of JMJ International's financial performance

Year	*2019*	*2020*	*2021*	*2022*	*2023*	*2024*
Sales	100	110	115	125	135	150
EBIT	100	105	125	150	165	170
Debt	100	100	130	160	170	180
Equity	100	110	120	130	150	150
Fixed assets	100	102	125	120	175	190

Note: All the absolute figures have been reduced to small and comparable relative figures. For example, sales of the year 2020 which was ₹3,08,000 have been reduced to 110 assuming sales of the year 2019 as 100.

It is evident from Exhibit 7.1 that JMJ's sales have steadily increased over the years from 100% in 2019 to 150% in 2024. EBIT for the said period too has gone up by 70%. As regards debt and equity capitals, it is seen that the firm has infused additional capitals into the business both in terms of debt and equity with an increase of 80% in case of the former and 50% in case of the later when compared with the base year. Investments in the form of fixed assets by the company too have gone up by almost double from 100% to 190% for the period under consideration.

Vertical Analysis

Vertical analysis, also referred to as common size analysis, is one under which financial statements of firms of different sizes are compared and analyzed against a 'common base' rather than based on the absolute figures themselves. The general practice is to express each components of the balance sheet as a percentage of the total assets or liabilities and so also of the components of income statement as a percentage of total sales. The common size analysis is found useful to inter-firm comparisons.

ILLUSTRATION 7.2

The balance sheets of three companies – A, B and C as on 31.03.2024 are as follows:

(Fig. in ₹'000)

Liabilities	A	B	C	*Assets*	A	B	C
Share capital	203	180	310	Gross block *less* depreciation	870	940	1,880
Reserves and surpluses	400	300	750	Stock in trade	325	275	1,020
Loans	650	450	1,040	Debtors	445	185	305
Creditors	462	520	1,220	Cash and bank balance	75	50	115
	1,715	1,450	3,320		1,715	1,450	3,320

You are required to make a vertical (common size) analysis of the companies' financial positions.

SOLUTION

Under the common size analysis as the name itself suggests we have to convert each of the components of assets and liabilities of all the three companies are to be converted into percentage by taking the assets and liabilities of the respective companies as 100. For instance, if total assets of company A, i.e., ₹17,15,000 is taken as 100%, its gross block will be 50.73% approximately, i.e., (870 ÷ 1715 × 100). In the same manner all other components of assets and liabilities of company A as well as those of B and C can be converted into percentage as given in Exhibit 7.2.

EXHIBIT 7.2 Common size (vertical) analysis of company A, B and C's financial positions

(Fig. in %)

Liabilities	A	B	C	*Assets*	A	B	C
Share capital	11.84	12.41	9.34	Gross block less depreciation	50.73	64.83	56.63
Reserves and surpluses	23.32	20.69	22.59	Stock in trade	18.95	18.97	30.72
Loans	37.90	31.04	31.33	Debtors	25.95	12.76	9.19
Creditors	26.94	35.86	36.74	Cash in hand and bank balance	4.37	3.44	3.46
	100	100	100		100	100	100

In absolute terms gross block of C (₹18,80,000) is 2.16 times higher than that of A (₹8,70,000) and 2 times higher than that of B (₹9,40,000), in percentage terms the gross block of B (64.83%) is higher than that of both A (50.73%) and C (56.63%) in relation to the total assets of the respective companies. As the size (in terms of total assets for example) of the companies vary, any inferences drawn based on absolute figures would not be logical. It is therefore the relative figures based on a common percentage that would lead to drawing useful inferences as regards the performance of the companies. Given this backdrop, it is seen that company C maintains higher volume of inventory (stock in trade) as a percentage to total assets i.e., 30.72% against 18.95% and 18.97% respectively of A and B. Apparently company C's inventory management is poor compared to that of A and B. Similar interpretations can be offered to other components of assets and liabilities of the three companies.

Ratio Analysis

Accounting ratios, which are simply the relationships between two accounting figures, have been the most popular, widely acclaimed and extensively used tools of financial statement analysis. Since late 1800s, ratio analysis has been the major tool used in the interpretation and evaluation of financial statements for investment decision making [1]. A ratio, defined as 'the indicated quotient of two mathematical expressions' and as 'the relationship between two or more things [2] helps reduce large quantity of financial data to small quantity which in turn aids to making a qualitative judgment about the firm's financial performance.

Types of Ratios

For all practical purposes financial ratios may be classified into five broad categories:

1. Liquidity ratios
2. Profitability ratios
3. Solvency ratios
4. Activity (or turnover) ratios
5. Valuation ratios

Exhibit 7.3A depicts an overview of these ratios, their components (by names as they are generally called), and their purpose as to who are interested in such ratios. Exhibit 7.3B represents the formula (e) for their calculations.

A. Liquidity Ratios

As contained in the Exhibit (7.3-A), included in the activity ratios are current ratio, quick ratio, absolute liquidity ratio, defensive interval ratio and working capital ratio.

1. Current ratio: Current ratio, calculated by dividing total current assets by total current liabilities, is a measure of the firm's short-term liquidity position, i.e., the firm's ability to meet its short-term obligations. The higher the current ratio, the greater is the firm's ability to meet its current obligations. Short-term creditors would always favour a higher current ratio as this would provide more safety to the funds they have made available to the firm. Higher liquidity ratio would mean lower profitability, a situation that would be least favoured by the firm. It is therefore that a standard of 2:1 has been prescribed as the ideal current ratio. A 2:1 current ratio implies that for every one rupee of current liabilities, two rupees of current assets are available. Beside the rule of thumb, inter-firm and intra-firm comparisons of current ratios would lead to drawing meaningful inferences about the liquidity position of the firm.

EXHIBIT 7.3-A Classification of financial ratios

			Ratio types		
Col. 1	*Liquidity ratios* *Col. 2*	*Profitability ratios* *Col. 3*	*Solvency ratios* *Col. 4*	*Activity ratios* *Col. 5*	*Valuation ratios* *Col. 6*
Objectives	To determine the ability of the firm to meet its day-to-day obligations.	To judge the ability of the firm to generate profits that would be adequate to support its operations (i.e., to meet its operating expenses) and also to ensure a fair return on its investment.	To judge the ability of the firm to meet its long-term obligations.	To judge the managerial efficiency in terms of assets management	To judge the profitability of and the reward on shareholders) investment
Who are interested	Short-term creditors, banks and financial institutions, bond holders, management.	Management, owners, creditors, lenders, potential investors and takeover bidders.	Management, bond holders, banks and financial institutions providing long-term capital, shareholders	Shareholders' potential takeover bidders, management	Shareholders' management, potential investors and takeover bidders
What are included in components	1. Current ratio 2. Quick ratio 3. Absolute liquid ratio 4. Defensive interval ratio 5. Net working capital ratio	A. *Based on profit margin:* 6. Gross profit ratio 7. Operating profit ratio 8. Net profit ratio B. *Based on expenses:* 9. Cost of goods sold ratio 10. Operating expenses ratio 11. Administrative expenses ratio 12. Selling expenses ratio 13. Operating ratio 14. Financial expenses ratio C. *Based on return on investment:* 15. Return on total assets (ROTA) 16. Return on capital employed (ROCE) 17. Return on shareholders' equity (ROSE) *D. Based on Du Pont's overall profitability analysis:* 18. Return On Investment (ROI)	19. Debt equity ratio 20. Debt to total capital 21. Debt to total assets 22. Proprietary ratio 23. Capital gearing ratio 24. Interest coverage ratio 25. Dividend coverage ratio 26. Total coverage ratio 27. Total cash flow coverage ratio 28. Debt service coverage	29. Inventory turnover ratio 30. Debtors turnover ratio 31. Average collection period 32. Creditors turnover ratio 33. Assets turnover ratio: (i) Total assets turnover (ii) Fixed assets turnover (iii) Current assets turnover (iv) Capital turnover (v) Working capital turnover	34. Earning per share (EPS) 35. Dividend per share (DPS) 36. Payout ratio 37. Price earning (P/E) ratio 38. Yield 39. Market value to book value ratio

EXHIBIT 7.3-B Formula (e) for calculation of the ratios

Sl. No.	*Name of the Ratio*	*Formula*
1	Current ratio	Current assets/Current liabilities
2	Quick ratio (or liquid ratio or acid test ratio)	Quick assets/quick liabilities = (Current assets stock)/(Current liabilities-Bank overdraft)
3	Absolute liquid ratio	(Quick assets-debtors)/(Quick liabilities – liabilities foregone by creditors + any new liabilities subsequently reported)
4	Defensive interval ratio	Quick assets/projected daily cash requirements = Quick assets/(Projected cash operating expenses of the year ÷ No. of days in a year)
5	Net working capital ratio	Net working capital/Net assets = Current assets – Current liabilities)/(Gross block + Net working capital)
6	Gross profit ratio	(Gross profit/sales) × 100
7	Operating profit ratio	(EBIT/Sales) × 100
8	Net profit ratio	(PAT/Sales) × 100
9	Cost of goods sold ratio	(Cost of goods sold/Net sales) × 100
10	Operating expenses ratio	{(Administrative expenses + Selling expenses)/Net sales} × 100
11	Administrative expenses ratio	(Administrative expenses/Net sales) × 100
12	Selling expenses ratio	(Selling expenses/Net sales) × 100
13	Operating ratio	{(Cost of goods sold + Operating expenses)/Net sales} × 100
14	Financial expenses ratio	(Financial expenses/Net sales) × 100
15	Return on total assets (ROTA)	(PAT/Average total assets) × 100. Also, {EBIT (1 – t)/Average total assets} × 100
16	Return on capital employed (ROCE)	(PAT/Average capital employed) × 100 Also, {EBIT (1 – t)/Average capital assets} × 100
17	Return on shareholders' equity (ROSE)	PAT/Average shareholders' equity* × 100 (*Note: Shareholders' equity includes equity share capital, Reserves and surpluses, share premium, reduced by accumulated losses)
18	Return On Investment (ROI)	Net profit margin × Investment turnover $\frac{\text{PAT}}{\text{Sales}} \times \frac{\text{Sales}}{\text{Total assets}}$
19	Debt equity ratio	Long-term debt/shareholders equity = (Bonds + Debentures + Long-term loans)/Equity share capital + Reserves and surpluses + profits.
20	Debt to total capital	Long-term debt/(Equity + Preference + Long-term debt capital)
21	Debt to total assets	Long-term debt/total assets
22	Proprietary ratio	Proprietor's fund/total assets
23	Capital gearing ratio	Net worth fixed interest bearing funds including preference share capital
24	Interest coverage ratio	EBIT/Interest
25	Dividend coverage ratio	PAT/Dividend on preference share capital
26	Total coverage ratio	(EBIT + Lease payment)/(Interest + Lease payments + {(Preference dividend + Installment of principal) ÷ (1 – t)}

(*Contd.*)

Sl. No.	Name of the Ratio	Formula
27	Total cash flow coverage ratio	(EBIT + Lease payment + Depreciation + Non-cash expenses)/ [(Lease payment + Interest) + {(Principal payment) ÷ (1 – t)}]
28	Debt service coverage ratio	PAT + Depreciation + Interest + Other non-cash expenses)/ (Interest + Term loan installment)
29	Inventory turnover ratio	Cost of goods sold/Average inventory Also, Sales/closing stock
30	Debtors turnover ratio	Credit sales/Average debtors Also, credit sales/(Average bills receivable)
31	Average collection period	Months (or days) in a year/Debtors turnover ratio
32	Creditors turnover ratio	Average creditors/Average daily purchases
33	(i) Total assets turnover (ii) Fixed assets turnover (iii) Current assets turnover (iv) Capital turnover (v) Working capital turnover	(i) Cost of goods sold (or sales)/Average total assets (ii) Cost of goods sold (or sales)/Average fixed assets (iii) Cost of goods sold (or sales)/Average current assets (iv) Cost of goods sold (or sales)/Average capital employed (v) Cost of goods sold (or sales)/Net working capital
34	Earning per share (EPS)	PAT/No. of equity shares outstanding
35	Dividend per share (DPS)	Profit distributed as dividend/No. of equity share outstanding
36	Payout ratio	DPS/EPS
37	Price earning (P/E) ratio	Market value of share/EPS
38	Yield	(Dividend + Price change)/initial price Also, DPS/Market price per share
39	Market value to book value ratio	Market price per share/book value per share

ILLUSTRATION 7.3

From the following current assets and current liabilities positions of firm A and firm B as on 31st March 2023 and 2024, comment on the two firms' short-term liquidity position in terms of current ratio:

(Fig. in ₹'000)

Current Liabilities					*Current Assets*				
Items	A		B		*Items*	A		B	
	2023	2024	2023	2024		2023	2024	2023	2024
Creditors	120	155	186	290	Stock	150	120	200	220
Bills payable	100	75	124	105	Debtors	120	170	250	250
Bank overdraft	—	20	—	—	Bills receivables	30	60	120	180
					Cash in hand and at bank	50	10	80	150

SOLUTION

Current ratio is calculated by dividing current assets by current liabilities. Exhibit 7.4 contains totals of the current assets, current liabilities and current ratios in respect of firm – A and B for the years 2023 and 2024.

EXHIBIT 7.4 Current assets, current liabilities and current ratios of A and B

	Firm A		*Firm B*	
	2023	*2024*	*2023*	*2024*
Current assets (₹)	3,50,000	3,60,000	6,50,000	8,00,000
Current liabilities (₹)	2,20,000	250	3,10,000	3,95,000
Current ratio	1.59:1	1.44:1	2.10:1	2.03:1

If current ratio is taken as the only measure of short-term liquidity, it is obvious that firm B maintains a sound short-term liquidity position compared to firm A. Firm B maintains its short-term liquidity position little over the rule of thumb of 2:1 in both the years whereas firm A has not been able to do so. Moreover, the short-term solvency position of firm A has further deteriorated in the year 2024, i.e., 1.44:1 as against 1.59:1 in 2023. Comparatively, firm B is in stronger position to meet its current obligations than firm A.

2. Quick ratio: Quick ratio, also called as acid-test ratio or liquid ratio, is a stringent measure of the firm's short-term liquidity position. It is calculated by dividing quick assets by quick liabilities. Quick assets are current assets *less* inventories and quick liabilities are current liabilities *less* bank overdraft. A standard ratio of 1:1 is considered as ideal quick ratio. The logic behind calculating quick ratio is to judge the ability the firm to convert its current assets quickly into cash so as to meet its current liabilities.

ILLUSTRATION 7.4

Taking Illustration 7.3, calculate and comment on the quick ratios of firm A and B.

SOLUTION

The calculated values of quick assets, quick liabilities and quick ratios for the year 2023 and 2024 for firm A and B may be arranged as in Exhibit 7.5:

EXHIBIT 7.5 Quick assets, quick liabilities and quick ratios of firm A and B

	Firm A		*Firm B*	
	2023	*2024*	*2023*	*2024*
Quick assets (₹)	2,00,000	2,40,000	4,50,000	5,80,000
Quick liabilities (₹)	2,20,000	2,30,000	3,10,000	3,95,000
Quick ratio	0.91:1	1.04:1	1.45:1	1.47:1

Short-term solvency position, measured in terms of quick ratio, has been well above the rule of thumb of 1:1 in case of firm B. For firm A too the quick ratio is close to the acceptable standard (0.91:1) in the year 2023 and is marginally above the standard (1.04:1) in 2024. Therefore, short-term solvency positions of both firm A and B in terms of quick ratio may be considered as satisfactory although firm B maintains a stronger liquidity position in comparison to firm A.

3. Absolute liquidity ratio: Absolute liquidity ratio, often called as super quick ratio, is the most vigorous measure of the firm's short-term liquidity position. It is calculated by dividing absolute liquid assets by absolute liquid liabilities. Absolute liquid assets are quick assets *less* debtors, i.e., current assets *less* stock less debtors and absolute liquid liabilities are quick liabilities *less* any unclaimed liabilities i.e., current liabilities *less* bank overdraft *less* any portion of the current liabilities that might be foregone by the creditors. A ratio of 0.5:1 is considered as satisfactory absolute liquidity ratio. This because not all the short-term liabilities fall due for payment on the same date, and therefore a firm which maintains 50 paise of most liquid assets such cash and marketable securities can serve 100 paise of current liabilities.

ILLUSTRATION 7.5

Considering illustration 7.3, absolute liquidity ratios for firm A and firm B may be calculated as given in Exhibit 7.6.

Exhibit 7.6 Absolute liquid assets, absolute liquid liabilities and absolute liquidity ratio of firm A and B

	Firm A		*Firm B*	
	2023	*2024*	*2023*	*2024*
Absolute liquid assets (₹)	80,000	70,000	2,00,000	3,30,000
Absolute liquid liabilities(₹)	2,20,000	2,30,000	3,10,000	3,95,000
Absolute liquidity ratio	0.36:1	0.30:1	0.65:1	0.84:1

Exhibit 7.6 clearly shows that the short-term solvency position measured in terms of absolute liquidity ratio is strong in case of firm B and is weak in case of firm A.

4. Defensive internal ratio: Defensive internal ratio is calculated to determine the firm's liquidity position in terms of its ability to meet projected daily expenditure from operations. It is calculated by dividing quick assets by projected daily cash requirements, where projected daily cash requirements is the projected cash operating expenses of the whole year divided by number of days in the year. Cash operating expenses include cost of goods sold without depreciation and administrative and selling expenses payable in cash. The defensive interval ratio measures the time period for which the firm can operate on the basis of present liquid assets without resorting to the next year's revenue. The higher the ratio, the better it is, since it reflects the ability of the firm to meet its cash requirements for a longer period of time.

ILLUSTRATION 7.6

The projected cash operating expenses of two firms – F_1 and F_2 for the year 2024 are ₹80,00,000 and ₹216,00,000, respectively. If the quick assets of the two firms for the said year are ₹20,00,000 and ₹30,00,000, respectively, what is their liquidity position in terms of defensive interval ratio?

SOLUTION

Defensive interval ratio = Quick assets ÷ Projected daily cash requirements
= Quick assets ÷ (Annual cash operating expenses ÷ No. of days in a year).

Therefore, defensive interval ratio for firm F_1 is 40 days, i.e., ₹20,00,000 ÷ (₹1,80,00,000 ÷ 360 days), assuming that a year has 360 working days.

For firm F_2, the defensive interval ratio is 50 days, i.e., ₹30,00,000 ÷ (₹2,16,00,000 ÷ 360 days).

In terms of defensive interval ratio, it is found that the liquidity position of firm F_2 is stronger than that of firm F_1 as the former can support its operations for 50 days as against the latter's 40 days without having recourse to the next year's revenue.

5. Net working capital ratio: Net working capital ratio is calculated by dividing net working capital, i.e., current assets *less* current liabilities by net assets (or by capital employed), to assess the firm's liquidity position and its potential reservoir of funds. Between two firms, the one having the larger net working capital will have greater ability to meet its current obligations.

ILLUSTRATION 7.7

The current assets, current liabilities and capital employed in two firms – P and Q are as follows:

	Firm P	*Firm Q*
	₹	₹
Current assets	65,000	35,000
Current liabilities	39,000	20,000
Current employed	1,30,000	1,00,000

Calculate and comment on the two firms' net working capital ratios.

SOLUTION

The net working capital of firm P is ₹26,000 and of firm Q is ₹15,000. Their corresponding net working capital ratio is 0.20 and 0.15. As firm P has got higher net working capital in comparison to firm Q, its liquidity position is considered to be more stronger than Q. Working capital ratio of firm P too is greater than that of firm Q. The liquidity position of firm P is therefore stronger than that of Q.

B. Profitability ratios

The various ratios calculated under the profitability ratios category as contained in Exhibit 7.3 are: gross profit ratio, operating profit ratio, next profit ratio, cost of goods sold ratio, operating expenses ratio, administrative expenses ratio, selling expenses ratio, operating ratio, financial expenses ratio, return on total asset ratio, return on capital employed ratio, return on shareholders' equity and return on investment (ROI) based on Du Pont's analysis.

6. Gross profit ratio: Gross profit ratio is a measure of the firm's profitability wherein the owner, management, creditors as well as competitors are interested. It is calculated by dividing gross profits by sales, expressed in percentage.

Mathematically, gross profit ratio = (Gross profits ÷ Sales) × 100.

Gross profit is the outcome of the relationship between volume of sales, prices and costs of production. A change in any of these factors can cause a corresponding change in the gross profit margin.

A high gross profit ratio generally mean better management of the firm in terms of its lower cost of production other things such as inventory valuation and pricing being fair. A low gross profit ratio may be taken as a warning signal for the management and hence may call for a careful and detailed consideration of the factors responsible for such low margin. There is no rule of thumb for the gross profit ratio as such, but a trend analysis and/or inter firm comparison would lead to drawing useful inferences.

ILLUSTRATION 7.8

Gross profits of firm K for the year 2020 through 2024 has been ₹45,000, ₹66,600, ₹78,000, ₹92,400 and ₹1,08,000 respectively as against the corresponding sales of ₹1,50,000, ₹1,80,000, ₹2,00,000, ₹2,10,000 and ₹2,40,000 said for the period. Calculate and comment on the firm's profitability position measured in terms of gross profit ratio.

SOLUTION

Exhibit 7.7 may be constructed to display firm K's gross profit ratios for the period 2020–2024:

EXHIBIT 7.7 Gross profits, sales and gross profit ratios of firm K

Year	*2020*	*2021*	*2022*	*2023*	*2024*
Gross profits (₹)	45,000	66,600	78,000	92,400	1,08,000
Sales (₹)	1,50,000	1,80,000	2,00,000	2,10,000	2,40,000
Gross profit ratio (%) [(=Gross profit/sales) × 100]	30	37	39	44	45

The firm's profitability, measured in terms of gross profit ratio, has improved over the years from 30% in 2020 to 45% in 2024. This improvement in the profitability could be due to decreased cost of production as a result of managerial efficiency and/or increased market price of the product.

7. Net profit ratio: Net profit ratio, calculated as net profit to sales, and also profit after tax to sales, and expressed in percentage, is a measure of the firm's managerial ability to provide reasonable compensation to the owners for providing their capital at risk and also to withstand adverse economic conditions due to falling demand, reduced selling price and increased cost of production.

A higher net profit ratio is preferred to a lower ratio as it would mean higher managerial efficiency and better ability of the firm to recover from its revenues the cost of merchandise or services, the operating expenses and the cost of borrowed funds, leaving reasonable margin on the capital invested.

ILLUSTRATION 7.9

Other things remaining constant as in Illustration 7.8, if the net profits of the firm for the period happens to be ₹27,000, ₹45,000, ₹60,000, ₹67,200, and ₹84,000, what is the net profit ratio of firm K?

SOLUTION

Applying the formula for net profit ratio as 'net profit/sales × 100', firm K's net profit ratios for the year 2020 through 2024 are found to be 18%, 25%, 30%, 32% and 35%, respectively. This implies that the firm's profitability has improved over the years and it is now in a better position to reward its owners.

8. Expenses ratio: A variation of the profitability ratio in relation to sales of the firm is the expenses ratio. In general expenses ratio is derived by dividing expenses by sales and expressing it in terms of percentage. As expenses are often categorized into cost of goods sold, administrative, selling, operating and financial expenses, ratios in relation to each of them can be calculated as under:

(i) Cost goods sold ratio = (Cost of goods sold/Net sales) × 100
(ii) Administrative expenses ratio = (Administrative expenses/Net sales) × 100
(iii) Selling expenses ratio = (Selling expenses/Net sales) × 100
(iv) Operating expenses ratio = (Administrative + Selling expenses)/Net sales × 100
(v) Financial expenses ratio = (Financial expenses/Net sales) × 100

In addition, operating ratio is often calculated as:

(Cost of goods sold + Operating expenses/Net sales) × 100.

Each of the above (expenses) ratios has a bearing on the profit margin of the firm. Higher the expenses ratios, lower will be the profitability ratio of the firm. Further, the expenses ratios have their own internal relationship as well. For example, the cost of goods sold ratio would mean the percentage of sales consumed by it for its recovery and the portion of sales it leaves for recovery of administrative, selling and financial expenses.

For the firm, lower these expenses ratios, better it is. There is no rule of thumb of course for these ratios, but a trend analysis, inter-firm and intra-firm comparisons and comparison with industry average will help the analyst drawing meaningful inferences.

ILLUSTRATION 7.10

The following figures relate to Heavy Weight Industries Ltd. as on 31st March 2022, 2023 and 2024.

(*Fig. in* ₹' 000)

	2022	*2023*	*2024*
Sales	550	660	725
Cost goods sold	264	297	348
Administrative expenses	88	132	174
Selling and distribution expenses	44	99	87
Interest	22	33	25

You are required to calculate appropriate expenses ratios and comment as the same.

SOLUTION

Exhibit 7.8 may be constructed to display calculated expenses ratios of Heavy Weight Industries Ltd. for the year 2022 through 2024:

EXHIBIT 7.8 Expenses ratios of Heavy Weight Industries Ltd.

Ratios (%)	*2022*	*2023*	*2024*
Cost of goods sold ratio	48	45	48
Administrative expenses ratio	16	20	24
Selling and distribution expenses	8	15	12
Financial expenses (interest) ratio	4	5	8
Operating expenses ratio	24	35	36
Gross profit ratio	52	55	52
Net profit ratio	24	15	8

It is observed from Exhibit 7.8 that operating expenses of the firm has increased over the years from 24% to 36%. This increase has been due mainly to a clear cut increase in the administrative expenses (from 16% to 24%). The cost of goods sold of the firm has remained 45% and above (48% in case of year 2022 and 2024). This implies that the gross profit ratio of the firm varies between the range of 52% to 55% against which total of the operating and financial expenses are to be adjusted to get the surplus profit (net profit) before tax. The net profit margin of the firm has got drastically reduced from 24% in 2022 to 8% in 2024. This is because of increased operating and financial expenses. A fall in the profit before tax is an indicative of the existence of financial risk in the business and consequently the managerial inefficiencies.

9. Return on total assets (ROTA): Return on total assets is another measure of the firm's profitability in relation to its investment on assets. Depending upon the variations in the concepts used to defining net profits and assets, return on total assets (ROTA) assume the following forms:

(i) ROTA = (Net profits after tax/Average total assets) × 100
(ii) ROTA = [(Net profit after tax + Interest)/Average total assets] × 100
(iii) ROTA = [(Net profit after tax + Interest)/Average tangible assets] × 100
(iv) ROTA = [(Net profit after tax + Interest)/Average fixed assets] × 100
(v) ROTA = [{(Net profit after tax + Interest (1 – t)}/Average total assets or tangible assets or fixed assets] × 100

The ratios calculated as above would help the firm determine how efficient its management is in terms of assets productivity. There is no standard benchmark as to what should be an ideal ROTA ratio. However, industry average and intra and inter-firm comparisons would therefore be useful for judging the performance of the firm with respect to ROTA.

ILLUSTRATION 7.11

Following is the abstracts of the balance sheets of Electronics Co. Ltd:

(Fig. in ₹' 000)

	31.03.2023	3.03.2024
Fixed assets	260	320
Total assets	400	550
Net profit after tax	—	75

You are required to comment on the company's return on investment based on ROA.

SOLUTION

The company's average fixed assets and average total assets are found to be ₹2,90,000 and ₹4,75,000, respectively. Therefore, its return respectively on fixed assets and on total assets shall be 25.86% and 15.79%. These figures indicate that the company's fixed assets are more productive than the total assets.

10. Return on capital employed (ROCE): Return on capital employed is a measure of the firm's profitability based on long-term capital employed contrary to total assets. Long term capital employed is long term liabilities plus owners' equity, or alternatively, net working capital plus fixed assets.

Depending upon the concepts used to defining profits and also capital employed, the following variations are generally observed in calculating return on capital employed (ROCE) ratios:

(i) ROCE = (PAT ÷ Average capital employed) × 100
(ii) ROCE = (EBIT ÷ Average capital employed) × 100
(iii) ROCE = [{PAT + Interest (1 – t)} ÷ Average capital employed] × 100
(iv) ROCE = [PAT + Interest) ÷ Average total capital employed – Average intangible assets)] × 100

A comparison of ROCE ratio with similar firms, with the industry average and over time, i.e., trend analysis would be ideal in judging the efficiency of the firm in using long-term funds. The higher the ROCE, the more efficient is the firm's management in the use of long term capital.

ILLUSTRATION 7.12

The assets and liabilities position of two firms P and Q as on 31.03.2024 are as follows:

(Fig. in ₹' 000)

Liabilities	A	B	*Assets*	A	B
Share capital	250	350	Intangible assets	108	88
Reserves and surplus	120	150	Fixed assets less depreciation	515	645
Profits	75	105	Current assets	202	192
Long-term debt	245	195			
Creditors	135	125			
Total	825	925	Total	825	925

If the EBIT of Company P and that of Q is calculated at ₹2,76,000 and ₹3,44,000 respectively, what is the ROCE of the companies?

SOLUTION

Based on the available data, ROCE for each of the company can be calculated as:

(EBIT/Capital employed) × 100, where capital employed shall be total of share capital, reserves and surpluses, profits and long-term debt, which amounts to ₹6,90,000 in case of P and ₹8,00,000 in case of Q.

ROCE for P and Q shall therefore be 40% (i.e., ₹2,76,000/₹6,90,000 × 100) and 43% (i.e., ₹3,44,000/₹8,00,000 × 100).

The return on investment, expressed as EBIT in relation to capital employed, is higher in case of company Q as compared to company P.

11. Return on shareholders' fund: Return on shareholders' fund, often called as shareholders' equity, is a step forward in determining the profitability of the firm in relation to the return exclusively on shareholders' equity unlike ROCE where return on total capital employed i.e., debt and equity taken together is calculated.

Depending further upon the concept used to defining shareholders' equity such as equity share capital, reserves and surpluses and preference share capital taken together or only the net worth, return on shareholders' can be:

(i) Return on total shareholders' equity, which is equal to (PAT/Average total shareholders' equity) × 100.

(ii) Return on ordinary shareholders' equity, i.e., return on Net worth, which is equal to {(PAT – Preference dividend)/(Average ordinary shareholders' equity or net worth)} × 100.

Both the ratios are important measures of the firm's profitability and its managerial efficiency in providing satisfactory return on the owners' capital used. A trend analysis, inter-firm and industry average comparisons of the ratio(s) will help in drawing useful inferences about the performance of the firm. A higher ratio of ROCE however would always be favoured.

ILLUSTRATION 7.13

The following figures have been extracted from the financial statements of two firms – Z_1 and Z_2:

(Fig. in ₹'000)

	Z_1	Z_2
Equity share capital	150	150
15% preference share capital	200	300
Reserves and surpluses	75	80
Profit after tax (PAT)	70	95

Calculate and comment on the two firms' return on shareholders' equity.

SOLUTION

Exhibit 7.9 contains the calculated ratios in respect of the two firms' return on shareholders' equity:

EXHIBIT 7.9 Return of shareholders' equity

	Firm Z_1	*Firm Z_2*
(a) Profit after tax	70,000	95,000
(b) Profit after tax and preference dividend	40,000	50,000
(c) Total shareholders' equity (Equity share capital + Reserves and surpluses + Preference share capital)	4,25,000	5,30,000
(d) Equity shareholders' fund (Equity share capital + Reserves and surpluses)	2,25,000	2,30,000
(i) Return on total shareholders' equity, (i.e., (a)/(c) × 100)	16.47%	17.92%
(ii) Return on ordinary shareholders equity, (i.e., (b)/(d) × 100)	17.78%	21.74%

It is evident from Exhibit 7.9 that firm Z_2 gives higher rewards both to total shareholders and to ordinary shareholders compared to the return given by firm Z_1 to both the categories of investors in context. The efficiency of Z_2 in terms of return on shareholders' equity is therefore higher than that of Z_1.

12. Du Pont analysis: Du Pont analysis is an analysis of the overall profitability and operational efficiency of the firm. The analysis is based on the pioneering work of the US based Du Pont company wherein the earning power of the firm is judged through calculation of return on investment (ROI) by decomposing the net profit margin and the total assets turnover. ROI as per Du Pont is given by:

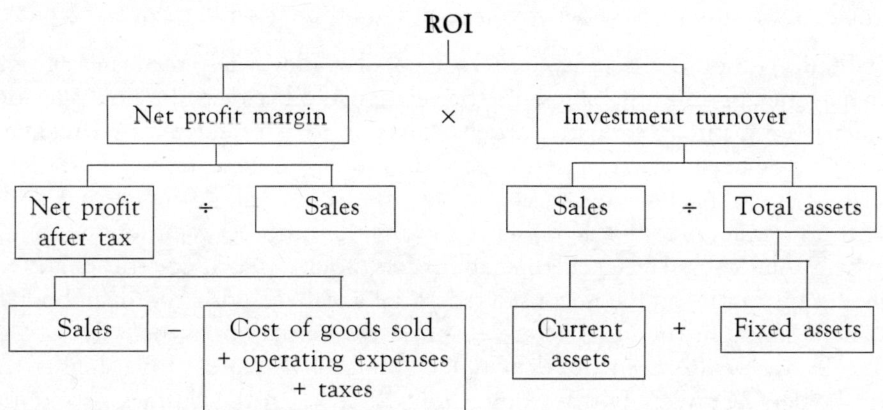

The ratio and the corresponding relationship presented under Du Pont analysis indicates that the performance of the firm can be improved by generating more profit margin per rupee of sales or by generating more sales per rupee of investment or by both.

ILLUSTRATION 7.14

The following figures relate to three firms A, B and C:

	Firm A	*Firm B*	*Firm C*
Total assets (₹)	2,50,000	2,50,000	2,50,000
Total sales (₹)	10,00,000	20,00,000	15,00,000
Total profit after tax (₹)	5,00,000	5,00,000	6,00,000

Make a Du Pont analysis on the earning power of the three firms.

Du Pont analysis of the ROIs in respect of firm A, B and C has been presented in Exhibit 7.10:

SOLUTION

EXHIBIT 7.10 Du Pont analysis

	Du Pont analysis		
	Firm A	*Firm B*	*Firm C*
(a) Net profit margin = (PAT ÷ sales) × 100	50%	25%	40%
(b) Investment turnover = (Sales ÷ total assets) × 100	400%	800%	600%
(c) Return on investment = {(a) × (b)} × 100	200%	200%	240%

It is evident from Exhibit 7.10 that the overall earning power of firm A and B is the same, i.e., 200% each and that of firm C is higher at 240%. Whereas, firm A has higher profit margin 50% as against firm B's 25% and firm C's 40%, firm B has higher investment turnover 800% compared to firm A's 400% and firm C's 600%. It is further clear form the ROI equation that earning powers of firms can be affected by two variable, profit margin and investment turnover.

C. Solvency Ratios

Solvency ratios are calculated to judge the long-term liquidity position of the firm. As indicated in Exhibit 7.3-A, included under the solvency ratios are the debt-equity ratio, debt to total capital, debt to total assets, propitiatory ratio, interest coverage ratio, dividend coverage ratio, total coverage ratio, total cash flow coverage ratio and debt service coverage ratio.

13. Debt-Equity ratio: Debt-equity ratio is a popular and widely used measure of the firm's long-term solvency position. It represents the relationship between the firm's borrowed capital and its ownership capital. Normally, a debt-equity ratio is calculated by dividing long-term debt by shareholders' equity. A variation of the ratio is the inclusion of short-term debt, i.e., current liabilities in the long term debt to get total debt and to divide it by shareholders' equity. A third variation of the debt equity ratio is the ratio between long-term debt to total capital, where total capital is equal to shareholders' equity plus long-term debt.

A debt equity ratio of 1:1 is considered to be ideal for both the debt holders' and the equity holders' stakes in the business are equal. Any alternation to this such as a debt-equity ratio of 2:1 or 3:1 would mean the debt holders' stake is twice or thrice higher than that of the equity holders'. Conversely, the equity holders' stake in the business is one-half or one-third of that of the debt holders'. A higher debt-equity ratio would be favoured by the equity holders in order to derive the benefits associated with financial leverage. The debt holders would however favour inclusion of more and more equity capital in the capital structure so that of their investments are safe should the firm go for liquidation. It is for this reason that a debt equity ratio of 1:1 is recommended which puts both the debt holders and the equity holders on equal footing.

ILLUSTRATION 7.15

The balance sheets of Sharada Associates for the years 2020 to 2024 are as follows:

(Fig. in ₹'000)

Liabilities	2020	2021	2022	2023	2024
Share capital	150	150	200	200	200
Reserves and surpluses	100	120	135	180	195
Long-term loan	60	–	–	80	65
Debentures	250	300	315	340	300
Current liabilities	140	230	250	300	340
	700	800	900	1100	1100
Assets:					
Fixed assets *less* depreciation	460	500	575	700	705
Current assets	240	300	325	400	395
	700	800	900	1100	1100

You are required to calculate and comment on the long-term solvency position of the firm.

SOLUTION

Associate's long-term solvency position calculated in three different forms of debt-equity ratios, has been reflected in Exhibit 7.11.

EXHIBIT 7.11 Long-term solvency position of Sharada Associates

(Fig. in ₹'000)

	2020	2021	2022	2023	2024
(a) Long-term debt (Long-term loan plus debentures)	310	300	315	420	365
(b) Total debt (Long-term debt plus current liabilities)	450	530	565	720	705
(c) Shareholders' equity (Share capital plus reserves and surpluses)	250	270	335	380	395
(d) Total capital (Shareholders' equity plus long term debt)	560	570	650	800	760
Debt-equity ratios:					
(i) Long-term debt to shareholders' equity (a ÷ c)	1.24:1	1.11:1	0.94:1	1.11:1	0.92:1
(ii) Total debt to shareholders' equity (b ÷ c)	1.80:1	1.96:1	1.69:1	1.89:1	1.78:1
(iii) Long-term debt to total capital (a ÷ d)	0.55:1	0.53:1	0.48:1	0.53:1	0.48:1

Evidently, Sharada Associate's long-term debt in relation to shareholders' equity has remained almost close to the recommended standard of 1:1. In fact three out of the five years under consideration, the firm's long-term debt in relation to shareholders' equity has been little over 1 and in the remaining two years it is slightly under 1. As regards, total debt to shareholders' equity, total debt has remained over 169% of the shareholders' equity throughout. In the year 2008, the said ratio was the highest at 1.96:1. The long-term debt in relation to total capital has been around 50% in all the years. Overall, the firm's long-term solvency position has been satisfactory.

14. Debt to total assets ratio: Debt to total assets ratio, calculated by dividing total debt by total assets, is a measure of the portion of total assets financed by debt. In case of Sharada Associate, the said ratio is found to be 44.29%, 37.5%, 35%, 38.18% and 33.18% respectively for the years 2020 through 2024.

15. Proprietary ratio: Proprietary ratio is calculated by dividing proprietors' fund (i.e, the owners' fund) by total assets to known the portion of total assets financed by ownership fund. For Sharada Associate, the said ratio is found to be 35.71%, 33.75%, 37.22%, 34.55%, and 35.91% respectively for the years 2020 through 2024.

16. Interest coverage ratio: Interest coverage ratio, also called as time-interest earned ratio, is calculated by dividing EBIT by interest, and is used as a measure of the firm's ability to make interest payments. The ratio, expressed in 'times' indicates as to how many times the interest charges are covered by EBIT from which they will be paid. From the creditors' point of view, higher the coverage ratio, better it is, as higher interest coverage ratio would mean better ability of the firm to meet fixed interest charges.

ILLUSTRATION 7.16

If a firm reports ₹4,25,000 as its EBIT and ₹1,35,000 as its interest liabilities on bonds and debenture, and further ₹1,60,000 as its depreciation, comment on the firm's ability to meet its interest liabilities.

SOLUTION

The firm's ability to handle its fixed interest charges liabilities are best judged through interest coverage ratio which is EBIT divided by interest.

For the firm in context, interest coverage ratio based on 'EBIT/Interest' is found to be 3.15 times, i.e., ₹4,25,000 ÷ ₹1,35,000. This indicates that even if the firm's EBIT falls by three times, i.e., it becomes just one-third of the present amount, still the firm would be able to pay its interest liabilities. There is of course no benchmark as to what value of interest coverage (ratio) will ideal be except for the fact that higher the ratio, better it is for the creditors. A higher interest coverage ratio may also mean unused debt capacity which the firm's management should check in.

Treatment of depreciation: Depreciation being a non-cash item does not result in the outflow of cash. As such an amount equal to depreciation may also be taken as additional fund available for serving the debt. Interest coverage ratio in such case becomes (EBIT + Depreciation)/ Interest or EBDIT/Interest.

In the above illustration therefore interest coverage ratio, after incorporation of the value of depreciation, becomes 4.33 times, (i.e., ₹4,25,000 + ₹1,60,000)/₹1,35,000, which is still higher than the interest coverage ratio calculated under EBIT/Interest.

17. Dividend coverage ratio: Dividend coverage ratio, calculated by dividing PAT by preference dividend, is a measure of the firm's ability to pay preference dividend which carry a pre-fixed rate of return. As such, preference shareholders would favour a higher dividend coverage ratio.

ILLUSTRATION 7.17

Verification of the books of account of a firm reveals that its post tax profit was ₹1,95,000 against an equity capital of ₹1,00,000 divided into 10,000 equity shares of ₹10 each and a preference capital of ₹5,00,000 divided into 50,000 12% preference shares of ₹10 each. Comment on the firm's ability to pay preference dividend.

SOLUTION

The firm's ability to pay preference dividend can be judged through its dividend coverage ratio which is PAT ÷ preference dividend.

In the given illustration, profit after tax (PAT) is ₹1,95,000 and preference dividend is 12% of ₹5,00,000, i.e., ₹60,000. Hence, its dividend coverage ratio is ₹1,95,000 ÷ ₹60,000 or 3.25 times. This indicates that even if the firm's post tax profit gets reduced to one-third of its present level, it will still be able to pay its preference dividend.

18. Total coverage ratio: Total coverage ratio helps determine the firm's ability to meet all its long-term obligations such as interest on term loans, repayment of principals, preference dividend, and lease payments, as against the interest coverage or dividend coverage ratio which satisfies a specific segment only, i.e., either the bond holders or the preference holders.

Calculated as (EBIT + lease payment) / {Interest + lease payment + (Preference dividend + Installment of principal) ÷ (1 – t)} a higher total coverage ratio would mean a stronger position of the firm in meeting its total long-term obligations.

ILLUSTRATION 7.18

A firm provides the following details:

EBIT	₹4,18,000	Interest	₹50,000
Preference dividend	₹95,000	Lease rentals	₹1,20,000
Repayment of principal	₹85,000	Applicable tax rates	25%

What is the firm's total coverage ratio?

SOLUTION

Total coverage ratio is given by (EBIT + lease payment) / {Interest + lease payment + (Preference dividend + Installment of principal) ÷ (1 – t)}.

The firm's total coverage ratio therefore is 1.31., i.e., (₹4,18,000 + ₹1,20,000) ÷ [(₹50,000 + ₹1,20,000) + {(₹95,000 + ₹85,000) ÷ (1 – 0.25)}].

Whereas the firm having a total coverage ratio of 1.31:1 can meet its obligations, any improvement to 1.31 will put it in more comfortable position as regards serving total debts.

19. Total cash flow coverage ratio (CFCR): Total cash flow coverage ratio calculated as, (EBIT + Lease payment + Depreciation + Non-cash expenses) / [(Lease payment + Interest) + {(Principal payment) ÷ (1 – t)}], is taken as an ideal test of the firm's ability to meet its long term obligations *on time*. A timely payment of the obligation is possible only when the firm's earnings are supported by immediate cash. It is for this reason that the cash flow coverage ratio is calculated. A higher ratio of the kind is preferred as higher the cash flow coverage ratio, better is the firm's ability to serve its long-term obligations.

ILLUSTRATION7.19

Following are the extracts from the books of S. Mittal & Sons:

EBIT	₹6,80,000	Interest	₹1,80,000
Depreciation	₹3,70,000	Principal repayment	₹3,60,000
Preference dividend	₹60,000	Applicable tax rates	25%

Comment on its total cash flow coverage ratio.

SOLUTION

Total cash flow coverage ratio (CFCR) is given by (EBIT + Lease payment + Depreciation + Non-cash expenses)/[(Lease payment + Interest) + {(Principal payment) ÷ (1 – t)}].

For S. Mittal & Sons, the total cash flow coverage ratio is found to be 1.71:1, i.e., (₹6,80,000 + ₹3,70,000) ÷ [₹1,80,000 + {₹3,60,000 ÷ (1 – 0.4)} + {₹60,000 ÷ (1 – 0.4)}] or ₹10,50,000 ÷ ₹9,80,000.

Although there is no prescribed rule of thumb as regards total cash flow coverage ratio, Mittal & sons' CFCR of 1.71:1 may be considered satisfactory as because it is able to maintain ₹1.71 cash inflows as against every ₹1.00 long-term financial obligations. Any improvement over 1.71:1 will put the firm in further stronger position to meet its fixed financial obligations.

20. Debt service coverage ratio (DSCR): Debt service coverage ratio, calculated as PAT + Depreciation + Interest + Other non-cash expenses)/(Interest + Term loan installment), is considered as a more comprehensive and apt measure of the firm's ability to serve its debt. Higher the debt service coverage ratio, better it is for the firm. A ratio of 2:1 is however taken as satisfactory DSCR by lending financial institutions.

ILLUSTRATION 7.20

If profit after tax, depreciation, interest on term loans, and the corresponding amount of loan installment as reported by a firm for a year are ₹8,50,000, ₹2,50,000, ₹2,20,000 and ₹4,30,000, respectively, comment on its debt service coverage ratio.

SOLUTION

Debt service coverage ratio is given by PAT + Depreciation + Interest + Other non cash expenses)/(Interest + Term loan installment).

For the given firm, debt service coverage ratio comes to 2.03:1, i.e., (₹8,50,000 + ₹2,50,000 + ₹2,20,000) ÷ (₹2,20,000 + ₹4,30,000).

The firm's debt service coverage ratio is marginally higher then 2:1, the benchmark followed by lending financial institutions. The ratio may therefore be taken as satisfactory.

D. Activity Ratios

Activity ratios are calculated to judge the managerial efficiency in terms of asset management of the firm. As contained in Exhibit 7.3-A, included under the activity ratios are inventory turnover, debtors turnover, average collection period, creditors turnover and assets turnover ratios.

21. Inventory turnover ratio: Inventory turnover ratio, often called as stock turnover ratio, is calculated by dividing cost of goods sold by average inventory to measure the firm's selling efficiency. The ratio which is expressed in 'times' indicates how quickly inventory is replaced, i.e., converted into sales during the year. Whereas, there is no rule of thumb as to what should be an ideal inventory turnover ratio, a trend analysis and/or a comparison with industry average would lead to drawing a better inference of the firm's performance as regards inventory turnover. A high inventory turnover ratio though implies better inventory management and is therefore preferred to a low inventory turnover, a very high inventory turnover may also mean low inventory holding and stock out. Similarly, a very low inventory turnover may signify excessive inventory holding and slow inventory movement. Hence, both high and low inventory turnover should be avoided.

ILLUSTRATION 7.21

Following figures have been extracted from the books of firm A and B:

	A ₹	B ₹
Cost of goods sold	12,00,000	15,00,000
Opening stock	2,00,000	5,00,000
Closing stock	3,50,000	3,50,000

Comment on the two firms' inventory management efficiency.

SOLUTION

A firm's inventory management efficiency is primarily assessed through its inventory turnover ratio. The inventory turnover ratio is calculated by dividing cost of goods sold by average inventory, where average inventory is (opening stock + closing stock) ÷ 2. Inventory turnover ratio for firm A and B thus comes out to be 4.36 times and 3.53 times, respectively, i.e., ₹12,00,000 ÷ {(₹2,00,000 + ₹3,50,000)/2} for A and ₹15,00,000 ÷ {(₹5,00,000 + ₹3,50,000)/2} for B. The calculated ratios indicate that inventory moves faster in firm A (i.e., 3.53 times) compared to firm B and therefore the management of firm A is more efficient than that of B in managing its inventory.

Inventory of raw materials and work in progress: Inventory for manufacturing firms normally includes raw materials and work-in-progress. It therefore makes sense even to calculate raw materials inventory turnover and work-in-progress turnover as:

Raw material inventory turnover = Materials consumed/Average raw materials inventory.

Work-in-progress inventory turnover = Cost of production/Average work-in-progress inventory.

22. Debtors turnover ratio: Debtors' turnover ratio is a measure of the credit management efficiency of the firm. It is calculated by dividing credit sales by average debtors. Higher the debtors turnover ratio, better it is for the firm as this will indicate that the firm is able to quickly convert its debtors and receivables into cash.

ILLUSTRATION 7.22

The credit sales of M/S Vision & Vision for the year ended 31.03.2024 amounts to ₹7,50,000 and its debtors in the beginning and at the end of the year were ₹80,000 and ₹1,70,000, respectively.

What is its credit management efficiency if the industry average debtors turnover ratio is 4.5 times?

SOLUTION

Credit management efficiency of firms are best judged through debtors turnover ratios where debtors turnover ratio which is calculated by dividing credit sales by average debtors.

For Vision & Vision, debtors turnover is found to be 6 times, i.e., ₹7,50,000 ÷ {(₹80,000 + ₹1,70,000)/2}, which is well above the industry average. As there is no benchmark as regards debtors' turnover ratio, and as Vision & Vision's debtors' turnover ratio is above industry average, it may be concluded that the firm is efficient in managing its debtors.

23. Average collection period: Average collection period is an extended measure of the firm's liquidity and credit management efficiency insofar as it helps in determining for how long the firm's debtors remain outstanding and for that purpose how fast the firm is able to collect from its debtors.

Continuing with Illustration 7.22 for calculation of debtors' turnover ratio, we find that the average collection period for Vision Care has been 2 months (i.e., 12 months/6) or 60 days. Although, there is no rule of thumb as to what should be an ideal collection period, firms would favour a shorter collection period as it would mean quicker conversion of debtors and receivables into cash.

24. Creditors' turnover ratio: Creditors' turnover ratio is a measure of the promptness with which the firm makes payments to its creditors. A low creditors' turnover ratio would means quick payments to the creditors which would be welcome by the creditors and would also increase the firm's goodwill. A high creditors' turnover ratio would mean delayed discharge of the creditors' claim which would not be at the firm's interest at least in the long run.

ILLUSTRATION 7.23

The following figures relate to RKR & Co.

	Year 1	*Year 2*	*Year 3*
Opening creditors (₹)	80,000	1,20,000	1,50,000
Closing creditors (₹)	1,20,000	1,50,000	1,60,000
Total credit purchases (₹)	7,20,000	8,28,000	8,82,000

Comment on the Company's ability to liquidate claims of the creditors.

SOLUTION

The company's ability to liquidate claims of the creditors can be judged through creditors' turnover ratio which is calculated by dividing average creditors by average daily purchases.

For RKR & Co., the average creditors for the year 1, 2, and 3 comes to be ₹1,00,000, ₹1,35,000 and ₹1,55,000, respectively. The average daily purchases for the said period, taking 360 working days a year, comes to ₹2,000, ₹2,300 and ₹2,450.

Creditors' turnover ratio for the company therefore is 50 days, 58.70 days and 63.27 days respectively for year 1, 2 and 3. The calculated ratios indicate that payments to creditors by RKR & Co. has become slower over the years as it has taken over 63 days in year 3 to liquidate creditors' claim as against 50 days in year 1.

25. Assets turnover ratio: Assets turnover ratio is also known as investment turnover ratio. It is a measure of the firm's managerial efficiency in terms of assets utilization. It is calculated by dividing cost of goods sold (or sales) by total assets. A higher assets turnover ratio would mean higher managerial efficiency and a lower ratio would mean underutilization of the assets and existence of idle capacity leading to inefficiency of the management in utilizing the available assets. There is no prescribed standard as to what should be taken as an ideal assets turnover ratio. Hence a trend analysis and/or comparison with industry average would help in drawing meaningful inferences. Further the depending upon the concepts used to define assets, there can be variations in the calculated assets turnover ratio such as total assets turnover, fixed assets turnover, current assets turnover, capital turnover and working capital turnover ratios. Care should be taken to see that the assets are net of depreciation. In addition, sales may be taken as the numerator in the absence of cost of goods sold to calculate the assets turnover ratios.

ILLUSTRATION 7.24

Following balance sheets relate to Alpha & Alpha Ltd. as on 31st March:

Balance Sheets *(Fig. in ₹' 000)*

Liabilities	*2022*	*2023*	*2024*	*Assets*	*2022*	*2023*	*2024*
Equity share capital	200	200	300	Gross block			
Reserves and surpluses	100	120	180	*Less:* depreciation	400	480	680
Loans	300	330	420	Current assets	200	290	310
Creditors	150	120	140	Preliminary expenses	–	–	50
	650	770	1040		650	770	1040

If the goods sold for 2022, 2023 and 2024 were ₹10,45,000, ₹12,25,000 and ₹18,00,000, respectively, what was the company's efficiency in managing its fixed assets vis-à-vis total assets?

SOLUTION

The company's assets management efficiency is best judged through its assets utilization capabilities which in turn are measured through various assets turnover ratios.

For Alpha & Alpha, the fixed assets turnover ratio (i.e., cost of goods sold/average fixed assets) is found to be 2.78 (i.e., 1225/{(400 + 480)/2} for the year 2023 and 3.10 (i.e., 1800/{(480 + 680)/2} for the year 2024.

The total assets turnover for Alpha & Alpha for the year 2023 and 2024 is found to be 1.73 and 2.05, respectively, as per the following calculations:

$$\text{Total assets turnover} = \frac{\text{Cost of goods sold}}{\text{Average total assets}} = \underset{\textit{Year 2023}}{\frac{1225}{(650+770)/2}} \qquad \underset{\textit{Year 2024}}{\frac{1800}{(770+990^*)/2}}$$

(***Note:** Preliminary expenses being fictitious assets have been excluded from the scope of total assets for computation of total assets turnover ratios).

The calculated ratios indicate that Alpha & Alpha Ltd. has improved in its assets utilizing efficiency both in terms of fixed assets and total assets over the years under consideration. Further, Alpha & Alpha is more efficient in utilizing fixed assets compared to total assets.

E. Valuation Ratios

The valuation ratios are calculated in order to judge the profitability of and the reward on shareholders' investments. As shown in Exhibit 7.3-A, EPS, DPS, payout ratio, yield and market value to book value are the ratios which are included under the valuation ratios.

26. Earnings per share (EPS): Earnings per share, calculated as PAT divided by total number of outstanding equity shares, is a widely used profitability index that measures the firm's profitability in terms of its earnings power per share, i.e., the amount of profits after tax available to equity holders per share held. There is no fixed standard available as to what should be considered as an ideal EPS ratio. For the purpose of drawing meaningful inferences on EPS trend ratios, inter-firm comparison and comparison with industry average may be used.

ILLUSTRATION 7.25

Following are the abstracts of the income statements and balance sheets of M/S Steelace Ltd:

Details	*31.03.2021*	*31.03.2022*	*31.03.2023*	*31.03.2024*
PAT (₹)	80,000	1,20,000	1,00,000	1,35,000
Equity shares (Nos.)	50,000	60,000	60,000	60,000
Dividend distributed (₹)	65,000	90,000	90,000	1,15,000
Equity capital (₹)	1,00,000	1,20,000	1,20,000	1,20,000
Reserves (₹)	35,000	65,000	75,000	95,000
Market value per share (₹)	5	6	5.5	6.9

Comment on the EPS of Steelace Ltd. as a measure of profitability.

SOLUTION

EPS is calculated by dividing PAT by number of outstanding equity shares. For Steelace Ltd., Exhibit 7.12 table may be constructed to show EPS, besides ratios like DPS, payout ratio, P/E ratio, yield and market value (MV) to book value (BV) ratio.

EXHIBIT 7.12 EPS, DPS, Payout ratio, P/E, Yield and MV to BV ratios of Steelace Ltd.

Ratio(s)		*2021*	*2022*	*2023*	*2024*
EPS = PAT/No. of equity shares	(₹)	1.60	2.00	1.67	2.25
DPS = Dividend/No. of equity shares	(₹)	1.30	1.50	1.50	1.92
Payout ratio = DPS / EPS	%	81.25	75.00	89.82	85.33
P/E ratio = Market value per share/EPS	Times	3.13	3.00	3.29	3.07
Yield = [(Dividend + price change)/initial price)]	%	26.00	50.00	16.67	60.36
Market value to book value ratio = Market value per share to book value per share	Times	1.85	1.95	1.69	1.93

Note: Book value per share = Book value of equity plus reserves and surpluses divided by No. of equity shares

It is found that EPS of Steelace Ltd. has been fluctuating between ₹1.60 to ₹2.25 for the years 2021 to 2024.

27. Dividend per share: Dividend per share is a measure of the real cash income that is made available to, i.e., distributed among the equity shareholders as against the EPS, for companies do not normally distribute their entire EPS as dividend. As such, a majority of the present and potential investors would be interested in DPS of the company rather EPS.

DPS is calculated by dividing the total amount distributed as dividend by the number of ordinary shares outstanding. For Steelace Ltd. the DPS have been found to be ₹1.30, ₹1.50, ₹1.50 and ₹1.92 respectively for the years 2021, 2022, 2023 and 2024, as against the EPS of ₹1.60, ₹2.00, ₹1.67 and ₹2.25 for the corresponding years.

28. Payout ratio: Payout ratio, calculated as DPS divided by EPS, is an indicative of the retention policy of the firm. Higher the payout ratio, lower the retention and the vice versa. A firm having growth opportunity would favour higher retention ratio than a declining firm.

In case of Steelace Ltd., the payout ratio has been 81.25%, 75%, 89.82% and 85.33% respectively for the year years 2021, 2022, 2023 and 2024.

29. Price-Earning ratio (P/E Ratio): Pricing-earning ratio, measured as the relationship between market price per share and the earning per share is the most popular and widely used financial statistics in the stock market. The market price per share may be the price prevailing on a specific day or the average price for a given period. P/E ratio is a summary measure which primarily reflects the growth prospects, risk characteristics, shareholder orientation, corporate image and degree of liquidity. [3] Higher the P/E ratio, higher is the growth prospects of the firm. A lower P/E ratio on the other hand is attributed to the firm having higher risk complexion and poorer growth prospects. In other words, riskier firms will report lower P/E ratio. For better judgment therefore, P/E ratio for the same firm for several years or for several firms for the same year is calculated to see if the firm is improving in terms of its growth prospects over the years or in comparison to other firms in the same industry.

The P/E ratio of Steelace Ltd. for the year years 2021, 2022, 2023 and 2024 has been found to be 3.13, 3.00, 3.29 and 3.07 times, respectively, which indicates that the firm has not been able to improve upon its growth prospects.

30. Yield: Yield is a measure of the rate of return earned by the shareholders. It is calculated by dividing 'dividend plus change in the market price of the share' by initial market price of the share.

Mathematically,

$$\text{Yield} = \frac{\text{Dividend per share} + \text{Change in share price}}{\text{Initial share price}}$$

$$= \frac{\text{Dividend per share}}{\text{Initial share price}} + \frac{\text{Change in share price}}{\text{Initial share price}}$$

Whereas the first part of the equation is dividend yield, the second part is the capital gains (or losses) yield. The total yield to the shareholder therefore is the dividend yield plus the capital gains yield. For drawing inferences on yield, trend percentage, inter-firm and industry average comparisons would be required as there is no such available benchmark against which a comparison could otherwise be made. It is at the same time important to keep in mind that company with low growth prospects generally offers high dividend yield and low capital gains yield.

For Steelace Ltd., as can be seen from Exhibit 7.12, yield for the year years 2021, 2022, 2023 and 2024 has been found to be 26%, 50%, 16.67% and 60.36% respectively, based on the previous year's market price.

31. Market value to book value ratio (MV-BV ratio): Market value to book value per share is yet another popular ratio mostly used in the stock market which helps an analyst to judge how much the firm has contributed to the society's wealth. If the MV-BV ratio is greater than 1 it would mean that the firm has contributed to the wealth of the society by the same amount by which it exceeds 1, for every rupee invested in the firm. For example, if the MP-BV ratio is 3, it implies that the firm has contributed ₹2 for everyone rupee investment. If the ratio is 1 it would mean that the firm has not contributed to nor detracted from the wealth of the society. And if the ratio is less than 1, it implies that the firm has detracted the society's wealth to the extent it is short of one.

For Steelace Ltd., the MP-BV ratio has been 1.85, 1.95, 1.69 and 1.93 meaning thereby that the firm has contributed to the creation of the society's wealth each year ranging from 0.69 paise at the lowest to 0.93 paise at the highest per every rupee (100 paise) invested in it.

Modern Techniques

A few contemporary techniques of financial statement analysis in vogue are the EVA, MVA and MDA.

Economic Value Added (EVA)

Developed in the early 1980's by Stern Stewart & Co, a New York based consulting firm, EVA is considered as an absolute measure of the firm's performance. Peter Ducker has put EVA as 'a measure of total factor productivity'. EVA is a measure of real economic value created for shareholders by a firm's management for a given year [4]. EVA is essentially the surplus left after making an appropriate charge for the capital employed in the business [5].

Mathematically,

$$\text{EVA} = \text{NOPAT} - (k \times \text{capital employed}) \quad (1)$$

$$= \{\text{EBIT}\ (1 - t)\} - \{k \times \text{capital employed})\} \quad (2)$$

$$= \{\text{PAT} + \text{I}\ (1 - t)\} - \{k \times \text{capital employed}\} \quad (3)$$

$$= \text{PAT} - (k_e \times \text{Equity capital employed}) \quad (4)$$

$$= \text{Capital employed} \times (r - k) \quad (5)$$

Where,

NOPAT ⇒ Net operating profit after tax = EBIT (1 – k).
⇒ EBIT (1 – k)
k ⇒ Weighted average cost of capital (WACC).
Capital employed ⇒ Total capital (i.e., Debt plus equity) invested.
I ⇒ Total interest liability.
t ⇒ Tax rate (%).
k_e ⇒ Cost of equity capital.
PAT ⇒ Profit after tax.
r ⇒ Return on total capital employed = NOTPAT ÷ total capital (Debt + Equity) invested.

EVA can thus be calculated by applying any of the formulae, 1 through 5, listed above.

ILLUSTRATION 7.26

The summarized income statement and balance sheet of Shipyard and Co. Ltd. for the financial year ended 2024 are as follows:

Income Statement

	(₹'000)
Sales	525
Less: Cost of Goods Sold	415
EBIT	110
Less: Interest	20
EBT(or PBT)	90
Less: Tax	27
PAT	63

Balance Sheet

Liabilities	*₹'000*	*Assets*	*₹'000*
Equity Share Capital	100	Net Block	190
Bonds	25	Inventories	20
Debenture	35	Debtors	40
Fixed Deposits	60	Receivables	15
Term Loans	80	Cash at bank	20
		Cash in hand	15
Total	300	Total	300

If the company's cost of equity capital is 14% and pre-tax cost of debt capital is 10%, what is its EVA?

SOLUTION

Let us find out the values of NOPAT, k and r before applying any of the formulae for EVA.

$$\text{NOPAT} = \text{EBIT}\ (1 - t) = 110 \times (1 - 30\%)$$
$$= 110 \times 0.7 = ₹77{,}000.$$

$$k = \text{WACC} = \frac{[(110 \times 13\%) + 200 \times \{10 \times (1-t)\}\%]}{(100 + 200)} = \frac{13 + 14}{300} = 9\%$$

$$r = \text{NOPAT} \div \text{Total capital employed} = 77 \div 300 = 25.67\%$$

Hence, $\text{EVA} = \text{NOPAT} - k \times \text{capital employed}$

$$= 77 - (9\% \times 300) = 77 - 27 = ₹50{,}000$$

Alternatively,

(1) $\text{EVA} = \{\text{PAT} + I\ (1 - t)\} - (k \times \text{capital employed}\}$
$= \{63 + (20 \times 0.7)\} - (9\% \times 300) = 77 - 27 = ₹50{,}000$

(2) $\text{EVA} = \text{PAT} - (k_e \times \text{Equity capital})$
$= 63 - (13\% \times 100) = ₹50{,}000$

(3) $\text{EVA} = \text{Capital employed} \times (r - k)$
$= 300 \times (25.67\% - 9\%) = ₹50{,}000$ approximately

Shipyard and Co's EVA has been found to be ₹50,000. This is the surplus that the company has generated after making payments towards cost of capital. As EVA is an absolute measure of the company's success, higher the EVA is, better is the company's overall performance.

Moreover, as EVA is a function of NOPAT, k and capital employed, it can be improved by (i) improving operating performance (EBIT and NOPAT) without infusing additional capital, (ii) investing additional capital so long as r continues to be greater than k (i.e., r > k), (iii) withdrawing capital such as projects / activities that earn inadequate returns, and (iv) adopting alternative financing strategy that reduces k (or WACC).

Market Value Added (MVA)

MVA is considered as an indicator of the firm's managerial performance in terms of the shareholders value creation. Calculated as the difference between the market value of the firm's equity and the equity capital invested and/or the difference between the current market value of the firm's total capital (debt + equity) and the economic book value of the capital invested; MVA is a real measure of the shareholders value creation over the firm's life time.

Mathematically,

MVA = Market value of the firm's equity – Equity capital invested (1)

Also, MVA = Market value of the firm's debt and equity – Economic book value of the capital invested (2)

where,

Market value of equity = Average market price per share during the year x No. of outstanding equity shares.

Market value of debt = Average market price per debt instrument during the year x No. of outstanding debt instruments.

Economic book value of capital invested = Share capital + Reserve and surpluses + Profit + Debt capital.

ILLUSTRATION 7.27

The balance sheet of Sans India Ltd. as on 31.03.2024 is as follows:

(*Fig. in* ₹'000)

Liabilities	₹	*Assets*	₹
Equity capital:		Gross block *less* depreciation	2100
20,000 shares of ₹100 each	2000	Investments	400
Reserves and surpluses	300	Current assets	1200
Debentures:			
10,000 15% debentures of ₹100 each	1000		
Current liabilities	400		
	3700		3700

If the company's average market price per unit of equity and debenture for the year ended 31.03.2024 is ₹145 and ₹110, respectively, what is its market value added (MVA)?

SOLUTION

MVA = Market value of the company's equity and debt minus economic book value of the capital invested = (market value of equity + market value of debt) – Book value of equity, reserves and surplus and debentures.

For Sans India Ltd. therefore MVA = {(20,000 Equity shares × ₹145) + 10,000 debentures × ₹110)} – (₹20,00,000 + ₹3,00,000 + ₹10,00,000)
= ₹40,00,000 – ₹33,00,000
= ₹7,00,000

The company's performance in term of market value added is ₹7,00,000.

Multiple Discriminate Analysis

Multiple Discriminate Analysis (MDA) is a multivariate technique used by E.I. Altman [6] to predict corporate failure. Under this technique, a single discriminant score, called Z, is calculated for each year by using five financial ratios variables as follows:

$$Z = 0.012x_1 + 0.014x_2 + 0.033x_3 + 0.006x_4 + 0.999x_5$$

where,

x_1 = Working capital/total assets (a measure of liquidity)
x_2 = Retained earnings/total assets (a measure of reinvested earnings and past profitability)
x_3 = EBIT/total assets (a measure of profitability)
x_4 = Market value of equity/Book value of total debt (a measure of financial structure or leverage)
x_5 = Sales/total assets (a measure of asset efficiency)

As regards prediction of corporate bankruptcy, firms having a Z score of 2.99 and above are considered to be healthy and those having a Z score of 1.81 or less are considered to be potentially sick. Firms operating within the Z score of 1.81 to 2.99 are taken as operating in the 'risk zone'. Altman's MDA is thus a very useful technique which can be applied to judging the firm's total solvency position.

ILLUSTRATION 7.28

The following financial data relate to M/s Sunlite Ltd. for the last seven years that the firm is in operation:

(*Fig. in* ₹'000)

Year/Item	*2018*	*2019*	*2020*	*2021*	*2022*	*2023*	*2024*
Working capital	200	205	235	300	325	400	450
Total assets	800	880	900	955	1035	1100	1200
Retained earnings	75	115	145	145	160	180	200
EBIT	700	800	880	900	1025	1045	1050
Market value of equity	250	280	300	340	400	450	500
Book value of debt	500	550	700	700	750	800	850
Sales	950	1080	1200	1550	2100	2535	2200

You are required to comment on the firm's solvency position on the basis Altman's multiple Discriminant Analysis (MDA).

SOLUTION

Altman's MDA is a predictive model that helps in determining the firm's overall solvency position over the years, through calculation of a single Discriminant score (Z score) by using five variables as follows:

$$Z = 0.012x_1 + 0.014x_2 + 0.033x_3 + 0.006x_4 + 0.999x_5$$

where,

x_1 = Working capital/total assets
x_2 = Retained earnings/total assets
x_3 = EBIT/total assets
x_4 = Market value of equity/Book value of total debt
x_5 = Sales/total assets

Given the above, values of x_1, x_2, x_3, x_4, x_5 and Z for M/s Sunlite Ltd. may be computed as given in Exhibit 7.13.

EXHIBIT 7.13 Sunlite Ltd.'s MDA

Year \ Values of	*2018*	*2019*	*2020*	*2021*	*2022*	*2023*	*2024*
X_1	0.250	0.233	0.261	0.314	0.314	0.364	0.375
X_2	0.094	0.131	0.161	0.152	0.155	0.164	0.167
X_3	0.875	0.909	0.978	0.942	0.990	0.950	0.875
X_4	0.500	0.509	0.429	0.486	0.533	0.563	0.588
X_5	1.188	1.227	1.333	1.623	2.029	2.305	1.833
Z	1.223	1.264	1.372	1.661	2.069	2.342	1.859

Exhibit 7.13 reveals that M/s Sunlite Ltd.'s Z score for the years 1 through 4 were below 1.81. This indicates that the firm was potentially sick for the period 1st to 4th year. The firm though improved its solvency position thereafter, did not however reach the healthy zone of 2.99 or above. The Z scores from the 5th year onwards has remained between the 'suspect' zone of 1.81 to 2.99. M/s Sunlite Ltd.'s solvency position, determined through Altman's MDA, as such is far from satisfactory as it has been operating in the potentially sick and the suspect zones.

Z scores of Sunlite Ltd. may also be displayed in the form of the following as is shown in Fig. 7.1.

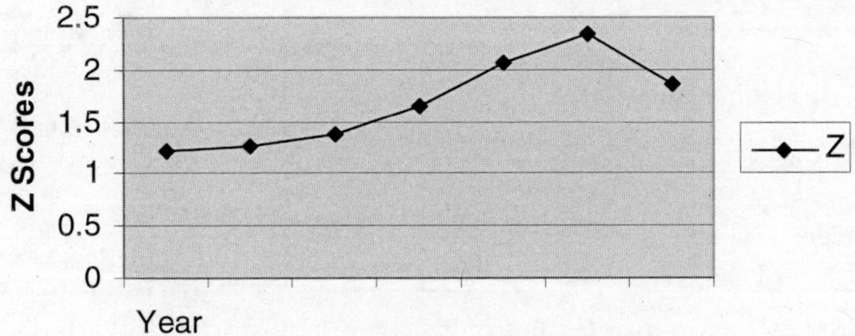

Figure 7.1 Z scores of M/s Sunlite Ltd.

Figure 7.1 clearly shows that M/s Sunlite Ltd. operated in the potentially sick zone till the 4th year and is operating in the suspect zone thereafter.

DIFFICULTIES IN ANALYZING FOREIGN FINANCIAL STATEMENTS

The major difficulties faced by analysists in analyzing foreign financial statements are:

1. Language, terminology and format,
2. Timeliness of data,
3. Availability and reliability.

Language, Terminology and Format

Analysists find difficulties in the analysis of foreign financial statements in the form of (1) the language in which the financial statements are presented especially by non-English speaking countries like France, Mexico, Spain, South Korea and Austria who use their own national language for the purpose; (2) the variation in accounting terminology, for example what is *inventory* in the US is *stock* in the UK or what is sales in the US is turnover in the UK; and (3) the format variation, i.e., the manner in which assets and liabilities are represented in the financial statements. In the US, for example, assets of the companies are reflected in the balance sheets in order of declining liquidity (i.e., most liquid assets followed by the least) and in the UK and Germany the arrangement is the reverse. Variations in the language and terminology, if not the format, to a great extent affect the analysis of foreign financial statements. Reasonable care should therefore be exercised by the analysists therefore in dealing with foreign financial statements for analysis.

Exhibit 7.14 represents a variation in the terminology as is used in the US, the UK and India to mean the same thing:

EXHIBIT 7.14 Variation in the accounting terminology used

The US	*The UK*	*India*
Inventory	Stock	Inventory
Sales	Turnover	Sales
Receivables	Debtors	Debtors
Payables	Creditors	Creditors
Retained earnings	Reserves	Provisions
Statement of operations	Profit & loss A/c	Profit & loss A/c

Timeliness of Data

Non-availability of international financial data on time has been a constraint for the analysts and investors. Baring a few countries such as the United States where strict regulations on the timing and mode of dissemination of financial information exist, in many other countries the case is not the same. Exhibit 7.15 constructed on the basis of a survey conducted by Choi[7] indicates the time lag that exists between the country specific company's year-end and the publication of its audited financial statements and annual reports.

EXHIBIT 7.15 Time lag between company's year-end and Publication of financial statements and annual report

Country	Time lag (in days)
Brazil, Canada, Mexico, South Korea and the United States	30–60
Argentina, Australia, Netherlands, New Zealand, Singapore, Sweden, Denmark, Finland, Norway and the UK	60–90
Austria, France, Germany, Italy, India and Nigeria	90–120

Although the IT revolution is expected to help companies reduce the time gap between their year-end financial reporting and the ultimate publication of the statements and reports, as long as the time lag continues to prevail, hindrance to analysis of foreign financial statements will continue.

Availability and Reliability of Data

Foreign financial data are often not easily available and accessible and when available are not reliable as well. This leads to the third major dimension of the difficulties that the analysists confront with. Except for companies who are in the public domain and who are required to file their financial information with the regulatory agencies of the country, say for example, the Reserve Bank of India (RBI) and the Securities and Exchange Board of India (SEBI); obtaining financial information about companies who are not in the public domain or about the companies operating in the debt-oriented economy remains a difficult task. As such analysts are more often than not forced to resort to private data base industry which collects, compiles and sells financial information with varied degree of coverage, reliability and price.

With the advent of IT and internet although these menace are expected to come down, non-availability and unreliability of data still hunts the analysts.

SUMMARY

The basic purpose of *foreign financial statement analysis* is to provide the analysts and the investors with financial data which are appropriate and useful to decision making with regard to the firm's current economic situation and predicting its future course. The decision makers are varied in nature, so also their requirements. Investors, for example, are concerned with portfolio decisions; creditors for determining the firm's credit worthiness; and employees for establishing economic bases for collective bargaining. The regulatory and policy formulating bodies of the state are interested in 'controlling' decisions; environmentalists and social activists on 'social accounting' issues; researchers for studying firm vis-à-vis industry behaviour; and the management for evaluating the operational and financial efficiency of the firm and its subunits.

To satisfy these stakeholders, financial statements of the MNCs with foreign affiliates are needed to be consolidated first and then the techniques of financial statement analysis be applied for drawing inferences as to the financial position of the firm(s).

The techniques widely used for financial statement analysis, both of domestic and foreign companies are basically the same. Prominent among these techniques are the horizontal (trend) analysis, vertical (common size) analysis, ratio analysis. Of late techniques like EVA,

MVA and MDA have also been found useful to financial statement analysis by virtue of their conceptual superiority.

Whereas horizontal analysis helps in analyzing financial statements of a number of years concerning the firm against a common base; vertical analysis helps in analyzing financial statements of firms of different sizes against a common base rather than based on the absolute figures. Ratio analysis, a major tool of financial statement analysis in use from late 1800s, helps in judging the *liquidity*, *profitability and solvency* positions of the firm. The technique also helps in judging the *managerial efficiency* of the firm in terms of assets utilization and earning power of the capital investment through calculation of activity and valuation ratios. Similarly, EVA helps in measuring the *real economic value created* for the shareholders by the firm's management for a given year; MVA measures the firm's managerial performance in terms of *shareholders' value creation* over the firm's life time. And MDA is a multivariate technique used to predict corporate failure by considering the firm's overall performance.

Despite the fact that several tools and techniques of financial statement analysis are available to the analysts, the real difficulties faced by them with regards to analyzing foreign financial statements are the *language*, the *terminology*, and the *format* in which the financial statements are prepared; the *non-availability* of these statements right on time for analysis and the *reliability* of the data contained in them.

KEY TERMS

Financial Statement Analysis: Financial statement analysis refers to an information processing system that is meant for providing financial data which are appropriate and useful to decision makers who are concerned with evaluating the economic situation of the firm and predicting its future course.

Horizontal analysis: Horizontal analysis also known as trend analysis or dynamic analysis is a technique of financial statement analysis under which financial statement of a number of years of the firm are analyzed against a common base.

Vertical analysis: Vertical analysis, also known as common size analysis is a technique of financial statement analysis under which financial statements of firms of different sizes are compared and analyzed against a common base rather than based on absolute figures.

Ratio analysis: Ratio analysis is a technique of financial statement analysis under which series of ratios are calculated to determine the liquidity, solvency profitability and asset utilization (activity) efficiency of the firm.

Current ratio: Current ratio is the relationship between the firm's current assets and current liabilities. It indicates the firm's ability to meet is short-term obligations.

Defensive interval ratio: Defensive interval ratio indicates the firm's liquidity position in terms of its ability to meet projected daily expenditure from operations. It is calculated by dividing quick assets by projected daily cash requirements.

Profitability ratio: Profitability ratio indicates the ability of the firm to generate profits that would be adequate to support the firm's operations.

Return on total assets (ROTA): ROTA indicates the managerial efficiency of the firm in terms of assets utilization.

Return on capital employed (ROCE): ROCE is a measure of the firm's profitability based on long term capital employed.

Du Pont analysis: Du Pont analysis is an analysis of the firm's overall profitability where in the firm's return on investment (ROI) is calculated based on decomposition of net profit margin and total assets turnover.

Solvency ratio: Solvency ratio is a measure of the firm's long-term liquidity position.

Interest coverage ratio: Interest coverage ratio refers to the 'times' the interest changes are covered by EBIT form which they will be paid.

Debt service coverage ratio: Debt service coverage ratio is a comprehensive measure of the firm's ability to serve its debt.

Earning per share (EPS): EPS is a profitability index that measures the firm's profitability in terms of its earnings per share, i.e., the amount of profits after tax available to equity holders per share held.

Dividend per share (DPS): DPS is a measure of the real cash income that is made available to the equity shareholders.

Payout ratio: Payout ratio is the relationship between DPS and EPS. It indicates the retention policy of the firm.

Price-Earning (P/E) Ratio: P/E ratio is the relationship between market price per share and the EPS.

Yield: Yield is a measure of the rate of return earned by the shareholders.

Economic Value Added (EVA): EVA is a measure of real economic value created for shareholders by a firm's management for a given year.

Market Value Added (MVA): MVA is a measure of the shareholders' value creation over the firm's life time. It is an indicator of the firm's managerial performance in terms of the shareholders' value creation.

Multiple Discriminate Analysis (MDA): MDA is a multivariate technique used to predict corporate failure.

REVIEW QUESTIONS

1. Discuss the utility of financial statement analysis from the point of view of the decision makers.
2. What are the various techniques used for financial statement analysis? Explain with suitable examples.
3. What do you understand by 'financial statement analysis'? Who may undertake such analysis and why? Explain with examples.
4. How does EVA differ from MVA? How do they help in financial statement analysis?

5. Explain the concept and process of Altman's MDA. Bring out its utility in financial statement analysis.
6. Discuss the steps you would follow in analyzing foreign financial statements.
7. Explain in detail and with suitable example(s) the ratios that you will calculate in determining the solvency position of a firm.
8. How is the profitability position of a firm judged? Explain with example(s).
9. 'Activity ratios are basically calculated to judge the managerial efficiency of the firm in terms of its asset productivity' – Elucidate.
10. What do you mean by valuation ratios? Who are benefited out of such ratios and how?
11. How will you assess the short-term solvency position of a firm? Explain with example(s).
12. Explain the following:
    (a) Du Pont analysis
    (b) EVA Vs MVA
13. Write short on:
    (a) Multiple Discriminate Analysis
    (b) Economic Value Added
    (c) Market Value Added
14. Differentiate between horizontal analysis and vertical analysis of financial statements.
15. What are the major difficulties faced in analyzing foreign financial statements? How will you address to such difficulties?
16. Give a brief note on the techniques available for foreign financial statement analysis.
17. The following balance sheet and abstract of income statement relates to M/S Moon & Moon as on 31.03.2024:

Liabilities	₹	*Assets*		₹
Equity share capital	1000	Fixed assets	₹3,600	
7% Preference share capital	200	Less: Depreciation	₹1,000	2600
Reserves and surplus	800	Cash		100
7% Mortgage debenture	1400	Investments		300
Current liabilities:		Debtors		600
Creditors	120	Stock		400
Bills payable	200			
Outstanding expenses	20			
Taxation provision	260			
Total	4000	Total		4000

Abstract of income statement	*(Fig. in ₹)*
Net sales	6000
Cost of goods sold	5160
Net income before tax	400
Net income after tax	200

Comment on the firm's short-term solvency, long-term solvency, profitability and activity positions.

18. From the following data extracted from the published reports of Black & Barry Ltd., prepare a comparative statement of ratios in relation to the firm's:

(a) liquidity
(b) solvency
(c) profitability
(d) activity positions

Also comment on the calculated ratios.

(*Fig. in* ₹'000)

	31.03.2022	*31.03.2023*	*31.03.2024*
Sales	2931	3260	3000
Profit after tax	115	120	150
Equity capital (₹10 per share fully paid)	800	800	800
General reserves	210	282	602
Long term debt	920	800	660
Creditors	299	382	549
Bank credit (short-term)	160	160	200
Fixed assets	1510	1589	1500
Inventories	300	331	809
Other current assets	305	504	402

19. The balance sheets of Sugar India Ltd. and its foreign subsidiary Sweets Ltd. as on 31.03.2024 are as follows:

Balance sheet of Sugar India as on 31.03.2024 (*Fig. in* ₹'000)

Liabilities	₹	*Assets*	₹
Equity share capital (20,000 shares of ₹100 each)	2000	Land and buildings	1900
		Plant and machinery	1700
Reserves and surpluses	1500	Furniture and fittings	1300
Profits	2100	Vehicles	1150
Debentures	2200	Investments in Sweets Ltd.	1350
Creditors	1050	Stock	1150
Payables	1030	Debtors	1150
Outstanding expenses	1020	Receivable	1200
Total	10900	Total	10900

Balance sheet of Sweets Ltd. as on 31.03.2024 (*Fig. in* ₹'000)

Liabilities	₹	*Assets*	₹
Equity share capital (8000 shares of ₹100 each)	1800	Land and buildings	1450
		Plant and machinery	350
Reserves and surpluses	200	Stock	200
Profits	100	Receivables	250
Creditors	150		
Total	**2250**	**Total**	**2250**

Additional Information

Sugar India had acquired 3,000 equity shares of Sweets Ltd. on 01.04.2022 when the latter had ₹1,40,000 to the credit of its Reserves Account.

You are required to comment on the financial position of the firms before and after consolidation, assuming that the consolidation takes place as per 'Equity method'.

20. Balance sheets of Movers India Ltd. and its foreign subsidiary Shakers & Co. Ltd. of Sri Lanka as on 31.03.2024 are as follows:

Movers India Ltd. (*Fig. in* ₹' 000)

Liabilities	₹	*Assets*	₹
Equity share capital	1300	Plant and machinery	1250
Reserves & surpluses	150	Furniture and fittings	1100
Long-term loan	1050	Investment in Shakers & Co. Ltd.	
Sundry creditors	520	(9000 shares)	108
		Sundry debtors	515
		Receivables	47
Total	3020	Total	3020

Shakers & Co. Ltd. (*Fig. in* ₹' 000)

Liabilities	₹	*Assets*	₹
Equity share capital (shares of ₹10 each)	120	Plant and machinery	700
Reserves	136	Sundry debtors	160
Term loans	600	Receivables	120
Creditors	124		
Total	**980**	**Total**	**980**

You are required to:

(a) Consolidate the balance sheets under 'pro-rata method' assuming that on 1st April, 2023 Movers India Ltd. acquired 75% of the shares of Shakers and Co. Ltd. and on which date the later had ₹16,000 to the credit of its reserve account;

(b) Comment on the financial position of the firms before and after the consolidation.

21. The balance sheets of ABC Ltd. and XYZ Ltd. as on 31.03.2024 are as follows:

(*Fig. in* ₹' 000)

Liabilities	*ABC Ltd.*	*XYZ Ltd.*	*Assets*	*ABC Ltd.*	*XYZ Ltd.*
Equity shares	150	150	Fixed assets		
Reserves/surplus	120	122	Less depreciation	275	290
Secured loan	140	145	Stock	138	266
Unsecured loan	—	108	Debtors	130	127
Bank overdraft	130	140	Cash in hand	112	102
Creditors	115	120			
Total	655	785	Total	655	785

You are given the following additional information:

	ABC Ltd.	*XYZ Ltd.*
Sales	₹1200	₹1175
Profit after Tax	₹115	₹108

You are required to indicate the overall efficiency of the firms and their financial position.

22. The Income Statement of ABC Ltd. for the year ended 31.03.2024 and the Balance Sheet as on that date are as follows:

Income Statement

Details	₹	₹
Sales	28,00,000	
Other incomes	30,000	
Total income		28,30,000
Less: Cost of goods sold		10,10,000
Opening stock	1,20,000	
Add: Purchases	11,00,000	
Less: Closing stock	2,10,000	
Gross profit		18,20,000
Less: Operating expenses		6,30,000
(a) Administrative:		
Office	4,40,000	
Depreciation	1,50,000	
(b) Selling:		
Advertising	40,000	
Profit before tax		11,90,000
Less: Tax(25%)		2,97,500
Profit after tax		8,92,500

Balance Sheet

Liabilities	₹	*Assets*	₹
Equity shares	25,00,000	Fixed assets	
Reserves / surpluses	12,00,000	*Less:* depreciation	36,50,000
Preference Share Capital	14,00,000	Stock	13,80,000
Secured loan	10,00,000	Debtors	18,00,000
Unsecured loan	13,00,000	Bills receivable	10,00,000
Creditors	11,50,000	Short term Investment	10,08,000
Bank overdraft	4,00,000	Cash in hand	1,12,000
Total	89,50,000	Total	89,50,000

You are required to comment on the overall efficiency and financial position of the firm.

23. The following financial data relate to M/s SPS Ltd. for the last 10 years that the firm is in operation:

(*Fig. in* ₹'000)

Year \ Item	*2015*	*2016*	*2017*	*2018*	*2019*	*2020*	*2021*	*2022*	*2023*	*2024*
Working capital	150	170	190	220	235	265	300	355	430	550
Total assets	600	680	760	800	890	960	1005	1095	1180	1300
Retained earnings	75	115	145	145	160	180	200	250	345	485
EBIT	700	800	880	910	1025	1045	1060	1140	1270	1425
Market value of equity	250	280	300	340	400	480	520	640	820	1075
Book value of debt	500	550	700	700	750	800	850	1090	1230	1470
Sales	950	1080	1200	1550	2100	2535	2200	2410	2720	3030

You are required to comment on the firm's solvency position on the basis of Altman's Multiple Discriminant Analysis (MDA).

24. From the following extracts of financial data, comment on the financial health of the two firms, ABC Ltd and XYZ Ltd:

(Fig. in ₹'000)

	ABC Ltd.					*XYZ Ltd.*				
Year \ Item	*2015*	*2016*	*2017*	*2018*	*2019*	*2020*	*2021*	*2022*	*2023*	*2024*
Working capital	175	195	230	400	535	665	800	995	1130	1450
Current assets	520	780	960	1020	1190	1460	1605	1995	2180	2600
Total assets	750	1150	1450	1450	1600	1880	2200	2200	2845	2985
Share capital (Shares of ₹10 each)	2500	2500	3000	3000	3000	4800	4800	4800	5200	5200
Retained earnings	800	950	1020	1100	1150	1200	1350	1490	1530	1570
EBIT	1050	1280	1400	1850	2000	2105	2290	2460	2740	2830
PAT	870	980	1150	1460	1620	1830	1950	2010	2340	2420
Market value of equity	2670	2750	3210	3270	3340	4940	5060	5110	5500	5680
Book value of debt	820	1015	1075	1130	1470	1580	1690	1770	1880	1990
Sales	3310	3375	3433	3600	3835	3908	4040	4345	4642	4855

25. The Balance sheets of Moon Light Ltd. and Sun Light Ltd. as on 31.03.2024 are given below:

The balance sheet of Moon Ltd. as on 31.03.2024

Liabilities	₹	*Assets*	₹
Equity Capital	18,00,000	Land and building (net of depreciation)	10,00,000
Reserves	5,00,000	Plant and Machinery (net of depreciation)	14,00,000
Profit	4,00,000	Furniture and fixture	8,00,000
Debentures	12,00,000	Loose tools	4,00,000
Term loan	13,00,000	Inventories	8,70,000
Creditors	8,00,000	Bills receivable	10,00,000
Bills payable	3,00,000	Cash at bank	9,00,000
Outstanding	2,70,000	Cash in hand	2,00,000
Total	65,70,000	Total	65,70,000

The balance sheet of Sun Light Ltd. as on 31.03.2024

Liabilities	₹	*Assets*	₹
Equity Capital	1,18,00,000	Land and building (net of depreciation)	1,20,00,000
Reserves	35,00,000	Plant and Machinery (net of depreciation)	1,44,00,000
Profit	24,00,000	Furniture and fixture	38,00,000
Debentures	1,12,00,000	Loose tools	24,00,000
Term loan	1,13,00,000	Inventories	56,00,000
Creditors	38,00,000	Bills receivable	50,00,000
Bills payable	25,00,000	Cash at bank	29,00,000
Outstanding	3,00,000	Cash in hand	7,00,000
Total	4,68,00,000	Total	4,68,00,000

You are required to advice an investor which of the two companies to invest in supported by your justifications.

26. Given the following Income Statements and Balance Sheets of three firms—A Ltd., B Ltd. and C Ltd., comment on the firms' profitability, liquidity and solvency positions: Income Statements of A Ltd., B Ltd. and C Ltd.

Details	*A Ltd.*	*B Ltd.*	*C Ltd.*
	₹	₹	₹
Sales	35,45,000	25,45,000	65,20,000
Less: Cost of goods sold	10,55,000	8,55,000	30,05,000
Operating income	24,90,000	16,90,000	35,15,,000
Less: Expenses:			
Manufacturing	6,30,000	3,10,000	10,60,000
Administrative	3,25,000	1,05,000	4,45,000
Selling and Distribution	2,40,000	1,30,000	3,18,000
Less: Depreciation	2,15,000	1,60,000	4,14,000
Net income	10,80,000	9,85,000	12,78,000

Balance Sheets of A Ltd., B Ltd. and C Ltd.

Particulars	*A Ltd.*	*B Ltd.*	*C Ltd.*
Liabilities	₹	₹	₹
Equity Share capital	25,00,000	45,00,000	30,55,000
Preference Share Capital	12,00,000	22,05,000	24,10,000
Profit	20,50,000	25,55,000	24,75,000
Bonds and debenture	14,00,000	34,10,000	28,21,000
Term loans	16,50,000	26,50,000	36,10,000
Creditors	9,10,000	19,15,000	17,20,000
Bills Payables	3,05,000	23,10,000	2,38,000
Total	1,00,15,000	1,95,45,000	1,63,29,000
Assets			
Land and building	23,50,000	33,52,000	37,79,000
Plant and equipment	15,00,000	55,13,000	35,60,000
Furniture and fixtures	8,25,000	18,35,000	13,45,000
Inventories	15,00,000	25,25,000	19,75,000
Debtors	22,25,000	23,15,000	29,25,000
Bills Receivables	11,00,000	25,60,000	18,75,000
Cash	5,15,000	14,45,000	8,70,000
Total	1,00,15,000	1,95,45,000	1,63,29,000

27. From the following Balance Sheets, calculate and comment on the liquidity and solvency position of the firms:

Liabilities	A Ltd.	B Ltd.	C Ltd.	D Ltd.
	₹	₹	₹	₹
Equity	5,00,000	6,00,000	8,00,000	5,00,000
Reserves	30,000	66,000	1,06,000	14,000
Bonds and debentures	6,36,000	4,14,000	7,16,000	5,36,000
Accounts payable	4,24,000	4,84,000	7,14,000	3,24,000
Outstanding	—	1,30,000	30,000	20,000
Total	15,90,000	16,94,000	24,66,000	13,94,000
Assets				
Land and building	5,30,000	5,50,000	7,20,000	5,20,000
Plants and equipment	3,18,000	3,42,000	5,12,000	3,12,000
Inventories (at market value)	4,24,000	4,34,000	6,16,000	3,24,000
Accounts receivable	2,12,000	2,42,000	4,12,000	1,12,000
Cash	1,06,000	1,36,000	2,06,000	1,26,000
Total	15,90,000	16,94,000	24,66,000	13,94,000

28. The Income Statement of Scientific Endeavours Ltd. for the year ended 31.03.2024 and the Balance Sheet as on that date are as follows:

Income Statement Scientific Endeavours Ltd. for the year ended 31.03.2024

Details	₹	₹
Sales	1,22,00,000	
Other incomes	61,000	
Total income		1,22,61,000
Less: Cost of goods sold:		65,30,000
Opening stock	11,26,000	
Add: Purchases	61,14,000	
Less: Closing stock	7,10,000	
Gross profit		57,31,000
Less: Operating expenses		23,70,000
(a) Administrative		
Office	14,45,000	
Depreciation	4,10,000	
(b) Selling		
Advertising	5,15,000	
Profit before tax		33,61,000
Less: Tax(25%)		8,40,250
Profit after tax		25,20,750

Balance Sheet of Scientific Endeavours Ltd. as on 31.03.2024

Liabilities	₹	*Assets*	₹
Equity shares	65,00,000	Fixed assets	
Reserves/surpluses	21,80,000	*Less:* depreciation	76,50,000
Preference Share Capital	34,50,000	Stock	33,80,000
Secured loan	20,20,000	Debtors	27,40,000
Unsecured loan	22,50,000	Bills receivable	20,60,000
Creditors	21,50,000	Short term Investment	20,08,000
Bank overdraft	4,25,000	Cash in hand	11,37,000
	1,89,75,000		1,79,75,000

You are required to comment on the overall efficiency and financial position of the firm by using appropriate accounting ratios.

29. Given the following Balance sheets of Eagle Enterprises, find out and comment on its long-term solvency position measured in terms of (i) Long-term debt to shareholders' equity, (ii) Total debt to shareholders' equity, and (iii) Long-term debt to total capital.

Liabilities	*2020*	*2021*	*2022*	*2023*	*2024*
	₹	₹	₹	₹	₹
Share capital	1500	1500	2500	2500	2500
Reserves and surpluses	700	820	1135	1080	1295
Profit	650	720	905	980	965
Long-term loan	460	660	720	820	700
Debentures	450	530	530	530	530
Current liabilities	840	830	1015	1055	1125
Total	4600	5060	6805	6965	7115
Assets					
Fixed assets *less* depreciation	2892	3445	4795	4860	4805
Current assets	1708	1615	2010	2105	2310
Total	4600	5060	6805	6965	7115

30. Balance Sheets of three firms- X Ltd., Y Ltd. and Z Ltd. as on 31st March 2024 are given here under:

Balance Sheet of X Ltd. as on 31st March 2024

Liabilities	₹	*Assets*	₹
Equity Share capital		Land and building	26,00,000
(Shares of ₹10 each)	29,50,000	Plant and equipment	20,52,000
Reserves	12,50,000	Long-term investment	8,50,000
Bonds and debenture	24,50,000	Inventories at market price	15,50,000
Term loans	15,50,000	Receivables	22,50,000
Payables	16,52,000	Cash	5,50,000
Total	98,52,000	Total	98,52,000

Balance Sheet of Y Ltd. as on 31st March 2024

Liabilities	₹	*Assets*	₹
Equity Share capital		Land and building	9,90,000
(Shares of ₹10 each)	12,80,000	Plant and Machinery	17,70,000
Reserves	8,20,000	Furniture and fittings	3,20,000
Profit	4,10,000	Long-term investment	8,81,000
Bonds and debenture	12,51,000	Inventories at market price	7,90,000
Term loans	9,90,000	Receivables	4,10,000
Payables	5,50,000	Short-term investments	1,80,000
Outstanding	1,30,000	Cash	90,000
Total	54,31,000	Total	54,31,000

Balance Sheet of Z Ltd as on 31st March 2024

Liabilities	₹	*Assets*	₹
Equity share capital		Land and building	19,90,000
(Shares of ₹10 each)	22,80,000	Plant and Machinery	24,70,000
Reserves	16,40,000	Furniture and fittings	5,20,000
Profit	14,10,000	Long-term investment	17,80,000
Bonds and debenture	16,50,000	Inventories at market price	9,90,000
Term loans	11,90,000	Receivables	8,20,000
Payables	6,50,000	Short-term investments	3,80,000
Outstanding	3,25,000	Cash	1,95,000
Total	91,45,000	Total	91,45,000

Abstract of the three firms' Income Statements for the year ended 31st March 2024 is given below:

Abstract of Income Statements for the year ended 31st March 2024

Particulars	*X Ltd.* (₹)	*Y Ltd.* (₹)	*Z Ltd.* (₹)
Sales	75,23,500	44,24,680	60,62,340
Other Income	6,17,100	2,32,300	5,19,600
Total Income	81,40,600	46,56,980	65,81,940
Total Expenses	51,10,340	22,07,100	41,02,780
EBDIT	30,30,260	24,49,880	24,79,160
Depreciation	5,01,120	2,07,520	4,14,270
EBIT	25,29,140	22,42,360	20,64,890
Interest	3,20,000	1,79,200	2,27,200
EBT	22,09,140	20,63,160	18,37,690
Tax (25%)	5,52,285	5,15,790	4,59,423

You are required to:

(i) Determine the overall financial health of the firms.

(ii) Find out the firm that maintains (a) better managerial performance, (b) better solvency position, and (c) better liquidity position.

(iii) Recommend the firm in which an investor who is interested in long term gain may invest his money.

REFERENCES

[1] Baruch, L., *Financial Statement Analysis: A New Approach*, Prentice Hall, Inc., Englewood Cliffs, N.J., 1974, p. 11.

[2] Webster's New Collegiate Dictionary, 8th Ed., Springfield, Mass: G & C, Merriam, 1975, p. 958.

[3] Chandra, P., *Financial Management*, 5th Ed., TMH, New Delhi, p. 736.

[4] McMenamin, J., *Financial Management—An Introduction*, Oxford University Press, p. 280.

[5] Chandra, P., Op. Cit., p. 280.

[6] Altman, E.I., Financial Ratios, *Discriminant Analysis and the Prediction of Corporate Bankruptcy*, *The Journal of Finance*, September 1968, pp. 589–609.

[7] Choi, F.D.S., Corporate Financial Data Bases for Empirical Research in Financial Management, *Financial Management*, Summer 1988, pp. 80–98.

8

Segment Reporting

LEARNING OBJECTIVES

After studying this chapter, you will be able to:

- Explain the concept and significance of segment reporting vis-à-vis- operating segment reporting
- Understand the different provisions of IFRS 8 on Operating Segment Reporting
- Know the applicability of IFRS 8
- Differentiate between Operating segment and Reportable segment
- Appreciate the terms Aggregation criteria and Quantitative threshold
- Understand the additional provisions of IFRS 8, Disclosure norms, Measurement, Reconciliation, and Restatement of previously reported information
- Understand provisions of IFRS 8 on Entity-wide disclosures, information about product and services, geographical areas, and major customers
- Know the provisions of Ind AS 108 on Operating Segment
- Appreciate operating segment reporting and disclosure in practice

INTRODUCTION

Business organizations have become more complex than what they were decades before. Even the conglomerate form of business has become more popular these days. With these changes, the utility of financial statements which present the full scope of an enterprise's operations had declined markedly. 'While it is certainly possible to access the overall financial health of the entity using such financial reports, it is much more difficult to evaluate management's operating and financial strategies, particularly with regard to its emphasis on specific lines of business' [1]. It was this reason that segment reporting was emphasized. The objective of presenting information by segments is to provide users of financial statements with information on the relative size, profit, contribution, and growth trend of the different industries and different geographical areas in which diversified enterprise operates to enable them to make more informed judgments about the enterprise as a whole [2]. Reporting on each segment of the business was felt a necessity to communicate to the users of financial statements about the operating performance of each segment of the business for better analysis and understanding of the enterprise's performance including its performance in dissimilar and diversified activities.

Accordingly, the International Accounting Standards Board (IASB) had adopted IAS 14: *Segment Reporting* in April 2001, which was originally issued by the International Accounting Standards Committee (IASC) in August 1997 as IAS 14 *Segment Reporting in* replacement to IAS 14: *Reporting Financial Information by Segment* issued in August 1981 by IASC.

Segment reporting refers to the disclosure of information about an enterprise's operation in different industries, its foreign operations and export sales, and its major customers. For the purpose of segment reporting, the standard provides for classifications of the products and services of the enterprise into (1) business segment, and (2) geographical segment. The standard further provides that classification of activities into segments would primarily depend on the enterprise's internal managerial decision making process. For example, if the management makes distinct decisions as regards the production, distribution and marketing of any specific product or service, then this would amount to a separate segment for disclosure purposes. The standard states 'An enterprise should look to its system of internal reporting to the board of directors and the chief executive officer for the purpose of identifying its business segments or geographical segments, for both primary and secondary reporting formats'.

***IAS 14 has now been replaced by IFRS 8: Operating Segment Reporting*. Similarly, in India, AS 17 which was the IAS 14 equivalent Indian Accounting Standard has now been replaced by Ind AS 108.** IFRS 8 was originally issued by IASB on 19th January, 2006. Further, IFRS 8 was made effective for annual period beginning on or after 1 January 2009, superseding IAS 14 Segment Reporting. IFRS 8 has further been amended on 16 April 2009, and subsequently on 12 December 2013 and has been made effective for annual periods beginning on or after 1 July 2014. Similarly, Ind AS 108 has been issued 16th February, 2015 vide notification G.S.R. 111(E).

IFRS 8 AND OPERATING SEGMENT REPORTING

International Financial Reporting Standard (IFRS) 8 provides for reporting of financial performance of an entity on its operating segments in order to enable the users of its financial statements to evaluate the nature and financial effects of the business activities in which the entity is engaged with and the economic environments in which it operates. 'An entity shall disclose information to enable users of its financial statements to evaluate the nature and financial effects of the business activities in which it engages and the economic environments in which it operates.'[3]

APPLICABILITY OF IFRS 8

IFRS 8 shall apply to:

(a) the separate or individual financial statements of an entity, (i) whose debt or equity instruments are traded in a public market (a domestic or foreign stock exchange or an over-the-counter market, including local and regional markets), or (ii) that files, or is in the process of filing, its financial statements with a securities commission or other regulatory organization for the purpose of issuing any class of instruments in a public market; and

(b) the consolidated financial statements of a group with a parent, (i) whose debt or equity instruments are traded in a public market (a domestic or foreign stock exchange or an over-the-counter market, including local and regional markets), or (ii) that files, or is in the process of filing, the consolidated financial statements with a securities commission or other regulatory organization for the purpose of issuing any class of instruments in a public market.

IFRS 8 further provides that, (1) if an entity that is not required to apply this IFRS chooses to disclose information about segments that does not comply with this IFRS, it shall not describe the information as segment information; and (2) if a financial report contains both the consolidated financial statements of a parent that is within the scope of this IFRS as well as the parent's separate financial statements, segment information is required only in the consolidated financial statements.

OPERATING SEGMENTS

IFRS 8 has laid down the following as operating segment:

(i) An operating segment is a component of an entity, that engages in business activities from which it may earn revenues and incur expenses (including revenues and expenses relating to transactions with other components of the same entity),

(ii) whose operating results are regularly reviewed by the entity's **chief operating decision maker** (CODM) to make decisions about resources to be allocated to the segment and assess its performance, and

(iii) for which discrete financial information is available. Further, an operating segment may engage in business activities for which it has yet to earn revenues, for example, start-up operations may be operating segments before earning revenues.

The following further clarifications have been provided by IFRS 8 on Operating Segment:

(iv) Not every part of an entity is necessarily an operating segment or part of an operating segment. For example, a corporate headquarters or some functional departments may not earn revenues or may earn revenues that are only incidental to the activities of the entity and would not be operating segments. For the purposes of this IFRS, an entity's post-employment benefit plans are not operating segments.

(v) The term 'chief operating decision maker' identifies a function, not necessarily a manager with a specific title. That function is to allocate resources to and assess the performance of the operating segments of an entity. Often the chief operating decision maker of an entity is its chief executive officer or chief operating officer but, for example, it may be a group of executive directors or others.

(vi) For many entities, the three defined characteristics of operating segments as stated above will clearly identify its operating segments. However, an entity may produce reports in which its business activities are presented in a variety of ways. If the chief operating decision maker uses more than one set of segment information, other factors may identify a single set of components as constituting an entity's operating segments, including the nature of the business activities of each component, the existence of managers responsible for them, and information presented to the board of directors.

(vii) Generally, an operating segment has a segment manager who is directly accountable to and maintains regular contact with the chief operating decision maker to discuss operating activities, financial results, forecasts, or plans for the segment. The term 'segment manager' identifies a function, not necessarily a manager with a specific title. The chief operating decision maker also may be the segment manager for some operating segments. A single manager may be the segment manager for more than one operating segment. If the three defined characteristics of operating segment apply to more than one set of components of an organization but there is only one set for which segment managers are held responsible, then that set of components constitutes the operating segments.

(viii) The three above defined characteristics which make an operating segment may also apply to two or more overlapping sets of components for which managers are held responsible. That structure is sometimes referred to as a matrix form of organization. For example, in some entities, some managers are responsible for different product and service lines worldwide, whereas other managers are responsible for specific geographical areas. The chief operating decision maker regularly reviews the operating results of both sets of components, and financial information is available for both. In that situation, the entity shall determine which set of components constitutes the operating segments by reference to the core principle.

REPORTABLE SEGMENTS

IFRS 8 provides that, an entity shall report separately information about each operating segment that (a) has been identified in accordance with provisions contained in (i) to (viii) above or results from aggregating two or more of those segments in accordance with the '*aggregation criteria*' as described in below, and (b) exceeds the quantitative thresholds as described here under.

Besides the above, clause 'i' through 'vi' described under 'additional provisions of IFRS 8' hereunder also specify other situations in which separate information about an operating segment is required to be reported by an entity.

AGGREGATION CRITERIA

IFRS 8 provides that operating segments often exhibit similar long-term financial performance if they have similar economic characteristics. For example, similar long-term average gross margins for two operating segments would be expected if their economic characteristics were similar. Two or more operating segments may be aggregated into a single operating segment if aggregation is consistent with the core principle of this IFRS, the segments have similar economic characteristics, and the segments are similar in each of the following respects:

(a) the nature of the products and services;

(b) the nature of the production processes;

(c) the type or class of customer for their products and services;
(d) the methods used to distribute their products or provide their services; and
(e) if applicable, the nature of the regulatory environment, for example, banking, insurance or public utilities.

QUANTITATIVE THRESHOLDS

An entity shall report separately information about an operating segment that meets any of the following quantitative thresholds:

(a) Its reported revenue, including both sales to external customers and intersegment sales or transfers, is 10 per cent or more of the combined revenue, internal and external, of all operating segments.
(b) The absolute amount of its reported profit or loss is 10 per cent or more of the greater, in absolute amount, of (i) the combined reported profit of all operating segments that did not report a loss, and (ii) the combined reported loss of all operating segments that reported a loss.
(c) Its assets are 10 per cent or more of the combined assets of all operating segments.

Operating segments that do not meet any of the quantitative thresholds may be considered reportable, and separately disclosed, if management believes that information about the segment would be useful to users of the financial statements.

ADDITIONAL PROVISIONS OF IFRS 8

IFRS 8 provides the following additional provisions:

(i) An entity may combine information about operating segments that do not meet the quantitative thresholds with information about other operating segments that do not meet the quantitative thresholds to produce a reportable segment only if the operating segments have similar economic characteristics and share a majority of the 'aggregation criteria'.
(ii) If the total external revenue reported by operating segments constitutes less than 75 per cent of the entity's revenue, additional operating segments shall be identified as reportable segments (even if they do not meet the 'quantitative criteria') until at least 75 per cent of the entity's revenue is included in reportable segments.
(iii) Information about other business activities and operating segments that are not reportable shall be combined and disclosed in an 'all other segments' category separately from other reconciling items in the 'reconciliations' as described under. The sources of the revenue included in the 'all other segments' category shall be described.
(iv) If management judges that an operating segment identified as a reportable segment in the immediately preceding period is of continuing significance, information about that segment shall continue to be reported separately in the current period even if it no longer meets the 'quantitative criteria' for reportability.

(v) If an operating segment is identified as a reportable segment in the current period in accordance with the quantitative thresholds, segment data for a prior period presented for comparative purposes shall be restated to reflect the newly reportable segment as a separate segment, even if that segment did not satisfy the quantitative criteria' for reportability in the prior period, unless the necessary information is not available and the cost to develop it would be excessive.

(vi) There may be a practical limit to the number of reportable segments that an entity separately discloses beyond which segment information may become too detailed. Although no precise limit has been determined, as to the number of segments that are reportable in accordance with increases above ten, the entity should consider whether a practical limit has been reached.

DISCLOSURE NORMS

IFRS 8 on disclosure provides that 'An entity shall disclose information to enable users of its financial statements to evaluate the nature and financial effects of the business activities in which it engages and the economic environments in which it operates'.

In order to give effect to the principle on disclosure stated in the aforesaid paragraph, an entity shall disclose the following for each period for which a statement of comprehensive income is presented:

(I) General information, comprising of:

(a) factors used to identify the entity's reportable segments, including the basis of organization, e.g., whether management has chosen to organize the entity around differences in products and services, geographical areas, regulatory environments, or a combination of factors and whether operating segments have been aggregated;

(b) the judgments made by management in applying the aggregation criteria. This includes a brief description of the operating segments that have been aggregated in this way and the economic indicators that have been assessed in determining that the aggregated operating segments share similar economic characteristics; and

(c) types of products and services from which each reportable segment derives its revenues.

(II) Information about profit or loss, assets and liabilities, comprising of:

(a) a measure of profit or loss for each reportable segment;

(b) a measure of total assets and liabilities for each reportable segment if such amounts are regularly provided to the chief operating decision maker;

(c) the following about each reportable segment if the specified amounts are included in the measure of segment profit or loss reviewed by the chief operating decision maker, or are otherwise regularly provided to the chief operating decision maker, even if not included in that measure of segment profit or loss:

(i) revenues from external customers; (ii) revenues from transactions with other operating segments of the same entity; (iii) interest revenue; (iv) interest expense; (v) depreciation and amortization; (vi) material items of income and expense disclosed in accordance with paragraph 97 of IAS 1 *Presentation of Financial Statements* (as revised in 2007); (vii) the entity's interest in the profit or loss of associates and joint ventures accounted for by the equity method; (viii) income tax expense or income; and (ix) material non-cash items other than depreciation and amortization.

An entity shall report interest revenue separately from interest expense for each reportable segment unless a majority of the segment's revenues are from interest and the chief operating decision maker relies primarily on net interest revenue to assess the performance of the segment and make decisions about resources to be allocated to the segment. In that situation, an entity may report that segment's interest revenue net of its interest expense and disclose that it has done so.

(d) An entity shall disclose the following about each reportable segment if the specified amounts are included in the measure of segment assets reviewed by the chief operating decision maker or are otherwise regularly provided to the chief operating decision maker, even if not included in the measure of segment assets:
   (i) the amount of investment in associates and joint ventures accounted for by the equity method, and
   (ii) the amounts of additions to non-current assets other than financial instruments, deferred tax assets, net defined benefit assets (see IAS 19 *Employee Benefits*) and rights arising under insurance contracts.

MEASUREMENT

For measurement, IFRS 8 provides that,

(i) The amount of each segment item reported shall be the measure reported to the chief operating decision maker for the purposes of making decisions about allocating resources to the segment and assessing its performance. Adjustments and eliminations made in preparing an entity's financial statements and allocations of revenues, expenses, and gains or losses shall be included in determining reported segment profit or loss only if they are included in the measure of the segment's profit or loss that is used by the chief operating decision maker. Similarly, only those assets and liabilities that are included in the measures of the segment's assets and segment's liabilities that are used by the chief operating decision maker shall be reported for that segment. If amounts are allocated to reported segment profit or loss, assets or liabilities, those amounts shall be allocated on a reasonable basis.

(ii) If the chief operating decision maker uses only one measure of an operating segment's profit or loss, the segment's assets or the segment's liabilities in assessing segment performance and deciding how to allocate resources, segment profit or loss, assets and liabilities shall be reported at those measures. If the chief operating decision maker uses more than one measure of an operating segment's profit or loss, the segment's assets or the segment's liabilities, the reported measures shall be those that management believes are determined in accordance with the measurement principles most consistent with those used in measuring the corresponding amounts in the entity's financial statements.

(iii) An entity shall provide an explanation of the measurements of segment profit or loss, segment assets and segment liabilities for each reportable segment. At a minimum, an entity shall disclose the following:

(a) the basis of accounting for any transactions between reportable segments.

(b) the nature of any differences between the measurements of the reportable segments' profits or losses and the entity's profit or loss before income tax expense or income and discontinued operations (if not apparent from the reconciliations described in paragraph 28). Those differences could include accounting policies and policies for allocation of centrally incurred costs that are necessary for an understanding of the reported segment information.

(c) the nature of any differences between the measurements of the reportable segments' assets and the entity's assets (if not apparent from the 'reconciliations'). Those differences could include accounting policies and policies for allocation of jointly used assets that are necessary for an understanding of the reported segment information.

(d) the nature of any differences between the measurements of the reportable segments' liabilities and the entity's liabilities (if not apparent from the 'reconciliations'). Those differences could include accounting policies and policies for allocation of jointly utilized liabilities that are necessary for an understanding of the reported segment information.

(e) the nature of any changes from prior periods in the measurement methods used to determine reported segment profit or loss and the effect, if any, of those changes on the measure of segment profit or loss.

(f) the nature and effect of any asymmetrical allocations to reportable segments. For example, an entity might allocate depreciation expense to a segment without allocating the related depreciable assets to that segment.

RECONCILIATIONS

IFRS 8 provides that an entity shall provide reconciliations of all of the following:

(i) Total of the reportable segments' revenues to the entity's revenue.

(ii) Total of the reportable segments' measures of profit or loss to the entity's profit or loss before tax expense (tax income) and discontinued operations. However, if an entity allocates to reportable segments items such as tax expense (tax income), the entity may reconcile the total of the segments' measures of profit or loss to the entity's profit or loss after those items.

(iii) Total of the reportable segments' assets to the entity's assets if the segment assets are reported in accordance with the provisions contained in '*Information about profit or loss, assets and liabilities*' *above*.

(iv) Total of the reportable segments' liabilities to the entity's liabilities if segment liabilities are reported in accordance with the provisions contained in '*Information about profit or loss, assets and liabilities*' *above*.

(v) Total of the reportable segments' amounts for every other material item of information disclosed to the corresponding amount for the entity.

(vi) All material reconciling items shall be separately identified and described. For example, the amount of each material adjustment needed to reconcile reportable segment profit or loss to the entity's profit or loss arising from different accounting policies shall be separately identified and described.

RESTATEMENT OF PREVIOUSLY REPORTED INFORMATION

1. If an entity changes the structure of its internal organization in a manner that causes the composition of its reportable segments to change, the corresponding information for earlier periods, including interim periods, shall be restated unless the information is not available and the cost to develop it would be excessive. The determination of whether the information is not available and the cost to develop it would be excessive shall be made for each individual item of disclosure. Following a change in the composition of its reportable segments, an entity shall disclose whether it has restated the corresponding items of segment information for earlier periods.
2. If an entity has changed the structure of its internal organization in a manner that causes the composition of its reportable segments to change and if segment information for earlier periods, including interim periods, is not restated to reflect the change, the entity shall disclose in the year in which the change occurs segment information for the current period on both the old basis and the new basis of segmentation, unless the necessary information is not available and the cost to develop it would be excessive.

ENTITY-WIDE DISCLOSURES

All entities that are subject to IFRS 8, including those entities that have a single reportable segment, will have to report on products and services, geographical areas, and major customers. Those entities whose business activities are not organized on the basis of differences in related products and services or differences in geographical areas of operations, their reportable segments may report revenues from a broad range of essentially different products and services, or more than one of its reportable segments may provide essentially the same products and services. Similarly, an entity's reportable segments may hold assets in different geographical areas and report revenues from customers in different geographical areas, or more than one of its reportable segments may operate in the same geographical area. Further, information required for reporting on products and services, geographical areas, and major customers shall be provided only if it is not provided as part of the reportable segment information required by this IFRS.

INFORMATION ABOUT PRODUCTS AND SERVICES

An entity shall report the revenues from external customers for each product and service, or each group of similar products and services, unless the necessary information is not available and the cost to develop it would be excessive, in which case that fact shall be disclosed. The amounts of revenues reported shall be based on the financial information used to produce the entity's financial statements.

INFORMATION ABOUT GEOGRAPHICAL AREAS

An entity shall report the following geographical information, unless the necessary information is not available and the cost to develop it would be excessive:

(a) Revenues from external customers (i) attributed to the entity's country of domicile and (ii) attributed to all foreign countries in total from which the entity derives revenues. If revenues from external customers attributed to an individual foreign country are material, those revenues shall be disclosed separately. An entity shall disclose the basis for attributing revenues from external customers to individual countries.

(b) Non-current assets other than financial instruments, deferred tax assets, post-employment benefit assets, and rights arising under insurance contracts (i) located in the entity's country of domicile and (ii) located in all foreign countries in total in which the entity holds assets. If assets in an individual foreign country are material, those assets shall be disclosed separately. For assets classified according to a liquidity presentation, non-current assets are assets that include amounts expected to be recovered more than twelve months after the reporting period.

The amounts reported shall be based on the financial information that is used to produce the entity's financial statements. If the necessary information is not available and the cost to develop it would be excessive, that fact shall be disclosed. An entity may provide, in addition to the information required herewith, subtotals of geographical information about groups of countries.

INFORMATION ABOUT MAJOR CUSTOMERS

An entity shall provide information about the extent of its reliance on its major customers. If revenues from transactions with a single external customer amount to 10 per cent or more of an entity's revenues, the entity shall disclose that fact, the total amount of revenues from each such customer, and the identity of the segment or segments reporting the revenues. The entity need not disclose the identity of a major customer or the amount of revenues that each segment reports from that customer. For the purposes of this IFRS, a group of entities known to a reporting entity to be under common control shall be considered a single customer. However, judgment is required to assess whether a government (including government agencies and similar bodies whether local, national or international) and entities known to the reporting entity to be under the control of that government are considered a single customer. In assessing this, the reporting entity shall consider the extent of economic integration between those entities.

Note: The above listed provisions have been taken from the published materials of IRFS Foundation on IFRS 8 Operating Segment.

INDIAN ACCOUNTING STANDARD (IND AS) 108 ON OPERATING SEGMENT

Ind AS 108 has replaced Accounting Stand (AS) 17 on segment reporting. Further, Ind AS 108 is an adoption of IFRS 8, in order to make the Indian entities report their financials in line with the international financial reporting for enhanced harmony.

However, extracts of Ind AS 108 on Operating segment are presented here for convenience and ease of comparison with that of IFRS 8.

Indian Accounting Standard (Ind AS) 108

Operating Segments

(This Indian Accounting Standard includes paragraphs set in ***bold*** *type and plain type, which have equal authority. Paragraphs in bold type indicate the main principles.)*

Core Principle

1. An entity shall disclose information to enable users of its financial statements to evaluate the nature and financial effects of the business activities in which it engages and the economic environments in which it operates.

Scope

2. This Accounting Standard shall apply to companies to which Indian Accounting Standards (Ind ASs) notified under the Companies Act apply.
3. If an entity that is not required to apply this Ind AS chooses to disclose information about segments that does not comply with this Ind AS, it shall not describe the information as segment information.
4. If a financial report contains both the consolidated financial statements of a parent that is within the scope of this Ind AS as well as the parent's separate financial statements, segment information is required only in the consolidated financial statements.

Operating Segment

5. An operating segment is a component of an entity:
   (a) that engages in business activities from which it may earn revenues and incur expenses (including revenues and expenses relating to transactions with other components of the same entity),
   (b) whose operating results are regularly reviewed by the entity's chief operating decision maker to make decisions about resources to be allocated to the segment and assess its performance, and
   (c) for which discrete financial information is available.

   An operating segment may engage in business activities for which it has yet to earn revenues, for example, start-up operations may be operating segments before earning revenues.
6. Not every part of an entity is necessarily an operating segment or part of an operating segment. For example, a corporate headquarters or some functional departments may

not earn revenues or may earn revenues that are only incidental to the activities of the entity and would not be operating segments. For the purposes of this Ind AS, an entity's post-employment benefit plans are not operating segments.

7. The term 'chief operating decision maker' identifies a function, not necessarily a manager with a specific title. That function is to allocate resources to and assess the performance of the operating segments of an entity. Often the chief operating decision maker of an entity is its chief executive officer or chief operating officer but, for example, it may be a group of executive directors or others.
8. For many entities, the three characteristics of operating segments described in paragraph 5 clearly identify its operating segments. However, an entity may produce reports in which its business activities are presented in a variety of ways. If the chief operating decision maker uses more than one set of segment information, other factors may identify a single set of components as constituting an entity's operating segments, including the nature of the business activities of each component, the existence of managers responsible for them, and information presented to the board of directors.
9. Generally, an operating segment has a segment manager who is directly accountable to and maintains regular contact with the chief operating decision maker to discuss operating activities, financial results, forecasts, or plans for the segment. The term 'segment manager' identifies a function, not necessarily a manager with a specific title. The chief operating decision maker also may be the segment manager for some operating segments. A single manager may be the segment manager for more than one operating segment. If the characteristics in paragraph 5 apply to more than one set of components of an organization but there is only one set for which segment managers are held responsible, that set of components constitutes the operating segments.
10. The characteristics in paragraph 5 may apply to two or more overlapping sets of components for which managers are held responsible. That structure is sometimes referred to as a matrix form of organization. For example, in some entities, some managers are responsible for different product and service lines worldwide, whereas other managers are responsible for specific geographical areas. The chief operating decision maker regularly reviews the operating results of both sets of components, and financial information is available for both. In that situation, the entity shall determine which set of components constitutes the operating segments by reference to the core principle.

Reportable Segment

11. An entity shall report separately information about each operating segment that:
    (a) has been identified in accordance with paragraphs 5–10 or results from aggregating two or more of those segments in accordance with paragraph 12, and
    (b) exceeds the quantitative thresholds in paragraph 13.

    Paragraphs 14–19 specify other situations in which separate information about an operating segment shall be reported.

Aggregation Criteria

12. Operating segments often exhibit similar long-term financial performance if they have similar economic characteristics. For example, similar long-term average gross margins for two operating segments would be expected if their economic characteristics were similar. Two or more operating segments may be aggregated into a single operating segment if aggregation is consistent with the core principle of this Ind AS, the segments have similar economic characteristics, and the segments are similar in each of the following respects:
    (a) the nature of the products and services;
    (b) the nature of the production processes;
    (c) the type or class of customer for their products and services;
    (d) the methods used to distribute their products or provide their services; and

    if applicable, the nature of the regulatory environment, for example, banking, insurance or public utilities.

Quantitative Thresholds

13. An entity shall report separately information about an operating segment that meets any of the following quantitative thresholds:
    (a) Its reported revenue, including both sales to external customers and intersegment sales or transfers, is 10 per cent or more of the combined revenue, internal and external, of all operating segments.
    (b) The absolute amount of its reported profit or loss is 10 per cent or more of the greater, in absolute amount, of (i) the combined reported profit of all operating segments that did not report a loss, and (ii) the combined reported loss of all operating segments that reported a loss.
    (c) Its assets are 10 per cent or more of the combined assets of all operating segments.

    Operating segments that do not meet any of the quantitative thresholds may be considered reportable, and separately disclosed, if management believes that information about the segment would be useful to users of the financial statements.
14. An entity may combine information about operating segments that do not meet the quantitative thresholds with information about other operating segments that do not meet the quantitative thresholds to produce a reportable segment only if the operating segments have similar economic characteristics and share a majority of the aggregation criteria listed in paragraph 12.
15. If the total external revenue reported by operating segments constitutes less than 75 per cent of the entity's revenue, additional operating segments shall be identified as reportable segments (even if they do not meet the criteria in paragraph 13) until at least 75 per cent of the entity's revenue is included in reportable segments.
16. Information about other business activities and operating segments that are not reportable shall be combined and disclosed in an 'all other segments' category

separately from other reconciling items in the reconciliations required by paragraph 28. The sources of the revenue included in the 'all other segments' category shall be described.

17. If management judges that an operating segment identified as a reportable segment in the immediately preceding period is of continuing significance, information about that segment shall continue to be reported separately in the current period even if it no longer meets the criteria for reportability in paragraph 13.
18. If an operating segment is identified as a reportable segment in the current period in accordance with the quantitative thresholds, segment data for a prior period presented for comparative purposes shall be restated to reflect the newly reportable segment as a separate segment, even if that segment did not satisfy the criteria for reportability in paragraph 13 in the prior period, unless the necessary information is not available and the cost to develop it would be excessive.
19. There may be a practical limit to the number of reportable segments that an entity separately discloses beyond which segment information may become too detailed. Although no precise limit has been determined, as the number of segments that are reportable in accordance with paragraphs 13–18 increases above ten, the entity should consider whether a practical limit has been reached.

Disclosure

20. An entity shall disclose information to enable users of its financial statements to evaluate the nature and financial effects of the business activities in which it engages and the economic environments in which it operates.
21. To give effect to the principle in paragraph 20, an entity shall disclose the following for each period for which a statement of profit and loss is presented:
    (a) general information as described in paragraph 22;
    (b) information about reported segment profit or loss, including specified revenues and expenses included in reported segment profit or loss, segment assets, segment liabilities and the basis of measurement, as described in paragraphs 23–27; and
    (c) reconciliations of the totals of segment revenues, reported segment profit or loss, segment assets, segment liabilities and other material segment items to corresponding entity amounts as described in paragraph 28.

    Reconciliations of the amounts in the balance sheet for reportable segments to the amounts in the entity's balance sheet are required for each date at which a balance sheet is presented. Information for prior periods shall be restated as described in paragraphs 29 and 30.

General Information

22. An entity shall disclose the following general information:
    (a) factors used to identify the entity's reportable segments, including the basis of organisation (for example, whether management has chosen to organise the entity around differences in products and services, geographical areas, regulatory

environments, or a combination of factors and whether operating segments have been aggregated);

(aa) the judgements made by management in applying the aggregation criteria in paragraph 12. This includes a brief description of the operating segments that have been aggregated in this way and the economic indicators that have been assessed in determining that the aggregated operating segments share similar economic characteristics; and

(b) types of products and services from which each reportable segment derives its revenues.

Information about Profit or Loss, Assets and Liabilities

23. An entity shall report a measure of profit or loss for each reportable segment. An entity shall report a measure of total assets and liabilities for each reportable segment if such amounts are regularly provided to the chief operating decision maker. An entity shall also disclose the following about each reportable segment if the specified amounts are included in the measure of segment profit or loss reviewed by the chief operating decision maker, or are otherwise regularly provided to the chief operating decision maker, even if not included in that measure of segment profit or loss:

    (a) revenues from external customers;
    (b) revenues from transactions with other operating segments of the same entity;
    (c) interest revenue;
    (d) interest expense;
    (e) depreciation and amortisation;
    (f) material items of income and expense disclosed in accordance with paragraph 97 of Ind AS 1, *Presentation of Financial Statements*;
    (g) the entity's interest in the profit or loss of associates and joint ventures accounted for by the equity method;
    (h) income tax expense or income; and
    (i) material non-cash items other than depreciation and amortisation.

    An entity shall report interest revenue separately from interest expense for each reportable segment unless a majority of the segment's revenues are from interest and the chief operating decision maker relies primarily on net interest revenue to assess the performance of the segment and make decisions about resources to be allocated to the segment. In that situation, an entity may report that segment's interest revenue net of its interest expense and disclose that it has done so.

24. An entity shall disclose the following about each reportable segment if the specified amounts are included in the measure of segment assets reviewed by the chief operating decision maker or are otherwise regularly provided to the chief operating decision maker, even if not included in the measure of segment assets:

    (a) the amount of investment in associates and joint ventures accounted for by the equity method, and

(b) the amounts of additions to non-current assets other than financial instruments, deferred tax assets, net defined benefit assets (see Ind AS 19, *Employee Benefits*) and rights arising under insurance contracts.

Measurement

25. The amount of each segment item reported shall be the measure reported to the chief operating decision maker for the purposes of making decisions about allocating resources to the segment and assessing its performance. Adjustments and eliminations made in preparing an entity's financial statements and allocations of revenues, expenses, and gains or losses shall be included in determining reported segment profit or loss only if they are included in the measure of the segment's profit or loss that is used by the chief operating decision maker. Similarly, only those assets and liabilities that are included in the measures of the segment's assets and segment's liabilities that are used by the chief operating decision maker shall be reported for that segment. If amounts are allocated to reported segment profit or loss, assets or liabilities, those amounts shall be allocated on a reasonable basis.
26. If the chief operating decision maker uses only one measure of an operating segment's profit or loss, the segment's assets or the segment's liabilities in assessing segment performance and deciding how to allocate resources, segment profit or loss, assets and liabilities shall be reported at those measures. If the chief operating decision maker uses more than one measure of an operating segment's profit or loss, the segment's assets or the segment's liabilities, the reported measures shall be those that management believes are determined in accordance with the measurement principles most consistent with those used in measuring the corresponding amounts in the entity's financial statements.
27. An entity shall provide an explanation of the measurements of segment profit or loss, segment assets and segment liabilities for each reportable segment. At a minimum, an entity shall disclose the following:
    (a) the basis of accounting for any transactions between reportable segments.
    (b) the nature of any differences between the measurements of the reportable segments' profits or losses and the entity's profit or loss before income tax expense or income and discontinued operations (if not apparent from the reconciliations described in paragraph 28). Those differences could include accounting policies and policies for allocation of centrally incurred costs that are necessary for an understanding of the reported segment information.
    (c) the nature of any differences between the measurements of the reportable segments' assets and the entity's assets (if not apparent from the reconciliations described in paragraph 28). Those differences could include accounting policies and policies for allocation of jointly used assets that are necessary for an understanding of the reported segment information.
    (d) the nature of any differences between the measurements of the reportable segments' liabilities and the entity's liabilities (if not apparent from the reconciliations described in paragraph 28). Those differences could include accounting policies and policies for allocation of jointly utilised liabilities that are necessary for an understanding of the reported segment information.

(e) the nature of any changes from prior periods in the measurement methods used to determine reported segment profit or loss and the effect, if any, of those changes on the measure of segment profit or loss.

(f) the nature and effect of any asymmetrical allocations to reportable segments. For example, an entity might allocate depreciation expense to a segment without allocating the related depreciable assets to that segment.

Reconciliations

28. An entity shall provide reconciliations of all of the following:

(a) the total of the reportable segments' revenues to the entity's revenue.

(b) the total of the reportable segments' measures of profit or loss to the entity's profit or loss before tax expense (tax income) and discontinued operations. However, if an entity allocates to reportable segments items such as tax expense (tax income), the entity may reconcile the total of the segments' measures of profit or loss to the entity's profit or loss after those items.

(c) the total of the reportable segments' assets to the entity's assets if the segment assets are reported in accordance with paragraph 23.

(d) the total of the reportable segments' liabilities to the entity's liabilities if segment liabilities are reported in accordance with paragraph 23.

(e) the total of the reportable segments' amounts for every other material item of information disclosed to the corresponding amount for the entity.

All material reconciling items shall be separately identified and described. For example, the amount of each material adjustment needed to reconcile reportable segment profit or loss to the entity's profit or loss arising from different accounting policies shall be separately identified and described[1].

Restatement of Previously Reported Information

29. If an entity changes the structure of its internal organisation in a manner that causes the composition of its reportable segments to change, the corresponding information for earlier periods, including interim periods, shall be restated unless the information is not available and the cost to develop it would be excessive. The determination of whether the information is not available and the cost to develop it would be excessive shall be made for each individual item of disclosure. Following a change in the composition of its reportable segments, an entity shall disclose whether it has restated the corresponding items of segment information for earlier periods.

30. If an entity has changed the structure of its internal organisation in a manner that causes the composition of its reportable segments to change and if segment information for earlier periods, including interim periods, is not restated to reflect the change, the entity shall disclose in the year in which the change occurs segment information for

---

[1] For assets classified according to a liquidity presentation, non-current assets are assets that include amounts expected to be recovered more than twelve months after the reporting period.

the current period on both the old basis and the new basis of segmentation, unless the necessary information is not available and the cost to develop it would be excessive.

Entity-wide Disclosures

31. Paragraphs 32–34 apply to all entities subject to this Ind AS including those entities that have a single reportable segment. Some entities' business activities are not organised on the basis of differences in related products and services or differences in geographical areas of operations. Such an entity's reportable segments may report revenues from a broad range of essentially different products and services, or more than one of its reportable segments may provide essentially the same products and services. Similarly, an entity's reportable segments may hold assets in different geographical areas and report revenues from customers in different geographical areas, or more than one of its reportable segments may operate in the same geographical area. Information required by paragraphs 32–34 shall be provided only if it is not provided as part of the reportable segment information required by this Ind AS.

Information about Products and Services

32. An entity shall report the revenues from external customers for each product and service, or each group of similar products and services, unless the necessary information is not available and the cost to develop it would be excessive, in which case that fact shall be disclosed. The amounts of revenues reported shall be based on the financial information used to produce the entity's financial statements.

Information about Geographical Areas

33. An entity shall report the following geographical information, unless the necessary information is not available and the cost to develop it would be excessive:
    (a) revenues from external customers (i) attributed to the entity's country of domicile and (ii) attributed to all foreign countries in total from which the entity derives revenues. If revenues from external customers attributed to an individual foreign country are material, those revenues shall be disclosed separately. An entity shall disclose the basis for attributing revenues from external customers to individual countries.
    (b) non-current assets[2] other than financial instruments, deferred tax assets, post-employment benefit assets, and rights arising under insurance contracts (i) located in the entity's country of domicile, and (ii) located in all foreign countries in total in which the entity holds assets. If assets in an individual foreign country are material, those assets shall be disclosed separately.

    The amounts reported shall be based on the financial information that is used to produce the entity's financial statements. If the necessary information is not available and the cost to develop it would be excessive, that fact shall be disclosed. An entity

---

[2] For assets classified according to a liquidity presentation, non-current assets are assets that include amounts expected to be recovered more than twelve months after the reporting period.

may provide, in addition to the information required by this paragraph, subtotals of geographical information about groups of countries.

Information about Major Customers

34. An entity shall provide information about the extent of its reliance on its major customers. If revenues from transactions with a single external customer amount to 10 per cent or more of an entity's revenues, the entity shall disclose that fact, the total amount of revenues from each such customer, and the identity of the segment or segments reporting the revenues. The entity need not disclose the identity of a major customer or the amount of revenues that each segment reports from that customer. For the purposes of this Ind AS, a group of entities known to a reporting entity to be under common control shall be considered a single customer. However, judgement is required to assess whether a government (including government agencies and similar bodies whether local, national or international) and entities known to the reporting entity to be under the control of that government are considered a single customer. In assessing this, the reporting entity shall consider the extent of economic integration between those entities.

Note: This Appendix is not a part of the Indian Accounting Standard. The purpose of this Appendix is only to bring out the major differences, if any, between Indian Accounting Standard (Ind AS) 108 and the corresponding International Financial Reporting Standard (IFRS) 8, Operating Segments, issued by the International Accounting Standards Board.

IFRS 8 VS IND AS 108: A QUICK COMPARISON

A quick comparison between IFRS 8 and Ind AS 108 on Operating Segments has been given in Table 8.1

TABLE 8.1 IFRS 8 Vs Ind AS 108 on *Operating Segments*: A quick Comparison

Sl. No	*Broad description*	*IFRS 8*	*Ind AS 108*
1	Transitional provisions	Given in IFRS 8	Not given in Ind AS 10. However, all transitional provisions related to Ind ASs, where considered necessary, have been included in Ind AS 101: First-time Adoption of Indian Accounting Standards, corresponding to IFRS 1: First-time Adoption of International Financial Reporting Standards.
2	Use of different terminology	Statement of financial position Statement of comprehensive income	Balance Sheet Statement of profit and loss

(*Contd.*)

TABLE 8.1 IFRS 8 Vs Ind AS 108 on *Operating Segments*: A quick Comparison (*Contd.*)

Sl. No	*Broad description*	*IFRS 8*	*Ind AS 108*
3	Paragraph 2	Paragraph 2 of IFRS 8 requires that the standard shall apply to: (a) the separate or individual financial statements of an entity: (i) whose debt or equity instruments are traded in a public market (a domestic or foreign stock exchange or an over-the-counter market, including local and regional markets), or (ii) that files, or is in the process of filing, its financial statements with a securities commission or other regulatory organization for the purpose of issuing any class of instruments in a public market; and (b) the consolidated financial statements of a group with a parent: (i) whose debt or equity instruments are traded in a public market (a domestic or foreign stock exchange or an over-the-counter market, including local and regional markets), or (i) that files, or is in the process of filing, the consolidated financial statements with a securities commission or other regulatory organisation for the purpose of issuing any class of instruments in a public market.	Contents of Paragraph 2 of IFRS 8 (as given in Column 3) has not been included in Paragraph 2 of Ind AS 108. In other words, Paragraph 2 of IFRS 8 has been deleted in Ind AS 108. This is because applicability or exemptions to the Indian Accounting Standards is governed by the Indian Companies Act and the Rules made thereunder. However, in order to maintain consistency in terms of number of paragraphs in both IFRS 8 and Ind AS 108 that Ind AS 108 does contain Paragraph 2 but with different contents.

OPERATING SEGMENT REPORTING IN PRACTICE

In order to appreciate how operating segment reporting is done in practice that the published Annual Report of Steel Authority of India (SAIL) Ltd. for the year 2022-23 and the published Integrated Annual Report of Oil and Natural Gas Corporation (ONGC) Ltd. for the year 2022-23 have been taken as examples.

Table 8.2 highlights the operating segment reporting of SAIL Ltd. SAIL has considered its five Integrated Steel Plants and three Alloy Steel Plants, being manufacturing units, as the primary business segments for reporting under Ind AS 108—'Operating Segments' issued by Ministry of Corporate Affairs, Government of India. The abbreviations, namely, BSP, DSP, RSP, BSL, ISP, ASP, SSP, and VISL contained in Table 8.2 stands for Bhilai Steel Plant, Durgapur Steel Plant, Rourkela Steel Plant, Bokaro Steel Plant, IISCO Steel Plant, Alloy Steels Plant, Salem Steel Plant, Visvesvaraya Iron and Steel Plant, respectively. Others include Chandrapur Ferro Alloy Plant and others.

TABLE 8.2 Operating Segment reporting in SAIL for the year 2022–23

Particulars	*BSP*	*DSP*	*RSP*	*BSL*	*ISP*	*ASP*	*SSP*	*VISL*	*Others*	*Inter Segment Sales*	Total
REVENUE											
– External sales											
Current Year ended 31st March 2023	28670.03	12133.21	24090.46	23155.90	13002.13	731.60	1798.55	144.00	41.66	—	103767.54
Previous Year ended 31st March 2022	26299.91	11146.83	24130.47	25680.67	11495.65	699.32	2632.13	243.21	476.94	—	102805.13
– Inter segment sales											
Current Year ended 31st March 2023	1693.79	1062.64	1380.61	2938.16	494.31	258.54	76.36	161.36	1356.57	(9422.34)	—
Previous Year ended 31st March 2022	1499.17	659.19	2591.85	2607.65	687.31	190.43	16.79	128.19	2808.56	(11189.14)	—
– Total Revenue from sale of products											
Current Year ended 31st March 2023	30363.82	13195.85	25471.07	26094.06	13496.44	990.14	1874.91	305.36	1398.42	(9422.34)	103767.73
Previous Year ended 31st March 2022	27799.08	11806.02	26722.32	28288.32	12182.96	889.75	2648.92	371.40	3288.91	(11189.14)	102808.54
RESULTS											
– Operating Profit/(Loss) before Interest and exceptional items											
Current Year ended 31st March 2023	954.33	502.49	1191.23	1218.79	558.03	(121.79)	(203.06)	(50.57)	366.94	—	4416.39
Previous Year ended 31st March 2022	2853.35	1157.02	6347.65	6386.86	827.14	(71.46)	97.79	(35.88)	527.54	—	18090.01
Finance Costs											
Current Year ended 31st March 2023	—	—	—	—	—	—	—	—	—	—	2037.47
Previous Year ended 31st March 2022	—	—	—	—	—	—	—	—	—	—	1697.88
– Exceptional Items											
Current Year ended 31st March 2023	—	—	—	—	—	—	—	—	—	—	(257.99)
Previous Year ended 31st March 2022	—	—	—	—	—	—	—	—	—	—	353.41

(*Contd.*)

TABLE 8.2 Operating Segment reporting in SAIL for the year 2022–23 (*Contd.*)

Particulars	*BSP*	*DSP*	*RSP*	*BSL*	*ISP*	*ASP*	*SSP*	*VISL*	*Others*	*Inter Segment Sales*	Total
Tax Expenses											
Current Year ended 31st March 2023	—	—	—	—	—	—	—	—	—	—	733.84
Previous Year ended 31st March 2022	—	—	—	—	—	—	—	—	—	—	4023.68
Profit for the year											
Current Year ended 31st March 2023	—	—	—	—	—	—	—	—	—	—	1903.07
Previous Year ended 31st March 2022	—	—	—	—	—	—	—	—	—	—	12015.04
Other Information											
Segment Assets											
Current Year ended 31st March 2023	34203.09	7440.11	28204.33	22190.44	15867.84	619.15	2515.84	238.26	16435.93	—	127714.99
Previous Year ended 31st March 2022	31351.06	6283.17	25844.95	20785.61	15750.29	565.31	2211.64	271.24	14677.87	—	117741.14
Segment Liabilities											
Current Year ended 31st March 2023	9300.61	3547.08	9203.46	6065.67	1602.70	258.03	501.46	60.45	45036.35	—	75575.81
Previous Year ended 31st March 2022	9195.16	3016.83	8367.33	7016.39	1752.99	250.07	534.20	63.54	35527.49	—	65724.00
Capital Expenditure											
Current Year ended 31st March 2023	1030.31	865.13	2011.35	1047.64	338.94	1.45	12.58	3.45	58.80	—	5369.65
Previous Year ended 31st March 2022	1214.86	270.84	3525.48	848.48	268.09	0.03	2.01	2.76	(405.31)	—	5727.24
Depreciation											
Current Year ended 31st March 2023	1242.26	292.98	1528.47	923.53	810.93	8.56	96.68	6.42	52.69	—	4962.52
Previous Year ended 31st March 2022	1177.46	278.72	935.29	888.10	798.07	8.60	99.00	7.32	81.61	—	4274.17
Non-Cash expenses other than Depreciation											
Current Year ended 31st March 2023	124.97	33.26	31.44	23.78	14.19	17.19	8.34	3.97	95.66	—	352.80
Previous Year ended 31st March 2022	75.23	25.73	120.26	33.02	22.83	1.18	0.83	0.29	77.47	—	356.84

The figures of previous periods have been re-grouped, wherever necessary, so as to conform to the current periods classification.

For and on behalf of the Board of Directors

Sd/-	Sd/-	Sd/-
(MB Balakrishnan)	(Anil Kumar Tulsiani)	(Anirban Dasgupta)
Company Secretary	Director-Finance	Director incharge, BSP

In terms of our report of even date

Sd/-	Sd/-	Sd/-	Sd/-
For Tej Raj & Pal	For SK Jaykishan	For Walker Chandiok & Co LLP	For KASG & Co.
Chartered Accountants	Chartered Accountants	Chartered Accountants	Chartered Accountants
Sd/-	Sd/-	Sd/-	Sd/-
[Dinakar Mohanty]	**[Ritesh Agarwal]**	**[Nalin Jain]**	**[Raj Kumar Agarwal]**
Partner	Partner	Partner	Partner

(*Source:* SAIL Annual Report 2022–23)

RELATED PARTY DISCLOSURE

As per Ind AS 24, related parties for SAIL comprise of Subsidiary, Joint venture, Associate, and Other companies with the details as given in Table 8.2(a).

TABLE 8.2(a) Related parties of SAIL Ltd.

Subsidiaries	*Joint Venture*	*Associate*	*Others*
SAIL Refractory Company Limited Chhattisgarh Mega Steel Limited	NTPC-SAIL Power Company Limited Bokaro Power Supply Company Private Limited SAIL Bansal Service Centre Limited Mjunction Services Limited Bhilai Jaypee Cement Limited International Coal Ventures Private Limited SAIL SCL Kerala Limited SAIL-RITES Bengal Wagon Industry Private Limited SAIL Kobe Iron India Private Limited Prime Gold-SAIL JVC Limited VSL SAIL JVC Limited Romelt-SAIL (India) Limited Bastar Railway Private Limited GEDCOL SAIL Power Corporation Limited	Almora Magnesite Limited	ICVL Mauritius Riverdale Mining (PTY) Limited (RML) Minas De Banga ICVL Zambeze Mauritius Limited Benga Power Plant (Mauritius) Limited IISCO Ujjain Pipe & Foundry Co. Limited UEC-SAIL Information Technology Limited

Source: SAIL Annual Report 2022–23

POST-EMPLOYMENT BENEFIT PLAN

The Post-Employment Benefit Plans of SAIL for the year 2022–23 has been reflected in Table 8.2(b).

TABLE 8.2(b) Post-Employment Benefit Plan of SAIL

HSL BSP Provident Fund, Bhilai	SAIL Provident Fund, New Delhi
DSP Provident Fund, Durgapur	Hindustan Steel Provident Fund, Ranchi
Hindustan Steel Ltd. Contributory Provident Fund, Rourkela	Hindustan Steel Limited, Central Purchase Organisation, Sales & Transport, Calcutta Provident Fund
Bokaro Steel Employees Provident Fund, Bokaro	Bharat Refractories Provident Fund, Bokaro
IISCO Limited Provident Institution, Burnpur	IFICO Provident Fund, Ramgarh CCSO Provident Fund, Dhanbad
Coal Provident Fund Trust, Collieries	SAIL RMD Establishment and Administrative Offices Employees Provident Fund, Kolkata
IISCO Limited Works Provident Fund, Burnpur	Bolani Ores Mines Provident Fund , Bolani
SAIL ASP Provident Fund, Durgapur	SAIL Employees' Superannuation Benefit Fund
Salem Steel Provident Fund, Salem	SAIL Gratuity Fund
Visvesvaraya Iron and Steel Plant Employees Provident Fund Trust, Bhadravati	SAIL Pension Fund

KEY MANAGEMENT PERSONNEL

Table 8.2(c) contains the list of key management personnel of SAIL for the year 2022-23.

TABLE 8.2(c) Key Management Personnel

1	Smt. Soma Mondal	15	Shri A.K. Tulsiani
2	Shri Harinand Rai	16	Shri B.P. Singh
3	Smt. Sukriti Likhi	17	Shri K.K. Singh
4	Shri Puneet Kansal	18	Smt. K. Raman
5	Shri A K Tripathi	19	Shri Jagdish Arora
6	Shri Kanhaiya Sarda	20	Shri Sanjeev Taneja
7	Smt. Neelam Sonkar	21	Shri S. Subbaraj
8	Shri S.K.V. Raju	22	Shri Rajeev Sehgal
9	Dr. G.S. Bhati	23	Shri Surajit Mishra
10	Shri N. Shankarappa	24	Shri Nirvik Banerjee
11	Shri A. Dasgupta	25	Shri M.V. Zode
12	Shri V.S. Chakravarthy	26	Shri M.B. Balakrishnan
13	Shri Amarendu Prakash	27	Shri Subhashis Sengupta
14	Shri Atanu Bhowmick		

RELATED PARTY TRANSACTIONS

Details of transactions between SAIL and the Related Parties during the Year 2022–23 have been given in Table 8.2(d).

TABLE 8.2(d) Details of transactions between SAIL and the Related Parties during the Year 2022–23

(₹ *in crore*)

Sl. No.	*Particulars*	*Subsidiary/Associate/Joint Ventures*	*Key Management Personnel*	*Total*
(i)	Investments	– (5.00)		– (5.00)
(ii)	Advance for Purchase of Shares	–3.52 (5.00)		–3.52 (5.00)
(iii)	Services Rendered	18.98 (8.28)		18.98 (8.28)
(iv)	Rental Income	0.06 (–)		0.06 (–)
(v)	Dividend Received	414.49 (192.70)		414.49 (192.70)
(vi)	Sale of Goods	37.59 (6.63)		37.59 (6.63)
(vii)	Other Operating Revenues	18.37 (16.11)		18.37 (16.11)
(viii)	Purchase of Goods	2075.54 (2158.80)		2075.54 (2158.80)
(ix)	Purchase of Power	3085.72 (2374.04)		3085.72 (2374.04)
(x)	Services Received	56.25 (64.11)		56.25 (64.11)
		1.88 (0.96)		1.88 (0.96)
(xi)	Interest Income	– (0.01)		– (0.01)
(xii)	Managerial Remuneration		15.84	15.84
			(13.18)	(13.18)

BALANCES WITH RELATED PARTIES

Table 8.2(e) reflects SAIL's balances with Related Parties as at the end of the Year 2022–23.

TABLE 8.2(e) Balances with Related Parties as at the end of the Year 2022–23

(In Rs Crore)

Sl. No.	Particulars	Total
(i)	Investments	1459.72 (1459.72)
(ii)	Provision for investments	23.77 (5.03)
(iii)	Other Loans and Advances	107.40 (64.70)
(iv)	Provision for Loans and Advances	15.95 (11.92)
(v)	Advance for Purchase of shares	–(3.52)
(vi)	Trade Receivable	8.41 (15.35)
(vii)	Trade Payable	591.67 (414.07)
(viii)	Security Deposit	0.37 (0.37)

DISCLOSURE OF MATERIAL TRANSACTIONS WITH RELATED PARTIES

Table 8.2(f) reveals information on Material Transactions with Related Parties.

TABLE 8.2(f) Disclosure of Material Transactions with Related Parties

(₹ in Crore)

Name of Struck off Company	*For the Year ended 31st March, 2023*	*For the Year ended 31st March, 2022*
Dividend Income		
SAIL Refractory Co. Ltd.	12.52	5.30
Bokaro Power Supply Co. Pvt. Ltd.	66.97	12.40
NTPC-SAIL Power Supply Co. Ltd.	325.00	100.00
Mjunction Services Limited	10.00	75.00
Investments		
ICVL		4.61
S&T Mining Co Ltd.		0.39
Advance for Purchase of Shares		
ICVL		4.61
SAIL SCL Kerala Ltd.	–3.52	
S&T Mining Co Ltd.		0.39
Sale of Goods		
BhilaiJaypee Cement Ltd.	0.06	4.57
SAIL Refractory Co. Ltd.	2.35	2.06
SAIL Rites Bengal Wagon Pvt Ltd.	30.69	
NTPC-SAIL Power Supply Co. Ltd	4.49	

Name of Struck off Company	*For the Year ended 31st March, 2023*	*For the Year ended 31st March, 2022*
Other Operating Revenues		
NTPC-SAIL Power Supply Co. Ltd.	18.37	16.11
Purchase of Goods		
SAIL Refractory Ltd.	197.15	202.30
Almora agnesite Ltd.	6.11	6.19
Minas De anga	1872.28	1950.31
Purchase of Power		
Bokaro Power Supply Co. Pvt. Ltd.	1022.55	901.52
NTPC-SAIL Power Supply Co. Ltd.	2063.17	1472.52
Services Rendered		
Bhilai Jaypee Cement Limited Mjunction Services Limited	3.21	0.54
SAIL-Bansal	0.09	0.11
Services Centre Ltd.	0.08	0.04
Bokaro Power Supply Co. Pvt. Ltd.	0.29	0.38
NTPC SAIL Power Supply Co. Ltd.	10.87	–2.65
SAIL Refractory Co. Ltd.	1.48	4.56
SAIL RITES Bengal Wagon	56.25	64.11
Auction services		
Mjunction Services Limited	1.88	0.96
PF Trusts	**1024.53**	1120.47

OPERATING SEGMENT REPORTING OF ONGC LTD.

ONGC Ltd. has identified two geographical segments, namely, 'Offshore' and 'Onshore' segments as the 'Reportable Segments' for the year 2022-23. The bases on which ONGC Ltd. has identified them as 'Reporting Segments' are the different risks and returns involved in their operations; the organization structure and the internal reporting systems associated with'.

Table 8.3(a), 8.3(b), 8.3(c), 8.3(d) and 8.3(f) respectively contain details of 'Segment revenue and results', 'Segment assets and liabilities' , 'Impairment loss' , 'Exceptional items', and 'Additions to non-current assets', for the identified reportable segments as given in ONGC Ltd.'s Integrated Annual Report 2022-23.

TABLE 8.3(a) Segment revenue and results

(₹ *in Million*)

Particulars	*Segment revenue*		*Segment profit/(loss)*	
	Year ended March 31, 2023	*Year ended March 31, 2022*	*Year ended March 31, 2023*	*Year ended March 31, 2022*
Offshore	1,041,138.04	715,413.31	430,095.99	325,066.64
Onshore	514,035.11	388,040.67	61,830.19	70,430.85
Total	1,555,173.15	1,103,453.98	491,926.18	395,497.49
Unallocated corporate expense (Net)			(14,257.92)	(15,792.03)
Finance costs			(26,996.01)	(23,598.62)
Interest/Dividend income			53,280.98	54,293.02
Profit before tax			503,953.23	410,399.86

TABLE 8.3(b) Segment assets and liabilities

(₹ *in Million*)

Particulars	*As at March 31, 2023*	*As at March 31, 2022*
Segment assets		
Offshore	1,499,830.13	1,494,378.00
Onshore	734,526.53	737,311.96
Total segment assets	2,234,356.66	2,231,689.96
Unallocated	1,436,014.27	1,140,952.42
Total assets	3,670,370.93	3,372,642.38
Segment liabilities		
Offshore	551,996.87	481,069.86
Onshore	176,394.76	159,088.66
Total segment liabilities	728,391.63	640,158.52
Unallocated	363,520.89	361,003.00
Total liabilities	1,091,912.52	1,001,161.52

Notes:

(i) Aforesaid segments are used for the purpose of monitoring performance and allocation of resources.

(ii) All assets are allocated to reportable segments other than investments in subsidiaries, associates and joint ventures, other investments, loans and current and deferred tax assets.

(iii) All liabilities are allocated to reportable segment other than borrowing, current and deferred tax liabilities.

(iv) Segment revenue, results, assets and liabilities include the respective amounts identifiable to each of the segments and amount allocated on reasonable basis. Unallocated expenditure includes common expenditure incurred for all the segments and expenses incurred at the corporate level. Finance cost includes unwinding of discount on decommissioning provisions not allocated to segment.

TABLE 8.3(c) Depreciation, depletion and amortization and other non-cash items—impairment and write off

(₹ *in Million*)

Particulars	*Depreciation, depletion and amortization*		*Other non-cash items- impairment and write off*	
	Year ended March 31, 2023	*Year ended March 31, 2022*	*Year ended March 31, 2023*	*Year ended March 31, 2022*
Offshore	120,307.60	110,071.25	19,207.83	4,343.86
Onshore	60,655.59	55,085.56	13,704.63	926.29
Unallocated	1,785.91	1,373.87	38.37	35.01
Total	182,749.10	166,530.68	32,950.83	5,305.16

TABLE 8.3 (d) Impairment loss

Particulars	*Year ended March 31, 2023*	*Year ended March 31, 2022*
Offshore	(12,969.73)	21,258.01
Onshore	(1,827.82)	(12,331.68)
Total	(14,797.55)	8,926.33

TABLE 8.3(e) Exceptional items

Particulars	*Year ended March 31, 2023*	*Year ended March 31, 2022*
Offshore	50,810.33	–
Onshore	41,540.81	–
Total	92,351.14	–

TABLE 8.3(f) Additions to non-current assets

Particulars	*Year ended March 31, 2023*	*Year ended March 31, 2022*
Offshore	54,488.58	39,923.32
Onshore	20,151.89	46,983.27
Unallocated	336.32	(385.69)
Total	74,976.79	86,520.90

The Company, as part of its reporting practices, as provided the following further information in its Annual Report 2022–23 for better comprehension of the stakeholders:

Information about major customers: Company's significant revenues, i.e., more than 85% are derived from sales to Public Sector Undertakings. The total sales to such companies amounted to ₹1,385,309.74 Million in 2022–23 and ₹930,188.42 Million in 2021–22. No other single customer contributed 10% or more to the Company's revenue for 2022–23 and 2021–22.

INFORMATION ABOUT GEOGRAPHICAL AREAS

The Company is domiciled in India. The amount of its revenue from sale of products from external customers broken down by location of customers has been shown in Table 8.3(g). Similarly, the total of non-current assets other than financial instruments, deferred tax assets, post-employment benefit assets, broken down by location of assets has been depicted in Table 8.3(h).

TABLE 8.3(g) Revenue from External Customers

Location	*Year ended March 31, 2023*	*Year ended March 31, 2022*
India	1,484,018.42	1,022,999.71
Other Countries (including SEZ)	63,522.93	76,623.27
Total	1,547,541.35	1,099,622.98

TABLE 8.3(h) Total of non-current assets other than financial instruments, deferred tax assets, post-employment benefit assets

Location	*As at March 31, 2023*	*As at March 31, 2022*
India	1,889,904.94	1,814,928.15
Other Countries (including SEZ)	—	—
Total	1,889,904.94	1,814,928.15

INFORMATION ABOUT PRODUCTS AND SERVICES

The Company generates its revenue from sale of crude oil, natural gas and value added products. The information about revenues from external customers about each product has been shown in Table 8.3(i).

TABLE 8.3(i) Details of Sales Revenue

Product	*Unit*	*Year ended March 31, 2023*		*Year ended March 31, 2022*	
		Quantity	*Value ₹ in Million*	*Quantity*	*Value ₹ in Million*
Crude Oil *	MT	19,193,843	1,061,631.55	20,295,439	867,712.64
Less: From Exploratory Wells in progress		38,742	1,411.75	1,151	33.02
Less: Government of India's share in Profit Petroleum			30,144.15		31,067.38
			1,030,075.65		836,612.24
Natural Gas *	000M 3	16,676,842	379,297.46	16,753,037	128,596.91
Less: From Exploratory Wells in progress		17,051	410.87	1,660	26.65
Less: Government of India's share in Profit Petroleum			4,718.41		4,156.16
			374,168.18		124,414.10
Liquefied Petroleum Gas	MT	883,847	55,542.72	883,425	46,751.77
Naphtha	MT	921,281	49,613.69	963,870	50,640.14
Ethane-Propane	MT	119,404	4,909.03	314,771	9,078.41
Ethane	MT	280,690	13,310.75	499,578	10,814.60
Propane	MT	147,177	8,713.61	196,574	10,636.58
Butane	MT	80,508	4,667.68	115,927	6,185.22
Superior Kerosene Oil	MT	732	67.54	18,434	879.64
LSHS	MT	27,610	1,217.78	22,968	838.77
HSD	MT	13,275	1,366.17	12,152	1,018.36
Aviation Turbine Fuel (ATF)	MT	39,349	3,691.81	26,124	1,543.64
MTO	MT	2,082	196.74	4,257	206.64
Others (Note No. 17.1)			-		2.87
Total			1,547,541.35		1,099,622.98

* Quantity includes share from Joint Operations as per the Participating interest and/or Entitlement interest, whichever is applicable.

RELATED PARTY DISCLOSURE

Name of the related parties and the relationship with ONGC Ltd has with has been given in Table 8.3(j).

TABLE 8.3(j) Disclosure on Related parties

A	*Subsidiaries*	A	*Subsidiaries*
1	ONGC Videsh Limited (OVL)	1.6.9	LLC Allianceneftegaz
1.1	ONGC Nile Ganga B.V. (ONGBV)	1.6.10	LLC Nord Imperial
1.1.1	ONGC Campos Limited	1.6.11	LLC Rus Imperial Group
1.1.2	ONGC Nile Ganga (San Cristobal) B.V.	1.6.12	LLC Imperial Frac Services
1.2	ONGC Amazon Alaknanda Limited (OAAL)	1.7	Beas Rovuma Energy Mozambique Limited
1.3	ONGC Narmada Limited (ONL)	1.8	ONGC Videsh Rovuma Limited
1.4	ONGC (BTC) Limited	1.9	ONGC Videsh Atlantic Inc.
1.5	Carabobo One AB	1.10	ONGC Videsh Singapore Pte. Limited
1.5.1	Petro Carabobo Ganga B.V.	1.10.1	ONGC Videsh Vankorneft Pte. Limited
1.6	Imperial Energy Limited	1.11	Indus East Mediterranean Exploration Limited.
1.6.1	Imperial Energy Tomsk Limited	2	Mangalore Refinery and Petrochemicals Limited (MRPL)
1.6.2	Imperial Energy (Cyprus) Limited	3	Hindustan Petroleum Corporation Limited (HPCL)
1.6.3	Imperial Energy Nord Limited	3.1	Prize Petroleum Company Limited
1.6.4	Biancus Holdings Limited	3.1.1	Prize Petroleum International Pte. Limited
1.6.5	Redcliffe Holdings Limited	3.2	HPCL Biofuels Limited
1.6.6	Imperial Frac Services (Cyprus)Limited	3.3	HPCL Middle East FZCO
1.6.7	San Agio Investments Limited	3.4	HPCL LNG Limited (HPCLNG) formerly known as HPCL Shapoorji Energy Pvt. Limited (HSEPL)
1.6.8	LLC Sibinterneft	4	Petronet MHB Limited
B	*Joint Ventures*	*B*	*Joint Ventures*
1	Mangalore SEZ Limited (MSEZ)	12	HPOIL Gas Private Limited (through HPCL)
2	ONGC Petro additions Limited (OPaL)	13	HPCL Rajasthan Refinery Limited (through HPCL)
3	ONGC Tripura Power Company Limited (OTPC)	14	South Asia LPG Company Private Limited (through HPCL)
4	ONGC Teri Biotech Limited (OTBL)	15	HPCL Mittal Energy Limited (through HPCL)
5	Dahej SEZ Limited (DSEZ)	16	Godavari Gas Private Limited (through HPCL)
6	Indradhanush Gas Grid Limited (IGGL)	17	Petronet India Limited (through HPCL, in process of voluntary winding up w.e.f. August 30, 2018)

(*Contd.*)

TABLE 8.3(j) Disclosure on Related parties (*Contd.*)

7	ONGC Mittal Energy Limited (OMEL) (through OVL)	18	Mumbai Aviation Fuel Farm Facility Private Limited (through HPCL)
8	Mansarovar Energy Colombia Limited, Colombia (through OVL)	19	Aavantika Gas Limited (through HPCL)
9	Himalaya Energy Syria BV, Netherlands (through OVL)	20	Bhagyanagar Gas Limited (through HPCL)
10	Shell MRPL Aviation Fuels and Services Limited (SMASL) (through MRPL)	21	Ratnagiri Refinery & Petrochemicals Limited (through HPCL)
11	Hindustan Colas Private Limited (through HPCL)	22	IHB Limited (through HPCL)
C	*Associates*	C	*Associates*
1	Pawan Hans Limited	8	Tamba BV, Netherlands (through OVL)
2	Petronet LNG Limited	9	JSC Vankorneft, Russia (through OVL)
3	Rohini Heliport Limited	10	Falcon Oil & Gas BV, Netherlands (through OVL)
4	Petro Carabobo SA, Venezuela (through OVL)	11	Bharat Energy Office LLC, Russia (through ONGC Videsh Singapore Pte. Limited-OVL)
5	Carabobo Ingenieria Y Construcciones, SA, Venezuela (through OVL)	12	Moz LNG1 Holding Company Limited (through OVL)
6	Petrolera Indovenezolana SA, Venezuela (through OVL)	13	GSPL India Gasnet Limited (through HPCL)
7	South East Asia Gas Pipeline Limited, Hong Kong (through OVL)	14	GSPL India Transco Limited (through HPCL)
D	*Trusts*	*D*	*Trusts*
1	ONGC Contributory Provident Fund Trust	10	MRPL Gratuity Fund Trust (through MRPL)
2	ONGC CSSS Trust	11	MRPL Provident Fund Trust (through MRPL)
3	ONGC Sahyog Trust	12	MRPL Education Trust (through MRPL)
4	ONGC PRBS Trust	13	MRPL Janseva Trust (through MRPL)
5	ONGC Gratuity Fund	14	Ujjwala Plus Foundation (through HPCL)
6	ONGC Post-Retirement Medical Benefit Trust	15	Hindustan Petroleum Corporation Limited Provident Fund
7	ONGC Energy Center	16	Hindustan Petroleum Corporation Limited Employees Post-Retirement Med-Benefit Fund
8	ONGC Foundation	17	Hindustan Petroleum Corporation Limited Employees Group Gratuity Assurance Scheme
9	ONGC Start Up Fund Trust	18	Hindustan Petroleum Corporation Limited Employees Superannuation Benefit Fund Scheme

(***Source:*** ONGC Integrated Annual Report 2022–23)

KEY MANAGEMENT PERSONNEL

The key management personnel of ONGC Ltd. has been reflected in Table 8.3 (k).

TABLE 8.3(k) Key Management Personnel

Whole time Directors	*Company Secretary*	*Independent Directors*	*Government Nominee – Directors*
Shri Arun Kumar Singh, Chairman (w.e.f. December 7, 2022) and CEO (w.e.f. January 1, 2023)	Shri Rajni Kant, Company Secretary	Shri Amitava Bhattacharya (Up to July 7,2022)	Shri Amar Nath (Up to May 14, 2022)
Dr. Alka Mittal, Director (HR) and Chairman & Managing Director - Additional Charge (Up to August 31, 2022)	—	Shri Syamchand Ghosh	Shri Praveen Mal Khanooja (w.e.f. September 23, 2022)
Shri Rajesh Kumar Srivastava, Director (Exploration) (Up to December 31, 2022) and Chairman & Managing Director - Additional Charge (w.e.f. September 01, 2022 Up to December 6, 2022)	—	Shri V. Ajit Kumar Raju	Shri Shrinivas Gudey (w.e.f. June 14, 2022 to September 22, 2022)
Shri O.P. Singh, Director(T&FS)	—	Shri Manish Pareek	—
Shri Anurag Sharma, Director (Onshore) (Up to 28 February 2023) and Director (Finance) - Additional Charge (Up to April 18, 2022)	—	Ms. Reena Jaitly	—
Shri Pankaj Kumar, Director (Offshore) (upto 28 February 2023) now Director (Production) (w.e.f. March 01, 2023)	—	Dr Prabhaskar Rai	—
Ms. Pomila Jaspal, Director (Finance) (w.e.f. April 19, 2022)	—	Dr Madhav Singh	—
Ms. Sushma Rawat, Director (Exploration) (w.e.f. January 1, 2023)	—	—	—

DETAILS OF TRANSACTIONS

The details of transactions involving Subsidiaries, Associates, Joint ventures, Trust, and Transactions with Government Related Entities have been given in Table 8.4(a), 8,4(b), 8.4(c), 8.4(d), and 8.4(e),respectively.

TABLE 8.4 (a) Transactions with Subsidiaries

(₹ *in Million*)

	Name of related party	*Nature of transaction*	*Year ended March 31, 2023*	*Year ended March 31, 2022*
(i)	Sale of products to:			
	Mangalore Refinery and Petrochemicals Limited	Sale of crude oil	118,133.11	71,437.55
	Hindustan Petroleum Corporation Limited	Sale of crude oil and value added products	244,949.41	192,469.32
(ii)	Purchase of product from:			
	Mangalore Refinery and Petrochemicals Limited	Purchase of petroleum oil and lubricants/high speed diesel	9,403.30	11,047.25
	Hindustan Petroleum Corporation Limited		1,679.37	2,117.69
(iii)	Services received from:			
	Prize Petroleum Corporation Limited (Subsidiary of HPCL)	Development of Field	—	2.11
	ONGC Videsh Limited	Rent for Office	929.05	—
(iv)	Services provided to:			
	Mangalore Refinery and Petrochemicals Limited	Leasing of office and Maintenance	61.24	54.43
		Tanker/Vehicle hiring charges and other services	—	12.17
		Guarantee fee	35.64	19.55
		Manpower deputation and other reimbursements	2.17	—
	ONGC Videsh Limited	Reimbursement of Expenses incurred	574.17	415.34
		Guarantee fee (OVVL)	552.72	209.41
		Guarantee fee (BREML)	5.81	2.76
	Hindustan Petroleum Corporation Limited	Rent for Office	0.10	0.06
		Other expenses	39.14	35.84
(v)	Deemed Investments—Non-cash transaction (Ind AS fair valuations):			
	ONGC Videsh Limited	Deemed equity investment on issue of Financial guarantees by ONGC on behalf of OVL	—	239.97

	Name of related party	*Nature of transaction*	*Year ended March 31, 2023*	*Year ended March 31, 2022*
	ONGC Videsh Limited	Deemed equity investment on issue of Financial guarantees by ONGC on behalf of OVRL	—	11.13
	Mangalore Refinery and Petrochemicals Limited	Deemed equity investment for Financial guarantees of interest	9.83	—
(vi)	Dividend income from:			
	ONGC Videsh Limited	Dividend income	4,800.00	6,000.00
	Hindustan Petroleum Corporation Limited		10,903.84	17,718.73
	Petronet MHB limited		403.27	438.93
(vii)	Non-cash transaction (Ind AS fair valuations):			
	ONGC Videsh Limited	Guarantee fee in respect of financial guarantee (OVL)	427.69	370.41
		Guarantee fee in respect of financial guarantee (OVRL)	2.47	2.09
	Mangalore Refinery and Petrochemicals Limited	Deemed equity investment for Financial guarantees of interest on Compulsory Convertible Debentures for OMPL which is amalgamated with MRPL w.e.f April 01, 2021	—	0.62

OUTSTANDING BALANCES WITH SUBSIDIARIES

Outstanding balances with subsidiaries have been given in Table 8.4(a–i).

TABLE 8.4(a–i) Outstanding balances with subsidiaries

(₹ *in Million*)

	Name of related party	*Nature of transaction*	*Year ended March 31, 2023*	*Year ended March 31, 2022*
(i)	Amount receivable:			
	Mangalore Refinery and Petrochemicals Limited	Trade and other receivables	13,809.60	6,874.94
	ONGC Videsh Limited	Other receivables	273.74	365.58
		Guarantee Fees (OVVL)	550.15	209.41
		Guarantee Fees (OVRL)	0.76	0.38
		Guarantee Fee (BREML)	8.59	2.77

(*Contd.*)

TABLE 8.4(a–i) Outstanding balances with subsidiaries (*Contd.*)

	Name of related party	*Nature of transaction*	*Year ended March 31, 2023*	*Year ended March 31, 2022*
	Hindustan Petroleum Corporation Limited	Trade and other receivables	13,363.83	27,060.40
(ii)	Amount payable:			
	Mangalore Refinery and Petrochemicals Limited	Trade payables	521.99	642.69
	Hindustan Petroleun Corporation Limited		114.21	187.74
	Prize Petroleum Corporation Limited (Subsidiary of HPCL)		—	0.62
	ONGC Videsh Limited	Other payable	150.06	4.30
(iii)	Corporate Financial guarantee issued on behalf of subsidiaries:			
	ONGC Videsh Limited (including its subsidiaries)	Value of financial guarantee	3,99,201.49	366,614.37
	Mangalore Refinery and Petrochemicals Limited	Value of financial guarantee	—	207,804.98
(iv)	Outstanding value of commitment made:			
	ONGC Videsh Limited	Performance guarantee	8,601.11	8,688.53

TABLE 8.4(b) Transactions with Joint Ventures

(₹ *in Million*)

	Name of related party	*Nature of transaction*	*Year ended March 31, 2023*	*Year ended March 31, 2022*
(i)	Sale of products to:			
	ONGC Tripura Power Company Limited	Sale of natural gas	7,955.16	6,430.57
	ONGC Petro additions Limited	Sale of natural gas, naphtha and C_2-C_3	70,572.36	76,623.27
(ii)	Services received from:			
	ONGC Teri Biotech Limited	Bio-remediation services	375.86	172.99
	Dahej SEZ Limited	Lease rent for SEZ land and ROU charges for pipeline	19.88	16.96
(iii)	Services provided to:			
	ONGC Petro additions Limited	ROU Charges for pipeline received	0.44	0.22
		Charges for Operation and Maintenance	110.67	—
	ONGC Teri Biotech Limited	Field study charges and rent	0.60	0.56
		Manpower deputation	0.09	—

	Name of related party	Nature of transaction	Year ended March 31, 2023	Year ended March 31, 2022
	ONGC Tripura Power Company Limited	Rent of office space	24.44	23.77
	Indradhanush Gas Grid Limited	Manpower deputation	39.90	24.95
(iv)	Loans and Advances			
	ONGC Petro additions Limited	Advance received for transfer of Land	17.30	—
(v)	Subscription to equity shares			
	Indradhanush Gas Grid Limited	Subscription to Equity	1,130.00	240.00
(vii)	Dividend Income from:			
	ONGC Tripura Power Company Limited	Dividend income	392.00	392.00
	ONGC Teri Biotech Limited		12.50	
(x)	Deemed Investments—Non-cash transaction (Ind AS fair valuations):			
	ONGC Petro additions Limited	Deemed equity Investment—Financial Guarantee Obligation and Financial guarantees for interest on Compulsory Convertible Debentures	22.74	13.47
	Indradhanush Gas Grid Limited	Deemed equity Investment - Financial Guarantee Obligation and Amortisation of Financial Guarantee Fee	7.68	—

OUTSTANDING BALANCES WITH JOINT VENTURES

Outstanding balances with joint ventures have been reflected in Table 8.4(b-i):

TABLE 8.4(b–i) Outstanding balances with joint ventures

(₹ *in Million*)

	Name of related party	*Nature of transaction*	*Year ended March 31, 2023*	*Year ended March 31, 2022*
A.	Amount receivable:			
	ONGC Petro additions Limited	Trade and other receivables	3,732.06	5,001.19
	ONGC Tripura Power Company Limited		393.44	434.93
	Indradhanush Gas Grid Limited		3.16	14.00
B.	Amount payable:			
	ONGC Teri Biotech Limited	Trade payables	62.36	19.17
C.	Advance outstanding:			
	ONGC Petro addition Limited	Advance against subscription to share warrants	33,649.59	33,649.59
	Indradhanush Gas Grid Limited	Advance for subscription of equity shares	—	830.00

(*Contd.*)

TABLE 8.4(b–i) Outstanding balances with joint ventures (*Contd.*)

	Name of related party	*Nature of transaction*	*Year ended March 31, 2023*	*Year ended March 31, 2022*
D.	Commitments:			
	ONGC Petro addition Limited	Unpaid subscription of share warrants	862.81	862.81
		Backstopping support for Interest outstanding towards CCDs	1,766.85	1,699.28
	Indradhanush Gas Grid Limited	Loan taken by IGGL from OIDB	200.00	—
E.	Letter of Comfort:			
	ONGC Petro addition Limited	Letter of Comfort—Term Loan (Refer Note No. 11.1.3)	65,000.00	65,000.00
		Letter of Comfort—NCDs (Refer Note No. 11.1.3)	30,000.00	30,000.00

During the year 2019–20, the Company had approved the related party transaction for transfer of Hazira Dahez Naptha Pipeline (HDNPL) to OPaL on as-is basis for a consideration of ₹1,653.40 Million comprising ₹1,154.40 Million (excludes GST) towards the cost incurred by Company for partially completed HDNPL pipe line with associated facilities and ₹499.00 Million towards Arbitration award and other related legal expenses. The arbitration award was pronounced against the Company in the ongoing dispute with M/s Punj Llyod Limited, and the Company has challenged arbitral award in the Hon'ble High Court of Bombay. The matter was heard by Hon'ble High Court of Bombay on September 29, 2022 wherein the Company was directed to deposit ₹380 Million within 6 weeks. Accordingly the Company has deposited the aforesaid amount on February 1, 2023 in consultation with OPaL and obtained stay on the impugned arbitration award. Management of OPaL has agreed to reimburse the same to the Company in terms of the Asset Transfer Agreement for which the Company is in the process of raising a claim for reimbursement.

TABLE 8.4(c) Transactions with Associates

(*₹ in Million*)

	Name of related party	*Nature of transaction*	*Year ended March 31, 2023*	*Year ended March 31, 2022*
A.	Services received from:			
	Pawan Hans Limited (PHL)	Hiring of helicopter services	1,342.06	1,259.84
	Petronet LNG Limited	Purchase of LNG (Net of custom duty)	15,472.58	18,319.61
		Facilities charges	555.47	770.86

	Name of related party	*Nature of transaction*	*Year ended March 31, 2023*	*Year ended March 31, 2022*
B.	Services provided to:			
	Pawan Hans Limited (PHL)	Miscellaneous receipt	–	60.83
	Petronet LNG Limited	Miscellaneous charges	0.14	–
C.	Income received from:			
	Petronet LNG Limited	Dividend Income	2,156.25	1,968.75

OUTSTANDING BALANCES WITH ASSOCIATES

Outstanding balances with associates have been given in Table 8.4(c–i).

TABLE 8.4(c–i) Outstanding Balances with Associates

(₹ *in Million*)

	Name of related party	*Nature of transaction*	*Year ended March 31, 2023*	*Year ended March 31, 2022*
A.	Amount receivable:			
	Petronet LNG Limited	Trade and other receivables	0.16	—
B.	Amount payable:			
	Pawan Hans Limited (PHL)	Trade payables	129.27	250.55
	Petronet LNG Limited		1,869.79	652.49

TABLE 8.4(d) Transactions with Trusts

(₹ *in Million*)

	Name of related party	*Nature of transaction*	*Year ended March 31, 2023*	*Year ended March 31, 2022*
A.	Remittance of payment:			
	ONGC Contributory Provident Fund Trust	Contribution	11,605.08	12,369.79
	ONGC CSSS Trust		2,209.08	1,077.05
	ONGC Sahyog Trust		43.60	31.34
	ONGC PRBS Trust		8,983.56	8,510.23
	ONGC Gratuity Trust		423.45	1,097.73
B.	Reimbursement of Gratuity payment made on behalf of Trust:			
	ONGC Gratuity Fund	Reimbursement	4,545.17	2,088.10
C.	Services provided to:			
	ONGC Energy Center	Rental income	3.24	4.07

(*Contd.*)

TABLE 8.4(d) Transactions with Trusts (*Contd.*)

	Name of related party	*Nature of transaction*	*Year ended March 31, 2023*	*Year ended March 31, 2022*
D.	Payment to Trust			
	ONGC Energy Center	For research and development	195.00	75.00
	ONGC Start Up Fund Trust	Investment	250.00	365.00
	ONGC Foundation	Supply of Oxygen Concentrator	—	93.57
		CSR Activities	1,496.19	1,511.68
E.	Sale/Purchase of Securities			
	ONGC Start Up Fund Trust	Sale of Equity Share and Compulsory Convertible Preference Shares	—	235.76

TABLE 8.4 (e) Transactions with Government Related Entities

(₹ *in Million*)

Name of related party	*Nature of transaction*	*Year ended March 31, 2023*	*Year ended March 31, 2022*
Sale of products during year to:			
(a) Indian Oil Corporation Limited	Sale of Crude Oil C_2–C_3, SKO, HSD, LPG and related services	449,191.91	319,310.36
(b) Bharat Petroleum Corporation Limited	Sale of Crude Oil C_2–C_3, SKO, HSD, LPG	173,920.40	153,444.49
(c) Chennai Petroleum Corporation Limited	Sale of Crude Oil	102,464.42	72,808.50
(d) Numaligarh Refinery Limited	Sale of Crude Oil	49,426.79	33,717.05
(e) GAIL (India) Limited	Sale of Natural Gas	327,876.27	99,469.27
(f) Brahmaputra Cracker and Polymer Limited	Sale of Natural Gas	1,049.90	506.65
(g) North Eastern Electric Power Corporation Limited	Sale of Natural Gas	1,669.55	1,242.47
Purchase of product during year from:			
(a) Indian Oil Corporation Limited	Purchase of Petrol Oil & Lubricant	1,765.33	3,543.17
(b) Bharat Petroleum Corporation Limited		5,453.95	3,993.72
(c) GAIL (India) Limited	Purchase of LNG	11,532.31	5,142.94
(d) Bharat Heavy Electricals Limited	Purchase of drilling rig related items including spares and related services	2,030.99	1,627.94
(e) Numaligarh Refinery Limited	Purchase of HSD	14.04	6.73
(f) Bharat Electronics Limited	Purchase of product	308.75	1,023.20
(g) Bharat Pumps and Compressors Limited	Purchase of spare parts	—	53.11
Services Received from:			
(a) United India Insurance Company Limited	Insurance premium	2,359.22	1,263.74

Name of related party	*Nature of transaction*	*Year ended March 31, 2023*	*Year ended March 31, 2022*
(b) Life Insurance Corporation of India	Remittance for Post-Retirement Medical Benefit Scheme, Leave Encashment and others	29,269.91	33,327.80
(c) Balmer Lawrie & Co Limited	Travel expenses	1,373.65	552.45
(d) Shipping Corporation of India Limited	Hiring of vessels	5,135.54	4,854.12
(e) Oil India Limited	Pipeline service	181.69	237.77
Dividend Income received from:			
(a) Indian Oil Corporation Limited	Dividend income	4,813.97	14,040.76
(b) GAIL (India) Limited		1,524.68	1,960.30
Amount receivable:			
(a) Indian Oil Corporation Limited	Trade and other receivable	24,707.02	32,584.08
(b) Bharat Petroleum Corporation Limited		9,434.05	12,323.96
(c) Chennai Petroleum Corporation Limited		4,470.73	9,902.24
(d) Numaligarh Refinery Limited		2,882.79	3,114.44
(e) GAIL (India) Limited		23,271.37	9,995.77
(f) Oil India Limited		371.96	840.09
(g) Brahmaputra Cracker and Polymer Limited		69.40	89.26
(h) Kochi Refineries Limited		—	0.05
(i) Coal India Limited		992.37	897.44
(j) Life Insurance Corporation of India	Receivable against Post-Retirement Medical Benefit Scheme	3,990.86	—
Amount payable:			
(a) Indian Oil Corporation Limited	Trade and other payable	96.79	79.25
(b) Bharat Petroleum Corporation Limited		674.02	1,028.32
(c) GAIL (India) Limited		321.02	320.76
(d) Bharat Heavy Electricals Limited		424.89	112.70
(e) Balmer Lawrie & Co Limited		56.09	32.68
(f) Shipping Corporation of India Limited		1,905.08	1,971.23
(g) Bharat Electronics Limited		91.32	383.08
(h) Oil India Limited		580.93	4.35
(i) Bharat Pumps and Compressors Limited		—	4.30
(j) Life Insurance Corporation of India		79.64	—

The above transactions with the government related entities cover transactions that are significant individually and collectively. The Company has also entered into other transactions such as telephone expenses, air travel, fuel purchase, deposits, etc. with above mentioned and other various government related entities. These transactions are insignificant individually and collectively and hence not disclosed.

SEGMENT REPORTING IN HINDUSTAN UNILEVER LIMITED (HUL)

The following paragraphs contain the segment reporting practices being followed by Hindustan Unilever Limited (HUL) as indicated in the Company's Avnnual Report 2022–23:

Segment Information

The Operating Segment is the level at which discrete financial information is available. Business segments are identified considering:

(a) the nature of products and services,
(b) the differing risks and returns,
(c) the internal organisation and management structure, and
(d) the internal financial reporting systems.

Revenue and expenses directly attributable to segments are reported under each reportable segment. Exceptional items and other expenses which are not attributable or allocable to segments are disclosed separately. Assets and liabilities that are directly attributable or allocable to segments are disclosed under each reportable segment. All other assets and liabilities are disclosed as unallocable assets and liabilities.

Business Segments

The Group has determined following reporting segments based on the information reviewed by the Group's Chief Operating Decision Maker ('CODM').

(a) Home Care include detergent bars, detergent powders, detergent liquids, scourers, water business, purifiers business, etc.
(b) Beauty & Personal Care include products in the categories of oral care, skin care, soaps, hair care, deodorants, talcum powder, colour cosmetics, salon services, etc.
(c) Foods and Refreshment include culinary products (tomato based products, fruit based products, soups, etc.), tea, coffee, health food drinks, ice-cream and frozen desserts.
(d) Others include exports, consignment, etc.

The CODM, who is responsible for allocating resources and assessing performance of the operating segments, has been identified as the Management Committee.

Segment Results

Segment revenue relating to each of the above domestic business segments includes Income from Services provided to group companies, where applicable. Segment results relate to profit from continuing operations before other income, finance costs, exceptional items and tax.

Based on HUL's Annual Report 2022–23, Table 8.5(a), Table 8.5(b), Table 8.5(c), Table 8.5(d), and Table 8.5(e) Segment Revenue and Results, Segment Assets and Liabilities, Capital expenditure, Depreciation/ Amortization, Non-cash expenses other than depreciation, information by Geographies, respectively, has been constructed to manifest the segment reporting practices of the company.

TABLE 8.5(a) Segment Revenue and Results of HUL

(₹ *in Crores*)

	Year ended 31st March 2023			*Year ended 31st March 2022*		
	External	*Intersegment*	*Total*	*External*	*Intersegment*	*Total*
REVENUE						
Home care	21,223	—	21,223	16,570	—	16,570
Beauty and Personal care	22,022	—	22,022	19,567	—	19,567
Foods and Refreshment	14,876	—	14,876	14,105	—	14,105
Others (includes Exports, Consignment, etc.						
Total Revenue	60,580	—	60,580	52,446	—	52,446
RESULT		—				
Home care	3,913	—	3,913	3,183	—	3,183
Beauty and Personal care	5,647	—	5,647	5,392	—	5,392
Foods and Refreshment	2,662	—	2,662	2,623	—	2,623
Others (includes Exports, Consignment, etc.)	790	—	790	568	—	568
Total Segment Results	13,012	—	13,012	11,766	—	11,766
Finance Costs			(114)			(106)
Other Income			512			258
Profit from continuing operations before exceptional items and tax			13,410			11,818
Share of net profit/(loss) of investments accounted for using equity method (net of income tax)			(1)			—
Exceptional items-income/ (expenditure)			(64)			(44)
Profit before tax from continuing operations			13,345			11,874
Tax Expenses						
Current tax			(3,001)			(2,840)
Deferred tax charge/(credit)			(200)			(147)
Profit for the year from Continuing Operations (A)			10,144			8,887
Profit for the year from Discontinued Operations (B)			(1)			5
Profit For the Year (A + B)			10,143			8,892
Less: Non-Controlling Interest			(23)			(13)
Profit for the Year			10,120			8,879

Other Information:

(A) Segment Assets and Liabilities

Table 8.5(b) displays the Segment Assets and Liabilities of HUL.

TABLE 8.5(b) Segment Assets and Liabilities of HUL

(in ₹ crores)

	Segment Assets		*Segment Liabilities*	
	As at 31st March 2023	*As at 31st March 2022*	*As at 31st March 2023*	*As at 31st March 2022*
Home care	4,785	3,999	4,075	3,755
Beauty and Personal care	7,140	6,239	6,117	5,670
Foods and Refreshment	50,299	49,669	3,131	3,140
Others (includes Exports, Consignment, etc.)	1,435	1,413	722	682
Total	63,659	61,320	14,045	13,247
Unallocated Corporate Assets/(Liabilities)	9,428	9,197	8,520	8,183
Total Assets/(Liabilities)	73,087	70,517	22,565	21,430

(B) Capital expenditure, Depreciation/Amortisation, Non-cash expenses other than depreciation.

Table 8.5(c) shows information on Capital expenditure, Depreciation/ Amortisation, Non-cash expenses other than depreciation.

TABLE 8.5(c) Capital expenditure, Depreciation/ Amortisation, Non-cash expenses other than depreciation

(in ₹ crores)

	Year ended 31st March 2023			*Year ended 31st March 2022*		
	Capital expenditure	*Depreciation/ Amortization**	*Non-cash expenses other than depreciation*	*Capital expenditure*	*Depreciation/ Amortization**	*Non-cash expenses other than depreciation*
Home care	625	240	49	280	213	38
Beauty and Personal care	644	539	50	512	544	44
Foods and Refreshment	579	309	33	361	300	34
Others (includes Exports, onsignment, etc.)	96	49	18	59	34	12

* In addition to the above, ₹15 crores (2021–22: ₹15 crores) of accelerated depreciation has been charged to exceptional items under a restructuring project.

(C) Additional Information by Geographies

Table 8.5(d) depicts information about HUL's revenue and assets by Geographies, i.e., from India and outside India.

TABLE 8.5(d) Information by Geographies

(*in ₹ crores*)

	Year ended 31st March 2023	*Year ended 31st March 2022*
Revenue by Geographical Market		
India	58,172	50,327
Outside India	2,408	2,119
Total	60,580	52,446
Carrying Amount of Segment Assets		
India	63,117	60,771
Outside India	542	549
Total	63,659	6,320

Note: Although the Group's (i.e., HUL's) operations are managed by product area, the company provides additional information based on geographies.

(D) Revenue from major customers

The Group's (i.e., HUL's) is not reliant on revenues from transactions with any single external customer and does not receive 10% or more of its revenues from transactions with any single external customer. However, Table 8.5(e) has been drawn to indicate revenues coming from sale of products and sale of services for better comprehension.

TABLE 8.5(e) Revenue from major customers

	Year ended 31st March, 2023	*Year ended 31st March, 2022*
Sale of products	59,443	51,472
Sale of services	106	76
Income from services rendered	370	294
Commission income on consignment sales	333	315
Government grants (GST budgetary support and Production linked incentives)	179	140
Others (including scrap sales, rentals, etc.) sale of products and sale of services.	149	149
Total	60,580	52,446

Source: HUL's Annual Report 2022-23

SUMMARY

Reporting on each segment of the business has become a necessity over the recent years to communicate to the users of financial statements about the operating performance of each segment of the business for better analysis and understanding of the enterprise's performance including its performance in dissimilar and diversified activities. The objective of presenting information by segments is to provide users of financial statements with information on the relative size, profit, contribution, and growth trend of the different industries and different geographical areas in which diversified enterprise operates to enable them to make more informed judgments about the enterprise as a whole.

Segment reporting thus refers to the disclosure of information about an enterprise's operation in different industries, its foreign operations and export sales, and its major customers. For the purpose of segment reporting, IAS 14 and also AS 17 provide for classifications of the products and services of the enterprise into (1) business segment, and (2) geographical segments. Business segment is a distinguishable component of an enterprise which is engaged in providing an individual product or service or a group of products or services that is subject to risks and returns that are different from those of other business segments. Geographic segment is a distinguishable component of an enterprise which is engaged in providing products or services within a particular economic environment that is subject to risk and returns that are different from those components operating in other economic environment. The two standards, IAS 14 and AS 17 too have stipulations as regards the disclosures to be made in segment reporting.

IAS 14 has now been replaced by IFRS 8: Operating Segment Reporting. Similarly, in India, AS 17 which was the IAS 14 equivalent Indian Accounting Standard has now been replaced by Ind AS 108. IFRS 8 provides for reporting of financial performance of an entity on its **operating segments** in order to enable the users of its financial statements to evaluate the nature and financial effects of the business activities in which the entity is engaged with and the economic environments in which it operates.

An operating segment is a component of an entity, that engages in business activities from which it may earn revenues and incur expenses (including revenues and expenses relating to transactions with other components of the same entity), whose operating results are regularly reviewed by the entity's **chief operating decision maker** (CODM) to make decisions about resources to be allocated to the segment and assess its performance, and for which discrete financial information is available. Further, an operating segment may engage in business activities for which it has yet to earn revenues, for example, start-up operations may be operating segments before earning revenues.

KEY TERMS

Segment reporting: Segment reporting refers to the disclosure of information about an enterprise's operation in different industries, its foreign operations and export sales, and its major customers.

Operating segment: An operating segment is a component of an entity, that engages in business activities from which it may earn revenues and incur expenses (including revenues and expenses relating to transactions with other components of the same entity), whose operating results are regularly reviewed by the entity's **chief operating decision maker** (CODM) to make decisions about resources to be allocated to the segment and assess its performance, and for which discrete financial information is available. Further, an operating segment may engage in business activities for which it has yet to earn revenues, for example, start-up operations may be operating segments before earning revenues.

Business segment: Business segment is a distinguishable component of an enterprise which is engaged in providing an individual product or service or a group of products or services that is subject to risks and returns that are different from those of other business segments.

Geographic segment: Geographic segment is a distinguishable component of an enterprise which is engaged in providing products or services within a particular economic environment that is subject to risk and returns that are different from those components operating in other economic environment.

Reportable segment: Reportable segment is a business or geographical segment whose majority of revenue is earned from sales to external customers and further that its revenue from sales to external customers and from transactions with internal customers (i.e., other segments) is 10% or more of the total revenue of all segments, or its segment result (i.e., profit or loss) is 10% or more of the combined result of all segments recording a profit or of all segments recording a loss, whichever is higher in absolute monetary terms, or its assets are 10% or more of the total assets of all segments.

REVIEW QUESTIONS

1. What segment reporting? What are its utilities? Explain with example(s).
2. Discuss the important provisions of international GAAP on segment reporting.
3. State the disclosure requirements as contained in IFRS 8.
4. Distinguish between business segment and geographic segment.
5. Write a note on Ind AS 108 on segment reporting.
6. Bring out the disclosure norms as stipulated in Ind AS 108.
7. Highlight the important features of segment reporting as practiced by any Indian firms in recent times.
8. Write explanatory notes on:
   (a) Business segment
   (b) Geographic segment
   (c) Reportable segment
9. Explain the following:
   (a) Operating Segment.
   (b) Reportable segment
   (c) Business segment.

REFERENCES

[1] Epstein, B.J., and Mirza, A.A., IAS 2002, John Willey & Sons, Inc.

[2] Ghosh, T.P., Financial Accounting for Managers, 2nd Ed., Taxmann Allied Service (p) Ltd., India, 2004, p. 205.

[3] IRFS Foundation

9

Interim Financial Reporting

LEARNING OBJECTIVES

After studying this chapter, you will be able to:

- Explain the concept and importance of interim reporting
- Discuss the provisions of International GAAP on interim reporting
- Describe the disclosure norms stipulated under IAS 34 on interim reporting
- Explain the provisions of Indian GAAP on interim reporting
- Describe the provisions of Ind AS 34 on disclosure requirements in interim reporting
- Discuss SEBI guidelines on interim reporting and disclosure
- Understand interim reporting and disclosure in practice

INTRODUCTION

Interim financial reporting refers to the presentation of financial statements of the enterprise covering periods of less than a full financial year. The purpose of such presentation of financial statements is to provide the decision makers with frequent and timely information for taking investment and credit decisions, based on their ability to predict full year's financial results from the interim results. IAS 34 issued by IASC contains detailed provisions as regards interim financial reporting. ICAI too had issued guidelines for interim reporting by Indian firms through pronouncement of AS 25 which has now been replaced by Ind AS 34.

The salient features of the guidelines issued under IAS 34 and Ind AS 34 have been highlighted as under:

IAS 34 ON INTERIM FINANCIAL REPORTING

IAS 34 stipulates that an enterprise must present interim financial reports either in the 'complete form' or in a 'condensed form' of financial statements, in order to provide information which will be useful in making economic decisions. The standard provided that 'Interim financial report means a financial report containing either a complete set of financial statements (as described in IAS 1 Presentation of Financial Statements (as revised in 2007)) or a set of condensed financial statements (as described in this Standard) for an interim period'[1]. Interim period is a financial reporting period shorter than a full financial year.

CONTENT OF AN INTERIM FINANCIAL REPORT

IAS 1 defines a complete set of financial statements as including the following components:

(a) a statement of financial position as at the end of the period;
(b) a statement of profit or loss and other comprehensive income for the period;
(c) a statement of changes in equity for the period;
(d) a statement of cash flows for the period;
(e) notes, comprising significant accounting policies and other explanatory information;
(ea) comparative information in respect of the preceding period as specified in paragraphs 38 and 38A of IAS 1; and
(f) a statement of financial position as at the beginning of the preceding period when an entity applies an accounting policy retrospectively or makes a retrospective restatement of items in its financial statements, or when it reclassifies items in its financial statements in accordance with paragraphs 40A–40D of IAS 1.

MINIMUM COMPONENTS OF AN INTERIM FINANCIAL REPORT

An interim financial report shall include, at a minimum, the following components:

(a) a condensed statement of financial position;
(b) a condensed statement or condensed statements of profit or loss and other comprehensive income;
(c) a condensed statement of changes in equity;
(d) a condensed statement of cash flows; and
(e) selected explanatory notes.

If an entity presents items of profit or loss in a separate statement as described in paragraph 10A of IAS 1 (as amended in 2011), it presents interim condensed information from that statement.

FORM AND CONTENT OF INTERIM FINANCIAL STATEMENTS

As regards the *form and content* of interim financial statements, IAS 34 provides that:

1. If an entity publishes a complete set of financial statements in its interim financial report, the form and content of those statements shall conform to the requirements of IAS 1 for a complete set of financial statements.
2. If an entity publishes a set of condensed financial statements in its interim financial report, those condensed statements shall include, at a minimum, each of the headings and subtotals that were included in its most recent annual financial statements and the selected explanatory notes as required by this Standard. Additional line items or notes shall be included if their omission would make the condensed interim financial statements misleading.

3. In the statement that presents the components of profit or loss for an interim period, an entity shall present basic and diluted earnings per share for that period when the entity is within the scope of IAS 33 Earnings per Share.
4. If an entity presents items of profit or loss in a separate statement as described in paragraph 10A of IAS 1 (as amended in 2011), it presents basic and diluted earnings per share in that statement.
5. An interim financial report is prepared on a consolidated basis if the entity's most recent annual financial statements were consolidated statements.

IAS 34 further provides that an enterprise may also present interim financial reports for the parent company exclusively in addition to the consolidated interim reports.

DISCLOSURES IN INTERIM FINANCIAL REPORTING

IAS 34 stipulates, among others, the following minimum disclosures to be made in the interim financial reports:

1. Statements that the same accounting policies and methods have been applied in the interim financial statements as were applied in the most recent annual financial statements. In case any different policies or methods have been used, a description of the nature and the extent of the effect of such changes.
2. A description on the seasonality or cyclicality of interim operations.
3. The nature and extent of significant items affecting interim results which are unusual because of nature, size or incidence.
4. Dividend paid in aggregate or per share basis, separately for ordinary shares and other class(es) of shares.
5. Revenue and operating result for business segments or geographical segments whichever is the enterprise's primary reporting format.
6. Any significant events occurring subsequent to the end of the interim period.
7. Issuances, repurchases and repayments of debt and equity.
8. The nature and magnitude of changes in estimates of amounts reported in prior interim periods of the current financial year, or changes in estimates of amounts reported in prior financial years, if those changes have a material effect in the current interim period.
9. The effect of changes in the composition of the enterprise during the interim period, like business combinations, acquisitions or disposal of subsidiaries, and long-term investments, restructuring, and discontinuing operations.
10. The changes in contingent liabilities or contingent assets since the most recent annual financial statements.

Detailed provisions on disclosure as per IAS 34 have been given in Appendix-9(A) attached at the end of this Chapter

COMPARATIVE STATEMENTS

IAS 34 favours a comparative presentation of the interim financial statements which would be more useful than the presentation of information about any single period. The standard therefore recommends for presentation of a four-column income statement with comparative and year-to-date data. The four columns should reflect financial results of the first quarter of the current financial year in comparison to the first quarter result of the previous year along with the half yearly results of the current and the previous year. For the other components of interim reports, i.e., for the balance sheet, cash flow statement and the statement showing changes in equity, a two-column presentation of data would be considered ideal. These statements should present for two periods as follows:

1. The balance sheet as on the end of the current interim period and a comparative balance sheet as the immediately preceding financial year.
2. The cash flow statement cumulatively for the current financial year-to-date with a comparative statement for the comparable year-to-date period of the immediate preceding financial year.
3. The statement showing changes in equity cumulatively for the current financial year with a comparative statement for the comparable year-to-date period for the immediate preceding financial year.

IAS 34 also recommends for highly seasonal businesses to include additional column to the income statement columns in order to incorporate the result of the twelve months ending on the date of the most recent interim report in a view to eliminating the seasonality concerns. Such a reporting with additional columns to eliminate seasonality concerns is referred to be called as 'rolling twelve-month statements'.

INDIAN GAAP ON INTERIM FINANCIAL REPORTING

Indian Accounting Standard Ind AS 34 provides for presentation of interim financial reports. These interim financial reports may be either a complete set of financial statements as described in Ind AS 1 Presentation of Financial Statements, or a set of condensed financial statements for an interim period.

As per Ind AS 1, a complete set of financial statements shall include:

(a) a balance sheet as at the end of the period (including statement of changes in equity for the period which is presented as a part of the balance sheet);
(b) a statement of profit and loss for the period;
(c) [Refer to Appendix 1]
(d) a statement of cash flows for the period;
(e) notes, comprising a summary of significant accounting policies and other explanatory information; and
(f) a balance sheet as at the beginning of the earliest comparative period when an entity applies an accounting policy retrospectively or makes a retrospective restatement of items in its financial statements, or when it reclassifies items in its financial statements.

While preparing these statements all provisions contained in 'Appendix 1' of Ind AS 34 must be complied with.

The interim period shall be a period of less than a full year. As per the listing agreement, the listed companies in India are required to furnish quarterly unaudited financial results in the prescribed format to the stock exchange(s). However, Ind AS 34 provides that the information furnished to the stock exchange(s) under the listing agreement is not an interim financial report until and unless such reports are prepared in accordance with the provisions of Ind AS 34.

Ind AS 34 sets the following principles for interim financial reporting by Indian companies:

1. An entity may present a full set of financial statements or a set of condensed financial statements in an interim report.
2. In case the entity presents a complete set of financial statements, then the form and content of those statements should conform to the requirements of Ind AS 1 on presentation of financial statements.
3. If an entity publishes a set of condensed financial statements in its interim financial report, those condensed statements shall include, at a minimum, each of the headings and subtotals that were included in its most recent annual financial statements and the selected explanatory notes as required by this Standard. Additional line items or notes shall be included if their omission would make the condensed interim financial statements misleading.
4. In the statement that presents the components of profit or loss for an interim period, an entity shall present basic and diluted earnings per share for that period when the entity is within the scope of Ind AS 33 Earnings per Share.

Basic EPS = Net profit or loss for the period available to equity shareholders *divided by* weighted average number equity shares outstanding during the period; and diluted EPS = Net profit attributable to equity shareholders after adjustment for diluted earnings *divided by* average number of weighted equity shares outstanding during the period considering the conversion of diluted potential equity shares.

Details of the procedure for calculation of basic EPS and diluted EPS have been given in Appendix-9(B) at the end of this chapter.

5. An interim financial report is prepared on a consolidated basis if the entity's most recent annual financial statements were consolidated statements. The parent's separate financial statements are not consistent or comparable with the consolidated statements in the most recent annual financial report. If an entity's annual financial report included the parent's separate financial statements in addition to consolidated financial statements, this Standard neither requires nor prohibits the inclusion of the parent's separate statements in the entity's interim financial report.

Disclosure Requirements

Ind AS 34 provides for the following minimum *disclosures* to be made in interim reporting:

1. An entity shall include in its interim financial report an explanation of events and transactions that are significant to an understanding of the changes in financial position and performance of the entity since the end of the last annual reporting period information disclosed in relation to those events and transactions shall update the relevant information presented in the most recent annual financial report.
2. A user of an entity's interim financial report will have access to the most recent annual financial report of that entity. Therefore, it is unnecessary for the notes to an

interim financial report to provide relatively insignificant updates to the information that was reported in the notes in the most recent annual financial report.

3. The following is a list of events and transactions, though not exhaustive, for which disclosures would be required if they are significant:
   - (i) the write-down of inventories to net realizable value and the reversal of such a write-down;
   - (ii) recognition of a loss from the impairment of financial assets, property, plant and equipment, intangible assets, or other assets, and the reversal of such an impairment loss;
   - (iii) the reversal of any provisions for the costs of restructuring;
   - (iv) acquisitions and disposals of items of property, plant and equipment;
   - (v) commitments for the purchase of property, plant and equipment;
   - (vi) litigation settlements;
   - (vii) corrections of prior period errors;
   - (viii) changes in the business or economic circumstances that affect the fair value of the entity's financial assets and financial liabilities, whether those assets or liabilities are recognized at fair value or amortized cost;
   - (ix) any loan default or breach of a loan agreement that has not been remedied on or before the end of the reporting period;
   - (x) related party transactions;
   - (xi) transfers between levels of the fair value hierarchy used in measuring the fair value of financial instruments;
   - (xii) changes in the classification of financial assets as a result of a change in the purpose or use of those assets; and
   - (xiii) changes in contingent liabilities or contingent assets.
4. A statement that the same accounting policies were followed in interim financial statements as were followed in the enterprise's most recent annual financial statements, or if these policies have been changed, a description of the nature and effect of such changes.
5. Description about the seasonal or cyclical effect on interim financial reports.
6. Unusual factors that impacted assets, liabilities, equity, net income and cash flows.
7. Changes in debt and equity through issuance, repurchase and repayments.
8. Segment revenue and segment result for business or geographical segment whichever is the primary reporting format.
9. Effect of changes in estimates.
10. Details of dividend payment.
11. Material changes in contingent liability since the last balance sheet.
12. Effect of changes in composition of the enterprise (due to business combination, acquisition, restructuring, disposal of subsidiaries, etc.) during interim period.
13. Material event that occurred after the end of interim period.

Further details of the provisions laid down in Ind AS 34 on interim reporting has been given in Apendix-9(C)

SEBI on Interim Reporting

Based on the C.B. Bhave Committee's recommendations on bringing certain basic changes to interim reporting by listed companies in India, the Securities and Exchange Board of India (SEBI) vide its Circular No. SMD/POLICY/CIR-08/2000, had made the following stipulations as mandatory for the listed companies in India:

1. Companies have to furnish unaudited financial results on a quarterly basis in the prescribed format within one month of the expiry of the period to the stock exchange where they are listed. They are also to make an announcement within 48 hours of the conclusion of the Board meeting in at least one English daily newspaper circulating in the whole or substantially the whole of India, and a newspaper published in regional language where the companies' respective registered offices are situated.
2. The company's unaudited result should not differ substantially from the audited result. If the sum of the four quarters' result in respect of any given item differs more than 20% as compared to its full year's figure, the company shall explain the reason of such variance.
3. Companies have to prepare half-yearly results in the same format as the quarterly results. However, the half-yearly results are subject to limited audit review by the company auditor(s). The limited audit review report should be submitted to the stock exchange within two months from the expiry of the half-year period.
4. If the sum of the first and second quarter's unaudited results in respect of any item given in the same format varies 20% or more from the respective half-yearly results determined after limited audit review, the company has to explain the reasons thereof and such explanatory statement should be approved by the Board of Directors and submitted to the stock exchange along with the limited audit review report.
5. If the company intimates the stock exchange in advance that it will publish its audited result within three months from the end of the financial year, the company need not publish the last quarter's result.

SEBI on Disclosures

The quarterly financial reports should be accompanied by the following disclosures as stipulated by SEBI:

1. Any material event or transaction such as strike, completion of diversification/ expansion programmes, which have material impact in understanding quarterly results along with any occurrence of such events subsequent to the end of the quarter and their effect on the quarter's result.
2. The effect of changes in accounting policies.
3. Any items of non-recurring or abnormal gains/losses should be disclosed separately.
4. The effect of changes in the composition of the company during the quarter due to reasons such as acquisitions, combinations, restructuring or disposal of subsidiaries.
5. Information on dividend paid.

6. In case of companies whose revenues are subject to seasonal variations, the financial results of the twelve months ending should be reported on the last day of the quarter for the current year and the preceding year on a rolling basis.
7. The audit qualifications, if any, on the previous year's financial statements along with the quarterly results with explanations as to how such qualifications has been addressed in the unaudited financial results.
8. The unaudited financial statements should be prepared on the basis of the same set of accounting policies which were followed in the preparation of the previous year's financial statement.
9. The company which is yet to commence commercial production should in lieu of the quarterly reports provide details of the status of the project, its implementation and expected date of commissioning.

SEBI on Corporate Governance Report

SEBI vide its circular SMDRP/POLICY/CIR-03/01 (January 22, 2001), required the listed companies to furnish quarterly compliance report on corporate governance. The suggestive list of items to be included in the governance report is:

A. A brief description of the company's philosophy on the code of governance.
B. Composition of the Board of Directors (such as promoter, executive, non-executive, independent, nominee-director, the institutions represented, as lender or as equity investor); attendance of each director at the Board of Directors (BoD) Meetings and the last Annual General Meeting (AGM); number of other BoDs or board committees he/she is a member or chairperson; number of BoD Meetings held and the dates on which held.
C. Composition of the Audit Committee along with names of the members and the chairperson; description of the terms of references; meetings and attendance during the year.
D. Composition of the Remuneration Committee with names of the members and the chairperson; description of the terms of references; attendance during the year; remuneration policy; and details of remuneration to all the directors, as per the format in the main report.
E. Details of the Shareholders Committee with name of non-executive director heading the committee; number of shareholders' complaints received so far; number of complaints not solved to the satisfaction of shareholders; and number of pending share transfers.
F. Details of the General Body Meetings such as the location and time where the last *three* AGMs were held; whether there will be special resolutions; whether they were put through postal ballot the previous year with details of the voting pattern: person who conducted the postal ballot exercise; whether they are proposed to be conducted through postal ballot; and the procedure for postal ballot.
G. Disclosures on materially significant related party transactions (i.e., transactions of the company of material nature, with its promoters, the directors or the management, their subsidiaries or relatives, etc.) which may have potential conflict with the interests of the company at large; details of non-compliance by the company, penalties, strictures

imposed on the company by a stock exchange or SEBI or any statutory authority on any matter related to capital markets during the *three* previous years.

H. Means of Communication such as half-yearly report sent to each household of shareholders; quarterly results; newspapers in which it is normally published; any website where displayed; whether it also displays official news releases; the presentations made to institutional investors or to analysts; and whether the Management Discussion and Analysis (MD&A) is a part of the annual report or not.

I. General Shareholder Information in relation to the date, time and venue of AGM; financial calendar; date of closure of books; date of payment of dividend; listing on stock exchanges and stock code; market price data such as High and Low during each month in the previous financial year; performance in comparison to broad-based indices such as the BSE Sensex, CRISIL ratings, etc.; registrars and transfer agents; share transfer system; distribution of shareholding; dematerialization of shares and liquidity; outstanding GDRs/ADRs/warrants or any convertible instruments, conversion date and likely impact on equity; plant locations; and address for correspondence.

Amendments to SEBI Regulations

SEBI has come up with several Regulations and Amendments to some of the existing Regulations issued by it from 1992. Table 9.1 contains a list of such regulations and amendments.

EXHIBIT 9.1(A) List of SEBI Regulations

Year of Issue	*Regulations*
1992	Securities and Exchange Board of India (Merchant Bankers) Regulations, 1992 [Last amended on August 18, 2023]
1992	Securities and Exchange Board of India (Stock Brokers) Regulations, 1992 [Last amended on August 18, 2023]
1993	Securities and Exchange Board of India (Debenture Trustees) Regulations, 1993 [Last amended on August 18, 2023]
1993	Securities and Exchange Board of India (Registrars to an Issue and Share Transfer Agents) Regulations, 1993 [Last amended on August 18, 2023]
1994	Securities and Exchange Board of India (Bankers to an Issue) Regulations, 1994 [Last amended on August 18, 2023]
1996	Securities and Exchange Board of India (Custodian) Regulations, 1996 [Last amendment on July 4, 2023]
1996	Securities and Exchange Board of India (Mutual Funds) Regulations, 1996 [Last amended on August 18, 2023]
1999	Securities and Exchange Board of India (Collective Investment Scheme) Regulations, 1999 [Last amended on August 18, 2023]
1999	Securities and Exchange Board of India (Credit Rating Agencies) Regulations, 1999 [Last amended on July 4, 2023]
2000	Securities and Exchange Board of India (Foreign Venture Capital Investor) Regulations, 2000 [Last amended on February 07, 2023]
2001	SEBI (Procedure for Board Meetings) Regulations, 2001 [Last amended on December 9, 2022]

Year of Issue	*Regulations*
2001	Securities and Exchange Board of India (Employees' Service) Regulations, 2001 [Last amended on May 06, 2024]
2003	SEBI (Prohibition of Fraudulent and Unfair Trade Practices relating to Securities Market) Regulations, 2003 [Last amended on January 25, 2022]
2004	Securities and Exchange Board of India (Self Regulatory Organisations) Regulations, 2004 [Last amended on February 07, 2023]
2007	SEBI (Certification of Associated Persons in the Securities Markets) Regulations, 2007 [Last amended on February 07, 2014]
2008	Securities and Exchange Board of India (Intermediaries) Regulations, 2008 [Last amended on August 01, 2022]
2008	Securities and Exchange Board of India (Issue and Listing of Securitised Debt Instruments and Security Receipts) Regulations, 2008 [Last amended on August 18, 2020]
2009	Securities and Exchange Board of India (Investor Protection and Education Fund) Regulations, 2009 [Last amended on October 23, 2023]
2011	Securities and Exchange Board of India (Substantial Acquisition of Shares and Takeovers) Regulations, 2011 [Last amended on May 17, 2024]
2011	Securities and Exchange Board of India {KYC (Know Your Client) Registration Agency} Regulations, 2011 [Last amended on August 18, 2023]
2012	Securities and Exchange Board of India (Alternative Investment Funds) Regulations, 2012 [Last amended on April 25, 2024]
2013	Securities and Exchange Board of India (Investment Advisers) Regulations, 2013 [Last amended on April 26, 2024]
2014	Securities and Exchange Board of India (Infrastructure Investment Trusts) Regulations, 2014 [Last amended on October 23, 2023]
2014	Securities and Exchange Board of India (Real Estate Investment Trusts) Regulations, 2014 [Last amended on March 8, 2024]
2014	Securities and Exchange Board of India (Research Analysts) Regulations, 2014 [Last amended on April 26, 2024]
2015	Securities and Exchange Board of India (Issue and Listing of Municipal Debt Securities) Regulations, 2015 [Last amendment on August 18, 2023]
2015	Securities and Exchange Board of India (Listing Obligations and Disclosure Requirements) Regulations, 2015 [Last amended on May 17, 2024]
2015	Securities and Exchange Board of India (Prohibition of Insider Trading) Regulations, 2015 [Last amended on May 17, 2024]
2018	Securities and Exchange Board of India (Appointment of Administrator and Procedure for Refunding to the Investors) Regulations, 2018
2018	Securities and Exchange Board of India (Buy-back of Securities) Regulations 2018 [Last amended on May 17, 2024]

(*Contd.*)

Year of Issue	Regulations
2018	Securities and Exchange Board of India (Depositories and Participants) Regulations, 2018 [Last amended on May 10, 2024]
2018	Securities and Exchange Board of India (Issue of Capital and Disclosure Requirements) Regulations 2018 [Last amended on May 17, 2024]
2018	Securities and Exchange Board of India (Settlement Proceedings) Regulations, 2018 [Last amended on August 09, 2023]
2018	Securities Contracts (Regulation) (Stock Exchanges and Clearing Corporations) Regulations, 2018 [Last amended on May 10, 2024]
2019	Securities and Exchange Board of India (Foreign Portfolio Investors) Regulations, 2019 [Last amended on June 03, 2024]
2020	Securities and Exchange Board of India (Portfolio Managers) Regulations, 2020 [Last amended on August 18, 2023]
2021	Securities and Exchange Board of India (Delisting of Equity Shares) Regulations, 2021 [Last amended on August 3, 2021]
2021	Securities and Exchange Board of India (Issue and Listing of Non-Convertible Securities) Regulations, 2021 [Last amended on July 06, 2023]
2021	Securities and Exchange Board of India (Share Based Employee Benefits and Sweat Equity) Regulations, 2021
2021	Securities and Exchange Board of India (Vault Managers) Regulations, 2021 [Last amended on August 18, 2023]
2024	Securities and Exchange Board of India (Index Providers) Regulations, 2024

Source: https://www.sebi.gov.in

Furthermore, SEBI (Listing Obligations and Disclosure Requirements) Regulations, 2015, which was published in the official Gazette of India has also seen several amendments as indicated in Exhibit 9.1(B).

EXHIBIT 9.1(B) SEBI (Listing Obligations and Disclosure Requirements) Regulations, 2015 and its amendments

Date	SEBI Regulations 2015 and amendments
September 2, 2015	Securities and Exchange Board of India (Listing Obligations and Disclosure Requirements) Regulations, 2015. Published in the Government of India Gazette vide No. SEBVLAD-NRO/GN/2015-16/013.
December 22, 2015	Securities and Exchange Board of India (Listing Obligations and Disclosure Requirements) (**Amendment**) Regulations, 2015 vide notification No. SEBVLAD-NRO/GN/2015-16/27.
May 25, 2016	Securities and Exchange Board of India (Listing Obligations and Disclosure Requirements) (Amendment) Regulations, 2016 vide notification No. SEBVLAD-NRO/GN/ 2016-17/001.
July 8, 2016	Securities and Exchange Board of India (Listing Obligations and Disclosure Requirements) (Second Amendment) Regulations, 2016 vide notification No. SEBV LAD- NRO/GN/2016-17/008.

Date	*SEBI Regulations 2015 and amendments*
January 4, 2017	Securities and Exchange Board of India (Listing Obligations and Disclosure Requirements) (Third Amendment) Regulations, 2016 vide notification no. SEBV LAD-NRO/GN/2016-17/025.
February 15, 2017	Securities and Exchange Board of India (Listing Obligations and Disclosure Requirements) (Amendment) Regulations, 2017 vide notification No. SEBVLAD/NRO/GN/2016-17/029.
March 6, 2017	Securities and Exchange Board of India (Payment of Fees and Mode of Payment) (Amendment) Regulations, 2017 vide Notification No. LAD-NRO/GN/2016- 17/037 read with March 29, 2017 by Securities and Exchange Board of India (Payment of Fees and Mode of Payment) (Amendment) Regulations, 2017 vide notification No. SEBI/LAD/NRO/GN/2016-17/38.
May 9, 2018	Securities and Exchange Board of India (Listing Obligations and Disclosure Requirements) (Amendment) Regulations, 2018 vide notification No. SEBVLAD-NRO/GN/2018/10.
May 30, 2018	Securities and Exchange Board of India (Listing Obligations and Disclosure Requirements) (Second Amendment) Regulations, 2018 vide notification No. SEBVLAD NRO/GN/2018/13.
June 1, 2018	Securities and Exchange Board of India (Listing Obligations and Disclosure Requirements) (Third Amendment) Regulations, 2018 vide notification No. SEBVLAD NRO/GN/2018/21.
June 8, 2018	Securities and Exchange Board of India (Listing Obligations and Disclosure Requirements) (Fourth Amendment) Regulations, 2018 vide notification No. SEBVLAD NRO/GN/2018/24.
September 6, 2018	Securities and Exchange Board of India (Listing Obligations and Disclosure Requirements) (Fifth Amendment) Regulations, 2018 vide notification no. SEBVLAD NRO/GN/2018/30.
November 16, 2018	Securities and Exchange Board of India (Listing Obligations and Disclosure Requirements) (Sixth Amendment) Regulations, 2018 vide notification No. SEBVLAD NRO/GN/2018/47.
March 29, 2019	Securities and Exchange Board of India (Listing Obligations and Disclosure Requirements) (Amendment) Regulations, 2019 vide notification No. SEBVLAD-NRO/GN/2019/07.
May 7, 2019	Securities and Exchange Board of India (Listing Obligations and Disclosure Requirements) (Second Amendment) Regulations, 2019, vide notification No. SEBV LAD NRO/GN/2019/12.
June 27, 2019	Securities and Exchange Board of India (Listing Obligations and Disclosure Requirements) (Third Amendment) Regulations, 2019, vide notification no. SEBV LAD NRO/GN/2019/22.
July 29, 2019	Securities and Exchange Board of India (Listing Obligations and Disclosure Requirements) (Fourth Amendment) Regulations, 2019, vide notification No. SEBV LAD NRO/GN/2019/28.
December 26, 2019	Securities and Exchange Board of India (Listing Obligations and Disclosure Requirements) (Fifth Amendment) Regulations, 2019, vide notification No. SEBI/ LAD NRO/GN/2019/45.
January 10, 2020	Securities and Exchange Board of India (Listing Obligations and Disclosure Requirements) (Amendment) Regulations, 2020, vide notification No. SEBI/LAD-NRO/GN/2020/02.
April 17, 2020	Securities and Exchange Board of India (Regulatory Sandbox) (Amendment) Regulations, 2020 vide No. SEBI/LAD-NRO/GN/2020/10.
August 5, 2020	Securities and Exchange Board of India (Listing Obligations and Disclosure Requirements) (Second Amendment) Regulations, 2020, vide notification No. SEBI/ LAD NRO/GN/2020/25.
October 8, 2020	Securities and Exchange Board of India (Listing Obligations and Disclosure Requirements) (Third Amendment) Regulations, 2020, vide notification No. SEBI/ LAD NRO/GN/2020/33.
January 8, 2021	Securities and Exchange Board of India (Listing Obligations and Disclosure Requirements) (Amendment) Regulations, 2021, vide notification No. SEBI/ LAD-NRO/GN/2021/02.

(*Contd.*)

Date	*SEBI Regulations 2015 and amendments*
May 5, 2021	Securities and Exchange Board of India (Listing Obligations and Disclosure Requirements) (Second Amendment) Regulations, 2021, vide notification No. SEBI/ LAD NRO/ GN/2021/22.
August 3, 2021	Securities and Exchange Board of India (Regulatory Sandbox) (Amendment) Regulations, 2021 vide notification No. SEBI/LAD-NRO/GN/2021/30.
August 3, 2021	Securities and Exchange Board of India (Listing Obligations and Disclosure Requirements) (Third Amendment) Regulations, 2021, vide notification No. SEBI/ LAD NRO/GN/2021/35.
August 13, 2021	Securities and Exchange Board of India (Listing Obligations and Disclosure Requirements) (Fourth Amendment) Regulations, 2021, vide notification No. SEBI/ LAD NRO/GN/2021/42.
September 7, 2021	Securities and Exchange Board of India (Listing Obligations and Disclosure Requirements) (Fifth Amendment) Regulations, 2021, vide notification No. SEBI/ LAD NRO/GN/2021/47.
November 9, 2021	Securities and Exchange Board of India (Listing Obligations and Disclosure Requirements) (Sixth Amendment) Regulations, 2021, vide notification No. SEBI/ LAD NRO/GN/2021/55.

Source: https://www.sebi.gov.in (modified)

INTERIM REPORTING IN PRACTICE

The current trends in interim financial reporting practices of the Indian firms has been highlighted in Exhibit 9.2(A) and Exhibit 9.2(B) by taking into consideration the interim reports of Steel Authority of India Limited (SAIL); and through Exhibit 9.2(A) and Exhibit 9.2(B) by taking into consideration of the interim reports of Hindustan Unilever Limited.

EXHIBIT 9.2(A) Statement of Standalone Audited Financial Results for the Quarter and Year ended 31st March, 2024

(*₹ Crore unless stated otherwise*)

SI. No.	*Particulars*	*Quarter ended*			*Year ended*	
		31st March, 2024	*31st December 2023*	*31st March, 2023*	*31st March, 2024*	*31st March, 2023*
		Audited	*Unaudited*	*Audited*	*Audited*	*Audited*
1	Income					
	(a) avenue from operations	27957.99	23345.48	29130.58	105374.59	104447.36
	(b) Other income	353.36	178.54	487.47	1148.06	1354.84
	Total Income (a+b)	28311.35	23524.02	29618.5	106522.65	106802.20
2	Expense					
	(a) Cost of materials consumed	15105.25	13740.44	14842.51	57618.84	62091.10
	(b) Changes in inventories of finished goods, work-in-progress and by-products	(614.56)	(2550.29)	661.86	(3352.92)	5160.14
	(c) Employee benefits expense	2839.79	2938.19	3433.07	11747.92	12053.62
	(d) Finance costs	642.14	613.85	517.00	2473.81	2037.47
	(e) Depreciation and amortization expenses	1355.69	1320.59	1364.40	5277.45	4962.52
	(f) Other expenses	7152.13	7076.95	7279.28	28229.04	27438.71
	Total Expenses (a+b+c+d+e+f)	26480.44	23139.73	28098.12	101994.14	103423.28

Sl. No.	Particulars	Quarter ended			Year ended	
		31st March, 2024	31st December 2023	31st March, 2023	31st March, 2024	31st March, 2023
		Audited	Unaudited	Audited	Audited	Audited
3	Profit before Exceptional items and Tax (1–2)	1830.91	384.29	1619.93	4528.51	2378.92
4	*Add/less*: Exceptional items	1502.34	76.46	(40.42)	(840.841	257.99
5	Profit before Tax (3+4)	1328.67	460.76	1479.61	3687.67	2636.91
	Total tax expense (a+b)	317.35	129.35	430.49	954.56	733.84
6	Tax expense (a) Current tax (b) Deferred tax	 118.46 198.89	 16.13 113.22	 (49.46) 479.95	 605.54 349.02	 118.37 615.47
7	Net Profit for the period (5–6)	1011.22	331.40	1049.02	2733.11	1903.07
8	Other Comprehensive Income (OCI):					
	A (i) Items that will not be reclassified to profit or loss	30.53	(99.17)	(847.76)	(122.72)	(566.83)
	(ii) Income tax relating to items that will not be reclassified to profit or loss	2.60	9.25	160.53	0.55	128.22
9	Total Comprehensive Income for the overload (7+8)	1044.35	241.48	361.79	2610.94	1464.46
10	Paid-up Equity Share Capital/ face value of ₹10 each	4130.53	4130.53	4130.53	4130.53	4130.53
11	Reserves excluding revaluation reserve				50000.01	48008.65
12	Earnings per equity share (of ₹10 each) (not annualized) 1. Basic 2. Diluted	 2.45 2.45	 0.80 0.80	 2.54 2.54	 6.62 6.62	 4.61 4.61
13	Debt Equity Ratio				0.67	0.59
14	Debt Service Coverage Ratio/ number of times				2.08	2.66
15	Interest Service Coverage Ratio/ number of times				2.64	2.05

Source: SAIL- Quarter and Year ended 31st March, 2024.pdf[2]

EXHIBIT 9.2(B) Standalone Segment-wise Revenue, Results, Assets and Liabilities of SAIL

₹ Crore unless stated otherwise

	Quarter ended			Year ended	
	31st March, 2024	31st December, 2023	31st March, 2023	31st March, 2024	31st March, 2023
	Audited	Unaudited	Audited	Audited	Audited
Segment revenue from operations					
♦ Bhilai Steel Plant	9699.55	6499.99	9146.25	33298.07	30516.07
♦ Durgapur Steel Plant	3245.95	2903.13	3619.19	12445.35	13250.48
♦ Rourkela Steel Plant	6978.85	5863.28	6796.91	26269.37	25600.33
♦ Bokaro Steel Plant	6528.83	6003.58	6861.82	25755.25	26343.74
♦ IISCO Steel Plant	3379.09	2906.94	3774.29	12699.33	13520.93
♦ Alloy Steels Plant	300.96	281.38	260.54	1190.24	1000.55
♦ Salem Steel Plant	622.28	515.19	697.23	2406.75	1881.81
♦ Visvesvaraya Iron & Steel Plant	46.32	48.78	63.94	162.10	310.86
♦ Others	411.16	357.34	327.78	1431.06	1444.93
Total segment revenue	31212.99	25379.61	31547.95	115657.52	113869.70
Less: Inter-segment revenue	3255.00	2034.13	2417.37	10282.93	9422.34
Net revenue from operations	**27957.99**	**23345.48**	**29130.58**	**105374.59**	**104447.36**
Segment results (Profit/(Loss) before interest exceptional Items and tax)					
♦ Bhilai Steel Plant	1336.03	62.41	627.49	3548.54	954.33
♦ Durgapur Steel Plant	176.00	196.92	298.72	564.60	502.49
♦ Rourkela Steel Plant	292.15	401.01	430.11	1415.53	1191.23
♦ Bokaro Steel Plant	243.05	458.19	311.39	1365.89	1218.79
♦ IISCO Steel Plant	72.99	52.84	367.71	295.25	558.03
♦ Alloy Steels Plant	(30.83)	(20.70)	(26.51	(71.55)	(121.79)
♦ Salem Steel Plant	(63.94)	(56.36)	(43.33)	(227.36)	(203.06)
♦ Visvesvaraya Iron & Steel Plant	(7.96}	(8.81)	(6.84}	(48.57)	(50.57)
♦ Others	455.56	(87.36)	78.19	159.99	366.94
Total	**2473.05**	**998.14**	**2036.93**	**7002.32**	**4416.39**
Less: Finance costs	642.14	613.85	517.00	2473.81	2037.47
Less: Exceptional items	502.34	(76.46)	40.42	840.84	(257.99)
Profit before Tax	**1328.57**	**460.75**	**1479.51**	**3687.67**	**2636.91**
Segment Assets					
♦ Bhilai Steel Plant	35944.19	36935.59	34203.09	35944.19	34203.09
♦ Durgapur Steel Plant	8868.84	8336.49	7440.11	8868.84	7440.11
♦ Rourkela Steel Plant	29560.59	28851.15	28204.33	29560.59	28204.33
♦ Bokaro Steel Plant	23199.09	22570.84	22190.44	23199.09	22190.44
♦ IISCO Steel Plant	15984.81	16131.13	15867.84	15984.81	15867.84
♦ Alloy Steels Plant	694.96	669.15	619.15	694.96	619.15
♦ Salem Steel Plant	2798.12	2472.39	2515.84	2798.12	2515.84
♦ Vlsvesvaraya Iron & Steel Plant	224.85	205.38	238.26	224.85	238.26
♦ Others	17785.50	13440.64	14195.18	17785.50	14195.18
♦ Unallocated Assets	2471.50	2457.24	2240.75	2471.50	2240.75
Total	**137532.45**	**132070.00**	**127714.99**	**137532.45**	**127714.99**

	Quarter ended			*Year ended*	
	31st March, 2024	*31st December, 2023*	*31st March, 2023*	*31st March, 2024*	*31st March, 2023*
	Audited	*Unaudited*	*Audited*	*Audited*	*Audited*
Segment Liabilities					
♦ Bhilai Steel Plant	8404.92	8825.70	9300.61	8404.92	9300.61
♦ Durgapur Steel Plant	3314.00	3539.56	3547.08	3314.00	3547.08
♦ Rourkela Steel Plant	9550.00	9742.18	9203.46	9550.00	9203.46
♦ Bokaro Steel plant	5933.93	5539.75	6065.67	5933.93	6065.67
♦ IISCO Steel Plant	1584.96	1360.93	1602.70	1584.96	1602.70
♦ Alloy Steels Plant	320.95	277.37	258.03	320.95	258.03
♦ Salem Steel Plant	622.44	545.27	501.46	622.44	501.46
♦ Visvesvaraya Iron & Steel Plant	125.25	50.55	60.45	125.25	60.45
♦ Others	16586.07	14459.88	13646.93	16586.07	13646.93
♦ Unallocated Liabilities	36959.39	34229.57	31389.42	36959.39	31389.42
Total	**83401.91**	**78570.76**	**75575.81**	**83401.91**	**75575.81**

Note: Operating Segments have been identified in line with the Ind AS 108 • Operating Segments.
Source: SAIL- Quarter and Year ended 31st March, 2024.pdf

INDEPENDENT AUDITOR'S REPORT

An abstract of the Independent Auditor's Report on Standalone Annual Financial Results of the Company (SAIL) Pursuant to the Regulation 33 and Regulation 52 read with Regulation 63 of the SEBI (Listing Obligations and Disclosure Requirements) Regulations, 2015 (as amended) has been given below only to illustrate how SAIL has complied to SEBI regulation:

To the Board of Directors of Steel Authority of India Limited

Qualified Opinion

1. We have audited the accompanying standalone annual financial results ('the Statement') of Steel Authority of India Limited ('the Company') for the year ended 31 March 2024, attached herewith, being submitted by the Company pursuant to the requirements of Regulation 33 and Regulation 52 read with Regulation 63 of the SEBI (Listing Obligations and Disclosure Requirements) Regulations, 2015 (as amended) ('Listing Regulations'), including SEBI Circular SEBI/HO/DDHS/P/CIR/2021/613 dated 10 August 2021(as amended).
2. In our opinion and to the best of our information and according to the explanations given to us, and based on the consideration of the reports of the branch auditors as referred to in paragraph 15* below, the Statement:
   (i) presents financial results in accordance with the requirements of Regulation 33 and Regulation 52 read with Regulation 63 of the Listing Regulations, except for the effects of the matters described in paragraph 3 below; and
   (ii) gives a true and fair view in conformity with the recognition and measurement principles laid down in the applicable Indian Accounting Standards ('Ind AS') specified under section 133 of the Companies Act, 2013 ('the Act'), read with the Companies (Indian Accounting Standards) Rules, 2015, and other accounting

principles generally accepted in India, of the standalone net profit after tax and other comprehensive income and other financial information of the Company for the year ended 31 March 2024 except for the effects of the matters described in paragraph 3 below.

Basis for Qualified Opinion

3. (a) As referred to in note 7 to the accompanying statement, the constitutional validity of the Entry Tax Act has been upheld by the Hon'ble Supreme Court and the matters relating to levy of entry tax are now pending before regular benches of the Supreme Court/Jurisdictional High Courts/assigned authorities. Pending decision by the aforesaid courts, the management is of the view that no adjustment is required in the accompanying statement of the Company for the disputed entry tax demand in various states amounting to ₹724.02 crore (net *of* ₹137.72 crores recognised as a liability basis ongoing settlement proceedings as explained in the said note) as on 31 March 2024. However, in the absence of sufficient appropriate evidence to support management's view, we are of the opinion that a provision for entry tax liability should be recognized in the statement.

   (b) As referred in note 8 to the accompanying statement, current assets include advance of ₹587.72 crore paid under protest to Damodar Valley Corporation against the bills raised for supply of power for the period 2010–11 to 2016–17. The matter is under litigation and currently pending before Jharkhand State Electricity Regulatory Commission (JSERC) for finalization of tariff. The management is of the view that the amount is fully recoverable and thus no adjustment is required in the accompanying statement. However, in the absence of sufficient appropriate evidence to support the management's contention of recoverability of these balances, we are of the opinion that an allowance for possible non-recoverability of such advance should be created in the statement.

Impact of all the above qualifications on the accompanying Statement for the year ended 31 March 2024 is as under:

Particulars	*As at 31 March 2024 (₹ in Crore)*	
	Reported Results	*Results after impact of all the qualifications which are quantified*
Other equity	50,000.01	49,018.41
Deferred tax liabilitv	6,178.20	5,848.06
Other current assets	4,541.05	3,953.33
Other current liabilities	4 565.19	5,289.21

Our audit report on the financial results of the company for the quarter and year ended 31 March 2023 dated 25 May 2023 and review report for the quarter and year-to-date period ended 31 December 2023 dated 12 February 2024 were also qualified in respect of these matters.

4. We conducted our audit in accordance with the Standards on Auditing specified under section 143(10) of the Act. Our responsibilities under those standards are further described in the *Auditor's Responsibilities for the Audit of the Statement* section of our

report. We are independent of the Company in accordance with the Code of Ethics issued by the Institute of Chartered Accountants of India ('the ICAI') together with the ethical requirements that are relevant to our audit of the financial results under the provisions of the Act and the rules thereunder, and we have fulfilled our other ethical responsibilities in accordance with these requirements and the Code of Ethics. We believe that the audit evidence obtained by us together with the audit evidence obtained by the branch auditors, in terms of their reports referred to in paragraph 15* below, is sufficient and appropriate to provide a basis for our qualified opinion.

**Note:* Paragraph 15 of the Independent Auditor's report reads as under:
'We did not audit the financial statements/financial information of 11(eleven) branches/units/marketing regions included in the Statement, whose financial information reflects total assets of ₹64,560.81 crore as at 31 March 2024, and total revenues of ₹40,094.16 crore, total net loss after tax of ₹49.65 crore, and total comprehensive loss of ₹109.03 crore, and cash flows (net) of ₹4.29 crore for the year then ended, as considered in the Statement. These statements/financial information have been audited by the branch auditors, whose reports have been furnished to us by the management, and our opinion, insofar as it relates to the amounts and disclosures included in respect of these branches/units/marketing regions, is based solely on the audit report of such branch auditors. Our opinion is not modified in respect of the above matters with respect to our reliance on the work done by and the report of the branch auditors.

INTERIM REPORTING BY HINDUSTAN UNILEVER LIMITED

Interim financial reporting practices of Hindustan Unilever Limited have been indicated in Exhibit 9.3(A): Standalone Financial Results for the Quarter and Nine Months Ended 31st December, 2023, and Exhibit 9.3(B): Standalone Segment-wise Revenue, Results, Assets and Liabilities.

EXHIBIT 9.3(A) Standalone Financial Results for the Quarter and Nine Months Ended 31st December, 2023

(₹ *in Crore*)

Unaudited Results for the quarter ended 31st December		*Unaudited Results for the quarter ended 30th September*	*Particulars*	*Unaudited Results for nine months ended 31st December*		*Audited Results for the year ended 31st March*
2023	2022	2023	**Revenue from operations**	2023	2022	2023
14,928	14,986	15,027	Sale of products	44,886	43,516	58,154
260	242	249	Other operating revenue	726	735	990
285	228	283	Other income	753	480	640
15,473	15,456	15,559	TOTAL INCOME	**46,365**	**44,731**	**59,784**
			EXPENSES			
4,600	4,767	4,412	Cost of materials consumed	13,483	14,683	19,229
2,944	2,892	2,843	Purchases of stock-in-trade	8,680	8,958	11,968
(177)	338	(34)	Changes in inventories of finished goods, work-in-progress and Stock-in-Trade	13	(136)	(53)

(*Contd.*)

Unaudited Results for the quarter ended 31st December		*Unaudited Results for the quarter ended 30th September*	*Particulars*	*Unaudited Results for nine months ended 31st December*		*Audited Results for the year ended 31st March*
649	676	708	Employee benefits expense	2,008	1,982	2,665
81	26	72	Finance costs	200	77	101
282	260	269	Depreciation and amortization expense	808	768	1,030
			Other expenses			
1,593	1,200	1,720	Advertising and promotion	4,794	3,569	4,859
2,039	1,818	1,933	Others	5,879	5,034	6,844
12,011	**11,977**	**11,923**	**TOTAL EXPENSES**	**35,865**	**34,935**	**46,643**
3,462	**3,479**	**3,636**	**Profit before exceptional items and tax**	**10,500**	**9,796**	**13,141**
(30)	(102)	(5)	Exceptional items (net charge)	(72)	(142)	(62)
3,432	**3,377**	**3,631**	**Profit before tax**	**10,428**	**9,654**	**13,079**
			Tax expenses			
(877)	(832)	(873)	Current tax	(2,592)	(2,108)	(2,922)
(36)	(40)	(41)	Deferred tax charge	(128)	(136)	(195)
2,519	**2,505**	**2,717**	**PROFIT FOR THE PERIOD (A)**	**7,708**	**7,410**	**9,962**
			OTHER COMPREHENSIVE INCOME			
			Items that will not be reclassified subsequently to profit or loss			
2	9	9	Measurements of the net defined benefit plans	21	28	(17)
(0)	(2)	(3)	Tax on above	(5)	(7)	4
			Items that will be reclassified subsequently to profit or loss			
(1)	4	(1)	Fair value of debt instruments through other comprehensive income	0	(1)	(1)
0	(1)	0	Tax on above	(0)	0	0
(9)	31	(0)	Fair value of cash flow hedges through other comprehensive income	(5)	(15)	(21)
1	(10)	0	Tax on above	(1)	8	9
(7)	31	5	OTHER COMPREHENSIVE INCOME FOR THE PERIOD (B)	10	13	**(26)**
2,512	**2,536**	**2,722**	**TOTAL COMPREHENSIVE INCOME FOR THE PERIOD (A+B)**	**7,718**	**7,423**	**9,936**
235	**235**	**235**	**Paid up Equity Share Capital (Face value ₹1 per share)**	**235**	**235**	**235**
			Other Equity			**49,986**
			Earnings per equity share (Face value of ₹1 each)			
10.72	10.67	11.56	Basic (in ₹)	32.80	31.54	42.40
10.72	10.67	11.56	Diluted (in ₹)	32.80	31.54	42.40

Source: HUL -Qr-23-results.pdf[3]

EXHIBIT 9.3(B) Standalone Segment-wise Revenue, Results, Assets and Liabilities

(₹ *in Crore*)

Unaudited Results for the quarter ended 31st December		*Unaudited Results for the quarter ended 30th September*	*Particulars*	*Unaudited Results for nine months ended 31st December*		*Audited Results for the year ended 31st March*
2023	*2022*	*2023*		*2023*	*2022*	*2023*
			Segment Revenue (Sales and Other operating income)			
5,448	5,518	5,312	♦ Home Care	16,185	15,592	21,230
5,705	5,718	5,809	♦ Beauty & Personal Care	17,115	16,643	21,831
3,733	3,700	3,851	♦ Foods & Refreshment	11,381	11,082	14,876
302	292	304	♦ Others (includes Exports, Consignment, etc.)	931	934	1,207
15,188	**15,228**	**15,276**	**Total Segment Revenue**	**45,612**	**44,251**	**59,144**
			Segment Results			
966	1,061	995	♦ Home Care	2,952	2,819	3,875
1,461	1,437	1,581	♦ Beauty & Personal Care	4,514	4,244	5,597
711	661	720	♦ Foods & Refreshment	2,112	1,983	2,662
120	118	129	♦ Others (includes Exports, Consignment, etc.)	369	347	468
3,258	3,277	3,425	**Total Segment Results**	**9,947**	**9,393**	**12,602**
(30)	(102)	(5)	*Less:* Exceptional Items (net charge)	(72)	(142)	(62)
(81)	(26)	(72)	*Less:* Finance Costs	(200)	(77)	(101)
285	228	283	*Add:* Other Income	753	480	640
3,432	**3,377**	**3,631**	**Total Profit Before Tax**	**10,428**	**9,654**	**13,079**
			Segment Assets			
4,378	3,979	4,356	♦ Home Care	4,378	3,979	4,349
6,288	5,966	6,739	♦ Beauty & Personal Care	6,288	5,966	6,224
50,032	49,629	49,757	♦ Foods & Refreshment	50,032	49,629	50,299
506	671	713	♦ Others (includes Exports, Consignment, etc.)	506	671	675
14,520	9,732	14,886	♦ Unallocable corporate assets	14,520	9,732	10,278
75,724	**69,977**	**76,451**	**Total Assets**	**75,724**	**69,977**	**71,825**
			Segment Liabilities			
4,794	4,303	4,329	♦ Home Care	4,794	4,303	4,086
6,667	6,359	6,577	♦ Beauty & Personal Care	6,667	6,359	5,978
3,772	3,278	3,539	♦ Foods & Refreshment	3,772	3,278	3,131
251	425	280	♦ Others (includes Exports, Consignment, etc.)	251	425	429
11,691	7,902	11,466	♦ Unallocable corporate liabilities	11,691	7,902	7,980
27,175	**22,267**	**26,191**	**Total Liabilities**	**27,175**	**22,267**	**21,604**

Segment Revenue, Results, Assets and Liabilities represent amounts identifiable to each of the segments. Other Income mainly includes interest income, dividend income and income from current investments (net). Segment Assets and Segment Liabilities are as at 31st December 2023, 30th September 2023, 31st March 2023 and 31st December 2022. Unallocable corporate assets less Unallocable corporate liabilities mainly represent investment of surplus funds, cash and bank balances and tax assets and liabilities.

Source: HUL -Qr-23-results.pdf[4]

Notes to standalone financial results:

1. Total sales at ₹14,928 crores was marginally lower than DQ22.
2. Earnings before interest, tax, depreciation and amortization (EBITDA) for the quarter was ₹3,540 crores (DQ 22: ₹3,537 crores). EBITDA margin at 23.7% increased by 10 bps vs DQ 22.
3. Profit after tax before exceptional items for the quarter at ₹2,541 crores (DQ 22: ₹2,581 crores) declined by 2%.
4. Exceptional items in DQ 23 include restructuring expenses of ₹30 crores (DQ 22: ₹57 crores) and acquisition and disposal related cost Nil (DQ 22: ₹45 crores).
5. Profit after tax for the quarter at ₹2,519 crores (DQ 22: ₹2,505 crores) grew by 1%.
6. The above results have been reviewed by the Audit Committee and approved by the Board of Directors at their meeting held on 19th January 2024.
7. The statutory auditors have issued an unmodified report on the above results.
8. The text of the above statement was approved by the Board of Directors at their meeting held on 19th January 2024.

SUMMARY

Interim financial reporting refers to the presentation of financial statements of the enterprise covering periods of less than a full financial year. The purpose of such presentation of financial statements is to provide the decision makers with frequent and timely information for taking investment and credit decisions, based on their ability to predict full year's financial results from the interim results. IAS 34 provides details of the guidelines for interim financial reporting.

An enterprise must present interim financial reports either in the 'condensed' form or in the form of a 'complete set' of financial statements. An enterprise which opts for presenting a *condensed* interim financial report must present a condensed balance sheet, a condensed income statement, a condensed statement showing either all changes in equity or changes in equity other than those arising from capital transactions with owners and distributions to owners, a condensed cash flow statement and a selected set of footnote disclosures.

If the enterprise chooses a 'complete set of financial statements for interim reporting in place of a 'condensed' financial statements, then the form and content of these complete statements should be in conformity with the requirements of IAS 1 (revised) on presentation of financial statements.

The minimum disclosures to be made in interim reporting ranges from the statements about the (same) accounting policies and methods applied in the interim reports as were applied in the most recent annual financial statements to a description on the seasonality or cyclicality of interim operations, the nature and extent of significant items affecting interim results which are unusual because of nature, size or incidence, dividend paid in aggregate or per share basis, separately for ordinary shares and other class(es) of shares, revenue and operating result for business segments or geographical segments whichever is the enterprise's primary reporting format, any significant events occurring subsequent to the end of the interim period, issuances, repurchases and repayments of debt and equity, the nature and magnitude of changes in estimates of amounts reported in prior interim periods of the current financial year, or changes in estimates of amounts reported in prior financial years, if those changes have a material effect in the current interim period, the effect of changes in the composition of the enterprise during the interim period, like business combinations, acquisitions or disposal of subsidiaries, and long-term investments, restructuring, and discontinuing operations and the changes in contingent liabilities or contingent assets since the most recent annual financial statements.

The Indian Accounting Standard Ind AS 34 too has stipulations on presentation of interim financial reports containing either a complete set of financial statements or a set of condensed financial statements for an interim period. A complete set of financial statements shall include a balance sheet, a profit and loss account, a cash flow statement and selected explanatory notes on the accounts and the accounting policies adopted. The interim period shall be a period of less than a full year. As per the listing agreement, the listed companies in India are required to furnish quarterly unaudited financial results in the prescribed format to the stock exchange(s).

KEY TERMS

Interim financial reporting: Interim financial reporting refers to the presentation of financial statements of the enterprise covering periods of less than a full financial year. The purpose of such presentation of financial statements is to provide the decision makers with frequent and timely information for taking investment and credit decisions, based on their ability to predict full year's financial results from the interim results.

Basic EPS: Basic EPS = Net profit or loss for the period available to equity shareholders *divided by* weighted average number equity shares outstanding during the period.

Diluted EPS: Diluted EPS = Net profit attributable to equity shareholders after adjustment for diluted earnings *divided by* average number of weighted equity shares outstanding during the period considering the conversion of diluted potential equity shares.

REVIEW QUESTIONS

1. What is interim reporting? Why has interim reporting become so important these days?
2. Discuss the provisions of IAS 34 on interim reporting.
3. Write a note on the disclosures to be made in interim reporting.
4. Discuss the salient features of Indian Accounting Standard (Ind AS) 34 on interim reporting.
5. Discuss the provisions of SEBI as regards interim reporting and disclosure requirements.
6. Write a detailed note on the corporate governance report as stipulated by SEBI.
7. Discuss with suitable example(s) the calculation and significance of 'basic' and 'diluted' EPS.

8. Write explanatory notes on:
   (a) Interim reporting
   (b) Corporate governance report
9. Explain the following:
   (a) Basic EPS
   (b) Diluted EPS
   (c) Condensed financial reports
10. Discuss the role and responsibilities of Independent Auditor(s) on interim reporting by a firm.

REFERENCES

[1] IAS 34, IFRS Foundation.
[2] https://www.sebi.gov.in
[3] SAIL-Quarter and Year ended 31st March, 2024.pdf
[4] HUL-Qr-23-results.pdf

APENDIX-9(A)
IAS 34: INTERIM FINANCIAL REPORTING

Objective

The objective of this Standard is to prescribe the minimum content of an interim financial report and to prescribe the principles for recognition and measurement in complete or condensed financial statements for an interim period. Timely and reliable interim financial reporting improves the ability of investors, creditors, and others to understand an entity's capacity to generate earnings and cash flows and its financial condition and liquidity.

Scope

1. This Standard does not mandate which entities should be required to publish interim financial reports, how frequently, or how soon after the end of an interim period. However, governments, securities regulators, stock exchanges, and accountancy bodies often require entities whose debt or equity securities are publicly traded to publish interim financial reports. This Standard applies if an entity is required or elects

to publish an interim financial report in accordance with International Financial Reporting Standards (IFRSs). The International Accounting Standards Committee[1] encourages publicly traded entities to provide interim financial reports that conform to the recognition, measurement, and disclosure principles set out in this Standard. Specifically, publicly traded entities are encouraged:

(a) to provide interim financial reports at least as of the end of the first half of their financial year; and

(b) to make their interim financial reports available not later than 60 days after the end of the interim period.

2. Each financial report, annual or interim, is evaluated on its own for conformity to IFRSs. The fact that an entity may not have provided interim financial reports during a particular financial year or may have provided interim financial reports that do not comply with this Standard does not prevent the entity's annual financial statements from conforming to IFRSs if they otherwise do so.
3. If an entity's interim financial report is described as complying with IFRSs, it must comply with all of the requirements of this Standard. Paragraph 19 requires certain disclosures in that regard.

Definitions

4. The following terms are used in this Standard with the meanings specified:

Interim period is a financial reporting period shorter than a full financial year.

Interim financial report means a financial report containing either a complete set of financial statements (as described in IAS 1 *Presentation of Financial Statements* (as revised in 2007)) or a set of condensed financial statements (as described in this Standard) for an interim period.

Content of an Interim Financial Report

5. IAS 1 defines a complete set of financial statements as including the following components:

(a) a statement of financial position as at the end of the period;

(b) a statement of profit or loss and other comprehensive income for the period;

(c) a statement of changes in equity for the period;

(d) a statement of cash flows for the period;

(e) notes, comprising significant accounting policies and other explanatory information;

(ea) comparative information in respect of the preceding period as specified in paragraphs 38 and 38A of IAS 1; and

(f) a statement of financial position as at the beginning of the preceding period when an entity applies an accounting policy retrospectively or makes a retrospective restatement of items in its financial statements, or when it reclassifies items in its financial statements in accordance with paragraphs 40A–40D of IAS 1.

An entity may use titles for the statements other than those used in this Standard. For example, an entity may use the title 'statement of comprehensive income' instead of 'statement of profit or loss and other comprehensive income'.

6. In the interest of timeliness and cost considerations and to avoid repetition of information previously reported, an entity may be required to or may elect to provide less information at interim dates as compared with its annual financial statements. This Standard defines the minimum content of an interim financial report as including condensed financial statements and selected explanatory notes. The interim financial report is intended to provide an update on the latest complete set of annual financial statements. Accordingly, it focuses on new activities, events, and circumstances and does not duplicate information previously reported.
7. Nothing in this Standard is intended to prohibit or discourage an entity from publishing a complete set of financial statements (as described in IAS 1) in its interim financial report, rather than condensed financial statements and selected explanatory notes. Nor does this Standard prohibit or discourage an entity from including in condensed interim financial statements more than the minimum line items or selected explanatory notes as set out in this Standard. The recognition and measurement guidance in this Standard applies also to complete financial statements for an interim period, and such statements would include all of the disclosures required by this Standard (particularly the selected note disclosures in paragraph 16A) as well as those required by other IFRSs.

Minimum components of an interim financial report

8. An interim financial report shall include, at a minimum, the following components:
    (a) a condensed statement of financial position;
    (b) a condensed statement or condensed statements of profit or loss and other comprehensive income;
    (c) a condensed statement of changes in equity;
    (d) a condensed statement of cash flows; and
    (e) selected explanatory notes.

8A If an entity presents items of profit or loss in a separate statement as described in paragraph 10A of IAS 1 (as amended in 2011), it presents interim condensed information from that statement.

Form and content of interim financial statements

9. If an entity publishes a complete set of financial statements in its interim financial report, the form and content of those statements shall conform to the requirements of IAS 1 for a complete set of financial statements.
10. If an entity publishes a set of condensed financial statements in its interim financial report, those condensed statements shall include, at a minimum, each of the headings and subtotals that were included in its most recent annual financial statements and the selected explanatory notes as required by this Standard. Additional line items or notes shall be included if their omission would make the condensed interim financial statements misleading.

11. In the statement that presents the components of profit or loss for an interim period, an entity shall present basic and diluted earnings per share for that period when the entity is within the scope of IAS 33 *Earnings per Share*.

11A. If an entity presents items of profit or loss in a separate statement as described in paragraph 10A of IAS 1 (as amended in 2011), it presents basic and diluted earnings per share in that statement.

12. IAS 1 (as revised in 2007) provides guidance on the structure of financial statements. The Implementation Guidance for IAS 1 illustrates ways in which the statement of financial position, statement of comprehensive income and statement of changes in equity may be presented.

13. [Deleted]

14. An interim financial report is prepared on a consolidated basis if the entity's most recent annual financial statements were consolidated statements. The parent's separate financial statements are not consistent or comparable with the consolidated statements in the most recent annual financial report. If an entity's annual financial report included the parent's separate financial statements in addition to consolidated financial statements, this Standard neither requires nor prohibits the inclusion of the parent's separate statements in the entity's interim financial report.

Significant events and transactions

15. An entity shall include in its interim financial report an explanation of events and transactions that are significant to an understanding of the changes in financial position and performance of the entity since the end of the last annual reporting period. Information disclosed in relation to those events and transactions shall update the relevant information presented in the most recent annual financial report.

15A. A user of an entity's interim financial report will have access to the most recent annual financial report of that entity. Therefore, it is unnecessary for the notes to an interim financial report to provide relatively insignificant updates to the information that was reported in the notes in the most recent annual financial report.

15B. The following is a list of events and transactions for which disclosures would be required if they are significant: the list is not exhaustive.
   (a) the write-down of inventories to net realisable value and the reversal of such a write-down;
   (b) recognition of a loss from the impairment of financial assets, property, plant and equipment, intangible assets, assets arising from contracts with customers, or other assets, and the reversal of such an impairment loss;
   (c) the reversal of any provisions for the costs of restructuring;
   (d) acquisitions and disposals of items of property, plant and equipment;
   (e) commitments for the purchase of property, plant and equipment;
   (f) litigation settlements;
   (g) corrections of prior period errors;

(h) changes in the business or economic circumstances that affect the fair value of the entity's financial assets and financial liabilities, whether those assets or liabilities are recognised at fair value or amortised cost;
(i) any loan default or breach of a loan agreement that has not been remedied on or before the end of the reporting period;
(j) related party transactions;
(k) transfers between levels of the fair value hierarchy used in measuring the fair value of financial instruments;
(l) changes in the classification of financial assets as a result of a change in the purpose or use of those assets; and
(m) changes in contingent liabilities or contingent assets.

15C. Individual IFRSs provide guidance regarding disclosure requirements for many of the items listed in paragraph 15B. When an event or transaction is significant to an understanding of the changes in an entity's financial position or performance since the last annual reporting period, its interim financial report should provide an explanation of and an update to the relevant information included in the financial statements of the last annual reporting period.

16. [Deleted]

Other disclosures

16A. In addition to disclosing significant events and transactions in accordance with paragraphs 15–15C, an entity shall include the following information, in the notes to its interim financial statements or elsewhere in the interim financial report. The following disclosures shall be given either in the interim financial statements or incorporated by cross-reference from the interim financial statements to some other statement (such as management commentary or risk report) that is available to users of the financial statements on the same terms as the interim financial statements and at the same time. If users of the financial statements do not have access to the information incorporated by cross-reference on the same terms and at the same time, the interim financial report is incomplete. The information shall normally be reported on a financial year-to-date basis.
(a) a statement that the same accounting policies and methods of computation are followed in the interim financial statements as compared with the most recent annual financial statements or, if those policies or methods have been changed, a description of the nature and effect of the change.
(b) explanatory comments about the seasonality or cyclicality of interim operations.
(c) the nature and amount of items affecting assets, liabilities, equity, net income or cash flows that are unusual because of their nature, size or incidence.
(d) the nature and amount of changes in estimates of amounts reported in prior interim periods of the current financial year or changes in estimates of amounts reported in prior financial years.
(e) issues, repurchases and repayments of debt and equity securities.

(f) dividends paid (aggregate or per share) separately for ordinary shares and other shares.

(g) the following segment information (disclosure of segment information is required in an entity's interim financial report only if IFRS 8 *Operating Segments* requires that entity to disclose segment information in its annual financial statements):

(i) revenues from external customers, if included in the measure of segment profit or loss reviewed by the chief operating decision maker or otherwise regularly provided to the chief operating decision maker.

(ii) intersegment revenues, if included in the measure of segment profit or loss reviewed by the chief operating decision maker or otherwise regularly provided to the chief operating decision maker.

(iii) a measure of segment profit or loss.

(iv) a measure of total assets and liabilities for a particular reportable segment if such amounts are regularly provided to the chief operating decision maker and if there has been a material change from the amount disclosed in the last annual financial statements for that reportable segment.

(v) a description of differences from the last annual financial statements in the basis of segmentation or in the basis of measurement of segment profit or loss.

(vi) a reconciliation of the total of the reportable segments' measures of profit or loss to the entity's profit or loss before tax expense (tax income) and discontinued operations. However, if an entity allocates to reportable segments items such as tax expense (tax income), the entity may reconcile the total of the segments' measures of profit or loss to profit or loss after those items. Material reconciling items shall be separately identified and described in that reconciliation.

(h) events after the interim period that have not been reflected in the financial statements for the interim period.

(i) the effect of changes in the composition of the entity during the interim period, including business combinations, obtaining or losing control of subsidiaries and long-term investments, restructurings, and discontinued operations. In the case of business combinations, the entity shall disclose the information required by IFRS 3 *Business Combinations*.

(j) for financial instruments, the disclosures about fair value required by paragraphs 91–93(h), 94–96, 98 and 99 of IFRS 13 *Fair Value Measurement* and paragraphs 25, 26 and 28–30 of IFRS 7 *Financial Instruments: Disclosures*.

(k) for entities becoming, or ceasing to be, investment entities, as defined in IFRS 10 *Consolidated Financial Statements*, the disclosures in IFRS 12 *Disclosure of Interests in Other Entities* paragraph 9B.

(l) the disaggregation of revenue from contracts with customers required by paragraphs 114–115 of IFRS 15 *Revenue from Contracts with Customers*.

17-18 [deleted]

Disclosure of compliance with IFRSs

19. If an entity's interim financial report is in compliance with this Standard, that fact shall be disclosed. An interim financial report shall not be described as complying with IFRSs unless it complies with all the requirements of IFRSs.
    Periods for which interim financial statements are required to be presented
20. Interim reports shall include interim financial statements (condensed or complete) for periods as follows:
    (a) statement of financial position as of the end of the current interim period and a comparative statement of financial position as of the end of the immediately preceding financial year.
    (b) statements of profit or loss and other comprehensive income for the current interim period and cumulatively for the current financial year to date, with comparative statements of profit or loss and other comprehensive income for the comparable interim periods (current and year-to-date) of the immediately preceding financial year. As permitted by IAS 1 (as amended in 2011), an interim report may present for each period a statement or statements of profit or loss and other comprehensive income.
    (c) statement of changes in equity cumulatively for the current financial year to date, with a comparative statement for the comparable year-to-date period of the immediately preceding financial year.
    (d) statement of cash flows cumulatively for the current financial year to date, with a comparative statement for the comparable year-to-date period of the immediately preceding financial year.
21. For an entity whose business is highly seasonal, financial information for the twelve months up to the end of the interim period and comparative information for the prior twelve-month period may be useful. Accordingly, entities whose business is highly seasonal are encouraged to consider reporting such information in addition to the information called for in the preceding paragraph.
22. Part A of the illustrative examples accompanying this Standard illustrates the periods required to be presented by an entity that reports half-yearly and an entity that reports quarterly.

Materiality

23. In deciding how to recognise, measure, classify, or disclose an item for interim financial reporting purposes, materiality shall be assessed in relation to the interim period financial data. In making assessments of materiality, it shall be recognized that interim measurements may rely on estimates to a greater extent than measurements of annual financial data.
24. IAS 1 defines material information and requires separate disclosure of material items, including (for example) discontinued operations, and IAS 8 *Accounting Policies*,

Changes in Accounting Estimates and Errors requires disclosure of changes in accounting estimates, errors, and changes in accounting policies. The two Standards do not contain quantified guidance as to materiality.

25. While judgment is always required in assessing materiality, this Standard bases the recognition and disclosure decision on data for the interim period by itself for reasons of understandability of the interim figures. Thus, for example, unusual items, changes in accounting policies or estimates, and errors are recognized and disclosed on the basis of materiality in relation to interim period data to avoid misleading inferences that might result from non-disclosure. The overriding goal is to ensure that an interim financial report includes all information that is relevant to understanding an entity's financial position and performance during the interim period

Disclosure in annual financial statements

26. If an estimate of an amount reported in an interim period is changed significantly during the final interim period of the financial year but a separate financial report is not published for that final interim period, the nature and amount of that change in estimate shall be disclosed in a note to the annual financial statements for that financial year.
27. IAS 8 requires disclosure of the nature and (if practicable) the amount of a change in estimate that either has a material effect in the current period or is expected to have a material effect in subsequent periods. Paragraph 16A(d) of this Standard requires similar disclosure in an interim financial report. Examples include changes in estimate in the final interim period relating to inventory write-downs, restructurings, or impairment losses that were reported in an earlier interim period of the financial year. The disclosure required by the preceding paragraph is consistent with the IAS 8 requirement and is intended to be narrow in scope—relating only to the change in estimate. An entity is not required to include additional interim period financial information in its annual financial statements.
28. An entity shall apply the same accounting policies in its interim financial statements as are applied in its annual financial statements, except for accounting policy changes made after the date of the most recent annual financial statements that are to be reflected in the next annual financial statements. However, the frequency of an entity's reporting (annual, half-yearly, or quarterly) shall not affect the measurement of its annual results. To achieve that objective, measurements for interim reporting purposes shall be made on a year-to-date basis.
29. Requiring that an entity apply the same accounting policies in its interim financial statements as in its annual statements may seem to suggest that interim period measurements are made as if each interim period stands alone as an independent reporting period. However, by providing that the frequency of an entity's reporting shall not affect the measurement of its annual results, paragraph 28 acknowledges that an interim period is a part of a larger financial year. Year-to-date measurements may involve changes in estimates of amounts reported in prior interim periods of the

current financial year. But the principles for recognizing assets, liabilities, income, and expenses for interim periods are the same as in annual financial statements.

30. To illustrate:
    (a) the principles for recognizing and measuring losses from inventory write-downs, restructurings, or impairments in an interim period are the same as those that an entity would follow if it prepared only annual financial statements. However, if such items are recognized and measured in one interim period and the estimate changes in a subsequent interim period of that financial year, the original estimate is changed in the subsequent interim period either by accrual of an additional amount of loss or by reversal of the previously recognized amount;
    (b) a cost that does not meet the definition of an asset at the end of an interim period is not deferred in the statement of financial position either to await future information as to whether it has met the definition of an asset or to smooth earnings over interim periods within a financial year; and
    (c) income tax expense is recognized in each interim period based on the best estimate of the weighted average annual income tax rate expected for the full financial year. Amounts accrued for income tax expense in one interim period may have to be adjusted in a subsequent interim period of that financial year if the estimate of the annual income tax rate changes.
31. Under the Conceptual Framework for Financial Reporting (Conceptual Framework), recognition is the process of capturing, for inclusion in the statement of financial position or the statement(s) of financial performance, an item that meets the definition of one of the elements of the financial statements. The definitions of assets, liabilities, income, and expenses are fundamental to recognition, at the end of both annual and interim financial reporting periods.
32. For assets, the same tests of future economic benefits apply at interim dates and at the end of an entity's financial year. Costs that, by their nature, would not qualify as assets at financial year-end would not qualify at interim dates either. Similarly, a liability at the end of an interim reporting period must represent an existing obligation at that date, just as it must at the end of an annual reporting period.
33. An essential characteristic of income (revenue) and expenses is that the related inflows and outflows of assets and liabilities have already taken place. If those inflows or outflows have taken place, the related revenue and expense are recognized; otherwise they are not recognized. The *Conceptual Framework* does not allow the recognition of items in the statement of financial position which do not meet the definition of assets or liabilities.
34. In measuring the assets, liabilities, income, expenses, and cash flows reported in its financial statements, an entity that reports only annually is able to take into account information that becomes available throughout the financial year. Its measurements are, in effect, on a year-to-date basis.
35. An entity that reports half-yearly uses information available by mid-year or shortly thereafter in making the measurements in its financial statements for the first six-month period and information available by year-end or shortly thereafter for the

twelve-month period. The twelve-month measurements will reflect possible changes in estimates of amounts reported for the first six-month period. The amounts reported in the interim financial report for the first six-month period are not retrospectively adjusted. Paragraphs 16A(d) and 26 require, however, that the nature and amount of any significant changes in estimates be disclosed.

36. An entity that reports more frequently than half-yearly measures income and expenses on a year-to-date basis for each interim period using information available when each set of financial statements is being prepared. Amounts of income and expenses reported in the current interim period will reflect any changes in estimates of amounts reported in prior interim periods of the financial year. The amounts reported in prior interim periods are not retrospectively adjusted. Paragraphs 16A(d) and 26 require, however, that the nature and amount of any significant changes in estimates be disclosed.

Revenues Received Seasonally, Cyclically, or Occasionally

37. Revenues that are received seasonally, cyclically, or occasionally within a financial year shall not be anticipated or deferred as of an interim date if anticipation or deferral would not be appropriate at the end of the entity's financial year.
38. Examples include dividend revenue, royalties, and government grants. Additionally, some entities consistently earn more revenues in certain interim periods of a financial year than in other interim periods, for example, seasonal revenues of retailers. Such revenues are recognized when they occur.

Costs Incurred Unevenly during the Financial Year

39. Costs that are incurred unevenly during an entity's financial year shall be anticipated or deferred for interim reporting purposes if, and only if, it is also appropriate to anticipate or defer that type of cost at the end of the financial year.

Applying the Recognition and Measurement Principles

40. Part B of the illustrative examples accompanying this Standard provides examples of applying the general recognition and measurement principles set out in paragraphs 28–39.

Use of Estimates

41. The measurement procedures to be followed in an interim financial report shall be designed to ensure that the resulting information is reliable and that all material financial information that is relevant to an understanding of the financial position or performance of the entity is appropriately disclosed. While measurements in both annual and interim financial reports are often based on reasonable estimates, the preparation of interim financial reports generally will require a greater use of estimation methods than annual financial reports.

42. Part C of the illustrative examples accompanying this Standard provides examples of the use of estimates in interim periods.

Restatement of Previously Reported Interim Periods

43. A change in accounting policy, other than one for which the transition is specified by a new IFRS, shall be reflected by:
    (i) restating the financial statements of prior interim periods of the current financial year and the comparable interim periods of any prior financial years that will be restated in the annual financial statements in accordance with IAS 8; or
    (ii) when it is impracticable to determine the cumulative effect at the beginning of the financial year of applying a new accounting policy to all prior periods, adjusting the financial statements of prior interim periods of the current financial year, and comparable interim periods of prior financial years to apply the new accounting policy prospectively from the earliest date practicable.
44. One objective of the preceding principle is to ensure that a single accounting policy is applied to a particular class of transactions throughout an entire financial year. Under IAS 8, a change in accounting policy is reflected by retrospective application, with restatement of prior period financial data as far back as is practicable. However, if the cumulative amount of the adjustment relating to prior financial years is impracticable to determine, then under IAS 8 the new policy is applied prospectively from the earliest date practicable. The effect of the principle in paragraph 43 is to require that within the current financial year any change in accounting policy is applied either retrospectively or, if that is not practicable, prospectively, from no later than the beginning of the financial year.
45. To allow accounting changes to be reflected as of an interim date within the financial year would allow two differing accounting policies to be applied to a particular class of transactions within a single financial year. The result would be interim allocation difficulties, obscured operating results, and complicated analysis and understandability of interim period information.

Effective Date

46. This Standard becomes operative for financial statements covering periods beginning on or after 1 January 1999. Earlier application is encouraged.
47. IAS 1 (as revised in 2007) amended the terminology used throughout IFRSs. In addition it amended paragraphs 4, 5, 8, 11, 12 and 20, deleted paragraph 13 and added paragraphs 8A and 11A. An entity shall apply those amendments for annual periods beginning on or after 1 January 2009. If an entity applies IAS 1 (revised 2007) for an earlier period, the amendments shall be applied for that earlier period.
48. IFRS 3 (as revised in 2008) amended paragraph 16(i). An entity shall apply that amendment for annual periods beginning on or after 1 July 2009. If an entity applies

IFRS 3 (revised 2008) for an earlier period, the amendment shall also be applied for that earlier period.

49. Paragraphs 15, 27, 35 and 36 were amended, paragraphs 15A–15C and 16A were added and paragraphs 16–18 were deleted by *Improvements to IFRSs* in May 2010. An entity shall apply those amendments for annual periods beginning on or after 1 January 2011. Earlier application is permitted. If an entity applies the amendments for an earlier period it shall disclose that fact.
50. IFRS 13, issued in May 2011, added paragraph 16A(j). An entity shall apply that amendment when it applies IFRS 13.
51. *Presentation of Items of Other Comprehensive Income* (Amendments to IAS 1), issued in June 2011, amended paragraphs 8, 8A, 11A and 20. An entity shall apply those amendments when it applies IAS 1 as amended in June 2011.
52. *Annual Improvements 2009–2011 Cycle*, issued in May 2012, amended paragraph 5 as a consequential amendment derived from the amendment to IAS 1 *Presentation of Financial Statements*. An entity shall apply that amendment retrospectively in accordance with IAS 8 *Accounting Policies, changes in Accounting Estimates and Errors* for annual periods beginning on or after 1 January 2013. Earlier application is permitted. If an entity applies that amendment for an earlier period it shall disclose that fact.
53. *Annual Improvements 2009–2011 Cycle*, issued in May 2012, amended paragraph 16A. An entity shall apply that amendment retrospectively in accordance with IAS 8 *Accounting Policies, Changes in Accounting Estimates and Errors* for annual periods beginning on or after 1 January 2013. Earlier application is permitted. If an entity applies that amendment for an earlier period it shall disclose that fact.
54. *Investment Entities* (Amendments to IFRS 10, IFRS 12 and IAS 27), issued in October 2012, amended paragraph 16A. An entity shall apply that amendment for annual periods beginning on or after 1 January 2014. Earlier application of *Investment Entities* is permitted. If an entity applies that amendment earlier it shall also apply all amendments included in *Investment Entities* at the same time.
55. IFRS 15 *Revenue from Contracts with Customers*, issued in May 2014, amended paragraphs 15B and 16A. An entity shall apply those amendments when it applies IFRS 15.
56. *Annual Improvements to IFRSs 2012–2014 Cycle*, issued in September 2014, amended paragraph 16A. An entity shall apply that amendment retrospectively in accordance with IAS 8 *Accounting Policies, Changes in Accounting Estimates and Errors* for annual periods beginning on or after 1 January 2016. Earlier application is permitted. If an entity applies the amendment for an earlier period it shall disclose that fact.
57. *Disclosure Initiative* (Amendments to IAS 1), issued in December 2014, amended paragraph 5. An entity shall apply that amendment for annual periods beginning on or after 1 January 2016. Earlier application of that amendment is permitted.
58. *Amendments to References to the Conceptual Framework in IFRS Standards*, issued in 2018, amended paragraphs 31 and 33. An entity shall apply those amendments for

annual periods beginning on or after 1 January 2020. Earlier application is permitted if at the same time an entity also applies all other amendments made by *Amendments to References to the Conceptual Framework in IFRS Standards*. An entity shall apply the amendments to IAS 34 retrospectively in accordance with IAS 8 *Accounting Policies, Changes in Accounting Estimates and Errors*. However, if an entity determines that retrospective application would be impracticable or would involve undue cost or effort, it shall apply the amendments to IAS 34 by reference to paragraphs 43–45 of this Standard and paragraphs 23–28, 50–53 and 54F of IAS 8.

59. *Definition of Material* (Amendments to IAS 1 and IAS 8), issued in October 2018, amended paragraph 24. An entity shall apply those amendments prospectively for annual periods beginning on or after 1 January 2020. Earlier application is permitted. If an entity applies those amendments for an earlier period, it shall disclose that fact. An entity shall apply those amendments when it applies the amendments to the definition of material in paragraph 7 of IAS 1 and paragraphs 5 and 6 of IAS 8.

Source: IFRS Foundation (modified)

APPENDIX- 9(B)
CALCULATION OF BASIC EPS AND DILUTED EPS

Calculation of basic EPS

Basic Earnings Per Share = Net profit/loss for the period attributable to equity shareholder/ Weighted average number of equity shares outstanding during the period

Calculation of Net Profit/Loss for the period attributable to equity shareholder:

- Calculate the net profit/loss for the period including prior period items and extraordinary items and also deduct tax expense (Current tax + Deferred tax).
- Deduct the amount of preference dividend and any attributable tax on preference dividend from the figure calculated above. Dividend on non-cumulative preference share is deducted if dividend is provided, however in case of cumulative preference share dividend of current year is deducted even if not provided in accounts. Dividend paid during the current year in respect of previous periods is to be excluded.

Calculation of weighted average number of outstanding equity shares during the period:

Weighted average outstanding equity shares should be computed by adjusting for the change in equity shares, as per the following: If an enterprise has more than one class of equity shares, net profit or loss for the period is apportioned over the different classes of shares in accordance with their dividend rights.

List of shares issued, which are to be adjusted	*Weight to be considered from*
♦ Equity shares issued in exchange of cash	Date of cash receivable.
♦ Equity shares against conversion of debt instrument	Date of conversion.
♦ Equity shares against interest or principal of any financial instrument.	Date when interest ceases to accrue.
♦ Equity shares issued in exchange for the settlement of a liability of the enterprise.	Date on which settlement becomes effective.
♦ Equity shares issued in consideration of acquisition of assets other than cash.	Date on which acquisition is recognized.
♦ Equity shares issued against services rendered.	When service is rendered.
♦ Partly paid up share.	Partly paid up equity should be counted as fraction of equity shares in the ratio of amount paid up to the total face value of the share.
♦ Right issue.	Adjusted with Right factor.
♦ Equity shares issued as consideration in Amalgamation by way of:	
• Merger	Shares included in the calculation of weighted average from the beginning of the reporting period.
• Purchase	Included in the weighted average from the date of acquisition.
♦ Bonus shares	Shares included in weighted average from the beginning of the reporting period

Right Issue

Right issues are generally made at a price lower than fair value of share. Therefore, a right issue usually includes a bonus element. Since, right issue includes a bonus element, the number of equity shares to be used in calculating basic EPS for all periods prior to right issue is the number of equity shares outstanding prior to the issue multiplied by *right factor* which is calculated as under:

Right Factor = Fair value per share immediately prior to right issue/Theoretical ex-right fair value per share

Theoretical Ex-right fair value:

= Aggregate fair value of share immediately prior to the exercise of the rights + Proceeds from exercise of the rights/Number of shares outstanding immediately after the right issue

Diluted Earning Per Share

Diluted earnings per share is calculated when there are potential equity shares in capital structure of the enterprises. **Potential equity shares** are those financial instruments which entitle to its holder the right to acquire equity shares like convertible debentures, convertible preference shares, options, warrants, etc.

Diluted earnings per share = Net profit attributable to equity shareholders (after adjustment for diluted earnings)/Average number of weighted equity shares outstanding during the period (assuming the conversion of diluted potential equity shares)

Diluted Potential equity shares – Potential equity shares are diluted if their conversion into equity shares reduces the earning per share. If their conversion does not decrease the EPS rather it increases the EPS, then the potential equity shares are not to be considered dilutive.

Diluted Earning

- Compute net profit or loss for the period attributable to existing equity shareholder.
- Add back dividend along with distribution tax on convertible preference shares previously deducted.
- Add back interest net of tax effect charged on convertible debenture or loans.

Order in which potential equity share to be considered – Potential equity share should be ranked in order of dilutive effect. Dilutive effect is determined dividing incremental net profit by incremental net profit by incremental equity share arising out of conversion.

Re-statement

If the number of equity shares or potential equity shares outstanding is increased as a result of bonus issue, share split, consolidation of shares, the calculation of basic and diluted equity per share should be adjusted for all the period presented.

If changes occur after the balance sheet date but before the approval of financial statements by the component authority, the EPS calculation for these financial statements and any prior period financial statements should be restated on the basis of new number of shares.

APPENDIX-9(C)

INDIAN ACCOUNTING STANDARD (IND AS) 34 ON INTERIM FINANCIAL REPORTING

Objective

The objective of this Standard is to prescribe the minimum content of an interim financial report and to prescribe the principles for recognition and measurement in complete or condensed financial statements for an interim period. Timely and reliable interim financial reporting improves the ability of investors, creditors, and others to understand an entity's capacity to generate earnings and cash flows and its financial condition and liquidity.

Scope

1. This Standard does not mandate which entities should be required to publish interim financial reports, how frequently, or how soon after the end of an interim period. However, governments, securities regulators, stock exchanges, and accountancy bodies often require entities whose debt or equity securities are publicly traded to publish interim financial reports. This Standard applies if an entity is required or elects to publish an interim financial report in accordance with Indian Accounting Standards.
2. Each financial report, annual or interim, is evaluated on its own for conformity to Indian Accounting Standards. The fact that an entity may not have provided interim financial reports during a particular financial year or may have provided interim financial reports that do not comply with this Standard does not prevent the entity's annual financial statements from conforming to Indian Accounting Standards if they otherwise do so.
3. If an entity's interim financial report is described as complying with Indian Accounting Standards, it must comply with all of the requirements of this Standard. Paragraph 19 requires certain disclosures in that regard.

Definitions

4. The following terms are used in this Standard with the meanings specified:
   Interim period **is a financial reporting period shorter than a full financial year.**
   Interim financial report **means a financial report containing either a complete set of financial statements (as described in Ind AS 1 *Presentation of Financial Statements* or a set of condensed financial statements (as described in this Standard) for an interim period.**

Content of an interim financial report

5. Ind AS 1 defines a complete set of financial statements as including the following components:
   (a) a balance sheet as at the end of the period (including statement of changes in equity for the period which is presented as a part of the balance sheet);
   (b) a statement of profit and loss for the period;
   (c) [Refer to Appendix 1]
   (d) a statement of cash flows for the period;
   (e) notes, comprising a summary of significant accounting policies and other explanatory information; and
   (f) a balance sheet as at the beginning of the earliest comparative period when an entity applies an accounting policy retrospectively or makes a retrospective restatement of items in its financial statements, or when it reclassifies items in its financial statements.
6. In the interest of timeliness and cost considerations and to avoid repetition of information previously reported, an entity may be required to or may elect to provide

less information at interim dates as compared with its annual financial statements. This Standard defines the minimum content of an interim financial report as including condensed financial statements and selected explanatory notes. The interim financial report is intended to provide an update on the latest complete set of annual financial statements. Accordingly, it focuses on new activities, events, and circumstances and does not duplicate information previously reported.

7. Nothing in this Standard is intended to prohibit or discourage an entity from publishing a complete set of financial statements (as described in Ind AS 1) in its interim financial report, rather than condensed financial statements and selected explanatory notes. Nor does this Standard prohibit or discourage an entity from including in condensed interim financial statements more than the minimum line items or selected explanatory notes as set out in this Standard. The recognition and measurement guidance in this Standard applies also to complete financial statements for an interim period, and such statements would include all of the disclosures required by this Standard (particularly the selected note disclosures in paragraph 16) as well as those required by other Indian Accounting Standards.

Minimum components of an interim financial report

8. An interim financial report shall include, at a minimum, the following components:
   (a) a condensed balance sheet (including condensed statement of changes in equity for the period which is presented as a part of the balance sheet);
   (b) a condensed statement of profit and loss;
   (c) [Refer to Appendix 1];
   (d) a condensed statement of cash flows; and
   (e) selected explanatory notes.

Form and content of interim financial statements

9. If an entity publishes a complete set of financial statements in its interim financial report, the form and content of those statements shall conform to the requirements of Ind AS 1 for a complete set of financial statements.
10. If an entity publishes a set of condensed financial statements in its interim financial report, those condensed statements shall include, at a minimum, each of the headings and subtotals that were included in its most recent annual financial statements and the selected explanatory notes as required by this Standard. Additional line items or notes shall be included if their omission would make the condensed interim financial statements misleading.
11. In the statement that presents the components of profit or loss for an interim period, an entity shall present basic and diluted earnings per share for that period when the entity is within the scope of Ind AS 33 Earnings per Share.
12. An interim financial report is prepared on a consolidated basis if the entity's most recent annual financial statements were consolidated statements. The parent's separate

financial statements are not consistent or comparable with the consolidated statements in the most recent annual financial report. If an entity's annual financial report included the parent's separate financial statements in addition to consolidated financial statements, this Standard neither requires nor prohibits the inclusion of the parent's separate statements in the entity's interim financial report.

Significant events and transactions

13. An entity shall include in its interim financial report an explanation of events and transactions that are significant to an understanding of the changes in financial position and performance of the entity since the end of the last annual reporting period. Information disclosed in relation to those events and transactions shall update the relevant information presented in the most recent annual financial report.

13A. A user of an entity's interim financial report will have access to the most recent annual financial report of that entity. Therefore, it is unnecessary for the notes to an interim financial report to provide relatively insignificant updates to the information that was reported in the notes in the most recent annual financial report.

13B. The following is a list of events and transactions for which disclosures would be required if they are significant: the list is not exhaustive.

(a) the write-down of inventories to net realizable value and the reversal of such a write-down;
(b) recognition of a loss from the impairment of financial assets, property, plant and equipment, intangible assets, or other assets, and the reversal of such an impairment loss;
(c) the reversal of any provisions for the costs of restructuring;
(d) acquisitions and disposals of items of property, plant and equipment;
(e) commitments for the purchase of property, plant and equipment;
(f) litigation settlements;
(g) corrections of prior period errors;
(h) changes in the business or economic circumstances that affect the fair value of the entity's financial assets and financial liabilities, whether those assets or liabilities are recognized at fair value or amortized cost;
(i) any loan default or breach of a loan agreement that has not been remedied on or before the end of the reporting period; and
(j) related party transactions;
(k) transfers between levels of the fair value hierarchy used in measuring the fair value of financial instruments;
(l) changes in the classification of financial assets as a result of a change in the purpose or use of those assets; and
(m) changes in contingent liabilities or contingent assets.

14. An entity shall include the following information, in the notes to its interim financial statements, if not disclosed elsewhere in the interim financial report. The information shall normally be reported on a financial year-to-date basis:

(a) a statement that the same accounting policies and methods of computation are followed in the interim financial statements as compared with the most recent annual financial statements or, if those policies or methods have been changed, a description of the nature and effect of the change.
(b) explanatory comments about the seasonality or cyclicality of interim operations.
(c) the nature and amount of items affecting assets, liabilities, equity, net income or cash flows that are unusual because of their nature, size or incidence.
(d) the nature and amount of changes in estimates of amounts reported in prior interim periods of the current financial year or changes in estimates of amounts reported in prior financial years.
(e) issues, repurchases and repayments of debt and equity securities.
(f) dividends paid (aggregate or per share) separately for ordinary shares and other shares.
(g) the following segment information (disclosure of segment information is required in an entity's interim financial report only if Ind AS 108 *Operating Segments* requires that entity to disclose segment information in its annual financial statements).
   (i) revenues from external customers, if included in the measure of segment profit or loss reviewed by the chief operating decision maker or otherwise regularly provided to the chief operating decision maker.
   (ii) intersegment revenues, if included in the measure of segment profit or loss reviewed by the chief operating decision maker or otherwise regularly provided to the chief operating decision maker.
   (iii) a measure of segment profit or loss.
   (iv) total assets for which there has been a material change from the amount disclosed in the last annual financial statements.
   (v) a description of differences from the last annual financial statements in the basis of segmentation or in the basis of measurement of segment profit or loss.
   (vi) a reconciliation of the total of the reportable segments' measures of profit or loss to the entity's profit or loss before tax expense (tax income) and discontinued operations. However, if an entity allocates to reportable segments items such as tax expense (tax income), the entity may reconcile the total of the segments' measures of profit or loss to profit or loss after those items. Material reconciling items shall be separately identified and described in that reconciliation.
(h) events after the interim period that have not been reflected in the financial statements for the interim period.
(i) the effect of changes in the composition of the entity during the interim period, including business combinations, obtaining or losing control of subsidiaries and long-term investments, restructurings, and discontinued operations. In the case of business combinations, the entity shall disclose the information required by Ind AS 103 *Business Combinations*.

Disclosure of compliance with Indian Accounting Standards

15. If an entity's interim financial report is in compliance with this Standard, that fact shall be disclosed. An interim financial report shall not be described as complying with Indian Accounting Standards unless it complies with all of the requirements of Indian Accounting Standards.

Periods for which interim financial statements are required to be presented

16. Interim reports shall include interim financial statements (condensed or complete) for periods as follows:
    (a) (i) balance sheet as of the end of the current interim period and a comparative balance sheet as of the end of the immediately preceding financial year.
        (ii) (statement of changes in equity (which is presented as a part of the balance sheet) cumulatively for the current financial year to date, with a comparative statement for the comparable year-to-date period of the immediately preceding financial year).
    (b) statements of profit and loss for the current interim period and cumulatively for the current financial year to date, with comparative statements of profit and loss for the comparable interim periods (current and year-to-date) of the immediately preceding financial year.
    (c) [Refer to Appendix 1].
    (d) statement of cash flows cumulatively for the current financial year to date, with a comparative statement for the comparable year-to-date period of the immediately preceding financial year.
17. For an entity whose business is highly seasonal, financial information for the twelve months up to the end of the interim period and comparative information for the prior twelve-month period may be useful. Accordingly, entities whose business is highly seasonal are encouraged to consider reporting such information in addition to the information called for in the preceding paragraph.

Materiality

18. In deciding how to recognise, measure, classify, or disclose an item for interim financial reporting purposes, materiality shall be assessed in relation to the interim period financial data. In making assessments of materiality, it shall be recognised that interim measurements may rely on estimates to a greater extent than measurements of annual financial data.
19. Ind AS 1 and Ind AS 8 *Accounting Policies, Changes in Accounting Estimates and Errors* define an item as material if its omission or misstatement could influence the economic decisions of users of the financial statements. Ind AS 1 requires separate disclosure of material items, including (for example) discontinued operations, and Ind AS 8 requires disclosure of changes in accounting estimates, errors, and changes

in accounting policies. The two Standards do not contain quantified guidance as to materiality.

20. While judgement is always required in assessing materiality, this Standard bases the recognition and disclosure decision on data for the interim period by itself for reasons of understandability of the interim figures. Thus, for example, unusual items, changes in accounting policies or estimates, and errors are recognised and disclosed on the basis of materiality in relation to interim period data to avoid misleading inferences that might result from non-disclosure. The overriding goal is to ensure that an interim financial report includes all information that is relevant to understanding an entity's financial position and performance during the interim period.

Disclosure in Annual Financial Statements

21. If an estimate of an amount reported in an interim period is changed significantly during the final interim period of the financial year but a separate financial report is not published for that final interim period, the nature and amount of that change in estimate shall be disclosed in a note to the annual financial statements for that financial year.
22. Ind AS 8 requires disclosure of the nature and (if practicable) the amount of a change in estimate that either has a material effect in the current period or is expected to have a material effect in subsequent periods. Paragraph 16A(d) of this Standard requires similar disclosure in an interim financial report. Examples include changes in estimate in the final interim period relating to inventory write-downs, restructurings, or impairment losses that were reported in an earlier interim period of the financial year. The disclosure required by the preceding paragraph is consistent with the Ind AS 8 requirement and is intended to be narrow in scope—relating only to the change in estimate. An entity is not required.

Recognition and Measurement

23. An entity shall apply the same accounting policies in its interim financial statements as are applied in its annual financial statements, except for accounting policy changes made after the date of the most recent annual financial statements that are to be reflected in the next annual financial statements. However, the frequency of an entity's reporting (annual, half-yearly, or quarterly) shall not affect the measurement of its annual results. To achieve that objective, measurements for interim reporting purposes shall be made on a year-to-date basis.
24. Requiring that an entity apply the same accounting policies in its interim financial statements as in its annual statements may seem to suggest that interim period measurements are made as if each interim period stands alone as an independent reporting period. However, by providing that the frequency of an entity's reporting shall not affect the measurement of its annual results, paragraph 28 acknowledges that an interim period is a part of a larger financial year. Year-to-date measurements may involve changes in estimates of amounts reported in prior interim periods of the

current financial year. But the principles for recognising assets, liabilities, income, and expenses for interim periods are the same as in annual financial statements.

Revenues received seasonally, cyclically, or occasionally

25. Revenues that are received seasonally, cyclically, or occasionally within a financial year shall not be anticipated or deferred as of an interim date if anticipation or deferral would not be appropriate at the end of the entity's financial year.
26. Examples include dividend revenue, royalties, and government grants. Additionally, some entities consistently earn more revenues in certain interim periods of a financial year than in other interim periods, for example, seasonal revenues of retailers. Such revenues are recognised when they occur.

Restatement of previously reported interim periods

27. A change in accounting policy, other than one for which the transition is specified by a new Indian Accounting Standard, shall be reflected by:
    restating the financial statements of prior interim periods of the current financial year and the comparable interim periods of any prior financial years that will be restated in the annual financial statements in accordance with Ind AS 8; or
    when it is impracticable to determine the cumulative effect at the beginning of the financial year of applying a new accounting policy to all prior periods, adjusting the financial statements of prior interim periods of the current financial year, and comparable interim periods of prior financial years to apply the new accounting policy prospectively from the earliest date practicable.
28. One objective of the preceding principle is to ensure that a single accounting policy is applied to a particular class of transactions throughout an entire financial year. Under Ind AS 8, a change in accounting policy is reflected by retrospective application, with restatement of prior period financial data as far back as is practicable. However, if the cumulative amount of the adjustment relating to prior financial years is impracticable to determine, then under Ind AS 8 the new policy is applied prospectively from the earliest date practicable. The effect of the principle in paragraph 43 is to require that within the current financial year any change in accounting policy is applied either retrospectively or, if that is not practicable, prospectively, from no later than the beginning of the financial year.
29. To allow accounting changes to be reflected as of an interim date within the financial year would allow two differing accounting policies to be applied to a particular class of transactions within a single financial year. The result would be interim allocation difficulties, obscured operating results, and complicated analysis and understandability of interim period information.

Source: https//www.mca.gov.in (modified).

10

International Taxation

LEARNING OBJECTIVES

After studying this chapter, you will be able to:

- Explain the concept and importance of international taxation policy and planning
- Discuss the objectives of international taxation
- Describe the home government and host government's international tax policy
- Explain the concept of double taxation and tax treaties
- Discuss the salient features of Government of India's tax treaties with the USA and UK
- Draw the list of countries with which India has tax treaties
- Find out the applicable withholding tax rates in India
- Apply the knowledge of international taxation in deciding the manner and the destination of foreign investments

INTRODUCTION

Taxes have a significant bearing on business decisions ranging from designing a suitable capital structure, managing foreign exchange risk, determining cost of financing, deciding upon the mode and destination of foreign investments, to determining transfer prices, and managing inter-affiliated fund flows. The process of computation of taxable income and the corresponding taxes vary across nations depending on what 'costs' are deductible from the revenues. Tax rates too vary from country to country and from time to time. For instance, the present corporate tax rates in Bulgaria, Canada, Germany, Hong Kong, Hungary, Korea, Malaysia, Mauritius, Nepal, Norway, Poland, Romania, Singapore, Sweden and Taiwan is 19.5%, 22%, 25%, 17.5%, 18%, 27%, 28%, 25%, 25%, 28%, 19%, 25%, 22%, 28% and 25%, respectively. Tax rates are fixed by the Government as a function of domestic economic and political considerations. 'Government usually set tax rates as a function of domestic political considerations, but will sometimes treat foreign investors to the extent that they choose to encourage or discourage foreign investments[1]. 'It ought to be remembered that when the wisest government has exhausted all the proper subjects of taxation, it must, in cases of urgent necessity, have recourse to improper ones'[2]. Financial managers of multinational corporations operating in different countries therefore need to be aware about the broad dimensions of international taxation such as the objectives of taxation, tax credits, double taxation, tax havens and alike and their impact on various corporate decisions.

INTERNATIONAL TAX PLANNING

International tax planning in the context of Multi-National Corporations refers to the process of structuring foreign operations and remittances that would result in maximization of the firms' global after tax cash flows. 'International tax planning involves using the flexibility of the multinational corporation in structuring foreign operations and remittance policies in order to maximize global after tax cash flows' [3].

International tax planning process is a complex but essential phenomenon in international investment decisions of multinational corporations which calls for a close scrutiny and a careful consideration by the investing firm of all the provisions of a country in relation to taxation of foreign income before taking up the investment activities. This is because every sovereign country has the right to decide how to tax the foreign income of its residents and the income of foreigners originating from within its territories, and it is for the interest of the MNCs that they are aware about the overall tax laws and investment environment of the nation(s) where they would like to operate. 'Tax management is difficult because the ultimate tax burden on a multinational firm's income is the result of a complex interplay between the heterogeneous tax systems of home and host governments, each with its own fiscal objectives' [4].

The subject matter of international taxation as stated above is both vast and complex. A complete knowledge on international taxation therefore would warrant a detailed analysis of the tax laws and practices of every country concerned. Inclusion of a discussion on every country's tax laws and system is beyond the scope of this book. However, discussions have been attempted here on broad issues on international taxation like international tax objectives and policies, withholding taxes as found in general across nations. Selected provisions of the Indian Income Tax Act, 1961 in relation to tax treaties have also been highlighted.

OBJECTIVES OF INTERNATIONAL TAXATION

Taxation policies followed by most nations across the globe are characterized by two objectives—'tax neutrality' and 'tax equity'. Tax neutrality further assumes two forms: domestic neutrality, often called as capital export neutrality, and foreign neutrality, also known as capital import neutrality.

Tax Neutrality

Tax neutrality refers to a system of taxation which when adopted will not affect the investment decisions of the firms as regards the destination of the investment or the nationality of the investor. There are two forms of tax neutrality such as domestic neutrality and foreign neutrality.

Domestic neutrality or capital export neutrality is said to be existing when tax laws do not affect the capital owner's choice between investing in home country or in host (foreign) country. 'Taxation is export neutral if domestic and overseas investments that earn the same pre-tax rates of return also yield the same after tax rates of return. If capital export neutrality is violated, the capital owner will have an incentive to invest more where tax rate is lower, thereby realizing a higher after tax rate of return' [5].

Foreign neutrality or capital important neutrality exists when tax laws do not distort the after tax earnings to domestic and foreign investors. 'Taxation is import neutral if equal before tax returns to competing supplies of capital translate into equal after tax return' [6].

It is important to note that in any given situation it is either the export neutrality or the import neutrality that holds good, and not both. Moreover, a perfect neutral tax system will mean all countries have the same tax rates and that no double taxation occurs; a proposition almost impossible to achieve. It is for this reason that major capital exporting countries such as the United States, Japan, Germany, Sweden and Great Britain follow a mixed policy of capital export and capital import neutrality wherein they currently tax foreign branch profits but defer taxing the earnings from foreign subsidiaries till they are repatriated. Other countries like the Netherlands, France, Canada and Hong Kong fully exempt foreign incomes from domestic taxation, and Italy, Switzerland and Belgium exclude a part of the foreign income from computation of domestic tax liability.

Tax Equity

Tax equity refers to a system of taxation where equal sacrifices are made by the tax payers in bearing the tax burdens. The basic difference between tax neutrality and tax equity lies with the fact that the former is achieved by ensuring that investment decisions are unaffected due to the difference in tax laws, the latter is achieved by ensuring that equal sacrifices are made in bearing the tax burden under similar situations. Tax equity thus favours imposition of corporate income tax in the same manner and rates regardless of whether the income is generated through a foreign branch or a domestic branch. The rationale behind tax equity is to ensure that all, similarly situated tax payers must bear the cost of running a government.

INTERNATIONAL TAXATION POLICY IN PRACTICE

Given the broader objectives of international taxation of 'neutrality' and 'equity' as explained above, the tax policies in vogue at 'home' and 'host' countries may be outlined as in Fig. 10.1:

As depicted in Fig. 10.1, international taxation in practice has two broad dimensions—tax policies of the home government and tax policies of the host government. Tax policies of the home government are relatively complex in nature compared to that of the host government as because host country gets the first opportunity to tax incomes generated within its territory and based on the host country's policies, the home country's policies are adjusted.

Home Country's Tax Policies

The home country's tax policies have two dimensions:

(i) Treatment of foreign income and foreign taxes paid.

(ii) Timing of taxation.

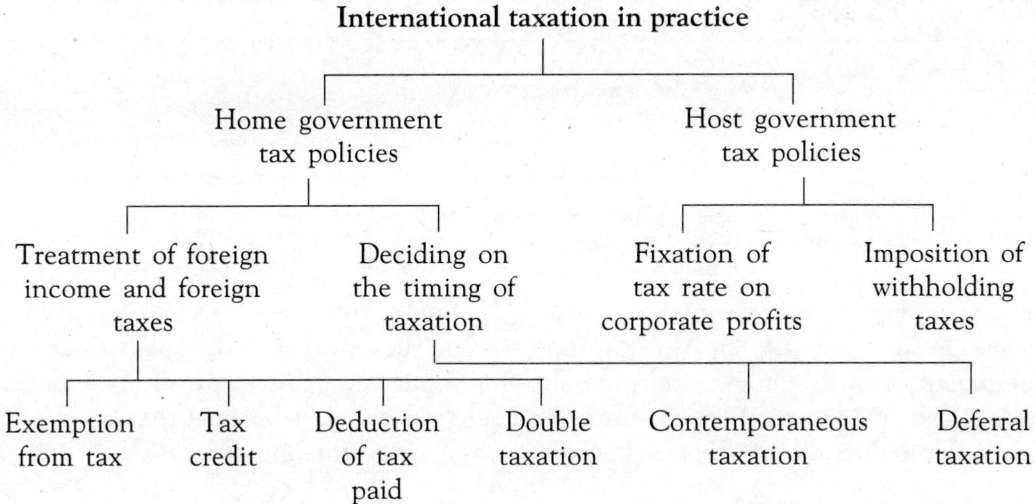

Figure 10.1 International taxation in practice.

These dimensions have been dealt with as follows:

(i) Treatment of foreign income and foreign taxes paid

There are four different ways in which a home government can treat foreign income earned and the taxes paid there on. These are

(a) *Exemption* of foreign income from domestic tax.
(b) Granting of full *tax credit* for the foreign taxes paid.
(c) Giving *deduction* for foreign taxes paid.
(d) Taxing foreign income by completely ignoring foreign taxes already paid on the income, i.e., taxing the income twice, first by the host government and then by the home government, resulting thereby in *double taxation.*

Let us examine each of the above cases as under:

Tax Exemption: Exemption of foreign income from domestic tax amounts to a situation where the foreign income accrued to a firm is taxed only by the host government and not by the home government. The home government may thus decide not to impose tax on foreign income, thereby exempting it from domestic tax.

ILLUSTRATION 10.1

Canon International Inc. of Japan has earned $2,25,000 through its Hong Kong subsidiary, the Scientific Inc. If the applicable corporate income tax rate in Japan and Singapore is 20% and 15%, respectively, and if the Japanese government decides to exempt the foreign income earned by its firm from tax, what is Canon International Inc.'s liability and post-tax income?

SOLUTION

Calculation of Tax liability and post-tax income of Canon International Inc. under 'Tax Exemption'

Particulars	($)
Foreign income *Less*: Foreign taxes paid (to Hong Kong government) @ 15%	2,25,000 33,750
Income after host government's tax *Less*: Home government's tax	1,91,250 Nil[1]
Net income after tax	1,91,250

Note: If the home government (Japan) has decides not to tax any foreign income, Canon Inc.'s tax liability will remain limited to the host (Hong Kong) government's imposition of 15% tax only.

Tax credit: Tax credit system emerges when the home government decides to tax foreign income at the domestic (tax) rate irrespective of the amount of tax paid to the host government on such income; and then allowing a full tax credit to the effect and extent of tax already paid to the host government. The ultimate tax liability of the firm therefore remains limited to the tax rate of the host or home government which over is higher.

ILLUSTRATION 10.2

Hi-Tech Inc. of Mauritius has earned $21,32,280 through its Malaysian subsidiary, the GreenTech Inc. If the applicable corporate income tax rate in Mauritius and Malaysia is 28.5% and 25%, respectively, and if the Mauritius government decides to exempt the foreign income earned by its firms from tax, what is Hi-Tech Inc.'s tax liability and post-tax income?

SOLUTION

Calculation of Tax liability and post-tax income of Hi-Tech Inc. under 'Tax Credit'

Particulars	($)
Foreign income *Less:* Foreign taxes paid (to Malaysian government) @ 25%	21,32,200 5,33,050
Income after host government's tax *Less:* Home government's tax	15,99,150 74,627[1]
Net income after tax	15,24,523

Note: The gross domestic tax liability of Hi-Tech Inc. comes to $6,07,677 (i.e., 28.5% of $21,32,200) of $5,33,050 paid to foreign government as tax (i.e., 25% of $21,32,200) is allowed as 'full tax credit'. The net domestic tax liability therefore comes to $74,627.

ILLUSTRATION 10.3

Jasmine Ltd. of Sri Lanka has earned $2000 through its Singapore subsidiary, the James Ltd. If the applicable corporate income tax rate in Sri Lanka and Singapore is 40% and 30%, respectively, and if the Sri Lankan government decides to (a) exempt the foreign income accrued to its firm, and (b) allow full credit in respect of the foreign taxes already paid, find out Jasmine Ltd.'s tax liability and after tax income.

SOLUTION

Computation of Jasmine Ltd.'s tax liability and after tax foreign income

Particulars	Tax liability and after tax income if given	
	'Tax Exemption' ($)	'Tax credit' ($)
Foreign income	2,000	2,000
Less: Foreign taxes paid (to Singapore government) @ 30%	600	600
Income after host government's tax	1,400	1,400
Less: Home government's tax	Nil[1]	200[2]
Net income after tax	1,400	1,200

Notes: 1. As the home government (Sri Lanka) decides not to tax foreign income, Jasmine Ltd.'s tax liability will remain limited to the host (Singapore) government's imposition of 30% tax alone.

2. The gross domestic tax liability of Jasmine Ltd. comes to $800 (i.e., 40% of $2,000) of which $600 paid to foreign government as tax (i.e., 30% of $2,000) is allowed as 'full tax credit'. The net domestic tax liability therefore comes to $200.

Tax Deduction: Deduction for foreign taxes paid amounts to a situation where the home country government allows the foreign taxes paid as 'deduction' from the foreign income and then imposes taxes on the 'reduced' income at the prevailing rate of domestic tax. The system varies from tax credit insofar as foreign taxes paid is directly deducted from the base income rather than being allowed as an adjustment against the calculated tax.

ILLUSTRATION 10.4

ComfortZone Inc. of UK has earned £4, 36,900 net surplus through its Canadian subsidiary InfiniteZone Inc. The corporate tax rate in UK is 18% and in Canada is 15%. If the UK government decides to allow deduction for foreign taxes paid, what will be post-tax foreign income of ComfortZone Inc?

SOLUTION

Computation of Comfort Zone Inc.'s tax liability and post-tax foreign income

Particulars	(£)
Foreign income	4,36,000
Less: Foreign taxes paid (to Canadian Government) @ 15%	65,400
Income after host government's tax	3,70,600
Less: Home government's tax	66,708[1]
Net income after tax	3,03,892

Note: When the home government allows deduction of foreign taxes paid, then tax by the home government will be levied at the applicable tax rate only on the income left after paying the amount of foreign tax. In the instant case therefore, tax by the UK government is levied on £3,70,600, i.e., £4,36,900–£56,400.

ILLUSTRATION 10.5

Continuing with Illustration 10.3 , if the Sri Lankan government decides to give a deduction for the tax already paid to the Singapore government instead of giving exemption or tax credit, what will be Jasmine Ltd.'s domestic tax liability and after tax income?

SOLUTION

When a deduction for foreign taxes paid is allowed, the domestic tax is levied at the applicable tax rate only on the income left after deducting the amount of foreign taxes paid from the base income, i.e., from the income before such payment of foreign taxes.

In the case of Jasmine Ltd. therefore, domestic tax of 40% will be levied on $1,400 (i.e., $2,000 – 30% of $2000 paid as tax to Singapore, the host government) and hence Jasmine Ltd.'s home government tax liability will be $560 (i.e., 40% of 1400), and its after tax income will be $840 (i.e., $2,000 – $600 – $560). This may also be presented in a tabular form as under:

Computation of tax liability and post-tax foreign income of Jasmine Ltd. when tax deduction is allowed

Particulars	($)
Foreign income	2,000
Less: Foreign taxes paid (to Singapore Government) @ 30%	600
Income after host government's tax	1,400
Less: Home government's tax	560[1]
Net income after tax	840

Note: 1. Home tax liability is 40% of $1,400

ILLUSTRATION 10.6

Supper Sales Ltd. of India has earned a foreign income of ₹24,48,96,000 through its affiliate, Universal Ltd. of Indonesia. If the corporate tax rate prevalent in Indonesia is 20% and in India is 25%, determine the post-tax foreign income of Supper Sales India Ltd. if the Government of India (i) gives exemption to foreign income from domestic tax, (ii) allows credit for tax paid on foreign income, and (iii) allows deduction for foreign taxes paid.

Computation of tax liability and post-tax foreign income of Supper Sales Ltd.

Particulars	*Under Tax options*		
	I *Tax exemption* ₹	*II* *Tax credit* ₹	*III* *Tax deduction* ₹
(A) Income from Universal Ltd. (A)	24,48,96,000	24,48,96,000	24,48,96,000
Less: (B) Tax paid to host Government, i.e., Indonesian Government @ 20%	4,89,79,200	4,89,79,200	4,89,79,200
(C) Income after foreign tax (i.e., A – B)	19,59,16,800	19,59,16,800	19,59,16,800
Less: (D) Tax paid/payable to home Government, i.e., Indian Government	Nil[1]	1,22,44,800[2]	4,89,79,200[3]
Net income after tax (C – D)	19,59,16,800	18,36,72,000	14,69,37,600

Notes:

1. Home tax liability is nil because the home government does not tax foreign income.
2. Gross tax liability is ₹6,12,24,000 (i.e., 25% of ₹24,48,96,000) *minus* ₹4,89,79,200 (i.e, the amount of tax paid to host government).
3. Foreign tax of ₹4,89,79,200 is allowed as 'deductible' expenses. Hence 25% tax is levied only on ₹19,59,16,800, i.e., ₹24,48,96,000 – ₹4,89,79,200.

Double taxation: Double taxation occurs when the home country government decides to tax foreign income at the domestic rate without taking into recognition the taxes already paid to the host government on such income. Under double taxation therefore domestic tax will be imposed on the original income, i.e., income before payment of foreign tax.

ILLUSTRATION 10.7

MaryMax, an FMCG Company registered in Philippines has generated an income of 55,45, 35,000 PHP (Philippines Peso) through its Indonesian subsidiary The SuperMax Ltd. If the corporate tax rate prevalent in Philippines and Indonesia is 30% and 25%, respectively, find out the post-tax foreign income of MaryMax if the Government of Philippines ignores the foreign taxes paid.

SOLUTION

Computation of tax liability and post-tax foreign income of MaryMax Ltd.

Particulars	*PHP*
Foreign income	55,45,35,000
Less: Foreign taxes paid (to Indonesian Government) @ 25%	13,86,33,750
Income after host government's tax	41,59,01,250
Less: Home government's tax @30% on 55,45,35,000 PHP	16,63,60,500[1]
Net income after tax	24,95,40,750

ILLUSTRATION 10.8

MM International Inc. of Italy has generated a profit of €78,87,700 in Sweden through its affiliate KKS Inc. The applicable tax rate in Sweden is 21.4% and in Italy is 24%. If the home government decides to (i) exempt any foreign income from tax, (ii) allow tax credit, (iii) allow deduction, and (iv) ignore any tax paid to host government on foreign income, what is the after tax income of MM International Inc.?

SOLUTION

Computation of MM International Inc.'s tax liability and after tax foreign income

Particulars	*Tax options*			
	I Tax exemption €	*II Tax credit* €	*III Tax deduction* €	*IV Double taxation* €
(A) Income from Italian affiliate, KKS Ltd. (A)	78,87,500	78,87,500	78,87,500	78,87,500
Less: (B) Foreign taxes paid, i.e, tax paid to the host government @21.4%	16,87,925	16,87,925	16,87,925	16,87,925
(C) Income after foreign tax (=A – B)	61,99,575	61,99,575	61,99,575	61,99,575
Less: (D) Tax paid/payable to Home Government @24%	Nil[1]	2,05,075[2]	14,87,898[3]	18,93,000[4]
Net income after tax (C – D)	61,99,575	59,94,500	47,11,677	43,06,575

Notes:

1. Home tax liability is nil because the home government has decided not to tax foreign income.

2. Gross tax liability is €18,93,000 (i.e., 24% of €78,87,500), of which €16,87,925 is already paid to foreign government which is now allowed as tax credit. Hence, the net domestic tax liability is €18, 93,000 – €16,87,925 = €2,05,075.
3. Foreign tax of €16,87,925 already paid to host government is allowed as 'deductible' expenses. Hence, 24% tax is levied only on differential amount which is €61,99,575 (i.e., €78, 87,500 – €16,87,925)
4. Tax paid to foreign government is ignored. Hence, 24% tax is levied on original income, i.e, income before foreign tax, irrespective of how much has been paid as tax to the host government; resulting thereby in double taxation, i.e., the same income is taxed twice, once by the host government and again by the home government.

ILLUSTRATION 10.9

Other things remaining unchanged in Illustration 10.3, if the Sri Lankan government decides to impose domestic tax on Jasmine Ltd.'s foreign earnings without recognizing the tax already paid to the Singapore government, what will be Jasmine Ltd.'s domestic tax liability and after tax income?

SOLUTION

As the Sri Lankan government decides to ignore the foreign tax already paid by Jasmine Ltd. and impose domestic tax of 40%, Jacks domestic tax liability will be 40% of $ 2000, or $ 800 and its after tax income will be $600 (i.e., $2,000 – $600 paid to Singapore government– $ 800 paid to Sri Lankan government).

ILLUSTRATION 10.10

Horizon Ltd. of Singapore has generated foreign income of $4,00,000 through its affiliate, Stevedors Ltd. of Malaysia. Corporate tax rate prevalent in Singapore and Malaysia is 35% and 30%, respectively. What will be Horizon's (a) foreign income tax liability, and (b) after tax foreign income if the Singapore government of decides to:

(i) exempt foreign income from domestic tax,
(ii) allow credit for tax paid on foreign income,
(iii) allow deduction for foreign taxes paid, and
(iv) tax foreign income without recognizing the taxes already paid.

SOLUTION

Computation of Stevedors Inc's tax liability and after tax foreign income

Fig. in $'000

Particulars	*Tax options*			
	I Tax exemption	*II Tax credit*	*III Tax deduction*	*IV Double taxation*
Income from Malaysian affiliate, Stevedors Ltd. (A)	400	400	400	400
Less: Foreign taxes @ 30% paid (B)	120	120	120	120
Income after foreign tax (i.e., A – B) = (C)	280	280	280	280
Less: Home tax @ 35% paid/payable (D)	Nil[1]	20[2]	98[3]	140[4]
Net income after tax (C – D)	280	260	182	140

Notes:

1. Home tax liability is nil because the home government does not tax foreign income.
2. Gross tax liability is $140 (i.e., 35% of $400), of which $120 already paid to foreign government is allowed as credit. Hence net domestic tax payable is $140 – $120 = $20.
3. Foreign tax of $120 is allowed as 'deductible' expenses. Hence 35% tax is levied only on $400 – $120 or on $280.
4. Tax paid to foreign government is not considered. Hence, 35% tax is levied on income before foreign tax, thereby resulting in double taxation.

ILLUSTRATION 10.11

Cosmo Ltd. of Sweden has earned a foreign income of $1,20,000 through its Philippines subsidiary, Protolab Ltd. The applicable corporate income tax rate in Sweden is 40% and in Philippines is 35%.

If the Government of Sweden decides to (i) exempt foreign income from tax, (ii) offer credit for foreign income tax paid, (iii) allows deductions for foreign income tax paid and (iv) ignores foreign income tax paid, determine Cosmo Ltd's tax liability on foreign income and also its after tax income.

SOLUTION

Computation of Cosmo Ltd's foreign income tax liability and after tax foreign income

Particulars	*Tax options*			
	I Tax exemption	*II Tax credit*	*III Tax deduction*	*IV Double taxation*
Income from Protolab Ltd.	1,20,000	1,20,000	1,20,000	1,20,000
Less: Foreign taxes @ 35% paid	42,000	42,000	42,000	42,000
Income after foreign tax	78,000	78,000	78,000	78,000
Less: Home tax @ 40% paid/payable	Nil[1]	6,000[2]	31,200[3]	48,000[4]
Net income after tax	78,000	72,000	46,800	30,000

Notes:

1. Home tax liability is nil as the home government (Sweden) decides to exempt foreign income from tax.
2. Gross tax liability comes to $48,000 (i.e., 40% of $1,20,000) of which $42,000 (i.e., 35% of $1,20,000) has already been paid by Cosmo Ltd. to Philippines government which is now allowed as 'tax credit'. Therefore the net tax payable to Sweden government by Cosmo Ltd. on its foreign income shall be $6,000 (i.e., $48,000 – $42,000).
3. Foreign tax of $ 42,000 already paid by Cosmo Ltd. to Philippines government is allowed as deduction from the total income and on the balance amount of $ 78,000 (i.e., $1, 20,000 – $42,000) a tax of 40% is levied which comes to $31,200.
4. Tax already paid to foreign government is ignored. Hence, Sweden government will impose 40% tax on $1,20,000 which will amount to $48,000.

(ii) Timing of taxation

Deciding upon the timing of taxation is the second important dimension of a home government's foreign tax policy. In practice, a home government has two choices before it for fixing the timing of taxing the foreign income. They are:

1. taxing foreign income in the same fiscal year in which it is earned, sometimes referred to be called as 'contemporaneous taxation', and
2. taxing only when incomes are repatriated, a phenomenon best known as 'tax deferral'.

The United States, for example, taxes incomes of foreign branches under contemporaneous taxation system, whereas for incomes from foreign subsidiaries it follows the tax deferral system. Branches of MNCs are foreign operation incorporated at home and subsidiaries are foreign operations incorporated in host countries. Therefore, branches are considered to have no separate legal existence than the parents and hence foreign income generated through branches are taxed by most countries like the USA in the same year in which they are earned. On the contrary, incomes generated through foreign subsidiaries are taxed only on their repatriation, for foreign subsidiaries are considered to have separate legal entity as being incorporated in the host countries.

Host Country's Tax Policies

The host government generally gets the first opportunity to tax corporate income generated in its territory as far as the international arrangement for taxation of corporate incomes goes. Further, the host government may also impose withholding taxes on repatriation of profits in the form of dividends and other incomes such as license fees, royalties and fees for technical services. These incomes do not attract withholding taxes as long as they are not repatriated from the host country and instead allowed to remain and get reinvested in the host country.

The host government thus enjoys the privilege of fixing corporate tax rate on returns on equity investments in its territories and also any withholding taxes on income that outflows.

DOUBLE TAXATION VS TAX TREATIES

Double taxation which occurs when the same income is taxed twice—first by the host government and second by the home government, works against the free flow of capital across nations. The efforts of developing countries in attracting foreign investments, better technologies and technical expertise from developed nations by introducing tax incentives also get nullified by double taxation. To avoid double taxation and to reduce overall tax burden therefore countries do undertake both unilateral and bilateral relief measures.

Unilateral relief measures are measures taken by one country alone as long as such measures continue to benefit the country concerned. Included under the unilateral measures are tax exemption, tax credit, and tax deduction as contained in Fig. 10.1 and explained in illustration 10.1 through 10.4. 'Investment credit' which permits deduction of a percentage of the capital investment in foreign country from the income so generated depending upon the expected rate of return on capital, too amounts to another measure of unilateral relief aimed at reducing the investors' tax liability and improving the after tax foreign income.

Under the *bilateral relief* measures included are the comprehensive and partial double tax avoidance treaties. These treaties are agreements between two countries to clearly demarcate their tax jurisdiction over a transaction and the percentage of tax on the income derived from such transaction(s). Depending upon the extent of coverage, these treaties can be comprehensive or partial. It is to the advantage of MNCs that they keep in view tax treaties while planning for foreign operations particularly on circumstances which give full tax advantage.

TAX TREATIES BY GOVERNMENT OF INDIA

Tax treaties aim at providing protection to tax payers against double taxation, and preventing the discouragement which taxation may cause in the free flow of international trade, international investment and international transfer of technology. Tax treaties also aim at preventing discrimination between the tax payers in the international field and providing a reasonable element of legal and fiscal certainty within a legal framework. In addition, tax treaties contain provisions for mutual exchange of information and for reducing litigation by providing for mutual assistance procedure.

The Government of India has been empowered under Section 90 of the Indian Income Tax Act, 1961 to enter into Double Tax Avoidance Agreements (tax treaties) with other countries. The object of such agreements is to evolve an equitable basis for the allocation of the right to tax different types of income between the 'source' and 'residence' country ensuring in the process tax neutrality in transactions between residents and non-residents.

A non-resident, under the scheme of income taxation, becomes liable to tax in India in respect of income arising here by virtue of its being the country of source and then again, in his own country in respect of the same income by virtue of the inclusion of such income in the 'total world income' which is the tax base in the country of residence. Tax incidence, therefore, becomes an important factor influencing the non-residents in deciding about the location of their investment, services; technology and alike.

Countries in Relation to India's DTA

Table 10.1 contains a list of countries with which Government of India has signed Double Tax Avoidance Agreements along with the effective assessment year:

TABLE 10.1 India's Double Tax Avoidance Agreements (tax treaties) with various countries

Sl. No.	*Name of the Country*	*Effective from Assessment Year*	*Sl. No.*	*Name of the Country*	*Effective from Assessment Year*
1	Australia	1993–94	30	Namibia	2000–2001
2	Austria	1963–64	31	Nepal	1990–91
3	Bangladesh	1993–94	32	Netherlands	1990–91
4	Belgium	1989–90; 1999–2000 (Revised)	33	New Zealand	1988–89
5	Brazil	1994–95		(1999–2000 amending notification) (2001–2002 Supp. Protocol)	
6	Belarus	1999–2000	34	Norway	1988–89
7	Bulgaria	1997–98	35	Oman	1999–2000

(*Contd.*)

TABLE 10.1 India's Double Tax Avoidance Agreements (tax treaties) with various countries (*Contd.*)

Sl. No.	*Name of the Country*	*Effective from Assessment Year*		*Sl. No.*	*Name of the Country*	*Effective from Assessment Year*	
8	Canada	1987–88; 1999–2000	 (Revised)	36	Philippines	1996–97	
9	China	1996–97		37	Poland	1991–92	
10	Cyprus	1994–95		38	Qatar	2001–2002	
11	Czechoslovakia	1986–87; 2001–2002	 (Revised)	39	Romania	1989–90	
12	Denmark	1991–92		40	Singapore	1995–96	
13	Finland	1985–86; 2000–2001	Amending protocol	41	South Africa	1999–2000	
14	France	1996–97	(Revised)	42	South Korea	1985–86	
15	F.R.G	1958–59	(Original)	43	Spain	1997–98	
	F.R.G.	1984–85	(Protocol)	44	Sri Lanka	1981–82	
	D.G.R.	1985–86		45	Sweden	1990–91; 1999–2000	 (Revised)
	F.R.G.	1998–99	(Revised)	46	Switzerland	1996–97	
16	Greece	1964–65		47	Syria	1983–84	
17	Hungary	1989–90		48	Tanzania	1983–84	
18	Indonesia	1989–90		49	Thailand	1988–89	
19	Israel	1995–96		50	Trinidad & Tobago	2001–2002	
20	Italy	1997–98	(Revised)	51	Turkmenistan	1999–2000	
21	Japan	1991–92	(Revised)	52	Turkey	1995–96	
22	Jordan	2001–2002		53	U.A.E.	1995–96	
23	Kazakhstan	1999–2000		54	U.A.R.	1970–71	
24	Kenya	1985–86		55	U.K.	1995–96	(Revised)
25	Libya	1983–84		56	U.S.A.	1992–93	
26	Malta	1997–98		57	Russian Federation	2000–2001	
27	Malaysia	1973–74		58	Uzbekistan	1994–95	
28	Mauritius	1983–84		59	Vietnam	1997–98	
29	Mongolia	1995–96		60	Zambia	1979–80	

Source: Compiled form Taxman's website

The tax treaties contained in Table 10.1 follow a near uniform pattern in as much as India has guided itself by the UN model of double tax avoidance agreements. The agreements allocate jurisdiction between the source and residence country. Wherever such jurisdiction is given to both the countries, the agreements prescribe maximum rate of taxation in the source country which is generally lower than the rate of tax under the domestic laws of that country. The double taxation in such cases are avoided by the residence country agreeing to give credit for tax paid in the source country thereby reducing tax payable in the residence country by the amount of tax paid in the source country.

These agreements give the right of taxation in respect of the income of the nature of interest, dividend, royalty and fees for technical services to the country of residence. However, the source country is also given the right but such taxation in the source country has to be limited to the rates prescribed in the agreement. The rate of taxation is on gross receipts without deduction of expenses.

Taxation on Different Types of Income

Capital gains: Gains arising from transfer of immovable properties are taxed in the country where such properties are situated. Gains arising from the transfer of movable properties forming part of the business property of a 'permanent establishment' or the 'fixed base' are taxed in the country where such permanent establishment or the fixed base is located. Different provisions exist for taxation of capital gains arising from transfer of shares. In a number of agreements the right to tax is given to the State of which the company is resident. In some others, the country of residence of the shareholder has this right and in some others the country of residence of the transferor has the right if the shareholding of the transferor is of a prescribed percentage. So far as the business income is concerned, the source country gets the right only if there is a 'permanent establishment' or a 'fixed place of business' there. Taxation of business income is on net income from business at the rate prescribed in the Finance Acts. Chapter X may be referred to for a discussion on the subject.

Professional services: Income derived by rendering of professional services or other activities of independent character are taxable in the country of residence except when the person deriving income from such services has a fixed base in the other country from where such services are performed. Such income is also taxable in the source country if his stay exceeds 183 days in that financial year.

Personal Services: Income from dependent personal services, i.e., from employment is taxed in the country of residence unless the employment is exercised in the other state. Even if the employment is exercised in any other state, the remuneration will be taxed in the country of residence if –

(i) the recipient is present in the source State for a period not exceeding 183 days;
(ii) the remuneration is paid by a person who is not a resident of that state; and
(iii) the remuneration is not borne by a permanent establishment or a fixed base.

Others: The agreements also provides for jurisdiction to tax Director's fees, remuneration of persons in Government service, payments received by students and apprentices, income of entertainers and athletes, pensions and social security payments and other incomes. For taxation of income of artists, entertainers, sportsman, etc., CBDT circular No. 787 dates 10.2.2000 may be referred to.

Special Clauses

Agreements also contain clauses for non-discrimination of the national of a contracting State in the other State vis-a-vis the nationals of that other State. The fact that higher rates of tax are prescribed for foreign companies in India does not amount to discrimination against the permanent establishment of the non-resident company. This has been made explicit in certain agreements such as one with U.K.

Provisions also exist for mutual agreement procedure which authorizes the competent authorities of the two States to resolve any dispute that may arise in the matter of taxation without going through the normal process of appeals, etc. provided under the domestic law.

Another important feature of some agreements is the existence of a clause providing for exchange of information between the two contracting States which may be necessary for carrying out the provisions of the agreement or for effective implementations of domestic laws concerning taxes covered by the tax treaty. Information about residents getting payments in other contracting States necessary to be known for proper assessment of total income of such individual is thus facilitated by such agreements.

Favourable Domestic Law

It may sometimes happen that owing to reduction in tax rates under the domestic law taking place after coming into existence of the treaty, the domestic rates become more favourable to the non-residents. Since the objects of the tax treaties is to benefit the non-residents, they have, under such circumstances, the option to be assessed either as per the provisions of the treaty or the domestic law of the land.

Tax Deducted at Source

In order to avoid any demand or refund consequent to assessment and to facilitate the process of assessment, it has been provided that tax shall be deducted at source out of payments to non-residents at the same rate at which the particular income is made taxable under the tax treaties. As a result of amendment made by the Finance Act, 1997 exempting from tax income from dividend declared after 1.6.1997, no deduction is required to be made in respect of such income.

Countries with which No Agreement Exists

(1) If any person who is resident in India in any previous year proves that, in respect of his income which accrued or arose during that previous year outside India (and which is not deemed to accrue or arise in India), he has paid in any country with which there is no agreement under section 90 for the relief or avoidance of double taxation, income-tax, by deduction or otherwise, under the law in force in that country, he shall be entitled to the deduction from the Indian income-tax payable by him of a sum calculated on such doubly taxed income at the Indian rate of tax or the rate of tax of the said country, whichever is the lower, or at the Indian rate of tax if both the rates are equal.

(2) If any person who is resident in India in any previous year proves that in respect of his income which accrued or arose to him during that previous year in Pakistan he has paid in that country, by deduction or otherwise, tax payable to the Government under any law for the time being in force in that country relating to taxation of agricultural

income, he shall be entitled to a deduction from the Indian income-tax payable by him:

- of the amount of the tax paid in Pakistan under any law aforesaid on such income which is liable to tax under this Act also; or
- of a sum calculated on that income at the Indian rate of tax; whichever is less.

(3) If any non-resident person is assessed on his share in the income of a registered firm assessed as resident in India in any previous year and such share includes any income accruing or arising outside India during that previous year (and which is not deemed to accrue or arise in India) in a country with which there is no agreement under section 90 for the relief or avoidance of double taxation and he proves that he has paid income-tax by deduction or otherwise under the law in force in that country in respect of the income so included he shall be entitled to a deduction from the Indian income-tax payable by him of a sum calculated on such doubly taxed income so included at the Indian rate of tax or the rate of tax of the said country, whichever is the lower, or at the Indian rate of tax if both the rates are equal.

Explanation of the terms used in this section:

- "Indian income-tax" means income-tax charged in accordance with the provisions of this Act;
- "Indian rate of tax" means the rate determined by dividing the amount of Indian income-tax after deduction of any relief due under the provisions of this Act but before deduction of any relief due under this Chapter, by the total income;
- "Rate of tax of the said country" means income-tax and super-tax actually paid in the said country in accordance with the corresponding laws in force in the said country after deduction of all relief due, but before deduction of any relief due in the said country in respect of double taxation, divided by the whole amount of the income as assessed in the said country;

The expression "income-tax" in relation to any country includes any excess profits tax or business profits tax charged on the profits by the Government of any part of that country or a local authority in that country.

Execution Process of Double Tax Avoidance Agreements

There are numerous terms in each of the Double Tax Avoidance treaties that India has signed with different countries. Reproduction of all these terms and for all the treaties is beyond the scope of this book except for one country, namely, the USA which has been taken to cite as an example. The execution process is self-contained in the agreement.

India's DTA Treaty with the USA

Whereas the annexed Convention between the Government of the United States of America and the Government of the Republic of India for the avoidance of double taxation and the prevention of fiscal evasion with respect to taxes on income has entered into force on the 18th December, 1990, after the notification by both the Contracting States to each other of the completion of the procedures required under their laws for bringing into force the said Convention in accordance with paragraph 1 of Article 30 of the said Convention.

Now, therefore, in exercise of the powers conferred by section 90 of the Income-tax Act, 1961 (43 of 1961), and section 24A of the Companies (Profits) Surtax Act, 1964 (7 of 1964), the Central Government hereby directs that all the provisions of the said Convention shall be given effect to in the Union of India.

Further, in exercise of the powers conferred by section 44A(b) of the Wealth-tax Act, 1957 (27 of 1957) and section 44(b) of the Gift-tax Act, 1958 (18 of 1958), the Central Government also directs that the provisions of Article 28 of the said Convention shall be given effect to in the Union of India.

[Notification No. G. S. R. 990(E), dated 20th December, 1990.]

ANNEXURE

The Government of the United States of America and the Government of the Republic of India, desiring to conclude a Convention for the avoidance of double taxation and the prevention of fiscal evasion with respect to taxes on income, have agreed as follows:

ARTICLE 1: General scope

1. This Convention shall apply to persons who are residents of one or both of the Contracting States, except as otherwise provided in the Convention.
2. The Convention shall not restrict in any manner any exclusion, exemption, deduction, credit, or other allowance now or hereafter accorded:
   (a) by the laws of either Contracting State; or
   (b) by any other agreement between the Contracting States.
3. Notwithstanding any provision of the Convention except paragraph 4, a Contracting State may tax its residents (as determined under article 4 (Residence)), and by reason of citizenship may tax its citizens, as if the Convention had not come into effect. For this purpose, the term "citizen" shall include a former citizen whose loss of citizenship had as one of its principal purposes the avoidance of tax, but only for a period of 10 years following such loss.
4. The provisions of paragraph 3 shall not affect:
   (a) the benefits conferred by a Contracting State under paragraph 2 of article 9 (Associated enterprises), under paragraphs 2 and 6 of article 20 (Private pensions, annuities, alimony, and child support), and under articles 25 (Relief From Double Taxation), 26 (Non-Discrimination), and 27 (Mutual Agreement Procedure); and
   (b) the benefits conferred by a Contracting State under articles 19 (remuneration and pensions in respect of Government service), 21 (payments received by students and apprentices), 22 (payments received by professors, teachers and research scholars) and 29 (diplomatic agents and consular officers), upon individuals who are neither citizens of, nor have immigrant status in, that State.

ARTICLE 2: Taxes covered

1. The existing taxes to which this Convention shall apply are:
   (a) in the United States, the federal income taxes imposed by the Internal Revenue Code (but excluding the accumulated earnings tax, the personal holding company

tax, and social security taxes), and the excise taxes imposed on insurance premiums paid to foreign insurers and with respect to private foundations (hereinafter referred to as "United States tax"); provided, however, the Convention shall apply to the excise taxes imposed on insurance premiums paid to foreign insurers only to the extent that the risks covered by such premiums are not reinsured with a person not entitled to exemption from such taxes under this or any other Convention which applies to these taxes; and

(b) in India:

(i) the income-tax including any surcharge thereon, but excluding income-tax on undistributed income of companies, imposed under the Income-tax Act; and

(ii) the surtax.

(hereinafter referred to as "Indian tax").

Taxes referred to in (a) and (b) above shall not include any amount payable in respect of any default or omission in relation to the above taxes or which represent a penalty imposed relating to those taxes.

2. The Convention shall apply also to any identical or substantially similar taxes which are imposed after the date of signature of the Convention in addition to, or in place of, the existing taxes. The competent authorities of the Contracting States shall notify each other of any significant changes which have been made in their respective taxation laws and of any official published material concerning the application of the Convention.

ARTICLE 3: General definitions

1. In this Convention, unless the context otherwise requires:

(a) the term "India" means the territory of India and includes the territorial sea and airspace above it, as well as any other maritime zone in which India has sovereign rights, other rights and jurisdictions, according to the Indian law and in accordance with international law;

(b) the term "United States", when used in a geographical sense, means all the territory of the United States of America, including its territorial sea, in which the laws relating to United States tax are in force, and all the area beyond its territorial sea, including the seabed and subsoil thereof, over which the United States has jurisdiction in accordance with international law and in which the laws relating to United States tax are in force;

(c) the terms "a Contracting State" and "the other Contracting State" mean India or the United States as the context requires;

(d) the term "tax" means Indian tax or United States tax, as the context requires;

(e) the term "person" includes an individual, an estate, a trust, a partnership, a company, any other body of persons, or other taxable entity;

(f) the term "company" means anybody corporate or any entity which is treated as a company or body corporate for tax purposes;

(g) the terms "enterprise of a Contracting State" and "enterprise of the other Contracting State" mean respectively an enterprise carried on by a resident of a Contracting State and an enterprise carried on by a resident of the other Contracting State;

(h) the term "competent authority" means, in the case of India, the Central Government in the Ministry of Finance (Department of Revenue) or their authorized representative, and in the case of the United States, the Secretary of the Treasury or his delegate;

(i) the term "national," means any individual possessing the nationality or citizenship of a Contracting State;

(j) the term "international traffic" means any transport by a ship or aircraft operated by an enterprise of a Contracting State, except when the ship or aircraft is operated solely between places within the other Contracting State;

(k) the term "taxable year" in relation to Indian tax means "previous year" as defined in the Income-tax Act, 1961.

2. As regards the application of the Convention by a Contracting State any term not defined therein shall, unless the context otherwise requires or the competent authorities agree to a common meaning pursuant to the provisions of article 27 (Mutual Agreement Procedure), have the meaning which it has under the laws of that State concerning the taxes to which the Convention applies.

ARTICLE 4: Residence

1. For the purposes of this Convention, the term "resident of a Contracting State" means any person who, under the laws of that State, is liable to tax therein by reason of his domicile, residence, citizenship, place of management, place of incorporation, or any other criterion of a similar nature, provided however, that

(a) this term does not include any person who is liable to tax in that State in respect only of income from sources in that State; and

(b) in the case of income derived or paid by a partnership, estate, or trust, this term applies only to the extent that the income derived by such partnership, estate, or trust is subject to tax in that State as the income of a resident, either in its hands or in the hands of its partners or beneficiaries.

2. Where by reason of the provisions of paragraph 1, an individual is a resident of both Contracting States, then his status shall be determined as follows:

(a) he shall be deemed to be a resident of the State in which he has a permanent home available to him; if he has a permanent home available to him in both States, he shall be deemed to be a resident of the State with which his personal and economic relations are closer (centre of vital interests);

(b) if the State in which he has his centre of vital interests cannot be determined, or if he does not have a permanent home available to him in either State, he shall be deemed to be a resident of the State in which he has an habitual abode;

(c) if he has an habitual abode in both States or in neither of them, he shall be deemed to be a resident of the State of which he is a national;

(d) if he is a national of both States or of neither of them, the competent authorities of the Contracting States shall settle the question by mutual agreement.

3. Where, by reason of paragraph 1, a company is a resident of both Contracting States, such company shall be considered to be outside the scope of this Convention except for purposes of paragraph 2 of article 10 (Dividends), article 26 (Non-discrimination), article 27 (Mutual agreement procedure), article 28 (Exchange of information and administrative assistance) and article 30 (Entry into force).
4. Where, by reason of the provisions of paragraph 1, a person other than an individual or a company is a resident of both Contracting States, the competent authorities of the Contracting States shall settle the question by mutual agreement and determine the mode of application of the Convention to such person.

ARTICLE 5 Permanent establishment

1. For the purposes of this Convention, the term "permanent establishment" means a fixed place of business through which the business of an enterprise is wholly or partly carried on.
2. The term "permanent establishment" includes especially;
   (a) a place of management; (b) a branch; (c) an office; (d) a factory; (e) a workshop; (f) a mine, an oil or gas well, a quarry, or any other place of extraction of natural resources; (g) a warehouse, in relation to a person providing storage facilities for others; (h) a farm, plantation or other place where agriculture, forestry, plantation or related activities are carried on; (i) a store or premises used as a sales outlet; (j) an installation or structure used for the exploration or exploitation of natural resources, but only if so used for a period of more than 120 days in any twelve-month period; (k) a building site or construction, installation or assembly project or supervisory activities in connection therewith, where such site, project or activities (together with other such sites, projects or activities, if any) continue for a period of more than 120 days in any twelve-month period; (l) the furnishing of services, other than included services as defined in article 12 (royalties and fees for included services), within a Contracting State by an enterprise through employees or other personnel, but only if:
   (i) activities of that nature continue within that State for a period or periods aggregating to more than 90 days within any twelve-month period; or
   (ii) the services are performed within that State for a related enterprise (within the meaning of paragraph 1 of article 9 (associated enterprises)).
3. Notwithstanding the preceding provisions of this article, the term "permanent establishment" shall be deemed not to include any one or more of the following:
   (e) the use of facilities solely for the purpose of storage, display, or occasional delivery of goods or merchandise belonging to the enterprise;
   (f) the maintenance of a stock of goods or merchandise belonging to the enterprise solely for the purpose of storage, display or occasional delivery;
   (g) the maintenance of a stock of goods or merchandise belonging to the enterprise solely for the purpose of processing by another enterprise;

(h) the maintenance of a fixed place of business solely for the purpose of purchasing goods or merchandise, or of collecting information, for the enterprise;

(i) the maintenance of a fixed place of business solely for the purpose of advertising, for the supply of information, for scientific research or for other activities which have a preparatory or auxiliary character, for the enterprise.

4. Notwithstanding the provisions of paragraphs 1 and 2, where a person other than an agent of an independent status to whom paragraph 5 applies is acting in a Contracting State on behalf of an enterprise of the other Contracting State, that enterprise shall be deemed to have a permanent establishment in the first-mentioned State, if:

   (a) he has and habitually exercises in the first-mentioned State an authority to conclude contracts on behalf of the enterprise, unless his activities are limited to those mentioned in paragraph 3 which, if exercised through a fixed place of business, would not make that fixed place of business a permanent establishment under the provisions of that paragraph;

   (b) he has no such authority but habitually maintains in the first-mentioned State a stock of goods or merchandise from which he regularly delivers goods or merchandise on behalf of the enterprise, and some additional activities conducted in that State on behalf of the enterprise have contributed to the sale of the goods or merchandise; or

   (c) he habitually secures orders in the first-mentioned State, wholly or almost wholly for the enterprise.

5. An enterprise of a Contracting State shall not be deemed to have a permanent establishment in the other Contracting State merely because it carries on business in that other State through a broker, general commission agent, or any other agent of an independent status, provided that such persons are acting in the ordinary course of their business. However, when the activities of such an agent are devoted wholly or almost wholly on behalf of that enterprise and the transactions between the agent and the enterprise are not made under arm's-length conditions, he shall not be considered an agent of independent status within the meaning of this paragraph.

6. The fact that a company which is a resident of a Contracting State controls or is controlled by a company which is a resident of the other Contracting State, or which carries on business in that other State (whether through a permanent establishment or otherwise), shall not of itself constitute either company a permanent establishment of the other.

ARTICLE 6: Income from immovable property (Real Property)

1. Income derived by a resident of a Contracting State from immovable property (real property), including income from agriculture or forestry, situated in the other Contracting State may be taxed in that other State.
2. The term "immovable property" shall have the meaning which it has under the law of the Contracting State in which the property in question is situated.
3. The provisions of paragraph 1 shall also apply to income derived from the direct use, letting, or use in any other form of immovable property.

4. The provisions of paragraphs 1 and 3 shall also apply to the income from immovable property of an enterprise and to income from immovable property used for the performance of independent personal services.

ARTICLE 7: Business profits

1. The profits of an enterprise of a Contracting State shall be taxable only in that State unless the enterprise carries on business in the other Contracting State through a permanent establishment situated therein. If the enterprise carries on business as aforesaid, the profits of the enterprise may be taxed in the other State but only so much of them as is attributable to (a) that permanent establishment; (b) sales in the other State of goods or merchandise of the same or similar kind as those sold through that permanent establishment; or (c) other business activities carried on in the other State of the same or similar kind as those effected through that permanent establishment.
2. Subject to the provisions of paragraph 3, where an enterprise of a Contracting State carries on business in the other Contracting State through a permanent establishment situated therein, there shall in each Contracting State be attributed to that permanent establishment the profits which it might be expected to make if it were a distinct and independent enterprise engaged in the same or similar activities under the same or similar conditions and dealing wholly at arm's length with the enterprise of which it is a permanent establishment and other enterprises controlling, controlled by or subject to the same common control as that enterprise. In any case where the correct amount of profits attributable to a permanent establishment is incapable of determination or the determination thereof presents exceptional difficulties, the profits attributable to the permanent establishment may be estimated on a reasonable basis. The estimate adopted shall, however, be such that the result shall be in accordance with the principles contained in this article.
3. In the determination of the profits of a permanent establishment, there shall be allowed as deductions expenses which are incurred for the purposes of the business of the permanent establishment, including a reasonable allocation of executive and general administrative expenses, research and development expenses, interest, and other expenses incurred for the purposes of the enterprise as a whole (or the part thereof which includes the permanent establishment), whether incurred in the State in which the permanent establishment is situated or elsewhere, in accordance with the provisions of and subject to the limitations of the taxation laws of that State. However, no such deduction shall be allowed in respect of amounts, if any, paid (otherwise than towards reimbursement of actual expenses) by the permanent establishment to the head office of the enterprise or any of its other offices, by way of royalties, fees or other similar payments in return for the use of patents, know-how or other rights, or by way of commission or other charges for specific services performed or for management, or, except in the case of banking enterprises, by way of interest on moneys lent to the permanent establishment. Likewise, no account shall be taken, in the determination of the profits of a permanent establishment, for amounts charged (otherwise than towards reimbursement of actual expenses), by the permanent establishment to the head office of the enterprise or any of its other offices, by way of royalties, fees or other similar

payments in return for the use of patents, know-how or other rights, or by way of commission or other charges for specific services performed or for management, or, except in the case of a banking enterprise, by way of interest on moneys lent to the head office of the enterprise or any of its other offices.

4. No profits shall be attributed to a permanent establishment by reason of the mere purchase by that permanent establishment of goods or merchandise for the enterprise.
5. For the purposes of this Convention, the profits to be attributed to the permanent establishment as provided in paragraph 1(a) of this article shall include only the profits derived from the assets and activities of the permanent establishment and shall be determined by the same method year by year unless there is good and sufficient reason to the contrary.
6. Where profits include items of income which are dealt with separately in other articles of the convention, then the provisions of those articles shall not be affected by the provisions of this article.
7. For the purposes of the Convention, the term "business profits" means income derived from any trade or business including income from the furnishing of services other than included services as defined in article 12 (royalties and fees for included services) and including income from the rental of tangible personal property other than property described in paragraph 3(b) of article 12 (royalties and fees for included services).

ARTICLE 8: Shipping and air transport

1. Profits derived by an enterprise of a Contracting State from the operation by that enterprise of ships or aircraft in international traffic shall be taxable only in that State.
2. For the purposes of this article, profits from the operation of ships or aircraft in international traffic shall mean profits derived by an enterprise described in paragraph 1 from the transportation by sea or air respectively of passengers, mail, livestock or goods carried on by the owners or lessees or chatterers of ships or aircraft including—
   (a) the sale of tickets for such transportation on behalf of other enterprises;
   (b) other activity directly connected with such transportation; and
   (c) the rental of ships or aircraft incidental to any activity directly connected with such transportation.
3. Profits of an enterprise of a Contracting State described in paragraph 1 from the use, maintenance, or rental of containers (including trailers, barges, and related equipment for the transport of containers) used in connection with the operation of ships or aircraft in international traffic shall be taxable only in that State.
4. The provisions of paragraphs 1 and 3 shall also apply to profits from participation in a pool, a joint business, or an international operating agency.
5. For the purposes of this article, interest on funds connected with the operation of ships or aircraft in international traffic shall be regarded as profits derived from the operation of such ships or aircraft, and the provisions of article 11 (Interest) shall not apply in relation to such interest.
6. Gains derived by an enterprise of a Contracting State described in paragraph 1 from the alienation of ships, aircraft or containers owned and operated by the enterprise, the income from which is taxable only in that State, shall be taxed only in that State.

ARTICLE 9: Associated enterprises

1. Where:
   (a) an enterprise of a Contracting State participates directly or indirectly in the management, control or capital of an enterprise of the other Contracting State; or
   (b) the same persons participate directly or indirectly in the management, control, or capital of an enterprise of a Contracting State and an enterprise of the other Contracting State,

   and in either case conditions are made or imposed between the two enterprises in their commercial or financial relations which differ from those which would be made between independent enterprises, then any profits which, but for those conditions would have accrued to one of the enterprises, but by reason of those conditions have not so accrued, may be included in the profits of that enterprise and taxed accordingly.
2. Where a Contracting State includes in the profits of an enterprise of that State, and taxes accordingly, profits on which an enterprise of the other Contracting State has been charged to tax in that other State, and the profits so included are profits which would have accrued to the enterprise of the first-mentioned State if the conditions made between the two enterprises had been those which would have been made between independent enterprises, then that other State shall make an appropriate adjustment to the amount of the tax charged therein on those profits. In determining such adjustment, due regard shall be had to the other provisions of this Convention and the competent authorities of the Contracting States shall if necessary consult each other.

ARTICLE 10: Dividends

Dividends paid by a company which is a resident of a Contracting State to a resident of the other Contracting State may be taxed in that other State.

1. However, such dividends may also be taxed in the Contracting State of which the company paying the dividends is a resident, and according to the laws of that State, but if the beneficial owner of the dividends is a resident of the other Contracting State, the tax so charged shall not exceed:
   (a) 15 per cent of the gross amount of the dividends if the beneficial owner is a company which owns at least 10 per cent of the voting stock of the company paying the dividends;
   (b) 25 per cent of the gross amount of the dividends in all other cases.

   Sub-paragraph (b) and not sub-paragraph (a) shall apply in the case of dividends paid by a United States person which is a Regulated Investment Company. Sub-paragraph (a) shall not apply to dividends paid by a United States person which is a Real Estate Investment Trust, and sub-paragraph (b) shall only apply if the dividend is beneficially owned by an individual holding a less than 10 per cent interest in the Real Estate Investment Trust. This paragraph shall not affect the taxation of the company in respect of the profits out of which the dividends are paid.
2. The term "dividends" as used in this article means income from shares or other rights, not being debt-claims, participating in profits, income from other corporate

rights which are subjected to the same taxation treatment as income from shares by the taxation laws of the State of which the company making the distribution is a resident; and income from arrangements, including debt obligations, carrying the right to participate in profits, to the extent so characterized under the laws of the Contracting State in which the income arises.

3. The provisions of paragraphs 1 and 2 shall not apply if the beneficial owner of the dividends, being a resident of a Contracting State, carries on business in the other Contracting State, of which the company paying the dividends is a resident, through a permanent establishment situated therein, or performs in that other State independent personal services from a fixed base situated therein, and the dividends are attributable to such permanent establishment or fixed base. In such case the provisions of article 7 (business profits) or article 15 (Independent Personal Services), as the case may be, shall apply.
4. Where a company which is a resident of a Contracting State derives profits or income from the other Contracting State, that other State may not impose any tax on the dividends paid by the company except insofar as such dividends are paid to a resident of that other State or insofar as the holding in respect of which the dividends are paid is effectively connected with a permanent establishment or a fixed base situated in that other State, nor subject the company's undistributed profits to a tax on the company's undistributed profits, even if the dividends paid or the undistributed profits consist wholly or partly of profits or income arising in such other State.

ARTICLE 11: Interest

1. Interest arising in a Contracting State and paid to a resident of the other Contracting State may be taxed in that other State.
2. However, such interest may also be taxed in the Contracting State in which it arises, and according to the laws of that State, but if the beneficial owner of the interest is a resident of the other Contracting State, the tax so charged shall not exceed:
   (a) 10 per cent of the gross amount of the interest if such interest is paid on a loan granted by a bank carrying on a bona fide banking business or by a similar financial institution (including an insurance company); and
   (b) 15 per cent of the gross amount of the interest in all other cases.
3. Notwithstanding the provisions of paragraph 2 of this article, interest arising in a Contracting State:
   (a) and derived and beneficially owned by the Government of the other Contracting State, a political sub-division or local authority thereof, the Reserve Bank of India, or the Federal Reserve Bank of the United States, as the case may be, and such other institutions of either Contracting State as the competent authorities may agree pursuant to article 27 (Mutual Agreement Procedure);
   (b) with respect to loans or credits extended or endorsed:
      (i) by the Export Import Bank of the United States, when India is the first-mentioned Contracting State; and

(ii) by the EXIM Bank of India, when the United States is the first-mentioned Contracting State; and

(c) to the extent approved by the Government of that State, and derived and beneficially owned by any person, other than a person referred to in sub-paragraphs (a) and (b), who is a resident of the other Contracting State, provided that the transaction giving rise to the debt-claim has been approved in this behalf by the Government of the first-mentioned Contracting State;

shall be exempt from tax in the first-mentioned Contracting State.

4. The term "interest" as used in this Convention means income from debt-claims of every kind, whether or not secured by mortgage, and whether or not carrying a right to participate in the debtor's profits, and in particular, income from government securities, and income from bonds or debentures, including premiums or prizes attaching to such securities, bonds, or debentures. Penalty charges for late payment shall not be regarded as interest for the purposes of the Convention. However, the term "interest" does not include income dealt with in article 10 (Dividends).
5. The provisions of paragraphs 2 and 3 shall not apply if the beneficial owner of the interest, being a resident of a Contracting State, carries on business in the other Contracting State in which the interest arises, through a permanent establishment situated therein, or performs in that other State independent personal services from a fixed base situated therein, and the interest is attributable to such permanent establishment or fixed base. In such case the provisions of article 7 (Business Profits) or article 15 (Independent Personal Services), as the case may be, shall apply.
6. Interest shall be deemed to arise in a Contracting State when the payer is that State itself or a political sub-division, local authority, or resident of that State. Where, however, the person paying the interest, whether he is a resident of a Contracting State or not, has in a Contracting State a permanent establishment or a fixed base, and such interest is borne by such permanent establishment or fixed base, then such interest shall be deemed to arise in the Contracting State in which the permanent establishment or fixed base is situated.
7. Where, by reason of a special relationship between the payer and the beneficial owner or between both of them and some other person, the amount of the interest, having regard to the debt-claim for which it is paid, exceeds the amount which would have been agreed upon by the payer and the beneficial owner in the absence of such relationship, the provisions of this article shall apply only to the last-mentioned amount. In such case the excess part of the payments shall remain taxable according to the laws of each Contracting State, due regard being had to the other provisions of the Convention.

ARTICLE 12: Royalties and fees for included services

1. Royalties and fees for included services arising in a Contracting State and paid to a resident of the other Contracting State may be taxed in that other State.
2. However, such royalties and fees for included services may also be taxed in the Contracting State in which they arise and according to the laws of that State; but if

the beneficial owner of the royalties or fees for included services is a resident of the other Contracting State, the tax so charged shall not exceed:

(a) in the case of royalties referred to in sub-paragraph (a) of paragraph 3 and fees for included services as defined in this article (other than services described in sub-paragraph (b) of this paragraph):
   (i) during the first five taxable years for which this Convention has effect,
      (A) 15 per cent of the gross amount of the royalties or fees for included services as defined in this article, where the payer of the royalties or fees is the Government of that Contracting State, a political sub-division or a public sector company; and
      (B) 20 per cent of the gross amount of the royalties or fees for included services in all other cases; and
   (ii) during the subsequent years, 15 per cent of the gross amount of royalties or fees for included services; and
(b) in the case of royalties referred to in sub-paragraph (b) of paragraph 3 and fees for included services as defined in this article that are ancillary and subsidiary to the enjoyment of the property for which payment is received under paragraph 3(b) of this article, 10 per cent of the gross amount of the royalties or fees for included services.

3. The term "royalties" as used in this article means:
   (a) payments of any kind received as consideration for the use of, or the right to use, any copyright of a literary, artistic, or scientific work, including cinematograph films or work on film, tape or other means of reproduction for use in connection with radio or television broadcasting, any patent, trademark, design or model, plan, secret formula or process, or for information concerning industrial, commercial or scientific experience, including gains derived from the alienation of any such right or property which are contingent on the productivity, use or disposition thereof; and
   (b) payments of any kind received as consideration for the use of, or the right to use, any industrial, commercial or scientific equipment, other than payments derived by an enterprise described in paragraph 1 of article 8 (Shipping and Air Transport) from activities described in paragraph 2(c) or 3 of article 8.
4. For purposes of this article, "fees for included services" means payments of any kind to any person in consideration for the rendering of any technical or consultancy services (including through the provision of services of technical or other personnel) if such services:
   (a) are ancillary and subsidiary to the application or enjoyment of the right, property or information for which a payment described in paragraph 3 is received; or
   (b) make available technical knowledge, experience, skill, know-how. or processes, or consist of the development and transfer of a technical plan or technical design.
5. Notwithstanding paragraph 4, "fees for included services" does not include amounts paid:
   (a) for services that are ancillary and subsidiary, as well as inextricably and essentially linked, to the sale of property other than a sale described in paragraph 3(a);

(b) for services that are ancillary and subsidiary to the rental of ships, aircraft, containers or other equipment used in connection with the operation of ships or aircraft in international traffic;

(c) for teaching in or by educational institutions;

(d) for services for the personal use of the individual or individuals making the payment; or

(e) to an employee of the person making the payments or to any individual or firm of individuals (other than a company) for professional services as defined in article 15 (Independent Personal Services).

6. The provisions of paragraphs 1 and 2 shall not apply if the beneficial owner of the royalties or fees for included services, being a resident of a Contracting State, carries on business in the other Contracting State, in which the royalties or fees for included services arise, through a permanent establishment situated therein, or performs in that other State independent personal services from a fixed base situated therein, and the royalties or fees for included services are attributable to such permanent establishment or fixed base. In such case the provisions of article 7 (business profits) or article 15 (Independent Personal Services), as the case may be, shall apply.

7. (a) Royalties and fees for included services shall be deemed to arise in a Contracting State when the payer is that State itself, a political sub-division, a local authority, or a resident of that State. Where, however, the person paying the royalties or fees for included services, whether he is a resident of a Contracting State or not, has in a Contracting State a permanent establishment or a fixed base in connection with which the liability to pay the royalties or fees for included services was incurred, and such royalties or fees for included services are borne by such permanent establishment or fixed base, then such royalties or fees for included services shall be deemed to arise in the Contracting State in which the permanent establishment or fixed base is situated.

(f) Where under sub-paragraph (a) royalties or fees for included services do not arise in one of the Contracting States, and the royalties relate to the use of, or the right to use, the right or property, or the fees for included services relate to services performed, in one of the Contracting States, the royalties or fees for included services shall be deemed to arise in that Contracting State.

8. Where, by reason of a special relationship between the payer and the beneficial owner or between both of them and some other person, the amount of the royalties or fees for included services paid exceeds the amount which would have been paid in the absence of such relationship, the provisions of this article shall apply only to the last-mentioned amount. In such case, the excess part of the payments shall remain taxable according to the laws of each Contracting State, due regard being had to the other provisions of the Convention.

ARTICLE 13: Gains

Except as provided in article 8 (Shipping and Air Transport) to this Convention, each Contracting State may tax capital gains in accordance with the provisions of its domestic law.

ARTICLE 14: Permanent establishment tax

1. A company which is a resident of India may be subject in the United States to a tax in addition to the tax allowable under the other provisions of this Convention.
   (a) Such tax, however, may be imposed only on:
      (i) the portion of the business profits of the company subject to tax in the United States which represents the dividend equivalent amount; and
      (ii) the excess, if any, of interest deductible in the United States in computing the profits of the company that are subject to tax in the United States and either attributable to a permanent establishment in the United States or subject to tax in the United States under article 6 (Income From Immovable Property (Real Property)), article 12 (Royalties and Fees for Included Services) as fees for included services, or article 13 (Gains) of this Convention over the interest paid by or from the permanent establishment or trade or business in the United States.
   (b) For purposes of this article, business profits means profits that are effectively connected (or treated as effectively connected) with the conduct of a trade or business within the United States and are either attributable to a permanent establishment in the United States or subject to tax in the United States under article 6 (Income From Immovable Property (Real Property)), article 12 (Royalties and Fees for Included Services) as fees for included services or article 13 (Gains) of this Convention.
   (c) The tax referred to in sub-paragraph (a) shall not be imposed at a rate exceeding:
      (i) the rate specified in paragraph 2(a) of article 10 (Dividends) for the tax described in sub-paragraph (a)(i); and
      (ii) the rate specified in paragraph 2(a) or (b) (whichever is appropriate) of article 11 (Interest) for the tax described in sub-paragraph (a)(ii).
2. A company which is a resident of the United States may be subject to tax in India at a rate higher than that applicable to the domestic companies. The difference in the tax rate shall not, however, exceed the existing difference of 15 percentage points.
3. In the case of a banking company which is a resident of the United States, the interest paid by the permanent establishment of such a company in India to the head office may be subject in India to a tax in addition to the tax imposable under the other provisions of this Convention at a rate which shall not exceed the rate specified in paragraph 2(a) of article 11 (Interest).

ARTICLE 15: Independent personal services

1. Income derived by a person who is an individual or firm of individuals (other than a company) who is a resident of a Contracting State from the performance in the other Contracting State of professional services or other independent activities of a similar character shall be taxable only in the first-mentioned State except in the following circumstances when such income may also be taxed in the other Contracting State:
   (a) if such person has a fixed base regularly available to him in the other Contracting State for the purpose of performing his activities, in that case, only so much of the income as is attributable to that fixed base may be taxed in that other State; or

(b) if the person's stay in the other Contracting State is for a period or periods amounting to or exceeding in the aggregate 90 days in the relevant taxable year.

2. The term "professional services" includes independent scientific, literary, artistic, educational or teaching activities as well as the independent activities of physicians, surgeons, lawyers, engineers, architects, dentists and accountants.

ARTICLE 16: Dependent personal services

1. Subject to the provisions of article 17 (Director's Fees), 18 (Income Earned by Entertainers and Athletes), 19 (Remuneration and Pensions in Respect of Government Service), 20 (Private Pensions, Annuities, Alimony and Child Support), 21 (Payments Received by Students and Apprentices) and 22 (Payments Received by Professors, Teachers and Research Scholars), salaries, wages, and other similar remuneration derived by a resident of a Contracting State in respect of an employment shall be taxable only in that State unless the employment is exercised in the other Contracting State. If the employment is so exercised, such remuneration as is derived there from may be taxed in that other State.
2. Notwithstanding the provisions of paragraph 1, remuneration derived by a resident of a Contracting State in respect of an employment exercised in the other Contracting State shall be taxable only in the first-mentioned State if:
   (a) the recipient is present in the other State for a period or periods not exceeding in the aggregate 183 days in the relevant taxable year;
   (b) the remuneration is paid by, or on behalf of, an employer who is not a resident of the other State; and
   (c) the remuneration is not borne by a permanent establishment or a fixed base or a trade or business which the employer has in the other State.
3. Notwithstanding the preceding provisions of this article, remuneration derived in respect of an employment exercised aboard a ship or aircraft operating in international traffic by an enterprise of a Contracting State may be taxed in that State.

ARTICLE 17: Director's fees

Director's fees and similar payments derived by a resident of a Contracting State in his capacity as a member of the board of directors of a company which is a resident of the other Contracting State may be taxed in that other State.

ARTICLE 18: Income earned by entertainers and athletes

1. Notwithstanding the provisions of articles 15 (Independent Personal Services) and 16 (Dependent Personal Services), income derived by a resident of a Contracting State as an entertainer, such as a theatre, motion picture, radio or television artiste, or a musician, or as an athlete, from his personal activities as such exercised in the other Contracting State, may be taxed in that other State, except where the amount of the net income derived by such entertainer or athlete from such activities (after deduction of all expense incurred by him in connection with his visit and performance) does not exceed one thousand five hundred United States dollars ($1,500) or its equivalent in Indian rupees for the taxable year concerned.

2. Where income in respect of activities exercised by an entertainer or an athlete in his capacity as such accrues not to the entertainer or athlete but to another person, that income of that other person may, notwithstanding the provisions of articles 7 (Business Profits), 15 (Independent Personal Services) and 16 (Dependent Personal Services), be taxed in the Contracting State in which the activities of the entertainer or athlete are exercised unless the entertainer, athlete, or other person establishes that neither the entertainer or athlete nor persons related thereto participate directly or indirectly in the profits of that other person in any manner, including the receipt of deferred remuneration, bonuses, fees, dividends, partnership distributions, or other distributions.
3. Income referred to in the preceding paragraphs of this article derived by a resident of a Contracting State in respect of activities exercised in the other Contracting State shall not be taxed in that other State if the visit of the entertainers or athletes to that other State is supported wholly or substantially from the public funds of the Government of the first-mentioned Contracting State, or of a political sub-division or local authority thereof.
4. The competent authorities of the Contracting States may, by mutual agreement, increase the dollar amounts referred to in paragraph 1 to reflect economic or monetary developments.

ARTICLE 19: Remuneration and pensions in respect of government service

1. (a) Remuneration, other than a pension, paid by a Contracting State or a political sub-division or a local authority thereof to an individual in respect of services rendered to that State or sub-division or authority shall be taxable only in that State.
   (b) However, such remuneration shall be taxable only in the other Contracting State if the services are rendered in that other State and the individual is a resident of that State who:
      (i) is a national of that State; or
      (ii) did not become a resident of that State solely for the purpose of rendering the services.
2. (a) Any pension paid by, or out of funds created by a Contracting State or a political sub-division or a local authority thereof to an individual in respect of services rendered to that state or sub-division or authority shall be taxable only in that State.
   (b) However, such pension shall be taxable only in the other Contracting State if the individual is a resident of, and a national of, that State.
3. The provisions of article 16 (Dependent Personal Services), 17 (Directors' Fees), 18 (Income Earned by Entertainers and Athletes) and 20 (Private Pensions, Annuities, Alimony and Child Support) shall apply to remuneration and pensions in respect of services rendered in connection with a business carried on by a Contracting State or a political sub-division or a local authority thereof.

ARTICLE 20: Private pensions, annuities, alimony and child support

1. Any pension, other than a pension referred to in article 19 (Remuneration and Pensions in Respect of Government Service), or any annuity derived by a resident of a Contracting State from sources within the other Contracting State may be taxed only in the first-mentioned Contracting State.
2. Notwithstanding paragraph 1, and subject to the provisions of article 19 (Remuneration and Pensions in Respect of Government Service), Social security benefits and other public pensions paid by a Contracting State to a resident of the other Contracting State or a citizen of the United States shall be taxable only in the first-mentioned State.
3. The term "pension" means a periodic payment made in consideration of past services or by way of compensation for injuries received in the course of performance of services.
4. The term "annuity" means stated sums payable periodically at stated times during life or during a specified or ascertainable number of years, under an obligation to make the payments in return for adequate and full consideration in money or money's worth (but not for services rendered).
5. Alimony paid to a resident of a Contacting State shall be taxable only in that State. The term "alimony" as used in this paragraph means periodic payments made pursuant to a written separation agreement or a decree of divorce, separate maintenance, or compulsory support, which payments are taxable to the recipient under the laws of the State of which he is a resident.
6. Periodic payments for the support of a minor child made pursuant to a written separation agreement or a decree of divorce, separate maintenance or compulsory support, paid by a resident of a Contracting State to a resident of the other Contracting State shall be taxable only in the first-mentioned State.

ARTICLE 21: Payments received by students and apprentices

1. A student or business apprentice who is or was a resident of one of the Contracting States immediately before visiting the other Contracting State and who is present in that other State principally for the purpose of his education or training shall be exempt from tax in that other State, on payments which arise outside that other State for the purposes of his maintenance, education or training.
2. In respect of grants, scholarships and remuneration from employment not covered by paragraph 1, a student or business apprentice described in paragraph 1 shall, in addition, be entitled during such education or training to the same exemptions, relieves or reductions in respect of taxes available to residents of the State which he is visiting.
3. The benefits of this article shall extend only for such period of time as may be reasonable or customarily required to complete the education or training undertaken.
4. For the purposes of this article, an individual shall be deemed to be resident of a Contracting State if he is resident in that Contracting State in the taxable year in which he visits the other Contracting State or in the immediately preceding taxable year.

ARTICLE 22: Payments received by professors, teachers and research scholars

1. An individual who visits a Contracting State for a period not exceeding two years for the purpose of teaching or engaging in research at a university, college or other recognized educational institution in that State, and who was immediately before that visit a resident of the other Contracting State, shall be exempted from tax by the first-mentioned Contracting State on any remuneration for such teaching or research for a period not exceeding two years from the date he first visits that State for such purpose.
2. This article shall apply to income from research only if such research is undertaken by the individual in the public interest and not primarily for the benefit of some other private person or persons.

ARTICLE 23: Other income

1. Subject to the provisions of paragraph 2, items of income of a resident of a Contracting State, wherever arising, which are not expressly dealt within the foregoing articles of this Convention shall be taxable only in that Contracting State.
2. The provisions of paragraph 1 shall not apply to income, other than income from immovable property as defined in paragraph 2 of article 6 (Income from Immovable Property (Real Property)), if the beneficial owner of the income, being a resident of a Contracting State, carries on business in the other Contracting State through a permanent establishment situated therein, or performs in that other State independent personal services from a fixed base situated therein, and the income is attributable to such permanent establishment or fixed base. In such case the provisions of article 7 (Business Profits) or article 15 (Independent Personal Services), as the case may be, shall apply.
3. Notwithstanding the provisions of paragraphs 1 and 2, items of income of a resident of a Contracting State not dealt with in the foregoing articles of this Convention and arising in the other Contracting State may also be taxed in that other State.

ARTICLE 24: Limitation on benefits

1. A person (other than an individual) which is a resident of a Contracting State and derives income from the other Contracting State shall be entitled under this Convention to relief from taxation in that other Contracting State only if:
   (a) more than 60 per cent of the beneficial interest in such person (or in the case of a company, more than 50 per cent of the number of shares of each class of the company's shares) is owned, directly or indirectly, by one or more individual residents of one of the Contracting States, one of the Contracting States or its political sub-divisions or local authorities, or other individuals subject to tax in either Contracting State on their worldwide incomes, or citizens of the United States; and
   (b) the income of such person is not used in substantial part, directly or indirectly, to meet liabilities (including liabilities for interest or royalties) to persons who are not residents of one of the Contracting States, one of the Contracting States or its political sub-divisions or local authorities, or citizens of the United States.

2. The provisions of paragraph 1 shall not apply if the income derived from the other Contracting State is derived in connection with, or is incidental to, the active conduct by such person of a trade or business in the first-mentioned State (other than the business of making or managing investments, unless these activities are banking or insurance activities carried on by a bank or insurance company).
3. The provisions of paragraph 1 shall not apply if the person deriving the income is a company which is a resident of a Contracting State in whose principal class of shares there is substantial and regular trading on a recognized stock exchange. For purposes of the preceding sentence, the terms "recognized stock exchange" means:
   (a) in the case of the United States, the NASDAQ System owned by the National Association of Securities Dealers, Inc. and any stock exchange registered with the Securities and Exchange Commission as a national securities exchange for purposes of the Securities Act of 1934;
   (b) in the case of India, any stock exchange which is recognized by the Central Government under the Securities Contract Regulation Act, 1956; and
   (c) any other stock exchange agreed upon by the competent authorities of the Contracting States.
4. A person that is not entitled to the benefits of this Convention pursuant to the provisions of the preceding paragraphs of this article may, nevertheless, be granted the benefits of the Convention if the competent authority of the State in which the income in question arises so determines.

ARTICLE 25: Relief from double taxation

1. In accordance with the provisions and subject to the limitations of the law of the United States (as it may be amended from time to time without changing the general principle hereof), the United States shall allow to a resident or citizen of the United States as a credit against the United States tax on income:
   (a) the income-tax paid to India by or on behalf of such citizen or resident; and
   (b) in the case of a United States company owning at least 10 per cent of the voting stock of a company which is a resident of India and from which the United States company receives dividends, the income-tax paid to India by or on behalf of the distributing company with respect to the profits out of which the dividends are paid.

   For the purposes of this paragraph, the taxes referred to in paragraphs 1(b) and 2 of article 2 (Taxes Covered) shall be considered as income taxes.
2. (a) Where a resident of India derives income which, in accordance with the provisions of this Convention, may be taxed in the United States, India shall allow as a deduction from the tax on the income of that resident an amount equal to the income-tax paid in the United States, whether directly or by deduction. Such deduction shall not, however, exceed that part of the income-tax (as computed before the deduction is given) which is attributable to the income which may be taxed in the United States;

(b) Further, where such resident is a company by which a surtax is payable in India, the deduction in respect of income-tax paid in the United States shall be allowed in the first instance from income-tax payable by the company in India and as to the balance, if any, from surtax payable by it in India;

3. For the purposes of allowing relief from double taxation pursuant to this article, income shall be deemed to arise as follows:
   (a) income derived by a resident of a Contracting State which may be taxed in the other Contracting State in accordance with this Convention (other than solely by reason of citizenship in accordance with paragraph 3 of article 1 (General Scope) shall be deemed to arise in that other State;
   (b) income derived by a resident of a Contracting State which may not be taxed in the other Contracting State in accordance with the Convention shall be deemed to arise in the first-mentioned State.

   Notwithstanding the preceding sentence, the determination of the source of income for purposes of this article shall be subject to such source rules in the domestic laws of the Contracting States as apply for the purpose of limiting the foreign tax credit. The preceding sentence shall not apply with respect to income dealt with in article 12 (Royalties and Fees for Included Services). The rules of this paragraph shall not apply in determining credits against United States tax for foreign taxes other than the taxes referred to in paragraphs 1(b) and 2 of article 2 (Taxes Covered).

ARTICLE 26: Non-discrimination

1. Nationals of a Contracting State shall not be subjected in the other Contracting State to any taxation or any requirement connected therewith which is other or more burdensome than the taxation and connected requirements to which nationals of that other State in the same circumstances are or may be subjected. This provision shall apply to persons who are not residents of one or both of the Contracting States.
2. Except where the provisions of paragraph 3 of article 7 (Business Profits) apply, the taxation on a permanent establishment which an enterprise of a Contracting State has in the other Contracting State shall not be less favourably levied in that other State than the taxation levied on enterprises of that other State carrying on the same activities. This provision shall not be construed as obliging a Contracting State to grant to residents of the other Contracting State any personal allowances, reliefs, and reductions for taxation purposes on account of civil status or family responsibilities which it grants to its own residents.
3. Except where the provisions of paragraph 1 of article 9 (Associated Enterprises), paragraph 7 of article 11 (Interest), or paragraph 8 of article 12 (Royalties and Fees for Included Services) apply, interest, royalties, and other disbursements paid by a resident of a Contracting State to a resident of the other Contracting State shall, for the purposes of determining the taxable profits of the first-mentioned resident, be deductible under the same conditions as if they had been paid to a resident of the first-mentioned State.

4. Enterprises of a Contracting State, the capital of which is wholly or partly owned or controlled, directly or indirectly, by one or more residents of the other Contracting State, shall not be subjected in the first-mentioned State to any taxation or any requirement connected therewith which is other or more burdensome than the taxation and connected requirements to which other similar enterprises of the first-mentioned State are or may be subjected.
5. Nothing in this article shall be construed as preventing either Contracting State from imposing the taxes described in article 14 (Permanent Establishment Tax) or the limitations described in paragraph 3 of article 7 (Business Profits).

ARTICLE 27: Mutual agreement procedure

1. Where a person considers that the actions of one or both of the Contracting States result or will result for him in taxation not in accordance with the provisions of this Convention, he may, irrespective of the remedies provided by the domestic law of those States, present his case to the competent authority of the Contracting State of which he is a resident or national. This case must be presented within three years of the date of receipt of notice of the action which gives rise to taxation not in accordance with the Convention.
2. The competent authority shall endeavour, if the objection appears to it to be justified and if it is not itself able to arrive at a satisfactory solution, to resolve the case by mutual agreement with the competent authority of the other Contracting State, with a view to the avoidance of taxation which is not in accordance with the Convention. Any agreement reached shall be implemented notwithstanding any time limits or other procedural limitations in the domestic law of the Contracting States.
3. The competent authorities of the Contracting States shall endeavour to resolve by mutual agreement any difficulties or doubts arising as to the interpretation or application of the Convention. They may also consult together for the elimination of double taxation in cases not provided for in the Convention.
4. The competent authorities of the Contracting States may communicate with each other directly for the purpose of reaching an agreement in the sense of the preceding paragraphs. The competent authorities, through consultations, shall develop appropriate bilateral procedure, conditions, methods and techniques for the implementation of the mutual agreement procedure provided for in this article. In addition, a competent authority may devise appropriate unilateral procedures, conditions, methods and techniques to facilitate the above-mentioned bilateral actions and the implementation of the mutual agreement procedure.

ARTICLE 28: Exchange of information and administrative assistance

1. The competent authorities of the Contracting States shall exchange such information (including documents) as is necessary for carrying out the provisions of this Convention or of the domestic laws of the Contracting States concerning taxes covered by the Convention insofar as the taxation there under is not contrary to the Convention, in particular, for the prevention of fraud or evasion of such taxes. The exchange of

information is not restricted by article 1 (General Scope). Any information received by a Contracting State shall be treated as secret in the same manner as information obtained under the domestic laws of that State. However, if the information is originally regarded as secret in the transmitting State, it shall be disclosed only to persons or authorities (including courts and administrative bodies) involved in the assessment, collection, or administration of, the enforcement or prosecution in respect of, or the determination of appeals in relation to, the taxes which are the subject of the Convention. Such persons or authorities shall use the information only for such purposes, but may disclose the information in public court proceedings or in judicial decisions. The competent authorities shall, through consultation, develop appropriate conditions, methods and techniques concerning the matters in respect of which such exchange of information shall be made, including, where appropriate, exchange of information regarding tax avoidance.

2. The exchange of information or documents shall be either on a routine basis or on request with reference to particular cases or otherwise. The competent authorities of the Contracting States shall agree from time to time on the list of information or documents which shall be furnished on a routine basis.
3. In no case shall the provisions of paragraph 1 be construed so as to impose on a Contracting State the obligation:
   (a) to carry out administrative measures at variance with the laws and administrative practice of that or of the other Contracting State;
   (b) to supply information which is not obtainable under the laws or in the normal course of the administration of that or of the other Contracting State;
   (c) to supply information which would disclose any trade, business, industrial, commercial or professional secret or trade process, or information the disclosure of which would be contrary to public policy (order public).
4. If information is requested by a Contracting State in accordance with this article, the other Contracting State shall obtain the information to which the request relates in the same manner and in the same form as if the tax of the first-mentioned State were the tax of that other State and were being imposed by that other State. If specifically requested by the competent authority of a Contracting State, the competent authority of the other Contracting State shall provide information under this article in the form of depositions of witnesses and authenticated copies of unedited original documents (including books, papers, statements, records, accounts, and writings), to the same extent such depositions and documents can be obtained under the laws and administrative practices of that other State with respect to its own taxes.
5. For the purposes of this article, the Convention shall apply, notwithstanding the provisions of article 2 (Taxes Covered):
   (a) in the United States, to all taxes imposed under title 26 of the United States Code; and
   (b) in India, to the income-tax, the wealth-tax and the gift-tax.

ARTICLE 29: Diplomatic agents and consular officers

Nothing in this Convention shall affect the fiscal privileges of diplomatic agents or consular officers under the general rules of international law or under the provisions of special agreements.

ARTICLE 30: Entry into force

1. Each Contracting State shall notify the other Contracting State in writing, through diplomatic channels, upon the completion of their respective legal procedures to bring this Convention into force.
2. The Convention shall enter into force on the date of the latter of such notifications and its provisions shall have effect:

(a) in the United States

(i) in respect of taxes withheld at source, for amounts paid or credited on or after the first day of January next following the date on which the Convention enters into force;

(ii) in respect of other taxes, for taxable periods beginning on or after the first day of January next following the date on which the Convention enters into force; and

(b) in India, in respect of income arising in any taxable year beginning on or after the first day of April next following the calendar year in which the Convention enters into force.

ARTICLE 31: Termination

This Convention shall remain in force indefinitely but either of the Contracting States may, on or before the thirtieth day of June in any calendar year beginning after the expiration of a period of five years from the date of the entry into force of the Convention, give the other Contracting State through diplomatic channels, written notice of termination and, in such event, this Convention shall cease to have effect:

(a) in the United States

(i) in respect of taxes withheld at source, for amounts paid or credited on or after the first day of January next following the calendar year in which notice of termination is given; and

(ii) in respect of other taxes, for taxable periods beginning on or after the first day of January next following the calendar year in which the notice of termination is given; and

(b) in India, in respect of income arising in any taxable year beginning on or after the first day of April next following the calendar year in which the notice of termination is given.

IN WITNESS WHEREOF, the undersigned, being duly authorized by their respective Governments, have signed this Convention.

DONE at New Delhi in duplicate, this 12th day of September, 1989, in the English and Hindi languages, both texts being equally authentic. In case of divergence between the two texts, the English text shall be the operative one.

(Sd.) N. K. Sengupta
Secretary to the Government of India.
For the Government of the Republic of India,
For the Government of the United States of America,
(Sd.)
John R. Hubbard, Ambassador.

PROTOCOL

At the signing today of the Convention, between the United States of America and the Republic of India for the Avoidance of Double Taxation and the Prevention of Fiscal Evasion with respect to Taxes on Income, the undersigned have agreed upon the following provisions, **which shall form an integral part of the Convention:**

I. Ad Article 5: It is understood that where an enterprise of a Contracting State has a permanent establishment in the other Contracting State in accordance with the provisions of paragraphs 2(j), 2(k) or 2(1) of article 5 (Permanent Establishment), and the time period referred to in that paragraph extends over two taxable years, a permanent establishment shall not be deemed to exist in a year, if any, in which the use, site, project or activity, as the case may be, continues for a period or periods aggregating less than 30 days in that taxable year. A permanent establishment will exist in the other taxable year, and the enterprise will be subject to tax in that other Contracting State in accordance with the provisions of article 7 (Business profits), but only on income arising during that other taxable year.

II. Ad Article 7: Where the law of the Contracting State in which a permanent establishment is situated imposes, in accordance with the provisions of paragraph 3 of article 7 (Business profits), a restriction on the amount of executive and general administrative expenses which may be allowed as a deduction, in determining the profits of such permanent establishment, it is understood that in making such a determination of profits the deduction in respect of such executive and general administrative expenses in no case shall be less than that allowable under the Indian Income-tax Act as on the date of signature of this Convention.

III. Ad Articles 7, 10, 11, 12, 15 and 23: It is understood that for the implementation of paragraphs 1 and 2 of article 7 (Business Profits), paragraph 4 of article 10 (Dividends), paragraph 5 of article 11 (Interest), paragraph 6 of article 12 (Royalties and Fees for Included Services), paragraph 1 of article 15 (Independent Personal Services), and paragraph 2 of article 23 (Other Income), any income attributable to a permanent establishment or fixed base during its existence is taxable in the Contracting State in which such permanent establishment or fixed base is situated even if the payments are deferred until such permanent establishment or fixed base has ceased to exist.

IV. Ad Article 12: It is understood that fees for included services, as defined in paragraph 4 of article 12 (Royalties and Fees for Included Services) will, in accordance with United States law, be subject to income-tax in the United States based on net income and, when earned by a company, will also be subject to the taxes described in paragraph 1 of article 14 (Permanent Establishment Tax). The total of these taxes which may be imposed on such fees, however, may not exceed the amount computed by multiplying the gross fee by the appropriate tax rate specified in sub-paragraph (a) or (b), whichever is applicable, of paragraph 2 of article 12.

V. Ad Article 14: It is understood that references in paragraph 1 of article 14 (Permanent Establishment Tax) to profits that are subject to tax in the United States under article 6 (Income from Immovable Property (Real Property)), under article 12 Royalties and Fees for Included Services), as fees for included services as defined in that article, or under article 13 (Gains) of this Convention, are intended to refer only to cases in which the profits in question are subject to United States tax based on net income (i.e., by virtue of being effectively connected, or being treated as effectively connected, with the conduct of a trade or business in the United States). Any income which is subject to tax under those articles based on gross income is not subject to tax under article 14.

IN WITNESS WHEREOF, the undersigned, being duly authorised by their respective Governments, have signed this Protocol.

DONE at New Delhi in duplicate, this 12th day of September, 1989, in the English and Hindi languages, both texts being equally authentic. In case of divergence between the two texts, the English text shall be the operative one.

(Sd.)
N. K. Sengupta
Secretary to the Government of India.
For the Government of the Republic of India,
For the Government of the United States of America,
(Sd.)
John R. Hubbard, Ambassador.
EMBASSY OF UNITED STATES OF AMERICA
New Delhi, September 12, 1989.

Excellency

I have the honour to refer to the Convention between the Government of the United States of America and the Government of the Republic of India for the avoidance of double taxation and the prevention of fiscal evasion with respect to taxes on income which was signed today (hereinafter referred to as "the Convention") and to confirm, on behalf of the Government of the United States of America, the following understanding reached between the two Governments:

Both sides agree that a tax sparing credit shall not be provided in article 25 (Relief from Double Taxation) of the Convention at this time. However, the Convention shall be promptly amended to incorporate a tax sparing credit provision if the United States hereafter amends its laws concerning the provision of tax sparing credits, or the United States reaches agreement on the provision of a tax sparing credit with any other country.

Both sides also agree that, for purposes of paragraph 4(c) of article 5 (Permanent Establishment) of the Convention, a person shall be considered to habitually secure orders in a Contracting State, wholly or almost wholly for an enterprise, only if

1. such person frequently accepts orders for goods or merchandise on behalf of the enterprise;
2. substantially all of such person's sales-related activities in the Contracting State consist of activities for the enterprise;
3. such person habitually represents to persons offering to buy goods or merchandise that acceptance of an order by such person constitutes the agreement of the enterprise to supply goods or merchandise under the terms and conditions specified in the order; and
4. the enterprise takes actions that give purchasers the basis for a reasonable belief that such person has authority to bind the enterprise.

I have the honour to request Your Excellency to confirm the foregoing understandings of Your Excellency's Government.

Accept, Excellency, the renewed assurances of my highest consideration.

(Sd.)

John R. Hubbard,
His Excellency Dr. N. K. Sengupta, Ambassador
Secretary (Revenue), Ministry of Finance, New Delhi.
SECRETARY
GOVERNMENT OF INDIA
MINISTRY OF FINANCE
(Department of Revenue)
New Delhi, September 12, 1989.

Excellency

I have the honour to acknowledge receipt of Your Excellency's Note of today's date, which reads as follows:

I have the honour to refer to the Convention between the Government of the United States of America and the Government of the Republic of India for the avoidance of double taxation and the prevention of fiscal evasion with respect to taxes on income which was signed today (hereinafter referred to as "the Convention") and to confirm, on behalf of the Government of the United States of America, the following understandings reached between the two Governments:

Both sides agree that a tax sparing credit shall not be provided in article 25 (Relief from Double Taxation) of the Convention at this time. However, the Convention shall be promptly amended to incorporate a tax sparing credit provision if the United States hereafter amends its laws concerning the provision of tax sparing credits, or the United States reaches agreement on the provision of a tax sparing credit with any other country.

Both sides also agree that, for purposes of paragraph 4(c) of article 5 (Permanent Establishment) of the Convention, a person shall be considered to habitually secure orders in a Contracting State, wholly or almost wholly for an enterprise, only if:

1. such person frequently accepts orders for goods or merchandise on behalf of the enterprise;
2. substantially all of such person's sales-related activities in the Contracting State consist of activities for the enterprise;

3. such person habitually represents to persons offering to buy goods or merchandise that acceptance of an order by such person constitutes the agreement of the enterprise to supply goods or merchandise under the terms and conditions specified in the order; and
4. the enterprise takes actions that give, purchasers the basis for a reasonable belief that such person has authority to bind the enterprise.

I have the honour to confirm the understandings contained in your Excellency's note on behalf of the Government of the Republic of India.

Accept, Excellency, the renewed assurances of my highest consideration.

(sd.)
N. K. Sengupta
His Excellency Dr. John R. Hubbard
Ambassador of the United States of America, New Delhi
EMBASSY OF THE UNITED STATES OF AMERICA
New Delhi, September 12, 1989.

Excellency

I have the honour to refer to the Convention signed today between the United States of America and the Republic of India for the avoidance of double taxation and the prevention of fiscal evasion with respect to taxes on income and to inform you on behalf of the United States of America of the following:

During the course of the negotiations leading to conclusion of the Convention signed today, the negotiators developed and agreed upon a memorandum of understanding intended to give guidance both to the taxpayers and the tax authorities of our two countries in interpreting aspects of article 12 (Royalties and Fees for Included Services) relating to the scope of included services. This memorandum of understanding represents the current views of the United States Government with respect to these aspects of article 12, and it is my Government's understanding that it also represents the current views of the Indian Government. It is also my Government's view that as our Governments gain experience in administering the Convention, and particularly article 12, the competent authorities may develop and publish amendments to the memorandum of understanding and further understandings and interpretations of the Convention.

If this position meets with the approval of the Government of the Republic of India, this letter and your reply thereto will indicate that our Governments share a common view of the purpose of the memorandum of understanding relating to article 12 of the Convention.

Accept, Excellency, the renewed assurances of my highest consideration.

(Sd.)
John R. Hubbard,
Ambassador.
His Excellency Dr. N. K. Sengupta,
Secretary (Revenue), Ministry of Finance, New Delhi.
GOVERNMENT OF INDIA
MINISTRY OF FINANCE
(Department of Revenue)
New Delhi, September 12, 1989.

Excellency

I have the honour to acknowledge receipt of Your Excellency's Note of today's date, which reads as follows:

I have the honour to refer to the Convention signed today between the United States of America and the Republic of India for the avoidance of double taxation and the prevention of fiscal evasion with respect to taxes on income and to inform you on behalf of the United States of America of the following:

During the course of the negotiations leading to conclusion of the Convention signed today, the negotiators developed and agreed upon a memorandum of understanding intended to give guidance both to the taxpayers and the tax authorities of our two countries in interpreting aspects of article 12 (Royalties and Fees for Included Services) relating to the scope of included services. This memorandum of understanding represents the current views of the United States Government with respect to these aspects of article 12, and it is my Government's understanding that it also represents the current views of the Indian Government. It is also my Government's view that as our Governments gain experience in administering the Convention, and particularly article 12, the competent authorities may develop and publish amendments to the memorandum of understanding and further understandings and interpretations of the Convention.

If this position meets with the approval of the Government of the Republic of India, this letter and your reply thereto will indicate that our Governments share a common view of the purpose of the memorandum of understanding relating to article 12 of the Convention.

I have the honour to confirm the understandings contained in Your Excellency's Note, on behalf of the Government of the Republic of India.

Accept, Excellency, the renewed assurances of my highest consideration.

(sd.)

N. K. Sengupta

His Excellency Dr. John R. Hubbard,

Ambassador of the United States of America, New Delhi.

May 15,1989

U.S.–INDIA TAX TREATY

Memorandum of understanding concerning fees for included services in Article 12

Paragraph 4 (in general):

This memorandum describes in some detail the category of services defined in paragraph 4 of article 12 (Royalties and Fees for Included Services). It also provides examples of services intended to be covered within the definition of included services and those intended to be excluded, either because they do not satisfy the tests of paragraph 4, or because, notwithstanding the fact that they meet the tests of paragraph 4, they are dealt with under paragraph 5. The examples in either case are not intended as an exhaustive list but rather as illustrating a few typical cases. For ease of understanding, the examples in this memorandum describe U.S. persons providing services to Indian persons, but the rules of article 12 are reciprocal in application.

Article 12 includes only certain technical and consultancy services. By technical services, we mean in this context services requiring expertise in a technology. By consultancy services, we mean in this context advisory services. The categories of technical and consultancy services are to some extent overlapping because a consultancy service could also be a technical service. However, the category of consultancy services also includes an advisory service, whether or not expertise in a technology is required to perform it.

Under paragraph 4, technical and consultancy services are considered included services only to the following extent: (1) as described in paragraph 4(a), if they are ancillary and subsidiary to the application or enjoyment of a right, property or information for which a royalty payment is made; or (2) as described in paragraph 4(b), if they make available technical knowledge, experience, skill, know-how, or processes, or consist of the development and transfer of a technical plan or technical design. Thus, under paragraph 4(b), consultancy services which are not of a technical nature cannot be included services.

Paragraph 4(a):

Paragraph 4(a) of article 12 refers to technical or consultancy services that are ancillary and subsidiary to the application or enjoyment of any right, property, or information for which a payment described in paragraph 3(a) or (b) is received. Thus, paragraph 4(a) includes technical and consultancy services that are ancillary and subsidiary to the application or enjoyment of an intangible for which a royalty is received under a licence or sale as described in paragraph 3(a), as well as those ancillary and subsidiary to the application or enjoyment of industrial, commercial, or scientific equipment for which a royalty is received under a lease as described in paragraph 3(b).

It is understood that, in order for a service fee to be considered "ancillary and subsidiary" to the application or enjoyment of some right, property, or information for which a payment described in paragraph 3(a) or (b) is received, the service must be related to the application or enjoyment of the right, property or information. In addition, the clearly predominant purpose of the arrangement under which the payment of the service fee and such other payment are made must be the application or enjoyment of the right, property, or information described in paragraph 3. The question of whether the service is related to the application or enjoyment of the right, property, or information described in paragraph 3 and whether the clearly predominant purpose of the arrangement is such application or enjoyment must be determined by reference to the facts and circumstances of each case. Factors which may be relevant to such determination (although not necessarily controlling) include:

1. the extent to which the services in question facilitate the effective application or enjoyment of the right, property, or information described in paragraph 3;
2. the extent to which such services are customarily provided in the ordinary course of business arrangements involving royalties described in paragraph 3;
3. whether the amount paid for the services (or which would be paid by parties operating at arm's length) is an insubstantial portion of the combined payments for the services and the right, property, or information described in paragraph 3;
4. whether the payment made for the services and the royalty described in paragraph 3 are made under a single contract (or a set of related contracts); and

5. whether the person performing the services is the same person as, or a related person to, the person receiving the royalties described in paragraph 3 (for this purpose, persons are considered related if their relationship is described in article 9 (Associated Enterprises) or if the person providing the service is doing so in connection with an overall arrangement which includes the payer and recipient of the royalties).

To the extent that services are not considered ancillary and subsidiary to the application or enjoyment of some right, property, or information for which a royalty payment under paragraph 3 is made, such services shall be considered "included services" only to the extent that they are described in paragraph 4(b).

(***Source:*** *Taxman's website*)

The above terms of reference are found to be contained in India's Double Tax Avoidance (DTA) treaty with the USA. Terms of a similar treaty with the UK have been given in Appendix 10-A to facilitate readers to draw a comparison between different treaties.

WITHHOLDING TAX RATES IN INDIA

The government of India imposes withholding taxes at different rates on repatriation of foreign incomes. Table 10.2 exhibits applicable withholding tax rates in vogue in case of countries with which India has double taxation avoidance agreements:

TABLE 10.2 Withholding tax rates in India

Country	*Dividends* %	*Interest* %	*Royalties* %	*Country*	*Dividends* %	*Interest* %	*Royalties* %
Albania	10	10	10	Malaysia	5	10	10
Armenia	10	10	10	Malta	10	10	10
Australia	15	15	10/15	Mauritius	5/15	7.5	15
Austria	10	10	10	Mexico	10	10	10
Bangladesh	10/15	10	10	Mongolia	15	15	15
Belarus	10/15	10	15	Montenegro	5/15	10	10
Belgium	15	10/15	10	Morocco	10	10	10
Bhutan	10	10	10	Mozambique	7.5	10	10
Botswana	7.5/10	10	10	Myanmar	5	10	10
Brazil	15	15	25/15	Namibia	10	10	10
Bulgaria	15	15	15/20	Nepal	5/10	10	15
Canada	15/25	15	10/15	Netherlands	10	10	10
Chile	10	10	10	New Zealand	15	10	10
China	10	10	10	Norway	10	10	10
Taiwan	12.5	10	10	Oman	10/12.5	10	15
Colombia	5	10	10	Philippines	15/20	10/15	15
Croatia	5/15	10	10	Poland	10	10	15
Cyprus	10	10	10	Portugal	10/15	10	10
Czech Republic	10	10	10	Qatar	5/10	10	10
Denmark	15/25	10/15	20	Romania	10	10	10
Egypt	20	20	30	Russian Federation	10	10	10
Estonia	10	10	10	Saudi Arabia	5	10	10

Country	*Dividends* %	*Interest* %	*Royalties* %	*Country*	*Dividends* %	*Interest* %	*Royalties* %
Ethiopia	7.5	10	10	Serbia	5/15	10	10
Fiji	5	10	10	Singapore	10/15	10/15	10
Finland	10	10	10	Slovak Republic	15/25	15	30
France	10	10	10	Slovenia	5/15	10	10
Georgia	10	10	10	South Africa	10	10	10
Germany	10	10	10	Spain	15	15	20
Greece	20	20	30	Sri Lanka	7.5	10	10
Hong Kong	10	10	10	Sudan	10	10	10
Hungary	10	10	10	Sweden	10	10	10
Iceland	10	10	10	Switzerland	10	10	10
Indonesia	10	10	10	Syria	5/10	10	10
Iran	10	10	10	Tajikistan	5/10	10	10
Ireland	10	10	10	Tanzania	5/10	10	10
Israel	10	10	10	Thailand	10	10	10
Italy	15	15	20	Trinidad and Tobago	10	10	10
Japan	10	10	10	Turkey	15	10/15	15
Jordan	10	10	20	Turkmenistan	10	10	10
Kazakhstan	10	10	10	Uganda	10	10	10
Kenya	10	10	10	Ukraine	10/15	10	10
Korea	15	10	10	United Arab Emirates	10	5/12.5	10
Kuwait	10	10	10	United Kingdom	10/15	10/15	10/15
Kyrgyzstan (Kyrgyz Republic)	10	10	15	United States	15/25	10/15	10/15
Latvia	10	10	10	Uruguay	5	10	10
Libya	20	20	30	Uzbekistan	10	10	10
Lithuania	5/15	10	10	Vietnam	10	10	10
Luxembourg	10	10	10	Zambia	5/15	10	10
Macedonia	10	10	10	Non-treaty countries	10	20	20

Source: Compiled from (1) http://taxsummaries.pwc.com/india/corporate/withholding-taxes; (2) India's Double Taxation Avoidance Agreements - India Guide | Doing Business in India (india-briefing.com), and (3) https://sbi.co.in/documents/21077/23246/DTAA+Country+List.pdf[7]

Note: Where two rates are mentioned, such as 10 % or 15 % for Dividend income from Bangladesh, selection of the applicable rate will depend on fulfilling the conditions as specified in the DTAA with the country concerned.

Withholding Tax Rates for non-treaty Foreign Companies

Withholding tax rates for non-treaty foreign companies in India are given in Table 10.3

TABLE 10.3 Withholding tax rates for non-treaty companies

	Withholding Tax Rate for non-treaty foreign companies
Dividends	10%
Interest Income	20%
Royalties	20%
Technical Services	30%
Other income	55%

Given the withholding tax rates and the listed incentives above, financial managers of MNCs need to plan their investments involving repatriation or non-repatriation of incomes from the host country.

TAX HAVEN

Tax haven in international taxation refers to a moderate or liberal taxation of foreign income by the host government. Consequently the tax liabilities of the MNCs get reduced when they operate in countries where such moderate tax policy exists. MNCs in turn manage to substantially reduce or defer taxation on income routed through tax haven countries.

The various tax havens in vogue across countries may be clubbed into four types as given below:

1. Tax havens that have no income or capital gains tax or gift and estate tax.
2. Tax havens that do impose taxes, but whose rate is very low.
3. Tax havens that tax income from domestic sources, but exempt all income from foreign sources.
4. Countries that allow special tax privileges and are suitable for tax havens only for selected purposes.

While choosing a particular tax haven, MNCs should keep in view factors like the political and economic stability of the country and the integrity of the government concern, tax treaties, tax laws other than income taxes, infrastructural facilities and the attitudes of the country towards tax haven business.

SUMMARY

Taxes have a significant bearing on business decisions ranging from designing a suitable capital structure to managing foreign exchange risk, determining cost of financing, deciding upon the mode and destination of foreign investments, determining transfer prices, and managing inter-affiliated fund flows. The process of computation of taxable income and the corresponding taxes and tax rates vary across nations depending on what 'costs' are deductible from the revenues. Tax rates are usually fixed by the government as a function of domestic economic and political considerations. The government's tax policy may sometimes encourage or discourage foreign investments. Financial managers of multinational corporations operating in different countries therefore need to be aware about the broad dimensions of international taxation such as the objectives of taxation, tax credits, double taxation, tax havens and alike and their impact on various corporate decisions before deciding upon the magnitude and destination of foreign investments.

International taxation policies across nations are characterized by twin objectives of 'tax neutrality' and 'tax equity'. Tax neutrality further assumes two forms: domestic neutrality and foreign neutrality. As long as imposition of taxes on foreign income is concerned, the various taxing policies followed by different countries ranges from tax exemption, to tax credit, tax deduction and double taxation.

In order to avoid double taxation thereby encouraging free flow of foreign investments, technology and expertise, countries do undertake unilateral and bilateral relief measures. The bilateral relief measures are in the form of Double Tax Avoidance Agreements or simply called as the Tax Treaties. India has signed such treaties with over 65 countries at present. Countries also impose withholding taxes on repatriation of foreign incomes with the ultimate intention of discouraging 'income outflows' and encouraging reinvestment of such incomes in the host country.

KEY TERMS

International tax planning: International tax planning refers to the process of structuring foreign operations and remittances that would result in maximization of the firms' global after tax cash flows. It involves using the flexibility of the multinational corporation in structuring foreign operations and remittance policies in order to maximize global after tax cash flows.

Tax neutrality: Tax neutrality refers to a system of taxation which when adopted will not affect the investment decisions of the firms as regards the destination of the investment or the nationality of the investor. There are two forms of tax neutrality—domestic neutrality and foreign neutrality.

Domestic neutrality: Domestic neutrality or capital export neutrality is said to be existing when tax laws do not affect the capital owner's choice between investing in home country or in host (foreign) country. 'Taxation is export neutral if domestic and overseas investments that earn the same pre-tax rates of return also yield the same after tax rates of return.

Foreign neutrality: Foreign neutrality or capital important neutrality exists when tax laws do not distort the after tax earnings to domestic and foreign investors. 'Taxation is import neutral if equal before tax returns to competing supplies of capital translate into equal after tax return.

Tax equity: Tax equity refers to a system of taxation where equal sacrifices are made by the tax payers in bearing the tax burdens.

Double taxation: Double taxation which occurs when the same income is taxed twice—first by the host government and second by the home government.

Tax treaties: Tax treaties are bilateral relief measures undertaken by countries to avoid double taxation and to reduce overall tax burden. Tax treaties aim at providing protection to tax payers against double taxation, and preventing the discouragement which taxation may cause in the free flow of international trade, international investment and international transfer of technology.

Unilateral relief measures: Unilateral relief measures are measures taken by one country alone to avoid or reduce double taxation as long as such measures benefit the country concerned.

Bilateral relief measures: Bilateral relief measures are measures taken by two countries to avoid or to reduce the burden of double taxation.

Withholding taxes: Withholding taxes are imposed by the host government at different rates on repatriation of foreign incomes in the form of dividends, interest, royalties and technical services.

Tax haven: Tax haven in international taxation refers to a moderate or liberal taxation of foreign income by the host government.

REVIEW QUESTIONS

1. What do you understand by international tax planning? What are its objectives and significance? Explain.
2. What do you understand by home and host country's tax policies in the context of international taxation? Explain with examples.
3. Give a sketch of the international taxation policies as practiced by different nations.
4. Give a detailed account of home country's tax policies in relation to treatment of foreign income and foreign taxes paid.
5. As the CEO of an India MNC, what factors in relation to international taxation should you consider before placing your investments abroad?
6. What do you understand by 'double taxation'? How do countries avoid double taxation?
7. What are tax treaties? Why and how are such treaties entered? Cite example(s) to supplement your answer.
8. What are unilateral relief and bilateral tax relief? What is their significance?
9. Bring out the salient features of India's Double Tax Avoidance (DTA) Agreement with the USA.
10. ABC Ltd. of Sweden has earned $ 12,000 through its Canddian subsidiary, the XYZ Ltd. If the applicable corporate income tax rate in Sweden and in Canada is 40% and 30%, respectively, and if the Sweden government decides to (a) exempt the foreign income accrued to its firm, and (b) allow full tax credit in respect of the foreign taxes paid, what will be ABC Ltd.'s tax liability and after tax income?
11. Black and Blue Co. Ltd. of Germany has generated a profit of $ 20,000 through its foreign subsidiary Red and White Ltd. of Australia. If the German government decides to give deduction for the tax already paid to the Australian government, what will be Black and Blue Ltd.'s domestic tax liability and after tax income? Will the company's post-tax income significantly vary if tax credit is allowed instead of deduction? Assume that the prevailing tax rate in Germany and in Australia is 25% and 20%, respectively.
12. Smith and Company of Hong Kong has earned a profit of $ 25,000 through its Taiwan subsidiary the Slim & Co. Ltd. The prevalent corporate tax rates in Hong Kong and Taiwan is 25% and 19%, respectively. If the Hong Kong government decides to impose domestic tax on Smith and Co.'s foreign earnings without recognizing the tax already paid to the Taiwan government, what will be Smith and Co. Ltd. domestic tax liability and after tax income?
13. Amro Ltd. of Singapore has generated foreign income of $ 24,00,000 through its affiliate, Stones Ltd. of Malaysia. Corporate tax rate prevalent in Singapore and Malaysia is 35% and 30%, respectively. What will be Amro Ltd.'s (a) foreign tax liability, and (b) after tax foreign income if the Singapore government of decides to:
    (i) exempt foreign income from domestic tax,

(ii) allow credit for tax paid on foreign income,
(iii) allow deduction for foreign taxes paid, and
(iv) tax foreign income without recognizing the taxes already paid?

14. Microcon Ltd. of Sweden has earned a foreign income of $ 16,20,000 through its Canadian subsidiary, Promotors Ltd. The applicable corporate tax rate in Sweden is 25% and in Canada is 20%.
If the Government of Sweden decides to (i) exempt foreign income from tax, (ii) offer credit for foreign income tax paid, (iii) allows deductions for foreign income tax paid, (iv) ignores foreign income tax paid, determine Cosmo Ltd.'s tax liability on foreign income and also its after tax income.

15. What are withholding taxes? How can such taxes be avoided? Explain in the light of provision of international taxation policy to the effect.

16. Write explanatory notes on:
(a) Tax neutrality
(b) Tax equity

17. Write notes on:
(a) Home country tax policies
(b) Host country tax policies

18. ABC Ltd. of Canada has earned $ 11,22,000 through its Italian subsidiary, the XYZ Ltd. Applicable corporate tax rate prevalent in Canada is 27.5% and in Italy is 30%. If the Canadian government decides to (a) allow 50% tax credit in respect of the foreign taxes paid, and (b) allow tax deduction, what will be ABC Ltd.'s tax liability and after tax income?

19. Brown Valley Ltd. of Italy has generated a profit of $ 21,12,000 through its German subsidiary Green Fields Ltd. If the Italian government decides to (i) give deduction for the tax already paid to the German government, and (ii) ignore any taxes paid to the host government, what will be domestic tax liability and after tax income of Brown Valley Ltd? Will the company's post-tax income significantly vary if tax credit is allowed instead of deduction? Assume that the prevailing tax rate in Germany and in Italy is 25% and 30%, respectively.

20. Blue Sky Ltd. of South Korea has earned a profit of $ 52,25,000 through its Malaysian subsidiary Fat & Fit Ltd. The applicable corporate tax rate prevalent in South Korea is 25% whereas in Malaysia it is 22.40%. If the South Korean government decides to impose domestic tax on Blue Sky Ltd.'s foreign earnings without recognizing the tax already paid to the host government, what will be Blue Sky Ltd.'s domestic tax liability and its post-tax foreign income?

21. Red Star Ltd. of India has generated a foreign income of $ 42,24,420 through its foreign affiliate, Bright Star Ltd. of Cambodia. The applicable corporate tax rate prevalent in Cambodia is 35% and India is 25%. Determine the (a) foreign tax liability and (b) post-tax foreign income of Red Star Ltd. if the Government of India decides to:
(i) exempt foreign income from domestic tax,
(ii) allow credit for tax paid on foreign income, and

(iii) impose tax on foreign income without recognizing the taxes already paid to host government.

22. White Woods Inc. of Mexico has earned $ 16,32,640 through its foreign subsidiary, Super Max Inc. of Spain. You are required to determine the (a) foreign tax liability, and (b) post-tax foreign income of White Woods Inc. if the Government of Mexico decides to:

(i) exempt foreign income from domestic tax,
(ii) allow deduction of taxes paid to the Government of Spain, and
(iii) levy tax on foreign income ignoring taxes already paid to the Mexican government.

Given further that, the applicable corporate tax rate in Mexico is 32.5% and Spain is 28%.

23. Maple Tree Inc. of Belgium has earned € 39,13,390 through its foreign subsidiary, SmartWorld Inc. of Denmark. The applicable corporate tax rate prevalent in Belgium is 32% and Denmark is 28%.

Determine the post-tax foreign income of Maple Tree Inc. if the Government of Belgium decides to:

(a) give credit for the tax paid to foreign government,
(b) allow tax deduction for foreign tax paid, and
(c) levy tax on foreign income ignoring taxes already paid to foreign government.

24. Marvel Wing International of Mauritius has generated $69,69,690 foreign income through its subsidiary in Hong Kong the Wonders Inc. The corporate tax rate prevalent in Mauritius is 31% and in Hong Kong is 25%.

You are required determine the post-tax foreign income of Marvel Wing International if the Government of Mauritius decides to:

(a) exempt foreign income from domestic tax,
(b) give credit for the tax paid to foreign government,
(c) allow tax deduction for foreign tax paid, and
(d) levy tax on foreign income irrespective of any tax already paid to foreign government.

25. Blue Star India Ltd. has earned $ 66,66,660 and $ 98,89,980 through its Mexican subsidiary Red Star Inc. and Canadian subsidiary Rising Star Inc., respectively. The applicable corporate tax rate in India is 25%, whereas in Mexico and Canada the rates are 22.5% and 23.5%, respectively. Determine the tax liability on foreign income and the post-tax income of Blue Star India Ltd. if the Government of India decides to

(i) exempt foreign income from tax,
(ii) offer 50% tax credit, and
(iii) allow deductions for foreign taxes paid.

26. Seven Hills India Ltd. has earned foreign income of $ 34,24,140 and $ 61,16,610 through its Malaysian subsidiary Green Hills Ltd. and Indonesian subsidiary Green Valley Ltd., respectively. If the applicable corporate tax rate in India, Malaysia and Indonesia is 25%, 21.5% and 23%, respectively, and if the Government of India decides to (i) exempt foreign income from tax, (ii) offer tax credit for foreign income tax paid, and (iii) allow 75% deductions for foreign tax paid, what will be Seven Hills India Ltd.'s tax liability on foreign income and its after tax income?

27. A-One Services of Sri Lanka has made pre-tax foreign income of $ 21,42,630 through its British subsidiary MaxPro Ltd., $ 11,22,440 through its Italian subsidiary McMillan Ltd., and $ 32,23,200 through its Malaysian subsidiary Infinity Ltd. The applicable corporate tax rate in Sri Lanka, UK, Italy and Malaysia is 32% 28%, 25% and 22%, respectively. Determine the after-tax foreign income of A-One Services Ltd. and its domestic tax liability under the following conditions:
    (a) Government of Sri Lanka decides to allow 75% tax credit
    (b) Government of Sri Lanka decides to allow tax deductions
    (c) Government of Sri Lanka decides to ignore any foreign tax paid.

28. The following information relates to GreenTech Inc. of Singapore in respect to its foreign income generated through four subsidiaries:

Subsidiaries	*GenNex Inc., Hong Kong*	*FutureTech Inc., Mauritius*	*Universal Tech, Malaysia*	*i-Tech Ltd, Mexico*
Pre-tax Earnings	$ 3,14,24,140	$ 2,31,40,240	$ 4,12,34,220	$ 1,24,45,100
Applicable tax rate in host country	26%	23.5%	21.5%	22.5%
Home government's tax policy for foreign income	Tax exemption	Tax credit	Tax deduction	Ignore any foreign taxes paid

You are required to determine the post-tax foreign income of Green Tech Inc. and its domestic tax liability, given further that the corporate tax rate in Sri Lanka is 28.5%.

29. Blue Bell Inc. of Taiwan furnishes the following information relating to its foreign earnings through four of its subsidiaries:

Subsidiaries	*Super Max Ltd., Mauritius*	*Rose Valley Ltd., Sri Lanka*	*United Corporation, Malaysia*	*Universal Ltd. Singapore*
Pre-tax Earnings	$ 6,09,27,345	$2,82,71,250	$ 4,86,54,230	$ 7,38,56,754
Applicable tax rate in host country	23%	28.5%	21.5%	25.5%
Home government's tax policy for foreign income	Tax exemption	Tax credit	Tax deduction	Ignore any foreign taxes paid

If the corporate tax rate in Taiwan is 30%, what will be Blue Bell Inc.'s post-tax foreign income and its domestic tax liability? Will there be any significant change in Blue Bell's post-tax income if the Government of Taiwan decides to levy tax on foreign income irrespective of any foreign taxes paid?

30. Maxwell & Co. of UK furnishes the following information relating to its foreign earnings through its five subsidiaries:

Subsidiaries	*GreenZone Ltd., Holland*	*Green View Inc. Netherland*	*GreenLine Inc. Norway*	*Green Marks Ltd, France*	*Ever Green Ltd., Belgium*
Pre-tax Earnings in €	12,24,36,480	10,20,30,400	15,30,45,600	17,34,51,680	8,16,24,320
Applicable tax rate in host country	22.5%	24.5%	26.5%	28.5%	30.5%
Home government's tax policy for foreign income	Tax deduction	Tax credit	Tax Exemption	Ignore any foreign taxes paid	60% Tax Credit

If the corporate tax rate in UK is 32%, what will be Maxwell & Co.'s after tax foreign income and its domestic tax liability? Will there be any significant change in Maxwell & Co.'s after tax income if the Government of UK decides to levy tax on all foreign incomes irrespective of any taxes paid to host government(s)?

REFERENCES

[1] Valla V.K., *International Financial Management—Text and Cases*, Anmol, New Delhi, 2003, p. 959.

[2] Adam Smith (1976), *Wealth of the Nation.*

[3] Allan C., Shapiro, *Multinational Financial Management*, PHI Learning, New Delhi, 2002, p. 535.

[4] Ibid

[5] Valla V.K., Op. Cit., p. 964.

[6] Ibid, p. 966.

[7] E-resources

(i) http://taxsummaries.pwc.com/india/corporate/withholding-taxes;

(ii) India's Double Taxation Avoidance Agreements - India Guide | Doing Business in India (india-briefing.com), and

(iii) https://sbi.co.in/documents/21077/23246/DTAA+Country+List.pdf

APPENDIX 10-A
TERMS OF REFERENCE OF INDIA'S DTA WITH UK

Convention between the Government of the Republic of India and the Government of the United Kingdom of Great Britain and Northern Ireland for the avoidance of double taxation and the prevention of fiscal evasion with respect to taxes on income and capital gains

Whereas the annexed Convention between the Government of the Republic of India and the Government of the United Kingdom of Great Britain and Northern Ireland for the avoidance of double taxation and the prevention of fiscal evasion with respect to taxes on income and capital gains has entered into force on 26th October, 1993, on the notification by both the Contracting States to each other of the completion of the procedures required by their respective laws, as required by Article 30 of the said Convention.

Now, therefore, in exercise of the powers conferred by section 90 of the Income-tax Act, 1961 (43 of 1961), the Central Government hereby directs that all the provisions of the said Convention shall be given effect to in the Union of India.

[Notification No. G.S.R. 91(E), dated 11th February, 1994.]

ANNEXURE

Convention between the government of the republic of India and the government of the United Kingdom of Great Britain and Northern Ireland for the avoidance of double taxation and the prevention of fiscal evasion with respect to taxes on income and capital gains

The Government of the Republic of India and the Government of the United Kingdom of Great Britain and Northern Ireland:

Desiring to conclude a new Convention for the avoidance of double taxation and the prevention of fiscal evasion with respect to taxes on income and capital gains:

Have agreed as follows:

ARTICLE 1: Scope of the convention

1. This Convention shall apply to persons who are residents of one or both of the Contracting States.
2. This Convention extends to the territory of each Contracting State, including its territorial sea, and to those areas of the exclusive economic zone or the continental shelf adjacent to the outer limit of the territorial sea of each State over which it has, in accordance with international law, sovereign rights for the purpose of exploration and exploitation of the natural resources of such areas, and references in this Convention to the Contracting State or to either of them shall be construed accordingly.

ARTICLE 2: Taxes covered

1. The taxes which are the subject of this Convention are:
   (a) in the United Kingdom; (i) the income-tax; (ii) the corporation tax; (iii) the capital gains tax; and (iv) the petroleum revenue tax; (hereinafter referred to as "United Kingdom tax");
   (b) in India: the income-tax including any surcharge thereon; (hereinafter referred to as "Indian tax").
2. This Convention shall also apply to any identical or substantially similar taxes which are imposed by either Contracting State after the date of signature of this Convention in addition to, or in place of, the taxes of that Contracting State referred to in paragraph 1 of this Article. The competent authorities of the Contracting States

shall notify each other of any substantial changes which are made in their respective taxation laws.

ARTICLE 3: General definitions

1. In this Convention, unless the context otherwise requires:
   (a) the term "United Kingdom" means Great Britain and Northern Ireland;
   (b) the term "India" means the Republic of India;
   (c) the term "tax" means United Kingdom tax or Indian tax, as the context requires but shall not include any amount which is payable in respect of any default or omission in relation to the taxes to which this Convention applies or which represents a penalty imposed relating to those taxes;
   (d) the term "fiscal year" in relation to Indian tax means "previous year" as defined in the Income-tax Act, 1961 (43 of 1961) and in relation to United Kingdom tax means a year beginning with 6th April, in one year and ending with 5th April, in the following year;
   (e) the terms "a Contracting State" and "the other Contracting State" mean India or the United Kingdom, as the context requires;
   (f) the term "person" includes an individual, a company and any other entity which is treated as a taxable unit under the taxation laws in force in the respective Contracting States, but, subject to paragraph 2 of this article, does not include a partnership;
   (g) the term "company" means anybody corporate or any entity which is treated as a company or body corporate for tax purposes;
   (h) the terms "enterprise of a Contracting State" and "enterprise of the other Contracting State" mean respectively an enterprise carried on by a resident of a Contracting State and an enterprise carried on by a resident of the other Contracting State;
   (i) the term "competent authority" means, in the case of the United Kingdom, the Commissioners of Inland Revenue or their authorized representative, and, in the case of India, the Central Government in the Ministry of Finance (Department of Revenue) or their authorized representative;
   (j) the term "international traffic" means any transport by a ship or aircraft operated by an enterprise of a Contracting State except when the ship or aircraft is operated solely between places in the other Contracting State;
   (k) the term "Government" means the Government of a Contracting State or a political sub-division or local authority thereof. In relation to the United Kingdom, the term "political sub-division" shall include Northern Ireland.
2. A partnership which is treated as a taxable unit under the Income-tax Act, 1961 (43 of 1961), of India shall be treated as a person for the purposes of this Convention.
3. As regards the application of this Convention by a Contracting State any term not otherwise defined shall, unless the context otherwise requires, have the meaning which it has under the laws of that Contracting State relating to the taxes which are the subject of this Convention.

ARTICLE 4: Fiscal domicile

1. For the purposes of this Convention, the term "resident of a Contracting State" means any person who, under the law of that State, is liable to taxation therein by reason of his domicile, residence, place of management or any other criterion of a similar nature.
2. Where by reason of the provisions of paragraph 1 of this Article an individual is a resident of both Contracting States, then his status shall be determined in accordance with the following rules:
   (a) he shall be deemed to be a resident of the Contracting State in which he has a permanent home available to him. If he has a permanent home available to him in both Contracting States, he shall be deemed to be a resident of the Contracting State with which his personal and economic relations are closer (centre of vital interests);
   (b) if the Contracting State in which he has his centre of vital interests cannot be determined, or if he has not a permanent home available to him in either Contracting State, he shall be deemed to be a resident of the Contracting State in which he has an habitual abode;
   (c) if he has an habitual abode in both Contracting States or in either of them, he shall be deemed to be a resident of the Contracting State of which he is a national;
   (d) if he is a national of both Contracting States or of neither of them, the competent authorities of the Contracting States shall settle the question by mutual agreement.
3. Where by reason of the provisions of paragraph 1 of this Article a person other than an individual is a resident of both Contracting States, then it shall be deemed to be a resident of the Contracting State in which its place of effective management is situated.

ARTICLE 5: Permanent establishment

1. For the purposes of this Convention, the term "permanent establishment" means a fixed place of business through which the business of an enterprise is wholly or partly carried on.
2. The term "permanent establishment" shall include especially:
   (a) a place of management; (b) a branch; (c) an office; (d) a factory; (e) a workshop; (f) premises used as a sales outlet or for receiving or soliciting orders; (g) a warehouse in relation to a person providing storage facilities for others; (h) a mine, an oil or gas well, quarry or other place of extraction of natural resources; (i) an installation or structure used for the exploration or exploitation of natural resources; (j) a building site or construction, installation or assembly project or supervisory activities in connection therewith, where such site, project or supervisory activity continues for a period of more than six months, or where such project or supervisory activity, being incidental to the sale of machinery or equipment, continues for a period not exceeding six months and the charges payable for the project or supervisory activity exceed 10 per cent of the sale price of the machinery and equipment; (k) the furnishing of services including managerial services, other than those taxable under Article 13 (Royalties

and fees for technical services), within a Contracting State by an enterprise through employees or other personnel, but only if:

(i) activities of that nature continue within that State for a period or periods aggregating to more than 90 days within any twelve-month period; or

(ii) services are performed within that State for an enterprise within the meaning of paragraph 1 of Article 10 (Associated enterprises) and continue for a period or periods aggregating to more than 30 days within any twelve-month period:

Provided that for the purposes of this paragraph an enterprise shall be deemed to have a permanent establishment in a Contracting State and to carry on business through that permanent establishment if it provides services or facilities in connection with, or supplies plant and machinery on hire used or to be used in, the prospecting for, or extraction or production of, mineral oils in that State.

3. The term "permanent establishment" shall not be deemed to include:
   (a) the use of facilities solely for the purpose of storage or display of goods or merchandise belonging to the enterprise;
   (b) the maintenance of a stock of goods or merchandise belonging to the enterprise solely for the purpose of storage or display;
   (c) the maintenance of a stock of goods or merchandise belonging to the enterprise solely for the purpose of processing by another enterprise;
   (d) the maintenance of a fixed place of business solely for the purpose of purchasing goods or merchandise, or for collecting information, for the enterprise;
   (e) the maintenance of a fixed place of business solely for the purpose of advertising, for the supply of information or for scientific research, being activities solely of a preparatory or auxiliary character 'in the trade or business of the enterprise. However, this provision shall not be applicable where the enterprise maintains any other fixed place of business in the other Contracting State for any purpose or purposes other than the purposes specified in this paragraph;
   (f) the maintenance of a fixed place of business solely for any combination of activities mentioned in sub-paragraphs (a) to (e) of this paragraph, provided that the overall activity of the fixed place of business resulting from this combination is of a preparatory or auxiliary character.
4. A person acting in a Contracting State for or on behalf, of an enterprise of the other Contracting State other than an agent of an independent status to whom paragraph 5 of this article applies shall be deemed to be a permanent establishment of that enterprise in the first-mentioned State if:
   (a) he has, and habitually exercises in that State, an authority to negotiate and enter into contracts for or on behalf of the enterprise, unless his activities are limited to the purchase of goods or merchandise for the enterprise; or
   (b) he habitually maintains in the first-mentioned Contracting State a stock of goods or merchandise from which he regularly delivers goods or merchandise for or on behalf of the enterprise; or
   (c) he habitually secures orders in the first-mentioned State, wholly or almost wholly for the enterprise itself or for the enterprise and other enterprises controlling, controlled by, or subject to the same common control, as that enterprise.

5. An enterprise of a Contracting State shall not be deemed to have 4 permanent establishments in the other Contracting State merely because it carries on business in that other State through a broker, general commission agent or any other agent of an independent status, where such persons are acting in the ordinary course of their business. However, if the activities of such an agent are carried out wholly or almost wholly for the enterprise (or for the enterprise and other enterprises which are controlled by it or have a controlling interest in it or are subject to same common control) he shall not be considered to be an agent of an independent status for the purposes of this paragraph.
6. The fact that a company which is a resident of a Contracting State controls or is controlled by a company which is a resident of the other Contracting State, or which carries on business in that other State (Whether through a permanent establishment or otherwise), shall not of itself constitute either company a permanent establishment of the other.
7. For the purposes of this article the term "control", in relation to a company, means the ability to exercise control over the company's affairs by means of the direct or indirect holding of the greater part of the issued share capital or voting power in the company.

ARTICLE 6: Income from immovable property

1. Income from immovable property may be taxed in the Contracting State in which such property is situated.
2. (a) The term "immovable property" shall, subject to the provisions of sub-paragraph (b) of this paragraph, be defined in accordance with the law of the Contracting State in which the property in question is situated.
   (b) The term "immovable property" shall in any case include property accessory to immovable property, livestock and equipment used in agriculture and forestry, rights to which the provisions of general law respecting landed property apply, usufruct of immovable property and rights to variable or fixed payment as consideration for the working of, or the right to work, mineral deposits, sources and other natural resources. Ships and aircraft shall not be regarded as immovable property.
3. The provisions of paragraph 1 of this article shall apply to income derived from the direct use, letting, or use in any other form of immovable property.
4. The provisions of paragraphs 1 and 3 of this Article shall also apply to the income from immovable property of an enterprise and to income from immovable property used for the performance of independent personal services.

ARTICLE 7: Business profits

1. The profits of an enterprise of a Contracting State shall be taxable only in that State unless the enterprise carries on business in the other Contracting State through a permanent establishment situated therein. If the enterprise carries on business as aforesaid, the profits of the enterprise may be taxed in the other State, but only so much of them as is directly or indirectly attributable to that permanent establishment.

2. Where an enterprise of a Contracting State carries on business in the other Contracting State through a permanent establishment situated therein, the profits which that permanent establishment might be expected to make if it were a distinct and separate enterprise engaged in the same or similar activities under the same or similar conditions and dealing wholly independently with the enterprise of which it is a permanent establishment shall be treated for the purposes of paragraph 1 of this Article as being the profits directly attributable to that permanent establishment.
3. Where a permanent establishment takes an active part in negotiating, concluding or fulfilling contracts entered into by the enterprise, then, notwithstanding that other parts of the enterprise have also participated in those transactions, that proportion of profits of the enterprise arising out of those contracts which the contribution of the permanent establishment to those transactions bears to that of the enterprise as a whole shall be treated for the purposes of paragraph 1 of this Article as being the profits indirectly attributable to that permanent establishment.
4. Insofar as it has been customary in a Contracting State according to its law to determine the profits to be attributed to a permanent establishment on the basis of an apportionment of the total profits of the enterprise to its various parts, nothing in paragraphs 1 and 2 of this Article shall preclude that Contracting State from determining the profits to be taxed by such an apportionment as may be necessary; the method of apportionment adopted shall, however, be such that the result shall be in accordance with the principles laid down in this Article.
5. Subject to paragraphs 6 and 7 of this Article, in the determination of the profits of a permanent establishment, there shall be allowed as deductions expenses which are incurred for the purposes of the business of the permanent establishment, including executive and general administrative expenses so incurred, whether in the State in which the permanent establishment is situated or elsewhere, which are allowed under the provisions of and subject to the limitations of the domestic law of the Contracting State in which the permanent establishment is situated.
6. Where the law of the Contracting State in which the permanent establishment is situated imposes a restriction on the amount of the executive and general administrative expenses which may be allowed, and the restriction is relaxed or overridden by any Convention between that Contracting State and a third State which is a member of the Organization for Economic Co-operation and Development or a State in a comparable stage of development, and that Convention enters into force after the date of entry into force of this Convention, the competent authority of that Contracting State shall notify the competent authority of the other Contracting State of the terms of the relevant paragraph in the Convention with that third State immediately after the entry into force of that Convention and, if the competent authority of the other Contracting State so requests, the provisions of this Convention shall be amended by protocol to reflect such terms.
7. Paragraph 5 of this article shall not apply to amounts, if any, paid (otherwise than towards reimbursement of actual expenses) by the permanent establishment to the head office of the enterprise or any of its other offices, by way of royalties, fees or

other similar payments in return for the use of patents or other rights, or by way of commission, for specific services performed or for management, or, except in the case of a banking enterprise, by way of interest on monies lent to the permanent establishment; nor shall account be taken in the determination of the profits of a permanent establishment of amounts charged (otherwise than towards reimbursement of actual expenses) by the permanent establishment to the head office of the enterprise or any of its other offices, by way of royalties, fees or other similar payments in return for the use of patents or other rights, or by way of commission, for specific services performed or for management, or, except in the case of a banking enterprise, by way of interest on monies lent to the head office of the enterprise or any of its other offices.

8. No profits shall be attributed to a permanent establishment by reason of the mere purchase by that permanent establishment of goods or merchandise for the enterprise.
9. Where profits include items of income which are dealt with separately in the other Articles of this Convention, then the provisions of those Articles shall not be affected by the provisions of this Article.

Article 8: Air transport

1. Profits derived from the operation of aircraft in international traffic by an enterprise of one of the Contracting States shall not be taxed in the other Contracting State.
2. The provisions of paragraph 1 of this Article shall likewise apply in respect of participation in pools of any kind by enterprises engaged in air transport.
3. For the purposes of this article the term "operation of aircraft" shall include transportation by air of persons, livestock, goods or mail, carried on by the owners or lessees or charterers of aircraft, including the sale of tickets for such transportation on behalf of other enterprises, the incidental lease of aircraft on a charter basis and any other activity directly connected with such transportation.
4. Gains derived by an enterprise of a Contracting State from the alienation of aircraft owned and operated by the enterprise, the income from which is taxable only in that State, shall be taxed only in that State.

ARTICLE 9: Shipping

1. Income of an enterprise of a Contracting State from the operation of ships in international traffic shall be taxable only in that State.
2. The provisions of paragraph 1 of this Article shall not apply to income from journeys between places which are situated in a Contracting State.
3. For the purposes of this article, income from the operation of ships includes income derived from the rental on a bare-boat basis of ships if such rental income is incidental to the income described in paragraph 1 of this Article.
4. Notwithstanding the provisions of Article 7 (Business profits) of this Convention, the provisions of paragraphs 1 and 2 of this Article shall likewise apply to income of an enterprise of a Contracting State from the use, maintenance or rental of containers (including trailers and related equipment for the transport of containers) used for the transport of goods or merchandise.

5. The provisions of this Article shall apply also to income derived from participation in a pool, a joint business or an international operating agency.
6. Gains derived by an enterprise of a Contracting State from the alienation of ships or containers owned and operated by the enterprise shall be taxed only in that State if either the income from the operation of the alienated ships or containers was taxed only in that State, or the ships or containers are situated outside the other Contracting State at the time of the alienation.

ARTICLE 10: Associated enterprises

1. Where:
   (a) an enterprise of a Contracting State participates directly or indirectly in the management, control or capital of an enterprise of the other Contracting State, or
   (b) the same persons participate directly or indirectly in the management, control or capital of an enterprise of a Contracting State and an enterprise of the other Contracting State,

   and in either case conditions are made or imposed between the two enterprises in their commercial or financial relations which differ from those which would be made between independent enterprises, then any profits which would, but for those conditions, have accrued to one of the enterprises, but, by reason of those conditions, have not so accrued, may be included in the profits of that enterprise and taxed accordingly.
2. Where a Contracting State includes in the profits of an enterprise of that State and taxes accordingly profits on which an enterprise of the other Contracting State has been charged to tax in that other State and the profits so included are profits which would have accrued to the enterprise of the first-mentioned State if the conditions made between the two enterprises had been those which would have been made between independent enterprises, then that other State shall make an appropriate adjustment to the amount of the tax charged therein on those profits. In determining such adjustment, due regard shall be had to the other provisions of this Convention and the competent authorities of the Contracting States shall if necessary consult each other.

ARTICLE 11: Dividends

1. (a) A dividend paid by a company which is a resident of the United Kingdom to a resident of India may be taxed in India.
   (b) Where under paragraph 2 of this Article, a resident of India is entitled to a tax credit in respect of that dividend, tax may also be charged in the United Kingdom and according to the laws of the United Kingdom on the aggregate of the amount or value of the dividend and the amount of the tax credit, at a rate not exceeding 15 per cent.
   (c) Except as provided in sub-paragraph (b) of this paragraph, a dividend derived from a company which is a resident of the United Kingdom by a resident of India, who is the beneficial owner of that dividend, shall be exempt from any tax in the United Kingdom which is chargeable on dividends.

2. An individual who is a resident of India and who receives a dividend from a company which is a resident of the United Kingdom shall, provided he is the beneficial owner of the dividend, be entitled to the tax credit in respect of that dividend which an individual resident in the United Kingdom would have been entitled to had he received that dividend, and to the payment of any excess of that tax credit over his liability to United Kingdom tax.
3. A dividend paid by a company which is a resident of India to a resident of the United Kingdom may be taxed in the United Kingdom. The dividend may also be taxed in India but the Indian tax so charged shall not exceed 15 per cent of the gross amount of the dividend.
4. The preceding paragraphs of this Article shall not affect the taxation of the company in respect of the profits out of which the dividend is paid.
5. The provisions of paragraphs 1 and 2 or, as the case may be, paragraph 3 of this Article shall not apply if the beneficial owner of the dividend, being a resident of a Contracting State, has, in the other Contracting State of which the company paying the dividend is a resident, a permanent establishment or fixed base with which the holding by virtue of which the dividend is paid is effectively connected. In such a case the provisions of Article 7 (Business profits) or Article 15 (Independent personal services) of this Convention, as the case may be, shall apply.
6. Where a company which is a resident of a Contracting State derives profits or income from the other Contracting State, that other State may not impose any tax on the dividends paid by the company, except insofar as such dividends are paid to a resident of that other State or in so far as the holding in respect of which the dividends are paid is effectively connected with a permanent establishment or a fixed base situated in that other State, nor subject the company's undistributed profits to a tax on the company's undistributed profits, even if the dividends paid or the undistributed profits consist wholly or partly of profits or income arising in that other State.
7. As used in this Article the term "dividend" means income from shares or other rights, not being debt-claims, participating in profits, as well as income from other corporate rights treated in the same manner as income from shares by the taxation law of the State of which the company making the distribution is a resident and any other item treated as a dividend or distribution under that law.

ARTICLE 12: Interest

1. Interest arising in a Contracting State and paid to a resident of the other Contracting State may be taxed in that other State.
2. However, such interest may also be taxed in the Contracting State in which it arises and according to the law of that State, provided that where the resident of the other Contracting State is the beneficial owner of the interest the tax so charged shall not exceed 15 per cent of the gross amount of the interest.
3. Notwithstanding the provisions of paragraph 2 of this Article:
   (a) where the interest is paid to a bank carrying on a bona fide banking business which is a resident of the other Contracting State and is the beneficial owner

of the interest, the tax charged in the Contracting State in which the interest arises shall not exceed 10 per cent of the gross amount of the interest.

(b) where the interest is paid to the Government of one of the Contracting States or a political sub-division or local authority of that State or the Reserve Bank of India, it shall not be subject to tax by the State in which it arises.

4. Notwithstanding the provisions of Article 7 of this Convention and of paragraphs 2 and 3 of this Article:
   (a) interest arising in India which is paid to and beneficially owned by a resident of the United Kingdom shall be exempt from tax in India if it is paid in respect of a loan made, guaranteed or insured, or any other debt-claim or credit guaranteed or insured by the United Kingdom Export Credits Guarantee Department; and
   (b) interest arising in the United Kingdom which is paid to and beneficially owned by a resident of India shall be exempt from tax in the United Kingdom if it is paid in respect of a loan made, guaranteed or insured, or any other debt-claim or credit guaranteed or insured by the Export Credits and Guarantee Corporation of India and/or Export-Import Bank of India.
5. The term "interest" as used in this Article means income from debt-claims of every kind, whether or not secured by mortgage and whether or not carrying a right to participate in the debtor's profits, and in particular, income from Government securities and income from bonds or debentures, including premiums and prizes attaching to such securities, bonds or debentures but, subject to the provisions of paragraph 9 of this Article, shall not include any item which is treated as a distribution under the provisions of Article 11 (Dividends) of this Convention.
6. The provisions of paragraphs 1, 2 and 3(a) of this Article shall not apply if the beneficial owner of the interest, being a resident of a Contracting State, carries on business in the other Contracting State in which the interest arises through a permanent establishment situated therein, or performs in that other State independent personal services from a fixed base situated therein, and the debt-claim in respect of which the interest is paid is effectively connected with such permanent establishment or fixed base. In such case the provisions of Article 7 (Business profits) or Article 15 (Independent personal services) of this Convention, as the case may be, shall apply.
7. Interest shall be deemed to arise in a Contracting State when the payer is that State itself, a political sub-division, a local authority or a resident of that State. Where, however, the person paying the interest, whether he is a resident of a Contracting State or not, has in a Contracting State a permanent establishment or a fixed base in connection with which the indebtedness on which the interest is paid was incurred, and such interest is borne by that permanent establishment or fixed base, then such interest shall be deemed to arise in the Contracting State in which the permanent establishment or fixed base is situated.
8. Where, owing to a special relationship between the payer and the beneficial owner or between both of them and some other person, the amount of the interest paid exceeds for whatever reason the amount which would have been paid in the absence of such relationship, the provisions of this Article shall apply only to the last-mentioned amount. In that case, the excess part of the payments shall remain taxable according

to the law of each Contracting State, due regard being had to the other provisions of this Convention.

9. Any provision in the laws of either Contracting State relating only to interest paid to a non-resident company shall not operate so as to require such interest paid to a company which is a resident of the other Contracting State to be treated as a distribution or dividend by the company paying such interest or to be left out of account as a deduction in computing the taxable profits of the company paying the interest. The preceding sentence shall not apply to interest paid to a company which is a resident of one of the Contracting States in which more than 50 per cent of the voting power is controlled, directly or indirectly, by a person or persons who are residents of the other Contracting State.
10. The relief from tax provided for in paragraph 2 of this Article shall not apply if the beneficial owner of the interest:
    (a) is exempt from tax on such income in the Contracting State of which he is a resident; and
    (b) sells or makes a contract to sell the holding from which such interest is derived within three months of the date such beneficial owner acquired such holding.
11. The provisions of this Article shall not apply if it was the main purpose or one of the main purposes of any person concerned with the creation or assignment of the debt-claim in respect of which the interest is paid to take advantage of this Article by means of that creation or assignment.

ARTICLE 13: Royalties and fees for technical services

1. Royalties and fees for technical services arising in a Contracting State and paid to a resident of the other Contracting State may be taxed in that other State.
2. However, such royalties and fees for technical services may also be taxed in the Contracting State in which they arise and according to the law of that State; but if the beneficial owner of the royalties or fees for technical services is a resident of the other Contracting State, the tax so charged shall not exceed:
    (a) in the case of royalties within paragraph 3(a) of this Article, and fees for technical services within paragraphs 4(a) and (c) of this Article;
        (i) during the first five years for which this Convention has effect;
            (aa) 15 per cent of the gross amount of such royalties or fees for technical services when the payer of the royalties or fees for technical services is the Government of the first-mentioned Contracting State or a political sub-division of that State, and
            (bb) 20 per cent of the gross amount of such royalties or fees for technical services in all other cases; and
        (ii) during subsequent years, 15 per cent of the gross amount of such royalties or fees for technical services; and
    (b) in the case of royalties within paragraph 3(b) of this Article and fees for technical services defined in paragraph 4(b) of this Article, 10 per cent of the gross amount of such royalties and fees for technical services.

3. For the purposes of this Article, the term "royalties" means
   (a) payments of any kind received as a consideration for the use of, or the right to use, any copyright of a literary, artistic or scientific work, including cinematograph films or work on films, tape or other means of reproduction for use in connection with radio or television broadcasting, any patent, trademark, design or model, plan, secret formula or process, or for information concerning industrial, commercial or scientific experience; and
   (b) payments of any kind received as consideration for the use of, or the right to use, any industrial, commercial or scientific equipment, other than income derived by an enterprise of a Contracting State from the operation of ships or aircraft in international traffic.
4. For the purposes of paragraph 2 of this Article, and subject to paragraph 5 of this Article, the term "fees for technical services" means payments of any kind to any person in consideration for the rendering of any technical or consultancy services (including the provision of services of technical or other personnel) which:
   (a) are ancillary and subsidiary to the application or enjoyment of the right, property or information for which a payment described in paragraph 3(a) of this Article is received; or
   (b) are ancillary and subsidiary to the enjoyment of the property for which a payment described in paragraph 3(b) of this Article is received; or
   (c) make available technical knowledge, experience, skill, know-how or processes, or consist of the development and transfer of a technical plan or technical design.
5. The definitions of fees for technical services in paragraph 4 of this Article shall not include amounts paid:
   (a) for services that are ancillary and subsidiary, as well as inextricably and essentially linked, to the sale of property, other than property described in paragraph 3(a) of this Article;
   (b) for services that are ancillary and subsidiary to the rental of ships, aircraft, containers or other equipment used in connection with the operation of ships, or aircraft in international traffic;
   (c) for teaching in or by educational institutions;
   (d) for services for the private use of the individual or individuals making the payment; or
   (e) to an employee of the person making the payments or to any individual or partnership for professional services as defined in Article 15 (Independent personal services) of this Convention.
6. The provisions of paragraphs 1 and 2 of this Article shall not apply if the beneficial owner of the royalties or fees for technical services, being a resident of a Contracting State, carries on business in the other Contracting State in which the royalties or fees for technical services arise through a permanent establishment situated therein, or performs in that other State independent personal services from a fixed base situated therein, and the right, property or contract in respect of which the royalties or fees for technical services are paid is effectively connected with such permanent establishment

or fixed base. In such case, the provisions of Article 7 (Business profits) or Article 15 (Independent personal services) of this Convention, as the case may be, shall apply.

7. Royalties and fees for technical services shall be deemed to arise in a Contracting State where the payer is that State itself, a political sub-division, a local authority or a resident of that State. Where, however, the person paying the royalties or fees for technical services, whether he is a resident of a Contracting State or not, has in a Contracting State a permanent establishment or a fixed base in connection with which the obligation to make payments was incurred and the payments are borne by that permanent establishment or fixed base then the royalties or fees for technical services shall be deemed to arise in the Contracting State in which the permanent establishment or fixed base is situated.
8. Where, owing to a special relationship between the payer and the beneficial owner or between both of them and some other person, the amount of the royalties or fees for technical services paid exceeds for whatever reason the amount which would have been paid in the absence of such relationship, the provisions of this Article shall apply only to the last-mentioned amount. In that case, the excess part of the payments shall remain taxable according to the law of each Contracting State, due regard being had to the other provisions of this Convention.
9. The provisions of this Article shall not apply if it was the main purpose or one of the main purposes of any person concerned with the creation or assignment of the rights in respect of which the royalties or fees for technical services are paid, to take advantage of this Article by means of that creation or assignment.

ARTICLE 14: Capital gains

Except as provided in Articles 8 (Air transport) and 9 (Shipping) of this Convention, each Contracting State may tax capital gains in accordance with the provisions of its domestic law.

ARTICLE 15: Independent personal services

1. Income derived by an individual, whether in his own capacity or as a member of a partnership, who is a resident of a Contracting State in respect of professional services or other independent activities of a similar character may be taxed in that State. Such income may also be taxed in the other Contracting State if such services are performed in that other State and if:
   (a) he is present in that other State for a period or periods aggregating to 90 days in the relevant fiscal year; or
   (b) he, or the partnership, has a fixed base regularly available to him, or it, in that other State for the purpose of performing his activities;

   but in each case only so much of the income as is attributable to those services.
2. For the purposes of paragraph 1 of this Article an individual who is a member of a partnership shall be regarded as being present in the other State during days on which, although he is not present, another individual member of the partnership is so present and performs professional services or other independent activities of a similar character in that State.

3. The term "professional services" includes independent scientific, literary, artistic, educational or teaching activities as well as the independent activities of physicians, surgeons, lawyers, engineers, architects, dentists and accountants.

ARTICLE 16: Dependent personal services

1. Subject to the provisions of Articles 17 (Directors' fees), 18 (Artistes and athletes), 19 (Governmental remuneration and pensions), 20 (Pensions and annuities), 21 (Students and trainees) and 22 (Teachers) of this Convention, salaries, wages and other similar remuneration derived by a resident of a Contracting State in respect of an employment shall be taxable only in that State unless the employment is exercised in the other Contracting State. If the employment is so exercised, such remuneration as is derived there from may be taxed in that other State.
2. Notwithstanding the provisions of paragraph 1 of this Article, remuneration derived by a resident of a Contracting State in respect of an employment exercised in the other Contracting State shall not be taxed in that other State, if:
   (a) he is present in that other State for a period or periods not exceeding in the aggregate 183 days during the relevant fiscal year;
   (b) the remuneration is paid by, or on behalf of, an employer who is not a resident of that other State; and
   (c) the remuneration is not deductible in computing the profits of an enterprise chargeable to tax in that other State.
3. Notwithstanding the preceding provisions of this Article, remuneration in respect of an employment exercised aboard a ship or aircraft in international traffic may be taxed in the Contracting State of which the person deriving the profits from the operation of the ship or aircraft is a resident.

ARTICLE 17: Directors' fees

Directors' fees and similar payments derived by a resident of a Contracting State in his capacity as a member of the board of directors of a company which is a resident of the other Contracting State may be taxed in that other State.

ARTICLE 18: Artistes and athletes

1. Notwithstanding the provisions of Articles 15 (Independent personal services) and 16 (Dependent personal services) of this Convention, income derived by entertainers (such as stage, motion picture, radio or television artistes and musicians) or athletes, from their personal activities as such may be taxed in the Contracting State in which these activities are exercised.
2. Where income arising from personal activities are such as exercised in a Contracting State by an entertainer or athlete accrues not to that entertainer or athlete himself but to another person, that income may, notwithstanding the provisions of Articles 7 (Business profits), 15 (Independent personal services) and 16 (Dependent personal services) of this convention, be taxed in that Contracting State.
3. The provisions of paragraphs 1 and 2 of this Article shall not apply if the visit to a Contracting State of the entertainer or the athlete is directly or indirectly supported,

wholly or substantially, from the public funds of the other Contracting State, including a political sub-division or local authority of that other State.

ARTICLE 19: Governmental remuneration and pensions

1. Remuneration, other than a pension, paid by the Government of a Contracting State to any individual who is a national of that State in respect of services rendered in the discharge of governmental functions in the other Contracting State shall be exempt from tax in that other Contracting State.
2. Any pension paid by the Government of a Contracting State to any individual in respect of services rendered to that Government shall be taxable only in that Contracting State.
3. The provisions of this Article shall not apply to remuneration or pensions in respect of services rendered in connection with any trade or business.

ARTICLE 20: Pensions and annuities

1. Any pension, other than a pension referred to in Article 19(2) of this Convention, or annuity paid to a resident of a Contracting State shall be taxable only in that State.
2. The term "pension" means a periodic payment made in consideration of past employment or by way of compensation for injuries received in the course of performance of employment or any payments made under the social security legislation of either Contracting State.
3. The term "annuity" means a stated sum payable periodically at stated times during life or during a specified or ascertainable period of time under an obligation to make the payments in return for adequate and full consideration in money or money's worth.

ARTICLE 21: Students and trainees

1. An individual who is a resident of a Contracting State or was a resident of that State immediately before visiting the other Contracting State and who is temporarily present in that other State for the primary purpose of:
   (a) studying at a university or other accredited or recognized educational institution in that other Contracting State; or
   (b) securing training required to qualify him to practice a profession or a professional specialty; or
   (c) studying or doing research as a recipient of a grant, allowance, or award from a governmental, religious, charitable, scientific, literary or educational organization;

   shall not be subject to tax by that other Contracting State in respect of:
      (i) gifts from abroad for the purposes of his maintenance, education, study, research or training;
      (ii) the grant, allowance or award; an
      (iii) income from personal services rendered in that other Contracting State (other than any rendered by an articled clerk or other person undergoing professional training to the person or partnership to whom he is articled or who is providing the training) not exceeding the sum of 750 pounds sterling or its equivalent in Indian currency during any fiscal year.

2. The exemptions under paragraph 1 of this Article shall only extend for such period of time as may be reasonably or customarily required for the purpose of the visit, but in no event shall any individual have the benefit of paragraph 1 of this Article for more than five years.
3. An individual who is a resident of a Contracting State or was a resident of that State immediately before visiting the other Contracting State and who is temporarily present in that other State for a period not exceeding 12 months, as an employee of, or under contract with, a resident of the first-mentioned Contracting State, for the primary purpose of:
   (a) acquiring technical, professional or business experience from a person other than that resident of the first-mentioned Contracting State; or
   (b) studying at a university or other accredited or recognized institution in that other Contracting State;

   shall not be subject to tax by that other Contracting State on his income from personal services performed in the other Contracting State for that period in an amount not exceeding 1,500 pounds sterling or its equivalent in Indian currency.
4. An individual who is a resident of a Contracting State or was a resident of that State immediately before visiting the other Contracting State and who is temporarily present in that other State for a period not exceeding 12 months as a participant in a programme sponsored by the Government of the other Contracting State, for the primary purpose of training, research or study, shall not be subject to tax by that other Contracting State in respect of payments made by the Government of the first-mentioned Contracting State for the purposes of his maintenance, training, research, or study.

ARTICLE 22: Teachers

1. An individual who visits a Contracting State for a period not exceeding two years for the purpose of teaching or engaging in research at a university, college or other recognized educational institution in that State, and who was immediately before that visit a resident of the other Contracting State, shall be exempted from tax by the first-mentioned Contracting State on any remuneration for such teaching or research for a period not exceeding two years from the date he first visits that State for such purpose.
2. This Article shall only apply to income from research if such research is undertaken by the individual in the public interest and not primarily for the benefit of some other private person or persons.

ARTICLE 23: Other income

1. Subject to the provisions of paragraph 2 of this Article, items of income beneficially owned by a resident of a Contracting State, wherever arising, other than income paid out of trusts or the estates of deceased persons in the course of administration, which are not dealt with in the foregoing Articles of this Convention, shall be taxable only in that State.
2. The provisions of paragraph 1 shall not apply to income, other than income from immovable property as defined in paragraph 2 of Article 6, if the recipient of such

income, being a resident of a Contracting State, carries on business in the other Contracting State through a permanent establishment situated therein, or performs in that other State independent personal services from a fixed base situated therein, and the right or property in respect of which the income is paid is effectively connected with such permanent establishment on fixed base. In such case, the provisions of Article 7 or Article 15 of this Convention, as the case may be, shall apply.

3. Notwithstanding the provisions of paragraphs 1 and 2 of this Article, items of income of a resident of a Contracting State not dealt with in the foregoing articles of this Convention, and arising in the other Contracting State may be taxed in that other State.

ARTICLE 24: Elimination of double taxation

1. Subject to the provisions of the law of the United Kingdom regarding the allowance as a credit against United Kingdom tax of tax payable in a territory outside the United Kingdom (which shall not affect the general principle hereof):
   (a) Indian tax payable under the laws of India and in accordance with the provisions of this Convention, whether directly or by deduction, on profits, income or chargeable gains from sources within India (excluding, in the case of a dividend, tax payable in respect of the profits out of which the dividend is paid) shall be allowed as a credit against any United Kingdom tax computed by reference to the same profits, income or chargeable gains by reference to which the Indian tax is computed.
   (b) In the case of a dividend paid by a company which is a resident of India to a company which is a resident of the United Kingdom and which controls directly or indirectly at least 10 per cent of the voting power in the company paying the dividend, the credit shall take into account (in addition to any Indian tax for which credit may be allowed under the provisions of sub-paragraph (a) of this paragraph) the Indian tax payable by the company in respect of the profits out of which such dividend is paid.
2. Subject to the provisions of the law of India regarding the allowance as a credit against Indian tax of tax paid in a territory outside India (which shall not affect the general principle hereof), the amount of the United Kingdom tax paid, under the laws of the United Kingdom and in accordance with the provisions of this Convention, whether directly or by deduction, by a resident of India, in respect of income from sources within the United Kingdom which has been subjected to tax both in India and the United Kingdom shall be allowed as a credit against the Indian tax payable in respect of such income but in an amount not exceeding that proportion of Indian tax which such income bears to the entire income chargeable to Indian tax.
   For the purposes of the credit referred to in this paragraph, where the resident of India is a company by which surtax is payable, the credit to be allowed against Indian tax shall be allowed in the first instance against the income-tax payable by the company in India and, as to the balance, if any, against the surtax payable by it in India.
3. Subject to paragraph 5 of this Article, for the purposes of paragraph 1 of this Article the term "Indian tax payable" shall be deemed to include:

(a) any amount which would have been payable as Indian tax but for a deduction allowed in computing the taxable income or an exemption or reduction of tax granted for that year in question under the provisions of the Income-tax Act, 1961 (43 of 1961), referred to in paragraph 4(a) or (b) of this Article;

(b) that proportion of any amount which would have been payable as Indian tax by a resident of India but for a deduction allowed in computing the taxable income or an exemption or reduction granted for the year in question under the provisions of the Income-tax Act, 1961 (43 of 1961) referred to in paragraph 4(c) of this Article which corresponds to the proportion of that resident's total production in that year which was actually sold in the Indian Domestic Tariff Area under Orders issued by the Chief Controller of Imports and Exports bearing Nos. 21/90-93, 22/ 90-93, 23/90-93, 25/90-93, 26/90-93, 27/90-93 dated 30th March, 1990, and similar Orders from time to time published in the Official Gazette by the Central Government under power conferred on it by section 3 of the Import and Export (Control) Act, 1947 (18 of 1947).

4. The provisions referred to in this paragraph are:
   (a) Sections 10(4), 10(4B), 10(6)(viia), 10(15)(iv), 33AB, 80HHD, 80-I and 80-IA;
   (b) any other provision which may subsequently be enacted granting an exemption or reduction from tax which is agreed by the competent authorities of the Contracting States to be of a substantially similar character to a provision referred to in sub-paragraph (a) of this paragraph, if it has not been modified thereafter or has been modified only in minor respects so as not to affect its general character:
   (c) sections 10A and 10B.
5. Relief from United Kingdom tax shall not be given by virtue of this paragraph 3 of this Article in respect of income from any source if the income relates to a period starting more than 10 fiscal years after the deduction in computing taxable income or exemption from, or reduction of, Indian tax is first granted to the resident of the United Kingdom or to the resident of India, as the case may be, in respect of that source.
6. Income which in accordance with the provisions of this Convention is not to be subjected to tax in a Contracting State may be taken into account for calculating the rate of tax to be imposed in that Contracting State on other income.
7. For the purposes of paragraphs 1 and 2 of this Article profits, income and chargeable gains owned by a resident of a Contracting State which may be taxed in the other Contracting State in accordance with the provisions of this Convention shall be deemed to arise from sources in that other Contracting State.

ARTICLE 25: Partnerships

1. Where, under any provision of this Convention, a partnership is entitled, as a resident of India, to exemption from tax in the United Kingdom on any income or capital gains, that provision shall not be construed as restricting the right of the United Kingdom to tax any member of the partnership who is a resident of the United Kingdom on his share of the income and capital gains of the partnership; but any such income or

gains shall be treated for the purposes of Article 24 of this Convention as income or gains from sources in India.

2. Nothing in Article 2 of this Convention shall entitle a partnership which is a resident of India to a tax credit in respect of dividends paid to the partnership by a company which is a resident of the United Kingdom; but any member of the partnership who is a resident of India shall be regarded as entitled to the tax credit to which he would have been entitled under that Article, if his share of those dividends has been paid to him by the company which is a resident of the United Kingdom.

ARTICLE 26: Non-discrimination

1. The nationals of a Contracting State shall not be subjected in the other Contracting State to any taxation or any requirement connected therewith which is other or more burdensome than the taxation and connected requirements to which nationals of that other State in the same circumstances are or may be subjected.
2. The taxation on a permanent establishment which an enterprise of a Contracting State has in the other Contracting State shall not be less favourably levied in that other State than the taxation levied on enterprises of that other State carrying on the same activities in the same circumstances or under the same conditions. This provision shall not be construed as preventing a Contracting State from charging the profits of a permanent establishment which an enterprise of the other Contracting State has in the first-mentioned State at a rate of tax which is higher than that imposed on the profits of a similar enterprise of the first-mentioned Contracting State, nor as being in conflict with the provisions of paragraph 4 of Article 7 of this Convention.
3. Nothing contained in this Article shall be construed as obliging a Contracting State to grant to individuals not resident in that State any personal allowances, reliefs and reductions for taxation purposes which are bye-law available only to individuals who are so resident.
4. Enterprises of a Contracting State, the capital of which is wholly or partly owned or controlled, directly or indirectly, by one or more residents of the other Contracting State, shall not be subjected in the first-mentioned Contracting State to any taxation or any requirement connected therewith which is other or more burdensome than the taxation and connected requirements to which other similar enterprises of that first-mentioned State are or may be subjected.
5. In this Article, the term "taxation" means taxes which are the subject of this Convention.

ARTICLE 27: Mutual agreement procedure

1. Where a resident of a Contracting State considers that the actions of one or both of the Contracting States result or will result for him in taxation not in accordance with this Convention, he may, notwithstanding the remedies provided by the national laws of those States, present his case to the competent authority of the Contracting State of which he is a resident.
2. The competent authority shall endeavour, if the objection appears to it to be justified and if it is not itself able to arrive at an appropriate solution, to resolve the case by

mutual agreement with the competent authority of the other Contracting State, with a view to the avoidance of taxation not in accordance with the Convention.

3. The competent authorities of the Contracting States shall endeavour to resolve by mutual agreement any difficulties or doubts arising as to the interpretation or application of the Convention.
4. The competent authorities of the Contracting States may communicate with each other directly for the purpose of reaching an agreement in the sense of the preceding paragraphs.

ARTICLE 28: Exchange of information

1. The competent authorities of the Contracting States shall exchange such information as is necessary for carrying out the provisions of this Convention or of the domestic laws of the Contracting States concerning taxes covered by this Convention, insofar as the taxation thereunder is not contrary to this Convention, in particular for the prevention of fraud or evasion of such taxes. The exchange of information is not restricted by Article 1 of this Convention. Any information received by a Contracting State shall be treated as secret in the same manner as information obtained under the domestic laws of that State. However, if the information is originally regarded as secret in the transmitting State it shall be disclosed only to persons or authorities (including courts and administrative bodies) involved in the assessment or collection of the enforcement or prosecution in respect of, or the determination of appeals in relation to, the taxes which are the subject of this Convention. Such persons or authorities shall use the information only for such purposes but may disclose the information in public court proceedings or in judicial decisions. The competent authorities shall, through consultation, develop appropriate conditions, methods and techniques concerning the matters in respect of which such exchanges of information shall be made, including where appropriate, exchanges of information regarding tax avoidance.
2. In no case, shall the provisions of paragraph 1 of this Article be construed so as to impose on a Contracting State the obligation:
   (a) to carry out administrative measures at variance with the laws and administrative practice of that or of the other Contracting State;
   (b) to supply information which is not obtainable under the laws or in the normal course of the administration of that or of the other Contracting State;
   (c) to supply information which would disclose any trade, business, industrial, commercial or professional secret or trade process, or information, the disclosure of which would be contrary to public policy.

ARTICLE 29: Diplomatic and consular officials

1. Nothing in this Convention shall affect the fiscal privileges of diplomatic or consular officials under the general rules of international law or under the provisions of special agreements.
2. Notwithstanding the provisions of paragraph 1 of Article 4 (fiscal domicile) of this Convention, an individual who is a member of the diplomatic, consular or permanent mission of a Contracting State which is situated in the other Contracting State and

who is subject to tax in that other State only if he derives income from sources therein, shall not be deemed to be a resident of that other State for the purposes of this Convention.

ARTICLE 30: Entry into force

1. Each of the Contracting States shall notify to the other the completion of the procedures required by its law for the bringing into force of this Convention. This Convention shall enter into force on the date of the later of these notifications and shall thereupon have effect:
   (a) in the United Kingdom:
      (i) in respect of income-tax and capital gains tax, for any year of assessment beginning on or after 6th April, in the calendar year next following that in which the later of the notifications is given;
      (ii) in respect of corporation tax, for any financial year beginning on or after 1st April, in the calendar year next following that in which the later of the notifications is given;
      (iii) in respect of petroleum revenue tax, for any chargeable period beginning on or after 1st January, in the calendar year next following that in which the later of the notifications is given;
   (b) in India, in respect of income arising in any fiscal year beginning on or after the first day of April, next following the calendar year in which the later of the notifications is given.
2. Subject to the provisions of paragraph 3 of this Article, the Convention between the Government of the United Kingdom of Great Britain and Northern Ireland and the Government of India for the Avoidance of Double Taxation and the Prevention of Fiscal Evasion with Respect to Taxes on Income and Capital Gains signed in New Delhi on 16th April, 1981 (hereinafter referred to as "the 1981 Convention"), shall terminate and cease to be effective from the date upon which this Convention has effect in respect of the taxes to which this Convention applies in accordance with the provisions of paragraph 1 of this Article.
3. Where any provisions of the 1981 Convention would have afforded any greater relief from tax than is due under this Convention, any such provision as aforesaid shall continue to have effect:
   (a) in the United Kingdom, for any year of assessment or financial year; and
   (b) in India, for any fiscal year;

   beginning, in either case, before the entry into force of this Convention.

ARTICLE 31: Termination

This Convention shall remain in force until terminated by one of the Contracting States. Either Contracting State may terminate the Convention, through the diplomatic channel, by giving notice of termination at least six months before the end of any calendar year beginning after the expiration of ten years from the date of entry into force of the Convention. In such event, the Convention shall cease to have effect:

(a) in the United Kingdom:

(i) in respect of income-tax and capital gains tax, for any year of assessment beginning on or after 6th April, in the calendar year next following that in which the notice is given;

(ii) in respect of corporation tax, for any financial year beginning on or after 1st April, in the calendar year next following that in which the notice is given;

(iii) in respect of petroleum revenue tax, for any chargeable period beginning on or after 1st January, in the calendar year next following that in which the notice is given;

(b) in India, in respect of income arising in any fiscal year beginning on or after the first day of April, next following the calendar year in which the notice is given.

In witness whereof the undersigned, duly authorised thereto by their respective Governments, have signed this Convention.

Done on this 25th day of January, 1993, in New Delhi on two original copies each in the Hindi and English languages, both texts being equally authentic. In case of divergence between the two texts, the English text shall be the operative one.

For the Government of the United Kingdom, Republic of India, Great Britain and Northern Ireland.

(Sd.) (Sd.)
NICHOLAS FENN S. RAMAMURTI
BRITISH HIGH COMMISSION, NEW DELHI, JANUARY 25, 1993

Your Excellency:

I have the honour to refer to the Convention between the Government of the United Kingdom of Great Britain and Northern Ireland and the Government of the Republic of India for the Avoidance of Double Taxation and the Prevention of Fiscal Evasion with respect to Taxes on Income and Capital Gains which has been signed today and to propose on behalf of the Government of the United Kingdom of Great Britain and Northern Ireland:

(a) that, in applying sub-paragraph (j) of paragraph 2 of Article 5, for the purpose of determining whether a building site or construction, installation or assembly project or supervisory activity in connection therewith has continued for a period of more than six months, the Contracting States shall:

(i) take no account of time previously spent by employees of the enterprise on other sites or projects which have no connection with the site or project in question;

(ii) apply the more than six months test separately to each site or project which has no connection with any other site or project and to each group of connected sites or projects; and

(iii) regard a building site as a single site, even if several contracts have been entered into for the work being done, provided that it forms a coherent whole commercially and geographically;

(b) that, in applying paragraph 3 of Article 7, for the purpose of determining whether a permanent establishment has taken an active part in negotiating, concluding or fulfilling contracts entered into by the enterprise, the Contracting States shall take into consideration all relevant circumstances and, in particular, the fact that a contract or order relating to the purchase or provision of goods or services was negotiated or placed with the head office of the enterprise, rather than with the permanent establishment, shall not preclude them from determining that the permanent establishment did take an active part in negotiating, concluding or fulfilling that contract;

(c) that, in applying paragraph 1 of Article 8, for the purpose of determining the profits of an enterprise which are derived from the operation of aircraft in international traffic, the Contracting States shall treat interest derived from the investment or deposit of receipts arising directly from the operation of aircraft in international traffic as being included in those profits, but shall not treat interest derived from the reinvestment of such interest as being so included.

If the foregoing proposal is acceptable to the Government of the Republic of India I have the honour to suggest that the present Note and Your Excellency's reply to that effect should be regarded as constituting an agreement between the two Governments in this matter.

I avail myself of this opportunity to renew to Your Excellency the assurances of my highest consideration.

(Sd.)

Nicholas Fenn, High Commissioner.
His Excellency Mr. S. Ramamurti,
Chairman, Central Board of Direct Taxes,
Ministry of Finance, Government of India, New Delhi.
GOVERNMENT OF INDIA
MINISTRY OF FINANCE
(DEPARTMENT OF REVENUE)
CENTRAL BOARD OF DIRECT TAXES,
NEW DELHI, JANUARY 25, 1993.

Your Excellency:

I have the honour to acknowledge receipt of Your Excellency's Note of today which reads as follows:

"I have the honour to refer to the Convention between the Government of the United Kingdom of Great Britain and Northern Ireland and the Government of the Republic of India for the Avoidance of Double Taxation and the Prevention of Fiscal Evasion with respect to Taxes on Income and Capital Gains which has been signed today and to propose on behalf of the Government of the United Kingdom of Great Britain and Northern Ireland:

(a) that, in applying sub-paragraph (j) of paragraph 2 of Article 5, for the purpose of determining whether a building site or construction, installation or assembly project or supervisory activity in connection therewith has continued for a period of more than six months, the Contracting States shall:

   (i) take no account of time previously spent by employees of the enterprise on other sites or projects which have no connection with the site or project in question;

   (ii) apply the more than six months test separately to each site or project which has no connection with any other site or project and to each group of connected sites or projects; and

(iii) regard a building site as a single site, even if several contracts have been entered into for the work being done, provided that it forms a coherent whole commercially and geographically;

(b) that, in applying paragraph 3 of Article 7, for the purpose of determining whether a permanent establishment has taken in active part in negotiating, concluding or fulfilling contracts entered into by the enterprise, the Contracting States shall take into consideration all relevant circumstances and, in particular, the fact that a contract or other relating to the purchase or provision of goods or services was negotiated or placed with the head office of the enterprise, rather than with the permanent establishment, shall not preclude them from determining that the permanent establishment did take an active part in negotiating, concluding or fulfilling that contract

(c) that, in applying paragraph 1 of Article 8, for the purpose of determining the profits of an enterprise which are derived from the operation of aircraft in international traffic, the Contracting States shall treat interest derived from the investment or deposit of receipts arising directly from the operation of aircraft in international traffic as being included in those profits, but shall not treat interest derived from the reinvestment of such interest as being so included.

If the foregoing proposal is acceptable to the Government of the Republic of India I have the honour to suggest that the present Note and Your Excellency's reply to that effect should be regarded as constituting an agreement between the two Governments in this matter."

In reply, I have the honour to state that the Government of the Republic of India accepts the proposal made therein and agrees that Your Excellency's Note and the present reply shall constitute an agreement between the Government of the Republic of India and the Government of the United Kingdom of Great Britain and Northern Ireland in this matter.

I avail myself of this opportunity to renew to Your Excellency the assurances of my highest consideration.

(Sd.)

S. Ramamurti, Chairman, Central Board of Direct Taxes, India. His Excellency Sir Nicholas Fenn

British High Commissioner In India New Delhi.

(Sd.)

V. B. Srinivasan, Joint Secretary to the Government of India.

No. 9475/FN 505/3/86-FTD

Agreement for avoidance of double taxation and prevention of fiscal evasion with respect to duties on estates of deceased persons with United Kingdom of Great Britain text of agreement dated 3rd April, 1956 referred to above.

In exercise of the powers conferred by section 30 of the Estate Duty Act, 1953 (34 of 1953), the Central Government hereby fixes the 30th June, 1956, as the date on which the Agreement, dated the 3rd April, 1956, entered into between Government of India and the Government of the United Kingdom of Great Britain and Northern Ireland for the avoidance of double taxation and prevention of fiscal evasion with respect to duties on the estates of deceased persons and annexed hereto shall come into force.

[Notification: No. 38 ED, dated the 30th June, 1956]

ANNEXURE

The Government of India and the Government of the United Kingdom of Great Britain and Northern Ireland, desiring to conclude an Agreement for the avoidance of double taxation and the prevention of fiscal evasion with respect to duties on the estates of deceased persons, have agreed as follows:

ARTICLE I

The duties which are the subject of the present Agreement are:

(a) In India, the estate duty imposed under the Estate Duty Act, 1953 (34 of 1953); and

(b) In the United Kingdom, the estate duty imposed in Great Britain.

ARTICLE II

(1) In the present Agreement, unless the context otherwise requires,

- (a) the term 'India' means all the States and territories in the Union of India;
- (b) the term 'United Kingdom' means Great Britain and Northern Ireland;
- (c) the term 'Great Britain' means England, Wales and Scotland and does not include the Channel Islands and the Isle of Man;
- (d) the term 'territory' when used in relation to one of the other Contracting Govern ment means India or Great Britain, as the context requires;
- (e) the term 'duty' means the estate duty imposed in India or the estate duty imposed in Great Britain as the context requires.

(2) For the purposes of the present Agreement, the question where a deceased person was at the time of his death domiciled in any part of the territory of one of the Contracting Governments shall be determined in accordance with the law in force in that territory.

(3) In the application of the provisions of the present Agreement by either Contracting Government, any term not otherwise defined shall, unless the context otherwise requires, have the meaning which it has under the law of that Contracting Governments relating to duty.

ARTICLE III

(1) Subject to paragraph (2) of this Article, duty shall not be imposed in India on the death of a person who was not domiciled at the time of his death in any part of India but was domiciled in some part of Great Britain on any property situate outside India:

Provided that nothing in this paragraph shall prevent the imposition of duty in India on:

- (a) any settled property of which the deceased was life tenant where the settlor was domiciled in India at the time the settlement took effect; or
- (b) property that passes under a disposition or devolution regulated by the law of some part of India.

(2) Nothing in the present Agreement shall affect any provision of the law of India imposing duty on shares in or debentures of a company incorporated outside India

which carries on business in India and which has been treated for the purposes of the Indian Income-tax Act, 1922 (11 of 1922), as resident in India for two out of the three completed assessments immediately preceding the death; nor shall anything in the present Agreement be considered to confer a right to a credit against duty so imposed for any duty imposed in Great Britain on any such shares or debentures.

(3) Duty shall not be imposed in Great Britain on the death of a person who was not domiciled at the time of his death in any part of Great Britain but was domiciled in some part of India on any property situated outside Great Britain:

Provided that nothing in this paragraph shall prevent the imposition of duty in Great Britain on any property which passes under a disposition or devolution regulated by the law of some part of Great Britain.

ARTICLE IV

(1) Subject to paragraph (2) of this Article, where a person was at the time of his death domiciled in any part of the territory of one of the Contracting Governments, the suits of any property which for the purposes of duty passes or is deemed to pass on his death shall, for the purposes of the imposition of duty and of the credit to be allowed under Article VI, be determined exclusively in accordance with the rules in Article V of the present Agreement.

(2) Paragraph (1) of this Article shall apply if, and only if, apart from the said Article V:

  (a) duty would be imposed on the property under the law of each of the Contracting Governments; or

  (b) duty would be imposed on the property under the law of one of the Contracting Governments and would, but for some specific exemption, also be imposed thereon under the law of the other Contracting Government.

ARTICLE V

The rules referred to in paragraph (1) of Article IV are:-

(a) Rights or interests (otherwise than by way of security) in or over immovable property shall be deemed to be situated at the place where such property is located.

(b) Rights or interests (otherwise than by way of security) in or over tangible movable property other than such property for which specific provision is hereinafter made, and in or over bank or currency notes, other forms of currency recognised as legal tender in the place of issue, negotiable bills of exchange and negotiable promissory notes, shall be deemed to be situated at the place where such property, notes, currency or documents are located at the time of death of the deceased person or if in transit, at the place of destination.

(c) Debts, secured or unsecured and whether under seal or not, excluding the forms of indebtedness for which specific provision is made therein, shall be deemed to be situated at the place where the debtor was residing at the time of death of the deceased person:

Provided that, if the interest on any such debt was chargeable to income-tax under the Indian Income-tax Act, 1922 (11 of 1922), as having accrued or arisen in India, the debt shall be deemed to be situated in India.

(d) Bank accounts shall be deemed to be situated at the branch at which the account was kept.

(e) Securities issued by any Government or by any local or public authority shall be deemed, if in bearer form, to be situated at the place where they were located at the time of the deceased's death and if inscribed or registered, at the place of inscription or registration:

Provided that sterling securities issued by the Government of India or of any State in India, or by any local or public authority in India, shall be deemed to be situated in the territory in which the deceased was domiciled at the time of his death;

(f) Shares, stocks, debentures or debentures stock in a company (including any such property held by a nominee, whether the beneficial ownership in evidenced by scrip certificates or otherwise) shall be deemed to be situated at the place where the company was incorporated.

(g) Moneys payable under a policy of assurance or insurance, whether under seal or not, shall be deemed to be situated at the place where the policy provides that the moneys shall be payable or, in the absence of any such provision, at the head office of the company issuing the policy.

(h) An interest in a partnership shall be deemed to be situated at the place where the business is carried on; and if the business is carried on at more than one place an appropriate proportion of the interest shall be deemed to be situated at each of those places.

(i) Goodwill as a trade business of professional asset shall be deemed to be situated at the place where the trade, business or profession to which it pertains is carried on; and if a trade, business or profession is carried on at more than one place an appropriate proportion of the goodwill shall be deemed to be situated at each of those places.

(j) Ships and aircrafts and shares thereof shall be deemed to be situated at the place of registration of the ship of aircraft.

(k) Patents, trademarks and designs shall be deemed to be situated at the place where they are registered.

(l) Copyright, franchises and rights or licences to use any copyrighted material, patent trade mark or design shall be deemed to be situated at the place where the rights arising therefrom are exercisable.

(m) Rights or causes of action *ex-delicto* surviving for the benefits of the estate of a deceased person shall be deemed to be situated at the place where such rights or causes of action arose.

(n) A judgment debt shall be deemed to be situated where the judgment is recorded:

Provided that where the judgment was given in proceedings instituted to enforce a debt which, had it passed on the death, would have fallen within paragraph (c) of this Article, the judgment debt shall be deemed to be situated where that debt would have been situated;

(o) Any other right or interest shall:

(i) where the deceased person was domiciled at the date of his death in the territory of only one of the Contracting Governments, be deemed to be situated at the place determined by the law in force in the territory of the other Contracting Government;

(ii) where the deceased person was domiciled at the date of his death in the territory of both Contracting Governments, be deemed to be situated:

(aa) for the purposes of the imposition of duty in India, at the place determined by the law in force in India, and

(bb) for the purposes of the imposition of duty in Great Britain, at the place determined by the law in force in England or Scotland, as the case may be.

ARTICLE VI

(1) Where one Contracting Government imposes duty on any property which is not situated in its territory but is situated in the territory of the other Contracting Government, the former Government shall allow against so much of its duty (as otherwise computed) as is attributable to that property a credit (not exceeding the amount of the duty so attributable) equal to so much of the duty imposed in the territory of the other Contracting Government as is attributable to such property.

(2) Where each Contracting Government imposes duty on any property which is situated:

(a) in the territory of both Governments, or

(b) outside both territories,

each Government shall allow against so much of its duty (as otherwise computed) as is attributable to that property a credit which bears the same proportion to the amount of its duty so attributable or to the amount of the other Contracting Government's duty attributable to the same property, whichever is the less, as the former amount bears to the sum of both amounts.

(3) For the purposes of this Article, the amount of the duty of a Contracting Government attributable to any property shall be ascertained after taking into account any credit, allowance or relief, or any remission or reduction of duty, otherwise than in respect of duty payable in the territory of the other Contracting Government.

ARTICLE VII

(1) Any claim for a credit or for a refund of duty founded on the provisions of the present Agreement shall be made with six years from the date of death of the deceased person in respect of whose estate the claim is made, or, in the case of a reversionary interest where payment of duty is deferred until the date on which the interest falls into possession within six years from that date.

(2) Any such credit allowed or refund made shall be allowed or made without payment of interest on the amount credited or refunded.

ARTICLE VIII

(1) The taxation authorities of the Contracting Governments shall exchange such information (being information available under the respective taxation laws of the Contracting Governments) as is necessary for carrying out the provisions of the

present Agreement or for the prevention of fraud or the administration of statutory provisions against legal avoidance in relation to the duties which are the subject of the present Agreement. Any information so exchanged shall be treated as secret and shall not be disclosed to any person other than those concerned with the administration, assessment and collection of the duties which are the subject of the present Agreement. No information shall be exchanged which might disclose any trade secret or trade process.

(2) As used in this Article, the term 'taxation authorities' means:
   (a) in the case of India, the Central Board of Revenue or their authorized representative;
   (b) in the case of Great Britain, the Commissioners of Inland Revenue or their authorized representative;
   (c) in the case of Northern Ireland (to which the present Agreement applies under Article X), the Minister of Finance or his authorised representative;
   (d) in the case of any territory to which the present Agreement is extended under Article IX, the competent authority for the administration in such territory of the duties to which the present Agreement applies.

ARTICLE IX

(1) The present Agreement may be extended, either in its entirety or with modifications, to any territory for whose international relations the United Kingdom is responsible and which imposes duties substantially similar in character to those which are the subject of the present Agreement, and any such extension, shall take effect from such date and subject to such modifications and conditions (including conditions as to termination) as may be specified and agreed between the Contracting Governments in notes to be exchanged for this purpose.

(2) The termination in respect of India or the United Kingdom of the present Agreement under Article XII shall, unless otherwise expressly agreed by the Contracting Governments, terminate the application of the Agreement to any territory to which it has been extended under this Article.

ARTICLE X

The present Agreement shall apply in relation to the estate duty imposed in Northern Ireland as it applies in relation to the estate duty in Great Britain, but shall be separately terminable in respect of Northern Ireland by the same procedure as is laid down in Article XII.

ARTICLE XI

The present Agreement shall come into force on the date on which the last of all such things shall have been done in India and the United Kingdom as are necessary to give the Agreement the force of law in India and the United Kingdom, respectively, and the Agreement shall be effective only as to:

(a) the estates of persons dying on or after such date; and
(b) the estate of any person dying before such date and after the 15th October, 1953,

where the accountable person elects that the provisions of the present Agreement shall be applied to such estate.

ARTICLE XII

(1) The present Agreement shall remain in force for not less than three years after the date of its coming into force.

(2) If, not less than six months before the expiration of such period of three years, neither of the Contracting Governments shall have given to the other Contracting Government written notice through diplomatic channels of its intention to terminate the present Agreement, the Agreement shall remain in force after such period of three years until either of the Contracting Governments shall have given written notice of such intention, in which event the present Agreement shall not be effective as to the estates of persons dying on or after the date (not being earlier than the sixtieth day after the date of such notice) specified in such notice, or, if no date is specified, on or after the sixtieth day after the date of such notice.

In witness whereof the undersigned, duly authorized thereto, have signed the present Agreement.

Done at New Delhi, in duplicate, the 3rd Day of April, 1956.

Source: *Taxman website*

11

International Financial Management
An Overview

LEARNING OBJECTIVES

After studying this chapter, you will be able to:

- Understand the concept of international financial management
- Know the scope of international financial management
- Appreciate the functions of international finance
- Identify the role of international finance manager
- Differentiate between international financial management and domestic financial management

INTRODUCTION

The increased pace of globalization of business activities coupled with integration of national economy with world economy, and enhanced interdependence of countries for factors of production have lead to the development of international financial management as a separate and distinct branch of study today. With the WTO in place, international trade has registered an exponential growth during the turn of the twentieth century. The aggregate world export, for example, has increased from 59.6 billion USD in 1950 to 10239.8 billion USD in 2005 and to 1214 billion USD in 2010. Countries worldwide, including the developing ones such as India have joined the world trade more vigorously with the exchange of goods, services, capital, technology and management know-how than ever before thus contributing to the integration of national economy with the world economy. The commitments made by countries to the WTO on removal of trade barriers and as the resultant fall out leading to slashing of import restrictions by countries on the quantity; lowering of duties; and persuasion of policies to favour foreign direct investment (FDI) and foreign portfolio investment (FPI), have all resulted in dismantling of national boundaries in relation to trade and commerce, increased economic activities the world over, and the emergence of multinational corporations (MNC) with production and distribution centre spread across nations. Along with the growth in world trade, there has also been a significant innovation in the international credit and settlement system. Given the above, any talk on finance today by finance managers in general and of the MNCs in particular has to be in the line of a complex mechanism of international financial institutions, instruments and markets rather than in the line of the erstwhile domestic financial institutions, instruments and markets which by and large used to operate in a more protected environment.

CONCEPT OF INTERNATIONAL FINANCIAL MANAGEMENT

International financial management, also known as multinational financial management, refers to the *management of financial functions that are related to international trade and business*. 'International financial management is concerned with the management of international business related financial functions, commonly known as the international financial functions' [1] The international business related financial functions include, among others, recording of international (foreign) financial transactions; exchange rate forecasts; measurement and management of foreign exchange exposure; international investment decisions including foreign direct investment, foreign portfolio investment; management of political risk; international working capital management; international financial and monetary system, international taxation and derivatives market.

'The management of financial resources in the context of international business transactions is referred to as international financial management'. [2] A transaction, in relation to importing, exporting, foreign borrowings and lending, and forward contracts, taking place between parties belonging to two different countries, is said to be an international (business) transaction. International Accounting Standard (IAS) 21 provides that foreign transactions occur when an enterprise (a) buys or sells on credit goods or services whose prices are denominated in foreign currency, (b) borrows or lends funds and the amounts payable or receivable are denominated in foreign currency, (c) is a party to an unperformed foreign exchange contract, or (d) for other reasons, acquires or disposes of assets or incurs or settles liabilities denominated in foreign currency.

The basic principles of managing finance are just as equally applicable to international financial transactions as they are to financial transactions within the country. However, there are several features specific to international transactions which make international financial management a 'challenging task'. [3]

SCOPE OF INTERNATIONAL FINANCIAL MANAGEMENT

The scope of international financial management is both broad and complex. It includes all financial activities in relation to international business which in itself has three dimensions—international trade, foreign investments and contractual entry. International trade involves exports and imports, both direct, i.e., without the presence of intermediaries and indirect, such as through export houses, and is mainly of multilateral in character, although in certain cases can also be bilateral.

Foreign investments assume two forms, foreign direct investments and foreign portfolio investments. Foreign direct investments take three forms—greenfield investments, brownfield investments and mergers and acquisitions. Greenfield investment amounts to setting up of a new project by the MNC in the host country, opening up of branches in the host country and/or investment in the equity capital of firms in the host country, called financial collaboration. Greenfield projects are projects which are not constrained by prior work. Some examples of greenfield projects are new factories, new power plants or new airports which are built from scratch. These facilities when modified or upgraded become brownfield projects. Mergers and acquisition take the forms of the MNC's merging (amalgamating) with another firm aboard or buying an existing business in the host country. The mergers and acquisitions can be horizontal, i.e., merger of firms operating in the same line of business or vertical i.e., merger of firms on different line of business. Brownfield investments can be a combination of M&A and greenfield investment in as much as a foreign firm having acquired a business in the host country goes for capacity addition by undertaking subsequent investments.

Contractual entry, also known as technical collaboration, takes the forms of *franchising, management contracts, licensing, and turnkey projects*. Franchising refers to a company permitting the use of its brand by another company for consideration of some royalty payment. Licensing is the transfer of technology by a company to another company for consideration of some fees; whereas 'management contract' is the transfer of management know-how by a company to another company; and turnkey projects are the commissioning of projects/plants by a company on behalf of another company and handing over the keys for operation on successful execution upon consideration of some fees. In the context of international business that franchising, management contracts, licensing, and turnkey projects arrangements take place between the foreign companies mostly the MNCs and the domestic companies.

The complexities and the vastness of the scope of international financial management for any firm will depend on its involvement in some or all of the above mentioned kinds of international business activities. To appreciate the scope further, it is important to visualize the magnitude of foreign investments that flows into a country, the mode and the mechanism of such investments, the countries involved, the underlying laws and regulations and a host of related issues. For instance, FDI inflows to India over the period 2000–01 to 2010–11 has been 1,94,814 million USD as shown in Table 11.1(a). This Table also shows the investments made by FIIs in India amounting to 1,00,265 million USD in aggregate during the said period.

TABLE 11.1(a) India's FDI inflows over the period 2000-01 to 2010–11 (Estimate as per international best practices)

Fig. in Million USD

Sl No	*Financial year*	*Foreign Direct Investment (FDI)*					*Investment by FFIs (net)*
		FIPB route/ RBI's automatic route/ Acquisition route	*Equity capital of unincorporated bodies*	*+ Re-invested earnings*	*+ Other capital*	*Total FDI inflows*	
1	2000–01	2,339	61	1,350	279	**4,029**	1,847
2	2001–02	3,904	191	1,645	390	**6,130**	1,505
3	2002–03	2,574	190	1,833	438	**5,035**	377
4	2003–04	2,197	32	4,060	633	**4,322**	10,918
5	2004–05	3,250	528	1,904	369	**6,051**	8,686
6	2005–06	5,540	435	2,760	226	**8,961**	9,926
7	2006–07	15,585	896	5,828	517	**22,826**	3,225
8	2007–08	24,573	2,291	7,679	292	**34,835**	20,328
9	2008–09	27,329	702	9,030	777	**37,838**	–15,017
10	2009–10	25,609	1,540	8,669	1945	**37,763**	29,048
11	2010–11	19,430	657	6,703	234	**27,024**	29,422
Cumulative Total		1,32,330	7,523	48,861	6,100	**1,94,814**	1,00,265

Source: Fact Sheet on Foreign Direct Investment (FDI), Department of Industrial Policy & Promotion Ministry of Commerce and Industry, Government of India, 2011 available in www.dipp.nic.in/fdi_statistics/india_fdi_index.htm

Similarly, the overall inflows of FDI into India during 2011 to 2022 have been reflected in Table 11.1(b). This table also shows the FDI inflows to India as a percentage of India's total GDP over the period of 2011 to 2022.

TABLE 11.1(b) FDI inflow to India during 2011 to 2022–22 in aggregate

Year	*FDI in Billion USD*	*% of India's GDP*	*Year*	*FDI in Billion USD*	*% of India's GDP*
2011	36.50	2.00%	2017	39.97	1.51%
2012	24.00	1.31%	2018	50.61	1.78%
2013	28.15	1.52%	2019	50.61	1.78%
2014	34.58	1.70%	2020	64.36	2.41%
2015	44.01	2.09%	2021	44.73	1.42%
2016	44.46	1.94%	2022	49.92	1.47%

Source: https://www.macrotrends.net/global-metrics/countries/IND/india/foreign-direct-investment

The FDI inflows to India during 2000–01 to 2010–11 had come from 125 countries, of which contributions from the top ten countries alone had been to the tune of 80% of the total inflows as depicted in Table 11.2. This table also shows that the FDI inflows from Mauritius had been the highest at 54,227.06 million USD or 42% of the total inflows during the period under reference. The remaining 115 countries' contributions amounted to 20% of the total inflows during the said period.

TABLE 11.2(a): FDI inflows to India from top ten investing countries over the period 2000–01 to 2010–11

Fig. in Million USD

Rank	*Country*	*2000–01 to 2004–05*	*2005–06*	*2006–07*	*2007–08*	*2008–09*	*2009–10*	*2010–11*	*Cumulative 2000–2011*	*% to total inflows*
1	Mauritius	7,239	2,570	6,363	9,463	11,229	10,376	6,987	**54,227**	42%
2	Singapore	1,840	275	578	1,664	3,454	2,379	1,705	**11,895**	9%
3	USA	2,155	502	856	1,021	1,802	1,943	1,170	**9,449**	7%
4	UK	1,102	266	1,878	1,117	864	657	755	**6,639**	5%
5	Netherlands	1,384	76	644	601	883	899	1,213	**5,700**	4%
6	Japan	1,072	208	85	761	405	1,183	1,562	**5,276**	4%
7	Cyprus	84	70	58	773	1,287	1,627	913	**4,812**	4%
8	Germany	681	303	120	440	629	626	200	**2,999**	2%
9	France	505	18	117	120	467	303	734	**2,264**	2%
10	UAE	96	49	260	258	257	629	341	**1,890**	1%

Source: Compiled from Fact Sheet on Foreign Direct Investment (FDI) of the Department of Industrial Policy & Promotion Ministry of Commerce and Industry, Government of India, 2011, 2008, 2005 available in www.dipp.nic.in/**fdi**_statistics/**india_fdi**_index.htm

Similarly, the top countries in general from which FDI inflows to India continued to come during 2011–12 to 2022–23 were Mauritius, Singapore, USA, Japan, Netherlands, UK, Germany, South Korea, Cayman Islands, France, Cyprus and UAE; with Singapore taking over Mauritius from 2018–19 as the top most contributor. For example, in the year 2022–23, the FDI inflow to India in Million USD from the top 10 countries had been from Singapore, Mauritius, USA, Japan, Netherlands, UK, South Korea, Cayman Islands, UAE and Germany in the order of 14432, 6570, 2823, 2745, 2519, 1211, 982, 863, 853 and 817 (Million USD).

As regards the sector, i.e., the types of business that attracted FDI to India the most during 2000–01 to 2010–11 were the services sector as depicted in Table 11.3. It is evident from the Table that out of the total of 41 sectors that have attracted FDI in India; Services sector alone has pulled 21% of the total FDI inflows. Moreover, the Table also shows that the top ten sectors together accounted for 68% of the FDI inflows during 2000–01 to 2010–11.

TABLE 11.3 Sectors attracting highest FDI equity inflows in India

Fig. in Million USD

Rank	*Sector*	*2000–01 to 2007–08*	*2008–09*	*2009–10*	*2010–11*	*Cumulative inflows 2000–01 to 2010–11*	*% to total inflows*
1	Services Sector (financial and non-financial)	13,113	6,138	4,353	3,403	27,007	21
2	Computer software and hardware	7,343	1,677	919	784	10,723	8
3	Telecommunications (Radio paging, cellular mobile, basis telephone services	3,812	2,558	2,554	1,665	10,589	8
4	Housing and Real Estate	2,860	2,801	2,844	1,127	9,632	7
5	Construction activities (including roads and highways)	3,163	2,028	2,862	1,125	9,178	7
6	Automobile industry	2,236	1,152	1,208	1,331	5,927	5
7	Power	2,226	985	1,437	1,252	5,900	5
8	Metallurgical industries	1,762	961	407	1,105	4,235	3
9	Petroleum and Natural Gas	1,895	412	272	574	3,153	2
10	Chemicals (other than fertilizer)	1,383	749	362	398	2,892	2

Source: Compiled from FACT SHEET ON FOREIGN DIRECT INVESTMENT (FDI) of the Department of Industrial Policy & Promotion Ministry of Commerce and Industry, Government of India, 2011 available in www.dipp.nic.in/**fdi**_statistics/**india_fdi**_index.htm

In the year 2022–2023, the sectors who received the most FDI inflows were (i) computer software and hardware, (ii) services sector covering financial, banking, insurance, and business services, (iii) trading sector, (iv) drugs and pharmaceuticals, (v) automobile industry, (vi) Chemical, and (vii) construction (infrastructure) activities, attracting respectively, 9.39 billion USD, 8.70 billion USD, 4.79 billion USD, 2.05 billion USD, 1.90 billion USD, 1.85 billion USD and 1.70 billion USD worth of investments.

FDI inflows and cross-border Mergers and Acquisitions (M&A) across nations, based on UNCTAD estimates has been depicted in Table 11.4 for the years 2009 and 2010. Whereas the world over FDI inflows has marginally increased by 0.7% from 1,114.1 billion USD in 2009 to 1122 billion USD in 2010, the cross border M&A has registered a rise of 36.7% during the period under reference. This apart, the table also indicates the influence of FDI on every major economies of the world as enlisted in the Table. Further details on high value cross-border

TABLE 11.4 FDI inflows and cross-border M&A by region and major economy, 2009–2010

Fig. in Billion USD

Region/Economy	*FDI inflows*			*Net cross-border M&A*		
	2009	*2010*	*Growth Rate (%)*	*2009*	*2010*	*Growth Rate (%)*
World	**1,114.1**	**1122.0**	**0.7**	**249.7**	**341.4**	**36.7**
Developed economies	**565.9**	**526.6**	**–6.9**	**203.5**	**252.1**	**23.9**
Europe	378.4	295.4	–21.9	133.9	125.0	–6.6
European Union	361.9	289.8	–19.9	116.2	115.3	–0.8
Austria	7.1	12.6	78.8	1.8	4.9	174.2
Belgium	33.8	50.5	49.5	12.1	9.4	–22.3
Czech Republic	2.7	8.2	199.6	2.7	–0.5	—
Denmark	7.8	6.3	–119.2	1.7	1.4	–12.6
Finland	2.6	2.6	3.1	0.5	0.3	–36.3
France	59.6	57.4	–3.7	0.7	4.3	500.3
Germany	35.6	34.4	–3.5	12.8	10.8	–15.2
Greece	3.4	2.1	–38.3	0.5	–1.2	—
Ireland	25.0	8.4	–66.3	1.7	2.3	31.8
Italy	30.5	19.7	–35.5	1.1	7.7	590.2
Luxembourg	27.3	12.1	–55.7	0.4	2.1	368.9
Netherlands	26.9	–24.7	—	18.0	3.5	–80.8
Poland	11.4	10.4	–8.9	0.8	1.0	32.5
Portugal	2.9	3.4	17.8	0.5	2.2	338.1
Spain	15.0	15.7	4.3	32.2	8.5	–73.4
Sweden	10.9	12.1	11.6	1.1	0.8	–23.0
United Kingdom	45.7	46.2	1.2	25.2	56.3	123.5
United States	129.9	186.1	43.3	40.1	79.6	98.6
Japan	11.9	2.0	–83.3	–5.8	7.1	—
Developing economies	**478.3**	**524.8**	**9.7**	**39.1**	**85.1**	**117.6**
Africa	58.6	50.1	–14.4	5.1	7.7	49.3
Egypt	6.7	6.8	1.7	1.0	0.2	–80.4
Nigeria	5.9	2.3	–60.4	–0.2	0.4	—
South Africa	5.7	1.3	–77.9	4.2	3.9	–6.5
Latin America and other Caribbean	*116.6*	*141.1*	*21.1*	*–4.4*	*32.0*	–
Argentina	4.9	5.1	4.0	0.1	3.5	3001.5
Brazil	25.9	30.2	16.3	–1.4	9.4	—
Chile	12.7	18.2	43.4	0.8	1.8	121.0
Colombia	7.2	8.7	20.8	–1.6	0.6	—
Mexico	12.5	19.1	52.9	0.1	8.0	7616.1
Peru	4.8	6.9	44.7	0.0	0.7	1689.7
Asia and Oceania	*303.2*	*333.6*	*10.0*	*38.3*	*45.3*	*18.4*
West Asia	68.3	57.2	–16.2	3.5	4.8	34.5
Turkey	7.6	7.0	–8.0	2.8	2.1	–28.0
South, East and South East Asia	*233.0*	*274.6*	*17.8*	*34.7*	*31.5*	*–9.2*
China	95.0	101.0	6.3	10.9	6.0	–44.6
Hong Kong	48.4	62.6	29.2	3.0	12.2	301.5
India	34.6	23.7	–31.5	6.0	5.2	–14.3
Indonesia	4.9	12.8	162.7	1.3	0.9	–33.1

Region/Economy	*FDI inflows*			*Net cross-border M&A*		
	2009	*2010*	*Growth Rate (%)*	*2009*	*2010*	*Growth Rate (%)*
Malaysia	1.4	7.0	409.7	0.4	3.7	939.0
Singapore	16.8	37.4	122.7	9.7	4.7	–51.1
Thailand	5.9	6.8	14.2	0.3	0.5	32.0
South East Europe and the CIS	**69.9**	**70.5**	**0.8**	**7.1**	**4.3**	**–39.8**
Russian Federation	38.7	39.7	2.5	5.1	2.9	–43.6

Source: UNCTAD

M&A the world over during 2010 in terms of value (over three billion USD) along with the associated companies, industries and countries has been depicted in Table 11.5(a). This Table is indicative of, among others, the interdependence of nations and economies across the globe with regard to investments.

TABLE 11.5(a) Cross-border M&A deals with value over 3 billion USD in 2010

Value (Million USD)	*Acquired company*	*Industry of the acquired company*	*Host economy*	*(Ultimate) acquiring company*	*Ultimate acquiring nation*
7,603	Solvay Pharmaceutical SA	Pharmaceutical preparations	Belgium	Abbott Laboratories	United States
5,195	Unity Media GmbH	Cable and other pay television services	Germany	Liberty Media Corp	United States
4,469	Egyptian Co for Mobile services	Radiotelephone communications	Egypt	France Telecom SA	France
4,000	Liberty Global Inc-Subsidiaries	Cable and other pay television services	United States	KDDI Corp	Japan
3,700	Kraft Food Inc-North American Pizza Business	Frozen specialties, inc	United States	Nestle SA	Switzerland
3,363	Springer Science+ Business Media Deutschland GmbH	Books: Publishing, or publishing and printing	Germany	Group of Investors	Guernsey
18,769	Cadbury PLC	Candy and other confectionary products	United Kingdom	Kraft Foods Inc	United States
10,700	Zain Africa BV	Radiotelephone communications	Nigeria	Bharti Airtel Ltd.	India
8,496	T-Mobile(UK) Ltd	Radiotelephone communications	United Kingdom	France Telecom SA	France
7,325	Fomento Economico Mexicano SAB de CV-Beer Operations	Malt beverages	Mexico	Group of Investors	Netherlands
5,516	ZAO Kyiv star GSM	Radiotelephone communications	Ukraine	Vimpelkom	Russian Federation
4,848	Republic of Venezuela-Carabobo Block	Crude Petroleum and Natural Gas	Venezuela	Group of Investors	India
4,031	OSI Pharmaceuticals Inc	Pharmaceutical preparations	United States	Astellas Pharma Inc	Japan
3,800	Bunge Participacoes e Investimentos SA	Soybean Oil Mills	Brazil	Vale SA	Brazil

(Contd.)

TABLE 11.5(a) Cross-border M&A deals with value over 3 billion USD in 2010 (*Contd.*)

Value (Million USD)	*Acquired company*	*Industry of the acquired company*	*Host economy*	*(Ultimate) acquiring company*	*Ultimate acquiring nation*
3,426	Tandberg ASA	Radio and TV Broadcasting and communications equipments	Norway	Cisco Systems Inc	United States
3,160	Tommy Hilfiger Corp	Men's shirts and nightwear	Netherlands	Phillips-Van Heusen Corp	United States
3,100	Bridas Corp	Crude Petroleum and Natural Gas	Argentina	CNOOC	China
9,743	Brasilcel NV	Radiotelephone communications	Brazil	Telephonica SA	Spain
9,018	Lihir Gold Ltd.	Gold ores	Papua New Guinea	Newcrest Mining Ltd.	Australia
6,127	Millipore Corp	Laboratory analytical instruments	United States	Merck KGaA	Germany
5,959	Sybase Inc	Packaged software	United States	SAP AG	Germany
4,931	Ratiopharm International GmbH	Pharmaceutical preparations	Germany	Teva Pharm Inds Ltd.	Israel
4,380	Tomkins PLC	Mechanical Power transmission equipment, nec	United Kingdom	Onex Corp	Canada
4,110	Denway motors Ltd.	Motor Vehicle parts and accessories	Hong Kong, China	GAIG	China
4,052	AXA-SA Life Assurance Business, UK	Life Insurance	United Kingdom	Resolution Ltd.	Guernsey
3,717	Valeant Pharmaceuticals International Inc	Pharmaceutical preparations	United States	Valeant Pharmaceuticals	Canada
3,713	Piramal Health Care Ltd.–Health care Solutions Business	Pharmaceutical preparations	India	Abbott Laboratories	United States
3,679	Abertis Infraestucturas SA	Highway and Street Construction	Spain	CVC Capital Partners Ltd.	United Kingdom
3,330	Interactive Data Corp	Information retrieval services	United States	Interactive Data Corp SPV	United States
3,164	Arrow Energy Ltd.	Crude Petroleum and Natural Gas	Australia	Royal Dutch Shell PLC	Netherlands
3,100	BP PLC-Permian Basin Assets	Crude Petroleum and Natural Gas	United States	Apache Corp	United States
9,056	EDF Energy PLC-UK Power Distribution Business	Electric services	United Kingdom	Group of Investors	Hong Kong, China
7,625	E.ON US LLC	Natural Gas Distribution	United States	PPL Corp	United States
7,111	Repsol YPF Brasil SA	Crude Petroleum and Natural Gas	Brazil	Sinopec Group	China
4,540	Porsche Holding GmbH	Automobiles and other motor vehicles	Austria	Porsche Automobil Holding SA	Germany
4,517	Pactiv Corp	Plastics foam products	United States	Rank Group Ltd.	New Zealand

Value (Million USD)	*Acquired company*	*Industry of the acquired company*	*Host economy*	*(Ultimate) acquiring company*	*Ultimate acquiring nation*
3,397	HS1 Ltd.	Railroads, Line-haul operating	United Kingdom	Group of Investors	Canada
3,374	Andean Resources Ltd	Gold ores	United States	Goldcorp Inc	Canada
3,270	General Growth Properties Inc	Real Estate Investment Trusts	United States	Brookfield Asset Management Inc	Canada
3,269	Sunrise Communications AG	Radiotelephone communications	Switzerland	CVC Capital Partners Ltd.	Luxembourg
3,250	BP PLC-Western Canadian Upstream Gas Assets	Crude Petroleum and Natural Gas	Canada	Apache Corp	United States
3,119	Dimension Data Holdings PLC	Computer integrated systems design	South Africa	Nippon Telegraph and Telephone	Japan
3,090	Intoll Group	Investment offices, inc	Australia	Canada Pension Plan	Canada
3,019	RBS WorldPay	Functions related to depository banking, nec	United Kingdom	Group of Investors	United States

Source: UNCTAD

The number of M&A which has taken place worldwide during the period 2015 to 2022 has been depicted in Table 11.5(b), with the aggregate value of the M&A expressed in Billion USD for the said period being 4779, 3646, 3777, 3939, 3894, 3268, 5218 and 3390.

TABLE 11.5(b) Global M&A by numbers during 2015 to 2022

Region	*2015*	*2016*	*2017*	*2018*	*2019*	*2020*	*2021*	*2022*
North America	2409	2725	3723	3361	2937	2139	2451	2558
Europe	4927	5079	4920	4867	4360	3998	4485	4754
Asia Pacific	2381	2400	2418	2262	1905	1770	2105	2272
Latin America	616	571	555	532	405	387	427	474
Africa and Middle East	288	197	199	193	158	144	190	221

Source: www.statistica.com

Given the above, the scope of international financial management is vast which broadly includes the firm's decisions on international investment, financing, income distribution and repatriation, and international working capital management. Over and above, issues unique to international financial management shall be the functioning of the international financial system comprising of international financial institutions, international financial instruments and markets, international accounting and international taxation.

Finance managers of domestic companies with exposure to international operations too will have to redesign their financial structure in such a way as would result in maximization of value of the firm. In the context of international financial management it is therefore aptly said 'financial engineering is no more a fancy jargon but a reality. For those who are willing to master its complexities, the market provides endless opportunities for creative financial management; for the unwary, it is a minefield'. [4]

The core dimension of international financial management therefore shall include international investment decisions, international financing decisions, international financial system, international financial institutions, instruments and markets, international banking, IMF and World Bank, balance of payments, exchange rate forecasts and management, foreign exchange exposure-measurement and management, political risk , international accounting and recording of international transactions, transfer pricing, international taxation, management of interest rate risk, financing foreign trade, long-term and short-term sources of international financing, international indebtedness, FDI and foreign portfolio investments, and markets for financial derivatives like options, futures, swaps.

Of the several dimensions of international financial management listed above, management of foreign exchange exposure (Chapter-14) including exchange rate forecasting (Chapter-12), and measurement of foreign exchange exposure (Chapter-13) has been discussed at length in this book as exposure management is more linked to international accounting.

INTERNATIONAL FINANCE FUNCTIONS

The basic international finance functions remains the same as that of the finance functions performed in domestic environment, namely the treasury functions and the controlling functions, with one kind of functions affecting the other, for the two kinds of functions not being independent. The treasury functions broadly include financial analysis and planning, investment decisions, fund acquisition and financing decisions, cash management and risk management. Similarly, the controlling functions broadly include financial accounting and management accounting, budgeting and budgetary control, tax planning, management of accounts receivables, management information system and external reporting.

ROLE OF INTERNATIONAL FINANCE MANAGER

The major role of international finance manager shall be forecasting international financial environment such as the interest rate, exchange rate and inflation rates; managing the assets and liabilities of the firm; managing the foreign exchange exposure; and to evaluating and controlling the performance of the firm in order to achieve the stated objectives. Table 11.6 exhibits these roles in a seasonable detail without of course a full length discussion.

TABLE 11.6 Role of international financial manager

Forecasting the financial environment	Such as forecasting of the prices, inflation rates, interest rates, and exchange rates
Management of assets	Such as undertaking the international capital budgeting analysis decisions, cash management, at home and abroad, and in domestic and foreign currencies.
Management of liabilities	Such as international borrowing decisions, in domestic and foreign currencies, from domestic and foreign markets, long term and short term.
Management of exchange risk	Measuring the effect of exchange rate changes on the balance sheet items, and on the items of revenue and income, cash flows, and their effective management.
Performance evaluation, control, and reporting	Accounting and control of performance, for varied stakeholders, across countries and across currencies, without distortions.

INTERNATIONAL VS DOMESTIC FINANCIAL MANAGEMENT

International financial management is to a great extent the same as the domestic financial management, for the objectives of both the MNCs and the domestic firms being the same. The complexities involved in both the cases are however different in as much as domestic firms operate more in a protected environment with no or little exposure to political and exchange rate risks unlike the MNCs who operate in different political, economic, social and legal environments for having presence in different countries. 'Although both domestic firms and MNEs are exposed to foreign exchange risks, MNEs alone face certain unique risks that are not normally a threat to domestic operations, such as political risk'. [5] Table 11.7 depicts a broad comparison between the two against select parameters like the objectives, scope, complexities, risk factors, economic and competitive environment, desired liquidity and discounting rate.

TABLE 11.7 International Vs Domestic financial management

Sl. No	*Broad parameters*	*International financial management*	*Domestic financial management*
1	Objective	Maximization of owners' equity	Maximization of owners' equity
2	Scope	Broad	Narrow
3	Complexity	High	Low
4	Risk involvement (such as country risk, exchange risk, interest risk, political risk)	High	Low
5	Economic environment	Multinational	Mostly national
6	Competitive environment	Wide	Relatively narrow/ limited
7	Desired liquidity	Optimum	Optimum
8	Hurdle rate/discounting rate/ cost of capital (k)	Least	Least

Thus, international financial management and the domestic financial management have the same common broad objectives, namely, maximization of owners' equity. The cost of capital and desired level of liquidity are also the same for both. A marked difference however exists between the two as regards their scope, risk complexion, the economic, political and competitive environments in which they operate.

SUMMARY

The increased pace of globalization of business activities coupled with integration of national economy with world economy, and enhanced interdependence of countries for factors of production have lead to the development of international financial management as a separate and distinct branch of study.

International financial management, which is also known as multinational financial management, refers to the *management of financial functions that are related to international trade and business*. The international business related financial functions include, among others, recording of international (foreign) financial transactions; exchange rate forecasts; measurement and management of foreign exchange exposure; international investment decisions including foreign direct investment, foreign portfolio investment; management of political risk; international working capital management; international financial and monetary system; international taxation and derivatives market.

The scope of international financial management is both broad and complex. It includes all financial activities in relation to international business which in itself has three dimensions—international trade, foreign investments and contractual entry. Translated into specific activities, the scope of international financial management shall include international investment decisions, international financing decisions, international financial system, international financial institutions, instruments and markets, international banking, IMF and World Bank, balance of payments, exchange rate forecasts and management, foreign exchange exposure-measurement and management, political risk, international accounting and recording of international transactions, transfer pricing, international taxation, management of interest rate risk, financing foreign trade, long-term and short-term sources of international financing, international indebtedness, FDI and foreign portfolio investments, and markets for financial derivatives like options, futures, swaps.

The basic functions of international finance will remain the same as are performed in domestic environment, namely, the treasury functions and the controlling functions. The treasury functions will broadly include activities like the financial analysis and planning, investment decisions, fund acquisition and financing decisions, cash management and risk management; and the controlling functions will broadly cover the financial and management accounting activities, budgeting and budgetary control, tax planning, management of receivables, and management information and reporting system.

The major role of international finance manager shall be forecasting international financial environment such as the interest rate, exchange rate and inflation rates; managing the assets and liabilities of the firm; managing the foreign exchange exposure; and to evaluating and controlling the performance of the firm in order to achieve the stated objectives.

When compared, the international financial management and the domestic financial management have the same common broad objectives, namely, maximization of owners' equity. Their desired cost of capital is the least and the liquidity level is high. However, a marked difference exists between them in terms of their scope, risk complexion, and the economic, political and competitive environments in which they operate.

KEY TERMS

International financial management refers to the management of financial functions that are related to international trade and business.

Greenfield investment amounts to setting up of a new project by the MNC in the host country, opening up of branches in the host country and/or investment in the equity capital of firms in the host country, called financial collaboration.

Contractual entry, also known as technical collaboration, takes the forms of *franchising, management contracts, licensing, and turnkey projects*.

Franchising refers to a company permitting the use of its brand by another company for consideration of some royalty payment.

Licensing is the transfer of technology by a company to another company for consideration of some fees.

Management contract is the transfer of management know-how by a company to another company.

Turnkey projects are the commissioning of projects/plants by a company on behalf of another company and handing over the keys for operation on successful execution upon consideration of some fees.

REVIEW QUESTIONS

1. What is international financial management? What is its scope? Discuss.
2. What is international financial management? What is its scope and importance? Discuss.
3. What is international financial management? How it is different from domestic financial management? Discuss.
4. Discuss the complexities involved in international financial management.
5. Define international financial management and discuss the functions of international finance.
6. Give the role of international finance manager. Cite examples to justify your answer.
7. 'Financial engineering is no more a fancy jargon but a reality. For those who are willing to master its complexities, the market provides endless opportunities for creative financial management; for the unwary, it is a minefield'-Comment.
8. With the changing dimensions of international business, the complexities of international financial management have also increased. Discuss.
9. Discuss the scope and importance of international financial management keeping in view the changing business environment.
10. The role of international financial manager has become more complex and diversified than ever before. Do you agree with the statement? Justify your answer.

REFERENCES

[1] Sharan, V., *International Financial Management*, 4th Edn., PHI Learning, New Delhi, 2006, p. 3.

[2] Kevin, S., *Fundamentals of International Financial Management*, PHI Learning, New Delhi, 2009, p. 1.

[3] *Ibid.*

[4] Apte, P.G., *International Financial Management*, Tata McGraw-Hill Publishing Company Limited, New Delhi, 5th Edition, 2009, p. 4.

[5] David K. Eiteman, et al., *Multinational Business Finance*, 10th ed., Pearson, New Delhi, 2008.

SUGGESTED READINGS

1. Shapiro, Alan C., *Multinational Financial Management*, 4th Edition, PHI Learning, New Delhi, 2002.
2. Adrian Buckley, *Multinational Finance*, 3rd ed., PHI Learning, New Delhi, 1998.
3. John C. Hull, *Options, Futures and Other Derivatives*, 7th ed., Pearson, New Delhi, 2009.
4. Jeff Madura, *International Corporate Finance*, 8th ed., Thomson-South Western.

Relevant websites

www.imf.org	International Monetary Fund
www.worldbank.org	World Bank
www.bis.org	Bank of International Settlements
www.oecd.org	Organization for Economic Co-operation and Development
www.ecb.int	European Central Bank
www.federalreserve.gov	U.S. Federal Reserve System
www.fese.be	Federation of European Securities Exchanges
	https://www.macrotrends.net/global-metrics/countries/IND/india/foreign-direct-investment

12

Exchange Rate Forecasting

LEARNING OBJECTIVES

After studying this chapter, you will be able to:

- Understand the meaning of exchange rate forecasting
- Appreciate the need for exchange rate forecasting
- Know the techniques of exchange rate forecasting

INTRODUCTION

Exchange rate forecasting, which refers to forecasting or predicting/estimating the future exchange rate of a currency in the floating exchange rate regime, has remained an important dimension of multinational financial management insofar as a number of financial decisions such as the hedging decisions, the pricing decisions, the borrowings and lending decisions of the MNCs rest on some prediction of the future spot rate of the currency or currencies involved in the foreign transactions. The ability of the firm to predict the future exchange rate(s) more accurately will have a bearing on its performance in terms of managing the foreign exchange exposure vis-à-vis its overall performance. Besides the MNCs, financial and non-financial companies like the mutual and hedge fund businesses too find exchange rate forecasting a useful tool to make speculative gains in the foreign exchange market and enhance the shareholders value.

IMPORTANCE OF EXCHANGE RATE FORECASTING

Exchange rate forecasting, as stated above, is important for the MNCs in particular as based on the prediction of the rate(s) and assessment of the likely unfavorable variation(s) in the rates, they can formulate policy to effectively measure and manage the risk. The specific importances attached to exchange rate forecasting are the firm's hedging decision, financing decision, investment decision and evaluation of the subsidiaries' financial performance. An outline of these benefits is as under:

Hedging Decision

A firm importing goods from a foreign country will favour a forward market hedge when in the event its forecast rate is higher than the forward rate as this will help the firm eliminate or minimize the loss due to fluctuations in the exchange rate which in the absence of a forward hedge would have resulted in payment of higher amount of home currency. For example, ABC India Ltd. which has imported goods worth £ 50,000 from XYZ Ltd. of UK on a three month's term at the current exchange rate of ₹68, and a three month's forward rate of ₹69 will go for the forward contract to by £ 50,000 at ₹69 if it (ABC Ltd.) estimates (forecasts) the future spot rate to be (say) ₹70.20/£, as by so doing ABC can bring its loss down by ₹50,000 to ₹60,000 from ₹1,10,000 in the absence of a forward contract as calculated below:

Amount payable to fetch £50,000 on maturity…

£50,000 × ₹70.20 = ₹35,10,000

Amount payable to fetch £50,000 on the date of initiation…

£50,000 × ₹68.00 = ₹34,00,000

Excess amount payable in the absence of a forward contract …

₹35,10,000 – ₹34,00,000 = ₹1,10,000

Amount saved due to forward contract…

£50,000 × (₹70.20 – ₹69.00) = ₹60,000

The above calculations clearly indicate that it is beneficial for the firm to go for exchange rate forecasting.

Financing Decision

A firm borrowing in foreign currency(ies) as a part of its capital structure decision will find it beneficial to borrow in such currency(ies) whose value is/are expected to fall over maturity, i.e., the home currency becomes stronger compared to the foreign currency(ies) in context, resulting thereby in the borrowing firm paying less to settle the debt; the resultant effect being a reduced burden of repayment on the part of the borrowing firm.

EXAMPLE 12.1: ABC India Ltd. is contemplating to raise ₹45,00,000 overseas on a three years term, and has short listed five countries whose current and forecasted exchange rates are as follows:

Country	*US*	*UK*	*Australia*	*Canada*	*Japan*
Current rate	₹45/$	₹68/£	₹40/A$	₹35/C$	₹30/¥
Forecasted rate	₹44/$	₹67/£	₹42/A$	₹38/C$	₹34/¥

Given the above, it will be beneficial for ABC India Ltd. to go for borrowing in USD. The firm therefore will borrow 1,00,000 USD (i.e., ₹45,00,000/₹45) at present for which it will be required to pay off, at the time of redemption, ₹44,00,000 (i.e., 1,00,000 USD × ₹44), which is lesser by ₹1,00,000 to settle the debt.

A forecast of foreign currency therefore will be to the advantage of the firm trying to design its capital structure and finance its activities.

Investment Decision

Investment decisions of the MNCs, both short-term and long-term, get influenced by the forecasted exchange rate(s). For example, MNCs park their surplus cash in short-term investments in different foreign currency (ies) whose forecasted future spot rate(s) is/are higher than the forward rate(s), as this will maximize their earnings. The long-term investment decisions of the MNCs too get guided by similar principles as long as the cash inflows are the maximum.

Evaluation of the Subsidiaries' Financial Performance

Earnings of the subsidiaries expressed in forecasted exchange rate(s) will enable the MNCs evaluate performance of their subsidiaries' better. The forecasted exchange rate too will help the MNCs decide the direction and magnitude of their foreign investments. They will like to invest in countries whose currencies are expected to appreciate against the home currency as this will result in enhanced inflow of cash.

TECHNIQUES OF EXCHANGE RATE FORECASTING

The various techniques used for exchange rate forecasting may be divided into two broadly categories, (i) pure forecasting models, and (ii) economic structural models. The most popular techniques coming under the pure forecasting models are the (a) technical forecasting, and (b) market-based forecasting. The economic structural models, also known as the econometric models, like the purchasing power parity model and the current account monetary model, on the other hand are more fundamental and predictive models in nature which consider and use a number of macroeconomic variables like the inflation rate, interest rate, GDP with their forecasted values in the models to predict the exchange rate(s). The predictive value of these economic structural models thus depends more on the reliability of the forecasted values of the independent variables used in the models. Getting accurate forecasts for the independent variables being difficult, forecasts by economic structural models has also limitations.

Economic structural models have also failed to produce uniform results under two different situations, i.e., their out-of-sample predictive performance has been found to be far from satisfactory as the interrelationship between variables used in the models does not remain static in all the situations. Economic structural models have not been found to be uniformly satisfactory [1]. Their out-of-sample predictive performance is quite disappointing [2].

Despite of the limitations of economic structural models, we have used a simple fundamental technique of forecasting the exchange rate by taking a single variable, namely, the inflation rate, later in the discussion to explain how fundamental technique can be used to forecast the exchange rate, given that the more rigorous the technique is (by using more number of variables), the greater is the accuracy and reliability of the predictive value.

Further, to reduce the effect of errors in the estimations under any single technique of forecasting, a '*mixed*' forecasting technique is often recommended and also used. A mixed forecasting is a combination of all the three techniques, namely, technical, market based, and fundamental forecasting in so far as *a weighted average rate* is determined by taking into account all the individual rates as has been found under the three individual methods.

Thus, four methods of exchange rate forecasting, namely, the technical forecasting, market-based forecasting, fundamental forecasting and mixed forecasting are discussed hereunder which are considered as the most standardized methods of exchange rate forecasting in vogue:

Technical Forecasting

Under the technical forecasting method, future spot rate of exchange is forecasted by fitting the historical rates of exchange into (i) simple charts like the (a) line chart, (b) bar chart, (c) cylindrical (candle stick) chart, etc., and/or by using (ii) statistical and operation research tools like (a) the moving average—simple and weighted, (b) linear regression, and (c) other autoregressive models.

Technical forecasting is useful to short-term forecasting and to speculators who intend to make quick profits. It suffers from the limitations that it depends on a single factor, the historical rate alone; ignoring many other macroeconomic phenomena. Despite of this short-coming, technical forecasting is still a dominant technique among the professional forecasters. Surveys by Euromoney indicate that technical analysis has become the dominant methodology, at least among professional currency forecasters [3].

ILLUSTRATION 12.1

The exchange rates of USD against Indian rupee over the last six months period have been as follows:

Months	*April*	*May*	*June*	*July*	*August*	*September*
Current rate	₹44/$	₹46/$	₹45.10/$	₹47/$	₹44/$	₹48/$

What will be the exchange rate in the month of October?

SOLUTION

Let us find out a three months' moving average of the values and plot them the graph as below to determine the trend in the movement of the exchange rates over the period April to September.

The moving average for the months from June to September is found to be 45.03, 46.03, 45.37 and 46.33, respectively.

The moving average for the months from June to September is found to be 45.03, 46.03, 45.37 and 46.33, respectively.

Now a straight line between the coordinates through June to September may be drawn and extended to the month of October and the corresponding value in the Y-axis can be taken as the forecasted value of exchange rate for the month of October which in the graph comes to ₹46.10.

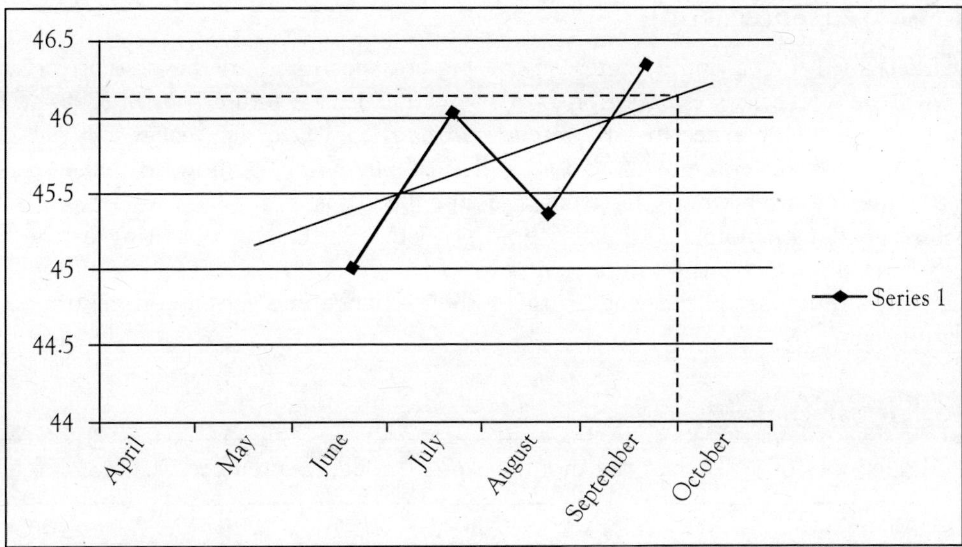

ILLUSTRATION 12.2

The exchange rate of Indian rupee against £ over the months April through October of a year has been 67, 71, 74, 78, 80, 79 and 76. Fit a 'least square' trend and find the value of exchange for the month of November.

SOLUTION

Let us assume that the linear trend under the least square takes the form '$y_c = a + bx$', with $\Sigma y = na + b\Sigma x$, and $\Sigma xy = a\Sigma x + b\Sigma x^2$, given $\Sigma x = 0$.

So, $a = \Sigma y/n$ and $b = \Sigma xy/x^2$

Month 't'	Rate(£) 'y'	$x = t$ –July	xy	x^2	Trend value $y_c = a + bx$
April	67	–3	–201	9	75 + (1.75) × (–3) = 69.75
May	71	–2	–142	4	75 + (1.75) × (–2) =71.50
June	74	–1	–74	1	75 + (1.75) × (–1) =73.25
July	78	0	0	0	75 + (1.75) × (0) = 75.00
August	80	1	80	1	75 + (1.75) × (1) = 76.75
September	79	2	158	4	75 + (1.75) × (2) = 78.50
October	76	3	228	9	75 + (1.75) × (3) = 80.25
	$\Sigma y = 525$ So $a = 75$	$\Sigma x = 0$	$\Sigma xy = 49$	$\Sigma x^2 = 28$	
November					75 + (1.75) × (4) = 82 Or trend value of October plus 1.75, i.e., 80.25 + 1.75 = 82

Note: $a = 525/7 = 75$ and $b = 49/28 = 1.75$

The estimated value of exchange for the month of November may be taken as ₹82/£.

Market-based Forecasting

The market-based forecasting operates on the present spot rate and the present forward rate along with the forecaster's expectation of a rise or fall in the future spot rate of the foreign currency. A speculator expecting the foreign currency, say £, to appreciate by 5% the next quarter against its current rate of ₹68/ £ will start buying the £ now to make speculative profit the next quarter when the exchange rate becomes ₹71.4/£ or something close to this value. Similar phenomena will also hold good to a speculator operating in the forward market who when expects the future sport rate of the currency to be higher will start buying currency forward now to offload when actually the exchange rate goes up on maturity to make speculative gain.

ILLUSTRATION 12.3

The exchange rate of USD over the months April through September, 2011 is as follows:.

Months	*April*	*May*	*June*	*July*	*August*	*September*
Current rate	₹45/$	₹45.80/$	₹46.50/$	₹47.20/$	₹48/$	₹48.30/$

It is expected that the dollar will be appreciated by 12% over the next quarter. What can be the exchange rate expected in the month of November 2011?

SOLUTION

The average spot rate during the months April–September 2011 is ₹46.8/USD. The exchange rate in November, 2011 is likely to be 12% above the average rate, hence will be (₹46.8 × 1.12)/USD or ₹52.42/USD.

The market-based forecasting too, like the technical forecasting, is useful to the speculators in the short run. For ***long-term forecasting*** however, the interest rate parity theory may be applied which states that 'if the interest rate of a country appreciates, its currency will depreciate'.

The value of currency appreciation or depreciation, in such case, involving two currencies, the Indian Rupee and Japanese Yen, for example, may be calculated as follows:

$$\text{Currency (Yen) appreciation (depreciation)} = [(1 + I_{India})^n/(1 + I_{Japan})^n] - 1,$$

where '*I*' is the interest rate and '*n*' is the period in years for which the forecast is to be made.

ILLUSTRATION 12.4

The current interest rate in India is 11% and that in Japan is 6%. What will be the exchange rate of Rupee against Yen 2 years down the line if the current exchange rate is ₹32/¥?

SOLUTION

The exchange rate two years down may be calculated by finding out the appreciation in ¥ over the two years period and then multiplying the current rate with the rate of appreciation, as under:

Appreciation in ¥ = $[(1+I_{India})^n/(1 + I_{Japan})^n] - 1$

$= [(1+0.11)^2/(1 + 0.06)^2] - 1$

$= 1.096 - 1 = 0.096 = 9.6\%$

The exchange rate will be ₹32 + 9.6% of ₹32, i.e., ₹35.07/¥

Fundamental Forecasting

The fundamental forecasting considers a number of macroeconomic variables while estimating the future spot rate of exchange. These variables can be inflation rate, interest rate, GDP, etc. However, with a single variable, say inflation, the exchange rate under the fundamental forecasting shall be determined as:

Future spot rate (say ₹/$) in the *n*th year = [(Current spot rate) × {(1+ % of Inflation in the home country)/(1 + % of Inflation in the host country)}^{n}]

ILLUSTRATION 12.5

(Fundamental forecasting with single variable)

The inflation rate in India at present is 9% and in USA 6%. If the current exchange rate is ₹45/$, what will be the exchange rate in two years next?

SOLUTION

Putting the values in the formula

Future spot rate (say ₹/$) in the *n*th year = [(Current spot rate) × {(1+ % of Inflation in the home country)/(1+ % of Inflation in the host country)}^{n}], we get ₹45 × $(1.09/1.06)^2$ = ₹47.25/$.

We may forecast the exchange rate with two variables, say inflation and interest rate by **regressing** the variables as:Future Spot Rate (₹/$) = s_0 + s_1 Inflation + s_2 Interest + μ where s_0 = constant; s_1 and s_2 are the sensitivity of the variables determined through running the regression equation and is the error term.

As stated before, the more the rigorous technique, the greater is the accuracy of the predictive value. In other words, more the number of variables used in the equation, more precise will be value of the estimates. However, the greatest limitation of the fundamental analysis is the validity of the assumptions/factors of forecast.

Mixed Forecasting

To overcome the limitations of the individual techniques of forecasting, i.e., the technical, market based and fundamental forecasting, and also to minimize the limitations of having any single forecasted rate of exchange (forecasted under individual methods), that the mixed forecasting technique is recommended which takes into account all the individual rates as forecasted under the three techniques and then finds a weighted average of the rates by assigning weights to a maximum of *unit or one* to the forecasted rates. In other words, the mixed forecast rate is a 'weighted average rate of exchange' obtained after assigning weights to the three forecast rates of exchange as found under the technical, fundamental and market-based forecasting.

Assuming that the weights are assigned in the proportion of 20%, 30% and 50% to the three rates, the mixed exchange rate would be

$$(R_t \times 0.2) + (R_m \times 0.3) + (R_f \times 0.5)$$

given that R_t, R_m, and R_f represents the forecasted exchange rate under the technical, market based and fundamental forecasting.

ILLUSTRATION 12.6

Given the exchange rate under the technical, market based and fundamental forecasting as ₹44/$, ₹47.25/$, and ₹49.50/$, what will be the rate under mixed forecasting?

SOLUTION

The rate under mixed forecasting shall be ₹47.73/$ calculated as:

(₹44 × 0.2) + (₹47.25 × 0.3) + (₹49.50 × 0.5) = ₹(8.80 + 14.175 + 42.75) or ₹47.73

SUMMARY

Exchange rate forecasting refers to the forecasting or predicting or estimating the future spot exchange rate of a currency in the floating exchange rate regime. It has become an important dimension of financial management of the MNCs in particular and other firms exposed to foreign transactions who are concerned with variety of financial decisions ranging from hedging decisions, investment decisions to pricing and borrowing and lending of funds. The performance of these firms will get significantly influenced by their ability to predict the future spot exchange rate(s) more accurately and manage the exposure. Speculators operating in the foreign exchange market and the mutual and hedge fund businesses too will find exchange rate forecasting a useful tool to make speculative gains and enhance shareholders value.

The techniques used for exchange rate forecasting are broadly of two categories, pure forecasting models and economic structural models. The popular techniques of pure forecasting models are technical forecasting which uses historical rates to find the trend by fitting into least square and a host of other similar techniques, and market-based forecasting that incorporates into the present spot rate of the home currency the forecaster's expectation of an upward or downward movement in the foreign currency to find the expected value of exchange. Under the economic structural models comes the fundamental forecasting which uses a number of macroeconomic factors like the interest rate, inflation rate and GDP to predict the future spot rate. A mixed forecasting technique is however used in practice by calculating the weighted average rate of the individual exchange rates as determined under the technical, market based and fundamental forecasting to eliminate the limitations of individual techniques in one hand and to increase the predictive value on the other.

KEY TERMS

Exchange rate forecasting refers to forecasting or predicting or estimating the future exchange rate of a currency in the floating exchange rate regime.

Technical forecasting is a method of exchange rate forecasting wherein the future spot rate is forecasted based on a single factor, the historical rates, by fitting a linear trend.

Market-based forecasting is a technique of exchange rate forecasting which appreciates or depreciates the present spot rate of home currency in proportion to the forecaster's expected depreciation or appreciation in the host currency.

Fundamental forecasting is a technique of exchange rate forecasting that considers a number of macroeconomic variables like the inflation rate, interest rate, GDP while estimating the future spot rate of exchange.

Mixed forecasting is a technique of exchange rate forecasting wherein a 'weighted average rate of exchange' is calculated by assigning weights aggregating to 'one' to the exchange rate determined individually under the technical, fundamental and market-based forecasting.

REVIEW QUESTIONS

1. What is exchange rate forecasting? What is its importance? Discuss.
2. What is exchange rate forecasting? What are different techniques of exchange rate forecasting? Explain.
3. Explain the need for and the techniques of exchange rate forecasting.
4. The exchange rates of USD against Indian rupee over the last five quarters have been as follows:

Quarter	1	2	3	4	5
Current rate	₹48/$	₹46.20/$	₹44.10/ $	₹49/$	₹50.90/$

   What can be the expected exchange rate in the sixth quarter?
5. The exchange rate of Indian rupee against ¥ over the months January through October of a year has been 37, 34, 32, 36, 39, 38, 39, 36, 35, and 37. Find the value of exchange for the month of November by fitting a 'least square' trend.
6. The exchange rate of £ over the months of January through June September has remained as follows:

Months	*January*	*February*	*March*	*April*	*May*	*June*
Current rate	₹65/£	₹65.80/£	₹66.50/ £	₹67.20/£	₹68/£	₹68.30/£

   It is expected that £ will be appreciated by 10% over the next quarter. What can be the exchange rate expected in the month of September?
7. The current interest rate in India is 11.5% and that in Japan is 5.6%. What will be the expected exchange rate of ¥ 3 years down the line if the current exchange rate is ₹34/¥?

8. The inflation rate in India at present is 10.56 % and in the US is 5.36%. If the spot rate exchange rate is ₹48.25/$, what will be the expected exchange rate in two years next?
9. What is mixed forecasting? How will you calculate mixed forecasting? What are its uses?
10. Write notes on:
    (a) Pure forecasting models
    (b) Economic structural models
11. Write explanatory notes on:
    (a) Fundamental forecasting
    (b) Technical forecasting
    (c) Market-based forecasting.
12. The exchange rate of £ over the months of March through August has remained as follows:

Months	*March*	*April*	*May*	*June*	*July*	*August*
Current rate	₹98.10/£	₹98.60/£	₹99.90/ £	₹100.10/£	₹100.70/£	₹101.20/£

It is expected that £ will be appreciated by 15% over the next quarter. What can be the exchange rate expected in the month of October?

13. The exchange rate of USD over the months of January through May has been as follows:

Months	*January*	*February*	*March*	*April*	*May*	*June*
Current rate	₹81.10/$	₹81.30/$	₹81.70/$	₹81.90/$	₹82.10/$	₹82.40/$

What can be the expected exchange rate in the month of July, if the USD will be appreciated by 10% over the next quarter?

14. The current interest rate in India is 7.60% and that in Singapore is 3.10%. What will be the expected exchange rate of Singapore Dollar 3 years down the line if the current exchange rate of Singapore Dollar is ₹61?
15. Write explanatory notes on:
    (a) Economic structural models
    (b) Market-based forecasting.
16. Differentiate between:
    (a) 'Fundamental forecasting' and 'Technical forecasting'.
    (b) 'Pure forecasting models' and 'Economic structural models'.
17. The present inflation rate in India is 4.85% and in Canada is 3.00%. If the spot exchange rate is ₹70/Canadian Dollar, what will be the expected exchange rate in two years next?
18. The exchange rate of Indian rupee against USD over the months February through November of a year has been 80.25, 80.55, 80.95, 81.30, 81.65, 81.95, 82.20, 82.45, 82.75 and 82.90. Find the value of exchange for the month of December by fitting a 'least square' trend.

19. The exchange rates of Australian Dollar against Indian rupee over the last five quarters have been as follows:

Quarter	I	II	III	IV	V
Current rate per Australian Dollar	₹52.00	₹52.80	₹53.10	₹53.70	₹53.90

What can be the expected exchange rate in the sixth quarter?

20. Given the exchange rate under technical forecasting, market-based forecasting and fundamental forecasting at ₹80.25/$, ₹81.75/$, and ₹82.50/$, what will be the exchange rate under mixed forecasting, if the weightage assigned is 0.20:0.30:0.50 ?

REFERENCES

[1] Mussa, M., *The Theories of Exchange Rate Determination*', National Bureau of Economic Research Conference Report, Chicago University Press, pp. 13–58.

[2] Meese, Richard A, and Rogoff, K, 'Empirical Exchange Models of the seventies, Do they fit?', *Journal of International Economics* 14 (1983), 3–24, North-Holland Publishing Company, 1982.

[3] Apte, P.G., *International Financial Management*, 5th Edn., Tata McGraw-Hill, New Delhi, 2009, p. 372.

SUGGESTED READINGS

1. Shapiro, Alan C., *Multinational Financial Management*, 4th Edition, PHI Learning, New Delhi, 2002.
2. David K Eiteman, et al., *Multinational Financial Management*, 10th Edition, Pearson, 2008.
3. Adrian Buckley, *Multinational Finance*, 3rd Ed., PHI Learning, New Delhi, 1998
4. Sharan, V., *International Financial Management*, 4th ed., PHI Learning, New Delhi, 2006.
5. John C. Hull, Options, *Futures and Other Derivatives*, 7th ed., Pearson, New Delhi, 2009.
6. Jeff Madura, *International Corporate Finance*, 8th ed., Thomson-South Western.

13

Measurement of Foreign Exchange Exposure

LEARNING OBJECTIVES

After studying this chapter, you will be able to:

- Understand the need for measurement of foreign exchange exposure
- Know the types of foreign exchange exposure
- Know the techniques of measurement of translation exposure
- Know the techniques of measurement of economic exposure comprising of transaction exposure and operating exposure
- Appreciate the difficulties in measuring real operating exposure

INTRODUCTION

Measurement of foreign exchange exposure is the second important dimension of exposure management, next to foreign exchange forecast in the sequence. An 'unanticipated change' in the exchange rate is termed as foreign exchange exposure. In other words, foreign exchange exposure occurs when there is an unexpected change in the exchange rate.

The importance of foreign exchange exposure to the firm lies with the fact that changes in exchange rate has direct impact on the value of the firm that undertakes international transactions due to a corresponding change in the value of their assets and liabilities and so also their present and future cash flows. In order to maximize their values, firms do undertake the exercise of determining the quantum of such foreign exchange exposure, followed by their efforts to manage the impact of such exposure to their advantage.

There are of course two schools of thought as regards the need for estimation of foreign exchange exposure, one supporting and the other opposing the move for such estimation. Those who oppose the move are of the opinion that the impact of any movement in the exchange rate is equally off set by the movement in the price because of the purchasing power parity (PPP) theory. PPP theory states that the change in exchange rate is matched by a reciprocal change in the price. For example, in a simple PPP mechanism involving two currencies, say the Indian rupee (INR) and the US dollar (USD), a higher inflation rate in India in comparison to that of the US will depreciate INR and as a result the cost of import by the Indian firm will go up, with the Indian firm losing its competitive advantage to the domestic firms producing and selling such products. At the same time, due to higher inflation, the cost of domestic firm too will increase. Consequently the domestic firms will also lose their competitive advantage. As a result, neither the importing firm nor the non-importing firm has the advantage. Their cash flows remain unaltered in the long run and hence 'exchange rate exposure is *irrelevant*'.

The supporters of the move feel that it is '*relevant*' for the firm to identify the sources of exchange rate exposure and measure their impact on the firm's cash flows because PPP theory does not hold good in the short-run. In the long-run too, PPP may not equally off set the exposure as there are many other factors like the GDP, political and/or economic factors, besides the inflation rate differential, that influence the exchange rate. As such, exchange rate exposure matters to the firms who need to adopt various strategies to handle the exposure and maximize their performance.

Empirical studies have also established that the value of the firm does get impacted by the firm's exposure to foreign exchange. Choi and Prasad [1], for example, have reported that the value of 60% of the 409 US multinational firms they studied have shown significant sensitivity to foreign exchange exposure. Glaum, Brunner and Himmet [2] have examined the economic exposure of German firms to report that German firms are significantly exposed to changes in DM/US dollar. Bodner and Gentry [3] who studied the industry exposure to exchange rate fluctuations on sample industries from three countries, the USA, Canada and Japan have found that some of these firms are significantly exposed to foreign exchange fluctuations. Stulz [4] has found that exchange rate fluctuations can affect firms' cash flow. Froot [5] et al. have also reported similar findings that the firm's cash flows can get influenced by exchange rate fluctuations. Sony, for instance had announced in 1999 that its profits fell 25% due to the effects of a yen appreciation on its foreign sales.

TYPES OF FOREIGN EXCHANGE EXPOSURE

Broadly speaking, there are two types of foreign exchange exposure—translation exposure and economic exposure. The economic exposure assumes two forms—transaction exposure and operating exposure. On the other hand, transaction exposure takes three forms—quotation exposure, backlog exposure and billing exposure. Figure 13.1 depicts the various kinds of foreign exchange exposure.

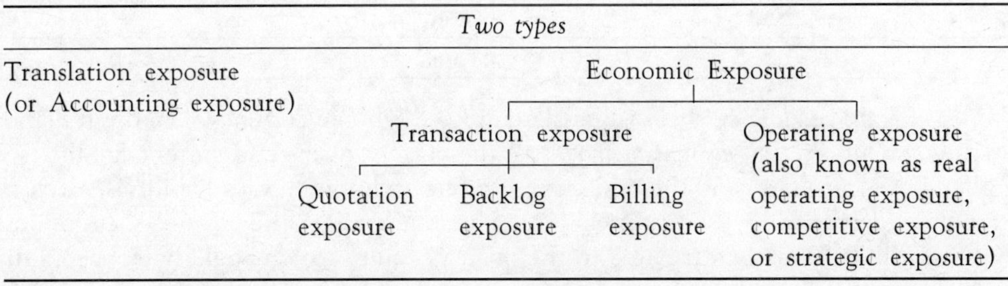

FIGURE 13.1 Types of Foreign Exchange Exposure

MEASUREMENT OF EXPOSURE

The following paragraphs deal with the concepts and quantifications of the different kinds of foreign exchange exposure a firm may be undertaking:

TRANSLATION EXPOSURE

Translation exposure, which is also known as the accounting exposure, arises on account of consolidation of financial statements. Consolidation of financial statements is the integration of financial data of the subsidiaries into the financial data of the parent, a phenomena more popular with the MNCs. Prior to consolidation, the financial statements of the subsidiaries are of course **translated** *under any of the four internationally recognized methods of translation, namely, the single rate (or the current rate) method, the current/non-current rate method, the monetary/non-monetary method, and the temporal method.*

A translation is the change in the expression of monetary units rather than a physical exchange of one currency against another. Translation, followed by consolidation, is made to know the net worth of the group, i.e., the parent and the subsidiaries taken together. ***Any increase or decrease in the net worth of the group indicates the amount and the nature of exposure associated with the translation***.

Whereas 'translation' has been dealt with in detail in Chapter 2 of this book, the following Balance Sheet of Simon & Co. of Canada, an Indian subsidiary may be taken as an example to explain the concept and the amount of translation exposure the Indian parent can be said to have on account of translation of the financial data of its Canadian subsidiary under the **current and non current method of translation**, assuming that the historical rate and current rate of 1 C $ is equal to ₹39 and ₹41, respectively.

The balance sheet of Simon & Co. of Canada, an Indian subsidiary, as on 31.03.2024 is as follows:

Liabilities	*Canada* (C $)	*Assets*	*Canada* (C $)
Equity & reserves	10,000	Land and building	10,000
Bonds and debentures	12,000	Plant and equipment	16,000
Accounts payable	10,000	Inventories (at market value)	8,000
Outstanding	8,000	Accounts receivable	4,000
		Cash	2,000
Total	40,000	Total	40,000

When the above balance sheet is translated into the home currency, i.e., the Indian Rupee, under the '*current and non-current method*', all the current assets and current liabilities will be multiplied by current rate, and the non-current assets and non-current liabilities, *except owner's equity* will be multiplied by the historical rate. The difference in the balance sheet representing **gain** or **loss** will be directly attributed to the owner's equity which could have been a different value under a straight multiplication. This gain or loss is thus due to translation. Whereas, a gain is going to increase the net worth of the firm and hence the management is certainly no concerned, a loss will decrease the net worth and will be a cause of concern needing the management's attention to manage the same, either to eliminate or to reduce the loss on translation. Now before going into the management part, let us find out the amount of loss or gain that is associated with translation of Simon & Co's balance sheet.

Balance sheet of Simon & Co. after translation

Liabilities	*Canada* (C $)	*Rate* ₹	*Translated amount* ₹	*Assets*	*Canada* (C $)	*Rate* ₹	*Translated amount* ₹
Equity & reserves	10,000		**3,82,000***	Land and building	10,000	39	3,90,000
Bonds and debentures	12,000	39	4,48,000	Plant and equipment	16,000	39	2,34,000
Accounts payable	10,000	41	4,41,000	Inventories (at market			3,28,000
Outstanding	8,000	41	3,28,000	value)	8,000	41	
				Accounts receivable	4,000	41	1,64,000
				Cash	2,000	41	82,000
Total	40,000		15,88,000	Total	40,000		15,88,000

Note: The value of equity and reserves, being non-current, if multiplied by ₹39 would have been ₹3,90,000, against which its value has been shown at ₹3,82,000 which is the balancing figure of the balance sheet after translation. The loss therefore is ₹8,000 which has been directly attributed to owner's equity under the logic that any gain or loss will go to the owner's pocket. This loss may even go up or down under the other two methods of translation, namely, monetary/monetary and temporal method.

Thus the translation loss in the instant case is ₹8,000, which needs to be managed in order to get eliminated or minimized to the extent possible. Management of exposure has been discussed separately in the chapter management of foreign exchange exposure.

ECONOMIC EXPOSURE

Economic exposure is the sensitivity of a firm's value to exchange rate movements. Economic exposure arises on account of the firm's exposure to foreign currency transactions already entered into. Economic exposure results in the alteration of the firm's cash inflows, whereas the translation exposure does not.

Economic exposure assumes two forms—the transaction exposure and operating exposure.

TRANSACTION EXPOSURE

Transaction exposure affects the firm's cash inflows. It arises due to the firm's financial obligations to be settled in foreign currency(ies). A transaction exposure arises whenever a company is committed to a foreign currency denominated transaction [6]. Transaction exposure measures changes in the value of outstanding financial obligations incurred prior to a change in exchange rates but due to be settled until after the exchange rates change [7]. Transaction exposure emerges mainly on account of export and import of commodities on open account, borrowings and lending in foreign currency and intra firm flows in an international company [8]. Transaction exposure thus occurs owing to the firm's:

(a) export and import of commodities on open account;
(b) borrowing and lending in foreign currency; and
(c) intra-firm transfer of funds, particularly in case of the MNCs.

The *gain* on exposure for an Indian firm due to export and import on open account shall be equal to 'rupee worth of accounts receivable on actual settlement *minus* rupee worth of accounts due receivable on initiation of the transaction. Similarly the *loss* shall be 'rupee worth of accounts payable on actual settlement *minus* rupee worth of accounts due payable on initiation of the transaction'.

The exposure due to borrowing and lending in foreign currency shall be to the extent that when a foreign currency appreciates, the burden of borrowings increases as more amount of domestic currency will be needed to settle the debt and the vice-versa.

Exposure associated with the intra-firm transfer of funds, say in the form of repatriation of income from one unit of the MNC located in a country X to another unit located in some other country Y, shall be high or low depending upon whether and to what extent the host country currency appreciates or depreciates against the home country currency.

The transaction exposure, as stated before, may take three forms—*quotation* exposure, *backlog* exposure and *billing* exposure. Quotation exposure is said to exist when the exporting firm quotes a price and the price continues remain valid till the importing firm places an order for supply of the commodities in context. Backlog exposure is said to exist in between the period of the placement of an order for supply by the importing firm and the actual shipment and billing by the exporting firm. Similarly, a billing exposure exists in between the billing of the shipment and the actual receipt of the payments from the importing firm.

'A transaction exposure is actually created at the first moment the seller quotes a price in foreign currency terms to a potential buyer. The quote can be either verbal, as in a telephone quote, or in the form of a written bid or even a printed price list. With the placing of an order, the potential exposure created at the time of quotation is converted into actual exposure, called the backlog exposure because the product has not yet been shipped or billed. Backlog exposure remains until actual payment is received by the seller'[9].

The transaction exposure should be the consolidated net exposure, i.e., the loss on account of one or more transaction(s) shall be set off against the gain on account of other transaction(s) involving inflow and outflow of funds so as to determine the net amount of transaction exposure.

OPERATING EXPOSURE

Operating exposure, **also called real operating exposure, competitive exposure, or strategic exposure**, arises when a change in the exchange rate coupled with inflation rate changes the amount and the risk complexion of the firm's stream of future revenue and costs. 'Real operating exposure arises when changes in exchange rate, together with rates of inflation, alter the amount and risk element of a company's future revenue and cost stream'[10].

The term real exchange rate refers to the 'inflation adjusted nominal exchange rate', i.e., the exchange rate after adjustment for inflation. For example, if the nominal exchange rate at time t_1 is ₹46/USD and the shift in inflation from t_1 to t_2 is 12% in India and 7% in the US, the *real exchange rate* is ₹48.15/USD, calculated as $₹46 \times \frac{112}{107}$ or $₹48.15/\text{USD}$. Further, the need for determining 'operating' exposure arises because of the fact that any change in the operating cash flow will change the 'value' of the firm.

Difficulties in Measuring Real Operating Exposure

Measuring real operating exposure may be difficult as forecast of inflation differential for future years is difficult. Precision of estimation of real operating exposure by the firm will depend on its ability to forecast the inflation rate. This will be clearer from the following example:

Suppose that the home currency of a country, say Indian rupee appreciates against a host currency, say USD by 5%. An appreciation of home currency will make the export uncompetitive because less amount of INR against Dollar will flow in. An appreciation of home currency will make the import attractive as less outflow of INR will take place against the Dollar. A reverse will be the case for depreciation in home currency. Now if inflation differential in India also comes down following a currency appreciation (or goes up when there is a currency depreciation) by the same amount, i.e., 5%, the resultant real operating exposure will be 0 (zero).

The firm's revenue and cost structure do also get influenced by the changes in the inflation and exchange rates. Its future flow of cash (revenue) will vary depending upon three different market conditions—the export market, domestic market with competition from import, and domestic market with no competition from import from foreign company. The cost structure will vary on three counts as well-on import of inputs, sourcing of inputs from domestic market with competition from foreign suppliers and sourcing of inputs from domestic market without competition from foreign suppliers.

For example, the exporting firm may well pass on to the importing firm abroad a rise in the domestic inflation, resulting thereby in earning increased revenue. But with competition from import, a rise in the inflation can't be passed on to the foreign customers as a result of which the revenue will fall. However, with no competition of import, a rise in inflation can be passed on to customers and the revenue can thus be increased.

As regards the cost structure, a rise in the inflation can impact the cost (i) *due to the import of inputs* with the exporting firm in monopoly passing on the burden to the importing firm which will increase the latter's cost; (ii) *due to the purchase of inputs from domestic supplier without competition* from foreign suppliers with the local manufacturer then raising the price for absence of competition. In case of *inputs from domestic supplier with competition from foreign firms*, the cost of the importing firm remains unaffected as a rise in inflation cannot be passed on.

Estimating the 'Real Operating Exposure'

The real operating exposure is the difference between the present values of cash inflows after adjustment against factors like the expected inflation rate differential, expected exchange rate differential, price-elasticity of demand, product features differential, import substitution (by domestically available input) and the ratio of imported input in the total input and the present value of cash inflows expected under stable real exchange rate.

Thus, estimation of real operating exposure is a complex phenomenon as is apparent from the above-mentioned process of calculation. The forecaster has to find the cash inflows under different conditions mentioned above, convert them into present values and then compared with the present values of the cash inflows that are expected under stable real exchange rate. The difference between the two is the real operating exposure. To illustrate the concept however a simple example may be taken as follows:

ILLUSTRATION 13.1

ABC Co. Ltd. expects cash inflows over the first five years period from its new foreign venture at \$8,000, \$10,000, \$14,000, \$15,000 and \$12,000. Due to changes in exchange rates to inflation rates, the cash inflows may be expected to accrue at \$6,500, \$8,500, \$12,000, \$14,000 and \$10,000, respectively over the said period.

What is the real operating exposure associated with the operation at 10% discount rate?

SOLUTION

(A) PV of cash flows before change:

$$\frac{\$8,000}{(1.10)^1}+\frac{\$10,000}{(1.10)^2}+\frac{\$14,000}{(1.10)^3}+\frac{\$15,000}{(1.10)^4}+\frac{\$12,000}{(1.10)^5}$$

$$=\$7,272.73+\$8,264.46+\$10,518.41+\$10,245+\$7,451.05=\$43,752$$

(B) PV of cash flows after change:

$$\frac{\$6,500}{(1.10)^1}+\frac{\$8,500}{(1.10)^2}+\frac{\$12,000}{(1.10)^3}+\frac{\$14,000}{(1.10)^4}+\frac{\$10,000}{(1.10)^5}$$

$$=\$5,909+\$7,025+\$9,016+\$9,562+\$6,209=\$37,721$$

(C) **Real operating exposure** = A – B = \$43,752 – \$37,721 = \$6,031 (down)

ILLUSTRATION 13.2

XYZ India Ltd. expects to generate cash inflows of \$18,000, \$28,000, \$45,000, \$35,000, and \$22,000 over the initial five years period from one of its new foreign ventures. However, due to exchange rate and inflation rate fluctuations, the firm cash inflows may come down to \$11,000, \$19,000, \$32,000, \$23,000, and \$14,000 respectively, for the said period.

You are required to determine the Firm's operating exposure at 10% discount rate?

SOLUTION

(A) PV of cash flows before change:

$$\frac{\$18,000}{(1.10)^1}+\frac{\$28,000}{(1.10)^2}+\frac{\$45,000}{(1.10)^3}+\frac{\$35,000}{(1.10)^4}+\frac{\$22,000}{(1.10)^5}$$

$$=\$16,363.64+\$23,140.50+\$33,809.17+\$23,905.47+\$13,660.27$$

$$=\$1,10,879.05$$

(B) PV of cash flows after change:

$$\frac{\$11,000}{(1.10)^1}+\frac{\$19,000}{(1.10)^2}+\frac{\$32,000}{(1.10)^3}+\frac{\$23,000}{(1.10)^4}+\frac{\$14,000}{(1.10)^5}$$

$$=\$10,000.00+\$15,702.48+\$24,042.07+\$15,709.31+\$8,692.90$$

$$=\$74,146.76$$

(C) **Operating exposure** = A – B = \$1,10,879.05 – \$ 74,146.76 = \$36,732.29 **(down)**

ILLUSTRATION 13.3

Double Star India Ltd. expects to generate cash inflows of \$29,000, \$38,000, \$52,000, \$40,000, and \$28,000 over the initial five years period from one of its new foreign ventures. However, due to fluctuations in the exchange rate and inflation rate, the firm's cash inflows may come down to \$21 ,000, \$29,000, \$42,000, \$28,000 and \$16,000 respectively, for the said period.

You are required to determine the Firm's strategic exposure at 10% discount rate?

SOLUTION

(A) PV of cash flows before change:

$$\frac{\$29,000}{(1.10)^1}+\frac{\$38,000}{(1.10)^2}+\frac{\$52,000}{(1.10)^3}+\frac{\$40,000}{(1.10)^4}+\frac{\$28,000}{(1.10)^5}$$

$$= \$26,363.64 + \$31,404.96 + \$39,068.37 + \$27,320.54 + \$17,385.80$$
$$= \$1,41,543.04$$

(B) PV of cash flows after change:

$$\frac{\$21,000}{(1.10)^1}+\frac{\$29,000}{(1.10)^2}+\frac{\$42,000}{(1.10)^3}+\frac{\$28,000}{(1.10)^4}+\frac{\$16,000}{(1.10)^5}$$

$$= \$19,090.91 + \$23,966.94 + \$31,555.22 + \$19,124.38 + \$9,934.74$$
$$= \$1,03,672.19$$

(C) **Strategic exposure** = A – B = \$1,41,543.04 – \$1,03,672.19 = \$37,870.85 **(down)**

Adler and Dumas [11] considered to be the pioneer in measuring exchange rate exposure have suggested the following simple regression model for measurement of the firm's exposure to exchange rate fluctuations:

$$r_{i,t} = \beta_{0,i} + \beta_{1,i}\, r_{x,t} + \varepsilon_{i,t}\, i = 1,\ 2,\ n$$

and
$$\varepsilon_{i,t}\, N(0,\ \delta^2)$$

where $r_{i,t}$ is return on firm *i*'s stock at time *t*; $r_{x,t}$ is percentage change in exchange rate at time *t*; $\beta_{1,i}$ is firm *i*'s exchange rate exposure coefficient (also known as exposure beta) which measures the sensitivity of a firm's returns to the exchange rate movements; and $\varepsilon_{i,t}$ is the residual that is unexplained by the regression. When exchange rate is expressed as the foreign currency price of home currency, there exists a negative relationship between the exchange rate changes and the firm value of an exporter. For instance, a depreciation of home currency (a negative value of $r_{x,t}$) may increase the firm's profitability which implies an increase in. For an importer the opposite is the case.

SUMMARY

Measurement of foreign exchange exposure is an important dimension of firm's exposure management. An unanticipated change in the exchange rate is termed as exchange rate exposure. There are three forms of foreign exchange exposure. They are the translation exposure, transaction exposure and operating exposure. Measurement of the exposure is important for the firm for a downward change in the cash inflows will decrease the firm's overall performance and 'value' to its stakeholders. Identification of the source(s) of exposure and its quantification will help the firm adopting strategies like the 'hedging' to eliminate or minimize such risk of exposure.

KEY TERMS

Foreign exchange exposure refers to an 'unanticipated change' in the exchange rate.

Translation exposure occurs on account of consolidation of financial statements.

Economic exposure arises on account of the firm's exposure to foreign currency transactions already entered into.

Quotation exposure is said to exist when the exporting firm quotes a price and the price continues remain valid till the importing firm places an order for supply of the commodities in context.

Backlog exposure is said to exist in between the period of the placement of an order for supply by the importing firm and the actual shipment and billing by the exporting firm.

Billing exposure exists in between the billing of the shipment and the actual receipt of the payments from the importing firm.

Real exchange rate refers to the 'inflation adjusted nominal exchange rate'.

REVIEW QUESTIONS

1. What is foreign exchange exposure? Why should a firm be concerned about foreign exchange exposure? Discuss.
2. Define foreign exchange exposure and discuss the various forms of foreign exchange exposure.
3. What do you mean by risk exposure? Explain the sources of operating and transaction exposure.
4. Discuss the arguments for and against the need for measurement of foreign exchange exposure.
5. Define foreign exchange exposure and discuss its importance to management.
6. How will you estimate translation exposure? Explain with example(s).
7. How is operating exposure estimated? Discuss with example(s) of your own.
8. A firm estimates cash inflows from one of its new foreign ventures over the initial six years period at $1,08,000, $1,20,000, $1,40,000, $1,75,000, $1,32,000 and $99,000. Due to exchange rate and inflation rate fluctuations however the firm anticipates its cash inflows to be down to $96,500, $1,08,500, $1,22,000, $1,45,000 , $1,10,000, and $88,000, respectively, for the stated period.

   What is the firm's operating exposure at 10% discount rate?

9. Discuss the difficulties a firm is likely to encounter in its endeavour to quantify its economic exposure.
10. The nominal exchange rate in the beginning of the first quarter of a year is ₹66/£. The inflation rate in India is likely to be 14% in the second quarter and 8% in the UK. What will be a firm's expectation of the real exchange rate in the second quarter?
11. Write notes on:
    (a) Transaction exposure
    (b) Translation exposure
12. Differentiate between transaction exposure and translation exposure. Discuss the techniques you will flow to measure translation exposure.
13. ABC Co. Ltd. expects to generate cash inflows over the first 6 years period from its new foreign venture at $18,000, $25,000, $40,000, $60,000, $44,000 and $29,000. Due to changes in exchange rates to inflation rates, the cash inflows may be expected to accrue at $15,500, $22,500, $37,500, $54,000, $39,000 and $25,000, respectively over the said period.
    What is the real operating exposure associated with the operation at 12% discount rate?
14. XYZ India Ltd. expects to generate cash inflows of $20,000, $30,000, $40,000, $35,000, and $25,000 over the initial five years period from one of its new foreign ventures. However, due to exchange rate and inflation rate fluctuations, the firm's cash inflows may come down to $18,000, $28,000, $38,000, $33,000, and $24,000, respectively, for the said period.
    Determine the Firm's strategic exposure at 12% discount rate.
15. Star and Shine India Ltd. expects to generate cash inflows of $19,000, $28,000, $42,000, $35,000, $29,000 and $22,000 over the initial six years period from one of its new foreign ventures. However, due to fluctuations in the exchange rate and inflation rate, the firm's cash inflows may come down to $18,500, $26,500, $40,000, $ 33,500, $27,000 and $29,500, respectively, for the said period.
    What is the Firm's real operating exposure underlying the project at 10% discount rate?

REFERENCES

[1] Choi, J.J., and Prasad, A.M, *Exchange rate sensitivity and its determinants: A firm and industry analysis of U.S. Multinational, Financial Management*, Vol. 24, No. 3,(1995), pp. 77–88.

[2] Glaum, M., Brunner, M., and Himmel, H., The DAX and the Dolar: The Economic Exchange Rate Exposure of German Corporation, *Journal of International Business Studies*, Vol. 31, No. 4, (2000), pp. 715–724.

[3] Bodnar, G.M., and Gentry, W. M. Exchange rate exposure and industry characteristics: Evidence from Canada, Japan and the USA, *Journal of International Money and Finance*, 12, (1993), pp. 29–45.

[4] Stulz, R. Optimal hedging policies, *Journal of Financial and Quantitative Analysis*, 19, (1984) pp. 127–140.

[5] Froot, K., Sharfstein, D., and J. Stein, Risk management: Coordinating corporate investment and financing decisions, *Journal of Finance*, 48, (1993) pp. 1629–1648.

[6] Shapiro, Alan C., *Multinational Financial Management*, 4th Edition, PHI Learning, New Delhi, 2002, p. 201.

[7] David K. Eiteman, et al., *Multinational Business Finance*, 10th Edition, Pearson, New Delhi, 2008, p. 240.

[8] Sharan, V., *International Financial Management*, 4th Edition, PHI Learning, New Delhi, p. 176.

[9] David K. Eiteman, et al., *Multinational Business Finance*, 10th Edition, Pearson, New Delhi, 2008, p. 245.

[10] Sharan, V., *International Financial Management*, 4th Edition, PHI Learning, New Delhi, p. 179.

[11] Adler, M., Dumas, B., *Exposure to currency risk: definition and measurement, Financial Management*, Summer, 13, (1984), 41–50.

14

Management of Foreign Exchange Exposure

LEARNING OBJECTIVES

After studying this chapter, you will be able to:

- Appreciate the need for management of foreign exchange exposure
- Know the different techniques of foreign exchange exposure management
- Comprehend the techniques of natural hedges and contractual hedges used for managing transaction exposure
- Understand the techniques used for hedging the operating exposure
- Understand the techniques used for hedging the translation exposure

INTRODUCTION

Exchange rate volatility has been a major source of macroeconomic uncertainty affecting the value of the firms in the floating exchange rate regime. Firms with low liquidity at times find themselves being pushed to financial distress due to exchange rate volatility. Effective and efficient management of exchange rate exposure has therefore become imperative for the firms in order to maximize their value. Management of foreign exchange exposure refers to the process of elimination and/or minimization of the loss accruing to the firms due to changes in the exchange rate. The process through which exchange rate exposure is managed is known as 'hedging'.

HEDGING TECHNIQUES

The various hedging techniques used for managing foreign exchange exposure may be clubbed into *three* categories, namely, those used for managing the *transaction exposure*, those used for managing the *operating exposure*, and those used for managing the *translation exposure*. Whereas, transaction exposure and operating exposure together result in economic exposure of the firm, translation exposure is the accounting exposure by nature as has been discussed in Chapter 13.

The hedging techniques used for managing the transaction exposure are broadly two—**natural hedges** and **contractual hedges**. Natural hedges are composed of *leads and lags, cross hedging, currency diversification, sharing of risk, pricing the transactions, back to back loans, currency swaps and 'matching the cash flows'*. These techniques are internal to the firm and hence are often called as the 'internal techniques' as they do not involve any contractual relationship with any parties outside the firm. Contractual hedges on the other hand are external in nature, hence called 'external techniques' at times as they result in creating contractual relationship with external agencies. Included under the contractual hedges are—*forward market hedge, hedging through currency futures, hedging through currency options* and *money market hedge*.

Similarly, the techniques used for managing the operating exposure are in the form of **financial, marketing and production strategy.** Whereas, financial strategy shall include *long-term transaction exposure hedging such as matching of cash flows, parallel loans* and *currency swaps*, and *matching of liabilities with assets*; marketing strategy shall comprise of strategies like selection of new market, product innovation/planning; and production strategy shall comprise of sourcing of product and product inputs, input mixing, plant location and productivity improvement.

The hedging techniques used for managing the translation exposure are the *balance sheet hedge* and a mixture of *balance sheet hedge with contractual and natural hedges*.

Figure 14.1 depicts the different hedging techniques as mentioned above.

HEDGING TECHNIQUES FOR TRANSACTION EXPOSURE

Natural Hedges (also known as internal techniques of hedging)

1. **Leads and lags:** Leads and lags are type of natural hedges which fall within the firm's internal financial management technique to manage its exposure to foreign exchange volatility. 'Lead' means advancing or accelerating the timing of receipt or of payment of foreign currency, 'Lag' means delaying or decelerating or postponing the timing of receipt a payment by modifying the credit terms. The purpose in both the cases is to reduce the burden of debt. For example, in the event of depreciation in the home currency, an importing firm can advance its payment to minimize outflow of cash and the reverse in case of appreciation of home currency.
2. **Cross-hedging:** 'Cross-hedging' as a technique for managing transaction exposure is adopted when a particular currency desired to be hedged can't be hedged in a forward market and as an alternative, a substitute currency whose volatility is highly correlated with the desired currency is identified and hedged.
3. **Currency diversification:** Currency diversification refers to a situation where the firm undertakes transactions involving a large number of foreign currencies rather than a relatively smaller number so that when there is depreciation in one or a few currency(ies), there may be appreciation in some other currency(ies) which will compensate the loss and the overall loss gets minimized. This may not be possible if the firm trades with a relatively small number of currencies involved in.
4. **Sharing of risk:** Sharing of risk is a contractual agreement wherein the buyer and the seller agree to share the foreign currency exposure. The arrangement is made in such a way that if the exchange rate falls below or goes above the agreed rate which

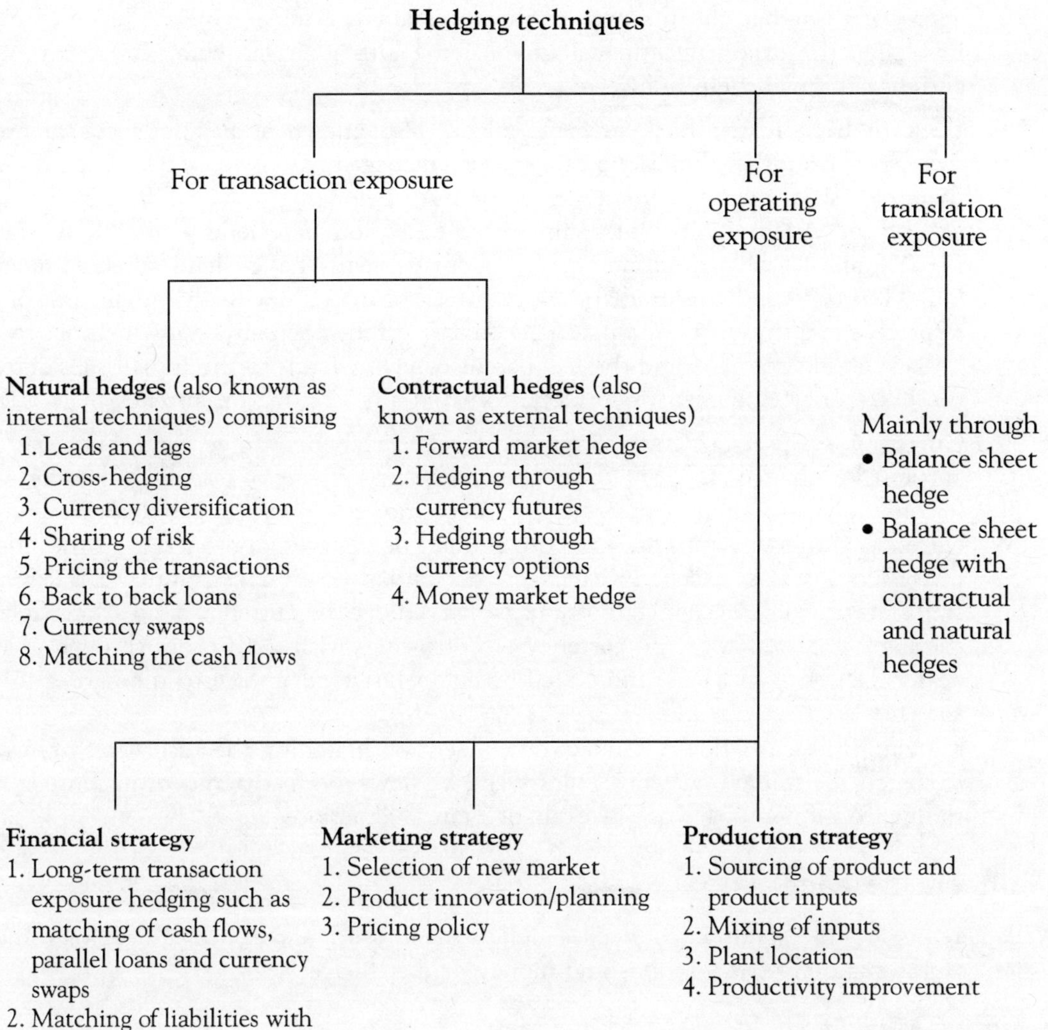

Figure 14.1 Different hedging techniques for managing exchange exposure.

is usually the spot rate plus or minus a certain percentage, the difference gets passed to either party. Consequently the burden of loss does not fall on any single party and the loss ultimately gets reduced.

5. **Pricing the transactions:** Foreign currency exposure can be managed through a variation in the pricing of the transactions. There are two ways to cause a variation in the pricing. They are price variation and currency invoicing. Price variation is effected by making up or down in the transaction price (sale price) to neutralize the adverse impact of any exchange rate changes. The exporter, upon the terms of agreement, may increase the selling price in terms of foreign currency when the home currency

appreciates so that the ultimate earnings remain the same. Under the currency of invoicing, the exporting firm will invoice the bills in home currency or any other currency that will help him recover his costs.

6. **Back to back loans:** Back to back a loan, also known as parallel loans or credit swap, is yet another technique of exposure management. It operates in such a way that the risk of exposure involving two parties belonging to two different countries gets off set. An Indian parent company for example has to lend to its UK subsidiary £10,000 and at the same time an UK parent company has to lend an equal amount (£10,000) to its Indian subsidiary. Now instead of the money really moving out of the respective country on remittances, the Indian parent company lends in India to the Indian subsidiary of UK and the UK parent company lends to the Indian subsidiary in the UK money equivalent to £10,000 to avoid any loss due to currency fluctuations.
7. **Currency swaps:** Currency swaps are foreign-exchange agreements between two parties to exchange the principal and/or interest payments of a loan in one currency for an equivalent amount of principal and/or interest payments of a loan in another currency. Currency swaps are over the counter derivatives, and operate in the line of interest rate swaps, except for the fact that unlike the interest rate swaps, currency swaps may involve exchange of the principal. Under the currency swap arrangements, the borrowers exchange the currency of borrowings with each other through a swap dealer. Currency swaps are motivated by comparative advantage to the parties to the agreement.
8. **Matching the cash flows:** Under the concept of 'matching the cash flows', firms try to match the foreign currency inflows and outflows, both in terms of magnitude and timing, to minimize the risk of exchange rate fluctuations.

Contractual Hedges

As depicted in Fig. 14.1, contractual hedges include the forward market hedge, hedging through currency futures and currency options and money market hedges.

Forward Market Hedge

The foreign exchange risk in terms of loss (or gain) to the trader (exporter or importer) may be managed (i.e., reduced, in case of loss) through forward market hedging where currencies are bought and sold forward. The forward buying and/or selling will depend on whether the trader, called the hedger, is taking the long or short position. An exporter is said to have taken long position if the exports are billed in foreign currency. Similarly, an importer takes short position when imports are billed in foreign currency.

Now in order to minimize the foreign currency exposure, exporter taking long position sales, i.e., agrees to sell under forward contract, a fixed sum of foreign currency at an agreed rate and on an agreed date. An importer, on the contrary, taking the short position, buys or agrees to buy under forward contract a certain amount of foreign currency at an agreed price and date.

Example of Long Position (by the exporter)

ABC Ltd., an Indian exporter sells goods to XYZ of Japan for 25,000 ¥ receivable three months hence. ABC Ltd. anticipates that the ¥ which is currently trading at ₹40/¥, (i.e., the spot rate is ₹40/¥) with the same (₹40/¥) as the forward rate, will depreciate (fall) by 10% after three months, i.e., the ¥ will be (₹40 – ₹4 or) 36/¥. Assuming that this anticipation holds good, the export earnings of ABC Ltd. will get reduced by ₹1,00,000, (i.e., 25,000¥ × ₹4). To avoid this, ABC Ltd. would enter into a forward contract for three months to sell 25,000¥ at ₹40/¥. By this arrangement, ABC Ltd. will earn ₹1,00,000 which will equally offset the loss due to fall in the exchange rate.

Example of Short Position (by the importer)

An importer who fears appreciation in the value of a foreign currency, say ¥, against the home currency, say Indian rupees, will enter into a forward contract to sell specified sum of ¥ at a predetermined rate and date. The following example illustrates the concept:

Basic Industries Ltd. an Indian importer buys goods from Fundamentals Ltd. of Japan for 50,000 ¥ payable three months hence. Basic Ltd. fears that ¥ which is currently trading at ₹40/¥ in the spot and forward market, will appreciate by 10% after three months, to become 44/¥. If the Yen really appreciates as anticipated, the import bill of Basic Ltd. will increase by ₹2,00,000 and its earnings will be down by ₹2,00,000, (i.e., 50,000¥ × ₹4). To counter this, Basic Ltd. will enter into a forward contract for three months to buy 50,000¥ at ₹40/¥. By so doing, it will save ₹2,00,000 which will equally offset the loss due to a rise in the exchange rate.

Hedging through Currency Futures

Under the currency futures, currencies are bought and sold like any other commodities, at a specified 'rate' of exchange and on a fixed maturity date, with the involvement of a clearing house and brokers with consideration of brokerage. Whereas, the mode of operation of currency futures is like that of forward contract, the basic difference between the two lies with fact that in a forward contract, there is no clearing house, no *fixed date of maturity*, no brokerage, and no fixed amount. In the currency futures, however, only a limited number of currencies and for relatively smaller amount are traded.

Under the currency futures arrangement, an importer buys currency futures whereas an exporter sells currency futures. The importer protects itself from the loss due to currency appreciation, and the exporter protects itself from the loss due to currency depreciation.

As for example, an exporter selling goods for 5,000 USD at the prevailing rate of ₹46/USD on a three months term may agree to sell currency futures at ₹46 or 47/USD on fear for depreciation in the USD that the USD will become ₹44/USD. Similarly, an importer will enter into a contract to buy currency futures on anticipation of a currency appreciation like ₹46/$ now to ₹51/$ later.

Hedging through Currency Options

Currency options are used for hedging risk and for making speculative profits. Like the futures market, currency option is a derivative market wherein large volume of currencies are bought and sold. Under the mechanism of currency options, the buyer has the option *but not the obligation* to the contract. The buyer exercises the option if the price is favourable to him after the expiry of the option terms/period. In order to have the privilege of exercising the option, the buyer pays a premium to the option-seller, in addition to the option price, i.e., an additional amount is paid to the option seller, in case the option price goes in favour of the buyer. The buyer may terminate the option by not performing the obligation, thus allowing it to expire. *The importer buys a call option and the exporter buys a put option.* Hedging through currency option is preferred to forward contract in case of a strong and highly volatile exchange market.

The Working of Currency Option

The working of currency option can be illustrated through the following examples of call option and put option:

Call option for the importer

An importer who anticipates appreciation in the foreign currency will buy a put option for selling the foreign currency. For example, ABC India Ltd. imports goods worth 50,000£ payable two months hence. The company expects an appreciation in £ and decides to purchase call option at ₹70/£ with ₹0.5/£ as premium. If the spot rate on maturity is ₹71.5/£, the Co. will go for exercising the call option as it will help the Co. gain by ₹50,000 or (₹50,000/71.5) calculated as follows:

The Company pays

$$(50{,}000 \times ₹70) + 50{,}000 \times ₹0.5$$
$$= ₹35{,}00{,}000 + ₹25{,}000$$
$$= ₹35{,}25{,}000$$

In the absence of (call) option, the Co. would have paid 50,000 × ₹71.5 = ₹35,75,000. Therefore, the Co. saves ₹35,75,000 – ₹35,25,000 = ₹50,000. Hence, ABC India Ltd. will exercise the call option.

Put option for the exporter

An exporter who fears depreciation in the foreign currency will buy a put option for selling the foreign currency. For example, Super Sales Ltd. has exported goods worth $50,000 to Privilege Inc. of USA on a three months term. Super Sales Ltd. expects that USD will depreciate over the period and therefore would go for a put option hedging by buying put option to sell USD on maturity at ₹49.5, with a commission of ₹0.5/USD. If the spot rate on maturity comes to ₹48.5/USD, Super Sales will receive 50,000 × ₹48.5 = ₹24,25,000.

When it goes for put option, it will receive (50,000 × ₹49.5) – (50,000 × ₹0.5) = ₹24,75,000 – ₹25,000 = ₹24,50,000. Under put option, Super Sales Ltd. gains by ₹25,000.

Money Market Hedge

Under the money market hedging mechanism, an importer, in order to cover foreign currency 'payables' will borrow local currency; convert the local currency so borrowed to desired foreign currency payables; and invest the converted amount of foreign currency for the payment period in such a way that the principal together with interest will be equal to the cost of the import.

For example, an importer has to make a payment of 50,000 USD four months hence.

If the rate of interest is 12% per annum, the foreign currency to be invested initially for four months shall be $\frac{50,000\,\text{USD}}{1.04}$ = 48,077 USD which will earn 50,000 USD on maturity. Going by the sequence of events therefore the importer has to borrow local currency (say, Indian Rupee) of 48,077USD × ₹40 or ₹19,23,080 which will be converted to ₹19, 23,080/₹40 = USD 48,077 and invested at 12% for 4 months to earn an interest of 1923 USD, and to generate 50,000 USD; with the principal amount of 48,077 USD and interest of 1923 USD taken together.

The exporter, in order to cover future receivables will first borrow foreign currency (48,077 USD), convert it to Indian currency (say 48,077 × ₹40/USD = ₹19,23,080) and invest ₹19,23,080 at 12% p.a. for 4 months to earn interest of ₹76,923 which, together with the principal amount of ₹19,23,080, will be equal to ₹20,00,003 or 50,000 USD.

HEDGING TECHNIQUES FOR OPERATING EXPOSURE

As stated before and depicted in Figure 14.1, the techniques used for managing operating exposure are in the form of **financial, marketing and production strategy.** 'Planning for operating exposure is a total management responsibility because it depends on the interaction of strategies in finance, marketing, purchasing and production' [1].

Financial strategy shall include *long-term transaction exposure hedging such as matching of cash flows, parallel loans* and *currency swaps*, and *matching of liabilities with assets*. Restructuring of assets and liabilities shall be undertaken in a way that any decline in the firm's earnings must also have a corresponding decline in the liabilities to be served.

Marketing strategy shall comprise of strategies like selection of new market, production planning and product pricing; and production strategy shall consist of alternative sourcing of product inputs, input mixing, and plant location.

Marketing Strategy

Selection of New Markets

Selection of new markets is a part of marketing strategy firms adopts to manage operating exposure. A firm, for example, exporting goods will not find exports competitive if the domestic currency of the firm appreciates (or the importing currency depreciates). Say, ABC Co. exports goods worth 10,000 USD on a 2 months term when the prevalent exchange rate is ₹48/USD. The export becomes uncompetitive if the exchange rate after two months becomes ₹44/USD. In such case, it would be ideal for ABC Co. to explore new market and withdraw from the present market, i.e., to stop exporting to the country against which the home currency is appreciating.

Product Innovation/Planning

If due to appreciation of home currency, export of firms becomes uncompetitive leading to a fall in export sales, firms can make up the decrease in sales by offering new and innovative products to their customers.

'Companies often respond to exchange risk by altering their product strategy, which deals with such areas as new product introduction, product line decisions, and product innovation. One way to cope with exchange rate fluctuations is to change the timing of the introduction of new products' [2].

Pricing Policy

The firm exporting the products may change its catalogue/listed price up or down depending upon whether the home currency appreciates or depreciates against a particular foreign currency in order to maintain the level of profit. For example, XYZ Co. with a break up of cost and profit of ₹39 and ₹6 against the selling price of ₹45 per unit, exports 1,000 units when the exchange rate is ₹45/USD, that is, the selling price is 1 USD per unit. Now, if Rupee appreciates against dollar at the time of settlement, say for example it becomes ₹40/USD; to maintain the same profit the selling price per unit has to be increased to 1.125 USD from 1 USD, so that the generate the same amount of sales, i.e., ₹45,000 at the new exchange rate of ₹40/USD which will bring ₹45,000/₹40 or 1125 USD for 1,000 units or 1.125 USD/unit.

Production Strategy

The production strategy that may be used by the MNCs for managing their foreign exchange exposure ranges from alternative sourcing of product and product inputs, mixing of inputs, plant location and productivity.

Sourcing of product and product inputs – Firms who import products and/or inputs from other countries will find it useful a strategy to look for alternative sources of supply in the event the exporting country's currency appreciates. In other words, when the currency of the country supplying product or inputs appreciates, the input buying firms have to find alternative sources of supply from other countries that may be cheaper.

Mixing of inputs—Firms experiencing unfavorable fluctuations in the exchange rates on import of inputs may, in order to contain cost, go for limited imports, while sourcing the rest of the requirements from indigenous sources. The exercise thus results in using a mix of imported and locally arranged inputs.

Plant location—Locating plants and production units in other countries whose currencies are either stable or are depreciating in comparison to home currency is yet another means of managing the adverse effect of foreign exchange risk. The option is particularly useful when the home currency appreciates and foreign currency depreciates, as an appreciated home currency increases the product costs and decreases the export earnings. 'Third country plant locations are also a viable alternative in many cases, depending especially on the labour intensity of production or the projections for further monetary realignments. Many Japanese firms, for example, have shifted production offshore—to Taiwan, South Korea, Singapore and other developing nations, as well as to the United States—in order to cope with the high yen'[3].

Productivity improvement—Productivity improvement, by adopting retrenchment strategy such as closing down of inefficient plants; resorting to large-scale automation; cost reduction and quality improvements, has also been seen as benefiting the MNCs in their efforts to managing the foreign exposure.

HEDGING TECHNIQUES FOR TRANSLATION EXPOSURE

Translation exposure or accounting exposure as it is also called is associated with the translation of financial statements of foreign subsidiaries into the parent's reporting currency for the purpose of consolidation of the financial performance of parent and the subsidiaries taken together. 'Translation exposure is the potential for an increase or decrease in the parent's net worth and reported net income caused by a change in exchange rates since the last transaction'[4]. The techniques used for managing translation exposure are mainly the *balance sheet hedge* and *balance sheet hedge with contractual and natural hedges*.

Balance Sheet Hedge

Balance sheet hedge is done by either reducing the 'exposed' assets without reducing the exposed liabilities or increasing the exposed liabilities without reducing the exposed assets. To illustrate the concept, the following balance sheet of Simplex & Co of Canada, an Indian subsidiary before translation may be taken into account:

Balance sheet of Simplex & Co. of Canada as on 31.03.2021(before translation)

Liabilities	*Canadian $*	*Assets*	*Canadian $*
Equity and reserves	10,000	Land and building	6,000
Bonds and debentures	12,000	Plant and equipment	8,000
Accounts payable	10,000	Long-term investments	12,000
Outstanding	8,000	Inventories (at market value)	8,000
		Accounts receivable	4,000
		Cash	2,000
Total	40,000	Total	40,000

When the above balance sheet is translated into the home currency, i.e., the Indian rupee, under the *'current and non-current methods'*, all the current assets and current liabilities will be multiplied by current rate, and the non-current assets and non-current liabilities *except owner's equity* will be multiplied by the historical rate. The difference in the balance sheet representing gain or loss will be directly attributed to the owner's equity which could have been a different value under the 'monetary/ non-monetary' or 'temporal' methods of translation as discussed in Chapter 2 under the title 'Foreign Currency Translation'. This gain or loss is thus due to translation.

A gain will increase the net worth of the firm and hence the management may not be concerned about such exposure, but a loss will decrease the net worth and hence will be a cause of concern for the management needing the management's attention to manage such exposure, either to eliminate or to reduce the loss on translation.

Now before going into the management part, let us find out the amount of loss or gain that is associated with translation of Simplex & Co's balance sheet under the *'current and non-current method' of* translation taking the current rate at ₹41 and historical rate at ₹39 per Canadian dollar (C $).

Balance sheet of Simplex & Co. after translation

Liabilities	C $	*Rate* ₹	*Translated amount* ₹	*Assets*	C $	*Rate* ₹	*Translated amount* ₹
Equity and reserves	10,000	39	**3,82,000***	Land and building	6,000	39	2,34,000
Bonds and debentures	12,000	41	4,68,000	Plant and equipment	8,000	39	3,12,000
Accounts payable	10,000	41	4,10,000	Long term investments	12,000	39	4,68,000
Outstanding	8,000		3,28,000	Inventories (at market value)	8,000	41	3,28,000
				Accounts receivable	4,000	41	1,64,000
				Cash	2,000	41	82,000
Total	40,000		15,88,000	Total	40,000		15,88,000

***Note:** The value of equity and reserves would have been ₹3,90,000 if multiplied by ₹39 which is the historical rate, against ₹3,82,000 which is the balancing figure on translation. The loss in the net worth therefore is ₹8,000 which has been directly attributed to owner's equity under the logic that any gain or loss will go to the owner's pocket. This loss may even go up or down under the two other methods of translation, namely, monetary/monetary and temporal method.

The translation loss in the instant case of ₹8,000 needs to be managed in order to get eliminated or minimized. Now, going by the balance sheet hedge, if the 'exposed' assets, namely, long-term investments of the subsidiary company is reduced by 4,000 C $ from the present 12,000 C $ to say 8,000 C $ and the inventories increased by 4,000 C $ from 8,000 C $ to 12,000 C $, all other things remaining unchanged, the new balance sheet and corresponding revised translated balance sheet would be as under:

Revised Balance sheet of Simplex & Co. of Canada as on 31.03.2011(before translation)

Liabilities	*Canadian $*	*Assets*	*Canadian $*
Equity and reserves	10,000	Land and building	6,000
Bonds and debentures	12,000	Plant and equipment	8,000
Accounts payable	10,000	Long term investments	8,000
Outstanding	8,000	Inventories (at market value)	12,000
		Accounts receivable	4,000
		Cash	2,000
Total	40,000	Total	40,000

Revised Balance sheet of Simplex & Co. after translation

Liabilities	C $	*Rate* ₹	*Translated amount* ₹	*Assets*	C $	*Rate* ₹	*Translated amount* ₹
Equity and reserves	10,000		**3,90,000***	Land and building	6,000	39	2,34,000
Bonds and debentures	12,000	39	4,68,000	Plant and equipment	8,000	39	3,12,000
Accounts payable	10,000	41	4,10,000	Long term investments	8,000	39	3,12,000
Outstanding	8,000	41	3,28,000	Inventories (at market value)	12,000	41	4,92,000
				Accounts receivable	4,000	41	1,64,000
				Cash	2,000	41	82,000
Total	40,000		15,96,000	Total	40,000		15,96,000

The revised translated balance sheet shows that the equity and reserves has become ₹3,90,000 which is just equal to the value that would have obtained by multiplying 10,000 C $ by ₹39 per C $ the historical rate without a loss in the net worth. This exercise amounts to balance sheet hedge wherein the 'exposed' assets, i.e., long-term investments was reduced and inventories increased without reducing the exposed liabilities, with the translation loss being 'nil'. A similar exercise may be undertaken to manage the translation loss by increasing the exposed liabilities without reducing the exposed assets.

Balance Sheet Hedge with Contractual and Natural Hedges

A combination of balance sheet hedge and contractual and natural hedge techniques may be applied by the MNCs to manage their translation loss. Whereas, balance sheet hedge technique may be the one as discussed above and the techniques of natural and contractual hedges may include leads and lags and forward contracts along with a host of other techniques as been discussed before.

NEED FOR HEDGING

The need for hedging has been subject to some debate with one school of thought holding the opinion that there is *no need* to go for hedging (the hedging irrelevant approach) and the other school of thought holding the opinion that there is a need for hedging (the hedging relevant approach) and firms must go for it. The hedging 'irrelevant' approach has its foundation on several grounds. *First*, the purchasing power parity (PPP) operates and therefore any movement in exchange rate will be equally matched by the movement in price as a result of which the financial performance of firm will not be affected. PPP states that 'the home currency price of a commodity in different countries, when converted into a common currency at the spot rate, is the same across countries'. *Second*, changes in the exchange rate cause both loss and gains to the firms involved in foreign transactions which in the long run tend to average out or off-set each other as a consequence of which the firms' performance remains unaffected in the long run. *Third*, shareholders are competent and rationale enough to minimize the currency risk by portfolio diversifications hence no need for hedging by the firm itself. *Fourth*, hedging does not add to the value of the firm and instead uses up its scarce resources because hedging involves costs and hence the firm's value gets reduced. *Fifth*, in case of market equilibrium in parity condition, the expected NPV of hedging is zero, and hence going for hedging will not be beneficial to the firm.

The arguments in support of hedging, on the other hand are, *first*, PPP does not hold good in the short run; *second*, hedging helps maintain cash flows; *third*, NPV of hedging is often positive and *fourth*, management can hedge the risk better than individual shareholders, hence hedging is essential to maximize value for the firm.

The benefits of hedging have been always higher than the limitations and hence in practice firms go for hedging by adopting all the aforesaid techniques of hedging.

SUMMARY

Exchange rate volatility has been a major source of macroeconomic uncertainty affecting the value of the firms in the floating exchange rate regime. Firms with low liquidity at times find themselves being pushed to financial distress due to exchange rate volatility. Effective and efficient management of exchange rate exposure has therefore become imperative for the firms in order to maximize their value. Management of foreign exchange exposure refers to the process of elimination and/or minimization of the loss accruing to the firms due to changes in the exchange rate. The process through which exchange rate exposure is managed is known as 'hedging'.

The techniques used for managing foreign exchange exposure broadly falls into *three* categories, those used for managing the *transaction exposure*, those used for managing the *operating exposure*, and those used for managing the *translation exposure*.

The hedging techniques used for managing the transaction exposure are broadly two-natural hedges and contractual hedges. Natural hedges are composed of *leads and lags*, *cross-hedging*, *currency diversification*, *sharing of risk*, *pricing the transactions*, *back to back loans*, *currency swaps* and '*matching the cash flows*'. These techniques are internal to the firm and hence are called the 'internal techniques'. They do not involve any contractual relationship with any external parties outside the firm. On the other hand, contractual hedges are external in nature, hence known as 'external techniques'. They result in creating contractual relationship with external agencies. Techniques like *forward market hedge*, *hedging through currency futures*, *hedging through currency options* and *money market hedges* fall under the contractual hedges.

The techniques used for managing the operating exposure are in the form of financial, marketing and production strategies. Financial strategy includes *long-term transaction exposure hedging such as the matching of cash flows*, *parallel loans* and *currency swaps*, and *matching of liabilities with assets*; marketing strategy includes strategies like selection of new market, product innovation/planning; and production strategy shall comprise of sourcing of product and product inputs, input mixing, plant location and productivity improvement.

The hedging techniques used for managing the translation exposure are the *balance sheet hedge* and a mixture of *balance sheet hedge with contractual and natural hedges*.

There are arguments for and against the use of 'hedging' as a tool for managing the foreign exchange exposure. However, as the benefits of hedging outplay the limitations, firms particularly the ones who are exposed to foreign currency volatility resort to hedging to minimize the effects of such volatility on their value.

KEY TERMS

Hedging refers to the process through which exchange rate exposure is managed.

Natural hedges are a set of hedging techniques used for managing the transaction exposure. They include techniques like leads and lags, cross-hedging, currency diversification, sharing of risk, pricing the transactions, back to back loans, currency swaps and 'matching the cash flows'.

Contractual hedges are techniques other than natural hedges used for managing the transaction exposure. Included under the contractual hedges are forward market hedge, hedging through currency futures, hedging through currency options and money market hedge.

Balance sheet hedge is the hedging technique used for managing the translation exposure.

Currency swaps are foreign-exchange agreements between two parties to exchange the principal and/or interest payments of a loan in one currency for an equivalent amount of principal and/ or interest payments of a loan in another currency.

Credit swap, also known as back to back a loan, or parallel loans is a technique of exposure management that operates in such a way that the risk of exposure involving two parties belonging to two different countries gets off set.

Currency future is a technique wherein currencies are bought and sold like any other commodities, at a specified 'rate' of exchange and on a fixed maturity date, with the involvement of a clearing house and brokers with consideration of brokerage.

Translation exposure or accounting exposure as it is also called is associated with the translation of financial statements of foreign subsidiaries into the parent's reporting currency for the purpose of consolidation of the financial performance of parent and the subsidiaries taken together.

Cross-hedging is a transaction exposure management technique which is adopted when a particular currency desired to be hedged can't be hedged in a forward market and as an alternative, a substitute currency whose volatility is highly correlated with the desired currency is identified and hedged.

REVIEW QUESTIONS

1. What is exchange rate volatility? Briefly discuss the techniques you will follow to manage such volatility.
2. What is transaction exposure? How will you manage the transaction exposure? Explain with appropriate example(s).
3. What is operating exposure? How will you manage such exposures? Discuss.
4. What is translation exposure? What are the techniques available for managing the translation exposure? Should MNCs be concerned about translation exposure? Discuss.
5. Discuss the arguments for and against the need for hedging as a tool for managing foreign exchange exposure.
6. Balance sheet of ABC Ltd. of UK, an Indian subsidiary, as on 31.03.2024 is as under:

Liabilities	£	*Assets*	£
Equity	70,000	Land and building	36,000
Reserves	12,000	Plant and machinery	88,000
Profits	10,000	Furniture and fittings	20,000
Bonds and debentures	58,000	Investments	42,000
Term loans	40,000	Inventories at market price	18,000
Accounts payable	35,000	Receivable	24,000
Outstanding	15,000	Cash	12,000
Total	2,40,000	Total	2,40,000

Given the current rate ₹80/£, and the historical rate ₹68/ £, (i) determine the translation exposure of the Indian parent, and (ii) suggest the best ways to manage the exposure.

7. Balance sheet of Systems Ltd. of USA, a subsidiary of Movers India Ltd., as on 31.03.2024 is as under:

Liabilities	$	*Assets*	$
Equity	1,80,000	Land and building	1,16,000
Reserves	92,000	Plant and machinery	1,88,000
Profits	60,000	Furniture and fittings	1,20,000
Bonds and debentures	1,48,000	Investments	1,22,000
Term loans	1,40,000	Inventories	1,08,000
Accounts payable	1,45,000	Receivable	1,14,000
Outstanding	1,15,000	Cash at bank	1,00,000
		Cash in hand	12,000
Total	8,80,000	Total	8,80,000

Given the current rate of exchange ₹51/$, and the historical rate ₹46/ $, (a) determine the translation exposure of Movers Indian Ltd. under the temporal method of translation, and (b) suggest the ways to manage the exposure.

8. An importer has to make a payment of 7,50,000 USD three months hence. If the rate of interest is 12% per annum, and the exchange rate is ₹50/USD, how much should the importer borrow from the local market to settle the dues?

9. Services India Ltd. has imported goods worth 70,000£ payable two months hence. The company expects an appreciation in £ and decides to buy call option at ₹75/£ with ₹0.5/£ as premium. If the spot rate on maturity becomes ₹77.5/£, will it be beneficial for the company to exercise the (call) option?

10. Write explanatory notes on:
    (a) Currency futures
    (b) Currency options

11. Write notes on:
    (a) Balance sheet hedge
    (b) Money market hedge

12. Write notes on:
    (a) Contractual hedges
    (b) Natural hedges

13. Balance sheet of S&S Ltd. of Netherlands, an Indian Subsidiary, as on 31.03.2024 is as under:

Liabilities	€	*Assets*	€
Equity	1,63,000	Land and building	1,46,000
Reserves	1,22,000	Plant and machinery	1,98,000
Profits	1,17,000	Furniture and fittings	1,10,000
Bonds and debentures	1,68,000	Investments	1,40,000
Term loans	1,30,000	Inventories at market price	1,18,000
Accounts payable	1,28,000	Receivable	1,26,000
Outstanding	1,12,000	Cash	1,02,000
Total	9,40,000	Total	9,40,000

Given the current rate of exchange ₹89/€, and the historical rate ₹86/€, (a) determine the translation exposure of S&S Ltd. under the temporal method of translation. Also give your opinion how you will manage this exposure.

14. Following is the Balance Sheet of Space Universe Ltd. of France, an Indian Subsidiary, as on 31.03.2024 is as under:

Liabilities	€	Assets	€
Equity	10,60,000	Land and building	20,43,000
Reserves	7,40,000	Plant and machinery	17,98,000
Profits	9,10,000	Furniture and fittings	5,10,000
Bonds and debentures	15,15,000	Inventories at market price	6,18,000
Term loans	10,80,000	Receivables	8,26,000
Accounts payable	6,15,000	Cash	1,25,000
Total	59,20,000	Total	59,20,000

If the current rate of exchange ₹89/€, and the historical rate ₹86/ €, determine the translation exposure of Space Universe Ltd. under the temporal method of translation. What are the ways available to manage such exposure?

15. On 10.01.2024, Star and Shine has imported goods for 9, 20,000 USD, payable three months hence. If the rate of interest is 9% per annum, and the exchange rate is ₹82/USD, how much should the importer borrow from the local market to settle the dues?

16. Write explanatory notes on:
(a) Currency options (b) Natural hedges

17. Explain the following with examples(s):
(a) Currency futures (b) Contractual hedges

18. Write explanatory notes on:
(a) Money market hedge (b) Currency futures

19. Explain the following with examples(s):
(a) Balance sheet hedge (b) Contractual hedges

20. Given below is the Balance Sheet of Universal Services Inc. of Singapore, an Indian Subsidiary:

Balance Sheet of Services Universal Inc.as on 31.03.2024

Liabilities	€	Assets	€
Equity	11,11,500	Land and building	16,16,160
Reserves	4,40,400	Plant and machinery	23,23,230
Profits	6,60,600	Furniture and fittings	6,06,060
Bonds	12,12,200	Inventories at market price	9,18,550
Term loans	17,17,700	Accounts Receivable	4,26,260
Accounts payable	8,80,800	Cash	1,32,940
Total	60,23,200	Total	60,23,200

If the current rate of exchange ₹61.80 per Singapore dollar and the historical rate ₹59.90 per Singapore dollar, determine the translation exposure of Universal Services

Inc. under the temporal method of translation. Also explain how you will manage such exposure.

REFERENCES

[1] David K. Eiteman, et al., *Multinational Business Finance*, Tenth ed., Pearson, New Delhi, 2004, p. 287.

[2] Allan C. Shapiro, *International Financial Management*, 4th ed., PHI Learning, New Delhi, 2002, p. 256.

[3] *Ibid.*, p. 259.

[4] David K. Eiteman, et al., op. cit., p. 313.

SUGGESTED READINGS

1. Apte, P.G., *International Financial Management*, 5th ed., Tata McGraw-Hill, New Delhi, 2009.
2. Adrian Buckley, *Multinational Finance*, 3rd ed., PHI learning, New Delhi, 1998.
3. Sharan, V., *International Financial Management*, 4th ed., PHI Learning, New Delhi, 2006.
4. John C. Hull, Options, *Futures and Other Derivatives*, 7th ed., Pearson, New Delhi, 2009.
5. Jeff Madura, *International Corporate Finance*, 8th ed., Thomson-South Western.

Glossary

Absolute Uniformity Model: Absolute Uniformity Model is a model suggested for preparing accounting and financial reports, without leaving any scope for alternative treatment of transactions and/or events, thus resulting in global harmony in accounting and financial reporting. The model is difficult to apply in practice for its rigidity.

Accounting standards: Accounting standards are policy documents issued by professional accountancy bodies at national and international levels, in relation to different aspects of measurement, treatment, disclosure and presentation of accounting information. The erstwhile International Accounting Standards Committee (IASC) has issued 41 IAS and the present International Accounting Standards Board (IASB) has issued 6 IFRS so far at the international level and the Institute of Chartered Accounts of India (ICAI) has issued 29 Accounting Standards in India as of now.

AS: AS are Indian Accounting Standards issued by ICAI.

Assets: As defined by IAS 1, Assets are probable future economic benefits to be obtained or controlled by a particular entity as a result of past transactions or events.

Basic EPS: Basic EPS = Net profit or loss for the period available to equity shareholders *divided* by weighted average number equity shares outstanding during the period.

Bilateral relief measures: Bilateral relief measures are measures taken by two countries to avoid or reduce the burden of double taxation.

Business segment: A distinguishable component of an enterprise which is engaged in providing an individual product or service or a group of products or services that is subject to risks and returns that are different from those of other business segments.

Circumstantial Uniformity Model: Circumstantial Uniformity Model has been suggested as the second model for accounting practices in order to achieve international harmony in financial reporting. The model leaves scope for certain alternative treatment of transactions depending upon the circumstances.

Consolidation: It is the presentation of the operating and financial results of the parent company and its subsidiary(ies) in a consolidated manner so as to help the users of the financial statements in getting a comprehensive view of the economic resources controlled by the group and also the group's obligations.

Convergence: Convergence, in the context of harmonization of practices, refers to bringing the accounting standards of a nation (say India) at par with the International Accounting Standards.

Cost of Sales Adjustment (COSA): COSA is an adjustment of the sales value in the context of price level accounting wherein the cost of sales as reported in the historical cost accounting method is brought to its current value.

Current Cost Accounting technique: CCA is a technique suggested by Sandilands statements against price level changes.

Current Purchasing Power (CPP) technique: CPP is a technique of adjusting financial statements against inflation. It is also known as the General Purchasing Power (GPP) technique.

Current ratio: The relationship between the firm's current assets and current liabilities is current ratio. It indicates the firm's ability to meet its short-term obligations.

Debt service coverage ratio: It is a comprehensive measure of the firm's ability to serve its debt.

Defensive interval ratio: This ratio indicates the firm's liquidity position in terms of its ability to meet projected daily expenditure from operations. It is calculated by dividing quick assets by projected daily cash requirements.

Diluted EPS: It is equal to net profit attributable to equity shareholders after adjustment for diluted earnings *divided by* average number of weighted equity shares outstanding during the period considering the conversion of diluted potential equity shares.

Distress price: The temporary fall in market price in comparison to the historical average owing to a situation where supply exceeds demand.

Dividend per share (DPS): DPS is a measure of the real cash income that is made available to the equity shareholders.

Domestic neutrality: Domestic neutrality or capital export neutrality is said to be existing when tax laws do not affect the capital owner's choice between investing in home country or in host (foreign) country. 'Taxation is export neutral if domestic and overseas investments that earn the same pre-tax rates of return also yield the same after tax rates of return.

Double taxation: Double taxation which occurs when the same income is taxed twice—first by the host government and second by the home government.

Du Pont analysis: This term refers to the analysis of the firm's overall profitability where the firm's return on investment (ROI) is calculated based on decomposition of net profit margin and total assets turnover.

Earning per share (EPS): EPS is a profitability index that measures the firm's profitability in terms of its earnings per share, i.e. the amount of profits after tax available to equity holders per share held.

Economic exposure: Economic exposure refers to the extent to which the value of the firm would be impacted by unexpected changes in the exchange rates. The managerial efforts to manage economic exposure would be to formulate long-term strategies so as to enhance and preserve its value in the event of unexpected exchange rate fluctuations.

Economic Value Added (EVA): EVA is a measure of the real economic value created for shareholders by a firm's management for a given year.

Equity: Equity as prescribed in IAS 1 is the residual interest in the assets that remains after deducting its liabilities. In a business enterprise, the equity is the ownership interest.

Exchange risk management: Exchange risk management aims at monitoring and managing the firm's foreign exchange exposure so as to maximize its profitability, cash flow and market value. Foreign exchange exposure primarily assumes *three* forms: Translation exposure, transaction exposure and economic exposure.

Financial statement analysis: An information processing system that is meant for providing financial data which are appropriate and useful to decision makers who are concerned with evaluating the economic situation of the firm and predicting its future course.

Foreign currency transactions: These are transactions whose terms are denominated in a foreign currency or which require settlement in a foreign currency. Foreign currency transactions arise when an enterprise buys or sells on credit goods or services whose prices are denominated in foreign currency; borrows or lends funds and the amounts payable or receivable are denominated in foreign currency; is party to an unperformed foreign exchange contract; or for other reasons, acquires or disposes of assets or incurs or settles liabilities denominated in foreign currency.

Foreign currency translation: Foreign currency translation refers to the change in the monetary expression of the financial data contained in financial statements.

Foreign neutrality: Foreign neutrality or capital important neutrality exists when tax laws do not distort the after tax earnings to domestic and foreign investors. 'Taxation is import neutral if equal before tax returns to competing supplies of capital translate into equal after tax return.

Forward exchange contracts: A forward exchange contract is a contract wherein a buyer agrees to buy a certain amount of foreign exchange at a future date and at a predetermined price. Conversely, a forward exchange contract is a contract where a seller agrees to sell a certain sum of foreign exchange at a future date and at a price agreed upon in advance.

Gearing adjustment: This refers to the equitable distribution of COSA.

General price level changes: General price level changes refer to the increase or decrease in the value of monetary unit measured in terms of a price index.

Geographic segment: A distinguishable component of an enterprise which is engaged in providing products or services within a particular economic environment that is subject to risk and returns that are different from those components operating in other economic environment.

Harmonization: Harmonization, in the context of accounting practices, refers to bringing down the disparities that exist in the financial reporting system practiced by nations. Harmonization is as good as standardization but with a certain degree of allowances.

Horizontal analysis: Also known as trend analysis or dynamic analysis it is a technique of financial statement analysis under which financial statement of a number of years of the firm are analyzed against a common base.

IAS: IAS are International Accounting Standards issued by IASC.

IFRS: IFRS (International Financial Reporting Standards) are accounting standards issued by IASB (the changed name of IASC after its restructuring).

Interest coverage ratio: This refers to the 'times' the interest changes are covered by EBIT form which they will be paid.

Interim financial reporting: This refers to the presentation of financial statements of the enterprise covering periods of less than a full financial year. The purpose of such presentation of financial statements is to provide the decision makers with frequent and timely information for taking investment and credit decisions, based on their ability to predict full year's financial results from the interim results.

International accounting: International accounting may be defined as that branch of accounting which deals with the recording and translation of foreign transactions, preparation and presentation of consolidated foreign financial statements, and presentation of international financial reporting in accordance with international GAAP and auditing practices.

International tax planning: International tax planning refers to the process of structuring foreign operations and remittances that would result in maximization of the firms' global after tax cash flows. It involves using the flexibility of the multinational corporation in structuring foreign operations and remittance policies in order to maximize global after tax cash flows.

Liabilities: Liabilities, as defined by IAS 1, are probable future sacrifices of economic benefits arising from present obligations of a particular entity to transfer assets or provide services to other entities in future as a result of past transactions or event.

Line-by-line consolidation: It is a technique of consolidation of financial statements wherein all the assets and liabilities of the subsidiary company are added to the corresponding items of the parent company. In case the parent company does not hold 100 per cent controlling interest, then minority interest is determined and shown in the balance sheet.

Market Value Added (MVA): MVA is a measure of the shareholders' value creation over the firm's life time. It is an indicator of the firm's managerial performance in terms of the shareholders' value creation.

Minimum transfer price: Incremental cost per unit incurred up to the point of transfer plus opportunity cost per unit to the selling division.

Minority interest: *Minority interest* is the proportion of values of assets and liabilities that belongs to shareholders outside the group.

Monetary assets and liabilities: Monetary assets and liabilities are those assets and liabilities that are not subject to reassessment of their recorded values due to changes in the purchasing power of money.

Multiple Discriminate Analysis (MDA): MDA is a multivariate technique used to predict corporate failure.

Net realizable value: Net realizable value in the context of inventory valuation as provided in IAS 2 is the difference between the net estimated selling price per unit (of the items of stock) in the ordinary course of business and the estimated cost of completion and estimated cost necessary to make the sale.

Non-monetary assets and liabilities: Non-monetary assets and liabilities are those that are subject to reassessment of their values due to changes in the purchasing power of money.

One line consolidation: *One line consolidation* is a technique of consolidation in which value of investment in subsidiary is determined and shown in the consolidated balance sheet unlike the line-by-line method.

Payout ratio: Payout ratio is the relationship between DPS and EPS. It indicates the retention policy of the firm.

Price level change: Price level changes refer to the changes in the value of monetary unit or simply the increase or decrease in the purchasing power of money.

Price-Earning (P/E) Ratio: P/E ratio is the relationship between market price per share and the EPS.

Profitability ratio: Profitability ratio indicates the ability of the firm to generate profits that would be adequate to support the firm's operations.

Prorata consolidation: Prorata consolidation refers to a technique of consolidation of financial statements wherein all the assets and liabilities and income and expenditure of the subsidiary are shown in the consolidated balance sheet and income statement in proportion to the controlling interest.

Purchasing power gains and losses: Purchasing power gains and losses occur on account of the treatment of trade debtors and creditors under inflationary situation.

Purchasing power of money: It is the ability of a given sum of money to buy goods or services now, in comparison to the amount of goods or services that the same sum could have bought at an earlier date.

Purposive Uniformity Model: Purposive Uniformity Model is the third model suggested for accounting practices in the context of harmonization. The model leaves scope for alternative treatment of certain transactions and events depending upon both the circumstances and the purpose.

Ratio analysis: A technique of financial statement analysis under which series of ratios are calculated to determine the liquidity, solvency profitability and asset utilization (activity) efficiency of the firm.

Relative price level changes: Relative price level changes refer to the change in the prices of one commodity in relation to the change in the prices of all commodities and services taken together.

Reportable segment: It is a business or geographical segment whose majority of revenue is earned from sales to external customers and further that its revenue from sales to external customers and from transactions with internal customers (i.e. other segments) is 10% or more of the total revenue of all segments, or its segment result (i.e. profit or loss) is 10% or more of the combined result of all segments recording a profit or of all segments recording a loss, whichever is higher in absolute monetary terms, or its assets are 10% or more of the total assets of all segments.

Return on capital employed (ROCE): ROCE is a measure of the firm's profitability based on long-term capital employed.

Return on total assets (ROTA): ROTA indicates the managerial efficiency of the firm in terms of assets utilization.

Segment reporting: It refers to the disclosure of information about an enterprise's operation in different industries, its foreign operations and export sales, and its major customers. It can be defined as the reporting of financial information in relation to different business activities of the firm classified as business segment or geographical segment.

Social disclosure: Social disclosure primarily aims at informing the general public about the social welfare measures taken by the firm and their effects on the society. The firm's ability and success in discharging social obligations also gets reflected in the process of social disclosure.

Solvency ratio: A measure of the firm's long-term liquidity position.

Specific Identification Method: Specific Identification Method is a method of determining the cost of inventory as per IAS 2.

Specific price level changes: This amounts to the changes in the prices of a specific good or service.

Standardization: In accounting context standardization refers to complete elimination of the disparities in accounting practices and reporting, by adopting a set of rigid rules and policy guidelines.

Tax equity: Tax equity refers to a system of taxation where equal sacrifices are made by the tax payers in bearing the tax burdens.

Tax haven: Tax haven in international taxation refers to a moderate or liberal taxation of foreign income by the host government.

Tax neutrality: Tax neutrality refers to a system of taxation which when adopted will not affect the investment decisions of the firms as regards the destination of the investment or the nationality of the investor. There are two forms of tax neutrality—domestic neutrality and foreign neutrality.

Tax treaties: Tax treaties are bilateral relief measures undertaken by countries to avoid double taxation and to reduce overall tax burden. Tax treaties aim at providing protection to tax payers against double taxation, and preventing the discouragement which taxation may cause in the free flow of international trade, international investment and international transfer of technology.

Transaction exposure: This arises due to the sensitivity of the firm's contractual cash flows denominated in foreign currency to exchange rate fluctuations. Transaction exposure arises from (1) buying and selling on credit goods or services whose prices are contractually denominated in foreign currency, (2) borrowing and lending funds in foreign currency, (3) forward exchange contracts, (4) acquisition or disposal of assets denominated in foreign currency, and (5) settlement of liabilities denominated in foreign currency.

Transfer price: The price that one segment (subunit, department, division) of an organization charges for a product or service supplied to another segment of the same organization.

Transfer pricing: Transfer pricing relates to the pricing of goods and services that change hands between entities engaged in inter-firm trade.

Translation exposure: Translation exposure refers to the potential of an increase or decrease in the parent company's networth and reported net income due to fluctuations in the exchange rates.

Unilateral relief measures: Unilateral relief measures are measures taken by one country alone to avoid or reduce double taxation as long as such measures benefit the country concerned.

Vertical analysis: Also known as common size analysis, vertical anslysis is a technique of financial statement analysis under which financial statements of firms of different sizes are compared and analyzed against a common base rather than based on absolute figures.

Withholding taxes: Withholding taxes are imposed by the host government at different rates on repatriation of foreign incomes in the form of dividends, interest, royalties and technical services.

Yield: Yield is a measure of the rate of return earned by the shareholders.

Index